A DOCUMENTARY HISTORY OF

The Negro People in the United States

Also by Herbert Aptheker

American Negro Slave Revolts (1943)

Essays in the History of the American Negro (1945)

The Negro People in America:
A Critique of Myrdal's "American Dilemma" (1946)

To Be Free: Studies in Afro-American History (1948)

Laureates of Imperialism: Big Business Re-Writes American History (1954)

History and Reality (1955)

Toward Negro Freedom (1956)

The Truth About Hungary (1957)

The Colonial Era (1959)

The American Revolution (1960)

The World of C. Wright Mills (1960)

Dare We Be Free?
The Meaning of the Attempt to Outlaw the Communist Party (1961)

American Foreign Policy and the Cold War (1962)

Soul of the Republic: The Negro Today (1964)

Mission to Hanoi (1966)

Nat Turner's Slave Rebellion (1966)

The Nature of Democracy, Freedom and Revolution (1967)

The Urgency of Marxist-Christian Dialogue (1970)

Afro-American History: The Modern Era (1971)

The Published Writings of W. E. B. Du Bois: An Annotated Bibliography (1973)

Edited by Herbert Aptheker

A Documentary History of the Negro People in the United States: From the Colonial Period to Establishment of the N.A.A.C.P. (1951)

Disarmament and the American Economy (1960)

And Why Not Every Man? A History of the Struggle against Slavery (1961)

Marxism and Democracy (1964)

Marxism and Alienation (1965)

One Continual Cry: Walker's Appeal to Colored Citizens (1965)

Marxism and Christianity (1968)

Autobiography of W. E. B. Du Bois (1968)

The Correspondence of W. E. B. Du Bois (Vol. I, 1879–1934) (1973)

The Education of Black People, by W. E. B. Du Bois (1973)

A Documentary History of the Negro People in the United States: From the Emergence of the N.A.A.C.P. to the Beginning of the New Deal (1973)

A DOCUMENTARY HISTORY

OF

The Negro People
in the
United States

1933-1945

Edited by
HERBERT APTHEKER

Preface by
WILLIAM L. PATTERSON

A Citadel Press Book
Published by Carol Publishing Group

A Citadel Press Book
Published by Carol Publishing Group
Citadel Press is a registered trademark of Carol Communications, Inc.

Editorial Offices: 600 Madison Avenue, New York, NY 10022
Sales & Distribution Offices: 120 Enterprise Avenue, Secaucus, NJ 07094
In Canada: Canadian Manda Group, P.O. Box 920, Station U, Toronto,
Ontario, M8Z 5P9, Canada

Queries regarding rights and permissions should be addressed to:
Carol Publishing Group, 600 Madison Avenue, New York, NY 10022

Manufactured in the United States of America
ISBN 0-8065-1007-2

Carol Publishing Group books are available at special discounts
for bulk purchases, for sales promotions, fund raising, or
educational purposes. Special editions can also be created to
specifications. For details contact: Special Sales Department,
Carol Publishing Group, 120 Enterprise Ave., Secaucus, NJ 07094

10 9 8 7 6 5 4 3 2

To the Memory of Sidney Finkelstein

Preface

THE APPEARANCE of the third volume of *A Documentary History of the Negro People in the United States (1932–1945)* is a matter of outstanding significance to those seriously concerned for a people's victory in the Black Liberation struggle.

This is a decisive period in the centuries-old conflict of Black Americans for liberation and full enjoyment of their rights and privileges. This volume reveals the continuity of the heroic struggles Black people have waged to civilize their country and to defeat its consistently vicious enemies of democracy. The picture sharpens the quest for a political strategy which, if implemented, must inevitably lead to a victory for the people.

This third volume carries us into a new era, for the world has been changed. New social forces have come to power. The battle of the Black people for the right to vote, to sit on juries and to enjoy the opportunities of free citizens has merged with the national liberation struggles of millions of the world's exploited and repressed masses. Those conflicts are in the main directed against U.S. reaction, now the main bulwark of world reaction, as shown in its support of South Africa, Rhodesia (Zimbabwe), the Portuguese African colonists and the Latin-American oligarchies.

The documents in the preceding two volumes of this monumental series showed that Black people are not newcomers to the fight for a better way of life in the United States. But as both the dignity and the human and constitutional rights of Blacks have been violated, so too have these valuable documents and what they show been denied proper place in most U.S. textbooks. The basic reason for this de facto censorship is that those who rule in this country did not want and do not want our youth to know of the magnificent contributions and massive struggles of the Black people. With such knowledge, youth would have a very high set of social values.

Surely we have now reached the stage in the liberation efforts of humanity when study of the volumes making up this *Documentary History* can constitute a giant step toward rectifying the conscious omissions and distortions characterizing dominant historiography.

This third volume brings to the fore, in particular, the great impact of the 1917 Socialist Revolution upon Black freedom fighters. That revolution and its impact helped release the militant and creative genius of the oppressed workers, peasants and oppressed nationalities in the former Czarist empire; it provoked also new trends of thought among U.S. Black people, as shown, for example, in the life of the late Dr. Du Bois. The continuing impact of that Revolution and of Marxism quite properly form a significant part of this third volume.

The third volume of the *Documentary History* illuminates a period of especially momentous events. It treats of the era of the great depression, and of the "New Deal"—which sought in the main to stabilize the capitalist economy with sops to the harried masses and with no substantial part of even those sops going to the Black masses in the plantation areas or in the ghettoes. This is the era during which the Scottsboro and Herndon Cases brought the Black liberation struggles into worldwide prominence. The genocidal policy of the government and its courts and the whole divide-and-rule policy of racism stood out in bold relief. The defenders of the victims in these cases called for united mass demonstrations, street actions, world-wide protests to accompany the court battles. A drive was organized against the sharecropping system and peonage. Jim Crow was sharply challenged and lynching fully exposed and excoriated.

While racism was intensified, struggles against it also intensified; while anti-Communism was whipped up, interest in Marxism and socialism grew. The militancy of Black millions reached unprecedented heights in this era.

The period saw the world-wide rise of fascism and its triumph in Italy, Japan and Germany, the ravishment of Ethiopia, the martyrdom of Spain and the collapse of the League of Nations—and the climax of World War II and the defeat of the Tokyo-Rome-Berlin axis. But the latter did not see the elimination of racism in the United States; on the contrary, in many ways chauvinism was intensified.

For the first time, Marxism-Leninism and the Communist Party motivated by that outlook played a really significant part in the Black Liberation movement. The invaluable character of Black-white, united mass political actions in the fight for full democracy was being recognized.

The documents reflect the mounting activity in the labor movement culminating in the creation and growth of the C.I.O.; they illuminate the growing politicalization of Black women. The three-dimensional nature of the Black liberation effort also is reflected in this volume: the class, racial and national character of the movement appears.

While the volume necessarily concentrates upon the thought and activities of Black people, the problems and concerns are problems and concerns of all people. These are problems made in the United States and the Black people of the United States are also made in this country. They are an amalgam out of Africa, Asia, Europe and the indigenous Americans—a people conceived in slavery but dedicating themselves to the proposition to which they have offered their lives—that all should have full equality and freedom.

Black resistance to the terror unleashed against liberation struggles just after the close of this volume reached such a level that President Truman was forced to establish an Advisory Committee on Civil Rights and then President Johnson also appointed such a committee. Briefing its members, the late President Johnson said: "Segregation and poverty have created in the racist ghetto a destructive environment totally unknown to white Americans through the distortion of history."

Who was at fault in this "distortion of history"? Mr. Johnson did not say, nor did the Presidents who preceded him, let alone the one who followed. Basic to undoing that distortion and properly placing the blame for its existence are the three volumes in this *Documentary History*. In making available these volumes Dr. Aptheker has performed a service of great value to all peoples in the United States and, indeed, in the world.

WILLIAM L. PATTERSON

Contents

In Appreciation

THE PUBLICATION of this third volume of the *Documentary History* completes a project first conceived in 1946. On the basis of an aspect of this idea, the granting of a Guggenheim Fellowship, 1946–47, was very helpful. After some four years of concentrated work, Volume I was completed, and Citadel Press undertook its publication. This was done back in 1951 when few publishers were interested in what is now called Black history and the same publisher has stayed with this work through the intervening generation. This faith and steadfastness are deeply appreciated.

Indeed, those directing Citadel have even kindly suggested that while three volumes complete the original conception, that itself might be expanded and that perhaps a fourth volume treating of the especially momentous decades since World War II might be prepared. If strength, and health hold up reasonably well, it is not impossible that this will be done.

Meanwhile this is done and Morris Sorkin and Allan Wilson of Citadel have my warmest thanks. Arthur Smith of Citadel has prepared Volumes II and III for the press and seen both of them through that fearsome process; he, too, has my great appreciation.

I am grateful to William L. Patterson—whose life is so integrally a part of the history of this volume—for having contributed a characteristically insightful and challenging preface.

In this entire project, as always, have been the sustaining strength and wise criticism of Fay P. Aptheker; here expressions of appreciation are altogether inadequate. One might as well thank his heart for beating away.

HERBERT APTHEKER

April, 1974

A DOCUMENTARY HISTORY OF

The Negro People in the United States

1

THE CASE OF ANGELO HERNDON

Angelo Herndon, a young Black Communist worker and organizer, was arrested in 1932 on a charge of "insurrection" since he had led in organizing Black and white unemployed people in Atlanta. His speech to the jury, delivered January 17, 1933, and the summary for the defendant delivered the next day by his chief attorney, Benjamin J. Davis, Jr. (1903–1964)— son of one of the most prominent Black men of Georgia, and later a national leader of the Communist Party and a New York City councilman— give the background and facts. Herndon was found guilty but the jury recommended mercy. Herndon was sentenced to eighteen to twenty years in prison, but a campaign of world-wide proportions and excellent preparations of appeals finally won him his freedom in 1936.

[a]

ANGELO HERNDON'S SPEECH TO THE JURY

Gentlemen of the Jury: I would like to explain in detail the nature of my case and the reason why I was locked up. I recall back about the middle of June 1932, when the Relief Agencies of the City of Atlanta, the County Commission and the city government as a whole, were cutting both Negro and white workers off relief. We all know that there were citizens who suffered from unemployment. There were hundreds and thousands of Negroes and whites who were each day looking for work, but in those days there was no work to be found.

The Unemployment Council, which has connection with the Unemployed Committees of the United States, after 23,000 families had been dropped from the relief rolls, started to organize the Negro and white workers of Atlanta on the same basis, because we know that their interests are the same. The Unemployment Council understood that in order to get relief, both races would have to organize together and forget about the question whether those born with a white skin are "superior" and those born with a black skin are "inferior." They both were starving and the capitalist class would continue to use this weapon to keep them further divided. The policy of the Unemployment Council is to organize Negroes and whites together on the basis of fighting for unemployment relief and unemployment insurance at the expense of the state. The Unemployment Council of Atlanta issued those leaflets after the relief had been cut off, which meant starvation for thousands of people here in Atlanta. The leaflets called upon the Negro and white workers to attend a meeting at the court house building on a Thursday morning. I forget the exact date. This action was initiated as the result of statements handed out to the local press by County Commissioners who said that there was nobody in the City of Atlanta starving, and if there were, those in need should come to the offices of the Commissioners and the matter would be looked into. That statement was made by Commissioner Hendrix.

The Unemployment Council pointed out in its circulars that there were thousands of unemployed workers in the City of Atlanta who faced hunger and starvation. Therefore, they were called upon to demonstrate in this court house building, about the middle part of June. When the Committee came down to the court house, it so happened that Commissioner Hendrix was not present that morning. There were unemployed white women with their babies almost naked and without shoes to go on their feet, and there were also Negro women with their little babies actually starving for the need of proper nourishment, which had been denied them by the county of Fulton and State of Georgia and City of Atlanta as well.

Well, the Negro and white workers came down to the Commissioners' office to show that there was starvation in the city of Atlanta and that they were in actual need of food and proper nourishment for their kids, which they never did receive. I think Commissioner Stewart was in the office at that time. The white workers were taken into his room and the Negroes had the door shut in their faces. This was done with the hope of creating racial animosity in order that they would be able to block the fight that the Negro and white workers were carrying on—a determined fight to get relief. The white workers were told: "Well, the county hasn't any money, and of course, you realize the depression and all that but we haven't got the money." We knew that the county did have money, but were using it for their own interest, and not for the interest of the Negro workers or white workers, either way. They talked to the white workers some considerable time, but when the white workers came out, they had just about as much results as the Negroes did—only a lot of hot air blown over them by the Commissioners, which didn't put any shoes on their little babies' feet and no milk in their stomachs to give them proper nourishment. No one disputed the fact they did keep the Negroes on the outside, but the white workers were in the same condition that their Negro brothers were in. In spite of the fact that the County Commissioners had published statements to the effect that there was no money in the county treasury to provide unemployment relief for the Negro and white workers, still the next day after the demonstration the County Commissioners voted $6,000 for relief, mainly because it was shown that for the first time in the history of Atlanta and the State of Georgia, Negro and white workers did join together and did go to the Commissioners and demand unemployment insurance. Have not they worked in the City of Atlanta, in different industries, different shops and other industrial concerns located in Atlanta for all their years, doing this work, building up the city where it is at the present time? And now, when they were in actual need of food to hold their bodies together, and when they came before the state and county officials to demand something to hold their bodies together, they were denied it. The policy of the Unemployment Council is to organize these workers and demand those things that are denied them. They have worked as slaves, and are entitled to a decent living standard. And, of course, the workers will get it if you ever organize them.

After the successful demonstration, the solicitor's office had two detectives stationed at the post office to arrest anyone who came to take the mail out of box 339. On Monday, July 11, 1932, I went to the post office to get mail from this box and was arrested by detectives, Mr. Watson and Mr. Chester. I had organized unemployed workers, Negro and white, of Atlanta, and forced the County Commissioners to kick in $6,000 for unemployment relief. For this I was locked up in the station house and held eleven days without even any kind of charges booked against me. I was told at the station house that I was being held on "suspicion." Of course, they knew what the charges were going to be, but in order to hold me in jail and give me the dirtiest kind of inhuman treatment that one could describe, they held me there eleven days without any charge whatsoever until my attorney filed a writ of habeas corpus demanding that they place charges against me or turn me loose. It was about the 22nd of July, and I still hadn't been indicted; there had been three sessions of the grand jury, and my case had been up before them each time, but still there was no indictment. This was a deliberate plot to hold me in jail. At the habeas corpus hearing, the judge ordered that if I wasn't indicted the next day by 2:30, I should be released. Solicitor Hudson assured the judge that there would be an indictment, which, of course, there was. Ever since then I have been cooped up in Fulton County Tower, where I have spent close to six months—I think the exact time was five months and three weeks. But I want to describe some of the horrible experiences that I had in Fulton Tower. I was placed in a little cell there with a dead body because I couldn't get out of the place. The man's name was William Wilson, who fought in the Spanish-American war for the American principles, as we usually call it. He was there on a charge of alimony. His death came as a result of the rotten food given to all prisoners, and for the want of medical attention. The county physician simply refused to give this man any kind of attention whatsoever. After three days of illness, he died, and I was forced to live there with him until the undertaker came and got him. These are just some of the things that I experienced in jail. I was also sick myself. I could not eat the food they gave me as well as hundreds of other prisoners. For instance, they give you peas and beans for one dinner, and at times you probably get the same thing three times a week. You will find rocks in it, and when you crack down on it with your teeth, you don't know what it is, and you spit it out and there it is. They have turnip greens, and just as they are pulled up out of the ground and put in the pot, with sand, rocks and everything else. But that's what you have to eat, otherwise you don't live. For breakfast they feed grits that look as if they were baked instead of boiled, a little streak of grease running through them, about two strips of greasy fatback. That is the main prison fare, and you eat it or else die from starvation. I was forced to go through all of this for five months without a trial. My lawyers demanded a trial time after time, but somehow the state would always find a reason to postpone it.

They knew that the workers of Atlanta were starving, and by arresting Angelo Herndon on a charge of attempting to incite insurrection the unity of Negro and white workers that was displayed in the demonstration that forced the County Commissioners to kick in with $6,000, would be crushed forever. They locked Angelo Herndon up on such charges. But I can say this quite clearly, if the State of Georgia and the City of Atlanta think that by locking up Angelo Herndon, the question of unemployment will be solved, I say you are deadly wrong. If you really want to do anything about the case, you must go out and indict the social system. I am sure that if you would do this, Angelo Herndon would not be on trial here today, but those who are really guilty of insurrection would be here in my stead. But this you will not do, for your role is to defend the system under which the toiling masses are robbed and oppressed. There are thousands of Negro and white workers who, because of unemployment and hunger, are organizing. If the state wants to break up this organization, it cannot do it by arresting people and placing them on trial for insurrection, insurrection laws will not fill empty stomachs. Give the people bread. The officials knew then that the workers were in need of relief, and they know now that the workers are going to organize and get relief.

After being confined in jail for the long period of time that I have already mentioned, I was sick for several weeks. I asked for aid from the county physician and was refused that; the physician came and looked through the bars at me and said: "What's the matter with you?" I told him, "I'm sick, can't swallow water, my chest up here is tight and my stomach absolutely out of order, seems as if I am suffering with ulcers or something." He could answer: "Oh, there's nothing the matter with you, you're all right." I explained: "I know my condition. I know how I'm feeling." He said: "You will be all right." Through friends I was able to get some medicine; otherwise I would have died.

On Christmas Eve I was released. My bail was once $3,000 but they raised it to $5,000 and from that up to $25,000, just in order to hold me in jail, but you can hold this Angelo Herndon and hundreds of others, but it will never stop these demonstrations on the part of Negro and white workers, who demand a decent place to live in and proper food for their kids to eat.

I want to say also that the policy of the Unemployment Council is to carry on a constant fight for the rights of the Negro people. We realize that unless Negro and white workers are united together, they cannot get relief. The capitalist class teaches race hatred to Negro and white workers and keep it going all the time, tit for tat, the white worker running after the Negro worker and the Negro worker running after the white worker, and the capitalist becomes the exploiter and the robber of them both. We of the Unemployment Council are out to expose such things. If there were not any Negroes in the United States, somebody would have to be used as the scapegoat. There would still be a racial question, probably the Jews, or the Greeks, or somebody. It is in the interest of the capitalist to play one race against the other, so greater profits can be realized from the working people of all races. It so happens that the Negro's skin is black, therefore making it much easier for him to be singled out and used as the scapegoat.

I don't have to go so far into my case, no doubt some of you jurymen sitting over there in that box right now are unemployed and realize what it means to be without a job, when you tramp the streets day in and day out looking for work and can't find it. You know it is a very serious problem and the future looks so dim that you sometimes don't know what to do, you go nuts and want to commit suicide or something. But the Unemployment Council points out to the Negro and white workers that the solution is not in committing suicide, that the solution can only be found in the unity and organization of black and white workers. In organization the workers have strength. Now, why do I say this? I say it because it is to the interest of the capitalist class that the workers be kept down all of the time so they can make as much profit as they possibly can. So, on the other hand, it is to the interest of Negro and white workers to get as much for their work as they can—that is, if they happen to have any work. Unfortunately, at the present time there are millions of workers in the United States without work, and the capitalist class, the state government, city government and all other governments, have taken no steps to provide relief for those unemployed. And it seems that this question is left up to the Negro and white workers to solve, and they will solve it by organizing and demanding the right to live, a right that they are entitled to. They have built up this country, and are therefore entitled to some of the things that they have produced. Not only are they entitled to such things, but it is their right to demand them. When the State of Georgia and the City of Atlanta raised the question of inciting to insurrection and attempting to incite to insurrection, or attempting to overthrow the government, all I can say is, that no matter what you do with Angelo Herndon, no matter what you do with the Angelo Herndons in the future, this question of unemployment, the question of unity between Negro and white workers cannot be solved with hands that are stained with the blood of an innocent individual. You may send me to my death, as far as I know. I expect you to do that anyway, so that's beside the point. But no one can deny these facts. The present system under which we are living today is on the verge of collapse; it has developed to its highest point and now it is beginning to shake. For instance, you can take a balloon and blow so much air in it, and when you blow too much it bursts; so with the system we are living under—of course, I don't know if that is insurrection or not!

From Angelo Herndon, *Let Me Live* (New York: Random House, 1937), pp. 342–48.

[b]

SUMMARY FOR ANGELO HERNDON, DEFENDANT, BEFORE FULTON COUNTY PETIT JURY
by Benjamin J. Davis, Jr.

Gentlemen of the Jury: Don't try to organize for better conditions, and—especially you who are unemployed—don't try to fight for bread for yourselves and starving families; for if you do, Mr. Hudson [the Prosecutor] will try to send you to the electric chair!

According to Mr. Hudson, it is a crime to ask for bread. It is a crime for poor Negro and white workers to exercise their constitutional rights to lawfully assemble and petition the government against their grievances. And, gentlemen of the Jury, Herndon, a heroic young Negro boy, must be sent to the electric chair because he organized black and white together—because Mr. Hudson must have his pound of flesh from the workers and the Negro people.

Mr. Hudson—I should say, Reverend Hudson—parades before you as a man of pure and holy principles. But let us examine his activities. On Sundays, Reverend Hudson preaches in a Methodist pulpit about a fair and just "God" who punishes injustice and iniquity with hell and damnation. But on Mondays, Tuesdays, Wednesdays—in short, on every other day of the week—he is busy sending innocent Negroes and poor whites to the infernal Georgia chain gang and the electric chair. Such a man cannot be rightfully called a "fair and impartial" prosecutor.

And how Mr. Hudson has tried to deceive you! He read amidst snorts and holy shrieks, from numerous pamphlets found in Herndon's possession, distorting their meaning, twisting their context to make it appear to you as if Communism is the doctrine of hatred between Negro and white workers.

In the first place, Reverend Hudson doesn't know any more about Communism than a pig knows about a full-dress suit. In the next place, he brazenly and dishonestly omitted all those passages which told of the lynchings of countless innocent Negro workers—all those passages which told of the ruthless manner in which you, many of whom are white workers, are placed against the Negro workers. Gentlemen of the Jury, the history of the South should be written in the blood of thousands of Negro lynch victims and in the sweat and suffering of the exploited poor whites.

Angelo Herndon is charged with attempting to incite insurrection. According to Reverend Hudson, it's insurrection to fight for bread— and when you fight, the Reverend Mr. Hudson, lord and master of the Methodist pulpit, wants to send you to the electric chair.

Gentlemen of the Jury, it is not Herndon who is the insurrectionist. It is the lynch mobs, the Ku Kluxers who are allowed to roam the land of this state burning innocent black people at the stake in defiance of every law of justice, humanity and right. If Reverend Hudson wants to send the insurrectionists to the electric chair, let him send the Ku Klux Klan to the electric chair; let him search out these terrorist bands who defy the laws of this state and of mankind right under his nose.

Gentlemen of the Jury, this is not a case of prosecution; it is one of persecution. Which one of you can say that he also will not be sitting in the scornful seat, listening at the righteous bellowing of Reverend Hudson, merely because you demanded food for your loved ones? Which one of you does not wish to clasp the hand of a young Negro boy who in the midst of every obstacle, every discrimination, dares to fight for the principles upon which this country was founded?

The Reverend Hudson says Herndon is stirring up racial hatred by advocating the doctrines of workers organizations. But I ask since when did it become racial strife for Negro and white workers to organize together for the betterment of their conditions? Is it not because young Herndon sat before you today and told you in the words of a man and not those of a cringing coward that he would never give up his principle of fighting for the workers and Negroes, that he sits framed before you today?

Gentlemen, this very case is a blot upon American civilization which boasts of liberty, democracy, freedom of speech and press.

And it is in the name of this very liberty and democracy that the Reverend Hudson is asking you to send this Negro youth to a horrible and unjustifiable death—merely because he fought for the rights of the poor and needy without regard to their race or color.

Gentlemen of the Jury, just as starvation, want and suffering knows no color or race line, neither does this injustice and exploitation. What happens to Herndon today as you ponder his fate in the jury room is going to determine what is going to happen to you when the sharp pains of hunger tug at the helpless emaciated forms of your loved ones tomorrow.

By every principle of justice and fair play Herndon must be acquitted.

It is difficult to dignify the testimony of the state's witnesses with the name of evidence. Every one of the witnesses called by the Reverend Hudson is on the payroll of the state, men who dare not testify against their higher-up officials—detectives, jailers, assistant solicitor generals. Herndon is charged with attempting to incite insurrection, but the evidence shows that Herndon organized a demonstration of Negro and white unemployed for adequate relief. The rest of the testimony appears to have been fabricated in the "pure and spotless" mind of the Reverend Hudson.

The issue is simply this: Consider in your minds when you retire to the jury room whether you want to see a man burn in the electric chair because he had the courage to fight for the Negroes and whites who are hungry and without bread or jobs. Consider in your minds whether you want to see a Negro boy executed in the electric chair at a trial where Negro citizens have been denied their constitutional rights to sit on juries, a right which is guaranteed to every defendant and citizen by the Constitution of the United States, the document upon which this country was founded.

Gentlemen of the Jury, you have but one course before you, if you would uphold your oath, to bring back a verdict in accordance with the facts and consonant with justice—and that is a verdict of acquittal. Any other verdict will be a mockery of justice; any other verdict will be catering to the basest passion of race prejudice which the Reverend Hudson has sought to conjure up in you all; any other verdict will be making a scrap of paper out of the Bill of Rights, the Constitution of the United States and the State of Georgia, out of the democratic rights which are the property of every citizen whether his skin is black or white.

From Herndon, *Let Me Live*, pp. 351–54. See the account of "The Herndon Case" by Benjamin J. Davis in his autobiography, *Communist Councilman from Harlem* (N.Y., 1969, International Publishers), pp. 53–81.

2

THE AMERICAN NEGRO AFRICAN MOVEMENT

In January, 1933, there was organized the above-named movement; the founding meeting was held in Pasadena, California. The officers were Elbert Wooley, president; James M. Jones, secretary; Samuel W. Guinn, treasurer. Jones, a graduate of Howard and long an admirer of Alain Locke and W. E. B. Du Bois, was the main force behind the effort. In a letter to Dr. Du Bois, dated January 18, 1933, Jones remarked that "a well-to-do white man is financing" the effort. Dr. Locke offered a somewhat tentative approval to the scheme but Du Bois was flatly opposed. It received some notice in the press for a time but then died away. Below is the text of a printed petition form issued by the American Negro African Movement.

PETITION

We, the undersigned American citizens, petition the United States Government through the American Negro African Movement that the United States Government favorably consider the program advocated by the American Negro African Movement, viz.:

That the United States Government take a firm stand against cancellation of the War debts owed to the United States by European countries, and advocate instead a readjustment of said debts on a new basis, namely that the European countries relinquish to the United States territory in Africa acquired by said debtor countries as a result of the World War, thereby making some return upon the War Debts.

Furthermore, we petition the United States Government that, if such territory be acquired in Africa, it shall be set aside for colonization by the American Negroes.

Furthermore, we petition the United States Government that adequate financial aid be given to the American Negroes in order to induce voluntary migration to said colony, to the following ends:

1. That the American Negroes may receive unrestricted opportunities to develop according to their abilities.
2. That the social problem caused by the presence of large numbers of Negroes in the United States, may be solved.
3. That large sums of money may be placed in circulation through American railways, steamships, and manufacturing concerns, who will supply the transportation, machinery, and building material to establish the new colony.

4. That unemployment may be relieved by the removal of millions of Negro laborers now employed in the United States.

5. That friendship of the darker races may be cemented by the aid that America can give in carrying out the project in an unselfish way.

From the original petition form in editor's possession; the cited letters are in the Du Bois Papers.

3

GETTING A SQUARE DEAL

by Oscar De Priest

On April 24, 1933, Judge James Lowell of the Federal District Court in Boston granted a writ of habeas corpus in the case of George Crawford, wanted for killing a white woman in Georgia in 1932. The governor of Massachusetts had already issued an extradition warrant at the request of the Virginia governor but the judge issued the writ on the ground that no Black person served on Virginia juries. For this act Judge Lowell was denounced by Southerners in Congress and an effort was made to impeach him. In October, 1933, the U.S. Supreme Court reversed Judge Lowell. Crawford was returned and in 1934 sentenced to life imprisonment. In December, 1933, Judge Lowell died. The Crawford case, the Lowell decision, and the southern attacks on the judge were the background for the following speech by Congressman De Priest in the House on May 3, 1933, presented in full except for some quoted matter and statistical data.

Mr. Chairman, no race of people in this country has ever been more loyal to America than the people of my race. In every period of war this country has been engaged in they have always served the American Government, and I hope they always will. They were emancipated by the proclamation issued by the immortal Abraham Lincoln in 1863. After that the Republican Party submitted to the people of this country three amendments, the thirteenth, the fourteenth, and the fifteenth amendments to the Constitution of the United States, which gave them their liberty, made them citizens, and gave them the right to vote.

Under the guise of Ku-Kluxism my people have been intimidated and bulldozed in certain neighborhoods; people who were trying to be intelligent citizens, and standing up for their manhood rights. I have seen those night-riders in Alabama, where I was born. Of course, the Ku-Klux died out shortly after that. It was reorganized a few years ago, not only fighting the American Negro but fighting the Jews and the Catholics also. Thank God they did not last very long.

Then when the Negroes were getting more power and more control in this country the hue and cry was raised in some Southern States of Negro domination. That was only a subterfuge. The Negro in America never was in the majority in any one State in the United States except the State of Mississippi. There never was any chance for Negro domination. It was only used as a subterfuge for other people to ride into office on.

Then came those days when they were deprived of their right to vote. After they had 23 Members of Congress in both bodies and for about 28 years no member of my group was able to be a Member of this Congress. If we had a right to exercise our franchise rights as the Constitution provides we should exercise them I would not be the only Negro on this floor. I hope to see the time come when the Federal Constitution will be actually enforced and that the Members of Congress who have sworn to support the Constitution will pass an act to enforce every section of the Constitution including the amendments to which I have referred.

But recently there has been some discussion on the floor of this Congress about Negroes getting a square deal over this country. There was a discussion here the other day when the resolution was introduced to impeach Judge Lowell, of Massachusetts, because of a decision which had nothing whatever to do with the innocence or guilt of this man Crawford. I know nothing about his guilt or innocence, but I do say one thing, that this House was misled. I do not say that excitedly, but this House was misled. There was not one scintilla of evidence introduced in that hearing in Massachusetts with regard to the innocence or guilt of this man charged with crime; not one. But the question was decided on its merits, on whether or not this man had been indicted by a legally drawn grand jury. The question was raised on the issue in the State of Virginia. It was proven that those of my racial group are not included in the jury system. No Member from the State of Virginia can rise on this floor and say that any Negro has served on a jury in Virginia in the last quarter of a century, whether petit jury or grand jury. That was the ground on which that decision was rendered, that the jury was drawn unconstitutionally, because a certain group of people had been excluded from jury service, and not on the guilt of this man Crawford. I do not know anything about that. If he is guilty, he should be punished, but for God's sake indict him with a legally drawn grand jury.

I am stating these things not because I want to stir up any racial animosity, but the American people ought to know that 12,000,000 people should not be tempted to join some organization that is not for the best interests of America. I do not think communism means any good to this country, either to me or anybody else in it.

There was another case down in Scottsboro, Ala., quite recently, down in the State where I was born, and I have often said that if God would forgive me for being born there I would never live there again. In reading some of the evidence in that trial it was shown that there were two white girls traveling as hoboes on a freight train dressed in over-alls. It happened some two years ago. I am not saying whether those boys are innocent or guilty. I could not say, for I have not read over the testimony, but I do know that one of the girls repudiated her testimony a very short time ago in the second trial of one of the defendants, and I do know that one of the white boys who was with her substantiated her repudiation, and that is a matter of record. Everybody can read it. I do know that those boys were first convicted in the courts. The case went to the United States Supreme Court and it was reversed, and I do know that the last Negro was convicted and sentenced to the electric chair, I presume. If not, he will be; and that case will go back to the United States Supreme Court also.

I do not want a condition to arise in this country where those of my group will become discouraged and think there is no chance in America for them. I know the great rank and file of American people are on the square. I know that. But I also know what is everybody's business is nobody's business, and I also know that the great body of Christian America and the great newspapers and periodicals of this country do not universally denounce this crime of injustice meted out to those of my particular group, especially when charged with crimes of that kind. They are convicted before they are tried. I have no brief for Negro criminals. I hold no brief for any kind of a criminal, but I do wish to say that I think the time will come when a Congress of the United States—I do not care whether it be Republican or Democrat; it will still be composed of American citizens—will take this question up and see that their rights are protected. They are beginning to feel that they cannot secure their constitutional rights in the courts of our land.

This country cannot survive by keeping one tenth of its population down. It is a dangerous frame of mind for people to get into, just as the people of Iowa thought they could not secure their constitutional rights in the courts, and they made the serious mistake of trying to go into

the court room and mete out so-called justice themselves by taking
that judge off the bench, dragging him out into the street, and man-
handling him and almost lynching him.

That is bordering on anarchy in this country. It was not brought
about by the voice of the Iowa farmer. It was brought about because he
thought he could not secure justice in the courts. He was wrong in this
assumption, of course he was; and the Governor of the State acted as a
human being ought to act. He called out the supreme power of the State
to put down that insurrection.

I am making these remarks because I want you to know that the
American Negro is not satisfied with the treatment he receives in
America, and I know of no forum where I can better present the matter
than the floor of Congress.

Down in Scottsboro conditions were so tense that it was necessary to
call out the militia to protect those boys during the first trial.

A few years ago in Arkansas five members of my group were convicted of plotting against the American Government. Who ever heard
of a Negro plotting against the American Government? The American
Government has never had better supporters than the Negroes. They
have supported it in every war. They have laid down their lives and
made the supreme sacrifice for America in the past, and I hope they
will do so in the future. You never heard of the assassination or attempted assassination of a President charged against members of my
group. No member of my race ever tried to commit assassination upon
any ruler in America.

If we are good enough to lay down our lives for this county, we are
good enough to enjoy the privileges of citizenship in this country.

I did not have anything to say on the floor the other day about the
judge in Massachusetts because I was not given the opportunity to
speak, but I did think it was uncalled-for; I did think it was premature
for this Congress to go on record and authorize an investigation while
the case was pending before the Federal courts.

No one is interested more than I in the continued loyalty of the
people of my racial group as citizens of the United States; and being
interested as I am, I want to take this opportunity to call the attention
of this body of lawmakers to certain untoward events, constantly re-
curring, that are, to say the least, turning the thoughts of my people
away from our democratic form of government and with perhaps hopeful but reluctant eyes on the dangerous communist theory in this
country. The treatment colored citizens receive in this country, and
especially in the courts in some parts of it, in some instances in the

North as well as the South, is having a bad effect on the minds of these people. The chief justice of the Supreme Court of the State of Alabama dissented from the decision in the first Scottsboro conviction, just as the United States Supreme Court threw out that conviction as a violation of the fourteenth amendment to the Constitution preventing States from depriving "any person of life, liberty, or property without due process of law."

I want particularly to discuss with you the now-famous Scottsboro case where nine youths of my race are accused of raping two white girls. The injustice imposed upon these boys in the first trial where they were convicted was such that the United States Supreme Court did not think they received a fair trial and set aside the verdict and ordered a new trial, on the ground that the fourteenth amendment to the Federal Constitution had been violated. This amendment says that no person shall be denied or deprived of life, liberty, or property without due process of law. In this connection I wish to quote as part of my remarks an editorial in the Washington *Daily News* of April 10, 1933, which reads as follows:

THE SCOTTSBORO VERDICT

The conviction of Haywood Patterson, first of the Negro defendants in the second trials of the Scottsboro cases, will be appealed. It should be.

Among other things prejudicial to a fair trial, the defense was able to show that the jury law apparently was administered to exclude Negroes from the panel for this case. On more than one occasion during the trial the State attorneys conducted themselves in such a way as to prevent orderly and judicious consideration of evidence by the jury.

In repudiating her testimony at the earlier trial, Ruby Bates swore that the other girl in the case, Victoria Price, had framed the Negro youths. Lester Carter, a white friend of the two girls, confirmed the testimony of Ruby Bates.

To execute boys on the discredited evidence of a woman of Victoria Price's character, and following a trial in which racial discrimination seemed to operate in the jury panel, would be unthinkable. Just as the chief justice of Alabama dissented from the first Scottsboro conviction, and just as the United States Supreme Court threw out that conviction as a violation of the fourteenth amendment of the Constitution preventing States from depriving "any person of life, liberty, or property without due process of law," so the Decatur verdict yesterday appears certain to be set aside by a higher court.

The action of courts and so-called "judicial procedure" in an atmosphere of intimidation, prejudice, and disturbance, as has happened in the Scottsboro case and as has frequently been the situation in other cases, creates disrespect of law and order and makes the Negro of America think it is impossible to get justice, especially in certain parts of the country.

May I quote again from the Washington *Daily News* of Tuesday, April 11, 1933, the words of Heywood Broun? He said, himself quoting—

We have no right to sit in the seats of the scornful. Nor is it the part of wisdom to think of the Scottsboro case as a local issue.

Continuing, he says:

Sunday, in Decatur, Ala., a jury of 12 white men brought in a verdict of death against Haywood Patterson. The attorney general of the great sovereign State referred to him as "that thing."

They say it was a quiet courtroom and a gentle day down in Morgan County when the jury filed in after 24 hours of deliberation. But could none of them hear the wind in the rigging of the slave ship, the creaking of her timbers, and the cries of the cargo?

Attorney General Knight could not even bring himself to admit that he was in the presence of a man on trial for his life. He had to take refuge in such a phrase as "that thing." He was afraid of the facts. He had reason to fear.

There was much panicky talk in the speeches of the men who pressed the case. "Show them that Alabama justice cannot be bought and sold with Jew money from New York!" cried Solicitor Wright at one point in the trial. And the attorney general, after deploring the injection of prejudice by his associate in the summation, went on to say: "If you acquit this Negro, put a garland of roses around his neck, give him a supper, and send him to New York City. There let Dr. Harry Fosdick dress him up in a high hat and morning coat, gray striped trousers and spats."

And that was because Dr. Fosdick had told Ruby Bates to face the danger of return and go back to confess that she lied when first she accused the Negro boys. And that was because the attorney general was afraid.

From the *Afro-American*, Baltimore, Md., April 8, 1933, I read the following in a news story from Decatur, Ala.:

Carter stated that he, the girls, and Orville Gilley, white, made the entire trip together and that the boys did not rape the girls. He was kept in jail at Scottsboro until the trial was over. He went to Albany to tell Governor Roosevelt about the case and then saw attorneys. He was kept in hiding.

Carter reached here at 2 A.M. Thursday. Ruby Bates is still expected.

The situation here is tense as the defense scatters the State's case.

*   *   *

A mob of 200 whites under Klan leadership was reported near here Tuesday night. Twenty extra guards were called out. The sheriff threatened to shoot to kill. The mob had planned to march on the jail, but dispersed when they saw they had formidable opposition.

From the Balitmore *Afro-American,* dated April 22, 1933, I read a news story as follows:

Decatur, Ala.—Another picture of Alabama justice flashed across the canvas here Monday when Bailiff E. R. Brittell admitted to Judge James E. Horton that he had allowed jurors to hold telephone conversations while serving in the Scottsboro case.

Joseph R. Brodsky, attorney, immediately entered a motion to set aside the verdict which condemned Haywood Patterson to death.

I want also to quote you a speech of my colleague, Congressman Tom Blanton, of Texas, delivered on the floor of the House March 27, 1933, following the impassioned plea of Representative [William] Sirovich, of New York, in behalf of the Jewish people, recent victims of attack in a foreign country. Mr. Blanton said:

I feel just as the gentleman does, and am unalterably opposed to any and all kinds of persecutions. If there is persecution against any people because of their race, it ought not to go unchallenged.

But is it not a matter that ought to be handled by our State Department? If we go to passing resolutions, unless we direct them to our own Executive and his Department of State, would we not be invading the Executive functions of the Government? We do not like to have the executive departments invade the legislative part of the Government. In this connection may I not call the attention of my friend to the fact that there is unreasonable, foolish, cruel persecution of the Jews right here in the Nation's Capital? I do not stand for that. I am against all persecutions. I have some very close personal friends of lifetime standing who are Jews. Why should we tolerate without protest the persecutions of Jews here in Washington?

There are very prominent apartment houses here in the Nation's Capital which refuse to permit Jews to rent apartments. There are apartment houses here where people can buy homes therein as they buy a residence. If my distinguished friend would go there and say, "I am a Jew," they would say, "We cannot sell to you." There is that ridiculous persecution, with which I have no sympathy whatever, right here in the gentleman's National Capital, but we ought to get that out of the way first before we go to foreign countries. Has my distinguished friend from New York any precedents for his resolution?

The remarks, quoted above, were uttered in the course of debate, when the subject of the persecution of the Jews in Germany was before the House. Mr. Blanton's speech pertaining to the Jews applies with equal force to all citizens alike in this country. I want to compliment him on the stand he took. I believe he is fair enough to want to mete out even-handed justice to all citizens, including the 12 million colored citizens of the United States, for I do not see how any Member of Congress can take any other stand when he remembers the oath of office he took to uphold the Constitution and our form of government.

I particularly want to call your attention to the Massie case that happened in the Hawaiian Islands. I am not pretending to say that the defendants over there, who were accused of raping Mrs. Massie, were innocent or guilty, but I do want to say that no jury had found them guilty. In their trial the jury was unable to agree on their guilt. Further, I want to call your attention to the apparent state of mind against all dark-skinned people where prejudice is allowed to defeat justice. About 140 Members of Congress signed a petition and cabled it to the Governor of the Hawaiian Islands asking the pardon of the Massies after they had been duly convicted of murdering one Kahahawai, one of the defendants accused of raping Mrs. Massie. There is no excuse that can be offered by any stretch of the imagination that will justify American citizens, either at home or abroad, or in our territorial possessions, in taking the law into their own hands.

I also wish to call attention to the fact that Lieutenant Massie is still holding a commission in the United States Navy despite conduct unbecoming a gentleman and prejudicial to the dignity of an officer of the Navy. He participated in a murder, and, according to his own testimony on the witness stand in his trial, an officer and an individual, admitted that he fired the fatal shot that killed Kahahawai. This officer of the United States Navy was convicted, sentence commuted to 1 hour, and which time was served.*

All these things have a tendency to drive into the American Negro the thought that he cannot secure justice in all parts of America and that dark-skinned people in its territorial possessions are subjected to the same prejudices. I call this to your attention, knowing full well the part colored American citizens have played in all the wars of this country where the dignity and honor of the United States have been assaulted by foes within and foes without.

No man of my racial group has ever been disloyal to our flag or to our country. I hope the time will never come when he may be goaded on to that extremity. I call your attention to dangerous possibilities lurking in a discouraged, dejected, despised, mob-ridden, and intimidated group

---

* Mrs. Thalia Massie, wife of a U.S. naval officer, alleged in 1931 that she had been raped by five young colored men. Five—a Chinese Hawaiian, two Japanese, and two Hawaiians—were tried but the jury could not agree. Mrs. Massie's testimony was quite vague; despite the jury's action, the Honolulu press, in vile racist terms, insisted on their guilt. One of the five was kidnapped by two sailors and Lieutenant Massie and shot dead by the latter. The three were found guilty and sentenced to ten years' imprisonment, but Governor Judd commuted the sentence to one hour and the murderers went free. Lieutenant Massie's defense was conducted by Clarence Darrow.

of citizens if this condition continues to prevail so that they are convinced there is no chance in this country to receive justice at the hands of our people.

I am appealing to the Christian, law-abiding people of America through its magazines, its newspapers, its periodicals, and its pulpit; through its fraternal organizations, labor organizations, church organizations, and all manner and kind of societies, to help maintain law and order in America and abolish this blight on our American jurisprudence and to help blot out the crime known as lynching. It becomes necessary also that the provisions in the Constitution must be safeguarded, so that no man shall be deprived of life, liberty, or property without due process of law; and due process of law means a fair and impartial trial for every citizen of our country.

He who stands idly by, knowing these conditions to exist, will be guilty of contributive negligence in not routing this monster of race prejudice evidenced in many places where it cannot be controlled but occupying too serious a place in our governmental and court procedure of the land. In the interest of America—great, shining, proud symbol of freedom and of liberty and of opportunity, of which 12,000,000 men and women, boys and girls, of my racial group are an integral part—let us stand up like men and women and uphold law and order and see that every man has a fair trial, equal opportunity, and a chance under the sun to have an existence. Only by such action on the part of the American people can America free itself of this odious institution and maintain the confidence and respect of that 12,000,000 American Negroes and also of the rest of the civilized world. It is already being said that we have no right to criticize Germany in her attitude toward the Jews, nor point the finger of scorn at Russia in her attitude against a certain class of her population, until we do justice here in America to every man, woman, and child who lives beneath the folds of the Stars and Stripes. We should remove the beam from out our own eyes before we try to take the mote from the eyes of the rest of the world.

It has not been my purpose here in this body to be radical on any question, especially on some phases of our American life that come close to me, but the time has come when someone must speak out against the damnable, lynching, menacing mob spirit which is depriving citizens of their just rights under the Constitution. This utter disregard of the rights of my people, reaching toward the doorway of our courts of justice, is all too prevalent in some parts of the country.

Let me again appeal to the American public—to you ladies and gentlemen, representatives of the people—that we strive to save America from this growing disregard of law and order. These are trying times in our political and economic life, as well as in our daily social contact, and I hazard to prophesy that the time will come when America may need every loyal citizen to defend our form of government. When that time does come, whether or not I am living, I am sure those of my racial group will stand loyally by this form of government under which we operate. That can only come about by the expressed will of the American people to see that justice is administered under all circumstances to all citizens alike, whether rich or poor, high or low, and without discrimination as to race, color, or creed.

And there now follows in rapid succession riotous demonstrations at the opening of the Mooney trial, whereby the presiding judge felt constrained to postpone the proceedings, and following this comes the assault upon a judge at the town of Le Mar, 20 miles north of Sioux City, Iowa, where the mob went so far as to place a noose, as is alleged, around the neck of the aged jurist. These riotous proceedings, coupled with a threat of impeachment of Judge Lowell, of Massachusetts, who did his duty as he saw it, contributes to a far-greater degree to the break-down of law and order than is healthy for this fair country of ours.

The issue in the Crawford case, which was discussed on the floor of this House by the gentleman from Virginia a few days ago, has nothing to do with whether or not Crawford will get a fair trial in Virginia. The sole issue involved in Judge Lowell's action was whether or not the indictment was constitutional in view of the express admission of the Virginia judge that Negroes had been excluded from the grand jury pursuant to established custom in the State of Virginia. Judge Lowell took the position that once the Virginia judge admitted he had excluded Negroes from the grand jury pursuant to the established custom, the case had been brought within the long line of precedents in the United States Supreme Court, particularly Neal against Delaware, which precedents establish that a conviction cannot be predicated upon an indictment returned by an unconstitutional grand jury. Judge Lowell said he had no doubt that Crawford would get a fair trial in Virginia but that a fair trial could not cure the illegality of the indictment which necessarily would have to serve as a foundation upon which all further proceedings would be based, and that it would be running around in a circle to send Crawford back to Virginia to answer to this particular indictment, when after trial and conviction and review up to the Supreme Court of the United States the United States Supreme Court would have to set the conviction aside in order to protect Crawford's constitutional rights as a citizen of the United States on the very same ground raised before him in the habeas-corpus proceedings, to wit, exclusion of Negroes from the grand jury pursuant to established custom. The judge, in substance, said that if the conviction would have to be set aside eventually on account of an unconstitutional exclusion of Negroes from the grand jury, it would be merely a matter of stage play to send Crawford back to Virginia to answer this unconstitutional indictment. The question of Crawford's innocence or guilt was never presented to the court or considered by it. . . .

Mr. Chairman, I ask unanimous consent that the Clerk may read a resolution which I send to the desk and I yield the rest of my time to the gentleman from New York [Mr. Fish].

The Chairman. Without objection, the resolution will be read.

There was no objection.

The Clerk read as follows:

House Joint Resolution 171

Resolved by the Senate and House of Representatives of the United States of America in Congress assembled (two thirds of each House concurring therein), That the fourteenth amendment to the Constitution is hereby amended, when ratified by the legislatures of three fourths of the several States, and shall be valid to all intents and purposes as a part of the Constitution, by adding to section 1 thereof the following sentence: "To insure to all citizens the equal protection of the laws and a fair trial when charged with crime, the courts of the United States are hereby given jurisdiction to determine, on proper application of any defendant who is charged with crime, whether such defendant's constitutional right to the equal protection of the laws and to a fair and impartial trial is prejudiced by considerations of race, color, or creed, or any other condition to the disadvantage of such defendant, and the said United States court shall have power, subject to the right of appeal as in other cases, to transfer the trial of such case to such other jurisdiction as in the judgment of the court will insure a fair and impartial trial."

Congressional Record, May 3, 1933; 73rd Cong., 1st sess., LXXVII, 2822–27.

4

A REQUEST OF F.D.R.

Mary Fitzbutler Waring, M.D., of Chicago, in her capacity as vice-president of the National Association of Colored Women, wrote President Roosevelt shortly after his inauguration suggesting a specific act on his part which would indicate his concern for the "forgotten man" who was Black.

May 11, 1933

Mr. Franklin D. Roosevelt,
President of the United States of America,

Honored Sir:

You have accomplished much, since you have been in office, for the general good of the masses. Politically, you realize that many of us are your friends and supporters. From a humane standpoint you must realize that we deserve to receive the same treatment as other citizens of the United States.

It would be a just act to put an end to discrimination against the millions of American citizens who are of African descent. Laws exist at the present time in the Southern States of this Union which compel the railroads to carry special coaches on all passenger trains. Colored people are forced to ride in these separate coaches. It matters not how cultured or refined members of our race may be, they are subjected to insult and rough treatment by the white people and railroad employees, because of this segregation, we speak from experience.

Your wise suggestion that railroads conserve by cutting out extra coaches makes this appeal opportune. In your address of May seventh, you spoke of the "Assistance of the government to eliminate the duplication and waste that is resulting in railroad receiverships and continuing operating deficits." We feel that the dropping of the separate coach would make a material difference in expense to the railroad. It would be a real economy.

When the World War broke out, our men answered the call. As loyal Americans, they gave their time, lives, all. Our women served, knit, saved, canteened and gave unstintingly to make a better world in which to live. We came here with emigrants to people this country in 1620. We can not be deported because we have no other country. Since we are loyal, law-abiding citizens; since we desire to instill self-respect and confidence in our youth, we ask that discrimination in public conveyances cease; we pray that discrimination in public places, because of the color of our skin, may end.

We believe that if the people of the white races would learn more about the achievements of the dark races in past ages they would understand that mentally and morally we are not naturally underlings. Continued ill-treatment has made many Negroes have an inferiority complex, and hence they have not measured up to as high a standard as they would have otherwise.

Mr. Roosevelt, we believe in you. You have expedited reconstruction and have given hope to despairing millions. Will you consider us? We appeal to you.

Respectfully yours,
Mary Fitzbutler Waring

This letter is located in the General Records of the Department of Commerce (Record Group 40) in the National Archives. It was referred to Secretary Roper's committee on transportation. On May 23, 1933, as those Records show, M. Kerlin, administrative assistant to the Secretary, thanked Dr. Waring for her suggestion "that considerable saving could be effected by the railroads by discontinuing the carrying of special coaches for the use of Colored people." He assured her that "careful consideration" would be given her letter. In fact, no further action of any kind was taken. (Appreciation is expressed to Jerome Finster of the National Archives and Records Service for data.)

5

WHAT DOES THE YOUNGER NEGRO THINK?

by Lawrence D. Reddick

Then a young graduate from Fisk University, L. D. Reddick—later in charge of the Schomburg Collection of the New York Library, biographer of Martin Luther King, Jr., and a professor at Temple University, Philadelphia —presents a brief but cogent view of his own generation in the opening period of the "New Deal."

In the pages of a recent issue of *The Nation* [June 21, 1933] Joseph Wood Krutch set down what to him the younger generation seems to be thinking. Waiving for the moment the question as to whether forty-year-old Krutch is a qualified spokesman for the generation in, or just out of, college, it is pertinent to inquire into the thought, if any, of a group which the report either melted into the mass or omitted entirely —the younger Negro.

From the outside it would seem that a failure on the part of such a group to think—and think hard—would represent an impossibility. Hemmed in and thwarted as a minority with a color badge of high visibility, the more awakened and refined the spirit of the Negro is made through books and learning, the more sensitive should this spirit be to the stifling meanness of American prejudice and crass ignorance. Then, in the year of our Lord 1933, there is the full implication of Scottsboro and the Crawford Case.

Before 1929 the black collegians used to bemoan and sometimes laugh over the fact that during college they were presidents of the Student Council, varsity debaters, and athletic stars, whereas in the Summer months these same "presidents" and "stars" were cuspidor cleaners and kitchen scullions. Now, even these jobs are gone. The student enrollment has dropped one-third in some instances, hundreds have "hit the road," and in Nashville, Washington, and Atlanta they may be seen clustered here and there about the corners—stuck, no money, no jobs, and conditions worse down home.

It should be expected that under the double pressure of such circumstances . . . the thought of the young Negro should be at once deep and revolutionary. Not so. As tragic as it may seem the thought and feeling is neither deep nor revolutionary; hardly articulate about matters which strike them as full in the face as high tuition (while teachers' pay is reduced), no jobs for *magna cum laudes,* and above all, the collapse of the preachment of three generations that "Education through participation, not violence, will write the new Emancipation Proclamation . . ." the cure to ills at once general and specific. In answer to these let-downs, most of the students are a little sad, a little disappointed, but still the safe, obedient, and believing pupils of their teachers.

The basic reasons for this phenomenon of apathy and rested acceptance defy satisfactory explanation. "Race temperament?" Hardly. The inertia and suppression of the faculty? Something of that. The cumulative effect of a Southern environment which seeks to control all expression, be it through word of mouth, attitude, or action? Yes, some of each. But the reason which seems to cover the most ground is the one that the Negro in college is a middle-class American and that as a respectable bourgeoisie he is infected with the characteristic hope of becoming a petty capitalist. Most of the students at Howard, Fisk, and Atlanta University have parents who are either doctors, school teachers, or "business men" and these same students aspire to be like their parents but with a finer car and a whiter collar. This deep-set faith persists though the present crisis has stripped the parents clean and plucked most of them to the bone. But there is hope. A few more read *The Nation* and *The New Republic.* There have always been small groups such as the *Wranglers* at Fisk who welcome any thinker, radical, or crank who comes to town. Earnest, intelligent, though sometimes sophomoric, young men who spend one evening each week tussling over the problems and seeking some way out. Out of the fog which blinds all of us. Out of the added soot which stifles black men. Socialists? Communists? Practically none, but the visits of Norman Thomas, the vice-presidential candidacy of James Ford, and the splendid activity of the I.L.D. at Decatur have made some dent. Moreover, if the hurricane continues to blow or the "New Deal" quiets the storm through a regimented order, many more will be shaken loose from this naive success-faith.

Opportunity, October, 1933.

6

YOUTH AND AGE AT AMENIA

by W. E. B. Du Bois

From August 18 through August 21, 1933 there occurred the Second Amenia Conference* held at the home of the Joel E. Spingarns in Troutbeck, New York. The roots of the Conference lay in the depression, the appearance of fascism on a world scale, the challenge of the USSR, and the mounting repression of Black people and the fight-back against this—as symbolized in the Scottsboro Case. The result was mounting discontent with the conventional civil liberties, non-economic, moderationist and legalistic features of the NAACP leadership; all this was being challenged from within notably by Dr. Du Bois.

Joel E. Spingarn, himself, however, President of the NAACP, in a confidential statement to its leadership, in February 1932, had remarked that the NAACP did not have the support of "young colored intellectuals"; that "our program needs reconsidering" and that therefore: "Has the time come for a new Amenia Conference?"** Du Bois was finally appointed chairman of the organizing committee—Spingarn had to threaten resignation to move the leadership (especially Walter White) to accept the idea of the Conference —and at the date and place stated, thirty-three young Black people met.

* For details on the First Amenia Conference held in 1916, see the present work, Vol. II (1973), pp. 130–35.
** Quoted in: B. Joyce Ross, *J. E. Spingarn and the Rise of the NAACP* (New York, 1972, Atheneum), p. 168.

Included were: Ira DeA. Reid, E. Franklin Frazier, Abram L. Harris, Ralph J. Bunche, Charles H. Houston, Elmer A. Carter (then editor of *Opportunity*, organ of the National Urban League), Emmett E. Dorsey of Howard, Harry W. Greene of West Virginia State, and Louis I. Redding, an attorney from Wilmington, Delaware. In addition to the host and Du Bois, Walter White, James Weldon Johnson and Mary White Ovington were present as observers from the Association. Visitors included Lewis Mumford and Henry J. Morgenthau, Jr., Roosevelt's Secretary of the Treasury; these are the "distinguished author" and the "Federal official" mentioned in the essay below.

The Conference reflected the movement of Black people in general away from the Republican Party and to the New Deal of FDR; the growing impact of Marxian concepts upon the Afro-American intelligentsia and its disenchantment with the traditional NAACP tactics; and the impending rise of the CIO with its great attention to the organization of Black and white workers in basic industry.

The essay that follows was written by Du Bois and published, unsigned, in *The Crisis*, October, 1933 (XL, pp. 226–27).

It was the great Jew, Benjamin Disraeli, who said: "Youth is a blunder; manhood a struggle; old age a regret." And so with blunder and regret and perhaps something of struggle, we came together last month in the second Amenia Conference.

The first conference at Joel Spingarn's beautiful country estate, took place in 1916. And after its few days of frank fellowship there was no adequate reason left for essential differences of opinion between the followers of Booker T. Washington, then just dead, and those younger men who had so vigorously opposed some of his policies.

The second Amenia conference held at Troutbeck, seventeen years later, had a definite object,—one much more usual in this world, and yet emphasized today both within ard without the Negro race because of World War and unemployment. It was an attempt to bring together and into sympathetic understanding, Youth and Age interested in the Negro problem. And more particularly Youth, with a fringe of Age; and not extreme youth. Eliminating four admittedly among the elders, the others ranged in age between twenty-five and thirty-five, with a median age of thirty, that is, they were well out of college and started on their life work, and yet, as the invitations suggested, they were still with inquiring minds and still unsettled as to their main life work.

These younger conferees may be classed in various ways:

There were 5 social workers; 5 college professors, 4 Y.W.C.A. workers, 3 teachers, 3 lawyers, 2 artisans, 2 librarians, a physician, a student and a Y.M.C.A. worker.

Representing age (more or less willingly), were 2 editors, a professor and a social worker. All were college graduates except one. There were two Doctors of Philosophy.

Among the visitors were a distinguished author, a Federal official, a social worker and a physician.

This, of course, was far from being a cross-section of the group represented. Those present were picked almost haphazard from a list of over 400 names sent to us from all parts of the country. The younger people were, however, very interesting. Among them 3 gave evidence of first-class scholarship, based on thoughtful study and reading; ten were clear-thinkers, able to state their thoughts succinctly and definitely, not at all settled in thought or opinion and frankly aware of the fact, and yet able to contribute to thought. Four were more emotional, not altogether clear in thought, but evidently in earnest and groping. Two were bright but cynical, and the rest were a miscellaneous group, some of whom lacked training and others were merely silent.

On the whole, they were inspiring. They had evidently been thinking and they had not stopped the process. Their difficulty was mainly the difficulty of all youth. Inspired and swept on by its vision, it does not know or rightly interpret the past and is apt to be too hurried carefully to study the present. For instance, one earnest young man told of the need of a Negro lobby in Washington and how certain persons were going to start one. The officials of the N.A.A.C.P. promptly told of the lobby which had been sustained there for five or more years; and the real solution of this apparent contradiction was: How efficient was the former lobby? Why was it not continued? And how far was the present proposal learning from the mistakes and successes of the first venture?

Only by such linking of past, present and future can real national and group advance be made, and this, I think, the Amenia conference was conscious of before it adjourned.

Of course, the difficulty with age and youth is to find a common language; an attitude in which they can approach each other. It is hard for age to admit or understand that it has not thought of everything or attempted everything, or done what it has done as efficiently as it might have done. It is equally difficult for youth to know that age has thought of some of the various problems which bother youth; has tried and failed and succeeded and for reasons not explained altogether by either stupidity or cowardice. In attitude, youth with its tongue in its cheek assumes very often a silent reverence for age which it does not in the slightest feel. And age recognizes the mockery, and on the other hand, it is exceedingly difficult for age not to patronize youth, and to say by silences and inflections: "You really know very little." Which is of course true but applies but little more to youth than to age.

We talked from Friday to Monday, interspersed with swimming and glorious food. Our general thesis was:

In view of the present world depression and the race problems which have exhibited themselves in Germany, India and Africa, the West Indies and the United States, what should be the ultimate goal of a young, educated American Negro with regard to:

A. Occupation and Income
B. Racial Organization
C. Inter-Racial Co-operation.

As a matter of fact most of the discussion confined itself to the economic conditions and the influence of education and politics on these conditions. There was little time left for the matter of racial organization, while the inter-racial aspects of the problem received practically no attention.

The discussion was interesting. There was not a single speech made; that is, there was no attempt at rounded periods and eloquence by persons who had nothing in particular to say. No one even attempted it. When anyone got the floor, they really took hold of the thought and did something with it. And in the end, the general consensus of agreement was rather startling. Far greater than most of us had thought. These were the resolutions:

This conference was called to make a critical appraisal of the Negro's existing situation in American Society and to consider underlying principles for future action. Such criticism at this stage does not involve the offering of concrete program for any organization for administrative guidance.

There has been no attempt to disparage the *older type of leadership*. We appreciate their importance and contributions but we feel that in a period in which economic, political, and social values are rapidly shifting, and the very structure of organized society is being revamped, the leadership which is necessary is that which will integrate the special problems of the Negro within the larger issues facing the nation.

The primary problem is economic. Individual ownership expressing itself through the control and exploitation of natural resources and industrial machinery has failed in the past to equalize consumption with production. As a result of which the whole system of private property and private profit is being called into question. The government is being forced to attempt an economic reorganization based upon a "copartnership" between capital, labor and government itself. The government is attempting to augment consumptive power by increasing wages, shortening hours and controlling the labor and commodity markets. As a consumer the Negro has always had a low purchasing power as a result of his low wages coming from his inferior and restricted position in the labor market. If the government program fails to make full and equal provision for the Negro, it cannot be effective in restoring economic stability.

In the past there has been a greater *exploitation of Negro labor* than of any other section of the working class, manifesting itself particularly in lower wages, longer hours, excessive use of child labor and a higher proportion of women at work. Heretofore there has been slight recognition by Negro labor or Negro leaders of the significance of this exploitation in the economic order. Consequently no technique or philosophy has been developed to change the historic status of Negro labor. Hence in the present governmental set-up there is grave danger that this historic status will be perpetuated. As a result the lower wages on the one hand will reduce the purchasing power of Negro labor and on the other be a constant threat to the standards and security of white labor.

The question then arises how far *existing agencies* working among and for Negroes are theoretically and structurally prepared to cope with this situation. It is the opinion of the conference that the welfare of white and black labor are one and inseparable and that the existing agencies working among and for Negroes have conspicuously failed in facing a necessary alignment between black and white labor.

It is impossible to make any permanent improvement in the status and the security of white labor without making an identical improvement in the status and the security of Negro labor.

The Negro worker must be made conscious of his relation to white labor and the white worker must be made conscious that the purposes of labor, immediate or ultimate cannot be achieved, without full participation by the Negro worker.

The traditional labor movement as based upon craft autonomy and separatism which is non-political in outlook and centering its attention upon the control of jobs and wages for the minority of skilled white workers is an ineffective agency for aligning white and black labor for the larger labor objectives. *These objectives* can only be attained through a new labor movement. This movement must direct its immediate attention to the organizing of the great mass of workers both skilled and unskilled, white and black. Its activities must be political as well as economic for the purpose of effecting such social legislation as old age pensions, unemployment insurance, child and female labor, etc. These social reforms may go to the extent of change in the form of Government itself. The Conference sees three possibilities:

(1) Fascism
(2) Communism
(3) Reformed Democracy.

The conference is opposed to *Fascism* because it would crystalize the Negro's position at the bottom of the social structure. *Communism* is impossible without a fundamental transformation in the psychology and the attitude of white workers on the race question and a change in the Negro's conception of himself as a worker. A *democracy* that is attempting to reform itself is a fact which has to be reckoned with. In the process of reform the interests of the Negro cannot be adequately safeguarded by white paternalism in government. It is absolutely indispensable that in this attempt of the government to control agriculture and industry, there be adequate Negro representations on all boards and field staffs.

While the accomplishment of these aims cannot be achieved except through the cooperation of white and black, the primary responsibility for the initiation, development and execution of this program rests upon the Negro himself. This is predicated upon the increased *economic independence* of the Negro. No matter what artificial class difference may seem to exist within the Negro group it must be recognized that all elements of the Race must weld themselves together for the common welfare. This point of view must be indoctrinated through the churches, educational institutions and other agencies working in behalf of the Negro. The first steps toward the rapprochement between the educated Negro and the Negro mass must be taken by the educated Negro himself. The Finding Committee recommends that the practical implications of this program be referred to a committee on continuation to be appointed at this conference.

There were some little sidelights that are of interest. First and foremost, I discovered that these young people could not sing. It was astonishing. It would be impossible to get thirty young Germans, Frenchmen, Spaniards, Haitians or Chinese together, who could not and would not sing enthusiastically songs that they all knew. But we did not know any songs and we could not sing them. We could not even try. We were too sophisticated. We had heard Hayes and Marian Anderson, not to mention the Metropolitan Opera, and we were dumb in both senses of the word.

In addition to that there was on the part of a few certain, not unexpected, but nevertheless startling lack of self-discipline. It has always been interesting to me to see how young people in many countries organize their government and discipline and enforce it with a certain ruthlessness. But here out of twenty-six, five did as they pleased with regard to noise, sleep and enjoyment with utter disregard of the perfectly evident desires of the rest, and to cap the climax, the rest uttered no protest. I have seen evidence of this sort of thing among young colored people elsewhere. It is for us and the race a new and pressing problem.

Perhaps the second Amenia conference will not be as epoch-making as the first, but on the other hand, it is just as possible that it will be more significant for the future than any conference which colored people have yet held. That depends entirely upon what reactions follow this meeting.

This sketch of the conference cannot close without reference to the hospitality of the host, Joel E. Spingarn, and the thoughtful co-operation of his wife, his two daughters and his two sons. It was withal a very beautiful experience.

See also, Du Bois, *Dusk of Dawn* (N.Y., 1940, Harcourt, Brace & World), pp. 299–302; Ross, *op. cit.*, pp. 169–85; and Irene Diggs, "The Amenia Conferences," in *Freedomways,* 2nd Quarter (1973), pp. 117–34. The day after the Conference concluded (August 22, 1933), Mary White Ovington wrote to Joel Spingarn that she had discerned a "leaning toward communism"—quoted by Elliott M. Rudwick in his *W. E. B. Du Bois* (Philadelphia, 1960, Univ. of Pa. Press), p. 274.

7

THE STRUGGLE FOR THE LENINIST POSITION ON THE NEGRO QUESTION IN THE UNITED STATES

by Harry Haywood

Throughout the nineteen-thirties in particular, one of the leading Afro-American Communists was Harry Haywood. In *The Communist* in 1933, monthly organ of the Party, Haywood presented in quite a lengthy essay the Party's theoretical position as of that time on the question of Black liberation. It is published below, in part, with the essential argumentation intact.

The present program of our Party on the Negro question was first formulated at the Sixth Congress of the Communist International, in 1928. On the basis of the most exhaustive consideration of all the peculiarities, historical development, economic, living and cultural conditions of the Negro people in the United States as well as the experience of the Party in its work among Negroes, that Congress definitely established the problem of the Negroes as that of an *oppressed nation* among whom there existed all the requisites for a national revolutionary movement against American imperialism.

This estimation was a concrete application of the Marxist-Leninist conception of the national question to the conditions of the Negroes and was predicated upon the following premises: first, the concentration of large masses of Negroes in the agricultural regions of the Black Belt, where they constitute a majority of the population; secondly, the existence of powerful relics of the former chattel slave system in the exploitation of the Negro toilers—the plantation system based on sharecropping, landlord supervision of crops, debt slavery, etc.; thirdly, the development, on the basis of these slave remnants, of a political superstructure of inequality expressed in all forms of social proscription and segregation; denial of civil rights, right to franchise, to hold public offices, to sit on juries, as well as in the laws and customs of the South. This vicious system is supported by all forms of arbitrary violence, the most vicious being the peculiar American institution of lynching. All of this finds its theoretical justification in the imperialist ruling class theory of the "natural" inferiority of the Negro people.

This whole vicious system of oppression, while being most sharply felt by the Negro masses in the South also affects their social status in the rest of the country. The Negro poor farmers and farm laborers fleeing from the misery and starvation of the Southern plantations to the industrial centers of the North, do not thereby obtain freedom. On the contrary, at their heels follows also the heritage of plantation slavery resulting in lower wages, worse living conditions, discrimination in social life even in the "liberal" North.

Thus the agrarian revolution, *i.e.* the struggle of the poverty-stricken and land-starved Negro sharecroppers and poor farmers on the Black Belt and in the South for the land, for the destruction of all vestiges of slave bondage—this, together with the general struggle for democratic rights of the Negro people all over the country, as well as for their rights to independent national existence on the Black Belt, constitute the chief axis of the Negro national liberation movement in the U.S.A.

The enslavement of the Negro masses in the United States is an important prop of American imperialism. American imperialism is fundamentally interested in the preservation of the slave remnants in Southern agriculture and the national oppression of the Negro people as a condition for the extraction of super profits. It is the force that stands behind the Southern white ruling classes (capitalists and landlords) in their direct and violent plunder of the Negro masses in the Black Belt. Therefore, the liberation struggles of the Negro masses are directed against the very foundation of the capitalist-imperialist social structure in the United States.

In the present epoch of imperialism and proletarian revolution the Negro question in the United States must be conceived as part of the national colonial problem, or, in other words, it is part of the general world-wide problem of freedom of the oppressed and dependent peoples from the shackles of imperialism. . . .

The Negro masses, once the allies of the Northern bourgeoisie (during the Civil War and Reconstruction), have now become the allies of the proletariat. In their struggle for national liberation these masses constitute an important part of the army of the revolutionary proletariat in the struggle for the overthrow of American capitalism. Hence, the victory of the proletarian revolution in the United States and the struggle of the Negro masses for national liberation demand the consummation of a united fighting front of the white toilers and the Negro people against the common enemy,—American imperialism. Such a united front can only be effective on the basis of direct and effective support by the white working class (as the working class of the oppressor nation) to the efforts of the Negro masses to free themselves from the imperialist yoke. In this connection it is important to keep in mind the dictum of Karl Marx to the English working class on the Irish question: "A people which oppresses another people cannot itself be free." . . .

The first real achievements of our Party in the leadership of the struggles of the Negro masses date from the beginnings of the application of this Leninist line. A historic landmark in the development of our Negro work was the public trial of August Yokinen. In this trial the case of discrimination by a white Party member against Negroes was made the occasion for a political demonstration in which the Party's program on the Negro question and the struggle against white chauvinism were dramatized with an unprecedented effect before the widest masses throughout the country. Comrade Browder in his report before American students, in estimating the political significance of this trial, declared "that it was a public challenge dramatically flung into the face of one of the basic principles of social relationships in America—the American institution of Jim-Crowism. . . . The expulsion of Yokinen, expressing our declaration of war against white chauvinism, exerted a tremendous influence to draw the Negro masses closer to us."

In this trial the Party achieved a great step forward in the education of its membership and the masses around the Party on our program on the Negro question. This was particularly exemplified in Comrade Yokinen himself who, after six months, came back into the Party as one of the staunchest fighters for its program of Negro liberation and who, as a result of his courageous and militant stand on this question, was deported by the Negro-hating imperialist government. The trial of Yokinen served to prepare the Party ideologically for a real interest in the struggle for Negro rights.*

The Yokinen trial was immediately followed by the organization of a mass movement to save the lives of the Scottsboro boys. On the basis of the political preparation through the Yokinen trial the Party was able to seize effectively upon the issue of the frame-up of these boys to develop a tremendous campaign of mass action and the ex-

---

* The Yokinen trial was held in February 1931; for details, see the present work, II (1973), pp. 674–76.

posure of the whole system of national oppression of the Negroes. The Scottsboro campaign marked the first real nation-wide mobilization of masses by the Party for a concrete struggle against one of the cornerstones of capitalist Negro oppression—the institution of lynching. Through the struggle on this issue the Party was able to bring its program before the widest masses of Negro and white toilers, arousing among them the greatest sympathy and confidence. Scottsboro, as the first big battle conducted by the Party on the front of Negro national liberation, did much to break down the traditional barriers of chauvinism and national distrust separating the Negro and white toilers. This struggle, which was coupled with a real political exposure of the treacherous role of the Negro bourgeois reformists of the N.A.A.C.P., hastened the process of class differentiation among the Negroes—the separation of the interests of the Negro proletarian and semi-proletarian masses from the general interests of "race solidarity" as propagated by the Negro bourgeois nationalists. The Negro toilers began to understand class divisions. They began to find out who were their friends and who their enemies.

Only through the vigorous application of our correct Leninist program on the Negro question could the Party carry through and lead such a struggle as the Scottsboro campaign. This campaign gave rise to the sudden movement of mass participation of Negro workers on an unprecedented scale in the general struggles of the working class throughout the country. The great strike of the Pennsylvania, Ohio and West Virginia coal miners which broke out in 1931, during the first part of the Scottsboro campaign, witnessed greater participation of Negro workers than any other economic action led by the revolutionary trade unions. Large masses of Negro workers rallied to the unemployed movement, displaying matchless militancy in the actions of the unemployed. Notable examples of this were the heroic demonstrations against evictions in the Negro neighborhoods of Chicago and Cleveland.

While the Negro masses were beginning to participate more and more in the class struggles in the North, an event of great historical significance occurred in the Black Belt—the organization of the Sharecroppers Union and the heroic resistance of the sharecroppers to the attacks of the landlords and sheriffs at Camp Hill, Alabama. In this struggle, the revolutionary ferment of the Negro poor farmers and sharecroppers received its first expression, resulting in the establishment of the first genuine revolutionary organization among the Negro poor farmers—the militant Sharecroppers Union. The agrarian movement of the Negro masses was further continued and developed in the Tallapoosa fight in which the sharecroppers gave armed resistance to the legalized robbery of the landlords and merchants.

This whole series of class and national liberation struggles was further deepened and politicalized through the Communist presidential election campaign of 1932. In this campaign the Party was able to further extend its program among the masses, rallying large numbers of Negroes behind its political slogans.

Thus the application of a Bolshevik program in conditions of sharpening crisis and growing radicalization of the Negroes has resulted in the extension of the political influence of the Party among broad masses of Negroes, and in the growth of the Party membership among them. Of outstanding importance in this period is the establishment of the Party in the South and in the Black Belt.

These struggles have led to a growing class consciousness of the Negro working class and its emergence upon the political arena as an independent class force in the Negro liberation movement. In the course of these struggles the Negro working class is rapidly liberating itself from the treacherous reformist influences. Thus the characteristic of the present stage of the development of the Negro movement is the maturing of this most important driving force of Negro liberation—the Negro industrial working class. The Negro workers, in close organic unity with the white working class and under the leadership of the Communist Party is the only force capable of rallying the masses of Negro toilers in a victorious struggle against capitalism. The struggle for Negro liberation is now taking place under conditions of growing proletarian hegemony and Communist Party leadership. . . .

The emphasis upon the development of economic struggles among the Negro toilers does not mean to slacken but on the contrary to increase in every way the struggle around the general issues of Negro liberation, such as Scottsboro and the fight against lynching. It is necessary to broaden out and deepen these struggles, bringing forward our full program of social equality and right of self-determination and building up the broadest united front on these issues. Our chief task, however, is to bring this struggle into the shops and factories and on the land, linking it up with the more immediate demands of the Negro toilers, making the factories the main base in the struggle for Negro liberation and our trade unions the main lever for the organization of the Negro working class. At the same time the revolutionary mass organizations and particularly the trade unions must come forward more energetically in the struggle on behalf of the political demands of the Negro toilers.

This must go hand in hand with the ruthless combatting of all forms of chauvinist and Jim Crow practices and the patient, systematic but persistent struggle against the ideology and influence of petty-bourgeois nationalists among the Negro toilers.

Only on this basis will the Party be able to give leadership to the rapidly developing upsurge of the Negro masses and to build this movement into a powerful weapon of the revolutionary proletariat for the weakening and destruction of the rule of American imperialism.

The Communist, September, 1933; XII, 888–901.

8

BLACK TEACHERS IN THE SOUTH

Reflective of the persistent and mounting militancy among Afro-American people—not least in the South—were the combined efforts of the North Carolina Negro Teachers Association and the branches of the N.A.A.C.P. in that state to lift teachers' salaries and to eliminate the differentiation in pay between Black and white teachers. Document [a] is the text of a mimeographed announcement concerning a mass meeting to be held in Raleigh late in October, 1933; document [b] is an article telling of that meeting and of the circumstances surrounding it. The author, George Streator (1902–1955), one of the leaders of the Fisk Student Strike a decade earlier, had taught at Bennett College; when writing this article he was a staff member of the N.A.A.C.P. Later, Streator was an organizer for the Amalgamated Clothing Workers, a reporter for *The New York Times*, and, finally, editor of *The Pilot*, organ of the National Maritime Union (C.I.O.).

[a]

NEGRO TEACHERS' SALARY

Dear Teacher:

As a teacher in North Carolina, you are already fully acquainted with the shamefully low wage that the newly created "Commission on Education" has decided to pay the Negro Teachers in the State.

As it now stands, the bulk of the Negro teachers in public schools in North Carolina are to be paid between $45.00 and $56.00 per month for eight months out of the year. When figured on a yearly basis this amounts to a wage of between $7.50 and $9.50 per week. This is not only unfair to the Negro teachers, but it is an insult to this group which represents one of our leading professions. Many Negro citizens are beginning to look upon it as an affront to the respect of the entire Negro citizenship of the State. Of course it is true that the White teachers have also received a heavy cut but even now the very lowest paid and lowest trained white teacher is to receive as much as the best trained and highest paid Negro teacher with the same experience.

What Can Be Done about the Situation?

The Negroes of the State have already employed every possible means of getting the "Commission" to correct the injustice without coercion. A delegation of Negroes called on the "Commission" at Raleigh and almost begged them to reconsider this rule. The "Commission" merely listened in silence to the pleadings, and after the delegation left they proceeded to authorize the various school boards to restrict Negro teachers' pay to the level mentioned.

Following this effort, the Executive Committee of the Negro Teachers' Association was called into a special session. This committee drafted a letter of resolutions to the Governor asking him to use his influence with the "Commission" in an effort to get the scale revised. In the face of this, the "Commission" has already begun the allocation of salaries to the various Superintendents with such restrictions that Superintendents are forced to the plan of limiting the Negro teachers' checks to the scale mentioned.

There seems to be but one remaining course that can be taken. As a final resort, the Negroes of the State have prepared to take the case to Court and follow it through even to the United States Supreme Court if necessary. *Now this is the plan!*

On October 28, 1933, all branches of the N.A.A.C.P. in North Carolina are sending delegates to Raleigh to a joint conference. The purpose of this conference is to organize all of these State branches into a State Federated branch of the N.A.A.C.P. This State-Wide branch will in turn push the case in court as far as it may be necessary to carry it—even if it has to be carried to the U.S. Supreme Bench for a just decision.

WHAT YOU ARE ASKED TO DO! ! !

Now frankly, this is what you are asked to do:

First, *we want you to be present in Raleigh on Sunday,* October 29, at 3:00 o'clock to attend a *state-wide mass meeting of Negroes*. This meeting, you will note, is on the day following the conference of the Branches of the N.A.A.C.P. and it is probable that detail plans will have been made and be ready to present to the public. We want as many teachers present as possible.

Mr. Walter White, Executive Secretary of the N.A.A.C.P., is to speak and acquaint the Negro citizens of the State with the whole plan.

A representative of the Executive Committee of the State Teachers' Association has also been asked to appear on the program.

Some of the most powerful legal advisers of the race will be present. This will include Atty. Charles H. Houston, Dean of the Howard University Law School, and Mr. Wm. H. Hastie of Washington, D.C. and also a member of the Howard University Law School. Mr. Hastie, as you know, is recognized as one of the ablest men, white or colored, of the American Bar. Mr. J. E. Spingarn, philanthropist and president of the N.A.A.C.P., and Dr. W. E. B. Du Bois will probably be present also.

Second, we want you to inform teachers and Negro citizens in your community about the Mass Meeting and urge them to attend. Try to get groups to bunch together and get automobiles to bring them to Raleigh for the Sunday afternoon meeting. Remember that the N.A.A.C.P. is launching the fight in defence of the Negro teachers. The least that we could expect is that the teachers will be there and become acquainted with the movement.

Since we can not write a personal letter to each teacher in your community, we are depending on you to pass the announcement on to all teachers with whom you come in contact.

Please don't forget!

It is true that this is a long message, but above all please don't forget what we have asked you to do. We repeat:

#1—Attend the Raleigh meeting yourself.

#2—Spread this information among others and encourage them to come.

We are depending on you.

Signed: H. C. Miller
Pres. Greensboro Branch, N.A.A.C.P.
Geo. E. Nightingale, M.D.
Pres. High Point Branch, N.A.A.C.P.
W. Avery Jones
Pres. Winston-Salem Branch N.A.A.C.P.

Leaflet in editor's possession.

[b]

THE COLORED SOUTH SPEAKS FOR ITSELF
by George W. Streator

James T. Taylor writes in the October *North Carolina Teachers Record:*

In North Carolina there is a dual salary schedule for teachers. One for white and the other for Negroes. The average annual salary paid to white elementary school teachers in 1928–1929: Rural, $724.38; city, $1,181.27. For Negro elementary school teachers: Rural, $410.25; city, $724.82. White high school teachers received an annual average salary of $1,256.69 and Negro high school teachers received $910.27.

Negro teachers are required to measure up to the same standard as white teachers for certification, but for an "A" grade certificate of any sort a white teacher receives approximately 30 per cent more salary than a Negro teacher holding the same sort of certificate. Under the 1933 school law the range in salaries for white teachers is $45–$90 per month and Negro teachers are to be paid 30 per cent less. It is certainly a reflection upon a State that those who teach the youth are so grossly underpaid, but the greater shame is our open espousal of salary discrimination based on race or color.

North Carolina in 1911–1912 spent for education of white pupils a per capita of $5.27 and for Negro pupils $2.02. A ratio in favor of the white child of 2.6 to 1. In 1922 $26.74 was spent on each white child and $10.13 on each Negro child. A ratio in favor of the white child of 2.7 to 1.

In 1928–1929 North Carolina spent $1,913,195.49 to transport white children to and from school; during the same period the State spent $14,-078.50 to transport Negro children to and from school.

Two thousand five hundred colored people, by far the most significant gathering of colored people ever held in the South, met in Raleigh on a beautiful October Sunday to voice their protest against the rising tide of white oppression, violence, and discrimination. Making known by their presence at a meeting sponsored by the National Association for the Advancement of Colored People that they were registering an open, courageous, and intelligent protest, these two thousand five hundred men and women from all walks of life made history for the South and for the nation. They made history not in a trivial, rhetorical sense. They made history because they came to give the lie to the oft-quoted libel that Southern Negroes are satisfied with their lot, and as an oppressed people are content to be led and advised at every turn of the road by those who hold for them the narrow vision of a submerged status.

They came to give silent assent to a revitalized Negro leadership for Negro people. Against the scandalous distribution of public money they raised their protest. Against a State that can spend more public money for enlarging a football stadium for one of the three truly big institutions for white students, than it spends annually to maintain the College for Negroes at Durham; against the exclusion from professional training of tax-paying colored citizens in tax-supported State institutions; against a State that could spend more money for ice-water for the last session of the legislature than it would give for the support of a school for delinquent colored girls (maintaining all the while two institutions for white girls), in short against the petty thievishness characteristic of this and every other Southern State in its treatment of the colored population.

More than a thousand of these people came from outside Raleigh. They came from the mountains in the Western portion where few Negroes dwell; they came from the Piedmont, new center of textile and tobacco industry; they came from down East, where the colored population is large. They came by car and bus and train; a hundred came from Greensboro, a hundred from Durham, from Charlotte, Winston-Salem, and the larger cities. They came in tens and fives from little villages and townships, stretched all the way from the Atlantic Ocean to the tapering Eastern highlands. From 300 towns they came, sometimes a single delegate half afraid of spying white folk and tattling Negroes. They came, and the ruling class in North Carolina was stirred by their coming.

Effective protest is in the long run to be judged by the results. But the gathering of two hundred Negroes at any time to a meeting not sponsored and approved by white people generally, is frequently unusual enough to provoke results. The gathering of *two and a half thousand* Negroes to hear speakers not always enjoying the approval of white people and their hand-picked colored yeomanry is sufficiently significant to be classed as miraculous even in these days and times.

Where were the old-line leaders? There were telegrams from many of these. One could recognize in the audience others who were not afraid to be seen at a meeting of intelligent colored people, gathered to protest. Some few came belligerently, determined to break up the meeting, it was said. Many stayed away, were ill, busy, out of town, or just plain incommunicado. One man who received an invitation to speak claims not to have heard of the meeting at all.

Some of the white "liberals" lament they were not consulted about the meeting and would have advised against it, if they had been consulted. Some allege that the intent of the meeting was to sabotage certain prominent figures who have played a part in the building up of the education system that made North Carolina a Southern State apart. Here and there "friends of the Negro" allege that they are being "put on the spot" by radical, "Northern Negroes." On the whole, the North Carolina white liberals were critical, and in a certain sense, inclined to be picayunish if not vindictive. Having formed the habit of dictating the program of Negro education and welfare, these men who were blazing new trails thirty years ago are reluctant to listen to the very people to whose training they have contributed.

Where stand the liberal white daily papers? Well, the Raleigh *News and Observer,* staffed by university graduates, in a confusion of rhetoric laments what the National Association for the Advancement of Colored People did to Judge J. Parker, and issues the warning that Negroes may be moved to rebellion. The editor rhapsodizes as usual about the leading white citizens in this State "who have done so much for Negro welfare. It may be noted also," he opines, "that every forward step for the Advancement of Negroes in North Carolina has been due to the leadership of white citizens." The young man who edits the *News and Observer* during his father's absence in Mexico has never heard of Price, O'Kelly, Merrick, Charles H. Moore, Dudley, and hundreds of other Negroes who achieved far more with greater handicaps than is common to North Carolina citizenry. In fact, the editor of the Raleigh *News and Observer* is a perfect example of the tea-pouring class of "friends of the Negro." Too few of them make an effort to learn about their subject. It is so much easier to be patronizing when one is ignorant!

Other papers, notably the High Point *Enterprise* and the Greensboro *Daily News,* do not commit themselves editorially, but allow the usual editorializing in the news columns. One learns from the erudite High Point paper that *The Crisis* sells for $2.00 a year, and most of the money garnered for its sales goes into the National Association treasury. The high school boy who reports for that worthy journal confuses the methods of financing the National Association and *The Crisis* with methods used in operating several well known High Point enterprises. The *Daily News,* usually fair and dignified, indulges its Raleigh correspondent in his wit and humor to the extent that the reader is persuaded that Negroes go about the State with little fetishes made in the likeness of certain officers of the National

Association and *The Crisis;* that the average North Carolina Negro in time of trouble will invoke one of these fetishes in the manner common to white people who try to yell and cheer themselves out of an economic slump like the present depression.

What about the liberals at Chapel Hill? After several months of hemming and hawing, they have discovered that North Carolina is not a paradise for the Negro, and in spite of the tendency to make themselves into a mutual admiration society, something good might come from Chapel Hill. The difficulty confronting a state supported institution arises from the childish fear that the legislature has a perennial snooping committee on the look-out for liberal sentiments. Of course the University is bedeviled by having David Clark at Charlotte constantly yapping at its academic heels, but even this arch-prelate of Textiles and Big Money is not the demon that timid men like to imagine him to be.

The North Carolina Committee on Interracial Cooperation strives to take on new life and has succeeded in adopting a resolution which any single colored person on the committee might have urged, it seems, fifteen years ago. But progress moves like that. It is still regrettable that one part of the life of this organization is to create friction between the races by castigating at every turn of the road those colored people who do not subscribe to the milk and honey theory of race relations.

It is amusing to note that the forces of reaction are attempting to spread the propaganda that the National Association for the Advancement of Colored People has a standing sneer for teachers. Nothing could be farther from the truth. The teachers themselves have a just fear of the Philistines who are put in the influential places. But so long as Negroes accept the thesis that white people must think for Negroes, so long will the race be saddled with sycophants who remain secure by truckling to gullible white folk.

It is tragic to observe that the school board led by Leroy Martin has declared that there is "nothing it can do about the problem." Here again we see the cheap subterfuge of the Southern politician and his whining cohorts. What Martin should have said is that there is nothing that he *will* do about it! The Negro has only one weapon to use against Martin and his ilk. That weapon is the ballot. North Carolina Negroes must be registered if it takes fifty law suits to do it. Negroes are voting in considerable number in Virginia, and they should vote in North Carolina in even larger numbers. With an intelligent ballot, the Negro may not be able immediately to remake North Carolina society, but he should seek to join forces with those elements of the white population who are willing to vote the rascals out! If the new crowd is guilty of the same disregard of the Negro, then vote the new crowd out. Uncle Toms and their like will caution against this, but if a people have no ballot in a democracy, they have no power. The battle cry of North Carolina teachers certainly should be "Register. Vote. Vote out Leroy Martin through the crowd that put him in office."

The North Carolina Negro Teachers Association must be built on a new pattern. Take the organization out of the hands of weasel-worded, petty school politicians and throw the organization into State politics. Make this band of 3000 teachers a power for the improvement of the lot of the whole race. Put in a courageous set of men and women; clean house. In the house cleaning keep those worth keeping and junk the rest. Teachers should begin at once to caucus. If 2500 Negroes can be assembled to listen at Raleigh, 2500 teachers can be marshalled for action next April. Stop these stupid back-slapping sessions. Dispense with the dance the night before election if the dance will prevent the attendance at voting sessions. No more nominating committees; no more reports to be accepted on the hubbub of adjournment!

It is a pleasure to read the editorial in the October number of the *North Carolina Teachers Record*. "These evil times have come upon us because both white and Negro teachers have been too indifferent to their rights. They have been content to follow along in the rear of movements of which they might have formed a part and over which they might have exercised some control. They have feared that the stigma of taking a position in such affairs might endanger their jobs. That time let us hope, is past."

The fight of school teachers for salaries is only one phase of the larger fight against discrimination. Those people who have pretended to believe that the Negro can enjoy life in the South without having a right to participate in the government have had the props knocked from under them in the recent developments in North Carolina. The lynching at Burgaw has received the usual official glossing over. The Governor is "powerless" to do anything about it for the simple reason that the Negro vote is not strong enough nor sufficiently concentrated to make him do something about it. Remember Ehringhaus at the polls!

The gunfire directed at the attorneys who went to the defense of the two boys held on a capital charge at Henderson proved that these things can happen wherever Negroes do not participate in the government. That several prominent colored people who interested themselves in this case have received letters from local "good Negroes" should not alter the defense. Such tactics are usual, and are necessary concomitants of puppet leadership.

The crimes of violence against colored people in Guilford county which have resulted in farcical trials, even to the point that the presiding judge saw fit to lecture the jury on its astounding disregard of evidence, is in severe contrast to the railroading of Negroes to the electric chair from the same enlightened district. One shudders at the confusion in the minds of people who abhor lynching at the hands of a mob and yet raise no voice against lynching at the hands of the court.

In the matter of jobless relief and employment under the codes, Negroes have fared poorly. The relief agencies have shouldered responsibility on untrained colored workers because these people could be hired more cheaply. In spite of organized protest, relief agencies in North Carolina as in every other Southern state have been guilty of the same violation of decency in the matter of relief given Negroes. If North Carolina has been guilty to a less degree, it is because North Carolina Negroes have been organized to protest.

The new State Federation of Branches of the National Association for the Advancement of Colored People has a representative set of officers. Old and young will serve. Women received splendid recognition in the election of Charlotte Hawkins Brown and Julia Brown Delaney. George E. Nightingale is an example of courage to all young men who despair of the reactionary forces in our Southern cities. Conrad Pearson, H. C. Miller, George E. Fisher, and a score of others whose names make news in North Carolina not only were willing to serve, but accepted their tasks with an enthusiasm uncommon to acceptances of such offices. Here was a task for strong men, and it appears that strong men have accepted the challenge.

The Crisis, December, 1933; XL, 374-75. The *Pittsburgh Courier*, November 4, 1933, p. 4, gave extensive coverage to the Raleigh meeting.

9

PAN-AFRICA AND NEW RACIAL PHILOSOPHY
by W. E. B. Du Bois

One of the seminal expressions of Dr. Du Bois' always questing mind was the following essay that concentrated on the socioeconomic realities of world-wide racism and the need for serious probing of the ways to face and alter those realities.

During the last ten months, we have tried in *The Crisis* magazine to make a re-statement of the Negro problem in certain of its aspects. We began with the question of health and disease among us. Then we took up in succession our physical rate of increase, "Karl Marx and the Negro," "The Problem of Earning a Living," "Marxism and the Negro Problem," "The Negro Vote," "The Class Struggle Within the Race," "Negro Education," and "Our Problems of Religion."

We have considered all these matters in relation to the American Negro but our underlying thought has been continually that they can and must be seen not against any narrow, provincial or even national background, but in relation to the great problem of the colored races of the world and particularly those of African descent.

There are still large numbers of American Negroes who in all essential particulars conceive themselves as belonging to the white race. And this, not on account of their color, which may be yellow, brown or black, but on account of their history and their social surroundings. They react as white Americans. They have all the racial prejudices of white America, not only against Asiatics and Jews, but even against Mexicans and West Indians. In all questions of human interest, they would flock to white America before they would flock to the brown West Indies or to black Africa or to yellow Asia.

This, of course, is quite natural, and in a sense proves how idiotic most of our racial distinctions are. Here is a boy, born in America, of parents who were born in America, of grandparents and great grandparents born in America. He speaks the American twang; he reads American history, he gets his news from American papers, and he understands American baseball. It is impossible for that boy to think of himself as African, simply because he happens to be black. He *is* an American. But on the other hand, as he grows up and comprehends his surroundings, he is going to be made to think of himself as at least a peculiar sort of American. Against this, he is going to protest, logically and emotionally, and dwell upon the anomaly of a person being outcast and discriminated against in his own home. Gradually, however, he is going to find that this protest has only limited effect; that to most white Americans of today, Negro prejudice is something that is beyond question and will. It is a stark, true fact and little or nothing can be done about it at present. In the future, the long future, things may change. But they are not going to change in the lifetime of those now living.

So long now as this is an academic question, a matter of attitudes and thoughts and spiritual likes and dislikes, we can leave it there. But when it becomes an economic problem, a stark matter of bread and butter, then if this young, black American is going to survive and live a life, he must calmly face the fact that however much he is an American there are interests which draw him nearer to the dark people outside of America than to his white fellow citizens.

And those interests are the same matters of color caste, of discrimination, of exploitation for the sake of profit, of public insult and oppression, against which the colored peoples of Mexico, South America, the West Indies and all Africa, and every country in Asia, complain and have long been complaining. It is, therefore, simply a matter of ordinary common sense that these people should draw together in spiritual sympathy and intellectual co-operation, to see what can be done for the freedom of the human spirit which happens to be incased in dark skin.

This was the idea that was back of the Pan-African Congresses; started in Paris directly after the war, and carried on for several years. These Congresses brought upon themselves the active enmity and disparagement of all the colony-owning powers. Englishmen, Frenchmen, Belgians and others looked upon the movement as a political movement designed to foment disaffection and strife and to correct abuse by force.

It may be that in the end nothing but force will break down the injustice of the color line. But to us who have seen and known the futility of war, the ghastly paradox of talking about Victor and Vanquished in the last world holocaust, there is a feeling that we must desperately try methods of thought and co-operation and economic readjustment before we yield to councils of despair. And in this program, all that has been said about economic readjustment in America for American Negroes can be said with even more emphasis concerning the Negroes of the world and concerning the darker peoples. These people raise everything necessary to satisfy human wants. They are capable of carrying on every process by which material, transported and re-made, may satisfy the needs and appetites of men. They are all of them willing and eager to work, and yet because their work is misdirected in order to make a profit for white people, these dark people must starve and be unemployed.

Here in the United States the net result of the National Recovery Act so far has been to raise wages for a small number of favored white workers and to decrease wages or push out of employment entirely the Negro. It is possible that this present result may in time be changed, and we note with interest what Secretary Ickes has said to the State Engineers and Public Works Administration:

"It is important to bear in mind that the Public Works Administration is for the benefit of all the people of the country. The established policy in the construction of public buildings and public works under its control is that in the employment of mechanics and labor, preference be given to local labor to the extent that it is available and competent, and that there be no discrimination exercised against any person because of color or religious affiliation."

Nevertheless, this we feel is going to make little difference so long as the American people believe that any white man of whatever character or education is better than any possible colored man.

It is, therefore, imperative that the colored peoples of the world, and first of all those of Negro descent, should begin to concentrate upon this problem of their economic survival, the best of their brains and education. Pan-Africa means intellectual understanding and co-operation among all groups of Negro descent in order to bring about at the earliest possible time the industrial and spiritual emancipation of the Negro peoples.

Such a movement must begin with a certain spiritual housecleaning. American Negroes, West Indians, West Africans and South Africans must proceed immediately to wipe from their minds the preconcepts of each other which they have gained through white newspapers. They must cease to think of Liberia and Haiti as failures in government; of American Negroes as being engaged principally in frequenting Harlem cabarets and Southern lynching parties; of West Indians as ineffective talkers; and of West Africans as parading around in breech-clouts.

These are the pictures of each other which white people have painted for us and which with engaging naiveté we accept, and then proceed to laugh at each other and criticize each other before we make any attempt to learn the truth. There are, for instance, in the United States today several commendable groups of young people who are proposing to take hold of Liberia and emancipate her from her difficulties, quite forgetting the fact that Liberia belongs to Liberia. They made it. They suffered and died for it. And they are not handing over their country to any group of young strangers who happen to be interested. If we want to help Liberia, our business is to see in what respect the Liberians need help, and the persons best able to give this information are the Liberians themselves.

It is a large and intricate problem but the sooner we put ourselves in position to study it with a vast and increasing area of fact and with carefully guided and momentarily tested effort, the sooner we shall find ourselves citizens of the world and not its slaves and pensioners.

The Crisis, November, 1933; XL, 247, 262.

10

WHAT PRICE NATIONAL RECOVERY?

by John P. Davis

The realities of the early "New Deal," so far as Black people were concerned, are brought out in the following essay. Its author was a leading force in bringing into being both the Negro Industrial League and, especially, the Joint Committee on National Recovery. The latter was a prime inspiration for the movement of unity which led to the creation, in 1936, of the National Negro Congress, with John P. Davis as its executive secretary.

Since the latter part of 1929 citizens of the United States have felt the effects of an economic condition which has steadily grown worse. The reasons given for this depression in our economic structure have been as varied as the persons giving them. All, however, have agreed to the outward manifestations occasioned by this condition.

The farmer raised live stock and farm produce in larger quantities than ever before, but found that he could not sell these increased quantities for enough to make a profit. On the other hand the urban worker in factory and mill was manufacturing goods for which there was a steadily diminishing market. The number of unemployed increased; the pay of industrial workers, collectively and individually, decreased. There was great reduction in the amount of goods inter-changed and this resulted in reduced freight car loadings, in lower valuation of stocks and bonds, in the wholesale failure of banks and insurance companies. These failures wiped out the savings of working people. Those who had money to lend feared to do so in a period of economic chaos. There was hoarding by individuals and by banks. This meant that credit was difficult to secure. Factories closed and men and women were thrown out of jobs. The depression continued and the normal agencies for charity and relief were unable to cope with the need of millions of jobless men and women, whose savings had become exhausted during an abnormal period of unemployment. The health and education of children suffered. Vagrancy and crime increased.

In all this picture the Negro suffered most. A marginal worker, he was the first to lose his job. A low paid worker, he had less reserve on which to live during unemployment. Often discrimination on the ground of color prevented him from securing his full share of the private and public charity furnished to unemployed workers generally. The so-called "Negro-jobs" were invaded by white workers who had been displaced from better jobs. In the South coercion and violence were used to drive Negro workers out of gainful employment. On the farm the Negro tenant farmer bore the brunt of low farm prices. The Negro farm owner was the first to lose his farm by foreclosure. Negro business, dependent almost entirely on Negro patronage, and operat-ing on a narrow margin of profit, also suffered most because of the extreme decrease in the buying power of its clientele. Although the Negro was but 12 out of every 100 persons in the population of the country, he represented about 30 out of every 100 sufferers in the depression.

Partially because of failure to realize the seriousness of the situation and partially because of callous indifference, officers of the govern-ment—federal, state and local—delayed in taking necessary remedies. And conditions became worse. Then came a change of administration and with it a new program for the solution of problems which had become acute. Whatever may be said in criticism of the remedies offered by the Roosevelt administration, it cannot be denied that, in theory at least, they were vigorous and concrete. Backed by an over-whelming congressional majority, the administration initiated brand new types of social legislation. "Brain trust" professors from Northern colleges were given the privilege of drafting legislation which had been the dream of their lives. For every ailment of the body politic there was a professor and a panacea.

There is little need for chronological analysis of the new legislation. Each enactment is but one part of a completed concept, a federal design for national recovery. The National Industrial Recovery Act stands out above all of these new devices for prosperity. Title I of this act created the National Recovery Administration. The function of this new agency is to bring back prosperity to industry and the industrial worker. The plan is to increase the buying power of workers in industry by increasing wages. Further by reducing the number of hours worked by each industrial wage earner, there will be created surplus man hours to be parcelled out to unemployed men and women. Naturally industry cannot take on more men and pay higher wages unless it increases the cost of products of their labor. This increase in price will be passed along to the consumer of the product. But this, it is said, will not be detrimental since the consumer will have more with which to buy. Thus in the scheme of things a circle of higher wages and higher prices leading to prosperity will take the place of the downward spiral of lower prices and lower wages.

There was every reason to hope that this new plan would destroy the inequality between white and black labor. The establishment of uniform minimum wages would normally result in the abolition of a system whereby black workers doing the same work as white workers and working longer hours received less pay than they. At all events it was not to be supposed that the new plan would create greater hardship to Negro labor than that to which it was subjected before the plan was put into effect. Indeed, assurance was glibly given by General Hugh S. Johnson, Administrator of the act, and others that this plan involved no race question.

Yet what has happened in the formation of the codes of fair competition, setting up wage and hours of service levels, has furnished ample proof that there is a problem of vicious discrimination to be faced.

The first code of fair competition approved by the administration was that for the cotton textile industry. This code established a minimum wage of $12 a week for the South and $13 a week for the North. Employees under the code were not to be employed more than 40 hours a week. Incidentally the cleaners, outside crews, and yardmen were not to be given benefits of a minimum wage or limitation of weekly hours of service. There was nothing on the surface of these provisions which indicated that Negro workers were to be treated any differently than white workers. But the reason for these exceptions are not hard to find, when it is realized that of the 14,000 Negro workers in this industry more than 10,000 of them come within the categories denied the benefits of the code. For these workers the NRA meant increases of from 10 to 40 per cent in the cost of everything they had to buy, without a single penny in increased wages, without a single hour subtracted from their working period. Because hours had not been reduced there were no available jobs for unemployed Negro workers.

Discrimination against Negro workers successfully achieved in the first code of fair competition lent courage to future efforts. In the same manner the discrimination in the cotton textile industry was extended to other branches of the textile industry. Thousands more Negro workers felt the effect of prejudice.

In the lumber industry a new type of discrimination was used. Here most of the Negro labor was to be found in the South. For this reason a wage of 23 cents an hour was established for the Southern branch of the industry while wages in other sections of the country, where the labor used was chiefly white, were set at 40 cents an hour. This meant that the Negro worker performing the same work in the South as the white worker was doing in the West would receive $6.80 a week less than the white saw mill operative. Calculated in terms of the total annual loss in wages which Negro workers suffered through the approval of this code, the astounding figure of more than 40 million dollars is reached. In codes affecting hundreds of thousands of Negro workers the same formula of discrimination has been used. In the steel code, Robert P. Lamont, president of the American Iron and Steel Institute, offered publicly to pay a wage of 30 cents an hour to steel workers in the Birmingham and Southern Districts in place of the 25 and 27 cents hourly rates previously offered. Despite this offer from the employer group the government finally approved the earlier minima with the consequent result that Negro steel workers in Jefferson County, Alabama, were denied pay increases of $484,000 annually; while those in the rest of the South were subjected to a potential loss of more than a million dollars yearly.

The plans for excluding most Negro industrial workers from the benefits of the increased wage and shorter hours have become bolder and bolder. Southern groups have started definite campaigns to secure government approval of a plan to pay Negro workers less than is paid whites. Even the establishment of the low wage in the lumber industry led to the open threats of saw mill owners to discharge Negro workers for the reason that "the payment of equal wages to whites and blacks would lead to social equality." In the North where Negro skilled workers were receiving wages in excess of the newly established minimum their wage in many instances has been reduced to that minimum. In other instances although bound by law to pay certain wages, white employers have openly violated the labor clauses of the code where Negroes are concerned and nothing has yet been done by the government.

As biting as has been the discrimination directed against Negro industrial workers, it has not presented one-half as serious a problem as that presented by the failure of the federal government to devise a way to improve the wage of household employees. There are more than two million domestics, most of them women, in the United States. Of this number 57 per cent are Negro. Of every 100 Negroes gainfully employed 26 are in this class of employment. They represent the lowest paid group in America, wages being as low in some cases as $1 a week for 60 or more hours of work. For these workers there is no code. They will feel just as much as any other consumer the burden of increased prices, yet they will receive no increase in wages, no shortening of hours.

It will serve no purpose to expand on the inequities appearing in the new federal design for recovery. There is neither space nor need for such analysis. It is sufficient to state that careful study of any of these measures will result in the blunt realization that Negro interests are in danger of serious impairment unless Negro organizations themselves become active and alert in opposition to discriminations as they appear.

It was an awakening to this fact that led to the formation of the Negro Industrial League. It was this organization that stood alone in protest at the public hearings held for the first code of fair competition. And it was through the effort of this organization that sixteen other national organizations joined in the formation of the Joint Committee on National Recovery.

The objectives of this new alliance are plain. It was the belief of those instrumental in its creation that all organizations seeking economic betterment of the Negro should come together and agree upon a policy for Negro advancement. It was further believed that recommendations should be made to those officers of the government who had authority to act. In no other way could responsibility for failure to act be definitely fixed. The efforts of the Joint Committee are non-partisan and non-political. It seeks the federal appointment of qualified colored men and women to positions of usefulness to the race, but it has no concern with the fate or fortunes of individual job-hunters or favor-seekers. In a word what has been attempted is the establishment of a group of fact finders in Washington to study the plans of the federal government for recovery and to seek to integrate the Negro into such plans. To accomplish this object there is need for intelligent cooperation of all persons and agencies interested in Negro welfare. Above all things the Joint Committee has but one cause to plead, and that cause is the economic advancement of colored people. It is responsible to but one interest, and that interest is the masses of Negro citizens of this country represented in the membership of one or more of the cooperating organizations. Today it is the machinery through which the elected representatives of more than three million organized Negro citizens have chosen to speak.

The work of the Joint Committee is many sided. It has studied codes of fair competition ferreting out by careful analysis clauses directed against Negro labor. It has filed briefs, made appearances at public hearings, buttonholed administrative officers relative to the elimination of unfair clauses in the codes. It has in the same way studied other major recovery measures and sought fair dealing at the hands of the press and to leaders of both races the inequities apparent in these measures. Dissatisfied with simple opinion as to the true facts of the discrimination, it has as far as possible made field investigations of labor conditions and cost of living among Negro workers; and has with a splendid corps of volunteer experts amassed a wealth of information about Negro labor.

Without question this work has had an effect on the problems faced by Negro citizens. It has made impossible casuistical treatment of Negro labor by administrative officers. These government officials have been brought face to face with the realities of race prejudice in industry. The appearance of the Joint Committee in public hearings has won for it the respect of labor leaders, of liberal federal officials, of the white press.

It is too early to state what the effect of this new unified force will be upon those who have power to alter or maintain the present economic condition of the Negro. But it does not seem too soon to state that the Unified and determined action of this federation of

Negro organizations represents a step forward in the fight for complete economic equality in agricultural and industrial America. To this purpose the organizations which compose the membership of the Joint Committee and the leadership to which its policies are entrusted, are unalterably committed. The fight has only just begun. That it shall continue until real dollars find their way into the pockets of jobless Negro men and women, until there is definite action taken to protect the economic interests of all citizens of the nation, is a determination that will not be destroyed.

The Crisis, December, 1933; XL, 271-72.

11

BLACK PEOPLE IN THE SOUTH AND "RELIEF" UNDER THE NEW DEAL: SOME LETTERS

In *The Crisis* (November, 1934) was published a series of letters from the South indicative of living conditions for Black people and of the administration of measures supposedly aimed at alleviating those conditions. These letters were introduced by *The Crisis* editor (unsigned, but Roy Wilkins held this post at that time) as follows: "These are human documents indicating how far the Federal Emergency Relief Administration will have to go beyond mere routine work if it is to bring even a bare existence to the forgotten colored people in the South, and especially the rural South."

.... , Ala.
April 27, 1934

N.A.A.C.P. Dear Sir:—Please allow me to present a question to you which with myself is very important because I am one of the persons of families that is in very bad need of aid an up to this date have been denied so it have retch the stage that something must be did. It is a well known fact that one cannot live without food and clothes so a friend and myself being among the unemployed and is not getting any aid so far from the public welfare of this county is asking for aid or information about aid from some sorce. Will you see after this matter at once. We get a small order some time and for months can't get anything. Its awful bad to wait for someone who does not care to give you food. Is not there some way or some sorce that we colored people can overcome being shadowed by starvation and depending on something that will not give you food. Please inform me at once if there is any other sorce of getting any relief. We are depending on you for relief or information as to where we might get food. We must have something at once. Please let me know at once.

We will be waiting an answer from you.

Very truly yours,

....

P.S. We are men of families.

.................., Ga.
Jan. 24. 1934

Dear Sir:—Sometime ago about 6 or 7 wekes ago my boy went up in town to sign to get on the releaf work to get some of the govnor money he was out of a job and I am a poor widder woman with a house full of little childrens and a cripple girl to take ceare of they woulden let him sign the white peoples knocked him down run him out of town woulden let him com back to town he went back to town in about 5 weakes they got after him agin about a hundred head of white mens with knives and they run him all ove town they cout him they throwed him in the back of a truck hog fashion he got out som way they put a Bulldog on him then he ran in a stor then som of the collord mens beg the cheef police to put him in jale to keepe the mob from killing him the cheaff say let them kill him just so they dont mobb him heare in town the night marshell put him in jale for safe keeping and I hade to pay him $5.00 to get him out and he had to leave town dont be see heare no more if they see him enny more they will sure kill him he left in the night walking with no money I wont able to gave him nothing and I want him to help me that is my sun he is just 17 years old.

Just write to help me if you all please take up far me and help me I am his mother my name is ....

................, Miss.
April 30, 1934

Dear Sir: This is .... asking for help for my mother her name is .... So she says that her age is 84. She says that she was 9 years old when Peace declaired you can tell from that just how ole she is she was large enough to carry water in the time of the War & now she is here sick in bed & has been since February the 25. & I have ben to the Red Cross & also the Relief

ofice asking for help & they would not help me with a Dr & neither did they fill a medical prescription for me after the Dr. come to my call she is yet sick & haven got shoes or close & a very little to eat & I am her daughter I haven got work to do to help my self out in paying house rent & nothing in my house to eat & no close to wear The relief has never give me one yrd of cloth & neither a pair of shoes since they started this work up here in . . . .
I have 3 in family my mother & myself & one child & the child only makes $1.50c one dollar & fifty cts (a week) & you knows without me telling you that will not pay rent & get close & make Grocery we are sufering here I will speak the truth. I haven got bread in my home to eat & nothing to buy it with. The relief give me 3 days work last week for the first time & no Grocery at all & I had to gave that to the rent man I ows him this morning $12.00 twelve dollars & he is telling me today if I cannot pay the rent to give him his house what must I do I am renting from a man by the name of . . . . Please help me & famely at once.
From . . . .

. . . . , Miss.
Mar. 22, 1934

N.A.A.C.P. Gentlemen:—In reply to yours of the 8th Inst. to making reports on conditions that exists against our people under the N.R.A. and other relief agencies in this City. I will say that they are very bad. One of the cases is that of a man of our race about 65 or 70 yrs. of age with 8 in family his name is . . . . He was threatened with arrest for pressing the relief agency for assistance. He wanted food for himself and family. He is in bad health, Miss. . . . ., who is managing the relief here is the one that threatened to arrest him because he insisted on them to give him food. Later she became more vexed at him and taken him in her Machine to a Pecan Factory. and offered him to the management for 60c per day. Which he refused and told her that the Factory was not working according to the Code. Mr. . . . . has been refused assistance on Two occasions that he applied. From the same office. He has also been registered with the Government Re-employment Office since the first opening, and up to now has not had a days work. He has a wife a Mother-in-law 77 yrs. old. and no job, no relief, he has not had work for 3½ yrs.

. . . .

..............., La.

Feb. 13, 1934

N.A.A.C.P. Your Honor:—I am writing you asking you if you will through your honorable organization assist me in procuring work on the C.W.A., P.W.A. or Direct relief. I have been deprived of work since Oct. 20th, 1933. All because I wrote several letters to Washington asking for work. I registered with the N.R.S. about Nov. 13, 1933. and just because I wrote those letters to Washington that office refused to call me out on any job. Being denied of work so long I was forced to apply for direct relief and the woman Parrish director of the E.R.A. told me because I had quit a job in Sept. that only paid me $2.00 per week 10-to-14 hours per day and because I had written several letters to Washington reporting this office she said you will not get any direct relief here. I will show you that you cannot run this office. You have been quarrelling with this office all the year. I will show you that you can't run this office. I have explained the situation to every legal authority I knew, even the President and the F.C.W.A. and the F.C.W.A. of La. and the E.R.A. of La. and the only thing that I can get is an answer as though I am seeking information. I am not seeking information I am asking for justice. Now since I cannot of myself get justice I am asking you to take this matter up with the legal authority of this country. I am enclosing a few letters received from Washington and New Orleans but such letters dont help me any I need food and raiment for my wife and children. I have not had one day of relief work since Oct. 20th 1933.

Please let me hear from you at your earliest convenience.

Yours sincerely,

....

..............., South Carolina

June 11, 1934

Dear Sir:—I am writing you these few lines ask you if it is any possible chance of you fining out just why F.E.R.A. office here in .... refuse to gave me work when I have six in family to care for and also my wife's mother who is over 65 years old and been under the Doctor care for the past seven years of course my wife has a little job but its not with the relief work which some weeks she make five dollars and some weeks less with four children to take care off which range in age 8–6–4–3 years old and we have $5 per month rent and also $1.74 per week Insurance which that dont enclude Food and Clothing and Fuel to burn. Now Mr.

White in the past two and half months I am being going to the relief office trying to get on the relief work and it seem like it is empossible and also just before the first of April I went up to the relief office and explain my case to Mr. ...., the man that gave out the work cards and he gave me a food order for the amount of $2—two dollars and also I got some work to do. But as soon as I got paid for the 24 hours work he came to me to collect $2 for the food order that he gave me and I refuse to gave him $2 and I havent been able to get any more work to do and I have been going up to the office each day sence. But they tell me at the office that they cant gave me work because my wife is working. Of course if that maybe the case I can gave you the name and the address of at least a hundred families where their is two and three in one family who are working on the relief project and I know of at least twenty single men with no one but theirself to take care of and are working 24 hours every week and they got to gave their foreman one dollar each every week if they want to stay on the job.

Now Mr. White the white man who my wife work for and my wife told him that they refuse to gave me work because she was working for me and he went up to relief office to see about it But they told him that they didnt cut me out of work because my wife were working but the cut me off because I were unable to do the work. and of course I know that to be very much untrue. The trouble is I refuse to be a fool like so many of my race here and else where around here to pay for a food order that is supose to be giving to the needy free of charge but lots are paying for them and also paying for their job. Of course Mr. White I am colored and when you go up to the relief office The Colored people is treated just as if they were dogs and not human beings. I have been up in the office and I have seen with my own eyes my color kicked and beaten down a whole flight of stairs. I have seen every thing done except been murder. Understand Mr. White the little job that my wife has isnt on the releif is a private and everybody that is head of any thing here in the releif office is kin to one another. Now Mr. White the lady that is head of the relief is Mrs. .... which I saw her once since I was cut off from work and I explained my case to her and she told that she would send a investigator around to my home the next morning whose name is Miss .... and she told me that when I gave Mr. .... the $2 for the food order she would O.K. my work card. Mr. White if possible will you please fine out for me just what is the reason they refuse to gave me work when I have six in family and rent to pay. Insurance, Doctor bill, milk bill, buy food and clothing with only my wife at work it is 'impossible Mr. White.

. . . .

. . . ., Ala.

June 21, 1934

N.A.A.C.P. Dear Sir. My name is . . . . I wrote you some time ago concerning the relief department an received a answer I received a grocer on the 8th of May an since that time I have ben completly without food since then so I received this one on the 20th of June I am sending it to you as a proof of how the relief system is carried on 93¢ just enough for a days eating before then I had not received nothing since Febuary they will expect me to live on this for more than a month please consider this as a serious matter an help us if it is possible to do so you may do what you think is best with this order I will be looking for a answer from you soon.

Very truly yours.

. . . .

. . . ., La.

April 3, 1934

Dear Sir:—Only few line to ask you to do something for us down hear in Plaquemines Parish. We have report to the E.R.A. and they dont gave us any work and dont gave relif to the colored people. so kindly got in tutch with Washington. See why they dont gave us work and dont wont to gave relif down hear in Plaquemines Parish. Miss Marjorie Rickey is Parish Director. Bad place to recave mail. No work to make a living, no money to leave. this will bee all for today kindly do this faver for us. From

. . . .

12

I HAVE SEEN BLACK HANDS

by Richard Wright

Up from Mississippi and into the Chicago ghetto came the young Richard Wright (1908–1960). Among his earlier work was this impassioned poem that captures so much of the anguish and hope of the 1930's. It was published in *New Masses*, June 26, 1934 (Vol. XI, No. 13, p. 16).

I

I am black and I have seen black hands, millions and millions of them—

Out of millions of bundles of wool and flannel tiny black fingers have reached restlessly and hungrily for life,

Reached out for the black nipples at the black breasts of black mothers,

And they've held red, green, blue, yellow, orange, white, and purple toys in the childish grips of possession,

And chocolate drops, peppermint sticks, lollypops, wineballs, ice cream cones, and sugared cookies in fingers sticky and gummy,

And they've held balls and bats and gloves and marbles and jack-knives and sling-shots and spinning tops in the thrill of sport and play,

And pennies and nickels and dimes and quarters and sometimes on New Year's, Easter, Lincoln's Birthday, May Day, a brand new green dollar bill,

They've held pens and rulers and maps and tablets and books in palms spotted and smeared with ink,

And they've held dice and cards and half-pint flasks and cue sticks and cigars and cigarettes in the pride of new maturity . . .

II

I am black and I have seen black hands, millions and millions of them—

They were tired and awkward and calloused and grimy and covered with hangnails,

And they were caught in the fast-moving belts of machines and snagged and smashed and crushed,

And they jerked up and down at the throbbing machines massing taller and taller the heaps of gold in the banks of bosses,

And they piled higher and higher the steel, iron, the lumber, wheat, rye, the oats, corn, the cotton, the wool, the oil, the coal, the meat, the fruit, the glass, and the stone until there was too much to be used,

And they grabbed guns and slung them on their shoulders and marched and groped in trenches and fought and killed and conquered nations who were customers for the goods black hands had made,

And again black hands stacked goods higher and higher until there was too much to be used,

And then the black hands held trembling at the factory gates the
dreaded lay-off slip,
And the black hands hung idle and swung empty and grew soft and
got weak and bony from unemployment and starvation.
And they grow nervous and sweaty, and opened and shut in anguish
and doubt and hesitation and irresolution . . .

III

I am black and I have seen black hands, millions and millions of
them—
Reaching hesitantly out of days of slow death for the goods they had
made, but the bosses warned that the goods were private and did
not belong to them,
And the black hands struck desperately out in defence of life and
there was blood, but the enraged bosses decreed that this too
was wrong,
And the black hands felt the cold steel bars of the prison they had
made, in despair tested their strength and found that they could
neither bend nor break them,
And the black hands fought and scratched and held back but a
thousand white hands took them and tied them,
And the black hands lifted palms in mute and futile supplication to
the sodden faces of mobs wild in the revelries of sadism,
And the black hands strained and clawed and struggled in vain at the
noose that tightened about the black throat,
And the black hands waved and beat fearfully at the tall flames that
cooked and charred the black flesh . . .

IV

I am black and I have seen black hands
Raised in fists of revolt, side by side with the white fists of white
workers,
And some day—and it is only this which sustains me—
Some day there shall be millions and millions of them,
On some red day in a burst of fists on a new horizon!

13

ON THE MEANINGS OF "SEGREGATION" AND THE STRUGGLE FOR AFRO-AMERICAN SURVIVAL

The persistence of the Great Depression, its terrible impact upon Black people and the generally racist application of New Deal measures—themselves very partial palliatives even where white people were concerned—led Dr. Du Bois to emphasize with increasing insistence the consequence of socioeconomic matters as against legal ones and the importance of a worldwide crusade against imperialism. Both these considerations brought him into mounting quarrels with the N.A.A.C.P. board and, finally, in the summer of 1934, to his resignation from the organization he had done so much to create and build. There follow several documents illustrating this important development. The first document [a] is a rather brief editorial statement by Du Bois in the January, 1934, *Crisis;* document [b] is a longer, signed essay by Du Bois in the following issue, reiterating his thinking and inviting discussion in the magazine; document [c] consists of the comments from three people, including Walter White, appearing in the March *Crisis;* document [d] is the commentary on these discussion pieces by Dr. Du Bois, appearing in the April *Crisis;* document [e] is the full text of Du Bois' letter of resignation from the N.A.A.C.P.

[a]

SEGREGATION
by W. E. B. Du Bois

The thinking colored people of the United States must stop being stampeded by the word segregation. The opposition to racial segregation is not or should not be any distaste or unwillingness of colored people to work with each other, to co-operate with each other, to live with each other. The opposition to segregation is an opposition to discrimination. The experience in the United States has been that usually when there is racial segregation, there is also racial discrimination.

But the two things do not necessarily go together, and there should never be an opposition to segregation pure and simple unless that segregation does involve discrimination. Not only is there no objection to colored people living beside colored people if the surroundings and treatment involve no discrimination, if streets are well lighted, if there is water, sewerage and police protection, and if anybody of any color who wishes, can live in that neighborhood. The same way in schools, there is no objection to schools attended by colored pupils and taught by colored teachers. On the contrary, colored pupils can by our own contention be as fine human beings as any other sort of children, and we certainly know that there are no teachers better than trained colored teachers. But if the existence of such a school is made reason and cause for giving it worse housing, poorer facilities, poorer equipment and poorer teachers, then we do object, and the objection is not against the color of the pupils' or teachers' skins, but against the discrimination.

In the recent endeavor of the United States government to redistribute capital so that some of the disadvantaged groups may get a chance for development, the American Negro should voluntarily and insistently demand his share. Groups of communities and farms inhabited by colored folk should be voluntarily formed. In no case should there be any discrimination against white and blacks. But, at the same time, colored people should come forward, should organize and conduct enterprises, and their only insistence should be that the same provisions be made for the success of their enterprise that is being made for the success of any other enterprise. It must be remembered that in the last quarter of a century, the advance of the colored people has been mainly in the lines where they themselves working by and for themselves, have accomplished the greatest advance.

There is no doubt that numbers of white people, perhaps the majority of Americans, stand ready to take the most distinct advantage of voluntary segregation and cooperation among colored people. Just as soon as they get a group of black folk segregated, they use it as a point of attack and discrimination. Our counter attack should be, therefore, against this discrimination; against the refusal of the South to spend the same amount of money on the black child as on the white child for its education; against the inability of black groups to use public capital; against the monopoly of credit by white groups. But never in the world should our fight be against association with ourselves because by that very token we give up the whole argument that we are worth associating with.

Doubtless, and in the long run, the greatest human development is going to take place under experiences of widest individual contact. Nevertheless, today such individual contact is made difficult and almost impossible by petty prejudice, deliberate and almost criminal propaganda and various survivals from prehistoric heathenism. It is impossible, therefore, to wait for the millennium of free and normal intercourse before we unite, to co-operate among themselves in groups of like-minded people and in groups of people suffering from the same disadvantages and the same hatreds.

It is the class-conscious working man uniting together who will eventually emancipate labor throughout the world. It is the race-conscious black man cooperating together in his own institutions and movements who will eventually emancipate the colored race, and the great step ahead today is for the American Negro to accomplish his economic emancipation through voluntary determined cooperative effort.

The Crisis, January, 1934; XLI, 20.

[b]

A FREE FORUM: THE N.A.A.C.P.
AND RACE SEGREGATION
by W. E. B. Du Bois

From the day of its beginning, more than twenty-three years ago, *The Crisis* has sought to maintain a free forum for the discussion of the Negro problem. The Editor has had advantage in time and space for expressing his own opinion, but he has tried also to let other and radically antagonistic opinions have place for expression. And above all, he has sought not to make the N.A.A.C.P. responsible for his individual ideas.

To some this has seemed an anomaly. They have thought that the National Organ of an organization should always express officially what that organization thinks. But a moment of reflection will show that this is impossible. The thought of an organization is always in flux and is never definitely recorded until after long consideration. Meantime, a living periodical reflects opinions and not decisions. And it is for this reason that the editorials of *The Crisis* have always appeared as signed individual opinions of the Editor and not as the recorded decisions of the N.A.A.C.P. This has given vividness and flexibility to the magazine and at the same time has allowed differences of opinion to be thoroughly threshed out.

This policy so long continued will be carried on, we trust, even more vigorously in the year 1934. And just as in earlier years we discussed Social Equality at a time when there was no unity of opinion within or without the organization, so this year we are going to discuss Segregation and seek not dogma but enlightenment. For this purpose, we are earnestly asking not only that our readers read carefully what is going to be said, but also that they contribute their thoughts and experiences for the enlightenment of other readers. It goes without saying that we cannot publish all these contributions but we shall read them over and try honestly to reflect in these pages a new and changing philosophy concerning race segregation in the United States.

There is a good deal of misapprehension as to the historic attitude of the National Association for the Advancement of Colored People and race segregation. As a matter of fact, the Association, while it has from time to time discussed the larger aspects of this matter, has taken no general stand and adopted no general philosophy. Of course its action, and often very effective action, has been in specific cases of segregation where the call for a definite stand was clear and decided. For instance, in the preliminary National Negro Convention which met in New York May 31st and June 1st, 1909, segregation was only mentioned in a protest against Jim-Crow car laws and that because of an amendment by William M. Trotter. In the First Annual Report, January 1, 1911, the Association evolved a statement of its purpose, which said that "it seeks to uplift the colored men and women of this country by securing to them the full enjoyment of their rights as citizens, justice in all courts, and equality of opportunity everywhere." Later, this general statement was epitomized in the well-known declaration: "It conceives its mission to be the completion of the work which the great Emancipator began. It proposes to make a group of ten million Americans free from the lingering shackles of past slavery, physically free from peonage, mentally free from ignorance, politically free from disfranchisement, and socially free from insult." This phrase which I first wrote myself for the Annual Report of 1915 still expresses pregnantly the object of the N.A.A.C.P. and it has my own entire adherence.

It will be noted, however, that here again segregation comes in only by implication. Specifically, it was first spoken of in the Second Report of the Association, January 1, 1912, when the attempt to destroy the property of Negroes in Kansas City because they had moved into a white section was taken up. This began our fight on a specific phase of segregation, namely, the attempt to establish a Negro ghetto by force of law. This phase of segregation we fought vigorously for years and often achieved notable victories in the highest courts of the land.

But it will be noted that the N.A.A.C.P. expressed no opinion as to whether it might not be a feasible and advisable thing for colored people to establish their own residential sections, or their own towns; and certainly there was nothing expressed or implied that Negroes should not organize for promoting their own interests in industry, literature or art. Manifestly, here was opportunity for considerable difference of opinion, but the matter never was thoroughly threshed out.

The Association moved on to other matters of color discrimination: the "Full Crew" bills which led to dismissal of so many Negro railway employees; the "Jim-Crow" car laws on railway trains and street cars; the segregation in government departments. In all these matters, the stand of the Association was clear and unequivocal: it held that it was a gross injustice to make special rules which discriminated against the color of employees or patrons.

In the Sixth Annual Report issued in March, 1916, the seven lines of endeavor of the Association included change of unfair laws, better administration of present laws, justice in the courts, stoppage of public slander, the investigation of facts, the encouragement of distinguished work by Negroes, and organizations.

Very soon, however, there came up a more complex question and that was the matter of Negro schools. The Association had avoided from the beginning any thorough-going pronouncement on this matter. In the resolutions of 1909, the conference asked: "Equal educational opportunities for all and in all the states, and that public school expenditure be the same for the Negro and white child." This of course did not touch the real problem of separate schools. Very soon, however, definite problems were presented to the Association: the exclusion of colored girls from the Oberlin dormitories in 1919; the discrimination in the School of Education at the University of Pennsylvania; and the Cincinnati fight against establishing a separate school for colored children, brought the matter squarely to the front. Later, further cases came; the Brooklyn Girls' High School, the matter of a colored High School in Indianapolis, and the celebrated Gary case.

Gradually, in these cases the attitude of the Association crystallized. It declared that further extension of segregated schools for particular races and especially for Negroes was unwise and dangerous, and the Association undertook in all possible cases to oppose such further segregation. It did not, however, for a moment feel called upon to attack the separate schools where most colored children are educated throughout the United States and it refrained from this not because it approved of separate schools, but because it was faced by a fact and not a theory. It saw no sense in tilting against windmills.

The case at Cheyney was a variation; here was an old and separate private school which became in effect though not in law a separate public normal school; and in the city of Philadelphia a partial system of elementary Negro schools was developed with no definite action on the part of the N.A.A.C.P.

It will be seen that in all these cases the Association was attacking specific instances and not attempting to lay down any general rule as to how far the advancement of the colored race in the United States was going to involve separate racial action and segregated organization of Negroes for certain ends.

To be sure, the overwhelming and underlying thought of the N.A.A.C.P. has always been that any discrimination based simply on race is fundamentally wrong, and that consequently purely racial organizations must have strong justification to be admissible. On the other hand, they faced certain unfortunate but undeniable facts. For instance, War came. The Negro was being drafted. No Negro officers were being commissioned. The N.A.A.C.P. asked for the admission of Negroes to the officers' schools. This was denied. There was only one further thing to do and that was to ask for a school for Negro officers. There arose a bitter protest among many Negroes against this movement. Nevertheless, the argument for it was absolutely unanswerable, and Joel E. Spingarn, Chairman of the Board, supported by the students of Howard University, launched a movement which resulted in the commissioning of seven hundred Negro officers in the A.E.F. In all the British Dominions, with their hundreds of millions of colored folk, there was not a single officer of known Negro blood. The American Negro scored a tremendous triumph against the Color Line by their admitted and open policy of segregation. This did not mean that Mr. Spingarn or any of the members of the N.A.A.C.P. thought it right that there should be a separate Negro camp, but they thought a separate Negro camp and Negro officers was infinitely better than no camp and no Negro officers and that was the only practical choice that lay before them.

Similarly, in the question of the Negro vote, the N.A.A.C.P. began in 1920 an attempt to organize the Negro vote and cast it in opposition to open enemies of the Negro race who were running for office. This was without doubt a species of segregation. It was appealing to voters on the grounds of race, and it brought for that reason considerable opposition. Nevertheless, it could be defended on the ground that the election of enemies of the Negro race was not only a blow to that race but to the white race and to all civilization. And while our attitude, even in the Parker case, has been criticized, it has on the whole found abundant justification. The final problem in segregation presented to us was that of the Harlem Hospital. Here was a hospital in the center of a great Negro population which for years did not have and would not admit a single Negro physician to its staff. Finally, by agitation and by political power, Negroes obtained representation on the staff in considerable numbers and membership on the Board of Control. It was a great triumph. But it was accompanied by reaction on the part of whites and some Negroes who had opposed this movement, and an attempt to change the status of the hospital so that it would become a segregated Negro hospital, and so that presumably the other hospitals of the city would continue to exclude Negroes from their staffs. With this arose a movement to establish Negro hospitals throughout the United States.

Here was an exceedingly difficult problem. On the one hand, there is no doubt of the need of the Negro population for wider and better hospitalization; and of the demand on the part of Negro physicians for opportunities of hospital practice. This was illustrated by the celebrated Tuskegee hospital where nearly all the Negro veterans are segregated but where an efficient Negro staff has been installed. Perhaps nothing illustrates better than this the contradiction and paradox of the problem of race segregation in the United States, and the problem which the N.A.A.C.P. faced and still faces.

The N.A.A.C.P. opposed the initial establishment of the hospital at Tuskegee although it is doubtful if it would have opposed such a hospital in the North. On the other hand, once established, we fought to defend the Tuskegee hospital and give it widest opportunity.

In other words, the N.A.A.C.P. has never officially opposed separate Negro organizations such as churches, schools and business and cultural organizations. It has never denied the recurrent necessity of united separate action on the part of Negroes for self-defense and self-development; but it has insistently and continually pointed out that such action is in any case a necessary evil involving often a recognition from within of the very color line which we are fighting without. That race pride and race loyalty, Negro ideals and Negro unity, have a place and function today, the N.A.A.C.P. never has denied and never can deny.

But all this simply touches the whole question of racial organization and initiative. No matter what we may wish or say, the vast majority of the Negroes in the United States are born in colored homes, educated in separate colored schools, attend separate colored churches, marry colored mates, and find their amusement in colored Y.M.C.A.'s and Y.W.C.A.'s. Even in their economic life, they are gradually being forced out of the place in industry which they occupied in the white world and are being compelled to seek their living among themselves. Here is segregation with a vengeance, and its problems must be met and its course guided. It would be idiotic simply to sit on the side lines and yell: "No segregation" in an increasingly segregated world.

On the other hand, the danger of easily and eagerly yielding to suggested racial segregation without reason or pressure stares us ever in the face. We segregate ourselves. We herd together. We do things such as this clipping from the *Atlanta Constitution* indicates:

A lecture on the raising of Lazarus from the dead will be delivered at the city auditorium on Friday night. The Big Bethel choir will sing and the Graham Jackson band will give additional music. Space has been set aside for white people.

The "Jim Crow" galleries of Southern moving picture houses are filled with some of the best Negro citizens. Separate schools and other institutions have been asked by Negroes in the north when the whites had made no real demand.

Such are the flat and undeniable facts. What are we going to do about them? We can neither yell them down nor make them disappear by resolutions. We must think and act. It is this problem which *The Crisis* desires to discuss during the present year in all its phases and with ample and fair representation to all shades of opinion.

The Crisis, February, 1934; XLI, 52–53.

[c]

COMMENTS ON SEGREGATION
David H. Pierce
Cleveland Heights, Ohio

Your article in the February *Crisis* must be elaborated. Otherwise you could easily be charged with advocating a policy of extreme reaction.

After reading your statement, my first question addressed to myself was, "When should the N.A.A.C.P. engage in a struggle and when should it refrain?" And frankly, were I to look to your recent pronouncements for guidance, I could not find an answer.

Let us make a concrete issue which concerns us in Ohio. A brilliant young colored girl was refused permission to take a course in home management at Ohio State University, even though the course was prescribed as necessary for a degree. The supreme court ruled against her. Negroes are entitled to "equal but not identical accommodations." She was graduated without the required course. I have in mind the Doris Weaver case, which, if properly advertised among Negroes and liberal whites, can wreck the Democratic party in Ohio.

If the Negro desires to erect a separate nation within these United States, there is much to say in support of such an endeavor. But he must make no concession whatever that will convey the impression he is willing to compromise with prejudice. Your position, I fear, involves too great a retreat. Furthermore it appears to embrace the belief that the present established order is the permanently established order.

My position is that the Negro in America should make his plight a subject for international consideration. He should give more thought to heretical political and social theories. But any concession must be followed by more concessions, and the end must be slavery.

The Negro has been altogether too respectful in the face of a social order which stacks the cards against him.

Walter White
Secretary, N.A.A.C.P.

Numerous requests have been made of the National Association for the Advancement of Colored People for a statement of the position of the Association on editorials by Dr. Du Bois on "Segregation" in the January and February issues of *The Crisis*. It is fitting and proper that the statement of the Secretary's position should first appear in *The Crisis,* the official organ of the Association.

Various interpretations have been placed upon Dr. Du Bois's editorial, a number of them erroneous and especially the one which interprets the editorial as a statement of the position of the N.A.A.C.P. The historic position of the N.A.A.C.P. has from the date of its foundation been opposed to segregation. Dr. Du Bois's editorial is merely a personal expression on his part that the whole question of segregation should be examined and discussed anew. There can be no objection to frank and free discussion on any subject and *The Crisis* is the last place where censorship or restriction of freedom of speech should be attempted. I wish to call attention to the fact that the N.A.A.C.P. has never officially budged in its general opposition to segregation. Since

Dr. Du Bois has expressed his personal opinion why this attitude might possibly have to be altered I should like to give my personal opinion why I believe we should continue to maintain the same attitude we have for nearly a quarter of a century, but I repeat that what I am about to say is merely my personal opinion just as Dr. Du Bois's editorial expressed his personal opinion.

Let us put aside for the moment the ethical and moral principles involved. It is my firm conviction, based upon observation and experience, that the truest statement in the January editorial is:

there is no doubt that numbers of white people, perhaps the majority of Americans, stand ready to take the most distinct advantage of voluntary segregation and cooperation among colored people. Just as soon as they get a group of black folk segregated, they use it as a point of attack and discrimination.

It is for this very reason that thoughtful colored people will be opposed to following the advice that "groups of communities and farms inhabited by colored folk should be voluntarily formed" where they involve government-financed and approved arrangements like the Homestead Subsistence projects.

It is unfortunate that Dr. Du Bois's editorial has been used, we learn, by certain government officials at Washington to hold up admission of Negroes to one of the government-financed relief projects. Protests have been made to Mrs. Roosevelt and others by the N.A.A.C.P. against such exclusion. Plans to admit Negroes as a result of the protest are being delayed with the editorial in question used as an excuse for such delay.

To accept the status of separateness, which almost invariably in the case of submerged, exploited and marginal groups means inferior accommodations and a distinctly inferior position in the national and communal life, means spiritual atrophy for the group segregated. When Negroes, Jews, Catholics or Nordic white Americans voluntarily choose to live or attend church or engage in social activity together, that is their affair and no one else's. But Negroes and all other groups must without compromise and without cessation oppose in every possible fashion any attempt to impose from without the establishment of pales and ghettoes. Arbitrary segregation of this sort means almost without exception that less money will be expended for adequate sewerage, water, police and fire protection and for the building of a healthful community. It is because of this that the N.A.A.C.P. has resolutely fought such segregation, as in the case of city ordinances and state laws in the Louisville, New Orleans and Richmond segregation cases; has opposed restrictive covenants written into deeds of property, and all other forms, legal and illegal, to restrict the areas in which Negroes may buy or rent and occupy property.

This principle is especially vital where attempts are made to establish separate areas which are financed by moneys from the federal or state governments for which black people are taxed at the same rate as white. No self-respecting Negro can afford to accept without vigorous protest any such attempt to put the stamp of federal approval upon discrimination of this character. Though separate schools do exist in the South and though for the time being little can be done towards ending the expensive and wasteful dual educational system based upon caste and color prejudice, yet no Negro who respects himself and his race can accept these segregated systems without at least inward protest.

I cannot agree with the statement made by Dr. Du Bois in the February crisis that the N.A.A.C.P. opposed the establishment of the Veterans' Hospital in Tuskegee "although it is doubtful if it would have opposed such a hospital in the North." The N.A.A.C.P. did oppose, and successfully, the recent attempt to establish a segregated Veterans' Hospital at Chester, Pennsylvania. It was the feeling of many of us then and now that the fight should be made for the acceptance of Negro physicians, specialists and nurses on the basis of equality to the staffs of *all* Veterans' Hospitals rather than to ask for jim-crow hospitals.

Nor can I agree that the failure of the citizens of Philadelphia to resist more persistently, intelligently and militantly the establishment of a partial system of elementary Negro schools is necessarily approval of the segregation which has been established. This opening wedge will undoubtedly result in *more* segregation in schools and other public institutions unless aggressively fought. Like cancer, segregation grows and must be, in my opinion, resisted wherever it shows its head.

It is admittedly a longer and more difficult road to full and unrestricted admission to schools, hospitals and other public institutions, but the mere difficulty of the road should not and must not serve as a deterrent to either Negro or white people who are mindful not only of present conditions but of those to which we aspire. In a world where time and space are being demolished by science it is no longer possible to create or imagine separate racial, national or other compartments of human thought and endeavor. The Negro must, without yielding, continue the grim struggle *for* integration and *against* segregation for his own physical, moral and spiritual well-being and for that of white America and of the world at large.

Leslie Pinckney Hill
President, Cheyney Training School for Teachers

The world in which we actually live today is not governed by truth or logic or reason. It is controlled chiefly by those prejudices, inherited and acquired, which have come down from prehistoric ages. The world is not a united world. It is definitely divided up into races and nations. And the feeling of race and nationality is deeper in human life everywhere today than ever before. This is in no way difficult to understand. We have only to remember that we are still in the long wake of the World War. War has always intensified the group feeling and developed the positive sense of belonging. We had thought for a while that transportation and communication, in all their subtle modern forms, nay, that the war itself, might break down the bars and give us a united world of brothers. That is what all good men want. That is the end and the dream. But the actual world is still completely divided up into self-conscious and intensified groups, races and nations.

It must be carefully understood, of course, that I am not considering now, in this brief statement, that marginal life of all people, wherein there is a perpetual blending and crossing, and where individuals are free from all group bonds. In the long reaches of unpredictable time this marginal life may come to be the universal life. I am speaking now strictly of men in the mass the world over. These masses everywhere, without regard to race or place, broadly speaking, are segregated. And it is not a question of whether this segregation has come about by force or by choice. No intelligent person is advocating it. It is simply a hard universal fact. My concern is that we Negroes shall recognize the fact and decide what we are going to do about it. Here, there should be one mind.

The first need is that we shall face the facts frankly and intelligently. And the first bitter fact is that races and nations in the crossing of their paths have always meant exploitation and war and hatred. This is because tribes and races and nations up to this moment have been motivated by the idea of dominance. All these separated world groups, through millenniums of time, have developed skills, services, behaviors, ways of looking at life, and richly varied expressions of the meaning to them of human existence. And all these things are, in themselves, good. The evil has lain always in the assumption, against all truth and reason, that one should profit at the expense of another, that the strong has a right to exploit the weak, that some are superior and others consequently inferior. The truth is that every people, every gift, is good and necessary. These varied gifts are the effective bridges from one group to another. They are proofs after all of a oneness of mankind in its response to whatever is good or beautiful or true. The enduring races of man thus far have failed of this perception. And right at this point we come to the sublime opportunity of the Negro, even in his segregated life. I am profoundly stirred when I contemplate this privilege, lest by division among ourselves we lose it.

Let us not be frustrated or stultified or split up, brothers, by the ugly force of this world curse known as segregation. We are bound to all men everywhere by the bond of suffering which the word connotes. Segregation operates upon us disastrously as it operates upon all people. It undermines health by keeping good people out of clean streets and sanitary houses. It shuts off a thousand enjoyments. It cheats our children out of a proper education. It prostitutes law. It corrupts government. It steals from the poor wages, shelter, clothing and food. It blinds men, stops their ears and hardens their hearts. It keeps white people and black people ignorant of one another and brings a spiritual impoverishment upon the land.

But the other side of the picture is to me the more important and compelling. If group life, segregated life, is at this moment inescapable for us and for all men, my counsel is that we organize our part of it for the highest racial and world ends. Let us keep a vision of a world of brothers. Let us cooperate and associate with all good hearts and all liberal minds round about us, building a new life under a new ideal from the ground on which we stand. Let us center ourselves in the great determination to develop a world service by showing in America, for instance, that twelve millions of us refuse to commit the follies by which so many other clans and tribes and nations have been destroyed.

My meaning here is very plain. While others have welded themselves together through the centuries for conquest and always failed, we may unite for *service*, the only banner under which defeat is impossible. While others have stood for hatred and exploitation and war, and sunk into less than nothingness, we may give our uttermost to good-will and cooperation—to that type of association which Mazzini preached. Instead of minimizing any other race of men, we may magnify all. In place of the doctrine of inferiority and superiority, we may exemplify and teach a fundamental equality. Instead of making money and creature comfort the measures of human worth, we may exalt again the imperishable things of the soul. If we are losing our bread-and-butter footing anywhere in the white world, let us stand together in supporting Negro business and the Urban League. If the law breaks down where Negroes are concerned, let us work, unitedly, without any wasteful conflict of leadership, for public servants who will advance the interests of all the people. Let us rally to the support of the N.A.A.C.P. So in education. If the great white colleges and universities are naturally centered in that learning which serves best the needs of the great white race, let us support the National Association for the Study of Negro Life and History, and build up by solid race support centres of learning where Negro youth shall have the still more liberal learning which they need today for survival and for progress. Let us support effective Negro schools of every type. Where the white stage, white literature, and white art conspire to represent us chiefly as zanies, or as defeated, helpless, dependents, let us compound our intellect and our genius to lift up our own vast drama in dignity and power. Let us have unity without a break in standing before the whole public school system everywhere on the great principle which insists that our children shall have teachers, whatever their color, who know these children and have a deep and consecrated will to serve them. No other teacher is fit, for in this proper education of our children we reach the very bed rock of all our hope. When the world goes bitter let us keep our poise, our native grace, our humor and our rhythm by an exalted resolution.

It is not isolation or segregation that men need any longer, but the association and cooperation of a world of friends. And these vast boons will come to us, I am convinced, in the degree in which we develop our own self-respect, self-reliance, and a wide world service. We have the challenging privilege of pointing out nothing less than a new way in unity for all the sons of man.

This is the sublime opportunity which even our present segregated existence affords. Nobody can do these great things for us but ourselves. And when we do build in unity, in mutual confidence, and in self-respect, refusing to let a word stalemate us or suspicion and internal strife divide us, we may by this high spiritual accomplishment go over the bars. We shall have defeated segregation. We shall find that we are united indissolubly to a multiplying world made up of like liberal mind and generous gift in every race. So may we construct at least the vanguard of the Kingdom.

The Crisis, March, 1934; XLI, 80–82.

[d]

SEGREGATION IN THE NORTH
by W. E. B. Du Bois

I have read with interest the various criticisms on my recent discussions of segregation. Those like that of Mr. Pierce of Cleveland, do impress me. I am not worried about being inconsistent. What worries me is the Truth. I am talking about conditions in 1934 and not in 1910. I do not care what I said in 1910 or 1810 or in B.C. 700.

The arguments of Walter White, George Schuyler and Kelly Miller have logic, but they seem to me quite beside the point. In the first place, Walter White is white. He has more white companions and friends than colored. He goes where he will in New York City and naturally meets no Color Line, for the simple and sufficient reason that he isn't "colored"; he feels his new freedom in bitter contrast to what he was born to in Georgia. This is perfectly natural and he does what anyone else of his complexion would do.

But it is fantastic to assume that this has anything to do with the color problem in the United States. It naturally makes Mr. White an extreme opponent of any segregation based on a myth of race. But this argument does not apply to Schuyler or Miller or me. Moreover, Mr. White knows this. He moved once into a white apartment house and it went black on him. He now lives in a colored apartment house with attendant limitations. He once took a friend to dine with him at the celebrated café of the Lafayette Hotel, where he had often been welcomed. The management humiliated him by refusing to serve Roland Hayes.

The attitudes of Schuyler and Kelly Miller are historically based on the amiable assumption that there is little or no segregation in the North, and that agitation and a firm stand are making this disappear; that obvious desert and accomplishment by Negroes can break down prejudice. This is a fable. I once believed it passionately. It may become true in 250 or 1000 years. Now it is not true. No black man whatever his culture or ability is today in America regarded as a man by any considerable number of white Americans. The difference between North and South in the matter of segregation is largely a difference of degree; of wide degree certainly, but still of degree.

In the North, neither Schuyler nor Kelly Miller nor anyone with a visible admixture of Negro blood can frequent hotels or restaurants. They have difficulty in finding dwelling places in better class neighborhoods. They occupy "Lower 13" on Pullmans, and if they are wise, they do not go into dining cars when any large number of white people is there. Their children either go to colored schools or to schools nominally for both races, but actually attended almost exclusively by colored children. In other words, they are confined by unyielding public opinion to a Negro world. They earn a living on colored newspapers or in colored colleges, or other social institutions. They treat colored patients and preach to colored pews. Not one of the 12 colored Ph.D.'s of last year, trained by highest American and European standards, is going to get a job in any white university. Even when Negroes in the North work side by side with whites, they are segregated, like the postal clerks, or refused by white unions or denied merited promotion.

No matter how much we may fulminate about "No segregation," there stand the flat facts. Moreover, this situation has in the last quarter century been steadily growing worse. Mr. Spingarn may ask judicially as to whether or not the N.A.A.C.P. should change its attitude toward segregation. The point that he does not realize is that segregation has changed its attitude toward the N.A.A.C.P. The higher the Negro climbs or tries to climb, the more pitiless and unyielding the color ban. Segregation may be just as evil today as it was in 1910, but it is more insistent, more prevalent and more unassailable by appeal or argument. The pressing problem is: What are we going to do about it?

In 1910, colored men could be entertained in the best hotels in Cleveland, Detroit and Chicago. Today, there is not a single Northern city, except New York, where a Negro can be a guest at a first-class hotel. Not even in Boston is he welcome; and in New York, the number of hotels where he can go is very small. Roland Hayes was unable to get regular hotel accommodations, and Dr. Moton only succeeds by powerful white influence and by refraining from use of the public dining room or the public lobbies.

If as Spingarn asserts, the N.A.A.C.P. has conducted a quarter-century campaign against segregation, the net result has been a little less than nothing. We have by legal action steadied the foundation so that in the future, segregation must be by wish and will and not law, but beyond that we have not made the slightest impress on the determination of the overwhelming mass of white Americans not to treat Negroes as men.

These are unpleasant facts. We do not like to voice them. The theory is that by maintaining certain fictions of law and administration, by whistling and keeping our courage up, we can stand on the "principle" of no segregation and wait until public opinion meets our position. But can we do this? When we were living in times of prosperity; when we were making post-war incomes; when our labor was in demand, we perhaps could afford to wait. But today, faced by starvation and economic upheaval, and by the question of being able to survive at all in this land in the reconstruction that is upon us, it is ridiculous not to see, and criminal not to tell, the colored people that they can not base their salvation upon the empty reiteration of a slogan.

What then can we do? The only thing that we not only can, but must do, is voluntarily and insistently to organize our economic and social power, no matter how much segregation it involves. Learn to associate with ourselves and to train ourselves for effective association. Organize our strength as consumers; learn to co-operate and use machines and power as producers; train ourselves in methods of democratic control within our own group. Run and support our own institutions.

We are doing this partially now, only we are doing it under a peculiar attitude of protest, and with only transient and distracted interest. A number of excellent young gentlemen in Washington, having formed a Negro Alliance, proceed to read me out of the congregation of the righteous because I dare even discuss segregation. But who are these young men? The products of a segregated school system; the talent selected by Negro teachers; the persons who can today, in nine cases out of ten, earn only a living through segregated Negro social institutions. These are the men who are yelling against segregation. If most of them had been educated in the mixed schools in New York instead of the segregated schools of Washington, they never would have seen college, because Washington picks out and sends ten times as many Negroes to college as New York does.

It would, of course, be full easy to deny that this voluntary association for great social and economic ends in segregation; and if I had done this in the beginning of this debate, many people would have been easily deceived, and would have yelled "No segregation" with one side of their mouths and "Race pride and Race initiative" with the other side. No such distinction can possibly be drawn. Segregation may be compulsory by law or it may be compulsory by economic or social condition, or it may be a matter of free choice. At any rate, it is the separation of human beings and separation despite the will to humanity. Such separation is evil; it leads to jealousy, greed, nationalism and war; and yet it is today and in this world inevitable; inevitable to Jews because of Hitler; inevitable to Japanese because of white Europe; inevitable to Russia because of organized greed over all the white world; inevitable to Ethiopia because of white armies and navies; inevitable, because without it, the American Negro will suffer evils greater than any possible evil of separation: we would suffer the loss of self-respect, the lack of faith in ourselves, the lack of knowledge about ourselves, the lack of ability to make a decent living by our own efforts and not by philanthropy.

This situation has been plunged into crisis and precipitated to an open demand for thought and action by the Depression and the New Deal. The government, national and state, is helping and guiding the individual. It has entered and entered for good into the social and economic organization of life. We could wish, we could pray, that this entrance could absolutely ignore lines of race and color. but we know perfectly well it does not and will not, and with the present American opinion, it cannot. The question is then, are we going to stand out and refuse the inevitable and inescapable government aid because we first wish to abolish the Color Line? This is not simply tilting at windmills; it is, if we are not careful, committing race suicide.

Back of all slogans lies the difficulty that the meanings may change without changing the words. For instance, "no segregation" may mean two very different things:

1. A chance for the Negro to advance without the hindrances which arise when he is segregated from the main group, and the main social institutions upon which society depends. He becomes, thus, an outsider, a hanger on, with no chance to function properly as a man.

2. It may mean utter lack of faith of Negroes in Negroes, and the desire to escape into another group, shirking, on the other hand, all responsibility for ignorance, degradation and lack of experience among Negroes, while asking admission into the other group on terms of full equality and with full chance for individual development.

It is in the first sense that I have always believed and used the slogan: "No Segregation." On the other hand, in the second sense, I have no desire or right to hinder or estop those persons who do not want to be Negroes. But I am compelled to ask the very plain and pertinent question: Assuming for the moment that the group into which you demand admission does not want you, what are you going to do about it? Can you demand that they want you? Can you make them by law or public opinion admit you when they are supreme over this same public opinion and make these laws? Manifestly, you 'cannot. Manifestly, your admission to the other group on the basis ot your individual desert and wish, can only be accomplished if they, too, join in the wish to have you. If they do so join, all problems based mostly on race and color disappear, and there remains only the human problems of social uplift and intelligence and group action. But there is in the United States today no sign that this objection to the social and even civic recognition of persons of Negro blood is going to occur during the life of persons now living. In which case there can be only one meaning to the slogan "No Segregation"; and that is, no hindrance to my effort to be a man. If you do not wish to associate with me, I am more than willing to associate with myself. Indeed, I deem it a privilege to work with and for Negroes, only asking that my hands be not tied nor my feet hobbled.

What is the object of those persons who insist by law, custom and propaganda to keep the American Negro separate in rights and privileges from other citizens of the United States? The real object, confessed or semiconscious, is to so isolate the Negro that he will be spiritually bankrupt, physically degenerate, and economically dependent.

Against this it is the bounden duty of every Negro and every enlightened American to protest; to oppose the policy so far as it is manifest by laws; to agitate against customs by revealing facts; and to appeal to the sense of decency and justice in all American citizens.

I have never known an American Negro who did not agree that this was a proper program. Some have disagreed as to the emphasis to be put on this and that method of protest; on the efficacy of any appeal against American prejudice; but all Negroes have agreed that segregation is bad and should be opposed.

Suppose, however, that this appeal is ineffective or nearly so? What is the Negro going to do? There is one thing that he can or must do, and that is to see to it that segregation does *not* undermine his health; does *not* leave him spiritually bankrupt; and does *not* make him an economic slave; and he must do this at any cost.

If he cannot live in sanitary and decent sections of a city, he must build his own residential quarters, and raise and keep them on a plane fit for living. If he cannot educate his children in decent schools with other children, he must, nevertheless, educate his children in decent Negro schools and arrange and conduct and oversee such schools. If he cannot enter American industry at a living wage, or find work suited to his education and talent, or receive promotion and advancement according to his deserts, he must organize his own economic life so that just as far as possible these discriminations will not reduce him to abject exploitation.

Everyone of these movements on the part of colored people are not only necessary, but inevitable. And at the same time, they involve more or less active segregation and acquiescence in segregation.

Here again, if there be any number of American Negroes who have not in practical life made this fight of self-segregation and self-association against the compulsory segregation forced upon them, I am unacquainted with such persons. They may, of course, explain their compulsory retreat from a great ideal, by calling segregation by some other name. They may affirm with fierce insistency that they will never, no never, under any circumstances, acquiesce in segregation. But if they live in the United States in the year of our Lord 1934, or in any previous year since the foundation of the government, they are segregated; they accept segregation, and they segregate themselves, because they must. From this dilemma I see no issue.

The Crisis, April, 1934; XLI, 115–16.

[e]

Dr. Du Bois Resigns: Full Text of His Letter

The Board of Directors of the National Association for the Advancement of Colored People at the June meeting took no action upon the resignation of Dr. Du Bois, tendered as of June 11, but named a committee to confer with Dr. Du Bois and see if some satisfactory settlement of differences could not be arranged.

Under date of June 26, however, Dr. Du Bois addressed the following letter to the Board and released it to the press as of July 1, eight days before it came officially to the notice of the Board at its regular meeting July 9:

In deference to your desire to postpone action on my resignation of June 11, I have allowed my nominal connection with *The Crisis* to extend to July 1, and have meantime entered into communication with the Chairman of the Board, and with your Committee on Reconciliation.

I appreciate the good will and genuine desire to bridge an awkward break which your action indicated, and yet it is clear to me, and I think to the majority of the Board that under the circumstances my resignation must stand. I owe it, however, to the Board and to the public to make clear at this time the deeper reasons for my action, lest the apparent causes of my resignation seem inadequate.

Many friends have truthfully asserted that the segregation argument was not the main reason for my wishing to leave this organization. It was an occasion and an important occasion, but it could have been adjusted. In fact, no matter what the Board of the National Association for the Advancement of Colored People says, its action towards segregation has got to approximate, in the future as in the past, the pattern which it followed in the case of the separate camp for Negro officers during the World War and in the case of the Tuskegee Veterans' Hospital. In both instances, we protested vigorously and to the limit of our ability the segregation policy. Then, when we had failed and knew we had failed, we bent every effort toward making the colored camp at Des Moines the best officers' camp possible, and the Tuskegee Hospital, with its Negro personnel, one of the most efficient in the land. This is shown by the 8th and 14th Annual Reports of the National Association for the Advancement of Colored People.

The only thing, therefore, that remains for us is to decide whether we are openly to recognize this procedure as inevitable, or be silent about it and still pursue it. Under these circumstances, the argument must be more or less academic, but there is no essential reason that those who see different sides of this same shield should not be able to agree to live together in the same house.

The whole matter assumed, however, a serious aspect when the Board peremptorily forbade all criticism of the officers and policies in *The Crisis*. I had planned to continue constructive criticism of the National Association for the Advancement of Colored People in *The Crisis* because I firmly believe that the National Association for the Advancement of Colored People faces the most gruelling of tests which come to an old organization: founded in a day when a negative program of protest was imperative and effective, it succeeded so well that the program seemed perfect and unlimited. Suddenly, by World War and chaos, we are called to formulate a positive program of construction and inspiration. We have been thus far unable to comply.

Today this organization, which has been great and effective for nearly a quarter of a century, finds itself in a time of crisis and change, without a program, without effective organization, without executive officers, who have either the ability or disposition to guide the National Association for the Advancement of Colored People in the right direction.

These are harsh and arresting charges. I make them deliberately, and after long thought, earnest effort, and with infinite writhing of spirit. To the very best of my ability, and every ounce of my strength, I have since the beginning of the Great Depression, tried to work inside the organization for its realignment and readjustment to new duties. I have been almost absolutely unsuccessful. My program for economic readjustment has been totally ignored. My demand for a change in personnel has been considered as mere petty jealousy, and my protest against our mistakes and blunders has been looked upon as disloyalty to the organization.

So long as I sit by quietly consenting, I share responsibility. If I criticize within, my words fall on deaf ears. If I criticize openly, I seem to be washing dirty linen in public. There is but one recourse, complete and final withdrawal, not because all is hopeless nor because there are no signs of realization of the possibilities of reform and of the imperative demand for men and vision, but because evidently I personally can do nothing more.

I leave behind me in the organization many who have long thought with me, and yet hesitated at action; many persons of large ideals who see no agents at hand to realize them, and who fear that the dearth of ability and will to sacrifice within this organization, indicates a similar lack within the whole race. I know that both sets of friends are wrong, and while I desert them with deep reluctance, it is distinctly in the hope that the fact of my going may arouse to action and bring a great and gifted race to the rescue, with a re-birth of that fine idealism and devotion that founded the National Association for the Advancement of Colored People.

Under these circumstances, there is but one thing for me to do, and that is to make the supreme sacrifice of taking myself absolutely and unequivocably out of the picture, so that hereafter the leaders of the National Association for the Advancement of Colored People, without the distraction of personalities and accumulated animosities, can give their whole thought and attention to the rescuing of the greatest organization for the emancipation of Negroes that America has ever had.

I am, therefore, insisting upon my resignation, and on July 1st, whether the Board of Directors acts or does not act, I automatically cease to have any connection whatsoever in any shape or form with the National Association for the Advancement of Colored People. I do not, however, cease to wish it well, to follow it with personal and palpitating interest, and to applaud it when it is able to rescue itself from its present impossible position and reorganize itself according to the demands of the present crisis.

Very respectfully yours,
(Signed) W. E. B. Du Bois

The Crisis, August, 1934; XLI, 245–46.

14

FOR A 49TH (ALL-BLACK) STATE

The forces that induced Dr. Du Bois to put forth the ideas elucidated in the preceding documents led at about the same time to the appearance of The National Movement for the Establishment of a 49th State, with headquarters in Chicago. This movement—with fairly exact parallels in Afro-American history going back into the nineteenth century—created considerable stir and discussion in the Black press for about six months; it is an idea which continues to have supporters as the twentieth century moves to a close. Reprinted is Bulletin No. 1 issued by the National Council of the movement; it was not dated but appeared early in 1934. The secretary of this movement was Oscar S. Brown, a Chicago attorney and president of the Howard University Alumni Association in that city.

THE NATIONAL MOVEMENT FOR THE
ESTABLISHMENT OF A 49TH STATE

In the United States of America, the Negro has been scorned as a social leper, denied reasonable protection under the law, prohibited from earning a decent living for himself, trampled upon because of his economic and numerical weakness, and maltreated in a thousand other ways. He has had many true friends, who have aided him during the years since the abolition of slavery, but such valued friends are definitely on the decrease, leaving the Negro standing almost alone in the midst of an unsympathetic or hostile crowd of ten times his number. It now appears absolutely certain that the Negro, himself, is his only source of salvation. The momentous question is, how can he save himself?

Most of the Negro population in the United States are found on farms and are dependent upon a landlord or someone else for an existence. Here, improved machinery and improved methods of intense cultivation of land have so increased agricultural production that there now is no market for much that has been and is being produced. It is estimated that in 1934 approximately thirty-three million acres of land will be taken out of production. The present trend indicates that from year to year more and more land will be taken out of production. Thus, millions of acres, heretofore a source of wealth, now become a surplus and a liability to the owners, and the men, who have been making their existence cultivating this land, now become "surplus men." The surplus acres may be allowed to grow up in grass and trees, but what of the "surplus men"? The marginal farmer—the farmer who has been able to make a bare existence—now drops below the margin of existence and will be eliminated. Most of the Negro farmers are found in this lowest or sub-marginal class.

In industry, improved machinery has so displaced men until now there are not enough jobs to go around. This displacement, in normal times, cut most heavily into the ranks of and eliminated the Negro worker. Labor unions and a general consensus of opinion in the United States seem definitely on the road to otherwise eliminate the Negro from many jobs which heretofore have been open to him. Thus, in industry as in farming, the Negro, who in normal times was the marginal worker, now becomes the sub-marginal worker, without an opportunity to earn an existence or to keep body and soul together.

Faced with this grim outlook, what can be done to forestall impending disaster? Whatever may be the difference of opinion among Negroes as to what ought to be done, all seem to be in definite agreement that something must be done and done quickly. We propose a definite program for the problem. This program may not be the ideal or most desirable way to meet the problem, yet it is definite and has in it the possibility for tremendous success. Thus, in the absence of anything else with such prospects of immediate alleviation of the Negro's suffering, we have adopted this program and will resolutely and vigorously press forward.

We propose, therefore, the ultimate establishment of a new state in the United States wherein colored people in the United States can have an opportunity to work out their own destiny, unbridled and unhampered by artificial barriers; wherein they can have a chance to raise the lot of their masses from exploitation, misery, wretchedness and insecurity; wherein they can become respected, industrious, thrifty citizens, self-governing, self-reliant and self-sustaining, always to be counted upon as unfalteringly loyal to their country and a credit to all that is noblest and best in it. Thus, we plan that the Negro secure an actual physical, geographic area for the establishment of a state like any other commonwealth in the United States.

The creation of a Forty-ninth state in the United States involves problems and ramifications that will require the utmost of intelligence and diplomacy, patience and determination. Legally it can be done, for Article 4, Section 3, of the Constitution of the United States provides:

New States may be admitted by the Congress into this Union; but no new State shall be formed or erected within the jurisdiction of any other State; nor any State be formed by the junction of two or more States, or parts of States, without the consent of the Legislatures of the States concerned, as well as of Congress.

Aid of the Federal Government will be sought in the acquisition of the territory, which must be adequate in size, moderate in climate and fertile as to soil. There are many reasons why the Government can afford to buy the area and be liberal and sympathetic in disposing of it to Negroes:

First. The Negro has been among his Country's most loyal and dependable citizens in peace and in war and as much as any other citizen deserves a True Deal. As any other people, similarly situated, he has a native ability and resourcefulness for self preservation and development. Though he has been burlesqued and called lazy, no people in the Nation have toiled as the Negro has. Whatever reasonable terms may be made to the Negro in selling him the land in the new State, there is reason to believe that such terms will be fully met.

Second. The Negroes themselves own hundreds of millions of dollars worth of property throughout the Country and many will be eager to dispose of it for property in a new state where they and their posterity can live in security, contentment and peace.

Third. As a slave, the Negro, was bound in chains and brought to America and for two hundred and fifty years was made to toil in the upbuilding of the Nation without adequate or reasonable compensation and without reasonable relative enjoyment of the progress of the Country. Thus, aid to the Negro in the establishment of his new state offers an opportunity for the Nation to reduce its debt to the Negro for past exploitation.

Fourth. The Negro in the United States is at the very bottom of the economic pyramid. By various devices of prejudice and injustice, he has been kept in subjection until now he is almost helpless to make a living or participate in the free and open market of employment. Yet, he is a citizen of the United States—a tenth part of it—and cannot be permitted to starve, if the Nation itself is to survive. In the life of America, the Negro thus becomes a future responsibility of the Government, and its duty is inescapable. It is as dangerous for a nation to neglect a tenth part of its body of citizens as it is for a person to neglect a tenth part of his own body. Any diseased part of the body will weaken and produce complications in the entire system. Whatever part of the Nation's body the Negro may be called, that part must be healthy if the whole body is to be healthy. Thus the necessity for helping the Negro warrants very substantial aid of the Government in order that the nation may make true and lasting progress.

The location of the area in which the state should be established need not be ascertained or pointed out at this time. The principal requirements are that it be adequate in size, hospitable in climate, and fertile as to soil, sufficient to produce most of the basic necessaries of life for its inhabitants. The new area could be carved out or cut from one or more existing states. It is proposed that the area be secured by the Federal Government upon the specific condition that the state or states selling the territory would approve of the future establishment of the new state. The area would then become a Territory of the United States and remain a territory during the period of preparation and organization for the establishment of the new independent commonwealth of the United States. As soon as the area is acquired by the Federal Government, we would ascertain, as far as possible, the Negroes who would go to the new state, their property holdings and their ability to work in the new community. Wherever the survey indicated deficiencies in certain fields of necessary activity in the new state, we would set out immediately to educate and train personnel sufficient to overcome the deficiencies and form a balanced economic and administrative unit.

If necessary, under the supervision of the Federal Government, the new area could pass into control of the new citizens of the state step by step until the entire functioning of the commonwealth would be under the dominant control of the citizens thereof.

The economic organization of the new state will be definitely planned in the direction of making the state, within its own borders, as nearly self-sustaining, with the necessaries of life, as it would be possible to do.

It is possible for the economic activity of a state to be so planned that the state will be almost self-sustaining, especially if the area is reasonably large, the soil is fertile and the climate moderate. It is likewise possible to direct the surplus production of a state or the exportable commodities of a state in such a way that many of them can be disposed of to the community or communities from which the state would need to import goods.

We shall proceed upon the theory that man's labors and the fruits of nature in our land of plenty are such that there need be no pauper class where the citizens are intelligent and industrious. Individual initiative, checked to prevent the exploitation of the weak, can produce a general well-being of the whole without limit. We shall strive for the attainment of sympathetic interest on the part of the individual for the welfare of the whole people. This coupled with an honest and intelligent balancing of economic activity will provide against privation and want for all who desire and are able to work.

As a highway to the new physical state and as a definite benefit to the Negro, we shall build in him a new State of Mind, of hope, of confidence, of a sympathetic interest and understanding in himself, and a state of unified action among Negroes in the United States, especially in the use of their buying power in the aggressive and effective support of industry, commerce, business and other agencies that are favorable in the employment of Negroes. Organized buying power is powerful, and the buying power of our thirteen million people can be made one of the most powerful factors in the nation, and has in it tremendous possibilities for good.

Our immediate task shall be to direct the Negroes' consumption into and through channels that will help Negroes to earn an honest, decent, reasonable living for themselves. We shall investigate the principal commodities produced and distributed in this country, and determine to what extent these producers and distributors employ Negroes and their attitude toward them as employees. This applies to every enterprise and agency that receives substantial patronage from Negroes. From the information thus gained, we shall give a rating or an unconditional approval of these businesses and of the commodities they produce or distribute or the services they supply. We will then go to our consuming public and urge aggressively and insistently that they favor only such enterprises as are favorable to Negroes. For example, if a certain chewing gum producer employs Negroes and another does not; or if a certain tooth paste company hires Negroes and another does not; or if a certain cigarette manufacturer gives jobs to Negroes and another does not; or if a certain automobile manufacturer hires Negroes and another does not, etc., etc., we will *know* that there is *reason* for our having a *preference, and we will have a preference, and make the preference effective.*

The existence of this new State of Mind can be made to materially lessen the economic imperativeness of the new physical state. Whatever the outcome of our effort for the establishment of a new physical state, the establishment of the new State of Mind will be of definite and far reaching benefit to us now and the good result will be directly in proportion to the degree of cooperation given by the Negro himself in putting it over.

It may not be out of place for the proponents of this movement to add a few general statements in an effort to make clear their motive in projecting the idea.

In the outset, it must be emphasized that the proponents of the movement favor for all citizens of the United States equal opportunity, equal enjoyment of and equal protection in all phases of the life of the Nation. We have never been and will never be satisfied with less. However, we believe that the temper of the dominant element of American life and the economic trend are such that the masses of the Negroes in this country must be rescued even if, for the present, we have to resort to technical un-American principles to do so. The insecurity and suffering of the masses of our poor people make it imperative that something be done for them now, to the extent of taking many of them from their present situation and transplanting them bodily into a New State that will be free, just and kind to them, offering to them a chance to live and move forward in peace as a part of a civilized nation.

There is no intention of compelling anyone to go to the New State. Only those who would desire to go will be desired there. There is reason to believe that several million people will go, and their going will relieve much of the economic stress throughout the country due to the vast oversupply of workers who can find no work.

Four-page leaflet, issued as Bulletin No. 1, The National Council, from Chicago, Ill.; in editor's possession. There is an article by Oscar S. Brown on the ideas of this movement in *The Crisis*, May, 1935; XLII, 134, 137.

15

NEGRO AMERICANS, WHAT NOW?

by James Weldon Johnson

In a brief book published in 1934, James Weldon Johnson faced up to the same problems tackled by Du Bois and by the 49th State Movement. He emerged with an answer summarized in that book's conclusion.

In these few pages I have made no attempt at a general consideration of social problems; rather have I sought to limit the discussion to the peculiar and immediate problems that confront us as a special group. I have also sought to project the discussion from the base of conditions as they are, and not from the base of conditions as we wish they were.

I have tried to show that the most logical, the most feasible and most worthwhile choice for us is to follow the course that leads to our becoming an integral part of the nation, with the same rights and guarantees that are accorded to other citizens, and on the same terms. I have pointed out that common sense compels us to get whatever and all the good we can out of the system of imposed segregation, to gather all the experience and strength that can be got from it; but that we should use that experience and strength steadily and as rapidly as possible to destroy the system. The seeming advantages of imposed segregation are too costly to keep. I have enumerated our principal forces and resources and set forth that none of these factors is a panacea; that we must correlate all our elements of strength to form a super-power to be centered on our main objective; that, knowing the rights we are entitled to, we must persistently use this power to defend those rights we hold, so that none may go by default, and to secure those we have not yet gained. I have stressed the vital need of plans and steps for uniting black and white workers. I have made plain the importance of interracial contact. I have pointed out the necessity of enlisting the energies of youth. I have shown that in addition to other factors there is an emotional factor to deal with. I have implied the fact that our policies should include an intelligent opportunism; by which I mean the alertness and ability to seize the advantage from every turn of circumstance whenever it can be done without sacrifice of principle. We require a sense of strategy as well as a spirit of determination.

To revolutionary elements it will no doubt appear that what I have outlined is too conservative. If it does, it is not because I am unconscious of the need of fundamental social change, but because I am considering the realities of the situation. Conservatism and radicalism are relative terms. It is as radical for a black American in Mississippi to claim his full rights under the Constitution and the law as it is for a white American in any state to advocate the overthrow of the existing national government. The black American in many instances puts life in jeopardy, and anything more radical than that cannot reasonably be required.

Much that I have here written I have stated before. In what I have said I have sought to avoid being either academic or lyric. I have spent no time with analyses of the psychology of race prejudice. I have suggested no quick or novel cure-all, for there is none. There is no one salient to be captured; our battle is along a wide front. What I have outlined is a plan for a long, hard campaign. A campaign that will demand courage, determination, and patience. Not, however, the patience to wait, but the patience to keep on working and fighting. This may seem far from a cheerful prospect; but why should we utter wails of despair? Our situation is luxuriously easy to what former generations have endured. We ought to gain fortitude from merely thinking of what they came through.

And we ought to gather inspiration from the fact that we are in the right. We are contending for only what we are entitled to under the organic law of the land, and by any high standard of civilization, of morality, or of decency. Black America is called upon to stand as the protagonist of tolerance, of fair play, of justice, and of good will. Until white America heeds, we shall never let its conscience sleep. For the responsibility for the outcome is not ours alone. White America cannot save itself if it prevents us from being saved. But, in the nature of things, white America is not going to yield what rightfully belongs to us without a struggle kept up by us. In that struggle our watchword needs to be, "Work, work, work!" and our rallying cry, "Fight, fight, fight!"

I offer now some words of caution. We are in constant danger of growing to feel that all the ills we suffer are due to race prejudice, and so, of falling into the habit of framing excuses for our own shortcomings. We must try to avoid that danger. We should squarely face our failings. And, too, we should remember that, if race prejudice were abolished today, there would remain to us tomorrow all the ills that are common to humanity. That, however, is exactly the point we are striving to reach, the point where we can enter the race, not handicapped back of the line, but starting from scratch.

In the situation into which we are thrown, let each one of us, let the whole race, be ceaselessly on guard against the loss of spiritual integrity. So long as we maintain *that* integrity we cannot be beaten down, not in a thousand years. For instance, we suffer the humiliations of Jim-Crowism; but we are not vitally injured so long as we are not Jim-Crowed in soul. If it is necessary for me to travel on the railroad in a Jim-Crow state, I am in all probability forced to climb into a Jim-Crow car; but the injury inflicted on me is only external, unless I should feel within myself that I am in my right place, that I am where I belong. Each time one of us *voluntarily* and *unnecessarily* Jim-Crows himself, he is undermining his spiritual integrity. We often permit mere timidity to undermine our spiritual integrity. We must throw off timidity and break through the barriers whenever we are able to do it. We often take discrimination for granted where there actually is none or where it is so indefinite that a little courage and pressure would sweep it away. Each time we break through or sweep away discrimination we make it easier for the next time and the next one.

This is a struggle in which time after time we are compelled to yield ground; let us never yield ground spiritually.

The pledge to myself which I have endeavored to keep through the greater part of my life is:

I will not allow one prejudiced person or one million or one hundred million to blight my life. I will not let prejudice or any of its at-

tendant humiliations and injustices bear me down to spiritual defeat. My inner life is mine, and I shall defend and maintain its integrity against all the powers of Hell.

J. W. Johnson, *Negro Americans, What Now?* (New York: Viking, 1934), pp. 98-103.

16

JIM CROW AND EATING: WASHINGTON, D.C.

In January, 1934, Representative De Priest's secretary, Morris Lewis, and a friend were refused service in the public restaurant operated within the Capitol building in Washington. For four months there ensued an effort by Representative De Priest to force Congress to mandate the elimination of this discrimination in a facility directly subject to its control. On March 17 some twenty or thirty Howard University students descended en masse upon the restaurant in order to "sit in," but police ejected them. Finally, on April 25, 1934, the House, by a vote of 237 to 114, ordered the creation of a committee to investigate the question of exclusion of Black people; that killed the matter and Washington remained a rather tightly jim-crowed city until World War II. Published below is the text of one of Congressman De Priest's speeches relative to this subject.

Mr. De Priest. Mr. Chairman and members of the Committee, I came to Washington as a Representative in Congress on the 15th of April 1929. Up until the 23d day of last January I never heard this question raised which has now been raised by the Chairman of the Committee on Accounts this year. On that day when my secretary went into the grillroom downstairs he was told by Mr. Johnson that by the orders of the Chairman of the Committee on Accounts he could not be served in that restaurant.

I read in the newspapers an interview where the Chairman of the Committee on Accounts said that no Negro had been served there and would not while he was here. I hope he was not quoted correctly.

I want to say that if the chairman was quoted correctly in that article "that Negroes had not been served there before" he was mistaken. I have seen them there in the grillroom several times. In the last 5 years I think I have seen them there 50 times.

I want to say further, after talking with some Members of the Committee on Accounts, that this question has never been raised in the committee before, and never was raised officially in the committee, if I am correctly informed.

It seems to be an arbitrary ruling on that question.

The restaurant of the Capitol is run for the benefit of the American people, and every American, whether he be black or white, Jew or gentile, Protestant or Catholic, under our constitutional form of Government, is entitled to equal opportunities.

I introduced a resolution on the 24th of January, asking for an investigation of this ruling by the chairman of the committee. That resolution went to the Committee on Rules. The Committee on Rules has not acted as yet. I waited 30 legislative days, and then I filed a petition with the Clerk of this House to discharge the Committee on Rules and to bring the resolution to the floor of the House.

That resolution calls for an investigation only. If the Chairman of the Committee on Accounts has that power, I should like to know it. If the Chairman of the Committee on Accounts has that power, the American people are entitled to know it.

I am going to ask every justice-loving Member in this House to sign that petition, as that seems to be the only way it can be threshed out on the floor of the House.

I come from a group of people—and I am proud of it and make no apology for being a Negro—who have demonstrated their loyalty to the American Government in every respect, making no exception. They have always proved to be good American citizens and have supported the Constitution. I challenge any man to contradict that assertion. If you are going to keep them good American citizens, like I pray they shall always be, it must be done by defending their rights as American citizens.

If we allow segregation and the denial of constitutional rights under the dome of the Capitol, where in God's name will we get them?

I appreciate the conditions that pertain in the territory where the gentleman comes from, and nobody knows that better than I do.

But North Carolina is not the United States of America; it is but a part of it, a one forty-eighth part. Then I expect, too, as long as I am a Member of this House, to contend for every right and every privilege every other American citizen enjoys; and if I did not, I would not be worthy of the trust reposed in me by constituents who have sent me here. [Applause.]

This is not a political problem. Someone said that I was trying to play politics. I did not instigate this; I did not start it; but, so help me God, I am going to stay to see the finish of it.

Mr. Blanton. Mr. Chairman, will our colleague yield to me for a question?

Mr. De Priest. Not now, Mr. Blanton; and I consider you one of the best friends I have on the Democratic side.

Mr. Blanton. I thought therefore you would yield for a question.

Mr. De Priest. I shall later on, but not now.

The Chairman. The gentleman declines to yield.

Mr. De Priest. I say to the Members of this House—and I have no feeling in the matter—this is the most dangerous precedent that could be established in the American Government. If we allow this challenge to go without correcting it, it will set an example where people will say Congress itself approves of segregation; Congress itself approves of denying 0.1 of our population equal rights and opportunity; why should not the rest of the American people do likewise? I have been informed that if I insisted on pressing this question it might hurt my usefulness down here. If I did not press it, I would not stay here very long. The people who sent me here would retire me next November, and they would rightly retire me because I should not be here if I did not stand up for a group of people who have always been on the square with this Government. I did not come here from a group of people who have committed treason against the Government; I did not come here from a group of people who are Communists or Socialists; I come here from the most loyal American citizens that we have.

During the World War when emissaries of the enemy were scattering pamphlets over the battlefields of Europe asking the colored people to desert the colors because they received inhuman treatment in America, no colored man deserted, and no man can say and history does not record when a Negro deserted the colors—not one. How do you expect them to go on giving loyal service to America, at a time when there is unrest over the whole world, when the Reds are trying to make inroads amongst my group because they are the lowest in the scale of society, from an economic standpoint, unless we give them something like a square deal in this country? I appreciate all that has been done so far, but the work has not been completed yet. And I say further, ladies and gentlemen of the Congress, that America never will be what it was intended to be until every citizen in America has his just rights under the Constitution. [Applause.] I would not have filed this petition if I could have gotten a hearing before the Committee on Rules. I asked for it. I was not even given the courtesy of a hearing before that committee.

Mr. Lundeen. Mr. Chairman, will the gentleman yield?

Mr. De Priest. Yes.

Mr. Lundeen. Will the gentleman tell us how many names are on that petition now?

Mr. De Priest. There were 93 names on it an hour ago.

Mr. Blanton. Mr. Chairman, will our colleague yield to me now?

Mr. De Priest. Yes; I yield with pleasure to the gentleman from Texas.

Mr. Blanton. The restaurant is for the benefit of the Members of the Congress because we have to be here at meal-time.

Mr. De Priest. I agree with the gentleman.

Mr. Blanton. Has not our colleague been allowed to go in there every time he wanted to? He can go in there right now and take anybody with him that he wishes to take.

Mr. De Priest. That is all true.

Mr. Blanton. What more do you ask? You go there at will and are allowed to take your friends with you at will. Is not that equal justice and right to you, the same as to the rest of us?

Mr. De Priest. I am asking for the same rights for my constituents that the gentleman from Texas wants for his, and that is all.

Mr. Blanton. But our colleague from Illinois does go in that restaurant whenever he wishes, and he takes his colored friends with him whenever he wishes to do so.

Mr. De Priest. I am not asking privileges for Oscar De Priest or proper treatment for him down there, because I will take care of that, but I am asking for those people who have no voice in this Congress, just like you, Mr. Blanton, would do if some of your constituents came here from Texas and were refused to be served in that restaurant. You would raise more hell than anybody I know of about it. [Laughter and applause.] I have been here long enough to know just what you would do, and I would vote with you on raising that hell. I would say that you were right, and that your constituents had a right to have the same treatment that I want for mine.

The Chairman. The time of the gentleman from Illinois has expired.

Mr. McLeod. Mr. Chairman, I yield the gentleman 10 minutes more.

Mr. Blanton. We have stood with you generously in helping to build up Howard University.

Mr. De Priest. Yes; and I expect you to stay with me.

Mr. Blanton. We have given it more than any white university in the United States.

Mr. De Priest. Do you want me to tell you why?

Mr. Blanton. Because the colored race sadly needs good teachers, and good nurses, and good dentists, and good doctors, and good preachers.

Mr. De Priest. All that is true, and I expect you to keep on doing it, you especially, to help. And while we are talking about Howard University, I might say that personally I am very sorry that those boys came down here from that university the other day as they did. If they had consulted me I would have told them to stay away from here. Another thing—I have investigated and I have found that the boy who has been locked up was not a student at Howard University. I do not know anything about the rest of them, but if they were from Howard University, they are just like the uncontrolled youth of any college or school. There are very few colleges which do not have some radicals in them.

I do not claim the Negro race is any better than anybody else. I know we have our criminal element, just like you have your criminal element. None of us is perfect, but it behooves all of us to do the best we can and respect the rights of the other fellow in America. Whether they be large or small, rich or poor, it makes no difference. Somebody said this was a peanut affair. Well, I agree with you. It ought to have been so small that no man in this House could have been small enough to bring it up. There was no occasion for it whatever.

The secretary who works for me I have known for 40 years. He is a Christian gentleman, a great deal better Christian than I ever thought of being or ever expect to be. There certainly can be no fault found with his personal conduct. He has been in that restaurant dozens of times. Perhaps he needs it worse than any other man down here. You know the condition in Washington and I know it. The public restaurants outside do not serve Negroes, and you know it. It is necessary for him to have some place to eat here, or else bring his lunch with him.

I appreciate the fact, as the gentleman said, that we have a restaurant for Members only, and that restaurant for Members only you cannot get into half the time on account of outsiders. Is that not true? I would like to see the Committee on Accounts bar everybody from the restaurant for Members only except Members and their friends who accompany them.

I was there with my wife and Professor Johnson's wife, and we had to wait 10 minutes to get a table because outsiders had crowded the restaurant. Every Member knows that is true.

To show you the subterfuge practiced; in the last 4 or 5 days they have taken down the sign which read "public restaurant," and placed there a sign "For Members only." I asked Mr. Johnson, the manager, personally, why it was done. He said, "I had orders to do it from the Chairman of the committee." I said, "Is it a subterfuge?" He said, "You understand what is going on." I certainly do. That sign was put there to keep only Negroes out. One man was asked if he was a foreigner. If he had said "Yes," he would have been served. Has the time come when American citizens cannot be served, and aliens can? Of course, every alien has every right that he is entitled to, so long as he is law-abiding, but at least we are entitled to the same treatment as every other American citizen, and we will be satisfied with nothing less than that.

Mr. Gavagan. Will the gentleman yield?

Mr. De Priest. I yield.

Mr. Gavagan. I am sorry to break into the gentleman's remarks, but I would like to take this opportunity to express my entire accord with the statements expressed and enunciated by you, and to say to you openly that I am trying to get sufficient signatures to your petition now on the Speaker's desk, so that we may discuss this question fully and openly on the floor. [Applause.]

Mr. De Priest. I thank the gentleman.

I want to say that all of my friends are not on the Republican side of the aisle, and all of my enemies are not on the Democratic side either. Since I have been in Congress I have tried so to conduct myself that I would command the respect of every Member of Congress. I have not imposed my society on any Member on either side of the House. I think every man has the right to select his own society. I would not say that, except that I received a letter from a Member of this Congress, which I am going to read into the *Record*. I would not do it if the gentleman had not published it himself first.

Hon. Oscar De Priest,
House Office Building, Washington, D.C.
Dear Sir: I have your letter of the 7th instant enclosing House Resolution 236. I presume you desire a reply to this letter.

Which I did.

I note the contents of the resolution and desire to state that I was raised among Negroes in the South and they have always been my personal friends. I work with them on my farm and pay them the same price that I pay white men for the same work. I treat them well and enjoy their confidence.

I am willing to allow them every right to which they are entitled under the Constitution and laws, but I am not in favor of social equality between the races.

And I do not give a damn about it, brother. It does not mean anything to me at all.

If there are enough Negroes around the Capitol to justify a restaurant for them to patronize, I would have no objection to establishing a restaurant for their use.

That we do not want and we will not accept.

I neither eat nor sleep with the Negroes, and no law can make me do so. I think this explains my position clearly.

George B. Terrell, of Texas

[Applause.]

I expected that applause. I expected certain gentlemen here to applaud that statement. I know what your feelings are and I understand them thoroughly. You did not disappoint me by applauding. I would have been surprised if you had not applauded.

Nobody asked the gentleman to sleep with him. That was not in my mind at all. I do not know why he thought of it. [Laughter.] I am very careful about whom I sleep with. [Laughter.] I am also careful about whom I eat with; and I want to say to you gentlemen that the restaurant down here is a place where one pays for what one gets. If I go in there, sit down to a table, I pay for what I get, and I am not courting social equality with you. That does not mean anything in America. Social equality is something that comes about by an exchange of visits from home to home and not appearing in the same public dining room. You might as well say I was seeking social equality if I rode in the same Pullman car with you. It would not be any special credit to me to be in there.

[Here the gavel fell.]

Mr. McLeod. Mr. Chairman, I yield the gentleman from Illinois 5 additional minutes

Mr. De Priest. I was down in Tennessee. I dropped into Knoxville one night, and the Chattanooga papers in southern Tennessee published a statement that I was coming there to talk about social equality. I had not thought of it. Nothing was further from my mind; but after they had made that charge and in order to make the papers of Chattanooga say something that was true, once in their lives, I did say something about it. This is what I said:

When the Negroes came to this country originally they were all black; they are not now, because somebody has had a good deal of social equality [laughter and applause]; social equality not sought by Negro women; social equality forced upon them because of the adverse economic situation down there.

I hope when I leave this Congress I shall leave with the respect of the Members; but if securing their respect means sacrificing my race, that respect I do not seek any longer. [Applause.]

I am sorry I have to devote my time trying to watch the needs of the American Negro. I wish I could devote my time, like you gentlemen devote your time, trying to watch the interests of all the American people instead of just 12,000,000 of them.

So far as Howard University is concerned, when the question came up here a year ago between the gentleman from Texas [Mr. Blanton] and myself about the talk made by President Johnson of that university and the charge that it was communistic, I repudiated communism everywhere. I think it is un-American; it is against our form of government; and whatever complaint I have to make against the treatment of my people, I am willing to stay here and fight it out with you, and not try to destroy our form of government.

Again, I ask every Member of this House who believes in a square deal, Democrats and Republicans alike, to sign this petition. I do not care where you live, you ought to be willing to give me and the people I represent the same rights and privileges under the dome of the Capitol that you ask for yourselves and your constituents. I do not think 90 percent of the people of America knew there was a restaurant in this building until this thing came up. The Negroes have not been imposed upon you; nobody can say they have. Had the thing come about as a result of action taken by the committee, perhaps I would not have said so much; but according to statements made by members of the committee, it has never been discussed or acted upon. It was just the arbitrary action of this gentleman who comes from North Carolina because prejudice prevails down there.

To my Democratic friends who said this was a political movement, or, as a Negro newspaper said, brought about to create an issue to get votes in Illinois, let me say I do not need an issue to get votes in Illinois; I will get them without any issue, if necessary. I could not have instigated this. The gentleman from North Carolina and myself never have even spoken to each other that I know of. I did not tell him to issue the order that the Negro could not be served. I do not need that kind of an issue. I would not go into a conspiracy to hurt the Negro race for 40 congressional seats. It is not necessary at all. *The New York Times* printed a statement like that the other day, that I was back of the movement to get the students from Howard University to come here. The truth of the matter is I did not know anything about it before it happened; but I have since learned that the boy who was arrested was not, as claimed, a student from Howard University. [Applause.]

Congressional Record, March 21, 1934; 73rd Cong., 2nd sess., LXXVIII, 5047–49. *The New York Times* reported this matter rather fully and with a distinct tone of annoyance at the "troublesome" Black people—issues of January 24, 25, 28, March 18, 24, 28, April 26, 1934.

17

COWARDS FROM COLLEGES

by Langston Hughes

Few articles were more reflective of the deep challenges arising from young Black men and women than the following essay by Langston Hughes.

Two years ago, on a lecture tour, I visited more than fifty colored schools and colleges from Morgan College in Baltimore to Prairie View in Texas. Everywhere I was received with the greatest kindness and hospitality by both students and faculties. In many ways, my nine months on tour were among the pleasantest travel months I have ever known. I made many friends, and this article is in no way meant as a disparagement of the courtesies and hospitality of these genial people—who, nevertheless, uphold many of the existing evils which I am about to mention, and whose very geniality is often a disarming cloak for some of the most amazingly old-fashioned moral and pedagogical concepts surviving on this continent.

At every school I visited I would be shown about the grounds, and taken to view the new auditorium or the modern domestic science hall or the latest litter of pigs born. If I took this tour with the principal or some of the older teachers, I would often learn how well the school was getting on in spite of the depression, and how pleasant relationships were with the white Southerners in the community. But if I went walking with a younger teacher or with students, I would usually hear reports of the institution's life and ways that were far from happy.

For years those of us who have read the Negro papers or who have had friends teaching in our schools and colleges, have been pretty well aware of the lack of personal freedom that exists on most Negro campuses. But the extent to which this lack of freedom can go never really came home to me until I saw and experienced myself some of the astounding restrictions existing at many colored educational institutions.

To set foot on dozens of Negro campuses is like going back to mid-Victorian England, or Massachusetts in the days of the witch-burning Puritans. To give examples, let us take the little things first. On some campuses grown-up college men and women are not allowed to smoke, thus you have the amusing spectacle of twenty-four year old men sneaking around to the back doors of dormitories like little boys to take a drag on a forbidden cigarette. At some schools, simple card playing is a wicked abomination leading to dismissal for a student—even though many students come from homes where whist and bridge are common amusements. At a number of schools, dancing on the campus for either faculty or students is absolutely forbidden. And going to dancing parties off campus is frequently frowned upon. At one school for young ladies in North Carolina, I came across an amusing rule which allowed the girls to dance with each other once or twice a week, but permitted no young men at their frolics. At some schools marching in couples is allowed instead of dancing. Why this absurd ban on ballroom dancing exists at colored schools, I could never find out—doubly absurd in this day and age when every public high school has its dances and "proms," and the very air is full of jazz, North and South, in inescapable radio waves.

One of the objects in not permitting dancing, I divined, seems to be to keep the sexes separated. And in our Negro schools the technique for achieving this—boys not walking with girls, young men not calling on young ladies, the two sexes sitting aisles apart in chapel if the institution is co-educational—in this technique Negro schools rival monasteries and nunneries in their strictness. They act as though it were unnatural for a boy and girl to ever want to walk or talk together. The high points of absurdity during my tour were campuses where young men and women meeting in broad daylight in the middle of the grounds might only speak to one another, not stand still to converse lest they break a rule; and a college in Mississippi, Alcorn,— where to evening lectures grown-up students march like school kids in and out of the hall. When I had finished my lecture at Alcorn, the chairman tapped a bell and commanded, "Young ladies with escorts now pass." And those few girls fortunate enough to receive permission to come with a boy rose and made their exit. Again the bell tapped and the chairman said, "Unescorted young ladies now pass." And in their turn the female section rose and passed. Again the bell tapped. "Young men now pass." I waited to hear the bell again and the chairman saying, "Teachers may leave." But apparently most of the teachers had already left, chaperoning their grown-up charges back to the dormitories. Such regimentation as practiced in this college was long ago done away with, even in many grammar schools of the North.

Apparently the official taboo on male and female companionship extends even to married women teachers who attend summer seminars in the South, and over whom the faculty extends a prying but protective arm. The wife of a prominent educator in the South told me of being at Hampton for one of their summer sessions a few years ago. One night her husband called up long distance just to hear his wife's voice over the phone. Before she was permitted to go to the phone and talk to a MAN at night, however, she had to receive a special permit from, I believe, the dean of women, who had to be absolutely assured that it really was her husband calling. The long distance phone costs mounted steadily while the husband waited but Hampton did its part in keeping the sexes from communicating. Such interference with nature is a major aim on many of our campuses.

Accompanying this mid-Victorian attitude in manners and morals, at many Southern schools there is a great deal of official emphasis placed on heavy religious exercises, usually compulsory, with required daily chapels, weekly prayer meetings, and Sunday services. Such a stream of dull and stupid sermons, uninspired prayers, and monotonous hymns—neither intellectually worthy of adult minds nor emotionally existing in the manner of the old time shouts—pour into students' ears that it is a wonder any young people ever go to church again once they leave college. The placid cant and outworn phrases of many of the churchmen daring to address student groups today makes me wonder why their audiences are not bored to death. I did observe many young people going to sleep.

But there are charges of a far more serious nature to bring against Negro schools than merely that of frowning on jazz in favor of hymns, or their horror of friendly communication between boys and girls on the campuses. To combine these charges very simply: Many of our institutions apparently are not trying to make men and women of their students at all—they are doing their best to produce spineless Uncle Toms, uninformed, and full of mental and moral evasions.

I was amazed to find at many Negro schools and colleges a year after the arrest and conviction of the Scottsboro boys, that a great many teachers and students knew nothing of it, or if they did the official attitude would be, "Why bring that up?" I asked at Tuskegee, only a few hours from Scottsboro, who from there had been to the trial. Not a soul had been, so far as I could discover. And with demonstrations in every capital in the civilized world for the freedom of the Scottsboro boys, so far as I know not one Alabama Negro school until now has held even a protest meeting. (And in Alabama, we have the largest colored school in the world, Tuskegee, and one of our best colleges, Talladega.)

But speaking of protest meetings—this was my experience at Hampton. I lectured there the week-end that Juliette Derricotte was killed. She had been injured in an automobile wreck on her way home from Fisk University where she was dean of women, and the white Georgia hospitals would not take her in for treatment, so she died. That same week-end, a young Hampton graduate, the coach of Alabama's A.&M. Institute at Normal was beaten to death by a mob in Birmingham on his way to see his own team play. Many of the Hampton students and teachers knew Juliette Derricotte, and almost all of them knew the young coach, their recent graduate. The two happenings sent a wave of sorrow and of anger over the campus where I was a visitor. Two double tragedies of color on one day—and most affecting to students and teachers because the victims were "of their own class," one a distinguished and widely-travelled young woman, the other a popular college graduate and athlete.

A note came to me from a group of Senior students asking would I meet with a student committee. When a young man came to take me to the meeting, he told me that it would concern Juliette Derricotte and their own dead alumnus. He said that the students wanted to plan a protest on the campus against the white brutality that had brought about their death.

I was deeply touched that they had called me in to help them, and we began to lay plans for the organization of a Sunday evening protest meeting, from which we would send wires to the press and formulate a memorial to these most recent victims of race hate. They asked me would I speak at this meeting and I agreed. Students were chosen to approach the faculty for permission to use the chapel. We were to consult again for final plans in the evening.

At the evening committee meeting the faculty had sent their representative, Major Brown, a Negro (who is, I believe, the dean of men), to confer with the students. Major Brown began by saying that perhaps the reports we had received of the manner of these two deaths had not been true. Had we verified those reports?

I suggested wiring or telephoning immediately to Fisk and to Birmingham for verification. The Major did not think that wise. He felt it was better to write. Furthermore, he went on, Hampton did not like the word "protest." That was not Hampton's way. He, and Hampton, believed in moving slowly and quietly, and with dignity.

On and on he talked. When he had finished, the students knew quite clearly that they could not go ahead with their protest meeting. (The faculty had put up its wall.) They knew they would face expulsion and loss of credits if they did so. The result was that the Hampton students held no meeting of protest over the mob-death of their own alumnus, nor the death on the road (in a Negro ambulance vainly trying to reach a black hospital) of one of the race's finest young women. The brave and manly spirit of that little group of Hampton students who wanted to organize the protest was crushed by the official voice of Hampton speaking through its Negro Major Brown.

More recently, I see in our papers where Fisk University, that great (?) center of Negro education and of Jubilee fame has expelled Ishmael Flory, a graduate student from California on a special honor scholarship, because he dared organize a protest against the University singers appearing in a Nashville Jim-crow theatre where colored people must go up a back alley to sit in the gallery. Probably also the University resented his organizing, through the Denmark Vesey Forum, a silent protest parade denouncing the lynching of Cordie Cheek who was abducted almost at the very gates of the University.

Another recent news item tells how President Gandy of Virginia State College for Negroes called out the cracker police of the town to keep his own students from voicing their protest as to campus conditions. Rather than listen to just grievances, a Negro president of a large college sends for prejudiced white policemen to break his students' heads, if necessary.

And last year, we had the amazing report from Tuskegee of the school hospital turning over to the police one of the wounded Negroes shot at Camp Hill by white lynchers because the share-croppers have the temerity to wish to form a union—and the whites wish no Negro unions in Alabama. Without protest, the greatest Negro school in the world gives up a poor black, bullet-riddled share-cropper to white officers. And awhile later Tuskegee's president, Dr. Moton, announces himself in favor of lower wages for Negroes under the N.R.A. and Claude Barnett, one of his trustees, voices his approval of the proposed code differentials on the basis of color

But then, I remember that it is Tuskegee that maintains a guest house on its campus for *whites only!* It also maintains a library that censors all books on race problems and economics to see that no volumes "too radical" get to the students. And during my stay there several young teachers whispered to me that a local white trustee of the school receives his Negro visitors only on the porch, not in his house. It is thus that our wealthiest Negro school with its two thousand six hundred students expects to turn out men and women.

Where then would one educate "Uncle Toms"?

Freedom of expression for teachers in most Negro schools, even on such unimportant matters as to rouge or not to rouge, smoke or not smoke, is more or less unknown. Old and mossbacked presidents, orthodox ministers or missionary principals, control all too often what may or may not be taught in the class rooms or said in campus conversation. Varied examples of suppression at the campuses I visited are too numerous to mention in full in a short article, but they range all the way from an Alabama secondary school that permitted no Negro weeklies like the *Chicago Defender* or the *Pittsburgh Courier* in its library because they were "radical," to the great university of Fisk at Nashville where I asked a nationally known Negro professor and author of several books in his field what his attitude toward communism was, and received as an answer, "When I discuss communism on this campus, I will have a letter first from the president and the board of trustees."

There is at the Negro schools in the South, even the very well-endowed and famous ones that I have mentioned, an amazing acquiescence to the wishes of the local whites and to the traditions of the Southern color-line. When programs are given, many schools set aside whole sections in their own auditoriums for the exclusive use of whites. Often the best seats are given them, to the exclusion of Negro visitors. (But to insert into this article a good note, Mary McLeod Bethune, however, permits no such goings-on at Bethune-Cookman Institute in Daytona, one of the few campuses where I lectured that had not made "special provisions" for local white folks. A great many whites were in the audience but they sat among the Negroes.)

Even where there is no official campus segregation (such as Tuskegee's white guest house, or Hampton's hospital where local whites are given separate service) both teachers and students of Negro colleges accept so sweetly the customary Jim-crowing of the South that one feels sure the race's emancipation will never come through its intellectuals. In North Carolina, I was given a letter to the state superintendent of the Negro schools, a white man, Mr. N. C. Newbold. When I went to his office in Raleigh to present my letter, I encountered in his outer office a white woman secretary busy near the window quite a distance from the door. She gave me a casual glance and went on with what she was doing. Then some white people came into the office. Immediately she dropped her work near the window and came over to them, spoke to them most pleasantly, and ignored me entirely. The white people, after several minutes of how-are-you's and did-you-enjoy-yo'self-at-the-outing-last-week, said that they wished to see Mr. Newbold. Whereupon, having arrived first and having not yet been noticed by the secretary, I turned and walked out.

When I told some Negro teachers of the incident, they said, "But Mr. Newbold's not like that."

"Why, then," I asked, "does he have that kind of secretary?"

Nobody seemed to know. And why had none of the Negro teachers who call at his office ever done anything about such discourteous secretaries? No one knew that either.

But why (to come nearer home) did a large number of the students at my own Lincoln University, when I made a campus survey there in 1929, declare that they were opposed to having teachers of their own race on the faculty? And why did they then (and probably still do) allow themselves to be segregated in the little moving picture theatre in the nearby village of Oxford, when there is no Jim-crow law in Pennsylvania—and they are some four hundred strong? And why did a whole Lincoln University basketball team and their coach walk docilely out of a café in Philadelphia that refused to serve them because of color? One of the players explained later, "The coach didn't want to make a fuss."

Yet Lincoln's motto is to turn out leaders! But can there be leaders who don't want to make a fuss?

And can it be that our Negro educational institutions are not really interested in turning out leaders at all? Can it be that they are far more interested in their endowments and their income and their salaries than in their students?

And can it be that these endowments, incomes, gifts—and therefore salaries—springing from missionary and philanthropic sources and from big Northern boards and foundations—have such strings tied to them that those accepting them can do little else (if they wish to live easy) but bow down to the white powers that control this philanthropy and continue, to the best of their ability, to turn out "Uncle Toms"?

A famous Lincoln alumnus, having read my undergraduate survey of certain deplorable conditions on our campus, said to me when I graduated there, "Your facts are fine! Fine! Fine! But listen, son, you mustn't say everything you think to white folks."

"But this is the truth," I said.

"I know, but suppose," continued the old grad patronizingly, in his best fatherly manner, "suppose I had always told the truth to white folks? Could I have built up that great center for the race that I now head in my city? Where would I have gotten the money for it, son?"

The great center of which he spoke is a Jim-crow center, but he was very proud of having built it.

To me it seems that the day must come when we will not be proud of our Jim-crow centers built on the money docile and lying beggars have kidded white people into contributing. The day must come when we will not say that a college is a great college because it has a few beautiful buildings, and a half dozen Ph.D.'s on a faculty that is afraid to open its mouth though a lynching occurs at the college gates, or the wages of Negro workers in the community go down to zero!

Frankly, I see no hope for a new spirit today in the majority of the Negro schools of the South unless the students themselves put it there. Although there exists on all campuses, a distinct cleavage between the younger and older members of the faculties, almost everywhere the younger teachers, knowing well the existing evils, are as yet too afraid of their jobs to speak out, or to dare attempt to reform campus conditions. They content themselves by writing home to mama and by whispering to sympathetic visitors from a distance how they hate teaching under such conditions.

Meanwhile, more power to those brave and progressive students who strike against mid-Victorian morals and the suppression of free thought and action! More power to the Ishmael Florys, and the Denmark Vesey Forum, and the Howard undergraduates who picket the Senate's Jim-crow dining rooms—for unless we develop more and ever more such young men and women on our campuses as an antidote to the docile dignity of the meek professors and well-paid presidents who now run our institutions, American Negroes in the future had best look to the unlettered for their leaders, and expect only cowards from the colleges.

The Crisis, August, 1934; XLI, 226–28.

18

A WAGE DIFFERENTIAL BASED ON RACE

by Robert C. Weaver

An incisive analysis of the impact of the National Recovery Act upon Black workers came from the pen of Robert C. Weaver, who had received a Ph.D. in economics in 1933 from Harvard and was, at this writing, an assistant to Clark H. Foreman, Advisor on Negro Affairs in the Department of the Interior.

No issue affecting Negroes under the recovery program is of more importance than that of wage policy under the N.R.A. There is no other question arising out of the New Deal which has excited more discussion among enlightened Negroes. Like most important controversies, this is a complicated matter. To discuss it intelligently, one must consider the philosophy of the recovery program and the implications of the Negro's position in American Life.

There are two observations which are fundamental. In the first place, Southern industrial life is personal and paternalistic. The employers like to keep in touch with the workers. This paternalism is especially present in the relationship between the white employer and his Negro workers. A manufacturer of the deep South explained why he preferred Negro workers saying that he could handle them easier—they felt close to the boss and he felt close to them. On the other hand, the philosophy behind minimum wage provisions (and all social legislation) is that of an impersonal and highly developed industrial life. Thus there is a fundamental conflict between the Southern system and the labor provisions of the N.R.A.

The very idea of a sub-marginal minimum for Negro workers is an expression of the second important feature in the situation—the tendency to lump all Negroes together and judge them by the least desirable and the least able in the group. This tendency is, of course, the most arbitrary and pernicious feature of race prejudice.

Since the inauguration of the N.R.A., there has been a series of attempts to establish lower minimum rates of wages for Negro workers. First it was said that Negroes have a lower standard of living. Then, lower wages were defended on the basis of the Negro's lower efficiency. Lastly, it was pointed out that lower wages for Negroes were traditional and should be incorporated as a feature of the New Deal. However, the most telling and important argument for a lower minimum wage for Negroes was the fact that they were being displaced from industry as a result of the operation of the labor provision of the N.R.A.

Long before the New Deal was thought of, there was a constant displacement of Negroes by white workers. Certain cities in the South replaced their colored workers with whites; in other places organizations were initiated to foster the substitution of white for black laborers in all positions. The minimum wage regulations of the N.R.A. accelerated this tendency. Indeed, it resulted in wholesale discharges in certain areas. More recently, the tendency has been arrested.

There are many causes for the failure of the program to be carried further. In the first place, there is reason to believe that employers resorted to the discharge of colored workers as a means of forcing the N.R.A. to grant a racial differential. They declared that if a man had to be paid as much as twelve dollars a week, they would pay a white worker that wage. Then, too, there are many instances where it is impossible to discharge a whole working force. Even modern industry with its automatic machinery requires workers of some training, and training is a time and money consuming process. Thus, where Negroes formed a large percentage of the total working force, it was often impracticable to displace them and hire a new all-white labor force.

Nevertheless, there have been many displacements of Negroes. All the available evidence seems to indicate, as one would expect, that perhaps the greater part of this substitution of white for Negro workers has occurred in small enterprises where the Negro is often the marginal worker. In such plants, the separation of Negro workers presented no important question of organizational integrity or of training.

Out of these developments a movement for a racial differential has arisen. The motivating force for such a campaign has come from the Southern employers who have, for the most part, shifted their emphasis from standard of living and tradition to efficiency and displacement.

The latter feature—the loss of job opportunities to Negroes—has been made much of in recent months. Appeals have been made to Negro leaders to endorse a lower minimum wage for Negroes on the ground that such action is necessary if Negroes are not to be forced out of industry. The colored leaders have been careful in their championing of this cause. A few have been convinced that it is the only possible way out; some have supported the policy because of local pressure in the South but most have tried to keep out of the discussion. Many are almost convinced that it is the proper choice but fear a loss of prestige among Negroes if they speak in favor of such a measure.

Briefly, the only possible argument for a racial wage differential is one based upon a *de facto* situation. Negroes have lost jobs as a result of the N.R.A., and a lower wage for them would counteract this tendency. It would assure Negroes of retaining their old jobs and perhaps it would lead to a few additional ones. It may be observed that this reasoning is correct as far as it goes. Certainly, a racial differential would do much to arrest and, perchance, offset the displacement of Negro workers. But there is more involved in this question than the arresting of Negro displacement. In it are the elements which combine to establish the whole industrial position of colored Americans.

The establishment of a lower minimum wage for Negroes would have far reaching effects. It would brand black workers as a less efficient and sub-marginal group. It would increase the ill-will and friction between white and colored workers. It would destroy much of the advance Negroes have made in the industrial North. It would destroy any possibility of ever forming a strong and effective labor movement in the nation. The ultimate effect would be to relegate Negroes into a low wage caste and place the federal stamp of approval upon their being in such a position.

It was pointed out above that the most damnable feature of racial prejudice in America is the tendency to judge all Negroes by the least able colored persons. Obviously, a racial minimum is an expression of such an attitude. Were this not true, why should Negroes be singled out for a special—and lower—rate of pay? There have been no satisfactory or convincing studies of racial efficiency. (Efforts along this line are even more crude than the measures we have which have been set up to gauge intelligence.) Indeed, it is absurd to talk about racial efficiency since Negroes, like every other group of human beings vary in their effectiveness. The efficiency of a worker depends upon his native ability, environment and specific training. These factors differ between individuals rather than between races. A racial differential on the other hand would say, in effect, that efficiency is based on race and the individual black worker—because he is a Negro—is less efficient.

Now, there is still another phase of this matter. The very attitude which dictates a racial differential would make such a provision most discriminatory against colored workers. Any minimum wage tends to become a maximum. In the case of Negro workers this tendency would be accentuated. Since all Negroes are usually considered the same regardless of their ability, a lower minimum for black labor would in fact, mean that practically all Negroes would receive wages lower than their white prototypes. Not only would this be manifestly unfair, but in certain areas it would undermine the race's industrial progress of the last twenty years. During this period, Negroes have entered the industries of the North and the West as never before. They came from the South, where they were treated with mercy (as opposed to justice), and faced a situation which was new to them. Standards of efficiency were higher and they had to measure up to these new standards. Some failed but the recent data on Negro participation in Northern industry show that many succeeded. It has been a difficult process of adaptation. The fruits have been higher wages and less racial discrimination in rates of pay. To establish a differential based on race, would be, in effect, to take away the fruits of this hard-won victory.

Nor would the white worker respond favorably to the notion of a lower minimum for Negro workers. His first response in the South would be favorable because his ego would be flattered. But when the lower minimum destroyed the effectiveness of the higher minimum, the white recipient of the latter would blame the Negro. The black worker, North and South, would be regarded as the force which rendered it impossible for workers to demand a decent wage and find employment. This would occasion no end of misunderstanding and hatred between the white and black worker.

It is clear that the unity of all labor into an organized body would be impossible if there were a racial differential. The essence of collective bargaining is an impersonal and standard wage. Unionism rests upon the cooperation of all workers. A racial wage differential prevents both of these developments. It would, therefore, destroy the possibility of *a real labor movement* in this country.

The Crisis, August, 1934; XLI, 236–37.

19

THEY COULD MAKE THE BIG LEAGUES
by W. Rollo Wilson

Mr. Wilson was sports columnist for the *Pittsburgh Courier* and Commissioner, Negro National Association of Professional Baseball Clubs. It will be noted that he felt racism "precludes the possibility" of Black players in the so-called Big Leagues; but his article reflects the growing pressure that finally did smash this feature of jim crow.

A few weeks ago I sat in the lofty press box in the White Sox park, Chicago, covering the second annual "East-West" baseball game. The opponents were picked, all star teams of Negro players, coming mostly from the National Association of Negro Baseball clubs.

Almost twenty-five thousand fans paid from fifty cents to one and a half dollars to sit in on the spectacle. It marked the "high" of attendance for a Negro sports event.

On Memorial Day, in Pittsburgh, more than 12,000 saw two baseball games between the Pittsburgh Crawfords and the Homestead Grays, both members of the league.

Not all of the fans who go to these games are colored; in Chicago it was estimated that at least 10% of the crowd was white. In Philadelphia and other cities sundown clubs attract large numbers of whites in their home parks and when they play white teams in white parks the attendance is largely white. Indeed, the best drawing cards on the sandlots are the high class Negro nines.

All of which leads up to the questions—why are there no colored players in Organized Baseball and will there ever be any colored players, as such, in Organized Baseball?

In recent years a symposium on the subject conducted by this writer and his associates on several weekly newspapers revealed the answer to the first question through the typewriters of many nationally known white sportswriters.

Racial prejudice which, according to Bill Dooly, of the Philadelphia *Record,* is harder to change than a lead quarter, precludes the possibility of a Negro team or Negro players in the major leagues.

Organized Baseball is built on a system of leagues of graduated ability. It is nation-wide. Not all Negro players would be eligible for the "big time" and would have to prove themselves in loops of less rating. Except in some northern spots they could never play on mixed teams. Big league teams must go South for their preliminary training and tell me a city in the South where colored athletes could live and work with their white companions.

Briefly, you have the reasons; now, whether there ever will be Negro players in the big leagues, I cannot answer. The economic conditions of the game, desperate efforts some time in the future to give it new color and added stars, may pave the way. I am hopeful —and fearful.

Denied their place in the baseball sun because of racial prejudice Negro players have gone along, playing for little or nothing and have made reputations which have endured. Here in Philadelphia you will find hundreds of white fans who will tell you that they prefer seeing colored league games to going out to watch either the A's or Phils. We have educated them to high grade baseball by colored athletes.

Many of the men I have seen playing the game in the years agone and during the current season might have been big league stars had they been given the chance.

Out in Chicago on that eventful Sunday a few weeks past was one hurler who stood head and shoulders—literally and figuratively— above his fellows. After the game the fans were full of praise for Leroy Paige, ace pitcher of the East who had turned back the West menace in critical times.

They didn't refer to him as "Paige"; to each and everyone he was "Satchell," so yclept because of his long feet. Satchell Paige is the Dizzy Dean, the Rube Waddell (except that he is a right-hander) of colored baseball. Today you have him pitching a low-hit game for you; when you want him again he is on his way to the Dakotas or Dahomey. Satchell has wandering feet—maybe that's why they are so large—and he is a real problem to his owner and manager.

Jim Bell of the Pittsburgh Crawfords, scored the only run of that game and his fleetness of foot did it. He walked and stole second and tallied on a little hit which rolled across second base. A great outfielder, major league stars have said that he is the fastest man in baseball. They ought to know for many of them play with or against him during the off seasons. (In Cuba, Porto Rico or on the Coast playing with Negro stars does not brand white players with the bar sinister, it seems.)

Even Babe Ruth, himself, has driven no baseball farther in the

Yankee Stadium than I have seen Josh Gibson, catcher, hit them. During a series several years ago between the Homestead Grays and the Lincoln Giants, Josh, then serving his first year in tophole Negro baseball, hit one homer over the extreme left wing of the grandstand in the "House That Ruth Built."

"Ted" Trent of the Chicago American Giants, is another pitcher who ought to be in the big leagues. He has everything which any big league club needs in the way of a hurler. Recently he held the hard-hitting Philadelphia Stars to two hits and lost a 3–2 game. Unfortunately for him both of the hits were home runs and one came after a runner had been put on the sacks by a teammate's error.

I have not seen a first baseman anywhere who has impressed me as much as "Buck" Leonard, of the Homestead Grays. He is a certain fielder and a hard, steady hitter who would mace as many four-masters in the big circuits as Jimmy Foxx and Lou Gehrig.

I could fill this magazine with tales of players who might have been in the big leagues but space is too limited.

For instance, there was Joe Mendez, the Cuban, nicknamed by John McGraw "the black Christy Matthewson" and Mac's statement that he would sign him for the Giants if it were possible.

Oscar Charleston fifteen or more years ago was hailed as a greater fielder and faster base runner than Max Carey, then the idol of the Pittsburgh Pirates. That praise from a white baseball writer caused Barney Dreyfuss, late president of the Pittsburgh National league club, to refuse the use of his park to Negro teams for many years.

Without any reasons I'll give the names of some of the stars of our game who might have been in the big leagues and maybe I'll get the space to explain later on. Here goes: John Henry Lloyd, Louis Santop, Dick Redding, Dave Brown, Nip Winters, Phil Cockrell, Joe Williams, Dan McClelland, Rube Foster, Willie Foster, "Chet" Brewer, Dick Lundy, Bill Monroe, Bullet Rogan, Willie Wells, Vic Harris, Clarence Williams, Pete Hill, Jess Barbour, Bill Holland, Walter Cannady and many others. Most of these lads, if given the chance—and if prejudice were not the powerful agent we know it to be—would be valuable decorations in any American or National league ballyard.

The Crisis, October, 1934; XLI, 305–6. For subsequent efforts to break jim-crow in baseball, see the document by William L. Patterson, this volume, p. 375.

20

UNCLE TOM IN HOLLYWOOD

by Loren Miller

An early and vigorous protest against the racism permeating the movie industry came from a young California attorney; it was published in *The Crisis,* November, 1934.

A few years ago I attended a showing of *Trader Horn,* a Metro-Goldwyn-Mayer film, at a Negro theater. One scene depicts the "beautiful"—of course, blond—heroine in the clutches of "savage" Africans. In typical Hollywood thriller style the girl is saved just as all hope is ebbing away. At this particular showing the audience burst into wild applause when the rescue scene flashed on the screen. I looked around. Those who were applauding were ordinary Negro working people and middle class folk. Hollywood's movie makers had made the theme so commonplace and glorious that it seemed quite natural white virtue should triumph over black vice. Obviously those spectators were quite unconscious of the fact that they were giving their stamp of approval to a definite pattern of racial relationships in which they are always depicted as the lesser breed.

Unwritten, but iron clad rules in the movie industry require that films in which racial relationships are depicted show the white man as the overlord. Ordinarily Negroes get servant parts in which they are either buffoons or ubiquitous Uncle Toms. A written section of the code forbids the showing of miscegenation. Where there is racial clash as in *Birth of a Nation* the Negro is pictured as vicious and depraved. Occasional pictures such as *Hallelujah* or *Hearts in Dixie* purport to treat Negro life seriously but even there the economic roots of the Negro question are carefully avoided and the Negro is shown as a lowly, loyal and contented fellow happy in his lot.

News reels poke fun at Negro revivals or baptisings and avoid such "dangerous" subjects as the Scottsboro case. I heard dozens of administration spokesmen pleading for pet Roosevelt legislation or unimportant special laws but I did not hear a single lawmaker plead for the anti-lynching bill during the past year.

The cumulative effect of constant picturization of this kind is tremendously effective in shaping racial attitudes. Hollywood products are seen in every nook and corner of the world. Millions of non-residents of the United States depend almost entirely on the movies for their knowledge of Negro life, as those who have been abroad can testify. Other millions of white Americans of all ages confirm their beliefs about Negroes at the neighborhood theaters while Negroes themselves fortify their inferiority complex by seeing themselves always cast as the underdog to be laughed at or despised.

Although the Hollywood portrayal of Negro life is so out of focus that it is in effect rabid anti-Negro propaganda, it would be unfair to tax the movie magnates with inventing their product out of whole cloth. It is easy enough to see that the movies but reflect the traditional American outlook on the Negro question. By giving that tradition wide and effective circulation and by implying its artistic truthfulness, the movie makers are certainly doing more than their share to whip up prejudice and making the breakdown of racial chauvinism more difficult. Of course, Hollywood excuses its actions on the grounds that it is merely supplying the audiences with what they want. The argument is ingenious and plausible enough until one remembers how the movies consciously set out to mold public sentiment, as they did in the last war in the face of an overwhelming pacifist spirit among the American people. The differences in treatment of the Massie and the Scottsboro cases also illustrate the fact that the movies are deliberately used to further causes dear to the hearts of those who control them.

At the present time the movie makers are being attacked by a group of moralists in an effort to force them to make "clean" films. Negroes can expect little from this crusade because the moralists themselves define "cleanliness" in traditional terms. The Catholics, for example, list the showing of miscegenation as objectionable along with perversion and sexual intercourse. Another plumed knight of the crusade is William Randolph Hearst, an accomplished race baiter whose newspapers are distinctly unfriendly to all colored peoples. Hardly an organization enlisted in the present purity drive is opposed to Jim Crow and all that it means. The Negro will have to fend for himself. And he will learn that the opposition is formidable.

Those who control the movies are powerful in other phases of American life. The Chase National Bank, controlled by the Rockefellers, has its hands on a half dozen studios. A manual of corporate directorates will reveal the fact that movie boards interlock with those of other basic monopolies. The political tie-up is as plain. Louis B. Mayer of the Metro-Goldwyn-Mayers, is the personal friend of Herbert Hoover and a power in Republican politics. Jack Warner of Warner Brothers is commonly reputed to be the Roosevelt spokesman in Hollywood. These all powerful businessmen-politicians direct the destinies of the film world. The pictures they produce accord roughly yet firmly with their politico-economic outlook. Certainly, these men are far-sighted enough to realize that the movies are valuable aids in preserving the status quo on which their own welfare and profits depend. An important factor in the preservation of the status quo is the continued subordination of the Negro people. White superiority has cash value to them.

What can the Negro do? The first impulse is to say that he should produce his own films. Something of that sort is attempted in the Micheaux pictures. However the run-of-mine films produced by Negro companies fail miserably because their producers simply ape the white movies. Thus, we have ridiculous productions depicting burnt cork Clark Gables and Norma Shearers living in mansions and ordering butlers about. All semblance of reality is eschewed in efforts to match the current white films. Negro pictures of the past have been as out of focus as those produced by Hollywood. Those faults could be overcome, but tremendous technical difficulties both in production and distribution would remain. The average owner of the small theater is under the thumb of Hollywood producers and must take the pictures they offer him. Doubtless these Hollywood producers would not look kindly on competition even if capital for production could be obtained. I believe that the cost of production would be prohibitive. The best that can be hoped for in that direction, I believe, is the production of 16 millimeter films that might be shown in small halls. A "little movie" movement comparable to the "little theater" might be started.

The second move lies in protest. Negroes have used this weapon in the past to some degree. Past protest has taken the form of appeals to authority to ban such shows as *Birth of a Nation*. Some success has been registered, but that method has its limitations. In a showdown the political and economic power of Hollywood is great enough to force permission to show any film that it may produce. Again, protest of that kind can never reach the pictures in which the anti-Negro propaganda is introduced by always showing him at his worst or as an inferior, nor can it compel favorable news reel showings. Protest to be of its greatest value must be inculcated in the great mass of Negro people. They must be taught to recognize and resent anti-

Negro sentiment in such a manner that their feelings can reach the box office. They must let Hollywood know that they object vigorously to being shown as buffoons, clowns or butts for jest. They must stop applauding for such imperialistic jingoism as *Trader Horn*.

The Negro masses will adopt a critical attitude only if organs of opinion and Negro leadership establish an adequate critique for their guidance. Criticism of the movies is in a deplorable state at the present time. Negro magazines give no attention to it at all until some monstrosity such as the *Birth of a Nation* is announced. Negro newspapers have pages devoted to the theater and the film, but those pages are jokes, or worse. Most of such a page is given over to re-printing blurbs at the request of theater owners. Not long since, I saw one of these blurbs in a Negro newspaper lauding a white woman for her success in maintaining her virtue on a South Sea island! What space is not given over to the publicity men is reserved for pumping some Negro bit actor up to the dimensions of a star. One not acquainted with American life and reading only a Negro newspaper theatrical page could believe easily enough that some 45-second Negro bit player, depicting a servant, was the star of the film being reviewed! Such criticism is worse than useless; it is the abjectness of a beggar fawning over a penny tossed him by his lord. It is acceptance of "our place."

Nor is it easy to over-emphasize the importance of the movies as agents in shaping public opinion. It is vitally important that immediate and active steps be taken to try and effect a change in their present attitude toward the Negroes they depict. The people who can change that attitude are the theatergoers themselves. And they can and will do it if they are armed with an intelligently critical spirit. These same people could become the base for the "little movie" movement if they were taught to demand pictures that reflect their own lives and aspirations. So long as we sit acquiescent and give either passive or active support to the Hollywood bilge of the present we are guilty of teaching ourselves, our own children and millions of white, yellow and brown movie-goers the world over that the Negro is an inferior. It's time we took up arms on the Hollywood front. We might get in some telling blows just now when the movie makers are already under fire.

21

SOUTHERN TERROR

by Louise Thompson

Strikes and demonstrations demanding jobs and relief—almost always with Left leadership—appeared everywhere in the nineteen-thirties, the South included. In Birmingham, Alabama, this was met by intense and officially supported terror. One representative of the International Workers Order who was in Alabama at this time was Louise Thompson, described by the editor who published her account of experiences as "the leading colored woman in the Communist movement in this country." Louise Thompson (Mrs. William L. Patterson) at the present writing heads the New York Committee to Free Angela Davis—a Black Communist woman out of Birmingham!

"Birmingham is a good place for good niggers—but a damn bad place for bad niggers."

Thus spoke the officialdom of Birmingham, Ala., to me last May, and in the course of my experience there I learned what they meant. I was arrested as I went to enter the apartment of a woman whom I had known in the North. It so happened that the red squad was raiding her apartment at the time, and as I knocked at the door it was opened by a policeman who brusquely ordered me in. I did so, and was immediately placed under arrest. As they fired questions at me, one officer interrupted to ask:

"Gal, where you from? I know you ain't from around here 'cause you don't talk like it."

"My home is California," I answered.

"California, hell! You're one of those —— yankee ——, that's what you are!"

And with a few more remarks quite in keeping with the above they loaded me into the "black wagon," along with the other persons in the apartment at the time, and off to the city jail we went. I was promptly locked up, with no chance given me to communicate with friends or an attorney. My attempts to question the procedure met with laughter or taunts from my jailers. "Held for investigation," I learned later from my cellmates.

I spent the night with fourteen other Negro women held on charges ranging from drunkenness and pickpocketing to murder. One of the women was demented, and the two of us kept vigil that night, she, walking the floor and raving; I, wondering what was to happen to me on the morrow and what my friends would think when I did not return home that night.

The long night finally ended. Breakfast of huge soda biscuits, beans and a colored water which passed for coffee. Then I was called out, again taken for a ride in the patrol to the identification department for fingerprinting and "mugging" for the rogues' gallery. Though I was being accorded the treatment of a criminal I had yet to know what I was being held for, and when I would be permitted to communicate with the outside world.

During the cross examination which followed, my questioners were inclined at first to make a joke of the affair, taunting me about "my comrades," slyly alluding to some intimate relationship with the men arrested with me, and the like. But upon my refusal to answer any more questions until I had an opportunity to consult an attorney, their taunts turned to open threats which ran something like this:

"What about turning this gal over to the Ku Klux Klan? I reckon they know how to handle her kind."

"Yeah, or a little tar and feathering might help."

"How about talking to her through the rubber tube. She might be glad to talk then." (I later learned that "talking through the rubber tube" meant beating with a rubber hose in the third degree.)

Again, one officer turned to me, pointing his finger and said: "See here, gal, you're arrested now, see. And you say 'yes sir' and 'no sir.' "

I was told later by some of the women prisoners that I was lucky not to have been slapped down when I refused to obey.

Later in the day my friends finally succeeded in getting an attorney in to see me, after reading in the papers of the raid. He immediately prepared a writ of habeas corpus to force the placing of a charge against me or my release. And again I rode from the city jail to Jefferson county courthouse where the Scottsboro boys are imprisoned. There I was turned over to the prize red baiter and "nigger" hater of the plainclothes squad, Moser, who boasts of eleven notches in his gun for helpless Negroes he has shot down. These were his words of welcome:

"So you're one of those ——— reds what thinks you are going to get social equality for niggers down here in the South. Well, we think Communists are lower than niggers, down here—fact is, we don't even allow them to sociate with white folks, let alone have white folks 'sociating with niggers. We know how to treat our niggers down here

and we ain't going to stand for no interference from you ———
yankee reds. We ought to handle you reds like Mussolini does 'em
in Italy—take you out and shoot you against a wall. And I sure
would like to have the pleasure of doing it."

With which this "protector of law and order" escorted me to the
courtroom where I was to meet my attorney for a hearing on the
habeas corpus proceedings. When my attorney read the writ, Moser
triumphantly stepped up to the judge with a warrant for my arrest
as a "vagarant." Vagrancy is that convenient catch-all which serves
all purposes.

My bail was set for $300 cash, my trial for ten days hence. On
the tenth day I entered the courtroom and took my seat on the side
for Negroes to await the calling of my case. Surrounding the judge
were a group of officers and others, whom I learned later to be
members of the White Legion. From time to time they would suggest
to the judge or prosecutor questions to be asked the Negro prisoners
appearing before the bar of "justice." The word "nigger" rang out
from lips of judge, solicitor, officers, White Legionnaires every second.
Any attempt on the part of a Negro prisoner to dispute testimony
against him was met by, "Nigger, do you dare to dispute the word
of a white man?", or simply by loud bursts of laughter. Here was
"southern justice" undisturbed by any militant interference!

My case was finally called and I stood before Judge Abernathy. The
White Legion boys drew a little nearer, the police officers stepped up
to testify. All eyes were focused upon me. The judge then listened
to the testimony of the arresting officer, embellished with a few points
to win the laughing approval of the crowd about the bench. Meanwhile
the judge fingered the documents which disproved any charge of
vagrancy against me, my status as a representative of the International
Workers Order, the articles of incorporation which permit my organization to operate under state law, cancelled checks for my weekly
wages. He looked at me intently and then asked of the crowd about
him:

"Wonder where this gal is from? Looks like she came from Mississippi—that's the way they mix up down there. Course it's got
nothing to do with the case, but I'm going to ask her where she was
born as I'm mighty interested in how these mixtures turn out." And
to me, "Where were you born, gal?"

With no further questioning, the case was dismissed with the Judge
declaring, "You can't arrest the gal for being an octoroon."

"No, she can't help that," was Moser's parting shot.

I was not yet entirely free for another warrant was produced to arrest me on the charge of concealing my identity. A few days later, however, this second case was thrown out of court without my having to appear again.

The Bourbon authorities learned that the workers throughout the country were ready to apply their weapon of mass pressure against my arrest—and their experience with the Scottsboro case, with the Herndon case, made them cautious. They wanted stronger grounds to prepare another frame-up against a Negro engaged in working class activity.

Thus did I learn from first hand experience of the kind of "justice" meted out to Negroes in the South, of the unswerving determination of the servants of the State and of vested interests to keep the Negro people in utter subjection. And more, of the treatment of those who would help the Negro people in their fight for emancipation from this oppression. All the others arrested with me were white, yet they fared no better than I did, for as Communist suspects they are bitterly hated and granted no more constitutional rights than are given Negroes in the South. Being a Communist in the South is synonymous with being a fighter for the rights of the Negro people, of being a "nigger lover," of trying to bring white and Negro workers and poor farmers together—of fighting against lynching, of challenging the southern ruling class' traditional manner of treating Negroes. John Howard Lawson, prominent Hollywood playwright, who came to Birmingham to write up the terror was arrested as he left Jefferson county courthouse, fingerprinted and "mugged" and ordered from town. When he returned later with a delegation of liberals he was arrested again and charged with libel for telling the truth about the terror of Birmingham's police and White Legion.

A word or two about the White Legion, this openly Fascist organization in Birmingham whose stated purpose is to fight communism and any move to lift oppression from the backs of the Negro people. Its membership fee is $5.00, which of course precludes any worker members. As a matter of fact it recruits its members from the officials of the city, merchants and other middle class elements. It maintains an office on one of the main streets of Birmingham and displays in the front window Communist leaflets and any material from the Negro or revolutionary press which advocates equal rights for Negroes. One week they displayed a picture of Langston Hughes with his poem *An Open Letter to the South*, in which Hughes appeals to Negro and white labor to unite in struggle for a better world. The comment scrawled along the margin was: "If this bird thinks we are going to have social equality in the South, he's crazy!"

During the height of the terror against the Negro and militant white workers, the White Legion issued highly inflammatory leaflets seeking to provoke white against Negro workers. One such leaflet included this statement: "How would you like to awaken one morning to find your wife or daughter attacked by a Negro or a Communist!" It wound up with an appeal to pay the membership fee so that the White Legion could handle such situations in the traditional manner. During the planning of action against the class-conscious workers of Birmingham, one wing of the Legion was for riding through the Negro neighborhood and shooting indiscriminately into the homes of innocent Negroes, but cooler heads in the gang realized that such an extreme form of terror was a bit premature.

The southern press also played its part well during the reign of terror which did not end with our arrests, but went on in a series of raids upon the homes of workers over the entire city. The mining strike was at its height in Birmingham and for the first time Negro and white workers were militantly picketing together. The daily press came out with scare heads of "red violence" and "red plots" and references to "social equality." One paper carried a story of a raid upon a Negro home which produced a "highly inflammatory" document—it was the Bill of Civil Rights calling for full political, economic and social equality for the Negro people. Yet those papers which went beyond the borders of the state carried not a line of the raids, the arrests, or the general terror.

That the press, the White Legion and the government officials always link the "reds" and Communism with the Negro question is not a mere coincidence. First of all, the International Labor Defense through the Scottsboro case has aroused the Negro people and rallied to their defense workers over the whole world. And it is the Communist Party which has analyzed the Negro question as that of an oppressed nation of people, defined the alignment of class forces for and against the Negro people's struggle for liberation, and begun the organization of white and Negro working masses together. Revolutionary leaders in the South are boldly defying all that the southern ruling class has striven to perpetuate, and terror and jail bars do not stop them. Down in the heart of Dixie, the Black Belt, some 8,000 share-croppers have organized a militant Sharecroppers Union to fight the starvation program of the A.A.A. which deputy sheriffs' bullets have been unable to stop.

It is another matter, however, when organizations within the Negro group come forward as vehemently against any show of militancy on the part of the Negro masses and with as great enmity against a revolutionary program and revolutionary organizations as is expressed in the White Legion of Birmingham. Such organizations disregard the economic roots of the Negro's oppression, and through collaboration with the ruling class seek to restrain the masses of Negroes from militant struggle. Such organizations accept the present system of capitalism and are willing to be satisfied with what hollow reforms may come without any fundamental change.

But it is impossible to take one step in the direction of winning for the Negro people their elementary rights that is not revolutionary. Capitalism developed in America upon the super-exploitation of the Negro people and through the division created between white and Negro labor. Any attempt to end this super-exploitation, to destroy the enmity and to unite Negro and white labor is a blow at American capitalism. So it is that the southern ruling class is not going to budge from its position of exploiting and oppressing the Negro people. And behind the southern Bourbons stand the amassed strength of American finance capital—U.S. Steel, Wall Street investments in the plantations of the South, and the like. Any organizations among the Negro people which do not point out these class alignments must therefore become the voice of reaction in the midst of a people struggling for freedom. So it is that the leadership among the Negro people must pass into new hands—into the hands of working class leaders, the Angelo Herndons, who will not be stopped by jail, by a desire to cling on to jobs, by death itself in leading the Negro people through the final conflict to complete emancipation.

The Crisis, November, 1934; XLI, 327–28.

22

MINORITY PEOPLES IN TWO WORLDS
by Langston Hughes

Visiting the Soviet Union in the midst of the depression that ravaged the capitalist world—and not least the United States—was the Black poet

Langston Hughes. His impression was published in *New Masses*, February 12, 1935 (XIV, No. 7, pp. 18–20).

In the South, two years ago, a well-known Negro woman, a teacher, was severely injured in an automobile wreck when her car turned over, throwing the passengers into a field beside a country road. The teacher's name was Juliette Derricotte. She was motoring with three students from Fisk University in Nashville, where she was Dean of Women, to the home of her parents in the state of Georgia. Suddenly an approaching car, in order to pass a slower vehicle, swerved toward the centre of the road. Miss Derricotte, to avoid a collision, turned quickly to the side of the highway. Her wheels sank into a ditch, and her car turned over. The Negro teacher and the three students accompanying her were all badly injured. Passing motorists carried them into the nearest town, a small southern farming centre. Here the white hospital refused point blank to give treatment to Negroes, so the bruised and bleeding victims were not admitted. Instead, they were taken to the house of a poor black woman of the town and there white doctors gave them attention, without the necessary instruments and anaesthetics that the hospital could have furnished.

Three of them were suffering intensely, but the least injured of the four, a young student, was able to find a telephone. He called the nearest city in which a Negro hospital was located, and asked that an ambulance be sent for them. Late in the night the ambulance arrived, but on the way to the distant Negro hospital Juliette Derricotte, the teacher, died. Thus one of the most brilliant of our younger colored women was lost to America. Had not a white hospital refused to treat black people—even in so grave an emergency as this automobile accident—her life might have been saved.

That same day in Birmingham, Alabama, another young teacher, a man but recently graduated from Hampton Institute, was beaten to death by a white mob, lynched in broad daylight in the streets of a big city.

That week-end I was lecturing at Hampton, one of the largest and best known of the schools for Negroes in the South. The students there, learning of the circumstances of Juliette Derricotte's death and of the lynching in Birmingham, were full of grief and anger—one of the finest Negro teachers refused treatment in a white village hospital, and one of their own graduates beaten to death.

"We will organize a protest meeting," said the students. "Not even dogs would be treated like that."

So a committee was formed and plans were made. I was asked to help with the organization, to speak at the protest meeting, and to aid in formulating telegrams to the newspapers. But word of the students' plans soon reached the faculty, and when we met in the evening for a final talk, a representative of the President's office was there. This Negro teacher immediately began to throw cold water on the students' plan. He said that perhaps the newpaper reports of Miss Derricotte's death were not true. That the students should wait and investigate first. That even if the reports were true, the students could go quietly about writing a letter of condolence to the parents of the victims, and not hold an open protest meeting.

"Hampton," he said, "never protests. That is not our kind of a word. We go slowly and carefully and investigate."

When this teacher had finished speaking, the students were afraid to go ahead with their plans for a protest meeting. They knew that they would surely be expelled from school. They knew that it would be difficult for them to get into other schools. They would be black-listed as agitators. That had happened at Hampton before when there had been a student strike against oppressive and inhuman rules concerning campus life. So now, almost without argument, the students abandoned the idea of having a meeting. One or two of them were bitter and defiant, but the rest were afraid—so the meeting was not held. A teacher for whom the word *protest* was too strong, had killed the spontaneous and healthy desire of his students to speak against a land that lets injured Negroes die before it will open its white hospitals to them, and that lets mobs beat black men to death in the streets.

Another famous industrial school for Negroes, Tuskegee, in Alabama (founded by Booker T. Washington) has an endowment of over a million dollars gained by begging from rich white folks. Here the president and all the teachers are Negroes—yet there is on the grounds of Tuskegee a guest house where black people may not eat or sleep! This guest house is for white visitors only. Against this the teachers say nothing. But this indicates to what an extent philanthropy has bought the pride and manhood of the "intellectuals" of the black South. Behold how the education of Negro youth is controlled and demeaned by capitalist charity!

And with these charity dollars go preachers and prayers and hymns. Most of the presidents of the Southern Negro schools are ministers, and a large part of the education is religious. Many harmless amusements are forbidden the students on religious grounds. A rigorous and unnatural separation is enforced between boys and girls. Modern and scientific attitudes of study are discouraged. A mid-Victorian atmosphere prevails.

The reason, of course, for the prevalence of these Negro philanthropic schools and colleges is this: The free public school system in the south extends only partially to Negroes. Throughout this section laws separate Negroes from whites in all public places—trains, street cars, theatres, hospitals, and schools. Most southern cities have excellent school buildings for whites, but small and inadequate shacks for Negroes, with oft-times no institutions of higher learning for them at all. For example, the average annual expenditure per child of school age in Alabama is as follows: For white children, $23.57; for Negro children $3.81. A startling difference! In South Carolina the state spends for each white child an average of $27.88 per school year; but on each Negro child only $2.74 is spent. (Scott Nearing's *Black America.*) With such discriminatory odds against him, the Negro child has a difficult time getting an education. Thus, without the religious philanthropic schools, in many localities Negro children would remain utterly illiterate.

In Soviet Asia

In Kazakstan and Turkestan, before the Revolution when they were colonies of czarist Russia, the native children were utterly illiterate. Conditions were even worse there than they are now in Alabama. In Asia the czar supplied no schools for the education of the conquered peoples. And in the cells of the established Mohammedan *medresses* practically nothing except religion was taught, the Koran being the main text book. Even this meagre knowledge was open only to boys and men, not to girls and women.

Now, of course, in Soviet Central Asia all that is changed. The world knows of this change. But the surprising thing to a visitor from abroad, coming to Uzbekistan or Turkmenia, is the rapidity with which this change has been brought about. In less than ten years a new system of education has been introduced—and not only introduced but put into amazing working order. Teachers have been developed; students have been graduated; and illiteracy, not only of children but of adults, has been greatly reduced. The cells of the *medresses* are empty, and the schools of the state are overcrowded. New books in a new alphabet have come into being. Already, to the youth today, Allah is only a legend, and the Koran is forgotten. Marx, Lenin, Stalin, chemistry, economics, mathematics, scientific agriculture, electricity, and hygiene are the new realities to millions who once knew only the sleepy teachings of the priestcraft.

"How have you done this?" I asked in wonder when I visited the offices of the Commissariat of Education in Ashkhabad, capital of the Turkomen Soviet Socialist Republic in the heart of Asia. "How in so short a time have you developed this new Soviet educational system, created teachers, built schools, and taught thousands of students, awakening the minds of the masses?"

They told me how it had been done. It had not been easy—building this path to education in a region where illiteracy had been so great. But in the early years many teachers came down from Russia to help. Bright young Turkomen workers were chosen and sent away to normal schools in Russia with all expenses paid. They returned bringing new light. Textbooks were translated from the Russian and other languages. New texts were written in the Turkomen tongue. Sometimes they were copied by hand when printing processes were unavailable. Students taught one another, taught their parents, taught the peasants and workers. There was a comradely exchange of knowledge. What would have been a tremendously hard task was made easier by the great eagerness of the people to learn—the hunger for knowledge that czarism had starved. Thousands of new books, magazines, and newspapers in the national languages, but in the new universal Latin alphabet, were published, thus encouraging the desire to read. And now in 1934 in Turkmenia, this once most backward of the czarist colonies, there are 6,100 teachers (85 percent of them native people) and 75,000 pupils and students!

This information came to me from a group of officials in the Turkomen Narcompros (Commissariat of Education)—a group that included Turkomen, Russian, Tartar, and Tyurk nationalities—all working for the common aim of enlightening the masses. Each man spoke to me with great enthusiasm of his work, one telling of the creation of text books, another of the village schools, another of the kindergartens, another of the theatres and art classes. I was told how teachers study in summer and are paid while studying. (And I thought of America where many teachers have not been paid at all for months.) I was told of the excursions and rest homes provided for educational workers in Turkmenia. I was told, too, how children here in Soviet Asia stay in school during the cotton gathering season. (And I contrasted in my mind Alabama where school bells may ring—but black children remain in the fields when cotton needs picking.) I was told how at present seven years' schooling is required for all Turkomen children but that, beginning next year, ten years will be the minimum. And I was told that the struggle now is for *quality* in teaching and that all forces are being pushed toward that end—since the broad basis of education is already established. Today the task is to make education as excellent as possible.

During the weeks that followed, I visited nearly all of the scholastic institutions of Ashkhabad and several of the surrounding villages. I was under the guidance of a most enthusiastic Soviet teacher and MOPR worker, Comrade Stephan, a political exile many years ago from Belgium, who now teaches in one of the large seven-year schools at Ashkhabad. Every morning before his teaching duties began, Comrade Stephan would call at the *Dom Sovietov* for me to go visit with him a school, a museum, a library, or a factory.

I met many teachers and students and had a chance to talk to them. How different, I discovered, was the Soviet students' attitude from that of the American student. At home, with most students, football and other sports occupy a leading place in their conversations. In Turkmenia, students held passionate conversations about the progress of life under the First Five-Year Plan, the growth of literature under the Soviets, the plans of the imperialists beyond the borders. Here in a remote corner of Asia, I found young people asking intelligent and penetrating questions about happenings in France, Cuba, Mexico, and other countries where I had been.

And everywhere in Ashkhabad there are schools—an amazing number! There are schools for Turkomen children, for Farci children, for Russian children, with the teaching in each case in their own language. There are high schools. There are colleges of pedagogy, commerce, science, transport, veterinary treatment. There are special research institutes, with laboratories of bacteriology, mineralogy and botany for graduate students. There is a library school every summer for village librarians held under the guidance of the Turkomen Central Library. And besides all these, there are night schools for workers, schools in clubs, schools in the Red Army barracks, and schools in factories. For instance, attached to the Eighth of March Silk Mill there is not only a seven-year school, but a silk high school, a liquidation of illiteracy school for grown-ups, and a Communist Party school for candidates to the Party. Children and adults all go to school. All this, mind you, in the comparatively small city of Ashkhabad in the heart of the Turkmenian desert north of Persia where once, under the czar, Turkomens were not even allowed on certain streets of the towns, let alone in the classrooms of the Russian schools; and as recently as 1920 not more than 1 percent of the whole country's population could read or write!

But now the masses are making up for lost time. Even in the dusty little villages of the desert, new school buildings are being built, larger and better than the small ones that served in the early years immediately after the Revolution. To these rural schools will come new young Turkomen teachers from the normal schools at Ashkhabad; some even from the larger institutions at Tashkent; and others who have been to far-away Moscow for their education. The light of learning is pouring in an intense blaze over Soviet Asia. Turkmenia welcomes this light with open arms.

I spent a day at the First Turkomen Normal School at Kishi. This is attached to a modern combinat containing within itself all grades from kindergarten through the normal courses. It is located in a sandy plain a short distance from the city of Ashkhabad. On one side the desert stretches away to the horizon, and on the other the mountains rise like a wall. Beyond is Persia.

The Director of the First Turkomen Normal School is a political immigrant from Persia. There he was a shoemaker. Here he has under his guidance three hundred and fifty students and thirty-eight teachers. He received his training at the Communist University in Tashkent. He is a dark, firm man who impresses one well. He did not talk a great deal, but he showed me through the wide halls and well-lighted class rooms of the main normal building—and what I saw was better than words, I saw the splendidly equipped laboratories, the museum of biological and geological specimens and charts, and the room where the live animals for student study are kept: white rats, turtles, frogs, and fish, and great lizards that swell their bodies with air to ferocious size. I listened to some of the classes being conducted. I remarked on the various nationalities among both teachers and students. The students were largely local Turkomen, Farci, Beluchi, and Berberi, but there were a few Russians, some Tartars and Armenians. The teachers were Russian, Turkomen and Farci. Among them were five women, one an assistant professor. This is a remarkable thing in a land where a decade ago women neither taught nor received teaching.

I was interested in the social origin of the students. The greatest number, the director explained to me, are from poor peasant parentage, one hundred and forty-one in actual figures. Sixty-six are from the kolkhozes, forty-six are workers, twenty-nine are from the militia, and the rest are from hired farm labour and small proprietor stock. One hundred and twenty-six students are Young Communists, and thirty-seven are either in the Party proper, or are candidates for membership.

The students who gathered to greet me were interested in learning of student life in America. I spoke to them in English, which Comrade Stephen translated into Russian, which was then re-translated into Turkomen. But even with these double translations we succeeded in effecting some interesting exchanges of background and opinion. I told them of the difficulties for poor students, especially of minority groups in America. And they in turn told me of their new life and gave me their revolutionary greetings to carry back to the proletarian youth in the United States who still live under capitalism, and to the Negro students caught in the tangled web of philanthropy and oppression.

But the little children of the seven-year school to whom I spoke later were not satisfied with sending mere verbal greetings so far away as America. When they gathered in the open yard in the sunshine about the steps of their building, they brought with them a beautiful wall newspaper that they had made themselves in the Turkomen language for me to carry back to the Young Pioneers of America.

I shall not soon forget that sea of little faces below me as I stood on the steps—yellow, brown, white faces of these children of the Turkomen Socialist Soviet Republic as represented in this school on the edge of the desert. I shall never forget the eager questions that they put to me for more than an hour about life in those utterly different lands abroad where workers' children may suffer hunger and cold and lack of schooling, while other children have everything. How can there be enough food, and yet all people do not eat? And do they actually burn wheat in America to keep from selling it cheaply? Why are Negroes lynched? And is there really an electric chair?

When the questions were finished, a little fellow came forward with their wall newspaper with its bright picture of a revolutionary sun at the top, which they entrusted to my care.

Then I went away. Their lusty young voices rang out in farewell as a horse and cart belonging to the school carried me back to Ashkhabad.

It was all very different from Alabama.

23

I BREATHE FREELY

by Paul Robeson

The visit to the U.S.S.R. of Langston Hughes was by no means unusual for Black people, especially during the depression years. Another account of such a visit came from Paul Robeson, in an interview in Moscow he granted to Julia Dorn. This was published in *New Theatre*, a magazine then issued in New York City, in July, 1935 (II, No. 7, p. 5).

Paul Robeson, looking for a medium and a starting-point from which to determine the true African culture, has found in Soviet Russia the closest and most friendly attitudes to his own. The internationally known Negro singer and actor, at the end of his first visit to the Soviet Union early this year, said, "In Soviet Russia I breathe freely for the first time in my life. It is clear, whether a Negro is politically a Communist or not, that of all the nations in the world, the modern Russians are our best friends."

Since he speaks Russian, Robeson was able to talk directly with children, peasants and workers. Everywhere, in tramways, buses, streets and parks, he met with the same reaction from the people, he told this interviewer. "I was rested and buoyed up by the lovely, honest, wondering looks which did not see a 'negro,'" he said. "When these people looked at me, they were just happy, and interested. There were no 'double looks,' no venom, no superiority. . . ."

Looking for roles and songs, he has reached the same conclusion as Professor Kislitsan, the Russian sociologist, who has announced facts to prove that all races are related in culture, differing in the degree of their development only so far as they are affected by natural resources or the hindrances of exploitation.

"I find," declared Paul Robeson, "that the handicraft of certain periods of the Chinese and African cultures are almost identical; and that the Negro is more like the Russian in temperament and character."

Robeson has taken a keen interest in the Soviet minorities, their culture and the policy on national minorities. During his short stay in Moscow, he talked with representatives of the Commissariat of Public Education, and saw the policy in action. He plans to return to the Soviet

Union to make a serious study of minority groups, which is to be linked with his intensive researches into Asiatic and African culture. He has insisted, in answer to press comments labelling his interest in Africa "jingoistic," that he is not trying to "escape" race oppression in America and Europe by taking a nationalist attitude.

"I came here," he says, "because the Soviet Union is the only place where ethnology is seriously considered and applied. . . . Africa does not realize that it has something to contribute, that it has a culture as clear as the European. The Africans, instead of preserving their own culture, are fighting the idea of 'be what you are,' and go European as soon as they can. . . . The African and American Negro problem is not purely racial. These cultures must be freed, formulated, and developed, and this cannot be done without a change in the present system. The Negro cannot develop his culture until he is free."

Africa must be taught to be proud of its contributions. "Stalin speaks of the cultures of the different nationalities of the Soviet Union as 'socialist in content and national in form.' . ."

Mr. Robeson was interested in the Eastern and Russian music, which he believes African music strongly resembles.

"The Negro folk songs and African music strongly resemble Eastern and Russian music. When I approached Russia, I found that I was interested in the Eastern part. I can't read Turgeniev, whose language is influenced by France and the West," said Mr. Robeson, who reads and speaks Russian fluently, "but I am interested in Gogol and Pushkin, who show more Eastern and Tartar influence. . . ."

Paul Robeson is vitally interested in the efforts of the Western Negroes to free themselves. He stated, "I believe there is no such thing in England and America as inter-racial *cooperation* from the NAACP point of view. Our freedom is going to cost so many lives that we mustn't talk about the Scottsboro case as one of sacrifice. When we talk of freedom, we don't discuss lives. Before the Negro is free, there will be many Scottsboros. The Communist emphasis in that case is right."

Becoming more personal, Mr. Robeson spoke of needing something to sing outside of Negro and English folk songs, and Western peasant folk material, and of discovering, about four years ago, the Hebrew and Russian songs. He learned the two languages, finding that they were both quite easy for him.

"There is little audience in England and America for the things I feel like singing or playing. They want Negro religious songs from which they take, not the suffering, but the comfort of the resignation they express (not heeding that the song's cry for heaven is only a reflex from the Negro's having suffered hell on earth). . . ."

Although he did not give any concerts during this visit, Mr. Robeson sang some of his most popular songs to the workers of the Kaganovitch Ball Bearing Plant, where he was applauded by a group including a great many foreign and American workers. He also broadcast; and on his return, he plans a concert tour of folk songs, and there is talk of a film with Eisenstein. He said, "The most important development in Soviet culture I have seen is in the moving picture field."

Among the theatres he visited, Mr. Robeson was most interested in the Moscow Children's Theatre, and the Realistic Theatre. At the former, he was pleased by *The Negro Boy and the Monkey,* a popular play about a little African who comes to the Soviet Union and is guided by his Pioneer comrades. The production method of Oxlopkhov (regisseur of the Realistic Theatre) impressed him with its similarity to motion picture technique, which he feels is best adapted to the tempo of life in the Soviet Union. Its plan, with the audience surrounding the stage platform, and participating in the performance, agrees with his own feeling that the artist should be in close contact with his audience.

Paul Robeson's activities have been put, with the enlargement of his interests, on an international scale, including studies and experiments in Eastern cultures along with his participation in African and American affairs. In correlating racial cultures, he sets a standard of awareness, saying, "The Negro must be conscious of himself and yet international, linked with the nations which are culturally akin to him."

24

GEORGIA TEACHERS AND EDUCATIONAL ASSOCIATION: A NEW DEAL FOR THE NEGRO SCHOOL CHILD

There was launched, in 1935, an association whose title is given above; the subtitle comes from a printed leaflet issued by the association at the time, the text of which is printed below. The association's president was Mrs. M. Agnes Jones, Supervisor of Negro Schools, Atlanta; other officers were principals of various elementary and high schools for Black children in the state and W. M. Hubbard, president of the state T & A College in Forsyth, as well as Henry A. Hunt, connected with the Federal Farm Credit Administration. On the Advisory Committee were John Hope, president of Atlanta University, and W. E. B. Du Bois, then a professor at Atlanta University.

I. What Is the Association?

It is an organization of teachers, associated with other professional workers, business men and all other men and women whose fundamental interest is the improvement of the educational opportunities for Negro children of Georgia.

II. What Is the Program of the Association?

We, the Georgia Teachers and Educational Association, in order to form a more perfect state and nation, establish interracial good-will, insure economic stability, provide for the development of the hidden resources of Negro life, promote the effective training of our people, to insure the enlightenment of the thousands of Negro children in the State of Georgia, do ordain and establish this Declaration of Principles for the education of Negroes in the State of Georgia.

1. *Qualified teachers.* The number of qualified Negro teachers must rapidly increase.

2. *Salary scale.* Correspondingly, the salary for qualified teachers in Negro schools must be raised.

3. *School buildings.* Equipment facilities for Negro children must be greatly improved, more consolidated schools provided and adequate expenditures made for transportation.

4. *School term.* Negro children need a nine-month term of which the State should guarantee a minimum of seven months.

5. *High school.* The State should provide high schools for those thirty-two counties where no secondary school work is now offered for Negroes and support four-year high schools wherever the need exists.

6. *Extension work.* Negro children need a multiplication of the various extension agencies, such as Jeanes Supervisors, Farm and Home Demonstration Agents and teachers of Vocational Agriculture, Home Economics, and Trades.

7. *Adult education.* There is great need for continued attack upon illiteracy and for increased vocational efficiency and training in citizenship.

8. *Higher education.* We urge the Board of Regents to so re-organize and strengthen state schools for Negroes as to support at least one fully accredited four-year college and at least two fully accredited junior colleges for acceptable training in Liberal Arts, Teacher-Training, Agriculture, Home Economics, and Building Trades.

III. How Will This Program Be Carried Out?

By a membership drive; the strengthening of the city, county and district organizations; the finding and disseminating to individual teachers the facts concerning both the Emergency and the regular educational program for Negro children; periodic publications for teachers and publicity; increased functioning of district president and county and city regents; by keeping our needs before the state relief administration and the officials of the State Department of Education; the cooperation of our universities and Advisory Committee, and, ultimately, through the activity of a competent Executive Secretary.

Six-fold leaflet, in editor's possession.

25

TRENDS IN NEGRO EDUCATION
by Williana J. Burroughs

As part of the Left-led organizations of the unemployed early in the nineteen-thirties, an association of unemployed teachers was formed and by 1933 it issued a monthly periodical, *The Unemployed Teacher*. Early in 1935 it published the following article by an Afro-American teacher and activist in efforts at organizing the unemployed.

Though it has always been clear that the separate Negro public school system of the South, with its unfair appropriation, ramshackle, makeshift, inadequate buildings, low teacher pay, short school term and backward educational practices was responsible for the low level of education in that region, the authorities, utterly indifferent, modified none of its reactionary features. Even the stigma of the largest illiteracy rate of any section did not shame them into any reforms.

It has always been the practice for southern communities to divide the funds unequally for the two sets of schools, Negro and white. In some states only $1.50 is spent per capita for Negro schools. Totally inadequate budgets such as this have all along been supplemented by extra funds. Two sources supplied this money, the colored people themselves, and northern missionary societies, and the three foundations, Rockefeller, Rosenwald and Jeannes, and Phelps-Stokes. This money maintains modern rural schools, colleges, and academies, which local authorities do not provide.

With the coming of the crisis the whole makeshift fabric of segregated schools, both public and private, was shaken. Whole counties in Tennessee, Alabama, and S. Carolina closed down their schools. Teachers were dismissed wholesale. Salaries were slashed. Teachers were unpaid. Terms were shortened further. Gifts from the North fell off. The Negro people, suffering mass unemployment and very much reduced in income because of the N.R.A. wage policy and A.A.A. acreage-reduction schemes, were less able to contribute their share. In such a situation (for which it was largely responsible), the Federal government, which heretofore had steadily refused to consider national aid for Negro education, was forced to act. At a conference called by the federal department of education, government officials outlined their plans to the many Negro educators present.

In brief, Washington proposed to contribute to the educational budgets of the southern states, "so that every Negro child might have its rightful heritage of training." No demands were made on the South that it change its policy of racial discrimination. On the contrary, one resolution stated definitely that "we have no intention of challenging the customs of the section." So Jim Crow remains with government sanction.

Following the fascist practices of the South, certain communities above the Mason-Dixon line have long maintained separate schools. Delaware, New Jersey, Ohio, and later Philadelphia have such systems. Today reactionary forces are making desperate efforts to extend the Jim Crow area. Recently in Jersey, Pennsylvania, and Chicago, Negro parents, citizens, and students have been forced to put up a vigorous battle against separate schools in these places.

Rich New York also fails to provide adequately for its large colored school population. Surveys here disclose old unsanitary buildings, fire-traps in some cases, overcrowded classes, few up-to-date laboratories or workshops, swimming pools or playgrounds. There is talk in official educational circles of the need for a special curriculum for Harlem. Residents say that their childern are kept out of the modern well-equipped schools nearby. Well-informed people say that the Board of Education does not considered Harlem one of the show places of the school system. No nursery schools have been placed by the N.R.A. management in Negro Harlem, and teachers in such a school in Spanish Harlem were instructed not to admit dark Porto Ricans.

America thinks so well of the results of her limited school program for Negroes that she shares this knowledge with other imperialist powers. Teachers College is one center of education for imperialists. Some colonial teacher or administrator can always be found there, studying under Miss Mable Carney, who directs this work. Later they confer with Dr. Thomas Jesse Jones, another expert in Negro education, who is the representative of various foundations, already mentioned above which are interested in Negro education. He pilots them around the country, showing them Hampton, Tuskegee, and other Negro units. The visitor views graphs, tests, and statistics, which prove the Negro to be inferior. He is convinced that America has the proper method by which to keep the Negro in his place.

From what has been said, it is apparent that the control of Negro Education by strong financial and industrial groups is open and direct. Stringent trustee and faculty direction result in an entire lack of freedom for both the teaching and student body.

No militant action has ever been taken by the organized teachers of America against these various forms of rank injustice practised against the largest minority in the country. Even a resolution against discrimination in schools has been voted down year after year in the A. F. of L. convention. The Progressive Education Ass'n has progressed as far as a round table discussion on "The Place of Minorities in America." Negro teachers themselves are organized for the most part in the Ass'n of Teachers in Colored Schools. Their criticism of conditions shows a keen realization of prevailing evils and an earnest desire to better the schools. Up to the present, however, they have failed to develop a program of action.

Negro students have shown more aggression in fighting vicious practices in school policy than have Negro teachers. Despite the severity of faculty rule, students at Hampton and Fisk have on occasion gone on strike. Students of Howard staged a protest against exclusion of Negro guests from the House dining room. Students from Negro schools have been delegates to every recent student conference. The presentation of demands for the freedom of the Scottsboro boys to President Roosevelt by students of Fisk is still in our minds.

Some teachers, too, see the necessity for action on their part. At a summer college discussion, the question was raised, "How can we smash Jim Crow in education?" These are signs of a willingness for action. Taken with the desire for militant organization expressed at the last N.E.A. convention, and the resolution against segregation passed at the last A. F. of L. gathering, these show the possibility of effective united action against the fascist imperialist tendencies in Negro education.

The Unemployed Teacher (New York City), January, 1935; III, 3.

26

THE HARLEM OUTBREAK OF 1935

On March 19, 1935, sparked by the arrest of a boy, thousands of Harlemites rebelled, directing their anger at police and at stores displaying commodities of which they were so largely deprived. A brief contemporary account of the event as given in a leading Black newspaper follows as document [a]. An investigating committee filed a Report to Mayor La Guardia on the outbreak in March, 1936. This was not made public until it was printed in full—all thirty-six thousand words—in the *Amsterdam News* of July 18, 1936, and from that newspaper is taken a summary of the Report (document [b]). The chief author of the Report was Dr. E. Franklin Frazier; on the committee were, in addition, Dr. Charles H. Roberts, a dentist, chairman; Eunice Hunton Carter, an attorney; Hubert T. Delany, then tax commissioner; Countée Cullen, the poet; A. Philip Randolph; Charles E. Toney, a judge of the Municipal Court; and four white people: Oswald Garrison Villard; William J. Schieffelin, a financier and a trustee of Tuskegee; and two attorneys of the American Civil Liberties Union, Morris Ernst and Arthur Garfield Hays. An illuminating essay on the event, by Alain Locke, forms document [c].

[a]

HARLEM IS SCENE OF BATTLE

One man is dead,* two others are reported dying and scores are suffering from battered heads as Harlem's worst race riot in 25 years continues. Property damage, the result of fires and the smashing of shop windows will amount way into the thousands, it is said.

In an effort to halt further bloodshed between members of both races, Commissioner of Police Valentine called out reserves to aid the regular Harlem police. Throughout Tuesday night and Wednesday morning patrolmen roamed the streets from 110th Street to 145th Street swinging their night sticks assaulting every member of the Race that crossed their paths.

Harlem Tuesday night was bedlam with shots, screeching sirens of police cars, clanging fire apparatus called out by numerous false alarms and the clamor of rioters.

The situation has become tense. At least a dozen policemen have

* The "man" was a high school youngster named Lloyd Hobbs.

been hurt in hand-to-hand battle with Harlemites who resisted their brutal tactics.

The trouble was the outgrowth of a false report said to have been started by a group of organized radicals that a fourteen year old youth, Lino Rivera, had been killed in the Kresge 5-and-10 cent store on 125th Street and 7th Ave. The boy was not killed, but was reprimanded for stealing a ten-cent knife. He was released after he had bitten two store clerks.

When the news spread of the child's death, several men and women started a fight in the store and later smashed the plate glass windows. Crowds coming from the Harlem Opera House and Apollo Theatre joined the fight and 200 shop windows from 125th Street to 139th Street were smashed.

Not until 2 A.M. Wednesday—ten hours after the trouble began—could police find the boy to prove he was alive.

At least a dozen men and women are under arrest; scores of suspects are being questioned, and a half dozen whites, victims of rocks, knives, and revolvers were given treatment by ambulance surgeons.

Chicago Defender, March 23, 1935.

[b]

COMPLETE RIOT REPORT BARED

Answering the public's demand to get the word-by-word report of the Mayor's Commission which investigated conditions in Harlem following the March, 1935, rioting, the *Amsterdam News,* in this issue, puts into print every word of this report which Mayor F. H. La Guardia has insistently refused to release, although His Honor has had it in his possession since March 19, 1936.

From time to time, segments of this 36,000-word document have reached the public, but this is the very first time that anyone, outside of the commission itself, and the Mayor, has been able to read the report.

More than the complete report, the *Amsterdam News* is here making public for the first time the original chapter of conclusions—Chapter IX—which was considered too hot, too caustic, too critical, too unfavorable by the Mayor, and was allegedly revamped by the commission to make it more to his liking. The Chapter Nine in the official report in the Mayor's hands is the softer, less biting chapter.

Word for word, paragraph by paragraph, some of the findings of the commission will be found to be nothing new—no facts that Harlemites and New Yorkers have not known, or could not have known long before the riots of March 19.

Here, however, these conditions are reviewed and uttered by a commission having the sanction of the head of the City government, and conclusions are made, not only by the social workers and reformers, but by the "salt of the earth," the man in the street, the men and women who feel most the rigors of starvation, the spiked heels of the police, and the crushing load of high rents and discrimination in employment most.

The Commission, headed by Dr. Charles H. Roberts, 233 West 139th Street, and consisting of both whites and Negroes, lawyers, preachers, civic and public servants, reviewed the occurrences of the March afternoon, when a teenage boy, Lino Rivera, stole a pocket knife from a 125th Street five and ten cents store. It tells again of the combination of circumstances which made people to believe the young Negro boy had been beaten to death, and of how the police, first, inefficiently, and next, ruthlessly, tried to meet the excitement of the people.

The report tells how the commission could not locate a "committee of women shoppers" which the police said it had allowed to go into the basement of the store to verify that the boy had not been killed, and infers that no such committee of shoppers ever existed.

It records how the police told inquiring Negroes that the Rivera affair was none of their business, and how honest, decent citizens were chased away both from the store and the nearby police station when they tried to get the truth.

On the question of the crowd-inciting leaflets issued by the Young Liberators and which were supposed to play a prominent part in fanning the riot flames, the Commission notes that the leaflets did not hit the streets until 7:30 P.M. and therefore, the group "were not responsible for the disorders and attacks on property which were already in full swing. Already a tabloid in screaming headlines was telling the city that a race riot was going on in Harlem," the report states.

Speaking on the part the Communists played in the rioting, the Commission declares:

"While one, in view of the available facts, would hesitate to give Communists full credit for preventing the outbreak from becoming a race riot, they deserve more credit than any other element in Harlem for preventing a physical conflict between whites and Negroes."

Long felt hostility to the police, resentment at the inability to get economic opportunities in the midst of plenty, were some of the reasons for the rioting, the report states, and then detailedly it records its findings under sections entitled:

"How Negro Harlem Makes a Living."

"The Relief Situation."

"Housing Problem."

"Education and Recreation."

"Crime and Police."

It reports that Negroes who long felt that they could not get adequate and sympathetic assistance from welfare agencies found no improvement of conditions when the city home relief bureaus were established.

Then into 110 typewritten pages, the document continues, ending with its "Conclusion and Recommendations." Here the original sentiment of the commission is given; later this chapter was given a veneer to please the Mayor.

The nearness of the relief situation to the rank and file of the people was shown at the public hearings held at the Seventh District Municipal Courthouse, 447 West 151st Street. These were the most hectic meetings, the spectators crowded the place, they demanded to be heard, they booed and heckled home relief functionaries. They frightened city and commission, and in the end, the commission had to call off open hearings. Today extra police stand guard on the corners and mounted patrolmen ride through the streets of Harlem; the closing chapter says after briefly reviewing the cause of the rioting:

"To the citizens of Harlem," it continues, "they (the police) symbolize the answer of the city authorities to their protest of March 19. To Harlem this show of force simply signifies that property will be protected at any cost; but it offers no assurance that the legitimate demands of the citizens of the community for work and decent living conditions will be heeded.

"Hence, this show of force only tends to make the conditions which were responsible for the occurrence last March 19 more irritating. And so long as these conditions persist, no one knows when they will lead to recurrence, with possibly greater violence, of the happenings of that night."

Then the Commission goes down the list of its recommendations.

It makes recommendations seeking to prevent the present broadgauged discrimination against Negroes in employment.

It suggests immediate improvements in relief administration, and future adjustments concerning relief policy.

It makes recommendations on education and recreation, specifically asking for new school buildings.

It asks that colored doctors be admitted to all city hospitals, that Harlem Hospital be given a cleaning out.

It requests for a citizens' committee to hear citizens' complaints against the police.

New York *Amsterdam News,* July 18, 1936.

[c]

HARLEM: DARK WEATHER-VANE
by Alain Locke

Eleven brief years ago Harlem was full of the thrill and ferment of sudden progress and prosperity; and *Survey Graphic* sounded the tocsin of the emergence of a "new Negro" and the onset of a "Negro renaissance." Today, with that same Harlem prostrate in the grip of the depression and throes of social unrest, we confront the sobering facts of a serious relapse and premature setback; indeed, find it hard to believe that the rosy enthusiasms and hopes of 1925 were more than bright illusions or a cruelly deceptive mirage. Yet after all there was a renaissance, with its poetic spurt of cultural and spiritual advance, vital with significant but uneven accomplishments; what we face in Harlem today is the first scene of the next act—the prosy ordeal of the reformation with its stubborn tasks of economic reconstruction and social and civic reform.

Curtain-raiser to the reformation was the Harlem riot of March 19 and 20, 1935; variously diagnosed as a depression spasm, a Ghetto mutiny, a radical plot and dress rehearsal of proletarian revolution. Whichever it was, like a revealing flash of lightning it etched on the public mind another Harlem than the bright surface Harlem of the night clubs, cabaret tours and arty magazines, a Harlem that the social worker knew all along but had not been able to dramatize, a Harlem, too, that the radical press and street-corner orator had been pointing out but in all too incredible exaggerations and none too convincing shouts.

In the perspective of time, especially if the situation is handled constructively, we shall be grateful for the lightning-flash which brought the first vivid realization of the actual predicament of the mass life in Harlem and for the echoing after-peals of thunder that have since broken our placid silence and Pollyanna complacency about it. For no cultural advance is safe without some sound economic underpinning, the foundation of a decent and reasonably secure average standard of living; and no emerging élite—artistic, professional or mercantile—can suspend itself in thin air over the abyss of a mass of unemployed stranded in an over-expensive, disease- and crime-ridden slum. It is easier to dally over black Bohemia or revel in the hardy survivals of Negro art and culture than to contemplate this dark Harlem of semi-starvation, mass exploitation and seething unrest. But turn we must. For there is no cure or saving magic in poetry and art, an emerging generation of talent, or in international prestige and interracial recognition, for unemployment or precarious marginal employment, for high rents, high mortality rates, civic neglect, capitalistic exploitation on the one hand and radical exploitation on the other. Yet for some years now Harlem has been subject to all this deep undertow as against the surface advance of the few bright years of prosperity. Today instead of applause and publicity, Harlem needs constructive social care, fundamental community development and planning, and above all statesman-like civic handling.

Immediately after the March riot, Mayor La Guardia appointed a representative bi-racial Commission of Investigation, headed by an esteemed Negro citizen, Dr. Charles H. Roberts. After 21 public and 4 closed hearings conducted with strategic liberality by Arthur Garfield Hays, and nearly a year's investigation by subcommissions on Health and Hospitalization, Housing, Crime and Delinquency and Police, Schools, the Social Services and Relief Agencies, a general report has been assembled under the direction of E. Franklin Frazier, professor of sociology at Howard University, which was filed with the Mayor March 31, 1936, just a few days after the first anniversary of the riots. A preliminary section on the causes of the riot has been published, and several other sections have found their way to publications, some regrettably in garbled form. The public awaits the full and official publication of what is, without doubt, an important document on the present state of Harlem. When published,* the findings will shock the general public and all but the few social experts already familiar with the grave economic need and social adjustment in Harlem and the inadequacies of short-sighted provisions in basic civic facilities of schools, hospitals, health centers, housing control and the like,—a legacy of neglect from the venal, happy-go-lucky days of Tammany-controlled city government. Now with a socially-minded city and national government the prospects of Negro Harlem—and for that matter all handicapped sections—are infinitely brighter.

* The report was issued as a 118-page work, *The Negro in Harlem . . . The Mayor's Commission on Conditions in Harlem* (New York, 1936).

But there is evidence that the present city administration is losing no time in acting to improve the Harlem situation; partly no doubt upon the specific findings and recommendations of the recent investigation, but largely from previous plans, seriously delayed by lack of capital funds or federal subsidies such as are now financing some of the major items of the reform program. Within recent months, in some cases weeks, Harlem's urgent community needs have been recognized in the reconditioning of its sorely inadequate and formerly overcrowded municipal hospital, the completion and equipment of a long delayed women's hospital pavilion approximately doubling the bed capacity of the Harlem Hospital, the remodelling of a temporary out-patient department, and the recommendation by the Commissioner of Hospitals of a new out-patient building and of plans for a new independent hospital plant. Similarly, in the school system's 1937 budget two new school plants for Harlem have been incorporated. On June 20, the Mayor and the Secretary of the Interior spoke at the dedication of the foundations of the new Harlem River housing project, which will afford model housing for 574 low income families with also a nursery school, community playground, model recreation and health clinic facilities—a $4,700,000 P.W.A. project. On June 24, the Mayor drove the last foundation piling for another P.W.A. project, the $240,000 district health clinic for the badly congested Central Harlem section, where the incidence of tuberculosis, social disease and infant mortality is alarmingly high, and announced the appointment of an experienced Negro physician as head officer. It has been announced that a stipulation had been incorporated in the contract specifications for these new public works that Negro skilled labor was to have its fair share of consideration.

All this indicates a new and praiseworthy civic regard for Harlem welfare, contrasting sharply with previous long-standing neglect. The Commission in complaining of present conditions is careful to make plain that the present city administration has inherited most of them and that, therefore, they are not to be laid at its door. Yet they are on its doorstep, waiting immediate attention and all possible relief. The conditions are a reproach not only to previous politically minded municipal administrations but also to the apathy and lack of public-mindedness on the part of Harlem's Negro politicians and many professional leaders who either did not know or care about the conditions of the masses.

Recent improvements will make some sections of the Commission's report contrary to present fact when it appears, but few will care to cavil about that. Yet, both for the record and for the sake of comparison, the situation as the Commission found it should be known. Harlem may not be disposed to look gift horses in the mouth, though a few professional agitators may. Clearly the present administration is now aware of Harlem's objective needs and is taking steps to meet some of them. Mayor La Guardia, speaking at the housing ceremony, said: "We cannot be expected to correct in a day the mistakes and omissions of the past fifty years. But we are going places and carrying out a definite program. While the critics have been throwing stones, I have been laying bricks." But admittedly the situation is still in-adequately provided for even when present plans and immediate prospects are carried out; compounding the actual need is a swelling sense of grievance over past civic neglect and proscription. A long-range plan of civic improvements in low-cost housing, and slum clearance, in further hospital and health clinic facilities, recreation, library and adult education centers, auxiliary school agencies is imperatively neces-sary. And in certain city departments a clearer policy of fair play is needed, not so much with regard to the inclusion of Negroes in municipal posts—though that too is important—as in their considera-tion for executive and advisory appointments where they can construc-tively influence municipal policies and remedial measures for the Har-lem constituency. One of the fatal gaps between good intentions and good performance is in this matter of local administrators, where often an executive policy officially promulgated gets short circuited into discrimination at the point of practical application. Negroes are often accused of race chauvinism in their almost fanatical insistence upon race representatives on executive boards and in councils of policy, but the principle of this vital safeguard is of manifest importance. Espe-cially in situations of accumulated wrong and distrust, mere practical expediency requires public assurance and reassurance.

The riot itself might never have occurred had such imponderables been taken into consideration. Its immediate causes were trivial,— the theft of a ten-cent pocket-knife by a Negro lad of sixteen in Kresge's department store on 125 Street. It was rumored that the boy had been beaten in the basement by store detectives and was gravely injured or dead; by tragic coincidence an ambulance called to treat one of the Kresge employees, whose hand the boy had bitten, seemed to confirm the rumor and a hearse left temporarily outside its garage in an alley at rear of the store to corroborate this. As a matter of fact the boy had given back the stolen knife and had been released through the base-ment door. But it must be remembered that this store, though the bulk of its trade was with Negroes, has always discriminated against Negroes in employment. Shortly before the riot it had been the objective of a picketing campaign for the employment of Negro store clerks, had grudgingly made the concession of a few such jobs and then transferred the so-called "clerks" to service at the lunch counter. While the original culprit slept peacefully at home, a community of 200,000 was suddenly in the throes of serious riots through the night, with actual loss of life, many injuries to police and citizens, destruction of property, and a serious aftermath of public grievance and anger. The careful report of the Commission on this occurrence correctly places the blame far beyond the immediate precipitating incidents. It was not the unfortunate rumors, but the state of mind on which they fell; not the inflammatory leaflets issued several hours after the rioting had begun by the Young Liberators, a radical Negro defense organization, or the other broadside distributed a little later by the Young Communist League, but the sense of grievance and injustice that they could depend on touching to the quick by any recital of fresh wrong and injustice.

The report finds that the outbreak was spontaneous and unpremeditated; that it was not a race riot in the sense of physical conflict between white and colored groups; that it was not instigated by Communists, though they sought to profit by it and circulated a false and misleading leaflet after the riots were well underway; that the work of the police was by no means beyond criticism; and that this sudden breach of the public order was the result of a highly emotional situation among the colored people of Harlem, due in part to the nervous strain of years of unemployment and insecurity. ". . . Its distinguishing feature was an attack upon property rather than persons, and resentment against whites who, while exploiting Negroes, denied them an opportunity to work." The report warns of possible future recurrences, offering as the only safe remedy the definite betterment of economic and civic conditions which, until improved, make Harlem a "fertile field for radical and other propaganda."

It is futile, [the report continues] to condemn the propagandists or to denounce them for fishing in troubled waters. The only answer is to eliminate the evils upon which they base their arguments. The blame belongs to a society that tolerates inadequate and often wretched housing, inadequate and inefficient schools and other public facilities, unemployment, unduly high rents, the lack of recreation grounds, discrimination in industry and the public utilities in the employment of colored people, brutality and lack of courtesy by police. As long as these conditions remain, the public order can not and will not be safe.

Despite this clear diagnosis, there are those even in official circles who insist upon a more direct connection between Harlem's restless temper and radical propaganda. To do so seriously misconstrues the situation by inverting the real order of cause and effect. Discrimination and injustice are the causes, not radicalism. But to neglect the symptoms, to ignore the grievances will be to spread radicalism. Violence will be an inevitable result. Eleven years ago, in the Harlem issue of *Survey Graphic*, the writer said:

Fundamentally, for the present, the Negro is radical only on race matters, in other words, a forced radical, a social protestant rather than a genuine radical. Yet under further pressure and injustice iconoclastic thought and motives will inevitably increase. Harlem's quixotic radicalisms call for their ounce of democracy today lest tomorrow they be beyond cure.

That statement needs underscoring today, when aspects of discrimination, chronic through the years, become acute under the extra pressure of the depression. At such a time special—perhaps even heroic—remedy becomes necessary where preventive long term treatment should and could have been the scientific course. It follows that at this stage both the basic disease and its many complications as well must be treated. Obviously both long and short term measures are indicated, from the temporary palliative that allays inflamed public opinion to the long range community planning which requires years for development and application. The Commission report spreads its recommendations over just such a wide range. It is particularly wise and sound, even at the risk of appearing doctrinaire, in pointing to the Negro's economic exploitation through the employment policy of the whole community as the basic economic disease, and to segregation as inducing the radical complications. Unlike many such reports this one does not overlook fundamentals, and in that respect renders a service of truly scientific and permanent value.

It follows then that Harlem's most acute problem is employment. Not mere job occupancy, but rather a lifting of its economic earning power through less discriminatory job distribution. A careful analysis of job categories and employment trends makes this clear and is the basis for the rather startling suggestion that the municipality grapple with the traditionally non-governmental problem of the right to work according to ability. Knowing of course that the city cannot directly control the private labor market, the report nevertheless suggests, as a long term policy, measures of indirect control. It suggests that the city enact an ordinance that no municipal contracts be given to firms or corporations that discriminate, racially or otherwise, against workers, and that in its contracts with the public utilities it make provisions and reservations which will prevent flagrant labor discrimination. It further suggests that the city itself as an employer set a good example, not merely by the number of Negroes employed but by widening the range of jobs filled by Negroes. This is a particularly pointed suggestion in view of the fact that the relatively small quota of Negroes in the New York city service, 2.2 percent in 1920 had fallen to 1.4 percent in 1930, the latest figure available. The P.W.A. housing project for Harlem sets the proper but daring precedent of specifying that the employment of less than one third skilled Negro labor will constitute *prima facie* evidence of discrimination, and furnish grounds for disciplinary action against the contractor. Revolutionary as all this may seem, it goes to the economic roots of the race issue, and boldly carries the principle of the Fourteenth Amendment into the economic field. Typical is the report of the New York Edison Company with 65 Negroes in its employ out of 10,000 and the Fifth Avenue Coach Co. with 213 Negroes out of a total of 16,000 employes. It is such an industrial policy that brings, in the words of the report, "a certain retribution upon a community that discriminates against the Negro worker through the money it must spend upon him in the form of relief."

The common sense and logic of such a position become obvious when a community has to pay the indirect costs of labor discrimination in relief to the victims of insecure and marginal employment. Definite proof of this economic inequality is seen in the disproportionate number of Negroes on New York City relief rolls. Ten percent of the Negro population is on relief, over double its relative population of 4 percent. It has been further evidenced in the difficulties encountered by Negro workers with skilled vocational training and experience in securing work relief assignments except as unskilled laborers. Negroes did not receive their proportionate share of work relief jobs even in sections predominantly Negro, and in sections predominantly white Negro home relief clients were not given their proportional share of referral assignments to work relief jobs. Many skilled Negro workers had either to accept places in the unskilled ranks or go back to the home relief rolls as "unemployables." Of the employables in New York City on relief the year preceding the riot, 14 percent or 58,950 were Negroes.

Most of the complaints of discrimination in the relief services have occurred in the work relief sections, where finally an advisory committee on Negro problems was appointed, and in the matter of personnel policies of the Emergency Relief Bureau itself. In home relief, the investigation found substantial fairness and little or no justifiable complaint. Negroes have been employed in the relief services at a ratio almost double their percentage in the city's population, incidentally affording indirect evidence of the disproportionate amount of unemployment among Negroes with relatively high grade qualifications. There was some complaint, according to the report, about their slow admission to higher administration grades, especially the strategic positions of occupational clerks, a type of position vital for initiating any broader policy of labor classification for Negro eligibles. Recently, Mayor La Guardia announced the appointment of Dr. John H. Johnson, rector of St. Martin's Episcopal Church, as the sixth member of the Emergency Relief Bureau.

Housing is the most serious special community problem of Harlem. The Negro's labor short dollar is further clipped by the exorbitant rentals characteristic of the segregated areas where most Negroes must reside. Whereas rents should approximate 20 percent of family income, and generally tend to do so, in Harlem they average nearly double or 40 percent. Model housing does not begin to touch the real mass need either as slum clearance or low cost housing until it brings the average rental down to $5 to $7 per room per month. The Dunbar Apartments, erected some years back with Rockefeller subsidy, could not meet this need although at the time it gave middle-class Harlem a real lift in the direction of decent housing and neighborhood conditions. The new Harlem River Houses, to be erected with federal subsidy, will be the first model housing to reach the class that needs it most. The New York Housing Authority deserves great credit for initiation and for the principle of local Negro advice and promised Negro management which it has adopted. Harlem's appreciative response was clearly evident at the recent cornerstone-laying when Secretary Ickes, Mayor La Guardia and Commissioner Langdon Post of the Tenement House Department endorsed the principle of bringing modern housing to the congested sections of Harlem. Secretary Ickes said: "The record of American housing is proof positive of one thing. Private initiative cannot, unaided, properly house our low income families. It is simply not in the cards. It can mulct unenviable profits by housing our people badly; it cannot make money by housing them well." That holds a fortiori for the Negro. But when the federally aided scheme has demonstrated its social and humane objectives, cut the cost of crime and juvenile delinquency, exerted its remedial influence on other negative social forces, including racial discontent, the subsidizing of still larger scale projects by the state and municipality will be wisely charged off to their proper balances in the saner bookkeeping of an intelligently social-minded community. The Commission's subcommission on housing under Morris L. Ernst was very active in its advocacy of progressive housing legislation before the State Legislature, and considerable progressive state legislation for which the Harlem investigation housing commission was directly responsible.

Health is the second great problem and disease the second grim link in the Ghetto chain which fetters Harlem life. Central Harlem's rate of infant mortality, tuberculosis, and venereal disease is expectedly high and in direct proportion to areas of congestion and poverty. Harlem's hospital and health facilities were handicapped over a period of years, directly by antiquated equipment, indirectly by political and racial feuds. Regrettable differences often brought the two professional organizations of Negro physicians in Harlem into conflict. Although these differences were often over divergent views as to the gains and losses of segregation, or of this or that tactic in securing the admission of Negroes to staff and internes' positions in the municipal hospitals, they were anything but conducive to the morale of Harlem Hospital or to any clear policy of the hospital authorities. It took years of agitation to get any Negroes on the staff and the governing medical board, and Negro internes were admitted to Harlem Hospital only within the last ten years. Until recently there was only one Negro on the Harlem Hospital Board, and one Negro physician of full staff rank. The situation both as to hospital facilities and staff personnel has shown material improvement recently under what promises to be a new and liberalized policy instituted by the present Commissioner of Hospitals, Dr. Goldwater. But that change was too recent to spare the Commissioner or his immediate subordinate in charge of the Harlem Hospital from adverse criticism by the Commission. Recent improvements offset some of the shocking and inadequate conditions that had existed for years.

On January 2 the opening of the new women's wing to Harlem Hospital increased its capacity from 325 to 665 beds. This pavilion, almost completed four years ago, had stood unfinished chiefly because of legal complications growing out of the failure of contractors. This relief from overcrowding, no doubt the basis for the most serious complaints as to previous maladministration, clears the way for remodelling and modernizing the older parts of the hospital, which is now proceeding under W.P.A. grants. A new nurses' home has recently opened; plans for a new $1,500,000 out-patient department have been drawn, and an additional entirely new hospital has been recommended as an urgent item in the impending capital outlay for city hospitals. In the meantime, the Department of Hospitals has, with the assistance of the W.P.A., modernized a two-story building on the Harlem Hospital block, which will provide more than four times the space of the old clinic. These last projects are made necessary by the fact that the recently enlarged facilities of Harlem Hospital already are approaching a crowded condition at times.

Only incessant agitation brought staff appointments in municipal hospitals to Negro physicians. Recently, by a laudable departure in the direction of fairer play, five Negroes were given staff appointments to Queens' General Hospital and one to Sea View; and in the first six months of 1936 seven Negro physicians have been promoted from assistant to associate visiting rank, five from clinical assistants to assistant visiting rank, and seven new clinical appointments have been made. This, with three members of full attending rank and an increase of two members on the Medical Board of Harlem Hospital, represents a spectacular gain in comparison with the slow progress of former years. The Commission report, however, recommends "the admission of Negro physicians, internes and nurses to all city hospitals on merit in accordance with law, and the withholding of municipal financial aid from any institution refusing equal treatment to Negroes."

With the completion of the new health unit, there will no longer be ground for the present complaint that in the two health areas where Negroes are concentrated there is "conspicuous absence of the very agencies which deal with the major problems of Negro health—infant mortality and tuberculosis."

Similarly, the announcement of two new school buildings for Harlem in the 1937 Board of Education program corrects in prospect the major plant deficiencies complained of in the Commission's school report. It leaves for further consideration the plea for some special provisions to offset the effects of demoralized home and neighborhood conditions upon a considerable section of the Harlem school population. Primarily this is not a school function or responsibility, even though it gravely affects its work. Classes for deficient and delinquent children, special vocational guidance, supervised play are recommended, and also greater protection of school children from the demoralized elements of the adjacent neighborhoods by the police department. Logically and practically, however, it is obvious that only wide-scale slum clearance will reach the roots of such conditions.

One of the rare bright spots in the situation is the fine policy of the New York City school system of entirely disregarding race in the appointment and assignment of Negro school teachers, which policy should point a convincing precedent to other city departments and, for that matter, to other great municipalities.

No field of municipal government is more tied in with a problem such as underlies the Harlem riots than the police department. Even at that time a spirit of general antagonism toward the police was evident, and the fatal shooting of a sixteen-year-old highschool student, Lloyd Hobbes, whom the police charge with looting during the riot (a charge which several witnesses dispute), did much to aggravate the bitterness. As the report aptly says, "A policeman who kills is prosecutor, judge and executioner." In fact a series of police shootings in Harlem, continuing down to two quite recent killings of children in the police pursuit of suspected criminals, has brought the community to the point of dangerous resentment toward the police. The frequent heavy mobilization of police forces in Harlem, however well based the fear or probability of public disorder and the recurrence of rioting, has the practical effect of stimulating the very thing it is meant to avert—abnormal tension, resentment, and disrespect for proper police authority. Every close student of the situation sympathizes with the police authorities in their difficult responsibilities, especially during the strenuous campaign against the vice and small-time racketeering which are all too prevalent in Harlem. But respect for and confidence in police authority are primary assets in such a houscleaning campaign, and the good-will and cooperation of the law-abiding, better class element are essential. Restored confidence and good-will are particularly vital in the situation fraught with possible racial antagonisms.

Surprising and convincing reason for suspecting police brutality and intimidation is the fact that many in the Harlem community feel as much resentment toward Negro police as toward white police, and even toward the Negro police lieutenant, who sometime back was a popular hero and a proud community symbol. The Commission's recommendations, therefore, that the police be given instructions to use greater caution and tact in emergencies and show the strictest regard for citizens' rights, and that a bi-racial Citizens' Public Safety Committee be appointed as an advisory body to the Police Commissioner and to hear possible complaints and grievances against undue use of police power or claims of police brutality and intimidation, are of crucial and constructive importance in a somewhat critical situation. For without restored confidence and unbroken public order, Harlem's wound will not heal.

Dark as the Harlem situation has been, and in a lesser degree still is, the depression in general and the riot in particular have served a diagnostic purpose which, if heeded and turned into a program of constructive civic reform, will give us improvement and progress instead of revolution and anarchy. After all, in these days of economic crisis and reconstruction the Negro has more than racial import. As the man farthest down, he tests the pressure and explores the depths of the social and economic problem. In that sense he is not merely the man who shouldn't be forgotten; he is the man who cannot safely be ignored.

Yet, in addition, Harlem is racially significant as the Negro's greatest and formerly most favorable urban concentration in America. The same logic by which Harlem led the Negro renaissance dictates that it must lead the economic reconstruction and social reformation which we have been considering. There are some favorable signs from within and without that it will: from without, in terms of the promise of the new concern and constructive policy of the Mayor and a few progressive city authorities; from within, in terms of a new type and objective of Negro civic leadership. The latter is evidenced in part by the Mayor's Harlem Commission and its sustained activities, by the ever increasing advisory committees of leading and disinterested citizens, and recently, quite significantly, by the organization of the bi-racial All Peoples' Party in Harlem for independent political action to "rid Harlem of the corrupt political control of the two major parties and end the tyranny of political bosses." Recently 209 delegates from 89 social, civic and religious organizations organized with this objective of substituting civic organization and community welfare for political support and party spoils. A Harlem community-conscious and progressively cooperative is infinitely to be preferred to a Harlem racially belligerent and distempered. Contrast the Harlem of the recent W.P.A. art festival, gaily and hopefully celebrating in a festival of music, art and adult education, dancing in Dorrance Brooks Square, with the Harlem of the riot, a bedlam of missiles, shattered plate glass, whacking night-sticks, mounted patrols, police sirens and police bullets; and one can visualize the alternatives. It is to be hoped that Harlem's dark weather-vane of warning can be turned round to become a high index of constructive civic leadership and reform.

Survey Graphic, August, 1936; XXV, 457–62, 493–95.

27

"THERE GOES GOD!"
THE STORY OF FATHER DIVINE
AND HIS ANGELS

by Claude McKay

There is no adequate study of the Father Divine Movement—one of the remarkable phenomena in U.S. history. George Baker, a Black man from Georgia, attracted some attention as early as 1919 as the leader of an all-Black communal group in Sayville, Long Island, in New York. His followers increased slowly in the nineteen-twenties, though whites had become adherents by 1926. With the depression it grew by leaps and bounds and, while overwhelmingly Afro-American, did contain many whites—especially women. Branches appeared in many cities in the East, Midwest, and Pacific states—these were known as Peace Missions or heavens. Until World War II Father Divine's followers numbered in the tens of thousands; his program was pacifistic and anti-racist and also called for government ownership and operation of all factories lying idle. An essay on his movement by Claude McKay is published below.

The most African characteristic of Harlem, after the color of its people, is the multitude of amazing cults. Native African churches (so-called), groups of Negro-Jews, and a host of straight Christian and revival sects pullulate in Harlem. To say that there is a cult to every block would be no exaggeration.

It is through religion, more than any other channel, that primitive African emotions find expression in our modern civilization. Indoors and along the pulpit pavements of Harlem, black men and women, some singularly robed, ecstatically prance and reel and writhe with a fervor that is tolerated simply because their exhibitions bear the label of religion. No Negro cabaret or Negro theater could permit the display of such very African antics.

Returning to Harlem after three years spent in North Africa, I had a queer, topsy-turvy sensation when I mingled with folk who were so similar physically to those of North Africa (and from the same cause —miscegenation) but in spirit so different, though they have precisely the same strenuous preoccupation with religion. My arrival in Harlem coincided with a big religious parade. The streets were massed with marching people, led by bands of music, shouting, singing, bearing banners proclaiming, "Father Divine Is God," "God Almighty Is Father Divine." Automobiles loaded with enthusiastic disciples were bright with pennants praising Father Divine. Spectators jammed the pavements. Excited black and brown faces, framed in apartment windows, beamed down on the scene. Suddenly an airplane droned through the clouds, and looking up the people shouted: "God! God! There goes Father! Father Divine is God! The true and living God." Never had I seen such excitement in Harlem except in the days of Marcus Garvey's Back-to-Africa movement.

Father Divine is God! With that one phrase Father Divine stands out above all the other leaders and their cults. God, who was invisible to all before, is now personified in him. He has created "Kingdoms" of Heaven in Harlem and elsewhere. "He is sweet, so sweet," chant his "angel" followers, "God, so sweet, Father Divine." According to them Father Divine is the source of all things. He gives his "angels" work, health, food, happiness, prosperity—everything. Accepting nothing, he gives all, being God.

Father Divine was a name unknown to the large public a little more than two years ago. As the leader of a holy-rolling kind of black-and-white cult, he was known only in Sayville, Long Island. There Father Divine had acquired property, upon which he had built a house. The house was called a "kingdom." He had lived there for about ten years. Actually he was supposed to be in retirement after many years of preaching. But some of his faithful white and colored disciples, mainly from New York, continued to visit him, eating, sleeping, and worshiping in his house. As their numbers increased, their presence disturbed the respectable white residents, and Father Divine was prosecuted for maintaining a public nuisance. That colored and white persons of both sexes were united under a Negro leader seemed particularly to incense the presiding judge. In his preliminary examination of Father Divine he laid special emphasis upon that fact.

Meanwhile the case had attracted wide attention, especially among Negroes, because of its white-with-black feature. A clever Negro lawyer with some political influence offered his services free to Father Divine. In Harlem his followers organized large protest meetings. At one of these meetings, held at the Rush Memorial Baptist Church, a leading disciple exhorted the assembled congregation to hold together and be not dismayed, for their Father Divine would sentence the judge to death if the judge dared to sentence him to prison.

The court was unable to elicit anything about the antecedents of Father Divine, since he insisted that he had been divinely projected into existence and had no record of his life. Thereupon the judge committed him to jail, to obtain further information and to have his mental condition determined by a psychiatrist. When the case came up for final trial, the judge sentenced Father Divine to a year in prison and $500 fine. Curiously, three days after the sentence the judge died suddenly. He was very old and had been stricken by heart disease. To the Divine disciples the hand of their Father had struck the judge dead. They even reported that Father Divine had said that he regretted having to make an example of the judge. The news spread through the country.

Father Divine's attorney appealed the sentence. The verdict was reversed by the Brooklyn Supreme Court, which ruled that the presiding judge had injected prejudice into the minds of the jurors. Upon being released, Father Divine entered into his apotheosis. Overnight his following had developed into a vast army. The man who had retired to Sayville emerged as God. He came to New York again and thousands flocked to the Rockland Palace to hear him speak.

"Peace!" he cried to them; "Good health, good appetite, prosperity, and a heart full of merriness. I give you all and everything." And his people responded: "God! It is wonderful! I thank you, Father." Such is the essence of the Divine message and the response it calls forth. And so greatly grew that response that Father Divine alone could not handle it as he had done at Sayville. More and greater "kingdoms" had to be created. Father Divine declares, and his followers believe, that he is in all of them at the same time. "I am here and I am there and I am everywhere," he says. "I am like the radio voice. Dial in and you shall always find me."

Fifteen Divine kingdoms are maintained in New York City alone. In fine buildings all. The finest is the former bath premises in 126th Street, now know as the Faithful Mary Kingdom. Other kingdoms are in Jamaica, Brooklyn, and White Plains, in New Jersey and Connecticut. From Washington, D.C., to Seattle, Washington, centers have been established by Father Divine enthusiasts. Headquarters Kingdom, where Father Divine has office and residence, is in 115th Street. In whichever "kingdom" he eats, Father Divine himself serves his flock. The food goes through his hands before it is served. He pours and passes the coffee and cream in the grand style of a maître d'hôtel. And he has more dignity and naturalness doing that than when he is haranguing an audience.

The kingdoms are sanitary and apparently well managed. They pay their way. The secret of their financing is Father Divine's. Rooms are rented to individuals at a dollar a week, but there is more than one person to a room. In the restaurants meals are served for ten and fifteen cents. The food is good and plentiful. A good piece of meat and two vegetables cost ten cents; a piece of cake or ice-cream, five cents; coffee or soft drink, three cents. There are separate kingdoms for men and women. For in the kingdoms sex is proscribed.

The decorative motif of all the kingdoms is the apotheosis of Father Divine. His enlarged photographs dominate the walls. Large posters with black and red lettering proclaim his virtues: "Father Divine is God." "Father Divine is the living Tree of Life, Father, Son and Holy Ghost." "We all may take of the words of Father Divine, eat and drink and live forever." Other posters make a queer mélange of social and religious statements. They reveal that Father Divine is aware of social problems and that he has a special approach to them. Framed newspaper clippings advertise Father Divine's letters to firms doing business with him, from which he solicits jobs for his people. Also displayed are letters to the mayor referring to Father Divine's secret service, which is investigating racial and color discrimination and segregation in New York City institutions. One poster reads:

We the Inter-racial, International, Inter-denominational and Inter-religious Coworkers . . . as being called Father Divine's Peace Mission Workers . . . do demand the release through commutation of the life sentence of the Scottsboro boys, and other means of releasing the nine boys. And also we demand freedom, and extermination of the mistreatment of the Jews in Germany and all other countries, and we demand the equal rights and religious liberty according to our Constitution.
I thank you, Father.

Enthusiastic masses of colored people, with a sprinkling of whites, West Indians, and Latin Americans, make up the kingdoms. Women predominate, forming about three-quarters of the whole number. It is largely a middle-aged crowd. No prayers are said at the meetings. Praise has taken the place of prayer in Father Divine's religion. He often quotes: "Prayer is the heart's sincere desire, unuttered or unexpressed." And instead of praying, his people testify, praising and thanking him. Of music and singing and dancing there is no end—a riotous, prancing, antic performance that "it is wonderful" indeed to see and to feel. Loosely the women fling themselves about, with a verve and freedom that would startle a cabaret. They toss up their skirts and contort their limbs, dancing and singing to Father Divine:

I don't know why, I don't know why,
I don't know why you love me so . . .
You put your arms around me and you took me in . . .

With nervous, petulant gestures they turn from the men, the forbidden, and dance extravagantly with one another, colored with colored and colored with white. After they are exhausted from singing and dancing in chorus, they give individual testimony—amazing testimony, whether openly given in the kingdoms or privately related.

At Headquarters Kingdom I saw a little, wiry black man cleave through the jam to reach and kneel a moment against the back of Father Divine's chair. Standing up again with uplifted hand he cried: "Peace —O Father, thank you, Father, for what you have done for me. Father, I used to think I was smart. But I was all wrong and bad. I used to take the Jew man's furniture and then change my address and sell it. But Father, you showed me where I was wicked and I don't do that no more. And I mean to pay back all what I stole. And Father, I used to make the women pay. I was a mean feller, Father. Until, I find one woman what was different and wouldn't pay off. And I wanted her, Father. And wanted her that bad I couldn't help falling for her. But I had to take it the way she wanted to give. And she made me go housekeeping together like an honest couple and I changed my ways and worked like a man. Then we both heard about you, Father. And we came to you. And you stopped us from living in sin, thank you, Father, it is wonderful. Peace. And you put me in one kingdom, Father, and put her in another. And you did right, for Father Divine is always right. But, oh, Father, she been coming to my room every night in my dreams. It was powerful awful, Father, and I was afraid and asked you to guide me. I concentrated on your spirit, Father, and last night when I was dreaming she come again and all at once you just descended into the room like a lightning bolt between us. Oh, thank you, Father. It was wonderful."

"It is wonderful!" everybody echoed and joined in singing: "All hail the power of Father's name, let angels prostrate fall."

From a mulatto young woman standing behind Father Divine's chair escaped a frightening yell. "Father, you did call me," she cried, "call me all the way from Seattle. Father, let me confess the truth that I had sinful thoughts about you, sinful, deceitful woman as I am. I imagined that you were just another colored minister. I said, Father can't be so different, he is just another one. For I have lived my life, Father, as a sample and example of a free woman among men and counted my victims. All the long way from Seattle I came, Father, thinking evil. And when I entered your presence and tried to fix you, you fixed me instead. You saw straight through me, Father, the lust that was in me, and you drove it out of me into the Gadarene swine. And, oh, Father, you were God in the place of the man I was looking for. You put your spirit in me and made me pure, one of your 'angels,' Father. I thank you, Father. It is truly wonderful."

California and other points west have supplied most of the white followers. An old man in his sixties said that he had left California doubting that Father Divine could be more than a prophet, because there is a passage from the Bible which says that no man can look upon God and live. But as soon as he saw Father Divine he was convinced that he was in the presence of God. And he immediately experienced a transformation from a mortal to an angel. He lives now in one of the kingdoms.

The skeptic part of Harlem's population, whatever its opinion of Father Divine, is excited over his success and the financing of it. Unlike other evangelists Father Divine never collects any money at his meetings; he delights in making a mystery about the source of the funds he uses to run his Divine Trust of large, well-appointed kingdoms, cheap restaurants (where hundreds of hungry out-of-work persons are fed free daily), and the splendid buses and automobiles which convey his disciples from kingdom to kingdom. He waxes sharply waggish when inquires are made. He told a group of white parsons, professors, and students that he got his money from the Treasury in Washington, just like other people. At his meetings he jokes with his followers about "people who want to know where I get my money." "They want to know how I get my money. But you all know I take absolutely nothing." "Right, Father! Yes, Father!" the people cry. "I give everything, because I am omnipotent. I give you plenty of good food, clothes, shelter, work. And you are fat and merry." "Yes, Father! Thank you, Father!" the people shout. "It is wonderful!"

Graciously granted an interview, I could not ask Father Divine how he got his money. His white secretary had explicitly stated to me beforehand: "Father Divine does not accept money from his followers. Rich people interested in his work have offered large sums of money which Father Divine has refused, because he does not want to be limited in the conception of his work." The secretary also intimated that inquiries about the source of his income were annoying to Father Divine. I said that primarily my interest was in Father Divine's work.

In his sumptuous living quarters, African in the gay conglomeration of colors, Father Divine in a large easy-chair appeared like a slumping puppet abandoned after a marionette show. He seemed to have shrunk even smaller than his five feet four, which is not unimpressive when he is acting. He pointed to a seat near him, and said he thought he had said enough at his meetings to give me an idea of his work and mission. I told him that I was interested mainly in his ideas about social problems and inter-racial relations and would like a special pronouncement from him as a Negro leader and pacifist. Father Divine replied: "I have no color conception of myself. If I were representing race or creed or color or nation, I would be limited in my conception of the universal. I would not be as I am, omnipotent."

I said that I accepted his saying that he was above race and color, but because he happened to have been born brown and was classified in the colored group, the world was more interested in him as a Negro. And I asked him what was his plan for the realization of peace and understanding between the masses and the classes. Father Divine said: "I am representative of the universal through the cooperation of mind and spirit in which is reality. I cannot deviate from that fundamental. The masses and the classes must transcend the average law and accept me. And governments in time will come to recognize my law."

I drew his attention to an editorial in the *Daily Worker* referring to the demonstration against war and fascism, in which the Communists had paraded in company with Father Divine at the head of thousands of his people carrying banners bearing Divine slogans. The editorial was an explanation to critical readers of the necessity of cooperating with Father Divine and his followers, "carrying such strange and foolish placards." Father Divine said that he was always willing to cooperate in his own way with the Communists or any group that was fighting for international peace and emancipation of people throughout the world and against my form of segregation and racial discrimination. But what the Communists were trying to do he was actually doing, by bringing people of different races and nations to live together and work in peace under his will. He had come to free every nation, every language, every tongue, and every people. He did not need the Communists or any other organization, but they needed him. For he had all wisdom and understanding and health and wealth. And he alone could give emancipation and liberty, for he was the victory. I thanked Father Divine for the interview, and he dismissed me with the gift of a pamphlet.

The followers of Father Divine are always ready to testify to his divinity, the glory of the kingdoms, the sweetness of the fellowship, and the wonders of his works. But ask a pertinent question about the Divine finance and immediately they clamp their lips. That is something as taboo with them as it is with Father Divine.

Some cabalistic thing, such as exists in a secret society, may be at the bottom of this. The Divine disciples are called "angels." And Father Divine has said, "Denial of money is Angelship degree." Even those who have ceased to be followers will not discuss it. There is a story of a Negro petty shopkeeper who disappeared taking $1,500 of his own money. Investigating, his wife discovered him in one of the kingdoms, but without the money. Finally he was persuaded to return home. But neither he nor his wife will discuss the incident or what has become of the money.

Perhaps a clue to the Divine method of finance may be found in Faithful Mary. She was the first disciple of Father Divine. At all his big meetings she sits at his right. In striking contrast to him, her brown-moon face shines with a disarming other-worldiness. She is middle-aged, a fine-fleshed, compact, and balanced motherly woman. She testifies that she had been insane from drink for ten years, had been discharged from hospitals as an incurable. She was living soddenly in the gutters of Broome Street in Newark, eating out of garbage cans, when she heard about Father Divine. She concentrated upon him, believing that he was God. He lifted her up and cured her. And now she belongs to God. Faithful Mary's sincerity strikes you; her story is convincing.

Father Divine's little white secretary, who unlike Father Divine does talk about the material side of the Peace Mission, had this to say of Faithful Mary: "She is blessed with the love of the people and they give her great gifts. They have given her houses to be converted into kingdoms, clothes, and automobiles." The largest kingdom in 126th Street was given her. If Father Divine as God takes absolutely nothing, his first disciple, Faithful Mary, is not like him. And she declares that she belongs to God.

"It is truly wonderful," even as the "angels" of Harlem sing-song, this frantic, prancing expression of black emotionalism in the heart of the great white city.

The Nation, February 6, 1935; CXL, 151–53. There is a useful essay, "Father Divine," by George Streator in *Commonweal,* December 15, 1939; XXXI, 176–78. In the nineteen-thirties, *The New York Times* tended to report his movement rather fully; see, for example, an account of a meeting of five thousand of his followers in that paper, January 13, 1936, p. 19. See also, Robert A. Parker, *The Incredible Messiah: The Deification of Father Divine* (Boston, 1937).

28

THE NEW DEAL AND BLACK PEOPLE

By 1935 the efforts and character of the "New Deal" had become fairly clear. Four essays published that year and treating of the impact of that Deal upon the Afro-American follow. Document [a] treats specifically the social security enactments and proposals and demonstrates their inadequacies where Black people were concerned; document [b] is an overall quite critical estimate of the F.D.R. administration; document [c], while critical, is simultaneously hopeful. The final document, [d], is from a speech by the newly elected Democratic Black congressman from Chicago, Arthur W. Mitchell; its laudatory quality is not surprising.

[a]

LILY-WHITE SOCIAL SECURITY
by George Edmund Haynes

President Roosevelt, in stating the principles for his social security program, said, "except in old age insurance, actual management should be left to the states subject to the standards by the federal government." The Economic Security bill now before congress is the first measure designed to carry out parts of this social security program. Its purpose is to alleviate the hazards of old age, unemployment, illness and dependency. The main features of its administration following the principle laid down by the President is to be left to state authorities. The states are required to submit plans to be approved by the federal administrator for old age assistance, for aid to dependent children, for extension and strengthening of service for health of mothers and children. The bill also provides for allotments from the federal treasury of funds for unemployment insurance and old age annuities, and for assistance in the development of health services.

What has been the experience of Negroes under the regular services furnished by the several states with such cooperative help of federal funds, as well as under the emergency services that have been developed through legislation for recovery? In seeking facts to answer this question our attention should not be confined wholly to the southern states although the most serious situations have arisen there where more than three-fourths of the Negro population still resides. Some of the complaints that have arisen during the recovery administration have come from border and northern states.

Under the Smith-Hughes act, federal appropriations for vocational education and the training of teachers are appropriated to the several states on the condition that each dollar of federal money is to be matched by the state, the local community or both. The basis of allotments of federal funds to each state is, for agriculture, the proportion the state rural population bears to the total rural population of the nation; for trades, home economics and industries, the proportion the urban population bears to the total urban population; and for teacher-training, the proportion which the total population of the state bears to the total population of the nation. Under the Smith-Lever act which provides for agricultural and home demonstration work the basis of allotment of federal funds is the proportion the rural population of the state bears to the total rural population of the nation. A fair test, therefore, of the justice with which these funds have been spent in several states where Negroes form a large percentage of the population is to compare the percentage of funds which have been spent for Negroes with the percentage the Negroes comprised of the rural, the urban, and the total populations of those states.

On this basis of comparison if we examine the share Negroes received of the vocational funds and the teacher-training funds for the fiscal year 1931–32 and the percentage of Negroes in the rural population, the urban population and the total population in 1930, we find that only one of the sixteen states for which figures are available spent the proportion of the vocational funds equitably on the basis of the proportion of Negroes. In several of the states the gap between the percentages was wide.

The seriousness and extent of the handicap of this unfair discrimination of Negroes may be seen from a typical expenditure of funds for cooperative extension work from sources for the fiscal year 1931–32. The grand total of such funds expended by seventeen states that year was $9,339,610. Of this $4,558,449 came from Federal sources and $4,799,111 from state sources. The total amount spent for Negroes was $77,995. On the basis of the proportion of Negroes in the rural population of those states, however, they should have received $2,293,532.

In contrast with the decided discrimination shown under the Smith-Lever and Smith-Hughes acts evidence shows that where there are provisions in the organic law against discrimination on account of race the funds have been fairly and equitably distributed between the races even in states where there are separate educational facilities. This is clear from what has happened in the administration of the Morrill-Nelson funds created by acts of congress July 2, 1862, as amended to prevent discrimination, August 30, 1890. This amendment provides that no money shall be paid out to any state or territory for the support or maintenance of a college where a distinction is made in the admission of students on account of race or color; the amendment allows allotments to separate colleges for white and Negro students "if the funds received be equitably divided" according to specifications set forth in the amendment. To illustrate, typical expenditures for the year ending June 30, 1934, in those states having separate land-grant colleges show that the distribution of these funds was equitable in proportion that the two races formed of the total population of the respective states. Florida spent about an equal amount for Negro and white land-grant colleges although the Negro population formed less than one-third of the total population and South Carolina spent the same amount for the Negroes as for whites although the Negroes were a little less than half of the population. None of these states, however, gave similar distribution of funds drawn from state sources.

This bill has also a serious general defect as it relates to Negroes because practically all domestic and personal servants are excluded from unemployment insurance provisions since the bill applies only to employers with four or more employees. Also it is proposed to exempt farmers from the plans, thus eliminating Negro tenant farmers, most of whom are no better off than hired laborers. Thus about three-fifths of all Negroes gainfully employed will not be benefited at all by the bill.

Furthermore, even where administration is not left to the states there is danger of discrimination on account of race or color unless there is provision in the organic law. There is considerable data showing discrimination in public works where contracts have been left to private contractors by the Federal government. For example, investigations in the labor camps of the Mississippi Flood Control operations show conclusive evidence of abuses and exploitation of Negro workers, in long hours, low wages, over-charging for supplies through a commissary system, unsanitary, over-crowded living conditions, and in some instances actual physical violence. Investigations and repeated complaints about the exclusion of Negroes from employment on the Boulder Dam project in Colorado disclosed the fact that the contracts as made so bound the Federal government that the contractor could continue his exclusion of Negroes to such an extent that an official of the Department of the Interior admitted that the government could not intervene "as long as the contractor complied with all the laws and provisions of its contract." Had there been such a non-discrimination clause in the law providing for the Boulder Dam project the contractor would have had to conform.

These facts make clear that where such provisions have been put into the organic law they have been effective in preventing discrimination: and that where they are lacking, unfair, inequitable distribution of funds and other benefits have been widespread and continuously practiced in at least eighteen states. The conclusion is sound that there should be specific provisions under several of the titles of the Economic Security Bill to prevent discrimination on account of race or color against persons otherwise eligible.

Facts to prove beyond a reasonable doubt the need for non-discrimination clauses in the Economic Security Bill were presented to both the House ways and means committee and the Senate finance committee by the writer to urge, that under Title I dealing with old age; under Title II dealing with allotments for dependent children; under Titles III and IV dealing with unemployment insurance and old age annuities; under Title VII having to do with maternal and child health; and under Title VIII providing for allotments to local and public health programs, there should be some clause or clauses which will require as a part of any plan submitted by a state for approval of the federal administrator, provisions against discrimination on account of race or color. This legislation is so vital to Negro men, women and children and to peaceable race relations that every lover of fair play should see that his congressmen and senators support provisions in the bill against racial discrimination.

The Crisis, March, 1935; XLII, 85–86.

[b]

A BLACK INVENTORY OF THE NEW DEAL
by John P. Davis

It is highly important for the Negro citizen of America to take inventory of the gains and losses which have come to him under the "New Deal." The Roosevelt administration has now had two years in which to unfold itself. Its portents are reasonably clear to anyone who seriously studies the varied activities of its recovery program. We can now state with reasonable certainty what the "New Deal" means for the Negro.

At once the most striking and irrefutable indication of the effect of the New Deal on the Negro can be gleaned from relief figures furnished by the government itself. In October, 1933, six months after the present administration took office, 2,117,000 Negroes were in families receiving relief in the United States. These represented 17.8 per cent of the total Negro population as of the 1930 census. In January, 1935, after nearly two years of *recovery measures,* 3,500,000 Negroes were in families receiving relief, or 29 per cent of our 1930 population. Certainly only a slight portion of the large increase in the number of impoverished Negro families can be explained away by the charitable, on the grounds that relief administration has become more humane. As a matter of fact federal relief officials themselves admit that grave abuses exist in the administration of rural relief to Negroes. And this is reliably borne out by the disproportionate increase in the number of urban Negro families on relief to the number of rural Negro families on relief. Thus the increase in the number of Negroes in relief families is an accurate indication of the deepening of the economic crisis for black America.

The promise of N.R.A. to bring higher wages and increased employment to industrial workers has glimmered away. In the code-making process occupational and geographical differentials at first were used as devices to exclude from the operation of minimum wages and maximum hours the bulk of the Negro workers. Later, clauses basing code wage rates on the previously existing wage differential between Negro and white workers tended to continue the inferior status of the Negro. For the particular firms, for whom none of these devices served as an effective means of keeping down Negro wages, there is an easy way out through the securing of an exemption specifically relating to the *Negro* worker in the plant. Such exemptions are becoming more numerous as time goes on. Thus from the beginning relatively few Negro workers were even theoretically covered by N.R.A. labor provisions.

But employers did not have to rely on the code-making process. The Negro worker not already discriminated against through code provisions had many other gauntlets to run. The question of importance to him as to all workers was, "as a result of all of N.R.A.'s maneuvers will I be able to buy more?" The answer has been "No." A worker cannot eat a wage rate. To determine what this wage rate means to him we must determine a number of other factors. Thus rates for longshoremen seem relatively high. But when we realize that the average amount of work a longshoreman receives during the year is from ten to fifteen weeks, the wage rate loses much of its significance. When we add to that fact the increase in the cost of living—as high as 40 per cent in many cases—the wage rate becomes even more chimerical. For other groups of industrial workers increases in cost of living, coupled with the part time and irregular nature of the work, make the results of N.R.A. negligible. In highly mechanized industries speed-up and stretch-out nullify the promised result of N.R.A. to bring increased employment through shorter hours. For the workers are now producing more in their shorter work periods than in the longer periods before N.R.A. There is less employment. The first sufferer from fewer jobs is the Negro worker. Finally the complete break-down of compliance machinery in the South has cancelled the last minute advantage to Negro workers which N.R.A.'s enthusiasts may have claimed.

The Agricultural Adjustment Administration has used cruder methods in enforcing poverty on the Negro farm population. It has made violations of the rights of tenants under crop reduction contracts easy; it has rendered enforcement of these rights impossible. The reduction of the acreage under cultivation through the government rental agreement rendered unnecessary large numbers of tenants and farm laborers. Although the contract with the government provided that the land owner should not reduce the number of his tenants, he did so. The federal courts have now refused to allow tenants to enjoin such evictions. Faced with this Dred Scott decision against farm tenants, the A.A.A. has remained discreetly silent. Farm laborers are now jobless by the hundreds of thousands, the conservative government estimate of the decline in agricultural employment for the year 1934 alone being a quarter of a million. The larger portion of these are unskilled Negro agricultural workers—now without income and unable to secure work or relief.

But the unemployment and tenant evictions occasioned by the crop reduction policies of the A.A.A. is not all. For the tenants and sharecroppers who were retained on the plantations the government's agricultural program meant reduced income. Wholesale fraud on tenants in the payment of parity checks occurred. Tenants complaining to the Department of Agriculture in Washington have their letters referred back to the locality in which they live and trouble of serious nature often results. Even when this does not happen, the tenant fails to get his check. The remainder of the land he tills on shares with his landlord brings him only the most meagre necessities during the crop season varying from three to five months. The rest of the period for him and his family is one of "root hog or die."

The past year has seen an extension of poverty even to the small percentage (a little more than 20 per cent) of Negro farmers who own their own land. For them compulsory reduction of acreage for cotton and tobacco crops, with the quantum of such reduction controlled and regulated by local boards on which they have no representation, has meant drastic reduction of their already low income. Wholesale confiscation of the income of the Negro cotton and tobacco farmer is being made by prejudiced local boards in the South under the very nose of the federal government. In the wake of such confiscation has come a tremendous increase in land tenantry as a result of foreclosures on Negro-owned farm properties.

Nor has the vast public works program, designed to give increased employment to workers in the building trades, been free from prejudice. State officials in the South are in many cases in open rebellion against the ruling of P.W.A. that the same wage scales must be paid to Negro and white labor. Compliance with this paper ruling is enforced in only rare cases. The majority of the instances of violation of this rule are unremedied. Only unskilled work is given Negroes on public works projects in most instances. And even here discrimination in employment is notorious. Such is bound to be the case when we realize that there are only a handful of investigators available to seek enforcement.

Recently a move has been made by Negro officials in the administration to effect larger employment of Negro skilled and unskilled workers on public works projects by specifying that failure of a contractor to pay a certain percentage of his payroll to Negro artisans will be evidence of racial discrimination. Without doubting the good intentions of the sponsors of this ingenious scheme, it must nevertheless be pointed out that it fails to meet the problem in a number of vital particulars. It has yet to face a test in the courts, even if one is willing to suppose that P.W.A. high officials will bring it to a test. Percentages thus far experimented with are far too low and the number of such experiments far too few to make an effective dent in the unemployment conditions of Negro construction industry workers. Moreover the scheme gives aid and comfort to employer-advocates of strike-breaking and the open shop; and, while offering, perhaps, some temporary relief to a few hundred Negro workers, it establishes a dangerous precedent which throws back the labor movement and the organization of Negro workers to a considerable degree. The scheme, whatever its Negro sponsors may hope to contrary, becomes therefore only another excuse for their white superiors maintaining a "do-nothing" policy with regard to discrimination against Negroes in the Public Works Administration.

The Negro has no pleasanter outlook in the long term social planning ventures of the new administration. Planning for subsistence home-steads for industrially stranded workers has been muddled enough even without consideration of the problem of integrating Negroes into such plans. Subsistence Homesteads projects are overburdened with profiteering prices for the homesteads and foredoomed to failure by the lack of planning for adequate and permanent incomes for pro-spective homesteaders.

In callous disregard of the interdiction in the Constitution of the United States against use of federal funds for projects which dis-criminate against applicants solely on the ground of color, subsistence homesteads have been planned on a strictly "lily-white" basis. The more than 200 Negro applicants for the first project at Arthurdale, West Virginia were not even considered, Mr. Bushrod Grimes (then in charge of the project) announcing that the project was to be open only to "native white stock." As far north as Dayton, Ohio, where state laws prohibit any type of segregation against Negroes, the federal government has extended its "lily-white" policy. Recently it has estab-lished two Jim-Crow projects for Negroes. Thus the new administration seeks in its program of social planning to perpetuate ghettoes of Negroes for fifty years to come.

An even more blatant example of this policy of "lily-white" re-construction is apparent in the planning of the model town of Norris, Tennessee, by the Tennessee Valley Authority. This town of 450 model homes is intended for the permanent workers on Norris Dam. The homes are rented by the federal government, which at all times maintains title to the land and dwellings and has complete control of the town management. Yet officials at T.V.A. openly admit that no Negroes are allowed at Norris.

T.V.A. has other objectionable features. While Negro employment now approaches an equitable proportion of total employment; the pay-roll of Negro workers remains disproportionately lower than that of whites. While the government has maintained a trade school to train workers on the project, no Negro trainees have been admitted. Nor have any meaningful plans matured for the future of the several thousand Negro workers who in another year or so will be left without employment, following completion of work on the dams being built by T.V.A.

None of the officials of T.V.A. seems to have the remotest idea of how Negroes in the Tennessee Valley will be able to buy the cheap electricity which T.V.A. is designed to produce. They admit that standards of living of the Negro population are low, that the introduction of industry into the Valley is at present only a nebulous dream, that even if this eventuates there is no assurance that Negro employment will result. The fairest summary that can be made of T.V.A. is that for a year or so it has furnished bread to a few thousand Negro workers. Beyond that everything is conjecture which is most unpleasant because of the utter planlessness of those in charge of the project.

Recovery legislation of the present session of Congress reveals the same fatal flaws which have been noted in the operation of previous recovery ventures. Thus, for example, instead of genuine unemployment insurance we have the leaders of the administration proposing to exclude from their plans domestic and agricultural workers, in which classes are to be found 15 out of every 23 Negro workers. On every hand the New Deal has used slogans for the same raw deal.

The sharpening of the crisis for Negroes has not found them unresponsive. Two years of increasing hardship has seen strange movement among the masses. In Chicago, New York, Washington and Baltimore the struggle for jobs has given rise to action on the part of a number of groups seeking to boycott white employers who refuse to employ Negroes. "Don't Buy Where You Can't Work" campaigns are springing up everywhere. The crisis has furnished renewed vigor to the Garvey Movement. And proposals for a 49th State are being seriously considered by various groups.

In sharp contrast with these strictly racial approaches to the problem, have been a number of interracial approaches. Increasing numbers of unemployed groups have been organized under radical leadership and have picketed relief stations for bread. Sharecroppers unions, under Socialist leadership in Arkansas, have shaken America into a consciousness of the growing resentment of southern farm tenants and the joint determination of the Negro and white tenants to do something about their intolerable condition.

In every major strike in this country Negro union members have fought with their white fellow workers in a struggle for economic survival. The bodies of ten Negro strikers killed in such strike struggles offer mute testimony to this fact. Even the vicious policies of the leaders of the A. F. of L. in discrimination against Negro workers is breaking down under the pressure for solidarity from the ranks of whites.

This heightening of spirit among all elements of black America and the seriousness of the crisis for them make doubly necessary the consideration of the social and economic condition of the Negro at this time. It was a realization of these conditions which gave rise to the proposal to hold a national conference on the economic status of Negroes under the New Deal at Howard University in Washington, D.C., on May 18, 19 and 20. At this conference, sponsored by the Social Science Division of Howard University and the Joint Committee on National Recovery, a candid and intelligent survey of the social and economic condition of the Negro will be made. Unlike most conferences it will not be a talk-fest. For months nationally known economists and other technicians have been working on papers to be presented. Unlike other conferences it will not be a one-sided affair. Ample opportunity will be afforded for high government officials to present their views of the "New Deal." Others not connected with the government, including representatives of radical political parties, will also appear to present their conclusions. Not the least important phase will be the appearance on the platform of Negro workers and farmers themselves to offer their own experience under the New Deal. Out of such a conference can and will come a clear-cut analysis of the problems faced by Negroes and the nation.

But a word of caution ought to be expressed with regard to this significant conference. In the final analysis it cannot and does not claim to be representative of the mass opinion of Negro citizens in America. All it can claim for itself is that it will bring together on a non-representative basis well informed Negro and white technicians to discuss the momentous problem it has chosen as its topic. It can furnish a base for action for any organization which chooses to avail itself of the information developed by it. It cannot act itself.

Thus looking beyond such a conference one cannot fail to hope that it will furnish impetus to a national expression of black America demanding a tolerable solution to the economic evils which it suffers. Perhaps it is not too much to hope that public opinion may be moulded by this conference to such an extent that already existing church, civic, fraternal, professional and trade union organizations will see the necessity for concerted effort in forging a mighty arm of protest against injustice suffered by the Negro. It is not necessary that such organizations agree on every issue. On the problem of relief of Negroes from poverty there is little room for disagreement. The important thing is that throughout America as never before Negroes awake to the need for a unity of action on vital economic problems which perplex us.

Such a hope is not lacking in foundation upon solid ground. Such an instance as the All India Congress of British India furnishes an example of what repressed groups can do to better their social and economic status. Perhaps a *"National Negro Congress"* of delegates from thousands of Negro organizations (and white organizations willing to recognize their unity of interest) will furnish a vehicle for channeling public opinion of black America. One thing is certain: the Negro may stand still but the depression will not. And unless there is concerted action of Negroes throughout the nation the next two years will bring even greater misery to the millions of underprivileged Negro toilers in the nation.

The Crisis, May, 1935; XLII, 141–42, 154–55.

[c]

THE NEW DEAL AND THE NEGRO:
A LOOK AT THE FACTS
by Robert C. Weaver

It is impossible to discuss intelligently the New Deal and the Negro without considering the status of the Negro prior to the advent of the Recovery Program. The present economic position of the colored citizen was not created by recent legislation alone. Rather, it is the result of the impact of a new program upon an economic and social situation.

Much has been said recently about the occupational distribution of Negroes. Over a half of the gainfully employed colored Americans are concentrated in domestic service and farming. The workers in these two pursuits are the most casual and unstable in the modern economic world. This follows from the fact that neither of them requires any great capital outlay to buy necessary equipment. Thus when there is a decline in trade, the unemployment of workers in these fields does not necessitate idle plants, large depreciation costs, or mounting overhead charges. In such a situation, the employer has every incentive to dismiss his workers; thus, these two classes are fired early in a depression.

The domestic worker has loomed large among the unemployed since the beginning of the current trade decline. This situation has persisted throughout the depression and is reflected in the relief figures for urban communities where 20 per cent of the employables on relief were formerly attached to personal and domestic service. Among Negroes the relative number of domestics and servants on relief is even greater. The data for 30 typical cities will be found in the table on the following page.

In these cities, 43.4 per cent of the Negroes on relief May 1, 1934, were usually employed as domestics. The demand for servants is a derived one; it is dependent upon the income and employment of other persons in the community. Thus, domestics are among the last rehired in a period of recovery.

The new works program of the Federal Government will attack this problem of the domestic worker from two angles. Insofar as it accelerates recovery by restoring incomes, it will tend to increase the demand for servants. More important, however, will be its creation of direct employment opportunities for all occupational classes of those on relief.

Although it is regrettable that the economic depression has led to the unemployment of so many Negroes and has threatened the creation of a large segment of the Negro population as a chronic relief load, one is forced to admit that Federal relief has been a godsend to the unemployed. The number of unemployed in this country was growing in 1933. According to the statistics of the American Federation of Labor, the number of unemployed increased from 3,216,000 in January, 1930 to 13,689,000 in March 1933. In November, 1934, the number was about 10,500,000 and although there are no comparable current data available, estimates indicate that current unemployment is less than that of last November. Local relief monies were shrinking; and need and starvation were facing those unable to find an opportunity to work. A Federal relief program was the only possible aid in this situation. Insofar as the Negro was greatly victimized by the economic developments, he was in a position to benefit from a program which provided adequate funds for relief.

It is admitted that there were many abuses under the relief set-up. Such situations should be brought to light and fought. In the case of Negroes, these abuses undoubtedly existed and do exist. We should extend every effort to uncover and correct them. We can admit that we have gained from the relief program and still fight to receive greater and more equitable benefits from it.

The recent depression has been extremely severe in its effects upon the South. The rural Negro—poor before the period of trade decline —was rendered even more needy after 1929. Many tenants found it impossible to obtain a contract for a crop, and scores of Negro farm owners lost their properties. The displacement of Negro tenants (as was the case for whites) began before, and grew throughout the depression. Thus, at the time of the announcement of the New Deal, there were many families without arrangements for a crop—an appreciable number without shelter. The following summary of conditions in one county of a southern state will serve as an illustration. In Greene

Relief Data—Southern Cities and Other Important Urban Centers
(May, 1934)

Cities	Total Negroes on Relief	Negroes in Domestic Service on Relief	Percentage Domestic Service
1. Bowling Green, Ky. ...	130	80	61.5
2. Biloxi, Miss.	360	217	60.2
3. Wheeling, W. Va.	438	200	45.6
4. Lake Charles, La.	886	328	37.0
5. Houston, Texas	6,839	3,829	56.2
6. Jackson, Miss.	1,714	964	56.2
7. Evansville, Ind.	1,647	810	49.2
8. Lexington, Ky.	1,491	644	43.2
9. Charlotte, N.C.	3,153	1,778	56.3
10. Norfolk, Va.	4,943	2,461	49.7
11. Cincinnati, Ohio	11,669	4,900	43.7
12. New Orleans, La.	14,749	5,600	38.0
13. Washington, D.C.	21,315	10,213	48.3
14. Kansas City, Mo.	4,935	2,807	56.8
15. Indianapolis, Ind.	8,477	4,263	50.2
16. St. Louis, Mo.	18,440	7,950	43.1
17. Wilmington, Del.	2,426	1,090	32.5
18. Atlanta, Ga.	16,541	10,248	61.9
19. Gastonia, N.C.	140	69	49.2
20. Birmingham, Ala.	15,806	7,742	48.9
21. Oakland, Calif.	735	375	51.0
22. New York City	58,950	27,330	46.3
23. Boston, Mass.	2,534	1,232	48.6
24. Reading, Pa.	483	158	32.8
25. Rochester, N.Y.	462	203	43.9
26. Detroit, Mich.	15,070	3,380	22.4
27. Pittsburgh, Pa.	13,930	5,544	39.8
28. Akron, Ohio	2,365	995	42.0
29. Duluth, Minn.	59	15	25.4
30. Milwaukee, Wis.	1,575	495	31.4
TOTAL	278,388	121,044	43.4

County, North Carolina (where the population in 1930 was 18,656 divided almost equally between whites and Negroes) the F.E.R.A. survey reported data as of January 1934 relative to the period of displacement of families. This material shows that for this county, displacement of tenants was most severe in 1931–1932. The figures are as follows:

Length of Time Without Tenant Status	Colored	White	Total
Less than a year	14	13	27
One year	18	8	26
Two years	21	19	40
More than two years	42	13	55
Always farmed as day laborers	5	5	10
TOTAL	100	58	158

The problems facing the Negro farmer of the South are not new. They have been accentuated by the crop reduction program. They are, for the most part, problems of a system and their resistance to reform is as old as the system. This was well illustrated by the abuses in the administration of the Federal feed, seed, and fertilizer laws in 1928–1929. These abuses were of the same nature as those which confront the A.A.A. in its dealings with Negro tenants.

The southern farm tenant is in such a position that he cannot receive any appreciable gains from a program until steps are taken to change his position of absolute economic dependence upon the landlord. Until some effective measure for rehabilitating him is discovered, there is no hope. The new program for land utilization, rural rehabilitation, and spreading land ownership may be able to effect such a change. Insofar as it takes a step in that direction, it will be advantageous to the Negro farmer. The degree to which it aids him will depend upon the temper of its administration and the extent to which it is able to break away from the *status quo*.

In listing some of the gains which have accrued to Negroes under the New Deal, there will be a discussion of three lines of activity: housing, employment, and emergency education. These are chosen for discussion because each is significant in itself, and all represent a definite break from the *status quo* in governmental activity, method, and policy. They do not give a complete picture; but rather, supply interesting examples of what is, and can be, done for Negroes.

The Housing Division of the Federal Emergency Administration of Public Works has planned 60 Federal housing projects to be under construction by December 31, 1935. Of these, 28 are to be developed in Negro slum areas and will be tenanted predominantly or wholly by Negroes. Eight additional projects will provide for an appreciable degree of Negro occupancy. These 36 projects will afford approximately 74,664 rooms and should offer accommodations for about 23,000 low income colored families. The estimated total cost of these housing developments will be $64,428,000, and they represent about 29 per cent of the funds devoted to Federal slum clearance developments under the present allotments.

Projects in Negro areas have been announced in seven cities: Atlanta, Cleveland, Detroit, Indianapolis, Montgomery, Chicago, and Nashville. These will cost about $33,232,000 and will contain about 20,000 rooms. Two of these projects, the University development at Atlanta, and the Thurman Street development in Montgomery, are under construction. These are among the earliest Federal housing projects to be initiated by the P.W.A.

After a series of conferences and a period of experience under the P.W.A., it was decided to include a clause in P.W.A. housing contracts requiring the payment to Negro mechanics of a given percentage of the payroll going to skilled workers. The first project to be affected by such a contractual clause was the Techwood development in Atlanta, Georgia. On this project, most of the labor employed on demolition was composed of unskilled Negro workers. About 90 per cent of the unskilled workers employed laying the foundation for the Techwood project were Negroes, and, for the first two-month construction period, February and March, 12.7 per cent of the wages paid skilled workers was earned by Negro artisans. The payroll figures for the monthly period, March 29 to April 24 inclusive, are as follows:

	White	Negro	Percentage Negro Wage
Skilled	$ 7,338.30	$1,185.50	13.9
Intermediate	430.20	25.50	5.6
Unskilled	2,779.45	3,356.00	54.7
TOTAL	$10,547.95	$4,567.00	30.0

Under the educational program of the F.E.R.A., out of a total of 17,879 teachers employed in 13 southern states, 5,476 or 30.6 per cent were Negro. Out of a total of 570,794 enrolled in emergency classes, 217,000 or 38 per cent were Negro. Out of a total of $886,300 expended in a month (either February or March, 1935) for the program, Negroes received $231,320 or 26.1 per cent. These southern states in which 26.1 per cent of all emergency salaries were paid to Negro teachers, ordinarily allot only 11.7 per cent of all public school salaries to Negro teachers. The situation may be summarized as follows: Six of the 13 states are spending for Negro salaries a proportion of their emergency education funds larger than the percentage of Negroes in those states. The area as a whole is spending for Negro salaries a proportion of its funds slightly in excess of the percentage of Negroes in the population. This development is an example of Government activity breaking away from the *status quo* in race relations.

There is one Government expenditure in education in reference to which there has been general agreement that equity has been established. That is the F.E.R.A. college scholarship program. Each college or university not operated for profit, received $20 monthly per student as aid for 12 per cent of its college enrollment. Negro and white institutions have benefited alike under this program.

In the execution of some phases of the Recovery Program, there have been difficulties, and the maximum results have not been received by the Negroes. But, given the economic situation of 1932, the New Deal has been more helpful than harmful to Negroes. We had unemployment in 1932. Jobs were being lost by Negroes, and they were in need. Many would have starved had there been no Federal relief program. As undesirable as is the large relief load among Negroes, the F.E.R.A. has meant much to them. In most of the New Deal setups, there has been some Negro representation by competent Negroes. The Department of the Interior and the P.W.A. have appointed some fifteen Negroes to jobs of responsibility which pay good salaries. These persons have secretarial and clerical staffs attached to their offices. In addition to these new jobs, there are the colored messengers, who number around 100, and the elevator operators for the Government buildings, of whom there are several hundred. This is not, of course, adequate representation; but it represents a step in the desired direction and is greater recognition than has been given Negroes in the Federal Government during the last 20 years. Or again, in the Nashville housing project, a Negro architectural firm is a consultant; for the Southwest side housing project in Chicago, a Negro is an associate architect. One of the proposed projects will have two Negro principal architects, a Negro consultant architect, and a technical staff of about six Negro technicians. In other cities competent colored architects will be used to design housing projects.

This analysis is intended to indicate some advantages accruing to the Negro under the Recovery Program, and to point out that the New Deal, insofar as it represents an extension of governmental activity into the economic sphere, is a departure which can do much to reach the Negro citizens. In many instances it has availed itself of these opportunities. An intelligent appraisal of its operation is necessary to assure greater benefits to colored citizens.

Opportunity, July, 1935; XIII, 200–2.

[d]

CONGRESSMAN MITCHELL ON THE "NEW DEAL"

. . . Mr. Roosevelt promised not only a "new deal" but a square deal to the Negro during his campaign. He knew then as he knows now that the Negro is the most forgotten of all forgotten men in this country. He has kept his promise. Every instance of race discrimination that has been properly brought to the attention of the President has not only received immediate attention but has been amicably adjusted as far as the authority of the Executive Office could go. Mr. Roosevelt has appointed more Negroes to responsible governmental positions than the last three Republican administrations taken together. Under this administration, Dr. Thompkins, an outstanding Negro physician and a life-long Democrat, has been appointed recorder of deeds of the District of Columbia. Robert L. Vann, lawyer and publisher has been appointed Special Assistant Attorney General with offices in Washington, D.C. Mr. Lawrence Oxley, an outstanding social worker of the State of North Carolina has been appointed special assistant and adviser in the Department of Commerce. Eugene Kinckle Jones, a social worker of New York has been appointed special adviser in the Department of Labor. Lester A. Walton of the city of New York has been appointed minister to Liberia. Outstanding lawyers such as Theopholius Mann and William H. Hastie, special solicitors in the Department of Interior. There have been scores of other appointments of high and important rank such as Negroes have not enjoyed under any Republican administration. It is not this that I am most interested in. It is what this administration has meant to the Negro further down in the scale of intelligence and economics. They, under this administration, have been given the biggest chance that has come to the Negro under any administration in my day.

I should like to speak of the Ship of State as an automobile formerly in the hands of the Republican Party with Mr. Hoover at the wheel. He either went to sleep at the wheel or drove in such reckless manner that the vehicle left the highway and found itself bogged down in the mud, where it remained from 1929 until 1932, when the American people arose up in their righteous indignation and rebuked the Republican Party and Mr. Hoover by selecting another driver for this vehicle. This driver was Mr. Roosevelt. . . .

Mr. Roosevelt, upon assuming control of the machine, found many important parts missing. Bearings were burned out, connecting rods were gone, and before anything could be done in operating the machine and placing it back upon the highway, expert governmental mechanics had to be called from various sections of the country to render the repairs necessary before even the motor could be started.

For 2½ years Mr. Roosevelt has been driving and guiding the machine back toward the highway, during which time the wreckers of the machine have not only refused to help, but they have placed impediments in the way of the progress of the machine. They have tried to puncture the tires and they have even thrown brickbats at the driver. But through it all, our great President has been able to save the American Nation and has brought us back to the highway, and no amount of criticism will cause the American people to forget that Franklin Delano Roosevelt is the present savior of the Nation.

There is no question in my mind but that the source of this Government at this time is absolutely pure. I have had many conferences with the President of the United States and know that he is without race prejudice and believes in an absolute square deal for all citizens. regardless of race, color, or previous condition. Whatever corruption there is in the governmental stream today does not come from the source and can, and I hope will be, corrected.

No President has been more outspoken against the horrible crime of lynching than has Mr. Roosevelt. In speaking of lynching sometime ago he characterized it as "collective murder" and spoke of it as a crime which blackens the record of America. This crime should and must be wiped out. I have introduced a bill in the House which would make lynching a Federal crime and make the perpetrators of the crime punishable in the Federal courts. I believe that the day is not far hence when this legislation will be enacted into law. I wish to say, however, that I have no delusions about this important legislation. While I believe it is absolutely necessary, and I shall work for its passage whole-heartedly, I do not believe that the mere passing of the law will eliminate the crime. I should like to call attention to the fact that no major crime on the statute books of this country has been reduced with one-tenth of the rapidity as has lynching during the past 45 years. . . .

I believe that under this administration the Negroes of the United States have the best opportunity that has come to them during my lifetime. It is my wish and prayer that we open our eyes and bend every effort toward making this Government what it should be—a Government of the people, for the people, and by the people.

Let me say again, the attitude of the administration at the White House is absolutely fair and without prejudice, insofar as the Negro citizenry is concerned.

Congressional Record, August 13, 1935; 74th Cong., 1st sess.; given in part.

29

TO NEGRO WRITERS

by Langston Hughes

The impact of the anti-fascist and Left movements in the country was great among its artists and writers. Reflecting this was the first American Writers' Congress held in New York City in April, 1935. At its opening night, an audience of four-thousand was present; included were 216 writer-delegates from twenty-six states and 150 writer-guests from foreign countries, including Germany, Japan, Mexico, and Cuba. At that meeting Langston Hughes said:

There are certain practical things American Negro writers can do through their work.

We can reveal to the Negro masses, from which we come, our potential power to transform the now ugly face of the Southland into a region of peace and plenty.

We can reveal to the white masses those Negro qualities which go beyond the mere ability to laugh and sing and dance and make music, and which are a part of the useful heritage that we place at the disposal of a future free America.

Negro writers can seek to unite blacks and whites in our country, not on the nebulous basis of an inter-racial meeting, or the shifting sands of religious brotherhood, but on the *solid* ground of the daily working-class struggle to wipe out, now and forever, all the old inequalities of the past.

Furthermore, by way of exposure, Negro writers can reveal in their novels, stories, poems, and articles:

The lovely grinning face of Philanthropy—which gives a million dollars to a Jim Crow school, but not one job to a graduate of that school; which builds a Negro hospital with second-rate equipment, then commands black patients and student-doctors to go there whether they will or not; or which, out of the kindness of its heart, erects yet another separate, segregated, shut-off, Jim Crow Y.M.C.A.

Negro writers can expose those white labor leaders who keep their unions closed against Negro workers and prevent the betterment of all workers.

We can expose, too, the sick-sweet smile of organized religion— which lies about what it doesn't know, and about what it *does* know. And the half-voodoo. half-clown, face of revivalism, dulling the mind with the clap of its empty hands.

Expose, also, the false leadership that besets the Negro people —bought and paid for leadership, owned by capital, afraid to open its mouth except in the old conciliatory way so advantageous to the exploiters.

And all the economic roots of race hatred and race fear.

And the Contentment Tradition of the O-lovely-Negroes school of American fiction, which makes an ignorant black face and a Carolina head filled with superstition, appear more desirable than a *crown* of gold; the jazz-band; and the O-so-gay writers who make of the Negro's poverty and misery a dusky funny paper.

And expose war. And the old My-Country-'Tis-of-Thee lie. And the colored American Legion posts strutting around talking about the privilege of dying for the noble Red, White and Blue, when they aren't even permitted the privilege of living for it. Or voting for it in Texas. Or working for it in the diplomatic service. Or even rising, like every other good little boy, from the log cabin to the White House.

White House is right!

Dear colored American Legion, you can swing from a lynching tree, uniform and all, with pleasure—and nobody'll fight for you. Don't you know that? Nobody even salutes you down South, dead or alive, medals or no medals, chevrons or not, no matter how many wars you've fought in.

Let Negro writers write about the irony and pathos of the *colored* American Legion.

"Salute, Mr. White Man!"

"Salute, hell! . . . You're a nigger."

Or would you rather write about the moon?

Sure, the moon still shines over Harlem. Shines over Scottsboro.

Shines over Birmingham, too, I reckon. Shines over Cordie Cheek's grave, down South.

Write about the moon if you want to. Go ahead. This is a free country.

But there are certain practical things American Negro writers can do. And must do. There's a song that says, "the time ain't long." That song is right. Something has got to change in America—and change soon. We must help that change to come.

The moon's still shining as poetically as ever, but all the stars on the flag are dull. (And the stripes, too.)

We want a new and better America, where there won't be any poor, where there won't be any more Jim Crow, where there won't by any lynchings, where there won't be any munition makers, where we won't need philanthropy, nor charity, nor the New Deal, nor Home Relief.

We want an America that will be ours, a world that will be ours— we Negro workers and white workers! Black writers and white!

We'll make that world!

In Henry Hart, ed., *American Writers' Congress* (New York: International Publishers, 1935), pp. 139–41.

30

DONALD G. MURRAY VS. MARYLAND

Graduate and professional training for Black youth was possible after World War I in Howard, Fisk, and Atlanta; and for very few at universities like Harvard and Columbia. But at the state universities of the South—where the mass of Black people lived and where their labor and taxes were decisive in maintaining the institutions—they were barred. Protest brought at first scanty appropriations from southern states for out-of-state higher education; in 1933 an effort by Thomas Hocutt of North Carolina to be admitted to the University School of Pharmacy was rejected by a technicality. The first successful breakthrough was in the suit brought by Donald G. Murray against the University of Maryland, with the N.A.A.C.P. through Charles H. Houston and Thurgood Marshall the successful team. This was followed, in 1936, by the Lloyd Gaines case, decided against Missouri by the U.S. Supreme Court in 1938. The document that follows is the page one story in a Black newspaper on the Murray case.

The University of Maryland cannot bar Donald Gaines Murray, Amherst College graduate, from its law school because of his color, according to a decision handed down in the Baltimore city court last Tuesday by Judge Eugene O'Dunne. Lawyers of the National Association for the Advancement of Colored People, led by Charles H. Houston, its special counsel, presented Mr. Murray's plea for a writ of mandamus, requiring the university to accept and pass on his qualifications. He had been turned down by the authorities of this tax-supported institution when it was discovered that he was a Race man.

The N.A.A.C.P. lawyers proved that the state's scholarship aid is inadequate and that no facilities equal to those available at the university are furnished to Race students. There is no separate college in the state offering law training and other professional courses.

This is the first case in the association's recently accelerated campaign, to force open tax-supported higher educational institutions to colored students through legal action. It is thus of far-reaching significance, since a practice that is illegal in the tax-supported educational institutions of one state is doubtless illegal elsewhere.

Atty. Charles H. Houston, of Washington, D.C., recently appointed special counsel of the association, is in charge of this phase of the N.A.A.C.P. program and is planning to institute similar suits throughout the United States, wherever Race students are excluded from equal facilities in tax-supported schools and colleges.

This decision will unquestionably stir authorities in the Southern states where the color bar surrounds all public institutions of higher learning which the Race supports with its taxes but cannot enter.

Assisting Attorney Houston in the Maryland University case was Attorney Thurgood Marshall of Baltimore.

Chicago Defender, July 6, 1935, p. 1.

31

NEGRO STUDENTS CHALLENGE SOCIAL FORCES
by Maurice Gates

The Campuses in the nineteen-thirties were beehives of sociopolitical activity and struggle, the emphasis being upon measures to fight the effects of the Depression and to oppose militarism, fascism, war, and manifestations of anti-Semitism and racism. The numbers of Black college students were still small and the proportion of Black to white infinitesimal. However, on the campuses of the Black institutions the reflections of the general student movement appeared, as well as features specific to the needs of Black youth. A member of the National Executive Committee of the radical and influential National Student League wrote of this in the organ of the N.A.A.C.P.

Young people have always claimed that they are living in an unique age. The terrible newness of maturity, and the equally terrible problem of the world into which they have been precipitated make it difficult for past and present students to realize that there have always been pressing problems to face and to solve.

When we say, therefore, that we are facing a world that gives us new tasks and the possibility of new achievements, we must substantiate our assertions by facts. Three years ago the crisis was something to be joked about, unless one was in need of relief and Hoover's optimistic promises almost believed. It was supposed to be only one of those recurrent apoplexies of the system, which was no worse, perhaps, than many America had seen. Now the situation is different. The sixth year of the crisis sees only the deepening of the shadow over the future facing youth. War and fascism are no longer theoretical problems. They are practical, concrete and pressing dangers. Wage cuts now apply to the student as well as to his family. The repression, which constitutes at least the initial skirmishes of fascism, has been increased until academic freedom has become more of an ideal than a right or privilege. We are living in an unique age, an age which surely must compel the attention of future historians.

It is therefore not surprising that three years ago discussion clubs and forums, which later grew into several national student organizations, were formed on college campuses. The phenomenal growth of these organizations can only be explained by the timeliness of their appearance; the objective factors were there.

Major questions which affected society had immediate repercussions on the campus. College enrollments began to decline steadily because parents were losing their jobs, having their wages cut, and were compelled to economize. Those who remained in school were also affected by this problem, and in addition the disorganization of American economy offered them no chance to enter their professions or use their technical skill and knowledge after they had been graduated. Year after year college graduates left the college rostrum with the pious unctions of a Nicholas Murray Butler ringing in their ears to present their graduation certificates to the nearest relief bureau.

But the grim paradox of it all! Educational funds began to disappear, a wave of economy swept the American school system, schools closed down, such schools as Crane Junior College at Chicago. Fees were levied where they had never existed before, and raised where they had previously existed. The institution of free text-books began to disappear at the College of the City of New York, Brooklyn College and elsewhere. But the war masters must be served! No funds for education, but billions for war and war preparations.

It was in this era that the Vinson Naval Bill, providing for the largest naval appropriation of any nation during peace time, was speeded through the two houses of Congress. Money intended for work projects was diverted to finance war preparations, by a President who time after time has declared his peaceful intentions. Huge amounts of money were expended for military and naval display; but for education, the myth of American Democracy, there were no funds. Schools and college departments began to tack up signs "Closed Until Further Notice."

Only if college students were inanimate automatons, could they remain immobile and silent. In no uncertain terms they began to speak out. No longer were they limited to discussions in isolated groups. Broad mass actions and demonstrations spread through the country. With mounting vigor the American college campus began to re-echo the cries "All War Funds for Needy Students!," "Down with Fascism!," "Equal Opportunity to Negro Students!," "Schools, not Battleships!"

Students who stood in the forefront of this birth of progress on the American campus, were faced with dire reaction. Mac Weiss, editor of *Frontier* and a leader in the Social Problems Club, was suspended from City College; Reed Harris, editor of the *Columbia Spectator,* was expelled for his support of a student delegation to the mining regions of Kentucky, for his investigation which revealed the professionalism of Columbia football, and for his investigation of the John Jay dining hall. A militant strike of Columbia students resulted in his reinstatement. Twenty-one students were expelled from the College of the City of New York for protesting against an R.O.T.C. demonstration. The American student movement began to grow. No longer could one refer to docile students and academic celibates. It was the awakening of a virile, healthy student attitude conditioned by social forces. The American college campus rejected that which was dead and decaying, and sought for life outside of its rotten environment. Let the Butlers, Colligans, and Robinsons fester; the cry of the students was, "We choose life. We choose to live!"

During all this the Negro student, isolated for the most part from the main current of American student life, because of one of the most damnable features of the American social set-up—the Jim-Crow educational system—remained nearly inarticulate. Old values still held for him. The old *laissez-faire* policy of dog eat dog competition, and the survival of the fittest, determined the ideology of the mass of Negro students. It mattered little that their parents at home suffered from the problems of unemployment and social discrimination, or that they themselves when they finished would find the sphere of Negro exploitation seriously restricted, and if they were to work at all it would probably have to be done as an elevator operator, janitor, or domestic servant. Certainly if any group had cause for protest and cause to remonstrate it was this group. Yet, the first few years except for few and isolated instances nothing was done, nothing was said. These few instances, however, were cheerful and heartening.

At Virginia Union a small group of socially-minded students formed a group called the Cooperative Independent Movement, led by James C. Jackson, now a member of the national executive committee of the National Student League. This group carried on a rather consistent campaign of education on such broad social questions as war and fascism, retrenchment in education, and Negro discrimination. It was on this latter point that they reached a very high level. Together with a like group of white students at the University of Virginia, they formed a delegation to the state legislature and demanded equal appropriations for Negro schools. This was a turn in the right direction; unity, a basic need, was achieved. Negro students together with their white student allies had challenged in the Jim-Crow state of Virginia, the monstrous segregation and racial inequality. The group at the University of Virginia was organized by the local chapter of the National Student League. It was but the carrying out of their clearly defined policy: "Because of their comparatively greater freedom, it is the duty of white students to take the initiative in the struggle to break down these barriers of race prejudice and discrimination which tend to divide the student body and weaken its fight. Only through the unity of Negro and white students can their common ends be attained."

At Fisk University there was formed the Denmark Vesey Forum, a student group which discussed contemporary sociological and economic questions. It was, however, also in the field of Negro discrimination and on lynching that they reached their highest level. When Cordie Cheek was lynched at the edge of the Fisk campus, it was this group which stimulated and organized the campus protest, staging a parade and open-air protest meeting. This group was mainly under the leadership of Ishmael Flory, a graduate student from the University of California. It was this same group which led the protests and picketing of a local theatre and prevented a group of Fisk singers from appearing at a theatre where Negroes would be forced to an entrance on an alley way and a seat in a top gallery. Dr. Thomas Elsa Jones, the president of Fisk University, expelled Flory for his activities "detrimental to the best interests of the University."

At Virginia State College, students, sickened by the Victorian atmosphere and the convent-like restrictions imposed upon them by that amiable czar, Dr. John M. Gandy, rebelled and called a student strike, which for organization far surpasses that of any other similar student activity in the history of the American student movement. The school administration was forced to accede to a part of the demands, and this year President Gandy, who does not believe in student government, but student participation in government, has announced a Student Self-Government plan.

I think the turning point in the attitude of the Negro student to the growing militant student movement was the December conference of the National Student League, held at Howard University in 1933. This conference was invited to the campus by the faculty committee and later it became known that President Mordecai Johnson objected to the sessions being held. The students of Howard were conspicuous by their absence. This no doubt was due to the fear of association with "radicals." The Negro newspapers, in not too good an imitation of the press of William Randolph Hearst, had attempted and did partly succeed in producing a "Red-scare."

However, a few students, who had been impressed with the importance of the social problems to be discussed at the conference did attend and contributed greatly to the wealth of the discussion. This small group of students certainly are entitled to the most profound respect, because it was they who set themselves the task of making the students at Howard conscious of vital, living forces around them, thus setting an example for other schools to follow. The difficulty and the vastness of this task can be easily gauged when one considers that hitherto for the most part the students at Howard despite their social and economic position, had contented themselves with a middle class outlook. It was slow work, and one watched and wondered. The effect is just now being felt.

The first outstanding event among Negro students during the past school year was the picket line thrown around the National Crime Conference last December in Washington, D.C. This conference, called by the administration to discuss crime, omitted from their agenda the crime of lynching. On the first day of the session, the picketing was carried on by the District of Columbia branch of the National Association for the Advancement of Colored People, but the four pickets were arrested and released on bail. More than sixty students at Howard met with the N.A.A.C.P. branch that night and the next day appeared at the conference hall in a dramatic picket line, each student wearing a noose of rope about his neck, grim reminders of the terror used against a whole people.

Facing the serious problem of militarism in the schools, students at Howard University met together with students from the University of Maryland, George Washington and John Hopkins, at the latter school for an anti-war conference, where they discussed the growing intensity of war preparations, war propaganda and fascist tendencies on the campus. Having thoroughly discussed the several questions, they formulated a wide program of action. Probably nothing else would serve as well to indicate their seriousness, as the sight of these some three hundred students, Negro and white, who stood at the end of the conference and recited in concert the Oxford Pledge: "We students, solemnly pledge ourselves, not to support the government of the United States in any war it may conduct."

The anti-war sentiment has not lagged at other colleges, for at Virginia Union University, a similar anti-war conference was held and the Oxford Pledge taken by a large group of students.

It remained, however, for the student anti-war strike of April 12 to crystallize that sentiment and direct it into organized channels. This was true not only for students in Negro schools, but for the American student Movement as a whole. The April 12 strike was called by six organizations including the Methodist Student Federation, and the National Student League, in answer to the call of the International Student Congress Against War and Fascism, held at Brussels, Belgium, during the Christmas holidays.

One hundred fifty thousand students struck for one hour against war and fascism. Of this number at least three thousand were Negro students. This, of course, is not a very large number but it certainly shows the direction the Negro students are beginning to take. This is more clearly emphasized when it is remembered that the previous school year, no Negro school took part in the strike.

The Negro colleges which took part in the strike of April 12 were Howard University, Virginia Union, Virginia State, Morgan College and several other shools which held small meetings during the strike hour.

The strike served as a warning to the war makers and those interested in the spread of fascism that if they persist in their course they do so at their own peril. Students, Negro and white, will not allow themselves to blindly be drawn into another war to become the fuel for the perpetuation of a system which, to put it extremely mildly, is inadequate for the great masses of people. Not only will they not be drawn into such a conflict, but they will actively resist any attempt in that direction with all the means at their disposal.

Important also is the attitude of the white student to his newly found allies. I cite a recent case which shows very clearly the potentialities of such an alignment.

At East Lansing, Michigan, Negro students taking teacher-training courses are not allowed to practice teaching in the East Lansing schools. The chapter of the National Student League at the Teacher's College circulated a petition among the college students to remove this form of discrimination and succeeded in getting six hundred signatures of white students out of the three thousand students enrolled.

Two hundred fifty out of the three hundred fifty students in the East Lansing high school spontaneously signed a petition to have the Negro students teach. Also one of the parent-teacher groups passed a resolution 72–3 to allow the Negro students to teach. The National Association for the Advancement of Colored People and the American Civil Liberties Union also participated in this fight.

Although the American Student Movement is making tremendous strides and positive achievements can be pointed out, it still lags far behind the needs and demands of the students. Nor can it be denied that the Negro student is far behind the white student in his awareness and challenge of social problems. Yet the development that has taken place in the past three years both among Negro students and among white students seems to indicate that the basis has been established for a broad powerful mass student movement.

The Negro student can and must form a vital section of that movement. To speak of a powerful student movement without speaking of the Negro student is impossible. The white student needs the Negro student in his struggle and the Negro student needs the white student. Success will be achieved in just such measures as this is realized. We move swiftly ahead to unity, forging new weapons, blazing new trails, challenging social forces, which before seemingly resisted all challenge. We move in the direction of freedom and security for all, in the direction of a student body fully conscious of the society in which we live and aware of the problems it presents and the historic tasks it imposes.

The Crisis, August, 1935; XLII, 232–33, 251.

32

ALABAMA'S BLOOD-SMEARED COTTON
by Albert Jackson

The Depression brought outright starvation to the farming Black masses in the South and such New Deal measures as the Agricultural Adjustment Act (AAA) actually favored the planters and worsened conditions for the millions of tenant farmers and sharecroppers. A result was efforts at organization among the latter, including Black men and women. Socialist-led Southern Tenant Farmers Union and Communist-led Share Croppers Union led strikes in the South but unity between these two efforts was not achieved. From Alabama, came the following report by the Secretary of the Share Croppers Union, then in hiding from murderous planters and their police.

"Your time has come, you black — — —!" screeched through the woods surrounding Ed Bracy's home. A few seconds later the gang of vigilantes broke into the house and shot him nineteen times in the neck and head. This was the second killing during the Cotton Pickers Strike. It happened on Labor Day.

Ed Bracy, militant Negro leader of the Share Croppers Union, around Hope Hill, had continued to lead the masses of strikers in spite of terror and murder threats. Sheriff R. E. Woodruff's vigilante gang sneaked in at night, like the cowards they are, to murder another leader. The masses have already answered this attack on leaders—"We are all leaders and we will fight on to victory," they say. Since August 19, through the most vicious terror the landlords could unleash, the strikers have held their ranks solid. Such determination can only be born of dire poverty, starvation and oppression.

The terror drive continues. As I write this, there is a look-out to warn me of the approach of lynchers. Constant vigil is kept at all times. Sleep is tortured with nightmares of lynching, terror and murder. Food settles in lumps in your stomach. But the struggle must go on! The attack of the lynchers must be answered!

On August 22 they murdered Jim Press Meriwether, a Negro strike leader near Sandy Ridge. He walked by the home of Bennie Calloway, another striker, where Sheriff Woodruff's gang was beating the women. John Frank Bates, a Fort Deposit landlord, shot him down without a word. They found Jim's wife, beat her and hanged her from the rafters of the house for awhile before releasing her. Then they carried Jim to C. C. Ryles' plantation to question him. Getting no information from the dying man, they carried him out on a hillside and riddled his body with bullets.

Night riders, carrying Negro strikers out from their beds to beat them almost to death and throw them in the swamps. No sleep, no rest, but always watching for the terror gang. More than six strikers were carried out to be beaten. Some of them were unable to wear clothes on their back because of their wounds.

The search is hottest for me. Charles Tasker and James Jackson, Negro workers of Montgomery, were arrested on August 30. They were questioned continually about where I am. Later an I.L.D. lawyer secured their release. Detective Moseley carried them to the county line and told them to "Keep going and never come back!" They are forced to leave their homes and families.

The strike spreads. Montgomery, Talapoosa, Chambers, Lee and Randolph Counties are out solid now. The masses are willing to struggle, willing to sacrifice.

The small demands of the strike—$1 a hundred for picking cotton, $1 for 10 hours' work for wage hands, 20 cents an hour, 40 hours a week with pay in cash for relief workers—are more than 100 percent above the present rates, a grim testimony to the starvation conditions existing in the farming sections of the South. To maintain these conditions the landlords murder, terrorize and beat the strikers. The ugly head of fascism is rearing up in Dixie, in the "Cradle of the Confederacy."

Strikers hide out in swamps in the daytime to avoid attacks of the vigilante gangs. The night Jim Meriwether was killed the strikers got their guns and waited for another vigilante attack. When the lynchers arrived the strikers sounded the battle cry, it was to be steel for steel on even terms. The lynchers, cowards at heart, turned and ran before a shot was fired.

In the meantime, the landlords are beginning to crack. In lower Montgomery County a landlord is paying his hands $1 a day. In Reeltown, scene of the heroic Reeltown struggle of 1932, the landlords agreed to pay 75 cents a hundred and two meals for picking cotton. Around Dadeville and other parts of Talapoosa County the price is rising, but the masses refuse to pick for less than their demands. Only the small farmers, tenants and croppers who pick their own cotton are carrying anything to the gin. The landlords' fields are heavy with cotton that has been ready to pick for three weeks. On J. R. Bell's plantation in Lowndes County, the strikers say "$1 a hundred or let the cows eat it."

In the meantime, the Share Croppers Union waits word from the Southern Tenant Farmers Union on the question of amalgamation. Now more than ever before the necessity for one powerful union in the cotton fields rings out. The murder and terror drive of the landlords is a clarion call for unity, for a powerful united struggle against the fascist attacks of the landlords and for raising the miserably low living standards of the southern rural masses.

In spite of all the odds, the strike goes on. It is historic, it is the greatest strike movement the landlords have ever witnessed. It is significant to all labor, it is raising the miserably low-wage standard on which Roosevelt based his wage-smashing Relief Wage Scale. It loosens the spirit of the Negro masses; they are struggling to the bitter end for their rights. It is imperative to America, it is battering down the ugly head of fascism in the "Cradle of American Fascism."

New Masses, September 24, 1935 (XVI, No. 13), p. 13. For a first-hand account of organizing activities among farm and industrial workers in Alabama in this period see Hosea Hudson, *Black Worker in the Deep South* (N.Y., 1972, International Publishers), esp. pp. 30–75. See also, John Beecher, "The Share Croppers' Union in Alabama," in *Social Forces,* October, 1934 (XIII, 124–32) and J. S. Auerbach, "Southern Tenant Farmers: Socialist Critics of the New Deal," in *Labor History,* Winter, 1966 (VII, 3–18).

33

JOE LOUIS UNCOVERS DYNAMITE

by Richard Wright

A young Black writer, recently out of Mississippi, described the scene in Chicago's ghetto when the young Joe Louis knocked out Max Baer and commenced his reign as Heavyweight Champion of the World; the essay appeared in *New Masses.*

"Wun-tuh-threee-fooo-fiive-seex-seven-eight-niine-thuun!"
Then:
"JOE LOUIS—THE WINNAH!"
On Chicago's South Side five minutes after these words were yelled and Joe Louis' hand was hoisted as victor in his four-round go with

Max Baer, Negroes poured out of beer taverns, pool rooms, barber shops, rooming houses and dingy flats and flooded the streets.

"LOUIS! LOUIS! LOUIS!" they yelled and threw their hats away. They snatched newspapers from the stands of astonished Greeks and tore them up, flinging the bits into the air. They wagged their heads. Lawd, they'd never seen or heard the like of it before. They shook the hands of strangers. They clapped one another on the back. It was like a revival. Really there was a religious feeling in the air. Well, it wasn't exactly a religious feeling, but it was *something,* and you could feel it. It was a feeling of unity, of oneness.

Two hours after the fight the area between South Parkway and Prairie Avenue on 47th Street was jammed with no less than twenty-five thousand Negroes, joy-mad and moving to they didn't know where. Clasping hands, they formed long writhing snake-lines and wove in and out of traffic. They seeped out of doorways, oozed from alleys, trickled out of tenements, and flowed down the street; a fluid mass of joy. White storekeepers hastily closed their doors against the tidal wave and stood peeping through plate glass with blanched faces.

Something had happened, all right. And it had happened so confoundingly sudden that the whites in the neighborhood were dumb with fear. They felt—you could see it in their faces—that *something* had ripped loose, exploded. Something which they had long feared and thought was dead. Or if not dead, at least so safely buried under the pretence of good-will that they no longer had need to fear it. Where in the world did it come from? And what was worst of all, how far would it go? Say, what's got into these Negroes?

And the whites and the blacks began to *feel* themselves. The blacks began to remember all the little slights, and discriminations and insults they had suffered; and their hunger too and their misery. And the whites began to search their souls to see if they had been guilty of something, some time, somewhere against which this wave of feeling was rising.

As the celebration wore on, the younger Negroes began to grow bold. They jumped on the running boards of automobiles going east or west on 47th Street and demanded of the occupants:

"Who yuh fer—Baer or Louis?"

In the stress of the moment it seemed that the answer to the question marked out friend and foe.

A hesitating reply brought waves of scornful laughter. Baer, huh? That was funny. Now, hadn't Joe Louis just whipped Max Baer?

Didn't think we had it in us, did you? Thought Joe Louis was scared, didn't you? Scared because Max talked loud and made boasts. We ain't scared either. We'll fight too when the time comes. We'll win, too.

A taxicab driver had his cab wrecked when he tried to put up a show of bravado.

Then they began stopping street cars. Like a cyclone sweeping through a forest, they went through them, shouting, stamping. Conductors gave up and backed away like children. Everybody had to join in this celebration. Some of the people ran out of the cars and stood, pale and trembling, in the crowd. They felt it, too.

In the crush a pocketbook snapped open and money spilled on the street for eager black fingers.

"They stole it from us, anyhow," they said as they picked it up.

When an elderly Negro admonished them, a fist was shaken in his face. Uncle Tomming, huh?

"What in hell yuh gotta do wid it?" they wanted to know.

Something had popped loose, all right. And it had come from deep down. And nobody could have said just what it was, and nobody wanted to say. Blacks and whites were afraid. But it was a sweet fear, at least for the blacks. It was a mingling of fear and fulfillment. Something dreaded and yet wanted. A something had popped out of a dark hole, something with a hydra-like head, and it was darting forth its tongue.

You stand on the border-line, wondering what's beyond. Then you take one step and you feel a strange, sweet tingling. You take two steps and the feeling becomes keener. You want to feel some more. You break into a run. You know it's dangerous, but you're impelled in spite of yourself.

Four centuries of oppression, of frustrated hopes, of black bitterness, felt even in the bones of the bewildered young, were rising to the surface. Yes, unconsciously they had imputed to the brawny image of Joe Louis all the balked dreams of revenge, all the secretly visualized moments of retaliation, *and he had won!* Good Gawd Almighty! Yes, by Jesus, it could be done! Didn't Joe do it? You see, Joe was the consciously-felt symbol. Joe was the concentrated essence of black triumph over white. And it comes so seldom, so seldom. And what could be sweeter than long nourished hate vicariously gratified? From the symbol of one's strength they took strength, and in that moment all fear, all obstacles were wiped out, drowned.

They stepped out of the mire of hesitation and irresolution and were free! Invincible! A merciless victor over a fallen foe! Yes, they had felt all that—for a moment. . . .

And then the cops came.

Not the carefully picked white cops who were used to batter the skulls of white workers and intellectuals who came to the South Side* to march with the black workers to show their solidarity in the struggle against Mussolini's impending invasion of Ethiopia; no, no, black cops, but trusted black cops and plenty tough. Cops who knew their business, how to handle delicate situations. They piled out of patrols, swinging clubs.

"Git back! Gawdammit, git back!"

But they were very careful, very careful. They didn't hit anybody. They, too, sensed *something.* And they didn't want to trifle with it. And there's no doubt but that they had been instructed not to. Better go easy here. No telling what might happen. They swung clubs, but pushed the crowd back with their hands.

Finally, the street cars moved again. The taxis and automobiles could go through. The whites breathed easier. The blood came back to their cheeks.

The Negroes stood on the sidewalks, talking, wondering, looking, breathing hard. They had felt something, and it had been sweet— that feeling. They wanted some more of it, but they were afraid now. The spell was broken.

And about midnight down the street that feeling ebbed, seeping home—flowing back to the beer tavern, the pool room, the café, the barber shop, the dingy flat. Like a sullen river it ran back to its muddy channel, carrying a confused and sentimental memory on its surface, like a water-soaked driftwood.

Say, Comrade, here's the wild river that's got to be harnessed and directed. Here's that *something,* that pent-up folk consciousness. Here's a fleeting glimpse of the heart of the Negro, the heart that beats and suffers and hopes—for freedom. Here's the fluid something that's like iron. Here's the real dynamite that Joe Louis uncovered!

New Masses, October 8, 1935; XVII, 18–19.

* This refers to an article by George Martin telling how police smashed an anti-war demonstration in Chicago which appeared in *New Masses,* September 17, 1935.

34

THE BRONX SLAVE MARKET

by Ella Baker and Marvel Cooke

The ecstasy of a Joe Louis victory faded quickly—as Richard Wright said; but the realities of the street and of earning a living never went away. Two Black newspaperwomen describe those realities as faced by domestic workers in the midst of the Depression.

The Bronx Slave Market! What is it? Who are its dealers? Who are its victims? What are its causes? How far does its stench spread? What forces are at work to counteract it?

Any corner in the congested sections of New York City's Bronx is fertile soil for mushroom "slave marts." The two where the traffic is heaviest and the bidding is highest are located at 167th street and Jerome avenue and at Simpson and Westchester avenues.

Symbolic of the more humane slave block is the Jerome avenue "market." There, on benches surrounding a green square, the victims wait, grateful, at least, for some place to sit. In direct contrast is the Simpson avenue "mart," where they pose wearily against buildings and lamp posts, or scuttle about in an attempt to retrieve discarded boxes upon which to rest.

Again, the Simpson avenue block exudes the stench of the slave market at its worst. Not only is human labor bartered and sold for slave wage, but human love also is a marketable commodity. But whether it is labor or love that is sold, economic necessity compels the sale. As early as 8 A.M. they come; as late as 1 P.M. they remain.

Rain or shine, cold or hot, you will find them there—Negro women, old and young—sometimes bedraggled, sometimes neatly dressed—but with the invariable paper bundle, waiting expectantly for Bronx housewives to buy their strength and energy for an hour, two hours, or even for a day at the munificent rate of fifteen, twenty, twenty-five, or, if luck be with them, thirty cents an hour. If not the wives themselves, maybe their husbands, their sons, or their brothers, under the subterfuge of work, offer worldly-wise girls higher bids for their time.

Who are these women? What brings them here? Why do they stay? In the boom days before the onslaught of the depression in 1929, many of these women who are now forced to bargain for day's work on street corners, were employed in grand homes in the rich Eighties, or in wealthier homes in Long Island and Westchester, at more than adequate wages. Some are former marginal industrial workers, forced by the slack in industry to seek other means of sustenance. In many instances there had been no necessity for work at all. But whatever their standing prior to the depression, none sought employment where they now seek it. They come to the Bronx, not because of what it promises, but largely in desperation.

Paradoxically, the crash of 1929 brought to the domestic labor market a new employer class. The lower middle-class housewife, who, having dreamed of the luxury of a maid, found opportunity staring her in the face in the form of Negro women pressed to the wall by poverty, starvation and discrimination.

Where once color was the "gilt edged" security for obtaining domestic and personal service jobs, here, even, Negro women found themselves being displaced by whites. Hours of futile waiting in employment agencies, the fee that must be paid despite the lack of income, fraudulent agencies that sprung up during the depression, all forced the day worker to fend for herself or try the dubious and circuitous road to public relief.

As inadequate as emergency relief has been, it has proved somewhat of a boon to many of these women, for with its advent, actual starvation is no longer their ever-present slave driver and they have been able to demand twenty-five and even thirty cents an hour as against the old fifteen and twenty cent rate. In an effort to supplement the inadequate relief received, many seek this open market.

And what a market! She who is fortunate (?) enough to please Mrs. Simon Legree's scrutinizing eye is led away to perform hours of multifarious household drudgeries. Under a rigid watch, she is permitted to scrub floors on her bended knees, to hang precariously from window sills, cleaning window after window, or to strain and sweat over steaming tubs of heavy blankets, spreads and furniture covers.

Fortunate, indeed, is she who gets the full hourly rate promised. Often, her day's slavery is rewarded with a single dollar bill or whatever her unscrupulous employer pleases to pay. More often, the clock is set back for an hour or more. Too often she is sent away without any pay at all.

We invaded the "market" early on the morning of September 14. Disreputable bags under arm and conscientiously forlorn, we trailed the work entourage on the West side "slave train," disembarking with it at Simpson and Westchester avenues. Taking up our stand outside the corner flower shop whose show window offered gardenias, roses and the season's first chrysanthemums at moderate prices, we waited patiently to be "bought."

We got results in almost nothing flat. A squatty Jewish housewife, patently lower middle class, approached us, carefully taking stock of our "wares."

"You girls want work?"

"Yes." We were expectantly noncommittal.

"How much you work for?"

We begged the question, noting that she was already convinced that we were not the "right sort." "How much do you pay?"

She was walking away from us. "I can't pay your price," she said and immediately started bargaining with a strong, seasoned girl leaning against the corner lamp post. After a few moments of animated conversation, she led the girl off with her. Curious, we followed them two short blocks to a dingy apartment house on a side street.

We returned to our post. We didn't seem to be very popular with the other "slaves." They eyed us suspiciously. But, one by one, as they became convinced that we were one with them, they warmed up to friendly sallies and answered our discreet questions about the possibilities of employment in the neighborhood.

Suddenly it began to rain, and we, with a dozen or so others, scurried to shelter under the five-and-ten doorway midway on the block. Enforced close communion brought about further sympathy and conversation from the others. We asked the brawny, neatly dressed girl pressed close to us about the extent of trade in the "oldest profession" among women.

"Well," she said, "there is quite a bit of it up here. Most of 'those' girls congregate at the other corner." She indicated the location with a jerk of her head.

"Do they get much work?" we queried.

"Oh, quite a bit," she answered with a finality which was probably designed to close the conversation. But we were curious and asked her how the other girls felt about it. She looked at us a moment doubtfully, probably wondering if we weren't seeking advice to go into the "trade" ourselves.

"Well, that's their own business. If they can do it and get away with it, it's all right with the others." Or probably she would welcome some "work" of that kind herself.

"Sh-h-h." The wizened West Indian woman whom we had noticed, prior to the rain, patrolling the street quite belligerently as if she were daring someone not to hire her, was cautioning us. She explained that if we kept up such a racket the store's manager would kick all of us out in the rain. And so we continued our conversation in whispered undertone.

"Gosh. I don't like this sort of thing at all." The slender brown girl whom we had seen turn down two jobs earlier in the morning, seemed anxious to talk. "This is my first time up here—and believe me, it is going to be my last. I don't like New York nohow. If I don't get a good job soon, I'm going back home to Kansas City." So she had enough money to travel, did she?

The rain stopped quite as suddenly as it started. We had decided to make a careful survey of the district to see whether or not there were any employment agencies in the section. Up one block and down another we tramped, but not one such institution did we encounter. Somehow the man who gave us a sly "Hello, babies" as he passed was strangely familiar. We realized two things about him—that he had been trailing us for some time and that he was manifestly, plain clothes notwithstanding, one of "New York's finest."

Trying to catch us to run us in for soliciting, was he? From that moment on, it was a three-cornered game. When we separated he was at sea. When we were together, he grinned and winked at us quite boldly. . . .

We sidled up to a friendly soul seated comfortably on an upturned soap-box. Soon an old couple approached her and offered a day's work with their daughter way up on Jerome avenue. They were not in agreement as to how much the daughter would pay—the old man said twenty-five cents an hour—the old lady scowled and said twenty. The car fare, they agreed, would be paid after she reached her destination. The friendly soul refused the job. She could afford independence, for she had already successfully bargained for a job for the following day. She said to us, after the couple started negotiations with another woman, that she wouldn't go way up on Jerome avenue on a wild goose chase for Mrs. Roosevelt, herself. We noted, with satisfaction, that the old couple had no luck with any of the five or six they contacted.

It struck us as singularly strange, since it was already 10:30, that the women still lingered, seemingly unabashed that they had not yet found employment for a day. We were debating whether or not we should leave the "mart" and try again another day, probably during the approaching Jewish holidays at which time business is particularly flourishing, when, suddenly, things looked up again. A new batch of "slaves" flowed down the elevated steps and took up their stands at advantageous points.

The friendly soul turned to us, a sneer marring the smooth round-ness of her features. "Them's the girls who makes it bad for us. They get more jobs than us because they will work for anything. We runned them off the corner last week." One of the newcomers was quite near us and we couldn't help but overhear the following conversation with a neighborhood housewife.

"You looking for work?"

"Yes ma'am."

"How much you charge?"

"I'll take what you will give me." . . .

What was this? Could the girl have needed work that badly? Prob-ably. She did look run down at the heels. . . .

"All right. Come on. I'll give you a dollar." Cupidity drove beauty from the arrogant features. The woman literally dragged her "spoil" to her "den." . . . But what of the girl? Could she possibly have known what she was letting herself in for? Did she know how long she would have to work for that dollar or what she would have to do? Did she know whether or not she would get lunch or car fare? Not any more than we did. Yet, there she was, trailing down the street behind her "mistress."

"You see," philosophized the friendly soul. "That's what makes it bad for the rest of us. We got to do something about those girls. Orga-nize them or something." The friendly soul remained complacent on her up-turned box. Our guess was that if the girls were organized, the incentive would come from some place else.

Business in the "market" took on new life. Eight or ten girls made satisfactory contacts. Several women—and men—approached us, but our price was too high or we refused to wash windows or scrub floors. We were beginning to have a rollicking good time when rain again dampened our heads and ardor. We again sought the friendly five-and-ten doorway.

We became particularly friendly with a girl whose intelligent replies to our queries intrigued us. When we were finally convinced that there would be no more "slave" barter that day, we invited her to lunch with us at a near-by restaurant. After a little persuasion, there we were, Millie Jones between us, refreshing our spirits and appetites with ham-burgers, fragrant with onions, and coffee. We found Millie an articulate person. It seems that, until recently, she had had a regular job in the neighborhood. But let her tell you about it.

"Did I have to work? And how! For five bucks and car fare a week. Mrs. Eisenstein had a six-room apartment lighted by fifteen windows. Each and every week, believe it or not, I had to wash every one of those windows. If that old hag found as much as the teeniest speck on any one of 'em, she'd make me do it over. I guess I would do anything rather than wash windows. On Mondays I washed and did as much of the ironing as I could. The rest waited over for Tuesday. There were two grown sons in the family and her husband. That meant that I would have at least twenty-one shirts to do every week. Yeah, and ten sheets and at least two blankets, besides. They all had to be done just so, too. Gosh, she was a particular woman.

"There wasn't a week, either, that I didn't have to wash up every floor in the place and wax it on my hands and knees. And two or three times a week I'd have to beat the mattresses and take all the furniture covers off and shake 'em out. Why, when I finally went home nights, I could hardly move. One of the sons had 'hand trouble' too, and I was just as tired fighting him off, I guess, as I was with the work.

"Say, did you ever wash dishes for an Orthodox Jewish family?" Millie took a long, sibilant breath. "Well, you've never really washed dishes, then. You know, they use a different dishcloth for everything they cook. For instance, they have one for 'milk' pots in which dairy dishes are cooked, another for glasses, another for vegetable pots, another for meat pots, and so on. My memory wasn't very good and I was always getting the darn things mixed up. I used to make Mrs. Eisenstein just as mad. But I was the one who suffered. She would get other cloths and make me do the dishes all over again.

"How did I happen to leave her? Well, after I had been working about five weeks, I asked for a Sunday off. My boy friend from Washington was coming up on an excursion to spend the day with me. She told me if I didn't come in on Sunday, I needn't come back at all. Well, I didn't go back. Ever since then I have been trying to find a job. The employment agencies are no good. All the white girls get the good jobs.

"My cousin told me about up here. The other day I didn't have a cent in my pocket and I just had to find work in order to get back home and so I took the first thing that turned up. I went to work about 11 o'clock and I stayed until 5:00—washing windows, scrubbing floors and washing out stinking baby things. I was surprised when she gave me lunch. You know, some of 'em don't even do that. When I got through, she gave me thirty-five cents. Said she took a quarter out for lunch. Figure it out for yourself. Ten cents an hour!"

The real significance of the Bronx Slave Market lies not in a factual presentation of its activities; but in focusing attention upon its involved implications. The "mart" is but a miniature mirror of our economic battle front.

To many, the women who sell their labor thus cheaply have but themselves to blame. A head of a leading employment agency bemoans the fact that these women have not "chosen the decent course" and declares: "The well-meaning employment agencies endeavoring to obtain respectable salaries and suitable working conditions for deserving domestics are finding it increasingly difficult due to the menace and obstacles presented by the slavish performances of the lower types of domestics themselves, who, unlike the original slaves who recoiled from meeting their masters, rush to meet their mistresses."

The exploiters, judged from the districts where this abominable traffic flourishes, are the wives and mothers of artisans and tradesmen who militantly battle against being exploited themselves, but who apparently have no scruples against exploiting others.

The general public, though aroused by stories of these domestics, too often think of the problems of these women as something separate and apart and readily dismisses them with a sigh and a shrug of the shoulders.

The women, themselves present a study in contradictions. Largely unaware of their organized power, yet ready to band together for some immediate and personal gain either consciously or unconsciously, they still cling to that American illusion that any one who is determined and persistent can get ahead.

The roots, then of the Bronx Slave Market spring from: (1) the general ignorance of and apathy towards organized labor action; (2) the artificial barriers that separate the interest of the relief administrators and investigators from that of their "case loads," the white collar and professional worker from the laborer and the domestic; and (3) organized labor's limited concept of exploitation, which permits it to fight vigorously to secure itself against evil, yet passively or actively aids and abets the ruthless destruction of Negroes.

To abolish the market once and for all, these roots must be torn away from their sustaining soil. Certain palliative and corrective measures are not without benefit. Already the seeds of discontent are being sown.

The Women's Day Workers and Industrial League, organized sixteen years ago by Fannie Austin, has been, and still is, a force to abolish the existing evils in day labor. Legitimate employment agencies have banded together to curb the activities of the racketeer agencies and are demanding fixed minimum and maximum wages for all workers sent out. Articles and editorials recently carried by the New York Negro press have focused attention on the existing evils in the "slave market."

An embryonic labor union now exists in the Simpson avenue "mart." Girls who persist in working for less than thirty cents an hour have been literally run off the corner. For the recent Jewish holiday, habitués of the "mart" actually demanded and refused to work for less than thirty-five cents an hour.

The Crisis, November, 1935; XLII, 330–31, 340.

35

OLD GUARD VS. A. F. OF L.

by Lester Granger

It was in the organized labor movement that the decisive struggle as to effective economic and political mass strength was waged in the nineteen-thirties. A basic question in this connection was the position of the Black workers. An article describing the growing battle within the A. F. of L. follows; it appeared in a then new magazine whose managing editor was Genevieve W. Schneider and whose board included Martha Gruening, Loren Miller, Henry Lee Moon, George Streator, and others.

On the surface, so far as Negro workers are concerned, the American Federation of Labor's convention at Atlantic City was "just another of those affairs." It is true that the stage was set for dramatic fireworks, with the San Francisco convention of 1934 as a background. Delegate A. Philip Randolph, president of the Brotherhood of Sleeping Car Porters and fiery leader of Negro workers, had demanded at that convention an end of evasive resolution-passing by the A. F. of L. on the question of racial discrimination in unions. He submitted a resolution which if adopted would have given unions the choice of dropping their barriers against Negroes or loss of their charters.

The resolutions committee of that convention, as was expected, reported non-concurrence, but when the eloquent Randolph took the floor in defense of his motion the response of delegates to his address was so enthusiastic that there seemed real danger of a defeat for the hitherto impregnable political machine of the old guard. A compromise, hurriedly adopted, appointed a committee to study the issue of racial discrimination and report its findings to the 1935 convention.

The Committee on Problems of Negro Labor met in Washington last July and called witnesses to present definite testimony. The National Urban League was represented at that hearing, as well as the N.A.A.C.P., the Joint Committee on National Recovery, and similar organizations, backing up the labor leaders who exposed subtle and flagrant Jim Crow tactics by local and international unions.

The findings of the committee were turned over to the Executive Council of the A. F. of L., which promptly buried them. No mention was made of the issue in the council's annual report to the convention, and the committee's report was referred to the tender care of George L. Harrison of the Brotherhood of Railway and Steamship Clerks, an international whose constitution specifically bars Negroes from membership. Randolph's efforts to get action from the floor of the convention were smothered with the usual parliamentary technicalities and the bland statement that "the Federation must not violate the autonomy of internationals with respect to their memberships." This attitude from a group of officers who had just been defeated in their attempts to expel communists from unions affiliated with the A. F. of L.!

Thus described, the convention seemed truly "just another of those affairs." But this bare report does not tell the real story. For instance, there is the fact that the Committee on Problems of Negro Labor, headed by John Brophy of the United Mine Workers, made an honest and courageous report to the Executive Council—much to that diplomatic body's dismay. The report verified the justice of Negroes' protests and recommended adoption of the Randolph resolution in substance.

Finally on September 15, 1935, another resolution which Randolph immediately submitted tied up business in the council and the resolutions committee for half a day, while their members debated on ways and means to bury this unwelcome ghost of a dusky Banquo. In the old days both report and resolution would have been brought out on the floor to be crushed speedily under the convention machine. This year, however, the old guard knew perfectly well that there were a hundred delegates at the convention who were waiting for a chance to support any resolution that would give a finishing blow to Jim Crow in organized labor. The politicians simply couldn't take the chance of bitter conflict and possible defeat on this issue, leading the way to further and more fatal defeats on other convention issues.

Several lessons to Negro workers, developed at the San Francisco convention, were brought out even more sharply at Atlantic City. First, that it is more and more inaccurate to speak of an "A. F. of L. attitude" as if it were fixed or unanimous. Within the Federation, on the Negro issue as on other matters, there is a constant conflict between progressive and reactionary forces, with the progressives steadily growing in strength. Negroes who blindly condemn "the A. F. of L." as being a Jim Crow body seriously embarrass their own champions within the ranks of organized labor. Intelligent and helpful criticism will distinguish between friends and foes and support the former.

Second, labor leaders are perfectly correct when they say that the problem of Negro workers will be solved eventually, not at the A. F. of L. conventions but within the internationals and locals. Though the Federation can and should set the pace toward labor democracy, the goal will not be reached without patient educational work in the ranks of organized labor. That work has been begun in the rank-and-file movement, so-called, in union locals, but it must be supported by active efforts on the part of Negroes themselves. The lobby conducted at Atlantic City by the Urban League disclosed many officers of internationals who were perfectly ready to vote for the Randolph resolution, but who were frank in stating that its results would be disappointing without thorough follow-up work in the internationals and locals.

Finally, Atlantic City showed again the need for a louder and better organized Negro voice within the Federation, on the floor of its conventions, taking part in its committee meetings. Six or eight colored delegates were in evidence this year, including A. Philip Randolph and Milton L. Webster of the Sleeping Car Porters. Every Federal local with at least a majority of colored workers should strain its resources to send a delegate to the convention. Merely the presence of Negroes, sprinkled throughout the meeting, is bound to influence the convention vote on issues affecting interests of Negroes.

On the Negro question, on the issue of industrial unionism, as on that of a Labor Party, the Atlantic City Convention resolved itself into a struggle between an entrenched Old Guard of politicians and a newly-arising progressive faction. The Old Guard stands for conservatism, protection of fat jobs, extirpation of every tendency that seems militant—and therefore threatening to the Old Guard. And yet, the welfare of labor today demands more militancy, more radical departure from old ways than ever before. The Old Guard therefore is opposed to the A. F. of L.—the real Federation. It should not be difficult for Negroes to decide on which side they will line up.

Race, Winter, 1935–1936; I, 46–47.

36

AMSTERDAM NEWS LOCKOUT

by Henry Lee Moon

The most widely read newspaper among Afro-American people in New York City was (and is) the *Amsterdam News.* Its stance was pro-labor—until its own workers demanded a union shop through the Newspaper Guild, whose president at this time was Heywood Broun. As the author prophesied in the following essay, the eleven-week-long strike was successful and a union shop was recognized.

Although only seventeen workers are directly affected, the lockout of the editorial staff of the New York *Amsterdam News* for activities as a unit of the American Newspaper Guild is of real significance to the labor movement among Negroes. Dramatically it focuses attention on the relationship between Negro employer and Negro employee. It exposes the essential hypocrisy of the Negro employer who, berating the American Federation of Labor for failure to organize the Negro worker, at the same time exploits his own unorganized employees. And it gives an opportunity for white workers to demonstrate their support of their Negro fellow craftsmen.

The lockout on October 9 followed repeated refusal of the publishers of this most widely read Harlem weekly to enter into any sort of negotiations with the Guild for a collective agreement. The demands of the organized editorial workers were for recognition of the Guild, vacations (which this year had been arbitrarily suspended), severance notices, a grievance committee and the preferential shop. It was stipulated expressly that no negotiations on wages would be attempted until three months after the signing of the agreement.

Confronted with these demands, the publishers refused even to discuss them and threatened to discharge all editorial workers who supported the Guild in its efforts for a collective agreement. A citizens' committee, seeking to intercede on behalf of the organized editorial workers, was flatly rebuffed.

The threats of the publishers were translated into action when on October 7 seven Guild members were fired, on five-day notice. "Economy" was the reason as given by the publishers. However, all other departments of the paper remained intact. The following day two more Guild members, the editor and the city editor, were discharged. The lockout was completed the next day when the management announced that it was dispensing with the services of the entire editorial staff. Four men on the staff, three of them Guild members, capitulated to the demands of the management and immediately were rehired as scabs. The remaining editorial workers, supported by the Newspaper Guild of New York, prepared for strike activities. They established a headquarters at 205 West 135th street, and promptly picketed the office of the *Amsterdam News* at 2293 Seventh avenue.

In this action, for the first time in the history of American labor, Negro employees have resorted to trade union tactics to protect themselves against the aggrandizement of Negro employers. The action makes clear the real relationship between the two classes—employers and workers—a relationship in no way altered by identity of race.

In its fight against the Guild, the publishers of the *Amsterdam News* have adapted the tactics common to anti-labor employers. The red scare has been raised. Communists and Socialists have been accused of a dire conspiracy to destroy the *News*. Police have been called in and nine pickets arrested. A girl picket has been attacked by a thug on the street in front of the newspaper office. In addition, the publishers have injected the color issue. A bitter editorial in its issue of October 26 denounces the Guild as "an organization of white newspapermen" and protests the joint action of Negro and white men and women on the picket line. Negro newspaper workers, the editorial contends, have no place in "the white man's Guild." The attempt is made to arouse the latent racialism of the community against the presence of whites cooperating with discharged employees.

Negro business firms have been chiefly small retail stores, newspapers and such financial institutions as insurance companies, banks and building and loan societies. Consequently their employees have been for the most part white collar workers, a class traditionally hard to organize. In addition, Negro employers have found it profitable to appeal to the racial loyalty of their workers. They, the employers, are never in business for the sordid purpose of making money. Rather they are out to "build race institutions" and to "create opportunities for Negro youth." Noble objectives for which race conscious Negroes should be willing to make any sacrifice in low wages, long hours and wretched working conditions.

Then too, the "one big happy family" propaganda has worked with remarkable plausibility. Among Negroes, class lines have not been so rigidly stratified as in the remainder of American society. If he knows how to wear a dinner jacket, if he plays a good game of bridge and conducts himself with reasonable decorum and if he is a college graduate, it is still possible for the Negro employee of a Negro firm to marry the boss' daughter and to get that much of an edge on his fellow workers.

It is significant that the American Newspaper Guild should lead the way in the organization of Negro workers employed by Negroes. The editorial workers of the *Amsterdam News* and the Baltimore *Afro-American* are the only Negro-employed groups, with the exception of certain building trades and lately building service workers, organized along trade union lines.

The *Amsterdam News* has been most articulate in its demand for the organization of Negro workers. It has flayed the A.F. of L. for its neglect of Negro labor. It has demanded admission of Negroes to all trade unions. It has supported the pullman porters in their fight for union recognition. It has fostered the organization of the Negro Labor Committee in Harlem. And now, ironically, it kicks out its own employees for organizing.

Unwittingly the *Amsterdam News* has sown the seed from which widespread support of the locked out workers has sprung. It has been a most powerful agency toward making Harlem labor conscious. And it is the awareness of the necessity for organized effort that makes the appeal of the locked out workers fruitful in Harlem. Churches, fraternal organizations, civic groups, professional organizations as well as trade unions have been quick to respond to the appeal of the Newspaper Guild for the support of the locked out workers.

The Newspaper Guild of New York has thrown the full weight of its membership into the fight for the Harlem unit. Heywood Broun, president of the American Newspaper Guild, has done picket duty, has addressed open air meetings, has spoken over the radio, and has made valuable contacts for the *Amsterdam News* unit of the Guild. Other members of the organization have contributed their services equally as generously. Indeed the white members of the Guild have, in the words of Broun, translated the printed words of their constitution into action. The Guild constitution forbids any discrimination on account of race, color, creed or political affiliation.

The publishers of the *Amsterdam News* through their continued refusal to enter into negotiations with representatives of the Guild or to submit their case to an impartial mediator have demonstrated to the readers of that paper their unalterable opposition to organized labor. This challenge labor-conscious Harlem must meet. At this writing indications are that the working class of this largest Negro city will meet that challenge by refusing to buy the *Amsterdam News* until that publication practices in its office the pro-labor policy it has advocated on its editorial page.

Race, Winter, 1935–1936; I, 41–42. Reportage on the strike was fairly full in *The New York Times,* commencing October 10 and terminating with the story of the strikers' victory in its issue of December 25, 1935.

37

THE NATIONAL NEGRO CONGRESS

The founding convention of the National Negro Congress was held in Chicago, February 14–16, 1936. Present were 817 delegates representing 585 organizations; they came from 28 states and represented a combined, unduplicated membership of one million, two hundred thousand people. Among those present were delegates from 81 churches and religious groups, 83 trade unions, 71 fraternal societies, 26 youth, 2 farm, 23 women's, and 14 educational groups, and various political parties and professional and business organizations. There were sixty-six men and women on the original Executive Council, including Ralph Bunche, Benjamin J. Davis, Jr., Arthur Huff Fauset, James W. Ford, Lester B. Granger, William H. Hastie, the Reverend W. H. Jernagin, Henry Lee Moon, Richard B. Moore, Florence Nelson, Floria Pickney, Louis I. Redding, Maude White, Edward E. Strong, and Max Yergan. The president was A. Philip Randolph; the secretary was John P. Davis; and the treasurer, Miss Marion Cuthbert.

In the public evening sessions of the congress as many as eight thousand people attended. The congress, combining many different personalities and organizations, had serious problems of unity; nevertheless, it functioned for a decade and it spearheaded significant efforts aimed at eliminating racism.

Published below are document [a], coming from John P. Davis, its national secretary and one of the main inspirers of the congress, and [b], the full text of the Keynote Address delivered by A. Philip Randolph, its first president.

[a]

THE UNDERLYING AIM OF THE CONGRESS
by John P. Davis

The National Negro Congress was called to meet the increasingly difficult economic and social problems which face the Negro people in America. The need for the establishment through united action of a strong movement against the social and economic repressions being experienced by the Negro made such a Congress imperative.

While major stress at the Congress was laid upon joint action by Negroes themselves, there remained very clearly in the minds of the delegates the need for cooperation with friendly organizations of members of other races to solve the common economic problems facing all. Likewise it was realized that the Negro Congress must exist as a federation of organizations for the purpose of pooling the strength of constituent groups in the attack upon the evils retarding the securing by the Negro of his manhood rights. The Congress was not formed and does not exist to duplicate the work of any existing organization. Rather it exists to add strength and to give support to every progressive and meaningful program in aid of the Negro people in their just demand for equal opportunity and complete social and economic rights.

The Congress had no desire to exclude any group that sincerely worked for the expressed aims of the Congress, and any group that so worked could not be charged with unduly influencing or dominating its activity. And of the constituent groups participating it can be accurately stated that none attempted such domination.

[b]

KEYNOTE ADDRESS
by A. Philip Randolph

(Mr. Randolph was confined to his home by illness; his address was read by Dr. Charles Wesley Burton, regional vice-president for Illinois and Indiana of the congress.)

Mr. Chairman, Officers of the National Sponsoring Committee of the National Negro Congress, Fellow Delegates, Fellow Workers and Friends:

Greetings and felicitations upon this great Congress. Though absent in the flesh, I am with you in the spirit, in the spirit of the deathless courage of the 18th and 19th century black rebels and martyrs for human justice, in the spirit of Frederick Douglass and Nat Turner, of Gabriel and Denmark Vesey, of Harriet Tubman and Sojourner Truth —those noble rebels who struck out in the dark days of slavery that Negro men and women might be free.

We have met in times of world wide storm and stress, of social confusion, economic chaos, political disorder and intellectual uncertainty. Social institutions, from the church to the family, evince change and instability.

Unemployment falls like a deadening pall upon every great power and machine nations.* Democracies and dictatorships vie for supremacy. Witness the march of Fascist Italy and Nazi Germany along their imperialistic paths of manifest destiny.

Note their utter and flagrant abolition of democratic institutions, claiming that democracy is not only futile, but a menace to progress. Observe, too, tendencies toward Fascist growth and development in existing countries with democratic governments, such as America, France and England. These are signs of grave and sinister portent to the world of workers, lovers of liberty and minority groups.

Of threatening and disturbing significance, another world war looms upon the horizon. Many danger spots of conflict between great world powers stand out. Japan is restive in the face of the constant growth and power of Soviet Russia and is steadily resorting to provocative acts of war. Hitler seeks to serve as a spearhead of modern monopoly capitalism against the workers' republic.

Already Fascist Italy is on the march to subjugate the Ancient kingdom of Ethiopia; while France and Germany are in a state of truce, still at bay, awaiting the hour to strike for another conflict. England and Italy are in competition for place and prestige in the Mediterranean and darkest Africa, while Japan threatens to close the open door to American investment and advance her claim to the adoption of a Monroe Doctrine over the Pacific which may bring "Uncle Sam" and Nippon to grips. Meanwhile, Tokio proceeds on its long conquering trek of China.

With the collapse of the naval conference, a frenzied armament race swings into a high pace and a war of world currencies, credits and trade is renewed. Thus the world is pregnant with the seeds of war,

* So the original reads; an apparent typographical error but the precise meaning remains obscure.

another war, a war in the air, on and under the water, with poison gas and high explosives, which may put an end to civilization as we know it.

Now what of the American scene. It is no less forbidding and full of contradictions, unsettlement and cross currents in our social, economic and political life.

Of the outstanding problems that confront us following the collapse of capitalist prosperity and seeming stabilization of 1929, unemployment, trenching hard upon 15 millions, is one of the most perplexing. It has been attacked by the New Deal with its myriad legions of alphabets, but to little avail.

Nor is there any solution offered either by the "rugged individualists" despite their cry for the restoration of the grand era of Coolidge and Hoover, with a mythical "chicken in every pot" and a "flivver for every family."

With the economic affliction of nation-wide joblessness stand the liquidation of the farmers, the small shop owners, the middle class, the poor sharecropper and tenant farmers and farm laborers, the foreclosure of hundreds of thousands of mortgages upon the homes of the workers and the lower strata of the middle class, with no prospects of permanent rehabilitation by the hectic, sketchy, patchy, and makeshift capitalist program.

But economic insecurity, though baffling, is not the only challenge to the American workers, black and white and the middle classes. There is also political and civil insecurity. Even the most credulous can sense an existing grave danger to democratic institutions and constitutional liberties.

This danger is fascism—fascism which seeks the complete abrogation of all civil and political liberties in the manner and method of Nazi Germany and Fascist Italy. It is a menace to America. It is a world menace, it is a menace to black workers. It is a menace to religious tolerance and to the freedom and security of all minority groups.

And war is the twin evil sister of Fascism. Its coming is not now improbable. It is a danger, an immediate danger, a danger to the American workers, black and white, who fight and pay for all wars in blood and taxes, while the bankers and munition makers, such as the Morgans and DuPonts, reap huge and fabulous profits.

This congress is called to attempt to meet the problems of black America, the submerged tenth of the population. While this is true, it is also true that the problems of the Negro peoples are the problems of the workers, for practically 99 per cent of the Negro peoples win their bread by selling their labor power in the labor market from day to day. They cannot escape the dangers and penalties of the depression, war or Fascism.

However, our contemporary history is a witness to the stark fact that black America is a victim of both class and race prejudice and oppression. Because Negroes are black they are hated, maligned and spat upon; lynched, mobbed, and murdered. Because Negroes are workers, they are browbeaten, bullied, intimidated, robbed, exploited, jailed and shot down. Because they are black they are caught between the nether millstones of discrimination when seeking a job or seeking to join a union.

Thus, voteless in 13 states; politically disregarded and discounted in the others; victims of the lynch terror in Dixie, with a Scottsboro frame-up of notorious memory; faced with the label of the white man's job and the white man's union; unequal before the law; jim-crowed in schools and colleges throughout the nation; segregated in the slums and ghettos of the urban centers; landless peons of a merciless white landlordism; hunted down, harassed and hounded as vagrants in the southern cities, the Negro people face a hard, deceptive and brutal capitalist order, despite its preachments of Christian love and brotherhood.

What has brought us to this is the insistent question? The answer in brief lies in the World War, the sharpening and deepening of capitalist exploitation of the workers of hand and brain, the acceleration of a technological revolution creating a standing army of unemployed, the ripening and maturing of monopoly capitalism through trustification, rationalization and the rapid march of financial imperialism, and the intensification of racial and religious hatreds, together with increasingly blatant and provocative nationalism.

But the war itself was the effect of a deeper cause and that cause was the profit system which provides and permits the enrichment of the few at the expense of the many, allowing two per cent of the people to own ninety per cent of the wealth of the United States, a condition not much different in other capitalist countries, and also makes for the robbery and oppression of the darker and weaker colonial peoples of the world.

But the diagnosis of the causes of social problems such as wars, economic depressions and Fascism is only designed to enable the victims to seek the remedies. However, let me speak briefly of what are not remedies:

First, the "New Deal" is no remedy. It does not seek to change the profit system. It does not place human rights above property rights, but gives the business interests the support of the state. It is no insurance against the coming of Fascism or the prevention of war or a recurrent depression, though it be more liberal than the Republican Tories.

Second, the restoration of Republican rule is no solution. It was during the rule of the "Grand Old Party" under which the depression came. Negroes have watched themselves disfranchised and lynched under both regimes, Republican and Democratic.

Third, the Townsend Plan is no panacea. While an adequate old age pension should be fought for, a pension far greater than that offered by the New Deal "Security" legislation, the Townsend Plan is well nigh impossible of execution, and if executed would not achieve its aim.

Moreover, its aim is not designed to modify the structure of organized profit-making private property, and any old age pension law will be so manipulated as to nullify its meritorious features so long as the workers have no effective voice in the councils of government.

Fourth, the "Share the Wealth" plan of the Huey Long movement is fantastic and superficial, since it pretends to seek to share wealth while also seeking to maintain inviolate the profit system of exploitation.

Fifth, the currency cant of the Radio Priest [Charles E.] Coughlin is a glittering mirage and not a remedy, for it would merely effect inflation, thereby creating more money which has no magic power to reapportion or reallocate goods or wealth among the people.

Money is merely the measure of value and has no causal power of effecting the distribution of values. This can only be done by the organized might of the workers. Practically every government of the world has at one time or another tried the experiment of inflation, only to its sorrow and the sharper victimization of the workers.

Nor is deflation or reflation of any basic value. The mere existence of varying amounts of money does not affect the empty pockets of unemployed workers.

But back to remedies. At the top of the list of remedies I wish to suggest the struggle of the workers against exploitation of the employers. Next, the struggle of the workers against Fascism and for the prevention* of democratic institutions, the arena in which alone their economic power may be built.

Third, the struggle to build powerful Negro civil rights organizations. Fourth, the struggle against war which wrecks the organizations of the workers, and stifles and suppresses freedom of speech, the press and assembly. Fifth, the struggle to strengthen the forces of the exploited sharecropper and tenant farmers. Sixth, the struggle to build mass consumers' movements to protect housewives against price manipulation.

But the struggle to apply the aforementioned remedies can only be achieved through definite social, economic and political instrumentalities. Thus the fight against the economic exploitation of the workers can only be effectively carried on through industrial and craft unions, with the emphasis on the former.

The industrial union is important in this stage of economic development because modern business has changed in structure and assumed the form of giant trust and holding companies, with which the craft union can no longer effectively grapple.

Moreover, the craft union invariably has a color bar against the Negro worker, but the industrial union in structure renders race discrimination less possible, since it embraces all the workers included in the industry, regardless of race, creed, color or craft, skilled or unskilled.

Thus, this congress should seek to broaden and intensify the movement to draw Negro workers into labor organizations and break down the color bar in the trade unions that now have it.

The next instrumentality which the workers must build and employ for their protection against economic exploitation, war and fascism, is an independent working class political party. It should take the form of a farmer-labor political organization. This is indispensable in view of the bankruptcy in principles, courage and vision of the old line parties, Republican and Democratic.

They are the political committees of Wall Street and are constructed to serve the profit making agencies and therefore can no more protect or advance the interests of the workers than can a sewing machine grind corn. It is poor working class wisdom to fight big business for economic justice on the industrial field and vote for it on the political.

With these two major instrumentalities, there should be built up great consumers' cooperatives which, while less fundamental, none

* Apparently a typographical error; probably the word should be "preservation."

the less provide the basis for mass, collective action on the part of the workers and lower middle classes.

They have stood the workers in good stead wherever they have been constructed, providing they are shaped and directed by working class and not bourgeois interests.

The fight for civil and political rights of the Negro peoples can effectively be carried on only if those organizations that are pushing the struggles are broadened and built with a wider mass base. Those organizations that are serving on the civil rights front effectively for the Negro are the National Association for the Advancement of Colored People, and the International Labor Defense.

It needs to be definitely understood, however, that the fight in the courts for civil and political rights cannot be effective except when backed by a broad, nation-wide, if not international mass protest through demonstrations in the form of parades, mass meetings and publicity.

But while the fight for civil and political liberties for the Negro peoples has been brilliantly waged by the N.A.A.C.P. and I.L.D., the gravity and complexity of the problems of civil and political liberties, accentuated and widened by the evil of fascist trends in America, demand that new tactics and strategy be employed to meet the situation.

The maneuvering and disposing of the forces of Negro peoples and their sympathetic allies against their enemies can only be effectively worked out through the tactics and strategy of the united front. The task of overcoming the enemies of democratic institutions and constitutional liberties is too big for any single organization. It requires the united and formal integrating and coordinating of the various Negro organizations, church, fraternal, civil, trade union, farmer, professional, college and what not, into the framework of a united front, together with the white groups of workers, lovers of liberty and those whose liberties are similarly menaced for a common attack upon the forces of reaction, backed by the embattled masses of black and white workers.

The united front strategy and tactics should be executed through methods of mass demonstration, such as parades, picketing, boycotting, mass protest, the mass distribution of propaganda literature, as well as legal action.

The united front does not provide an excuse for weakness or timidity, or reliance by any one organization upon the others who comprise it, but, on the contrary, it affords an opportunity for the contribution of strength by each organization to the common pool of organizational power for a common defense against the enemy. Thus the Negro peoples should not place their problems for solution down at the feet of their white sympathetic allies which has been and is the common fashion of the old school Negro leadership, for, in the final analysis, the salvation of the Negro, like the workers, must come from within.

The power and effectiveness of the united front will be developed by waging the struggles around definite, vital and immediate issues of life and living.

The issues should be obvious, clear and simple, such as prevention of stoppage of relief, cuts in relief allotments, lay-offs of relief workers, of workers in any industry, discrimination in the giving of relief, exorbitant brutality, denial of free assembly, freedom of the press, freedom of speech to unpopular groups, denial of civil rights to Negroes such as the right to be served in hotels and restaurants, to have access to public utilities and forms of transportation, such as the Pullman car.

Wage struggles around war upon Ethiopia by the fascist dictator Mussolini, strikes and lock-outs of black and white workers, the amendment to the federal Constitution, of the adoption of social legislation such the Retirement Pension Act for railroad workers, fight for the freedom of Angelo Herndon, the Scottsboro boys, the Wagner-Costigan anti-lynching bill, the violations of the Wagner Labor Disputes bill, the forcing of teachers to take a loyalty oath, the goose-stepping of students in the school system through the R.O.T.C., the abolition of the color bar in trade unions, the murder of Shoemaker in Tampa, Fla., exposing the menace of the American Liberty League, William Randolph Hearst and the Ku Klux Klan, and supporting the movement of John L. Lewis for industrial unionism.

Such is the task of Negro peoples. This task comes as a sharp and decisive challenge at a time when new atrocities and nameless terrorism are directed against black America and when the workers, black and white, are being goaded by oppression and intimidation, to resort to general strikes such as took place in San Francisco and in Pekin, Ill., as well as national strikes such as the textile workers, the miners, and the workers' revolts in Minnesota and Toledo.

To meet this task, the Negro peoples, pressed with their backs against the wall, must face the future with heads erect, hearts undaunted and undismayed, ready and willing and determined to pay the price in struggle, sacrifices and suffering that freedom, justice and peace [require, so that they] shall share and enjoy a more abundant life.

Forward to complete economic, political and social equality for Negro peoples. Forward to the abolition of this sinister system of jim-crowism in these United States! The united front points the way. More power to the National Negro Congress. The future belongs to the people.

The Official Proceedings of the National Negro Congress (Washington, 1936), p. 3, for the statement by Mr. Davis; pp. 7–12 for the address by Mr. Randolph. A useful recent account of the congress, representing something of an antidote for the vituperative Red-baiting productions that have tended to dominate the subject, is L. S. Wittner, "The National Negro Congress: A Reassessment," *American Quarterly,* Winter, 1970; XXII, 884–901.

38

THE NATIONAL NEGRO CONGRESS

by James W. Ford

The most prominent Black Communist in the United States and an outstanding leader of the Party for many years (its vice-presidential candidate in 1932, 1936, and 1940) was James W. Ford (1894–1957). The Party, and Mr. Ford personally, was important as a catalyst and uniting force in creating the National Negro Congress. In a series of articles written early in 1936, James W. Ford described the history of the creation of the Congress.

The National Negro Congress was proposed in May 1935, at a National Conference held in Washington, D.C. The economic and social causes for the plight of the Negro people were very clearly brought out at this conference. The various participants in the Conference dealt with these matters with dramatic forcefulness. Moreover, the speeches and reports of many of the participants indicated on their part a decidedly-growing clearness on the problems of the Negro in modern America, a broader outlook and a desire for united actions in the solution of these problems.

For example, Mr. Albion Hartwell, of the Interprofessional Association for Social Insurance, showed the position of the Negro in employment and unemployment:

The fifteenth census, taken in 1930, showed 11,891,143 Negroes in the United States, constituting 9.7 per cent of the total population. Of these

5,503,535 were listed as employed. Thirty-six per cent of all Negro workers were engaged in agriculture, nearly 29 per cent in manufacturing and mechanical pursuits. More than 3,500,000 Negro workers—a great majority of all those employed—are found within the categories of domestic and personal service and agriculture, representing approximately 65 per cent of all Negroes gainfully employed.

The figure for unemployment among Negroes in 1932 was placed at 1,500,000; in 1934, between two and three million. These figures mean that in 1934, 50 per cent of the working population were without jobs, whereas it is estimated that between 20 and 25 per cent of white workers were unemployed.

Mr. Edward Lewis, secretary of the Baltimore Urban League, indicated the increase of the above-mentioned terrific burden placed on the Negroes by discrimination in relief:

In the South there has been a sustained movement to keep relief standards for Negroes low and to discriminate on the basis of color. The budget for a family of five is $7.85. The price of milk is deducted from the budget when it is made out for the client. This means that $1.54 is subtracted from $7.85 and the balance of $6.31 sent for the purchase of food for five people.

An investigation of 75 white families on relief and 75 colored families showed that nine out of every ten colored families were below the standard set by the B.E.R.C. The North is not entirely free from discrimination of this sort, as was indicated in the recent Harlem investigation.

In the Southern sections of the nation the percentage of Negroes on relief is uniformly shown to be from two and one-half to three times larger proportionately than is the Negro population in this section. Although we represent less than 10 per cent of the total population of the United States, the number of Negroes on relief today is more than 20 per cent of the total number of families for the United States.

The plight of the Negro domestic workers was brought out by Mary Anderson, head of the Women's Bureau of the Department of Labor. Quoting a Y.W.C.A. secretary in Brooklyn, she gave the following alarming facts about Negro domestic workers:

The average monthly wage paid colored domestic help amounts to 25 dollars when they live on the premises. In some cases this amounts to as little as 20 dollars. The conditions under which these people work are terrible. Whereas before the depression the laundry work was taken care of outside, now this has been added to the work given to the domestic help. Where the work is done on a daily basis, 20 to 25 cents an hour is common as the maximum compensation.

The representatives of the sharecroppers told the Conference of their heroic experiences. The courageous and determined action of the sharecroppers has aroused the entire Negro people toward organized struggle. The heroic example of Angelo Herndon and results of the united front for his freedom has also brought a significant change in the approach to the solution of problems of the Negro people.

Other speakers at the Conference stressed the need for organization. Mr. T. Arnold Hill, of the National Urban League, stated that "if workers are to have organization to protect their special interests, they must organize as workers. This seems to me to be the only likely means of affecting the mass pressure necessary to achieve the concessions which are critically needed to protect the future of Negro labor."

A. Philip Randolph declared:

The cause of the organization of Negro workers into the trade union movement has suffered greatly and been incalculably hindered by Negro leadership. The old-guard conservative groups are simply opposed to organized labor for the same reason that Mellon or Morgan is opposed to it. As a matter of fact they would oppose a group of Negro workers organizing to fight for more wages and better working conditions. The Negro intellectuals, too, have rendered doubtful service to the cause of the organization of Negro workers, since they have been content merely to proclaim their opposition to the A. F. of L. because of the existence of prejudice in various unions affiliated with it which, of course, nobody denies or condones. . . . But along with a policy of destruction with respect to discrimination, segregation and Jim-Crowism in the trade unions, there should also be developed a program of construction. Obviously, the only sound constructive program in dealing with the problem of Negro workers is organization.

Dr. W. E. B. Du Bois, however, was in a quandary. On the one hand, he warned of the danger of war and fascism and, on the other, remonstrated with the Communists who are outstanding fighters against fascism and war.

Among other outstanding participants were Dr. Ralph J. Bunche, of Howard University; Lester Granger, of the Workers Council of the National Urban League; A. W. McPherson, of the Steel and Metal Workers Union; and Olive M. Stone, of the North Carolina Institute of Social Science.

We Communists were never doubtful about the significance or the outcome of the National Negro Congress. We were not deterred by the charges of "Communist domination." We were guided by what we knew of the desire of the Negro masses for united action.

The trade union delegates were easily the outstanding participants. They discussed: "Discrimination in the American Federation of Labor," "Industrial Unionism," "Organized and Unorganized Negro Labor," "Independent Political Action for Labor," "The Organization of Domestic Workers," "The Randolph Resolution to End Discrimination in the A. F. of L." They endorsed the proposal to support and build labor committees in Negro communities, such as the Harlem Labor Committee in New York.

Another important factor of the Congress was the favorable reception given the Farmer-Labor Party. The program and meaning of a Farmer-Labor Party, the tactics in building a people's Labor Party in Negro communities, the meaning of a Farmer-Labor Party in the South and the possibilities of a million-fold alliance of all the toilers and oppressed, were clearly indicated at the National Negro Congress.

The fight for peace occupied an important place in the Congress proceedings. A description of the danger of war and the fascist forces was given by A. Philip Randolph:

War looms on the horizon . . . already fascist Italy is on the march to subjugate the ancient kingdom of Ethiopia . . . France and Germany are in a state of truce, awaiting the hour to strike for another conflict. . . . Italy and England are in a competition for place and prestige in the Mediterranean and Africa, while Japan threatens to close the open door to American investments and advance her claim to the adoption of a Monroe Doctrine over the Pacific which may bring "Uncle Sam" and "Nippon" to grips. . . . Meanwhile Tokyo proceeds on its long conquering trek of China . . . Japan is restive in the face of the constant growth and power of Soviet Russia and is steadily resorting to provocative acts of war . . . Hitler seeks to serve as a spearhead of modern monopoly capitalism against the workers' republic.

The declaration of Mussolini that the Ethiopian war was necessary so that Italy might take the great civilization of Rome to the desolate land of Ethiopia, was never more dramatically given the lie before an American audience than on the opening night of the Congress. A special envoy of the London Legation of Ethiopia spoke to more than 6,000 people. He said:

We have been called barbarians, not able to govern our own land. But Ethiopia is not the only country today in which barbarism exists.
This war is not unlike the American War of Independence. Ethiopia is fighting for life, liberty and the pursuit of happiness in her own land. We are fighting to preserve our independence and integrity. Ethiopia's defeat may mean the downfall of the collective security system and perhaps the end of the League of Nations. If Ethiopia wins, as she will if she is supported, it will strengthen the League of Nations and show that world sentiment must be respected.

Compare this analysis and attitude towards the collective security peace policy of the Soviet Union with the barbaric actions of Mussolini, who rains bombs and poison gas down upon defenseless men, women and children; or with Hitler, who takes advantage of the situation to prepare war on a world scale; or with the Japanese militarist clique, in their drive to bring the entire Chinese people under the heel of Japanese imperialism and to penetrate into Soviet territory; or with the most reactionary forces in England, France and the United States, that actively urge on this slaughter.

The sham Neutrality Act of the United States directly aided Italian fascism against Ethiopia by facilitating the shipment of munitions of war to Italy; and the unwillingness of the United States government to join in collective actions to isolate Italy played into the hands of the most reactionary war forces in the country.

The Congress exposed the weakness of the Neutrality Act of the United States which operates to aid Italy, as against Ethiopia. It demanded that the Congress of the United States extend the Act to include a ban on oil, metals, cotton and other war materials, raw and finished; it called upon the workers in the transport industry to refuse to handle shipments of war supplies to Italy.

The Congress sponsored the setting up of a national organization to aid Ethiopia and issued an appeal for financial and moral support to aid the fight "against atrocities being committed upon Ethiopia by the invading armies of Mussolini and the fascist party."

One of the most dramatic incidents of the Congress occurred when a motion was made to endorse a resolution against the Hearst press. The whole Congress went into an uproar. Copies of Hearst papers were torn into shreds and flung into the air. This outburst came spontaneously from a people bitterly harassed by hostile, vicious and reactionary Hearst papers. A resolution was adopted which urged Negroes and other opponents of war and fascism to insist that business firms refuse to advertise in the Hearst press.

"Whereas, there is a section of the American press distinctly hostile to the interests of Ethiopia," read the resolution, "therefore, be it resolved that this Congress urge all Negroes and other Americans opposed to fascism and war, to refuse to purchase papers and publications of Hearst and other sections of the hostile press."

The presence of Mr. Max Yergan, from Capetown, South Africa, brought additional international interest and significance to the National Negro Congress. Mr. Yergan, an American Negro who has spent fifteen years in Africa observing the ravages of imperialism, painted a vivid picture of the conditions of Negroes in Africa. He said:

The capitalist trusts divide up the spoils and partition the territories of the world among themselves. This phase of imperialism has manifested itself in every part of the African continent. Britain, France and other European countries have taken much of the land. . . . Various new forms of labor are forced on the people, and labor is drained out of the country. . . .

Imperialism, then, means annexation of land and confiscation of labor . . . it destroys the culture—the basic social fabric of the people's life. In South Africa, through the color laws, Africans are kept out of many phases of skilled labor and on the lowest level, industrially. Laws limiting freedom of assembly make it difficult for them to organize to defend themselves. . . .

This Congress has the opportunity and responsibility to make it possible for all organizations here represented to subscribe to a minimum program—to fight for those things on which the organizations are in agreement.

The Congress was duly influenced by the active participation of these representatives from abroad. The Congress condemned all forms of discrimination against foreign-born Negroes in the United States and opposed any attempt to deport or drop them from relief or employment; it advised better relations between foreign-born and native-born Negroes and went on record to support people of African descent in their struggle for economic and political freedom in their respective countries.

The Congress mapped out a plan to unite the fight for civil liberties for Negroes, against lynching, Jim-Crowism, residential segregation and disfranchisement, with the struggle against gag-laws, such as the Tydings-McCormack Act, the Kramer Sedition Bill, the Washington Anti-Communist Rider, Criminal Syndicalism Laws and Teachers' Oath Laws.

The Negro people and their various organizations have waged years of battle against these evils. But this militancy is now being developed into a political program of united struggle with other toilers.

United action of the Negro people through their basic organizations was stressed by the leading sponsors of the Congress. The Negro people are the most commonly oppressed in every sphere of life. But this is not admitted by some of the so-called "friends of the Negro people," and even by some individuals in the ranks of the Negro people themselves. They cannot understand if, indeed, they desire to, why it is that the National Negro Congress "was solicitous about the needs of small Negro business people." The small business man hates big capital; even more so the small Negro business man hates big capital because of the discriminatory practices which crush his aspirations for livelihood and cultural advancement. The aim of the united front should be to get the widest section of the masses into struggle under the guidance of the working class and trade union organizations, even on the basis of the smallest grievance. That is why the National Negro Congress expressed the demands of small Negro business men, and also advocated the organization of consumers' and producers' cooperatives and the unionization of employees, as a progressive road toward the solution of the problems of all the Negro people.

In like manner, the Congress endorsed measures of advancing Negro culture and cultural workers. The fight against the caricaturing of Negro culture and the exploitation of Negro artists is no doubt what inspired Rose McClendon, outstanding Negro actress (now deceased), to declare in *The New York Times* of June 30, 1935, that "what makes a Negro theater is . . . the selection of plays that deal with Negroes, with Negro problems, with phases of Negro life, *faithfully presented and accurately delineated* . . . and that a theater can be developed and operated by Negroes as a cultural experiment based on a program of social realism," which "could in the course of time alone create a tradition that would equal the tradition of any national group."

There are thousands of Negro organizations, trade unions, fraternal societies, lodges, social clubs, student bodies, Greek Letter Societies and churches. The membership of these organizations is composed largely of working-class composition and background, and all members are affected by a Jim-Crow status. Hundreds of thousands of men and women, eligible for trade union membership, are members of these organizations.

It is estimated that the membership of the Negro church is five or six million. Some people, however, say: "Never mind the people in the church. Let the hundred thousand Negro trade unionists keep away from these people. We are pure!" But the Negro Congress did not take this position. Neither do really advanced Negro trade unionists. They say that church members should belong to trade unions. Let us get them into the unions!

The Negro church has solid contacts with the Negro masses. In the long history of the peculiar social life of the Negro people it has always been a center of social activity, at one time being the exclusive center for amusement, drama, club life, etc. Within the church there are study circles, auxiliary committees, Young People's Circles, Epworth

Leagues, Young People's Baptist Leagues, where religious and secular topics are discussed.

There are numerous small churches with a large aggregate membership. The leaders are usually very close to the masses and react to the needs of these poorer parishioners. A single talk by the leaders of these churches on the need of joining a trade union could result, for example, in building almost over night a Domestic Workers Union of five hundred members in Harlem alone. This is not a far-fetched possibility.

That is why much importance can be attached to the resolutions adopted by the church session of the National Negro Congress, participated in by influential churchmen. It calls for the church "to work out an adequate technique comprehending social and economic problems affecting our group and working with non-Christian groups whose economic and social ideas are of value to the solution of our economic and social problems."

Today the tactic of the united front is bringing together large masses of Negroes; yet the consolidation of the organized united front among the Negro people is still weak.

The responsibility for this must be lodged with those who stand in the way of unity. And as for those people who claim to represent the interests of the proletariat but who are so simonpure that they cannot or do not care to concern themselves with the problems of the miserable life of the Negro people as a whole,—let them remember the picture of an entire people, so poignantly depicted by the great Negro poet, Paul Laurence Dunbar:

> A crust of bread and a corner to sleep in,
> A minute to smile and an hour to weep in,
>
> A pint of joy to a peck of trouble,
> And never a laugh but the moans come double
> And that is life.

The National Negro Congress recorded progress made by Communists and the many delegates who supported our program, in the increasing work we are carrying on in the various organizations of the Negro people. Our modest successes are, however, just beginnings. We must now undertake to profit from our experiences, mistakes, shortcomings and successes, by showing what changes are necessary in our methods of work to build the National Negro Congress.

The Congress has shown how, by overcoming sectarian methods of work, we can help to develop still further the movement for Negro liberation already started by the American Negro Labor Congress, the

League of Struggle for Negro Rights and the International Labor Defense.

We must be very critical of our past work so that we may more easily make the change. It is necessary for the Party membership, particularly the Negro members, to see the need and possibility of strengthening our influence in the existing Negro organizations, by joining them where possible and becoming useful members. We can today unite the Negro people on the basis of their day-to-day needs, and for the preservation of democratic rights in such a way that the greatest number of people will be brought together in common struggle.

The National Negro Congress, if it is to have standing among the Negro people, will have to be active in political struggles. The task is going to become more difficult. The ruling class is not going to stand idly by and allow us to work freely in the organizations of the Negroes.

The desire for unity by leaders in the Universal Negro Improvement Association is being attacked by reactionary politicians of the two old parties. In some cases in Harlem we have seen the police department instigate provocations to disrupt united front actions of the Universal Negro Improvement Association.

The reactionaries of the old-line political parties fear the movement for independent political action which is taking form in a number of Negro communities.

The vicious attacks of the Liberty Leaguers and reactionary forces in the country against the Negro people were seen during the election campaign of 1936 in the campaign of Governor Talmadge in the state of Georgia. A copy of the *Georgia Woman's World,* edited in Atlanta, reached my hands. President Roosevelt is attacked for advocating social equality. The publication carries on a blood-curdling anti-Negro campaign in its columns. The contents show to what depths the reactionary Liberty Leaguers and their agents will stoop to stir up a lynch frenzy against the Negro people. It carries a large picture of Mrs. Roosevelt being escorted by two Negro students of the Howard University R.O.T.C., and labels this "social equality." Another picture, showing President Roosevelt receiving a delegation of Negro Masons, is labeled: "Are We Headed for Social Equality?" The paper is filled from cover to cover with attacks upon the Negro people and is aimed at dividing still more the ranks of the Negro and white toilers.

An editorial, "Social Equality by Force," warns against a so-called civilization of mulattoes. It states:

If the Negroes of the South after they were freed and took control had possessed wealth in the same degree as the white people, the South today would be a mulatto civilization. Not because the whites would have desired it, but because the Negroes would have possessed power to enforce social equality.

Such a civilization of mulattoes is not impossible nor improbable in the not distant future if the policies of the present administration in Washington continue.

It may be recalled that Mussolini a few years back, in an article dealing with the Negroes in the U.S., made a similar statement.

Such are the appeals of the ultra-reactionary Liberty League-Hearst-Talmadge clique to the basest passions in order to develop the near-fascist program of the Republican Party.

Although the Congress resolutions decided against partisanship in politics, the National Negro Congress cannot be neutral in politics. The vital interests of the Negro people demand that the Congress apply the test of its program of minimum demands to every party and every candidate, and determine which candidates and which parties are enemies of its program. The Congress should draw up a legislative program of the demands of the Negro people, and campaign to unite the various organizations to see that this program is realized. Such simple participation in politics will not endanger the broadest unity of the Congress, but on the contrary will bring forward the issues of the Negro people and thereby cement unity and make the Congress stronger as a fighter for economic and social, as well as political rights.

We must revive the best traditions of the Negro people and honor their highest aspirations, their national feelings and desire for cultural expression. But to be able to do this effectively it is necessary to give the greatest attention to immediate needs. This has always been our aim. We are alert to the daily specific problems facing the Negroes as an oppressed nation of people. To fail in alertness in this regard leads to the abandonment of the Negro masses to the wolves of capitalism. We do not contrapose immediate issues to the revolutionary objective; we are concerned daily, hourly, with the miserable life of the whole of the Negro people, as a part of the larger struggle for socialism.

We Communists stand one hundred per cent for the general advancement of the Negro people, against all forms of discrimination, against fascism and war, for equal rights, and on all issues in line with the interests of the toiling masses for advancing the fight against capital.

We recall that in 1932 *The Crisis,* official organ of the National Association for the Advancement of Colored People, organized a symposium on Communism, by several Negro editors in various parts of the country.* And while these gentlemen admitted the relentless struggle of the Communists for the immediate interests of the Negro people, yet most of them openly stated their opposition to Communism. But today there is an entirely different situation. We are not received with open arms everywhere now; but we must register such important developments as the United Front of the National Association for the Advancement of Colored People, the League for Industrial Democracy, the American Civil Liberties Union, the International Labor Defense, and other organizations for defense of the Scottsboro boys.

In the past, the work of the N.A.A.C.P. in the economic field can be characterized as incidental to its civil liberty program. But we note that certain very definite changes in the policy regarding labor were made at its St. Louis convention. It recognized "the Negro as a landless proletariat in the country and as a propertyless wage-earner in the city, a reservoir of cheap labor . . . more easily exploited than white labor." The N.A.A.C.P. convention took under consideration the setting up by its branches, in strategic industrial and agricultural centers, of councils whose function should be:

(1) To conduct classes in workers' education designed to create among Negroes a knowledge of their present role in industry and a realization of their identity of interests with white labor; (2) to foster the building of a labor movement which will unite all labor, white and black, skilled and unskilled, industrial and agricultural; (3) to lay the basis for united action between white and black workers for securing passage of adequate legislation on immediate problems, such as old age pensions, unemployment and sick insurance, widows' and orphans' pensions, child and female labor, lynching, discrimination and Jim-Crowism; (4) to serve as a force against every manifestation and form of racial chauvinism in the labor movement, and to attempt to break down discrimination on the job and in pay, and Jim-Crowism in local and national trade union bodies.

Indeed, this is a far departure from the previous activities of the N.A.A.C.P. and certainly offers opportunity for common action with

---

* For the text of this symposium see Vol. II, this work, pp. 700–715.

the National Negro Congress, as well as the possibility for Communists to work in local branches for the furtherance of this progressive program.

In like manner, certain progressive steps can be noted in the Workers' Councils of the Urban League, under the directorship of Mr. Lester B. Granger. The Workers' Councils of the National Urban League, with branches in more than 32 industrial centers throughout the country, numbering many thousands of members, have as their basic program:

To acquaint Negro workers with the economic nature of their problems, with the essential unity of white and Negro workers' interests, and with the history, technique and necessity of collective workers' action; and to establish understanding and intelligent co-operation among workers of both races, within and without the ranks of organized labor.

The possibility for united action among organizations of Negro people, I believe, is clear. We have had excellent experiences, not only with these organizations, but also with the Universal Negro Improvement Association.

From these observations may follow our approach to the National Negro Congress for extending development of the liberation struggle of the Negro people. This struggle has been in the making for a long time in various organizations of the Negro people. It was given its most vigorous start in such organizations as the American Negro Labor Congress and the League of Struggle for Negro Rights.

The American Negro Labor Congress was organized in Chicago in October, 1925. It began to champion the rights of thirteen million Negroes in the United States and "to lead the struggles of the Negro workers and farmers against terrorism, lynching, mob violence, police brutality, segregation and all forms of race hatred; for equal pay for equal work; for better working conditions; for the organization of Negro workers into trade unions on the basis of complete equality."

The preamble and program of the American Negro Labor Congress stated in detail the position of the Negroes in the U.S. and outlined the methods of struggle. It made a summary of the struggles of the Negro people internationally against capitalist imperialist oppression.

The American Negro Labor Congress laid special emphasis on the organization of Negro *workers* and *farmers*. It called for struggle for the admittance of Negroes into the existing trade unions and their full participation in all offices and affairs; it called for the organization of Negroes into unions and in industries where no unions existed; it organized Inter-Racial Labor Conferences for the "promotion of solidarity of all workers regardless of race or color and to take steps to unionize Negro workers."

The American Negro Labor Congress was almost entirely of working-class composition. It represented quite a departure from previous Congresses of national gatherings initiated by Negroes. It served the definite purpose, in line with the trend in the industrialization of the Negro, of bringing the Negro working class forward as the decisive force in the movement of the Negro people as a whole.

Although there was a large migration of Negroes into industry, their organization into trade unions was weak, and their class consciousness was not widespread. There was a natural suspicion of the trade unions among Negroes because in most cases these unions were led by white leaders who carried out the policies of the ruling class of Jim-Crowism and segregation in the labor movement. The American Negro Labor Congress was faced with a most difficult task which it undertook to the best of its ability.

There were shortcomings in meeting this task. The A.N.L.C. was too narrow in its approach. For the period of its existence it was almost completely isolated from the basic masses of the Negro people; this shortcoming was carried over into the League of Struggle for Negro Rights. The class content of the program of the A.N.L.C., which was essentially correct, was, however, not carefully adapted to the feelings and moods of the Negro people. The local councils were too rigid. Instead of uniting broad masses of the Negro people through their organizations, the councils were built on the basis of individual membership composed in almost all cases of those people and individuals who were dissatisfied with the existing organizations and were breaking away from them completely. In many cases members of the councils were class-conscious white workers but, together with their Negro brothers, were separated from the broad masses, and knew little or nothing about their problems and their life. The white workers quite sincerely desired to carry out their class duty of unity with the Negro people. But unfortunately the form and the methods of work were not fruitful. In many cases sincere Negroes were driven away from the organization by bad methods of work.

I recall particularly the strict and unyielding attitude taken by the leaders of the American Negro Labor Congress toward religion. This attitude prevented the Congress from becoming a mass influence among church people. At an A.N.L.C. meeting in Chicago, 1926, composed of a large number of religious people, a leader of the organization in the course of his remarks, said: "To hell with religion; damn the church." But today in the National Negro Congress church organizations and religious people work co-operatively with non-church people. Our Negro Communists are fraternizing with church people in order to organize them in the struggle for Negro liberation.

Despite its shortcomings, the A.N.L.C. served a useful purpose.* The last convention of the American Negro Labor Congress was held in St. Louis in November, 1930, where, by unanimous decision, the name was changed to the League of Struggle for Negro Rights. There was a change in program also. The program called for the destruction of the plantation system in the South, for confiscation without compensation of the land of the big landlords, and declared for the complete right of self-determination for the Negro people in the Black Belt of the South. Such a program prevented the development of a broad movement. The masses did not understand this full program. Furthermore, the L.S.N.R. fell into the same sectarian methods of work as the A.N.L.C. It did not base its activity sufficiently on immediate, daily needs of the people. Naturally, this narrowed down the L.S.N.R.

The most useful and practical part of the program of the L.S.N.R. was the "Bill of Negro Rights," which aimed to develop a movement to enforce the enactment of legislation for Negro rights and the suppression of lynching.

The organizational weaknesses of the L.S.N.R. were identical with those of the American Negro Labor Congress. Calling for affiliation on the basis of the complete program, the L.S.N.R. tended to make existing organizations suspicious. The by-laws provided for the leadership of struggle for the L.S.N.R. program of immediate and general demands. But many organizations could not be drawn into united front struggle on the basis of the full program of the L.S.N.R.

It is precisely on this point that the National Negro Congress has made a great step forward to the advantage of the united front and joint action of different organizations.

What actually happened was the following: branches of individual members of the L.S.N.R. became, invariably, as in the A.N.L.C., small sectarian groups, and, as such, remained isolated and even were unable to hold those people who were willing to break away from other organizations. These branches could have attraction only for

* Material on the A.N.L.C. can be found in Vol. II, this work, pp. 488–492, 656–671.

unorganized Negro people. But contrary to opinions held by many, the Negro people are an organized people, that is, they are members of churches, lodges, fraternal organizations, etc.

There were tendencies to organize into the L.S.N.R. individuals who were either eligible for trade union membership or unemployed organizations. This was a sectarian mistake of all L.S.N.R. branches. Practically no effort was made in any part of the country to build the L.S.N.R. as a united front, federating organization on joint actions around immediate issues.

The National Negro Congress has wisely avoided all these pitfalls. In the first place, it avoids usurping the program of affiliated organizations. It rather works with organizations. It was organized upon the basis of a united front around a minimum program worked out and agreed upon by delegates.

The National Negro Congress is being organized on a regional, or district, and local council basis. A region or district is composed of several states, with a vice-president in charge. There are to be also state organizations. These are made up of city bodies or local councils within the state. The local council is the basic form of organization. The local sponsoring committees, which initiate the movement for the National Negro Congress, automatically become local councils. These councils are to be federated bodies of already existing organizations which affiliate to the council on the basis of a part or the whole of the program adopted at Chicago. There can also be sustaining members.

The life of these local councils can be justified only by their taking up and acting jointly on the issues that affect the Negro people. They can become effective in the community only by developing campaigns and struggles around these issues and by involving the membership of each organization in these activities. The most important task to be undertaken is to unionize Negro labor and to develop a fight to break down Jim-Crow barriers in national and local trade union bodies.

These are the immediate issues, together with those general political issues, such as the struggle against fascism and war and for the defense of the independence of Ethiopia, which have already been dealt with, that should occupy the immediate attention of the National Congress and all of the supporters and sympathizers.

We Communists must organize all our forces to render great assistance to the National Negro Congress in carrying out its program. If we develop systematic work we shall be able to fulfill very soon the task of developing a broad People's Front among the Negro people in the United States against fascism and war and for the liberation of the Negro people.

Summary of a series of articles appearing in *The Communist* (New York), February–June, 1936, published in James W. Ford, *The Negro and the Democratic Front* (New York: International Publishers, 1938), pp. 66–85.

39

PROPOSED PROGRAM FOR THE EDUCATIONAL PROGRESS OF THE NEGRO IN KENTUCKY

by Kentucky Negro Educational Association

The program and style of a rather "old-fashioned" Black organization are illustrated in the educational and social proposals that follow for a border state. In addition to Mr. Blanton and Mr. Wilson mentioned in the document, others on the Board of Directors of the association were R. L. Dowery of Manchester; E. T. Buford of Bowling Green; V. K. Perry of Louisville; and J. L. Vean of Versailles. This document is not dated, but it was issued in 1937.

Proposed Educational Program

It has been voted by the Board of Directors of the K.N.E.A. to sponsor a program for the educational progress of the Negro through a committee to be known as the "State Committee on Negro Welfare." This committee will be composed of the major officers and directors of the K.N.E.A., the K.N.E.A. legislative committee and a representative of each of the main organizations for the social welfare of the Negroes that are now organized in the state. The activities of this committee shall be mainly along the lines of education, but shall also consist of some provisions for the general welfare of the Negro.

The president of the K.N.E.A., W. S. Blanton of Frankfort, Ky., is to be chairman of the above mentioned committee and a chief agent in the execution of the program outlined. The interest of our governor, superintendent of public instruction and our legislators is solicited in the program herein outlined.

Atwood S. Wilson,
Sec'y-Treas. of K.N.E.A.
Louisville, Kentucky

Committee Activities and Aims

1. That the state legislature be asked to provide graduate and professional education for Negroes in Kentucky. The bill embodying this provision has already been written and was adopted by the K.N.E.A. In the main it provided that the state shall provide the payment of tuition fees of Negroes for graduate and professional studies in schools outside the state over and above the fees a White student pays in the state in a state school. It is estimated that $10,000 will be needed for this purpose each year, or $20,000 for the biennium. This bill should be pushed by the Combined Committee and the K.N.E.A. Legislative Committee through a legislator. This matter should also be discussed with Supt.-Elect Peters and with the K.E.A.

2. That we look forward after the next 3 or 5 years to graduate work at K.S.I.C. and senior college work at W.K.I.C.

3. That the state legislature be asked to provide the necessary funds to make the Kentucky State Industrial College a Class A Senior College and the West Kentucky Industrial College a Class A Junior College, in the Southern Association. That both of these colleges be given needed buildings and that both be provided with funds for establishing courses in the trades and industries. This matter should be discussed in detail with the presidents of each college and then with Supt.-Elect Peters and then pushed by some interested legislators.

4. That a committee of the K.N.E.A. wait on Supt. H. W. Peters at an early date and seek to make the school code really effective, especially as it pertains to salary schedules for all teachers.

5. That a Committee of the K.N.E.A. wait on Supt. Peters in regard to the appointment of a Negro educator as an assistant supervisor for Negro public schools. That it make itself known as favorable to the retention of the present supervisor of Negro rural schools.

NOTE: These five items are purely educational and should be pushed by the K.N.E.A. The K.E.A. program of teacher retirement, the pupil per capita of $12, and no major changes in the school code are sought by the K.N.E.A. This information is also given out for Supt. Peters and the K.E.A.

General Welfare Program
Special Committee Objectives

1. That there be formed a Negro Company of the State National Guard. The Negro has proved himself to be one of America's best soldiers in many wars. He should be given the responsibility of aiding in the protection of the Commonwealth of Kentucky.

2. That a policy be adopted by the state giving Negro appointments in administering the W.P.A., N.Y.A., nursery schools, adult education, and any other federal programs that may come to the state.

3. That Negroes be appointed to teach and otherwise administer to Negroes in the State reformatories, and other eleemosynary institutions.

4. That the state provide more adequate facilities for the crippled Negro children and better hospitalization for the state tubercular cases among Negroes.

5. That the present anti-lynching laws of the State of Kentucky be strengthened.

NOTE: The items listed above tend to promote the general welfare of the Negro and therefore, might well suggest the main activities of the State Committee on Negro Welfare. This committee should, however, be equally as interested in the proposed educational program. The above mentioned matters should be discussed with Governor Chandler, our legislators, and social leaders of the state.

Four-page printed folder in editor's possession.

40

A BLACK CONGRESSMAN ON
POLITICAL PARTIES

The Democratic representative out of Chicago's ghetto, Arthur W. Mitchell, delivered himself of some remarks in the House in June, 1936, which conveyed both hard facts and high spirits. He commenced with remarks directed to the Republican Party.

. . . For 70 years we followed you blindly; for 70 years we perpetuated you in power; and for 70 long years you promised relief, and forgot your promises the minute you found yourself in office. You have had your day with the Negro vote.

Granting that all you contend is true—and I say it is not—has not the Negro paid you for what you did for him in 1861, 1863, and 1865? Is it your idea that because he was liberated during the administration of a Republican President he must still vote your ticket as a matter of gratitude, with his eyes closed toward his present and future needs? I deny that this should be the requirement of any party. Does not 70 years of unbroken loyalty to you and your party even up the debt, or is it your contention that this party loyalty you are claiming is to be an eternal thing? Can you not cease to talk about what your party did 70 years ago, and tell the aspiring youth of this country what your party proposes to do in 1936 and the years to follow? Do you think we are so blind and so dumb as to be led again to the political slaughter by Republicans seeking to hold office, whose record insofar as we are concerned is a chain of broken promises reaching across three-quarters of a century? . . .

Now, my friends, what is the matter with the gentlemen on this side? I sounded an alarm to you the other day, and whether you believe it or not, you are going to witness not only difficulty but an impossibility in putting the Negro vote in your vest pocket this year. You can no longer fool the Negroes as you have done for 70 years.

You have boasted that you carry us in your vest pocket. That boast, thank God, is no longer true. In 1928, over here in the Barr Building, when Hoover was running for President of the United States, his campaign manager was approached and asked to give some money to maintain a Negro headquarters in Chicago, and he said, "We will not give another dime; we have the Negro vote in our vest pocket, and we can win without spending another cent on them."

Now, the Negroes have learned you do not want them.

You have said here today that the Democratic Party does not want them. I am inclined to concede that neither party particularly wants us. You, the Republicans, had us for 70 years, and kicked us around like footballs, and showed you have no real respect for us.

It is not a question now of which party wants us; it is a question of which party offers us a better opportunity to rise in this country and live as citizens should live. In other words, the question is this, which party does the Negro want? And I say frankly that the Negro not only wants but he is going to work for that party that assures him of the largest opportunity to enjoy the blessings of freedom,

justice, and an opportunity to develop into the fullest degree of manhood. We shall not take either party altogether upon its past record;
we shall deal with both parties as they show an interest in us and
deal with us in 1936. For my part there is no question in my mind
but that the Democratic Party, as constituted today, offers the Negro
by far the best opportunity in this country, and I shall use all the
influence and all the power that I possess to drive this truth home to
the Negroes in this country.

Today the Negro refuses to stand by you simply on 60-year-old
promises still unfulfilled. Until you make good the promises that you
have made for the last 70 years, we shall try new political fields not
marked "G.O.P."

Mr. Robison of Kentucky. Will the gentleman yield?

Mr. Mitchell of Illinois. I refuse to yield. The gentleman from
Kentucky told you about conditions in Texas and what the Democratic
Party would do to you. I come from Alabama and I would like to
tell you what the Republican Party will do to you in Alabama.

I was a Republican and in a Republican convention in Alabama
when the "lily white" Republican Party came into existence. I, with
many others, was driven out of the Republican convention in City Hall
just across from the big Hilman Hotel in Birmingham. The "lily
white" marched into the hotel. The Negroes were told to go out where
they belonged, and no Negro could be admitted to the "lily white"
party.

There were a few of us who met the educational qualifications, a
few who met the property qualifications, and the Democrats registered
us. After we were registered it was left to the Republican Party of
Alabama to drive us out, although we were registered voters there.
They said they were going to have a real white party. It is high time
that you Republicans stopped playing the hypocrite. When the Democratic Party kicked us out they told us they did not want us. You
told us that you wanted us and then kicked us out of the party.

The Republican Party has conjured with the name of Lincoln long
enough. Lincoln has been dead for 70 years, and his party as the
party of human rights died years ago.

Now, I am going to conclude with this story: There were two
Irishmen—and I am making no reflections on the Irish; they are my
friends—there were two Irishmen walking through the cemetery and
reading the inscriptions on the tombstones. They came to one and
they read, "Not dead but sleeping." Mike said to Pat, "What does

it say there?" Pat says, "Not dead but sleeping." Mike says, "Listen, if I was dead I would confess it and not tell a lie about it, would you?"

Congressional Record, June 1, 1936; 74th Cong., 2nd sess., LXXX, 8551-52.

41

TWO AGAINST 5,000

by Roy Wilkins

The following essay was introduced in the original with the italicized paragraph, and it needs no additional introduction.

This article was written from Associated Press news dispatches. Since that time later reports have reached The Crisis *that William and Cora Wales were not occupying the caretaker's cottage at a cemetery, but were living in their own home at the edge of the cemetery. It is reported that efforts have been made over a period of thirteen years to oust them from their property. They refused to sell. Some years ago the city condemned a part of their land to expand the cemetery. Their final refusal to vacate their home is said to have led to the battle. The community was out to "get" them. It is also reported that the white woman alleged to have been threatened by Wales vigorously denied that he threatened her—after Wales was dead.*

Too often the story of the Southern Negro deals exclusively with those who are timid. The truth is that colored people in the South would not be where they are today if it were not for the colored men and women who dare to speak out and, if necessary, to act, at the right times.

Southern white people, almost unanimously, characterize such Negroes as "crazy." A colored man who refuses to be shoved into the pattern they have set for the race, who protests and who fights when fighting is called for is labeled a lunatic.

The newspapers of Saturday, May 16, and Sunday, May 17, carried a story of stubborn, thrilling, "crazy" bravery by an aging colored man and his sister, and of cruel, bestial, atavistic degeneracy by some white people in and around Gordonsville, Va.

A mob of 5,000 persons including all the sheriffs, constables, deputies and state police for miles around, armed with everything from machine guns on down, was held at bay by a 60-year-old Negro man and his 62-year-old sister for six hours. The pitched battle of two against five thousand was finally won by the mob only after a gasoline-soaked torch was tossed into the house and the occupants burned to death. Even as the flames ate away at their fortress, the man and woman within kept up their rifle and shot-gun fire until the blazing roof caved in upon their heads. Then, as Cora Wales was silhouetted mercilessly against the firelight, machine guns in the hands of the superior race cut her down in a hail of bullets. Her brother, with the walls of his home now toppling in the raging fire, appeared at a doorway only to be shot down.

It would appear to all normal persons that with death would come the end of the episode. But not so here. Impatiently the mob waited hours for the embers of the house to cool. Then, like a pack of maniacs the killers rushed in and chopped up the two bodies for souvenirs to carry home. Even pieces of bone were carried away. If the tradition of American lynchers was faithfully followed, there reposes now on the mantelpieces of many a Virginia home a bit of flesh or a bone preserved in a jar of alcohol to remind children and grandchildren of the indomitable courage of a brother, father or son of the family who battled to the death to prevent two Negroes from overcoming 5,000 white Virginians.

If one has a fancy for words, this killing was not a lynching. It was sport—sport on a grand scale. Hunting 'possum compared to this is tiddlywinks. Beside it fox-hunting, as practised by the F.F.Vs., pales into a child's game. Here were a man and a woman cooped up in a frame house and all one had to do was shoot. All rules were off. Anything went.

There was a slight flaw in the set-up, however. The man and woman had arms and they were not afraid to shoot. They had killed a sheriff and wounded five others. The leaders of the five thousand looked about and took counsel together. They had numbers. They had machine guns. They had sulphur bombs. They had tear gas bombs. But the two in the house had rifles, shotguns and perhaps a pistol or two. Not so good. Not half as good as one lone Negro with nothing but his bare hands, easily dangled at the end of a rope by two or three hundred men; his swaying body a snap target for dozens of guns in the mob. A hanging, manacled Negro cannot shoot back. No, this was a different proposition.

So, off went a request to the United States Marine Corps at Quantico, Va., for a few squads of Leathernecks, a few tanks and a few of Uncle Sam's machine guns. (And how those Marines would have loved to have gone!) You see, gentle reader, the federal government must *never* interfere with the citizens of a sovereign state who wish to stage lynchings, but it is all right for the sovereign states to call on United States troops when some Negro is crazy enough not to want to be lynched. What the hell is the government for, anyway?

This was laying it on a bit thick, however, not for the Marines, but for the government, and therefore the request was turned down. The 5,000 were left to shift for themselves. They fell back and waited for darkness. Under the helpful—and healthful—cover of night the torch was tossed and then it was only a matter of time before the famed G-Men had to take a back seat for real killers.

The story goes that one member of the mob was a 12-year-old boy armed with a .22 calibre rifle. His small sister is said to have gone among the 5,000 begging ammunition for her valiant kin.

The story behind the slaughter at Gordonsville is that William Wales and his sister, living in the caretaker's cottage of a cemetery, had been notified to move. For some reason not stated by them or their murderers, they chose not to move. It is reported that the two patrolled their yard with firearms to balk eviction. With such determined opposition, the local whites were forced to fall back upon what they are pleased to call strategy. This proved to be the time-worn device of dragging some white woman into the quarrel and charging Wales with threatening her.

We have no knowledge of whether Wales threatened to kill a white woman who remonstrated with him about remaining in the house. Wales is dead. His sister is dead. In the face of machine guns, bombs, arson and the carving of human flesh, the colored people in the vicinity who might know something are sensibly mute. We do know that the trick of involving a white woman with a Negro in some manner is an old one, trotted out time and time again as a preliminary to a lynching.

In May, 1930, George Hughes was working on a farm near Sherman, Tex. He complained to his white farm boss that his wages were short the agreed amount. By nightfall Hughes was in jail charged with "attempted rape" of the farm boss's wife. By the next morning Hughes was a roasted corpse in the steel vault of the courthouse, where he had been placed for "safekeeping" from a mob which halted at nothing—not even the burning down of the courthouse.

There are dozens of other similar stories. It is an old trick, this white woman business. Maybe it was true at Gordonsville, maybe. . . . Anyway the sheriff swore out a warrant charging Wales with lunacy. (As was stated above, any Negro in the South who talks back to white people or who wants to fight white people is regarded as a lunatic.) When the sheriff appeared to serve the warrant he was shot and killed. That set the stage. Here was a Negro who would not "act right." Furthermore he had killed a sheriff—a white man. The lid was off. It was a free-for-all. Anybody could do anything. The white race must be vindicated. White supremacy must be maintained. The ordained of God must not be challenged. The Negro must be kept in the place the Lord made for him. So the five thousand against two. So the machine guns against shotguns. So the carving of bloody, roasted flesh.

But William Wales did kill a sheriff, did he not? Are the colored people for law and order? Does *The Crisis* mean to imply by this article that its policy is to defend colored people who kill sheriffs?

The answer is that colored people have to be for law and order even though the law has given them little protection. They are a relatively helpless minority. They have to place their reliance in the law which the powerful majority has made. But that does not mean that they necessarily approve of the law or the way it is administered, or of the people who administer it. All too infrequently they express their disapproval and resentment in a forthright manner. They have good cause to resort to direct action. It is a marvel of the age that they have been so meek and mild. They know the law is stacked against all poor people, and especially against Negroes. Yet they turn to it, sensing with that insight that has enabled them to survive in a hostile land, that they as a group are not in a position to change the law by democratic means or defy it with arms.

William Wales had had his fill of white people and their ways as expressed around Gordonsville. He probably decided that he did not intend to stand any more from the system set up and maintained to exploit, humiliate and crush him. No one knows now the workings of his mind. He probably felt that in this matter he was right and that he was not going to "knuckle under" to the white folk no matter what happened. Death was preferable to life as he had been forced to live it.

As Wales looked back upon his sixty years what did he see? He saw courts controlled by whites, responsive to whites, giving verdicts pleasing to whites. He saw his race's children cheated out of the schooling for which their parents paid taxes to the state. He saw separation of the races everywhere, with his having always the little end of the deal. He saw jobs, health, opportunity, prestige, family life and success denied upon the flimsy excuse of skin color. He saw his people hanged, roasted and mutilated by mobs while legislators called points of order and an aspirant to the Presidency fiddled with clauses, phrases, periods and commas in the so-called Bill of Rights. All about him were restriction and frustration. The people who wanted him and his sister evicted, the sheriff who came to serve him with a warrant, outlining another of the white man's "crimes," epitomized the system which closed in always about him and his.

The system killed that sheriff. Wales was the agent. Exploitation brings about its own destruction. The system is killing the white people around Gordonsville, around the thousand Gordonsvilles in this country. The army of 5,000, foaming at the mouth, cursing and pot-shotting at two old people, the army which saw nothing unusual in calling for government troops to carry out its desires—that army is being killed. Its members already are half-dead. The dancing firelight from the burning cottage revealed the decay eating away at the system Wales thought to kill with rifle bullets.

Some white people, some, even in Virginia, are shamed by Gordonsville. They know there is more to the story than the killing of a sheriff and the destruction of a "crazy Negro."

Yes, *The Crisis* defends William and Cora Wales. We think we understand them. What is more important, we think we know the real criminals in these situations everywhere. Crazy? Wales was not crazy. The two sane people in all that array were in the house. It was the five thousand outside who were mad.

The Crisis, June, 1936; XLIII, 169–70.

42

ATTITUDES OF NEGRO FAMILIES ON RELIEF
by Thyra J. Edwards

A penetrating examination of Black people on relief during the Depression came from the pen of a leading Black woman social worker. Her comments on alleged "malingering," and so on, have a deeply contemporary quality– as do the facts on Afro-American impoverishment. The numbered footnotes are in the original essay.

Several years ago a distinguished agriculturist from Tuskegee Institute was presented to the secretary of the Negro Branch Y.M.C.A. at Gary, Indiana. The secretary, recently migrated from Texas, looked up at his tall, broad shouldered visitor, acknowledged the introduction, and added facetiously, "Alabama, eh, where there are the meanest white folks in the world."

"The meanest white folks and the meanest Negroes," was the agriculturist's unperturbed rejoinder. "Throughout the States I have found that the Negro community is in every instance a parallel reflection of the local white community. The variation is in degree only. The essential social pattern is the same."

Briefly this simple incident points the untenability of the thesis posed rather generally by Negro students and students of the Negro in treating the Negro as an isolated phenomenon rather than an integral unit of the community and national life. Any premise that sets apart certain attitudes, reactions and behavior patterns as particularly and peculiar to any one racial or cultural group, be it Negro, Aryan or Jewish, is sociologically and anthropologically unsound. There are no particular Negro emotions, reactions, or rhythms patterned by race exclusively. Unemployed Negroes and their families do not suffer a particularized hunger and exposure, nor do they react to it in a particular Negro fashion.

Unemployment has become, except for the Soviet Union, universal in extent. For the past seven years a very considerable segment of the American population has been sustained by public funds administered as Direct Relief, or as Work Relief Projects. In December 1935 there were, according to the conservative estimates of the American Federation of Labor, 11,401,000 employable persons in the United States separated from gainful employment.[1] Mass unemployment of Negroes became acute by 1927 and by 1929 there were 300,000 employable Negroes separated from employment. A number which has continued to rise. The percentage of Negroes in this category usually exceeds the whites by from 30 per cent to 60

[1] In January 1935 there were 13,058,215 unemployed, according to A. F. of L. figures. These figures are of necessity conservative since in the United States there are no central Labor Exchanges or Federal machinery for a continual and accurate check of unemployment figures.

per cent. There is a similar disproportion in the relief population. Negroes constitute 9.4 per cent of the population while comprising 18.4 per cent of all relief cases, 17.8 per cent of all the Negroes in America being maintained by Public Relief funds.[2] At present the Negro Relief population is 3,864,000.

And what is the source of this desperate disproportion between the Negro population and the Negro Relief population in relation to the total American population and the total American Relief population? It is generally recognized that the Negro, as a marginal and a minority group, suffers intenser employment hazards through discrimination in wages, in work allotment and in the disbursement of Relief. There is a prevailing sentiment that Negroes should not be hired as long as there are white men without jobs. There are in addition other basic factors: the introduction of machinery into unskilled functions formerly predominantly performed by Negroes has displaced a mass of Negro workers; the reduction of production in the automotive and steel industries in which large numbers of Negroes were employed, has displaced other thousands; cessation of activity in building construction which previously absorbed a great bloc of Negro skilled and unskilled labor; the reduction of incomes of families employing numbers of servants and the widespread use of electrical household machinery has thrown domestic servants on the labor market. The disappearance of small business into which category all Negro business fell, has not only created unemployment but destroyed and blasted the hope of a separate "Negro economy." The destitution of the southern farm population affects some 2,000,000 Negro farmers, largely share croppers and tenant farmers. And the government's removal of acreage from cotton cultivation has increased the destitution and intensified the insecurity of this group.

Even in the more liberal urban centers there is discrimination and segregation in the assignment of Negroes to certain work projects and to camps. Chicago uses the Batavia Camp, exclusively for white men. There are exclusive "white" projects.

Now after seven years, Unemployment and Unemployment Relief can no longer be classified as emergencies. Yet Federal and local governments continue establishing temporary procedures, made work, and work programs of a few months' life span only. Such procedure is mere wishful thinking. For as distasteful as are unemployment and relief to the American temperament and to the American philosophy

[2] These figures are taken from "Incidence Upon the Negro" by Charles S. Johnson, *The American Journal of Sociology,* May 1935. Relief statistics of 1933 used as the percentage base for computation.

of individual thrift and industry and individual success the permanency of unemployment and the problem of caring for the unemployed population are now recognized and accepted by the American public. If indeed then, the Negro, in the face of these preponderant odds, has recognized the potential permanence of sustained unemployment and has adjusted his attitudes to the enigma of want and suffering in the midst of an abundance ruthlessly destroyed under government authority, then he has displayed an astuteness that exceeds and anticipates that of the finance capitalists and the political administrators who continue tampering and pottering with half measures. For there is doubtful virtue in the gesture of pacing the sidewalks in a futile search for jobs that do not exist.

Despite this it is notable that men and women on relief beg for and accept jobs, project and work relief assignments—even when the wage offered is the mere equivalent of their relief budgets. It restores some of their self respect to handle cash and to purchase direct and be able to shop about without the stigma and discrimination attendant upon buying on disbursing orders.

With the establishment of the Works Progress Administration this job-eager attitude repeated itself. A few men have refused jobs under slight pretexts. But the great number have anxiously accepted jobs, any kind of jobs, most of them at the ridiculous wage of $55.00 a month for full time. In large families this amount was cruelly below even the relief budget and families suffered the delays attendant upon cases being reopened for supplementation. Men went to these jobs often so poorly clad that "unsocially minded" foremen sent them home off the outdoor jobs. Waiting rooms in some relief stations displayed a gruesome exhibit of crisping, cracked, frozen ears, bleeding hands and swollen, frost bitten feet.

These men, eagerly accepting any kind of work under any kind of circumstances, represent a trend, not a phenomenon. At the American Association of Social Workers' Delegate Conference in Washington, February 14th, Mrs. Roslyn Serota, Junior supervisor of the County Relief Board of Philadelphia, Pa., reported that an impartial study of four urban centers disclosed that a very small proportion of job refusal (by the unemployed) is without justification. Physical disability, inability to perform the job offered, current employment, substandard wages are revealed as the common reasons for job refusals. Philadelphia has used a Job Refusal committee to define a bona-fide work offer and a "justifiable" refusal, and to hear complaints.[3] Before

[3] See: *The Compass*, February, 1936, p. 10.

presuming to indict the unemployed such boards of impartial hearing should be set up in every community dispensing to large units of the unemployed.

"They were on the whole," complains Mr. Newell Eason, referring to Negro families on Relief, "averse to any suggestion of self help."

Well, Watts, California, is remote from the experience and knowledge of the bulk of the American population. But in Chicago—the second city in the world for Negro population—the self-help efforts among Negroes are bravely defiant.

Last year a congested strip of Chicago's Black Belt comprising approximately nine city blocks and containing 1,349 households, a total of 4,422 individual souls was intensively studied and analyzed. There was the accustomed run of ice cream and water melon venders and window washers and news hawkers. And in addition, up and down the walks were fish vendors, carrying long strings of perch hanging from their backs or pushing their "catch" in rude carts converted from discarded baby carriages. The "junk men" had the middle of the street. These latter have hitched themselves to carts which they have built out of wheels, usually found on dump heaps, and irregular scraps of board gotten from some building in the process of demolition.

A conversation with the fish vendor disclosed this: "Three pounds for two bits, Miss. But sometimes I walk all day to sell three pounds. They's so many o' us on the street, we jus' cuttin' each other's tho'ts. I works wid a partner. A white fellow from the West Side. He stays out to de Lake and sets the nets and catch 'em, an' I walk up an' down an' sells 'em. I gets a quarter outta ev'y dollar I sells. But fish don' bite ev'y day, Miss. 'Pends on how de wind blowin. Ef it ain't blowin' yo' way it jus' sweep de fish out toward de middle o' de Lake an dey don' bite. Fish don' bite ev'y day."

Behind the stone facade of the building down the street a colony of unemployed men and women have drifted in and settled. The building appears gruesomely debauched. Outside doors have disappeared so that it stands open always. Window apertures are stuffed with rags, old clothes, cardboard, wire netting, wooden doors, anything at hand. A side entrance formerly protected by a door is now barricaded by rusted bed springs, stoves and scraps of iron. Throughout the floors are rotted and in places broken out. On the stairways windows have become only great gaps where the cold packs in. All electric wiring has been torn out, all gas piping stripped. Various styles and sizes of coal stoves are used in the different individual "quarters." In the absence of flues these are piped through holes cut through to the outer walls of the building. Passing on the outside when several "quarters" have fires the adjoining vacant lot is a series of smoke puffs at various heights and levels.

Mr. Eason bemoans the wane of parental authority and the loss of prestige by the father.* He cites the miserable example of Mr. S. clinging to the last vestige of medieval male dominance by arbitrarily denying the necessary milk to undernourished Billie even when the money had been especially provided for this. His sole explanation, "the visitor has allowed the money but your father refuses to buy the milk!" That is the strongest indictment of the contemporary family pattern. Parental rule by blind, unreasoning might of authority bulwarked by school, pulpit, press and by the mores, and ultimately conquered by Relief!

For in the past the complete economic dependence of women upon their husbands, children upon their parents, and in turn in sickness and old age, parents upon their children has tended to warp every fine, free impulse in familial relationships. It has created the nagging wife wheedling an underpaid husband for the little luxuries of life which his inadequate wage cannot provide. It has created the demand upon older sisters and brothers to sacrifice their own education to help support younger sisters and brothers.

And so instead of decrying this overthrow of the tyrant-parent the sociologist should rather hasten the day when in addition sickness and invalidity insurance, a comprehensive unemployment insurance act and adequate assistance for the aged will relieve the burden of poor relations on other poor relations.

The fact is that professional social workers have been in intimate daily contact with large segments of the unemployed population for more than five years now. They have had continual access to the case records of thousands of these families. They are thus in possession of the facts to expose and explode these hair trigger conclusions branding the unemployed as malingerers, chiselers and indolent and hopeless parasites. Instead of the too ready indictment of the unemployed condemnation should, it would seem, be directed against the political economy that creates these conditions of mass unemployment and its attendant malnutrition, disease, overcrowding, immorality, delinquency and family disintegration.

* This refers to an article by Prof. Newell D. Eason, in *Opportunity* for December, 1935, to which Miss Edwards is replying in general.

43

YOUTH EXHIBITS A NEW SPIRIT

by Lyonel Florant

A useful account of developments among Afro-American youth—especially
on campuses—appeared in the following essay. Rather characteristically, it
tended to assume that militancy was born at the same time as this author
came of age, but the nineteen-thirties did see a mounting sense of urgency in
rejecting the racism characteristic of the social order.

A new spirit manifests itself among Negro youth. Dissatisfied with
those patterns of thought and action bequeathed them in the past,
they have set about to determine their own solution to their problems,
and to shape their own destiny. The recently formed youth section
of the National Negro Congress is not just another of the numerous
organizations which tend to crop up on the racial horizon ever so
often with a pet line of solution for this or that problem. It represents
an attempt of many organizations to combine their forces, for they
have learned from experience the need for united effort on a minimum
program—if the optimum good is to be achieved for the greatest
number.

It was at the historic National Negro Congress held in Chicago,
February 14–16, that two hundred youth delegates federated their
strength into a youth section. This was no new organization, but an
amalgamation of groups, all of which were interested in and struggling
for economic opportunity for Negro youth, better educational facilities,
adequate recreational provisions, decent living conditions, and a peaceful society—free from lynchings, fascist terror, and the imminence of
war. All types of organizations cast in their lots—church groups, Y's,
Jr. N.A.A.C.P.'s, alumni clubs of many colleges, student groups,
forums, trade unions, and political organizations.

To many, the importance of the undertaking has not yet struck
home. But it has had great significance to those who have worked in
the student movement for years and can recognize its historical origin.
This youth section concretizes a development which has recently
manifested itself in Negro student circles—a tendency to substitute
for a narrow racial outlook an orientation based on class composition.
Negro students are rapidly realizing their identity of interest with the
working class.

As far back as 1933, white and Negro students felt the need for calling a conference at Columbia University to discuss the problems of the Negro students. It was not the old interracial get-together at which hands were shaken "for Jesus' sake," and, after a few sessions of intellectual back-slapping, Negroes and whites returned to their isolated way of living. No, it was a fiery, militant conference, that brought students and professors out of the deep South. The sugary spirit was absent; instead there was a common resolve to go back to the South and, for that matter, many areas of the North, and tackle shoulder to shoulder the problems of discrimination.

Much has taken place since that conference. Most of the Negro students who attended have become militant leaders. both on the campuses and in the working class movement. A few of the events that show the trend of affairs will serve to indicate the development now reaching maturity. Several conferences held in 1933 had as their major topic race prejudice, but two meetings stand out as very significant. One was a conference of students from Negro colleges held at Howard, and the other was the meeting of the National Student League at the same university during the Christmas vacation. This latter conference was again predominantly white, but the fact that it was held on a Negro campus and that several Negro students attended, indicates that already students of both races were coming to the realization that those problems formerly considered wholly Negro were well interlaced with those of white youth and vice versa. The League resolved that only through common struggle against the forces of reaction could solutions be achieved. It proposed militant student organization on the various Negro and white campuses in close co-operation with the labor movement in the locality. About the same time, the Student League for Industrial Democracy, an organization which educated for socialism before its amalgamation with the National Student League to form the American Student Union, made overtures to Negro students to join its ranks.

The repercussions were many and interesting. In Richmond, white students from the University of Virginia and Negroes from Virginia Union went to the state legislature in a body and demanded increased appropriations for their schools. At Virginia State a militant strike was organized against the "Victorian and convent-like atmosphere" which prevailed under the administration. Students at Fisk, under the leadership of the Denmark Vesey Forum, rose as one body in protest against the lynching of Cordie Cheek. That spring saw students from Texas,

Louisiana, Tennessee, and Mississippi assembled at Gulfport, Mississippi under the auspices of the Student Christian Movement. Though not as fully aware of the nature and scope of their problems as were those students at the Columbia conference, there were many who then recognized the need for organized effort to combat many of the limitations on freedom of speech and thought which envelop campus life in the deep South. Even then there were stories of the unemployed sharecroppers taking over court houses in the state of Mississippi for organizational purposes.

National attention soon shifted to Fisk University, cream of the Negro colleges, when word circled the country of the dismissal of Ishmael Flory, a graduate student, who dared to lead students in a protest against jim-crowism at a local theatre. This tyrannical display of authority on the part of the administration and the Uncle Tomism of many Negro as well as white members of the Fisk faculty, shocked the whole student world—white and black. Protest after protest stormed Nashville, students of the Denmark Vesey Forum circulated a petition demanding that the faculty reinstate Flory, and Norman Thomas wired: "Unthinkable for Fisk to support policy of jim-crowism." Flory was never reinstated. Last word states that he is in California leading a day to day struggle in the labor movement.

In the spring of that year white and Negro students held an L.I.D. conference in jim-crow Knoxville, Tennessee. The spirit of united effort had grown by now from a hope to a reality. Here were students in the South crumbling the wall of discrimination with a single battering ram—progressive, determined action.

The year of 1935 found local chapters of the S.L.I.D. and the N.S.L. organized on several Negro college campuses. In almost every case activity had to be carried on underground. Membership in either organization was a basis for expulsion. Yet Negroes rallied to the new approach. Howard students sent a delegation to the Brussels Congress Against War and Fascism as well as carried on a campaign for the freedom of the Scottsboro boys and Angelo Herndon. Two hundred and fifty students marched on April 12 through pouring rain to the gymnasium where a mammoth strike against war and fascism was carried on between the hours of eleven and noon. More than six hundred students refused to attend classes.

At the first American Youth Congress called at New York University, Negro students from all parts of the country joined in the establishment of a bona fide youth organization which united for peace, freedom and security. Throughout the turbulent sessions, Negro youth played an important part. They contributed freely to the discussions which resulted in a complete analysis of racial prejudice and put into words the new ideology which had been evidencing itself at student conferences in the two previous years. There were two features of this new ideology which especially differentiated it from the old: first, was the "awakening" which revealed the economic basis of racial prejudice, and the second was the logical patterning of a class rather than a racial solution.

The reaction of Negro youth organizations has been increasingly favorable to the American Youth Congress. When the Congress met in Detroit last year demands were made by Negro delegates that a special session be devoted to the discussion of the problems of minority groups. At one of these sessions it was pointed out that although Negro organizations had responded to the Congress call in large numbers, in proportion to the problems confronting youth of this generation, the need for organizational activities had not yet been felt on a wide scale among Negroes. The National Negro Congress was then merely an idea born at the Conference on Minorities at Howard University, but not a reality. Yet, the delegates welcomed the proposed federation of organizations interested in the problems of Negro youth, and among the resolutions passed can be found one supporting the organization and its purposes.

It was Edward Strong, Negro vice-chairman of the American Youth Congress who rallied the youth to organize on February 15 at the National Negro Congress with his fiery speech "Youth Demands a Hearing." His concluding remarks are significant enough to warrant quotation:

Out of this crisis the present generation of youth was transformed. Instead of youth living on illusions, we have today a group that looks reality clearly in the face. An ever increasing number of young Negroes understand our basic problem to be an economic one. We have an ever increasing number of young Negroes that understand that these basic economic problems cannot be solved by Negroes alone, but through the cooperative efforts of all people searching for industrial freedom. We have an ever increasing number of young Negroes that understand the needs for unification in our efforts to produce a concrete program through which economic slavery, political disfranchisement, and social inequalities may be eradicated. . . .

How can we unify our efforts? It can be done through building an all-inclusive youth movement that will put a stick of dynamite under the industrial barons that rule this country. Before we leave here we ought to consider and consider very carefully the organizing of a National Federation of Negro youth to come under the general supervision of any permanent agency that it may set up. Such a Congress must include every sector of Negro youth. It must include both organized and unorganized. Youth from the church and the school, from the farm and the factory, from the settlement house and from every type of fraternal, social, and political group. It must include all of those forces of youth, white or black, that stand ready to unite with us in making impossible another Scottsboro. Such a federation would be a tremendous aid in making sure the freedom of Angelo Herndon. . . .

This is the "new spirit." Since February, the national organization has carried on with headquarters in Washington. It has grown tremendously; from every large city comes word of activity. Chicago youth demand a recreational center on the South side and have planned it in detail for the approval of city officials. They have carried their fight against discrimination to the public utilities and demanded jobs for their college graduates and skilled workers. Philadelphia youth as well as those in Atlantic City have led the campaign of the adult group. In the relief agencies they have waged a battle against discrimination and carried on a day to day fight with officials for more W.P.A. jobs for unemployed Negro workers. New York has been the scene of combat with the school board against zoning restrictions which herd Negro high school students into the oldest schools where emphasis is placed on industrial and domestic rather than academic training. These efforts have resulted in promises for two new schools.

As a forerunner to the Southern Youth Conference to be held at Richmond in November, a conference on "The Problems of Negro Students" was called at Howard University May 15–16 under the joint sponsorship of the Howard Committee of the National Negro Congress and the Student Council. Delegates from Columbia, C.C.N.Y., N.Y.U., Temple, Lincoln, Hampton, Bowie Normal, Virginia Union, De Sable High School (Chicago), Western Reserve, New Jersey Teachers College, St. Paul, Downington, A.&I., Ohio State, and several local schools attended. Answering the challenge of Langston Hughes that "Many of our institutions . . . produce spineless Uncle Toms uninformed and full of mental and moral evasions," they fearlessly attacked the outmoded dogmas that cloak student life at Negro schools. Among the most significant resolutions passed by the body were those setting up trade union committees on Negro campuses to function as a sector of the local National Negro Congress Committee, the support of the N.A.A.C.P.'s court struggle for equal educational opportunities and the expression of a willingness to lend that organization mass support in obtaining favorable decisions, the support of the American Youth Act formulated by the American Youth Congress and now pending in Congress, which is the only piece of legislation which adequately provides for the five to seven million youth now unemployed. But most significant of all, is the resolution which reads: "Though Negro students, our problems are not peculiar to Negroes. Throughout America we see our fellow white students become socially conscious and aware of their economic insecurity. In the American Student Union we see an amalgamated force of black and white students realistically facing these problems."

Even the most conservative person could not help but admit that something is taking place among Negro youth—something that has never occurred before. This "new spirit," which Langston Hughes prophetically wrote in 1934 would have to be put in the majority of Negro schools by the students themselves if any hope is to come from the colleges, is now quite evident. Witness the peace strikes and assemblies that took place April twenty-second in such conservative and reactionary colleges as Hampton Institute, Morehouse College, Spelman College, Johnson C. Smith, and several others. These were new centers of interest that added their activity to the veterans at Howard and Virginia Union, while students of five nations joined hands in a determined effort to unite for peace and balk the fascist tendencies brought on by the present economic crisis.

Born out of stark reality and dire necessity the ideology and program of the youth section is bound to penetrate into every corner of Negro life where youth gathers. The paradox of an older generation singing "Happy Am I" in the face of starvation or depending on a deaf and far off God to create a job in a closed-down factory no longer baffles the younger generation. Breaking with tradition which "fetters soul and will," youth is facing the challenge of modern society in increasing numbers and not only demanding a hearing, but forging the youth section of the National Negro Congress, a new weapon capable of attacking and mastering the problems confronting them.

The Crisis, August, 1936; XLIII, 237–38, 253–54.

44

THE STUDY OF THE NEGRO
by George Longe

As the preceding essay had a distinctly current tone, so does the one that follows; with some alteration in dates and names, one might think of it as a study of the interest in what is currently called "Black Studies."

The favorable attitude toward courses in Negro history and Negro literature is of recent development. There have been and are now some difficulties to be encountered in establishing these courses in the public high schools of the South. Some of these difficulties are: crowded curricula offerings in the public high school, overworked teaching staff (heavy schedules and increasing teaching loads), and the difficulty of getting a suitable Negro history textbook. However, the work of teaching Negro history in the Negro public high schools of the South has gone on because of the resourcefulness, zeal and initiative of Negro educators and teachers.

In a recent survey of 174 Negro public high schools in 21 states and the District of Columbia it was found that 50 of these schools were offering courses in Negro history, that most of the courses were established since 1927 and that all of the courses carried full credit.

The survey also showed that these courses were very popular in the densely populated Negro sections of the South. Because of the high degree of race consciousness found in the above mentioned sections, and the separate school system, the South led all sections of the country in the matter of teaching Negro history.

Most of the schools offered the courses for half year with classes meeting five times a week. Woodson's *The Negro in Our History,* and Brawley's *A Short History of the American Negro,* were the textbooks in use. Students after having had these courses showed much interest in Negro problems, had more race pride and self-respect, acquired different points of view of certain periods in American history and showed a pronounced cooperative attitude toward National Negro Health Week, Rosenwald Day, Interracial Sunday and Negro History Week.

In the teaching of Negro literature, as shown by the survey, very little progress had been made in the public high schools. Six Negro high schools out of 174 were offering courses in Negro literature. In all probability it will be a long while before the teaching of Negro literature will become a part of the curriculum in Negro public high schools.

In the Negro colleges the picture is almost complete. The survey reports that 46 of the 48 Negro colleges surveyed were offering courses in Negro history, 29 courses in Negro literature and 29 courses in race relations.

In the white colleges a great interest is being shown by certain white teachers who are taking advantage of the opportunities that some courses offer to acquaint their students with facts about Negro life and history. A government survey made in 1932 reported 95 white colleges of 580 surveyed were offering courses in race relations to their students. These courses were listed as Race Relations, Negro Problems, The American Negro, Immigration and the Negro, Race and Culture, and Problems of Race and Nationality. The coming generations of white Americans should have an enlightened attitude on race questions as a result of these courses.

In many of the advanced colleges and universities several liberal white professors are interested in research in race relations; Dr. Franz Boas and Dr. Melville J. Herskovits in physical anthropology and Dr. Howard Odum and Dr. Johnson in Negro music and folk-lore are among those who have done much toward the movement for the study of the Negro in white colleges and universities.

During 1934, 113 theses and dissertations on and about the Negro were accepted by graduate departments in 35 colleges and universities in 21 states and the District of Columbia.

Other agencies are at work fostering the study of the Negro. Some of these are: Department of Negro History at Xavier University; Department of Records and Research at Tuskegee; Association for the Study of Negro Life and History; Commission on Interracial Cooperation; Commission on Race Relations of the Federal Council of the Churches of Christ in America; and various forums, study groups, clubs, interracial conferences, seminars and public lecture courses.

Because of continuous petitioning on the part of the Federation of Civic Leagues under the leadership of Dr. J. A. Hardin, the Orleans Parish school board through its department of superintendence appointed the writer as chairman of a committee of principals and teachers to write a syllabus for the teaching of Negro history from the first through the eleventh grades, in the colored public schools. The committee set about this most gratifying task and today the work is complete and it is the hope of the committee that each teacher will be provided with a syllabus and that the teaching of Negro history in all of the grades to all of the colored boys and girls will become a reality.

The development of the syllabus in the first four grades was assigned to Miss Pearl Tasker, primary supervisor in the colored public schools, and the work from the fifth through the eleventh grades was under the supervision of the writer.

Grade meetings were called, instructions and assignments were given, and all teachers were encouraged to send in contributions. Central committees were formed and all principals of the colored schools were asked to act as advisers at assigned grade levels. The central committees were to collect and classify all material handed in, the advisers were to criticize that material and offer suggestions for improvements.

The general aims of the work for the first four grades are: to develop appreciation for Negro literature, to portray the beautiful in the Negro race, and to establish an aesthetic basis for future study. Suggestions are given teachers. The poems are classified as poems of nature, of holiday, of romance, of Arbor Day, of patriotism and miscellaneous. Stories about great Negroes are written by the teachers. All of these are graded for the teacher and many suggested activities are given. The music is arranged by grades and consists of songs to be taught (spirituals and secular), and vocal and instrumental recordings are listed for appreciation which offer suggestions for presenting the Negro spirituals.

In the upper grades, from the fifth through the eleventh, each grade has as its aims, outline of subject matter with indication as to when this subject matter should be taught, suggested activities, a bibliography with page references, and lesson plans and units showing the teacher how to correlate the facts of Negro life and history with the regular classroom work in history. Our method is to teach the Negro in history. The general chairman feels confident that the colored boys and girls in the public schools after having been taught these facts concerning Negro life and history will develop a sense of loyalty, and patriotism, and dependability in the Negro of today; greater race pride and self respect. They will be inspired to greater accomplishments, and the course will assist in bringing about a better racial adjustment.

The Crisis, October, 1936; XLIII, 304, 309.

45

PROCLAMATION OF SOUTHERN NEGRO YOUTH: FOR FREEDOM, EQUALITY, AND OPPORTUNITY

The headquarters of the Southern Negro Youth Congress was in Richmond, Virginia. In 1937, when this proclamation was issued, its officers were William F. Richardson, chairman; Edward E. Strong, secretary; Helen Gray, vice-chairman; James Cox, treasurer; Columbus Alston, field representative.

The first page of this printed message, in addition to the title, as given above, carried a photo of the smiling face of Claudia Jones—later victimized by the Smith Act and then deported to England.

We are the Negro youth of the South. We are proud of every inch of Southern soil. We, and our fathers before us, have given our toil and the sweat of our brow that the land of our birth might prosper. We are proud of the generations of the Negro people of the South. We are proud of the traditions of Frederick Douglass, Sojourner Truth, Nat Turner, Harriet Tubman, and other Negro sons and daughters of the South who gave their lives that all men might be free and equal. And we are no less proud of the heritage given to all Americans alike by such fighters for liberty and democracy as Thomas Jefferson and Patrick Henry.

We Negro youth of the South know that ours is the duty to keep alive the traditions of freedom and democracy. We know that ours must be the ceaseless task to win the status of citizenship for the Negro people. From Douglass and Lincoln our hands received the torch of freedom and we shall hold it high.

We realize that the majority of white Southerners are not responsible for the conditions under which we live. These conditions are caused, not by the many—but by the few, those who profit by pitting white labor against black labor to the harm of both. To all white youth of the South we extend our hand in warmest brotherhood. For we know, and we would make them know, that as one rises all must rise, and as one falls all must fall. The right to live as citizens, the right to education, the right to all the benefits of life in a democratic land cannot be fully theirs unless these things are fully ours. We would be friends with them, friends in the deepest sense of the word, working together for our common good.

We have a right to a school that is free and equal; to a home around which the spectre of poverty, sickness, and want does not hover; to playgrounds and swimming pools and all those recreations which build young bodies and make them strong. We have a right to jobs at equal pay for equal work, to jobs which end in no blind alley.

Our generation cannot and must not grow into manhood a voteless generation. We have the right to vote, to serve on juries, to share in the government of this land of ours. We cannot prosper and the South cannot prosper as long as lynching and mob violence shadow our path of progress and stain with the blood of innocent victims the Constitution of our land. Lynching must end. The Jim-Crow system must end. For these are shackles which bind Negro and 'white youth alike.

We who are the sharecroppers and tenant farmers must be freed from the relics of slavery. Peonage must be abolished. We, who till the soil, must be given the opportunity to own land. Negro girls of the South, who toil as domestics, as laundresses, and on the farms must be free from the degradation to which low-paid toil and unequal opportunity now condemn them.

We, who work in mine, mill and factory, must win improved conditions of work and a higher standard of living. We must win the right to organize, with white workers, into large and powerful trade unions —for the union makes us strong.

Our bodies and our souls are destined for higher things than cannon fodder in banker-made wars. For this reason we take our stand with those who fight for peace, with those who fight against war and fascism. The tragic lessons of Ethiopia and Spain teach us that it is the growing menace of fascism which breeds war. We have seen tendencies towards fascism in our own country: the Ku Klux Klan. Realizing that fascism presents a world-wide danger, particularly to minority groups, we must unite with all those forces throughout the world which strike out boldly for the preservation of peace and democracy.

These things must be ours because we know them to be right and just. In our churches and schools we have been taught to love and respect the ideals of the brotherhood of man and the equality of all Americans. We dedicate ourselves to the attainment of these things because we know that America cannot be America to us until we share its benefits as we have gladly shared its burdens.

But we are under no illusions. We know that to win these rights there must be endless work. We know that Negro youth of the South, from church and school, from the plantations, from mine and mill and factory must be united. And for that unity we pledge our lives. Unity for us is no mere phrase. It is the practical device through which we will win our freedom. We will build this unity to win free schools, decent American homes and the right to play. We shall join our hands together to build trade unions in the South free from prejudice. We shall unite in the struggle for the right to work.

We have no higher duty than to bend our backs and lend our joint energies in a struggle to end the Jim-Crow system, to wipe out lynching and mob violence. We will not stop until Angelo Herndon and the nine Scottsboro boys are completely free.

United with youth of every land and every nation we will fight for peace and democracy.

United we will struggle to improve the status of Negro girls—the future Negro womanhood of the South.

Hands locked together and with heads erect we march into the future, fearless and unafraid. We are Americans! We are the hope of our people! We have the right to live!

Four-page folder in editor's possession.

46

ON THE NEED FOR UNITY

by A. Philip Randolph

The keynote speech at the Second Annual Meeting, in 1937, of the National Negro Congress was made by its president, A. Philip Randolph. It exuded the spirit of unity in the struggle against racism and reaction and the sense of confidence coming from the great successes being scored in the work of the infant C.I.O. This was published in the *Proceedings* of that Meeting.

In this hour of crisis in the nation, in the whole wide world, in governments, in industry, in trade union movements and among oppressed minorities everywhere, the Second National Negro Congress, representing hundreds of thousands of Negroes in America, hails the Constitution on its 150th birthday. We hail it as a Magna Charta of human rights. The Negro people, oppressed and persecuted, especially look to the Constitution as an impregnable citadel of their liberties.

Caught between the powerful forces of the southern plantation economy, on the one hand, and the rising financial and industrial power of the north, on the other, the Constitution was a compromise on the question of slavery, but the 13th, 14th, and 15th Amendments sought to chart and establish the guarantees of their full citizenship rights of the Negro people.

Sinister tendencies toward the re-enslavement of the Freedmen manifested themselves soon after the Civil War had ended, and the uncompromising Sumner, and the valiant band of Abolitionists had lost their memorable fight to protect the newly emancipated slaves with federal troops in the south. This unhappy chapter in American history tells of the tragic loss of the liberty of an entire race following the breakdown of the great and inspiring experiment of Reconstruction, rendering the bourbon plantation owners and the former slave-masters free to use the shotgun, the tissue ballot and the Ku Klux Klan terror, to drive the Negro back into a semi-caste status. Indeed, the conditions calculated to achieve the full citizenship for the former slaves were never fulfilled by the Civil War, though the beginning was challenging. Verily, the Constitution, without the force of enlightened public opinion back of it, could not itself effect what a bourgeois revolution did not accomplish.

While the new South with its lumber, turpentine and cotton magnates, went out for cheap labor as its major interest, to pile up high profits, it also attacked the civil rights of the Negro with a view to breaking his hope and faith in the inner redemptive forces of the race so that they would undervalue their human worth and economic role in Southern industry and planting. This created the need and demand for the 14th and 15th Amendments to the Constitution. They were passed. But the due process clause has been employed more as a weapon for defending corporate wealth rather than the human rights of the Negro people. . . .

It is well nigh a truism that without the freedom of speech, of habeas corpus, of the freedom of worship, of the right to vote and be voted for, the basic institutions of modern society, such as the home, family, church, school, press, free business enterprise, trade union movements and associations seeking the liberation of all oppressed minority groups, could hardly exist and enjoy a healthy growth and development.

The Constitution stands as an imposing bulwark of these rights. But the Constitution is not an end in itself. Nor is it a perfect document. It possesses many grave limitations, and needs some fundamental and permanent change so as to make possible reforms for the protection and advancement of the workers. This worthy objective is now courageously sought by President Roosevelt, without the method of constitutional change, in his Supreme Court reorganization plan. Any such change through the method of legislation only, though desirable and timely, may not be so enduring as if wrought through change of the Constitution itself. But let us back the President's fight for judicial justice.

In very truth, the Constitution is a means to an end. The end is the attainment of an enlightened and humane government, and an economic order that will invest the people with the right and the power to live the good life, the more abundant life.

And today, in a world of storm and stress, of confusion and uncertainty, of arrogant cynicism and deadly pessimism, of war and Fascism, the American Constitution proudly reveals its deeper moorings of stability, assurance and hope for democracy.

While the Negro people, under the Constitution, because of nullification by the spirit of the Lost Cause, are still without the full measure of citizenship in the former Confederate States, the Constitution, at least, vouchsafes complete citizenship rights and provides the grounds of principle and promises to secure it.

Albeit, it is more and more becoming correctly understood that the task of realizing full citizenship for the Negro people is largely in the hands of the Negro people themselves. Assuring full citizenship rights to the Afro-American is the duty and responsibility of the State, but securing them is the task of the Negro; it is the task of Labor and the progressive and liberal forces of the nation. Freedom is never given; it is won. And the Negro people must win their freedom. They must achieve justice. This involves struggle, continuous struggle.

True liberation can be acquired and maintained only when the Negro people possess power; and power is the product and flower of organization—organization of the masses, the masses in the mills and mines, on the farms, in the factories, in churches, in fraternal organizations, in homes, colleges, women's clubs, student groups, trade unions, tenants' leagues, in cooperative guilds, political organizations and civil rights associations.

Organization is the purpose and aim of the Second National Negro Congress. While it does not seek, as its primary program, to organize the Negro People into trade unions and civil rights' movements, it does plan to integrate and coordinate the existing Negro organizations into one federated and collective agency so as to develop greater and more effective power. The Congress does not stress or espouse any political faith or religious creed, but seeks to formulate a minimum political, economic and social program which all Negro groups can endorse and for which they can work and fight.

The Congress supports the fight of the National Association for the Advancement of Colored People for a federal anti-lynching bill, for around this issue there is no basic difference of opinion among Negroes. All Negro people desire and seek fair opportunities for work and the right to join trade unions. No one can object to a proposal for more and better jobs, the abolition of Jim-crow labor unions, and for equal educational chances in public schools and universities.

It may not be amiss to add also, in this connection, that the Congress is not Communist or Republican, Democratic or Socialist. It is not Methodist, Baptist or Christian Scientist. It avoids control by any single religion or political party. It shuns the Scylla and Charybdis of the extreme left and the extreme right. But, in the true spirit of the united front, and in the pattern and purpose of integration and coordination, for mass strength, embraces all sections of opinion among the Negro people. It does not seek to impose any issue of philosophy upon any organization or group, but rather to unite varying and various organizations, with various and varying philosophies, left, center, and right among the Negro people upon a simple, minimum program so as to mobilize and rally power and mass support behind vital issues affecting the life and destiny of the race.

Be it also known that the Congress does not seek to change the American form of government, but rather to implement it with new and rugged morals and spiritual sinews to make its democratic traditions, forms and ideals more permanent and abiding and a living force.

Startling changes, economic, political and social, have come upon the world. The empire of the Kaiser, apparently rock-ribbed and as steadfast as the sun, has been replaced by the totalitarian Third Reich. The Italian democratic state has given way to a corporate, fascist system. And the Czar, of all the Russias, has been relegated to oblivion by the Soviets of the workers.

And even if the honored democracies of the United States, England and France, have not succumbed and capitulated to the drastic and dangerous pattern of the dictator, they are under constant, menacing stress and strain of tendencies toward the rule of fascist force. Deadlocked, withal, in a mighty struggle for supremacy are the governments by the rule of "The man on horseback" and governments by rule of a free people.

Add to our existing political disorder reflected in the amazing and rapid transformation of the structure and direction of modern governments, economic maladjustments as seen in world-wide chronic and permanent unemployment, monetary fluctuations and industrial instability, the ever rising threat of a widening sweep of the wave of war, then optimism and hope are shattered and replaced by pessimism and fear.

Already, large areas of the world are in the flames of war. The "little brown men" of militaristic Nippon are raining fire and destruction upon the land of Confucius, but the Chinese people, proud in their noble heritage, are defending their country with matchless courage and resolve, yielding no single inch of territory except under the imperative of superior force.

And when we turn our eyes to the West, to the Mediterranean, we witness the vile and vicious efforts of Mussolini and Hitler, in accordance with the terms of a Berlin-Rome axis seeking to encompass by open murder the destruction of democracy. Lulled and solaced in conscience by the non-intervention sham, the democratic nations, England, France and the United States, are observing defenseless women and children of the legitimate Loyalist government of Spain massacred in shocking barbarism by the hordes of Franco, backed by the money and men in Italy and Germany. Whither doth it lead, comes the query?

It is well nigh accepted quite generally by the thoughtful peoples everywhere that if the dikes of democracy break in the land of the little Iberian peninsula, a world flood of fascism may not be far behind, and imperil free peoples everywhere.

This may be the tragic price that mankind must pay for its complacent and timid spirit before the brutal and ruthless aggression by Japan upon China in creating the puppet kingdom of Manchukuo, and the cruel and savage invasion of the ancient kingdom of Ethiopia by the fascist legions of Italy. The independence of Ethiopia has been sold down the river by the League of Nations, while winked at by England and France.

And when we return to our shores, we find closer at home that all is not well. Despite signs of some recovery from the depression, unemployment trenches hard upon eight million. Unemployment has taken on the picture of permanency. Production in certain industries increases while the workers decrease. The development of the machine, the refinements in management and the concentration and centralization of economic power in trusts and holding companies make this possible. With grave warning, President Roosevelt has declared that one-third of the population is in ill health, underfed, underhoused and underclothed. Relief needs have not appreciably lessened, for jobs are still scarce for the workers.

Civil rights, in industrial areas, where conflict between labor and capital is on, are arrogantly disregarded and broken down by pliant municipal representatives, and extra-governmental organizations such as the Ku Klux Klan, the Black Legion and other vigilante movements.

But not only are the rights of the workers assailed by vigilante mobs at the behest of the Liberty League and the organized open-shop business interests of America, but in State Legislatures and Congress, die-hard tories, such as Senator Vandenberg and others, are seeking to enact legislation, forcing upon trade unions and corporations, compulsory arbitration and the elimination of strikes.

And as we look to Labor we find its house divided. Thus it is obvious that the great problem of the workers in America today is the problem of unity. . . . Craft and industrial unionism can and must go side by side in the struggle of the workers for industrial democracy. These forms of organization must develop and function in one house of labor. Now, what of the Negro in relation to these problems?

The Negro people are an integral part of the American commonwealth. They, like our white brothers, bleed and die in war. They suffer and hunger in the depression. Thus, theirs is the task of consolidating their interests with the interest of the progressive forces of the nation. Collective bargaining brings power to black as well as to white workers. The abolition of the company union frees the Negro workers from economic bondage and enables them to express their voice in the determination of wage rates, hours and working conditions the same as it does for white workers. Thus, the strengthening of the labor movement, the improvement of labor standards, brings comfort, health and decency to black as well as to white workers.

But there are other problems that the Negro people face. In the South there is a blight of Jim-crowism, segregation, disfranchisement through grandfather clauses and lily white primaries and the terror of the Ku Klux Klan.

Peonage, a form of involuntary servitude, in utter nullification of the 13th Amendment, holds the Negro in many Southern states in a condition of virtual slavery. Negro tenant farmers are browbeaten, persecuted and driven, when they evince any semblance of independence [they are driven] out of their miserable and squalid shacks onto the highway. Civil and political rights for them are virtually unknown. Differentials in wages and hours of work are a common practice. Relief, though given by the Federal Government is administered by whim of Southern prejudice in the mood of arrogant superiority. What can be done about this? The answer is:

Let us build a united front of all Negro organizations, of varying strata, purpose and outlook. Let us build a united front in cooperation with the progressive and liberal agencies of the nation whose interests are common with Black America.

With the spirit and strategy of the United Front, the five remaining Scottsboro Boys can be released from their dark dungeon in Alabama. With it peonage in the South can be wiped out and the share cropper and tenant farmers, black and white, can organize and improve their economic status through collective bargaining. With it the horror of lynching in America may be eliminated and mob terror relegated to oblivion.

Thus, on the occasion of the 150th Anniversary of the American Constitution, and the Second Anniversary of the National Negro Congress, the Negro peoples face the future, with heads erect and souls uncurbed, resolved to march forward in the van of progress, with hope and faith in the creation of a new and better world. And the Congress shall help to guide them, to lead them on!

What now of the stewardship of the Congress since its memorable bow to black and white America?

Can more be said than that it has fought a good fight? It has kept the faith. It has worked and not grown weary for a happier humanity.

On the far-flung battle lines of steel, it marshalled militant black men to march in the van with the C.I.O. to chalk up an enviable record in bringing workers into the field of industrial organization. And it has worked with the American Federation of Labor. Our men did not fail or faint before blood or bullets—in South Chicago, Detroit, Michigan, Ohio and Pennsylvania.

The Congress has brought eager and aggressive black youth to grapple with the problem of the organization of the tobacco workers in Virginia. And these youth are winning their spurs.

To the laundry workers in Washington, D.C., the Congress is carrying the message of trade union organization. And it enlisted Negro organizers to join C.I.O. forces to organize the automobile industry.

On the civil and political rights' front, the Congress joined the fighting forces of the National Association for the Advancement of Colored People, to battle for the Wagner-Gavagan federal anti-lynching bill.

And to the rescue of Herndon and the Scottsboro Boys, the Congress has carried its unflagging fighting spirit.

But not only has it fought in the front for the defense of the rights of the Negro People, the Congress has also thrown its might with the progressive forces in the land to aid in the cause of Spanish Democracy, the independence of China from the domination of Japan, and the restoration of Haile Selassie to an independent Kingdom of Ethiopia.

Yes it has joined the great demonstration of the nation against war and fascism. And, too, it is stirring the women and youth of the Negro people to join and struggle with the national and world agencies of their groups for a better world.

Therefore, with humble pride we cry out of the depths of our souls to mankind everywhere: Forward with the destruction of the imperialist domination and oppression of the great peoples of Africa! Forward to the abolition of the fascist rule of Italy over the noble, independent, and unconquerable men of Ethiopia! Forward to the creation of a united, free and independent China! Forward to victory of the valiant loyalist armies over the fascist brigands of Franco! Long live the cause of world peace! Long live the spirit of world democracy! Long live the memory and love of the Black Revolutionists of the 19th Century, led by Denmark Vesey, Nat Turner, Gabriel, Harriet Tubman, Sojourner Truth, and Frederick Douglass! Long live the valor of those black regiments of slaves and freedmen whose blood and courage made Lincoln's Emancipation Proclamation a living reality!

Forward to the unity of the workers! Forward to democracy and freedom, progress and plenty! Forward with the torch of Education, the instrument of agitation, the weapon of organization to a day of peace on earth and toward men, good will!

47

THE NEGRO WORKER
IN THE NINETEEN-THIRTIES
by T. Arnold Hill

The fullest contemporary description of economic conditions confronting the Afro-American people during the depression was the book *The Negro and Economic Reconstruction*, by T. Arnold Hill, who had been executive secretary of the Chicago Urban League and at this time was director, Department of Industrial Relations of the National Urban League. This work was part of a series edited by Alain Locke; it is of some interest that originally Locke asked Dr. Du Bois to write on this subject for the series. Du Bois did produce a study of "The Negro and the New Deal" but Locke rejected it—after paying Du Bois for his work. Du Bois' manuscript will soon be rescued from the unpublished condition to which its quite critical tone then consigned it.

Whether the plight of Negro workers began three centuries ago, or whether it is of more recent origin, the fact is that the Negro remains the most insecure man in a program planned for the protection and utilization of the millions of workers neglected and exploited in the broil between men and money. In latter years the traditional job insecurity has been intensified by pressure from conditions of comparatively recent beginning.

No group suffered more severe devastation in the depression period than did the workers in agriculture and household employment—the two major classifications in which Negroes predominate. Government reports teem with evidence of unemployment and dire want throughout the agricultural regions of the country. The number of workers in the domestic service classification who found themselves on relief during the whole period of unemployment, was greatly out of proportion to the rest of the workers.

The effect of unemployment upon these groups as revealed in a study of "Six Rural Problem Areas"[1] was summarized in a Government release which included the following quotations:

Approximately half of the heads of relief families in this area in June 1934, had usually been tenant farmers, sharecroppers or farm laborers. This area had the highest proportion of totally unemployed on rural relief of any problem area reflecting the great extent to which farmers had lost their land. About 70 percent of all relief family heads were unemployed. The other 30 percent were employed, but earning too little to live on their jobs or farming.

About 19 percent of the whites and about 38 percent of Negroes were regarded as incapable of self-support in any occupation.

Negroes got less relief than whites, and much less chance at work relief. While 35 percent of the whites had work relief only, but 18 percent of the Negroes had work relief only.

The white families received an average of $13 a month relief, and the Negroes received an average of $7, the lowest of any area except the Western cotton.

That the pressure among household employees worked havoc among the domestic and personal service employees is also proved from numerous Federal Government figures,[2] from which the following are extracted: Of one and a half million Negro workers in domestic and personal service, more than 275,000 of them were on relief in March

[1] Federal Emergency Relief Administration. *Six Rural Problem Areas.*
[2] Works Progress Administration. *Workers on Relief in the United States: March, 1935.* A Census of Usual Occupations. Table 3, p. 13.

1935. Included among these were 125,000 servants in private families, 42,000 laundresses outside of laundries, 15,000 porters, and 17,000 cleaners and charwomen.

The second factor which steered Negro workers into an unfavorable position, came from the impact of skilled workers who moved down into unskilled fields, as is customary during periods of business dislocation. Skilled workers, better paid in normal times, are willing in a crisis to accept semi-skilled or even unskilled jobs rather than give up entirely. Some 82 percent of all employed workers receiving urban relief in 1934 were working at jobs below their usual occupational level. Fully 90 percent of Negro workers in industry fall into the marginal or unskilled class. This accounts for the terrific amount of unemployment among Negroes in cities; which, as is commonly known, is out of proportion to their actual numbers in the population.

From a list of selected cities which follows,[3] it is clear that the percent of Negroes among employables on relief in 1935 was greatly in excess of the ratio of Negroes to the total population:

City	Percent Negro in total population: 1930	Percent Negro among employables on relief: 1935
Atlanta, Ga.	33.4	65.7
Birmingham, Ala.	38.2	63.3
Charlotte, N.C.	30.4	75.2
Cincinnati, O.	10.6	43.5
Kansas City, Mo.	9.6	37.2
New York, N.Y.	4.7	11.2
Norfolk, Va.	33.9	81.3
St. Louis, Mo.	11.4	41.5
Wilmington, Del.	11.3	43.9

By January 1935, these conditions had culminated in one-fourth of the total Negro population being on relief as compared with 15.5 percent of whites and other races on relief.

A report of the Federal Emergency Relief Administration[4] indicates that:

An analysis of twenty-three states, each having a total Negro population of 100,000 or more in 1930, revealed that the largest urban proportion occurred

[3] Federal Emergency Relief Administration. *Survey of Occupational Characteristics of Persons on Relief.* April, 1935.
[4] *Monthly Report of the Federal Emergency Relief Administration,* March 1 through March 31, 1936.

in Missouri, New Jersey, and Ohio, each having approximately four times as great a percentage of Negroes as of whites on urban relief rolls.

Altogether, while Negroes comprised one-tenth of the total population of the United States, they have comprised an average of approximately one-sixth of the relief population.

The results of the pressure of whites upon Negro workers are seen not only in the high percentage of the latter on relief, but in the loss of status in types of employment in which large numbers have heretofore been engaged. There was actual supplanting of Negroes in bulk on particular jobs or in particular factories where they were employed as household employees, bellmen, waiters, elevator operators, railroad track laborers, diggers of ditches, drivers of wagons and carts. Evidence of the replacement of Negroes in these accustomed fields is everywhere so noticeable that specific instances do not have to be mentioned.

So continuous has been this substitution of whites for Negroes that it has caused many leaders to proclaim that conditions are worse for Negroes than they have been at any time since 1860. It has baffled educational authorities, who, knowing that the public is not yet willing to accept Negroes in all fields, and realizing that business houses are switching from Negroes to whites, are wondering which fields students should prepare themselves to enter.

The impact of this rivalry for status has intensified racial friction at the point of greatest irritation—trade unionism. Negroes have vehemently criticized the American Federation of Labor because it has refused to intervene against the discrimination of its nationals and internationals. The A. F. of L. has retorted in the language it has always employed, namely, that it is not opposed to Negro membership, but cannot compel its autonomous bodies to follow the edict of democratic action it has set for itself. In 1918 the A. F. of L. was memorialized by a group representing the National Urban League. At frequent intervals since, this same organization, and the National Association for the Advancement of Colored People, have constantly called the attention of the A. F. of L. to flagrant abuses on the part of various nationals and locals. Numerous resolutions have been presented on the floor of recent Conventions by Negro labor leaders.

But the A. F. of L. continues to refuse Negro members, unmoved by the certainty that poorly-paid, unorganized Negro labor will ultimately depress the wages of white organized workers. Flagrant abuses against the workers of the nation, though nullified during the depression, were not sufficient to instill realism in a movement which needs the unification of all workers to secure decent guarantees and recognition as a bargaining unit.

The plight of the Negro employed in the railroad industry is a tragic illustration of union hypocrisy. Of the 162,630 Negroes employed on railroads, all except porters, maintenance of way workers and certain shop employees are excluded from membership in those unions that are the bargaining agencies for railroad employees, known as the Brotherhood of Railway Trainmen. The problems faced by Negroes in this field have been summarized by one authority:[5]

1. The non-inclusion of or discrimination against Negroes as practiced by the four transportation brotherhoods, several of the shop crafts, and the telegraphers and the maintenance of way employees;
2. The prejudicial contracts between railroads and certain unions that limit and tend to reduce the number of Negro employees;
3. The resorting to physical violence (and other unfair tactics) as methods of reducing the number of Negroes employed as trainmen and switchmen on certain roads.

The result of deliberate discrimination of railroad brotherhoods against Negro employees in their contractual relations with carriers is well illustrated by the extent those contracts "negotiated during the last few years have prevented Negroes from regaining the place which they held on Southern roads before War industries attracted so many of them to more remunerative jobs. The Southern Railroad, where the firing force was 80 percent black before the War now employs but 10 percent colored firemen on its central division. On the Atlantic Coast Line the percentage has been reduced from 90 to 80. On the Seaboard Air Line the ratio has fallen from 90 to 50 percent, and the Brotherhood has recently been seeking a contract to reduce it to 40 percent. On the Shreveport division of the Illinois Central, where white firemen worked on a fifty-fifty basis, the Brotherhood has also been seeking a contract confining blacks to 40 percent of the jobs."[6]

The following excerpt, taken from a 1927 agreement between the Atlanta Joint Terminals and its firemen and hostler helpers, illustrates how union strategy has been used to reduce Negro trainmen:

White firemen will be given preference over Negro firemen in filling all jobs when the following changes in conditions of work are made:
(1) A change of 30 minutes or more in the starting time of a job.
(2) Filling vacancies.
(3) Creation of new jobs.

[5] Reid, Ira De. A. *The Employment of Negroes on Railroads*. National Urban League. 1933. p. 1 (Unpublished study.)
[6] Spero, Sterling D., and Harris, Abram L., *The Black Worker*. p. 306.

Violence has been resorted to as a means of eliminating Negroes from employment in transportation. In 1932 a reign of terror, a revival of similar tactics used in 1919 and 1920, resulted in the murder of seven Negro trainmen and in injury to more than ten others in the employ of the Illinois Central Railroad. In addition, others have been falsely accused of violating rules and regulations and discharged after prejudiced trials. The "Big Four" Railroad Brotherhoods have been attempting to lobby a "full crew" bill through Congress, which, if passed, will hasten the elimination of Negroes from positions as trainmen. The bill calls for a full crew on a train, to consist of a front end brakeman, a flag man, conductor, engineer and fireman. Most of the 2,743 Negroes who do the tasks of a front-end brakeman are classified as porters and thus eliminated from union protection.

The organization of the Brotherhood of Sleeping Car Porters and Maids is the one advanced step in unionism among Negroes. It came after continuous and persistent activity extending over a period of twelve years. Before union recognition was granted, the minimum wage paid porters was never higher than $77.50 per month. Hours averaged from 400 to 600 a month, and overtime, if and when granted, began after a porter had traveled 11,000 miles during the month. Each porter was expected to report four hours before train time each trip without pay, to prepare his car for service.

Under the direction of A. Philip Randolph as president, the Brotherhood grew to that point where the Pullman Company was forced to recognize the right of the union to bargain collectively for porters and maids. The contract as recently signed grants a 240-hour month, time and one-half for overtime, a minimum wage of $89.50 a month for the first year with progressive increases to $100.50, and abolition of the company union known as the Pullman Porters and Maids Protective Association. Over 8,000 porters and maids benefited by a wage increase of $1,152,000 for 1937.

There are several other important efforts now under way to meet the problems of Negroes employed by railroads. A newcomer to this field is the Association of Railway Employees, an industrial union which is trying to serve Negro shopmen, brakemen, switchmen and firemen by challenging the legality of contracts that discriminate against those not party to the contract. Another is the International Brotherhood of Red Caps, formed in 1937, which has been successful in completing negotiations in several large cities for improved wages and hours for station employees. Dining car waiters and cooks have several organizations and numerous contracts giving them better wages and shorter hours. They are now attempting to merge with other transportation units for a solid national front in this field. The newly organized Transport Workers' Union, an industrial union affiliated with the Committee for Industrial Organization, includes a number of Negro workers. Its strength is now limited to electric railways and buses. The International Brotherhood of Firemen and Oilers, an American Federation of Labor affiliate, is now admitting Negro railroad employees, though the organization is not basically a transportation union.

The one bright star in an otherwise dark union firmament, is the democratic policy of the Committee for Industrial Organization. In the unions of workers in the manufacture of steel, automobiles and garments, Negro membership is large. They are also members of the unions for electrical, transport, laundry and food workers. In the professional unions such as those for clerks, social workers, and newspaper employees, Negroes are also to be found. The C.I.O. is unique among existing American labor movements, not only in its philosophy, but in its policy of equality for all workers, Negro as well as white.

How did the various Governmental agencies relieve the unemployment pressure among Negroes? The Recovery agencies were helpful in ameliorating the suffering of the total population, irrespective of race, color, or religion. When assistance involved direct relief, housing, commodities, or camping, it reached a larger proportion of Negro families than when it involved work relief. As to administrative positions, whether in Washington or in local areas, there was not the slightest approach to a fair balance between Negroes and whites. Clerks, investigators, interviewers, intake workers and supervisors were employed throughout the country in relief and W.P.A. offices, though each category was not everywhere represented. There were wide variations between Negroes and whites in the size of relief grants, the number of workers on projects and salaries paid staff members.

The regular or normal departments of the Federal Government, varied little from the established practices of racial discrimination which in one form or another have long permeated the Washington scene. Recently established permanent bureaus, continuing the pattern of racial segregation, have followed the precedent of equality in service but discrimination in employment.

Local units of government responsible for administration in their areas, are blamed by Washington for unfair racial practices, but they have been much more liberal in according professional and white collar opportunities than has the Federal Government itself. In succeeding paragraphs an attempt has been made to summarize briefly the relationship of the Negro to the emergency program.

The National Recovery Administration (N.R.A.), which acted on Codes presented by the employer group, permitted wage differentials to be so devised as to force Negro workers into a separate orbit by the payment of wages to them lower than those paid whites for comparable classes of employment. While the discharges of Negroes from customary occupations preceded the introduction of the N.R.A., it is a fact that as wages were raised by virtue of the N.R.A., employers dismissed their Negro workers in order to pay the higher wage to whites. This cannot be charged against the intent of the law as drafted, but it does raise the question as to whether or not the N.R.A. proved of benefit or of harm to Negroes engaged in unprotected occupations in the South. Further, it raises the question as to the efficacy of a measure which does not provide for effective standardized administration of the provisions contained therein. This is not true of the Wagner Labor Relations Act, for under it workers may not be dismissed because of their labor union affiliation. Had it been possible under the N.R.A. to prevent the dismissal of workers when the Codes forced a higher wage, the N.R.A. would not have played into the hands of prejudicial racial sentiment.

Similarly grants under the Agricultural Adjustment Act (A.A.A.), intended for Negro farmers, were often dissipated and misappropriated. The large farm owners took advantage of illiterate sharecroppers and tenant farmers, whose checks in most instances were paid direct to the owner or manager of the plantation, who in turn was never too careful that the proceeds reached the hands of the dependent farmers. It was the dishonesty of the plantation managers and farm owners, practiced against both white and Negro farm workers, and encouraged by the administrative procedures of the A.A.A., that was the occasion for the organization of unions among the sharecroppers in the South. The original regulations have been so changed that crop payments must be made directly into the hands of the farm workers; but rural relief, as administered by the Federal and local units of Government, still makes an unfavorable difference in relief grants as between Negroes and whites.

Not even relief as formerly administered by the Federal Emergency Relief Administration (F.E.R.A.), and later in the shape of jobs, as administered by the Works Progress Administration (W.P.A.), has been free from numerous inequalities. Relief in kind—food allowances, clothing, commodity surpluses and the like—approximated fairness in many communities, particularly in the North; but work relief has been unequal in the clerical and white collar positions, even when it was reasonably adequate for unskilled workers. Skilled workers have also had little opportunity, and objection to Negroes working in certain places while on W.P.A. was never too forcefully met. Several special national projects and many local ones provided employment to professional and white collar Negroes in a wide range of occupations. In the South, figures published by the various relief organizations prove conclusively that separate budget allowances for Negroes resulted in much smaller grants for them than for other people.

A program of major significance to the employment and housing of Negroes has been the slum clearance and low-cost housing activities conducted under the Public Works Administration (P.W.A.). Housing congestion has been somewhat relieved in Indianapolis, Atlanta, Cleveland, New York, and a number of other cities as a result of this program. Out of a total of 47 units, 26 will be used fully or partially by Negroes. Projects in which Negroes are to live will be staffed in whole or in part with Negro personnel, and are of fireproof or semi-fireproof construction. They will be furnished with modern electrical and gas appliances, and will have facilities for recreation and health.

Under the Public Works Administration, contracts drawn for housing construction stipulated that the proportion of Negroes in skilled trades in a given city in 1930 should serve as the basis for their employment. A Negro staff in the Housing Division, combined, along with other duties, the responsibility of checking and enforcing this regulation.

The National Youth Administration (N.Y.A.), has come the nearest to meeting adequately the relief situation among Negro youth, with a staff of assistants at the head of a Negro Department. There are State and local supervisors in the districts in which large numbers of Negroes live, and N.Y.A. educational and work grants have been widely distributed among Negro people eligible for such support.

Since it began in 1933, the Civilian Conservation Corps (C.C.C.), has made progress in its treatment of Negroes, although its policy of segregation is, of course, to be condemned. And, too, its methods of recruiting have been criticized in various sections of the country. The C.C.C. now employs Negro Educational Advisers, and other staff members in Negro camps, but there is still a shortage of technical employees. The colored work is supervised by a Negro who is a member of the Director's staff.

Throughout the whole process of Government subsidy, as illustrated especially by the Home Owners' Loan Corporation (H.O.L.C.), the

Federal Housing Administration (F.H.A.), the Tennessee Valley Authority (T.V.A.), there was either gross neglect of the claims of Negroes, or assignment to jobs within certain limited categories; although the Farm Security Administration (and its predecessor the Resettlement Administration) has shown a fairly liberal attitude in its employment of technicians and professional workers, and the program has likewise benefited Negroes. To a limited degree, architects, draftsmen and research specialists have been employed in several other Recovery bureaus.

Segregation or complete exclusion is a fixity in the older departments such as the Government Printing Office, the Army, and the Navy. Clerks and stenographers, when they qualify for positions in Government service, have been refused appointments when their racial identity became known.

Discrimination has been carried over into the administration of the Federal Civil Service. It is flagrantly apparent in the administration of the Social Security Board. Despite the fact that good grades were made by Negroes in recent examinations given by the Civil Service Commission, there probably is no full-time paid employee of the Social Security Board at its national headquarters, above the status of messenger, and only a handful in some 336 Regional and Field offices, save for a group of less than two hundred housed in Baltimore.

It should be mentioned that certain departments recognized the dilemma of Negroes and attempted to make adjustment through Negro Advisers, or Assistants, whose business it was to check complaints and restrict unfair practices as much as possible. Among the Recovery bureaus that adopted such a practice were the W.P.A., the Department of Interior in conjunction with the P.W.A., the N.Y.A., the A.A.A., the Farm Credit Administration, the C.C.C., and the Farm Security Administration. Among the regular branches of the Government were the Departments of Commerce, Justice and Labor, the Bureau of the Census, and the Office of Education. Up to the limit of their power, these officials have been helpful in receiving, reporting and adjusting complaints.

When it is remembered that Negroes form 11 per cent of the total working population, it should have been possible for the Department of Labor to place more people at work in the various Bureaus of its large office. The other Departments would appear equally culpable, except for the fact that the Department of Labor is committed by statute to improving conditions among working people. It does make studies of Negro workers, and knows all the conditions of their employment and unemployment; yet it fails to touch the problem at its most vital point, namely, offering them an equal chance for employment and thus setting an example for others. There is a Negro Assistant in the United States Employment Service who has several workers on his staff; but there is no one in the Women's Bureau, no one on the regular staff of the Children's Bureau, no one in the Conciliation Service, nor in the important Bureaus of Labor Statistics and Labor Standards. When Negroes have passed merit examinations given for the State Employment Services, the Department of Labor contends that it is without power to secure their appointments; despite the fact that the Federal Government contributes 50 percent of the funds when State Services have qualified by meeting the standards set by the Department of Labor.

The final answer to the effectiveness of Government support to Negroes during the depression is that while they were not neglected, they were also not helped in proportion to the degree of unemployment that existed among them. Prejudice was beaten back frequently, and flagrant abuses were often corrected, but there was no recognition of the magnitude of the problem and no unified comprehensive plan made to remove or adjust unfair racial practices. A Negro's chance of securing a position as bureau chief, division head, auditor, accountant, stenographer or clerk, has improved but little, and as a result the total number of colored employees in the Washington offices, aside from postal employees, messengers and elevator operators, is negligible.

A hurried glance at huge Government staffs in Washington—so large in many instances that buildings outside of the business area have to be rented to house them—will convince the most skeptical that the Federal Government, the largest employer of labor in the country, draws the color line against Negroes as effectively as do private corporations. How successful can Government officials be in increasing employment opportunities for Negroes in private industry, when their own policies result in such definite discriminatory practices?

Small wonder, therefore, that the relief figures in Washington, D.C., show a greater disparity as between whites and Negroes than in any place in the country. In 1933, out of a population of 132,068, 28,850 Negroes were on relief, or 21.8 percent of the total; whereas only 8,591 whites out of a total of 353,914, or 2.4 percent, were unemployed.[7]

[7] Federal Emergency Relief Administration. *Unemployment Relief Census: October 1933.* Report No. 1.

Negro workers are insecure and will remain insecure as long as individuals in positions to change habits and morals remain adamant and afraid. Private industry and Government employment are both in the hands of persons to whom democracy is a shibboleth and not a course of action. All important Federal officials have had their attention called repeatedly to discrimination against Negroes. Some defied it—still others shifted it—and some went reasonably far, considering the depths of restriction existing beforehand—but none entirely removed it.

With 24 percent of the total Negro population on relief, private industry (according to a special study in six selected cities),[8] absorbed Negroes from relief rolls only one-half as frequently as it did whites, although Negroes went on relief to a degree twice as great as whites.

A public assistance program relieving at the point of greatest stress and need; a Government serving its citizens justly and mercifully; a labor union movement endeavoring to protect the interests of the masses; business men eager to increase consumer purchases—each has a part to play in righting a social system so grossly uneconomic. Bad as the Negro's economic plight is, individually considered, it is even more grave and significant as a symptom of general unbalance and maladjustment.

T. Arnold Hill, *The Negro and Economic Reconstruction* (Washington, 1937) (Associates in Negro Folk Education; Bronze Booklet Series No. 3, edited by Alain Locke), pp. 50–66.

48

TOO MUCH OF RACE

by Langston Hughes

Langston Hughes, as a delegate from the United States, delivered the following speech to the Second International Writers Congress, held in Paris in July, 1937. It reflects something of the time to observe that it was published in full in the organ of the N.A.A.C.P.

Members of the Second International Writers Congress, comrades, and people of Paris: I come from a land whose democracy from the very beginning has been tainted with race prejudice born of slavery, and

[8] Federal Emergency Relief Administration. *Monthly Report of the F.E.R.A., March 1 through March 31, 1936.*

whose richness has been poured through the narrow channels of greed into the hands of the few. I come to the Second International Writers Congress representing my country, America, but most especially the Negro peoples of America, and the poor peoples of America—because I am both a Negro and poor. And that combination of color and of poverty gives me the right then to speak for the most oppressed group in America, that group that has known so little of American democracy, the fifteen million Negroes who dwell within our borders.

We are the people who have long known in actual practice the meaning of the word Fascism—for the American attitude towards us has always been one of economic and social discrimination: in many states of our country Negroes are not permitted to vote or to hold political office. In some sections freedom of movement is greatly hindered, especially if we happen to be sharecroppers on the cotton farms of the South. All over America we know what it is to be refused admittance to schools and colleges, to theatres and concert halls, to hotels and restaurants. We know jim-crow cars, race riots, lynchings, we know the sorrows of the nine Scottsboro boys, innocent young Negroes imprisoned some six years now for a crime that even the trial judge declared them not guilty of having committed, and for which some of them have not yet come to trial. Yes, we Negroes in America do not have to be told what Fascism is in action. We know. Its theories of Nordic supremacy and economic suppression have long been realities to us.

And now we view it on a world scale: Hitler in Germany with the abolition of labor unions, his tyranny over the Jews, and the sterilization of the Negro children of Cologne; Mussolini in Italy with his banning of Negroes on the theatrical stages, and his expedition of slaughter in Ethiopia; the Military Party in Japan with their little maps of how they'll conquer the whole world and their savage treatment of Koreans and Chinese; Batista and Vincent, the little American-made tyrants of Cuba and Haiti; and now Spain and Franco with his absurd cry of "Viva España" at the hands of Italians, Moors and Germans invited to help him achieve "Spanish Unity." Absurd, but true.

We Negroes of America are tired of a world divided superficially on the basis of blood and color, but in reality on the basis of poverty and power—the rich over the poor, no matter what their color. We Negroes of America are tired of a world in which it is possible for any group of people to say to another: "You have no right to happiness, or freedom, or the joy of life." We are tired of a world where forever we work for someone else and the profits are not ours. We are tired of a world where, when we raise our voices against oppression, we are immediately jailed, intimidated, beaten, sometimes lynched. Nicolas Guillen has been in prison in Cuba, Jacques Romaine, in Haiti, Angelo Herndon in the United States. Today a letter comes from the great Indian writer, Raj Anand, saying that he cannot be with us here in Paris because the British police in England have taken his passport from him. I say, we darker peoples of the earth are tired of a world in which things like that can happen.

And we see in the tragedy of Spain how far the world oppressors will go to retain their power. To them now the murder of women and children is nothing. Those who have already practiced bombing the little villages of Ethiopia now bomb Guernica and Madrid. The same Fascists who forced Italian peasants to fight in Africa now force African Moors to fight in Europe. They do not care about color when they can use you for profits or for war. Japan attempts to force the Chinese of Manchuria to work and fight under Japanese supervision for the glory and wealth of the Tokio bourgeoisie—one colored people dominating another at the point of guns. Race means nothing when it can be turned to Fascist use. And yet race means everything when the Fascists of the world use it as a bugaboo and a terror to keep the working masses from getting together. Just as in America they tell the whites that Negroes are dangerous brutes and rapists, so in Germany they lie about the Jews, and in Italy they cast their verbal spit upon the Ethiopians. And the old myths of race are kept alive to hurt and impede the rising power of the working class. But in America, where race prejudice is so strong, already we have learned what the lies of race mean—continued oppression and poverty and fear—and now Negroes and white sharecroppers in the cotton fields of the South are beginning to get together; and Negro and white workers in the great industrial cities of the North under John L. Lewis and the C.I.O. have begun to create a great labor force that refuses to recognize the color line. Negro and white stevedores on the docks of the West coast of America have formed one of the most powerful labor unions in America. Formerly the unorganized Negro dockworkers—unorganized because the white workers themselves with their backward ideology didn't permit Negroes in their unions—formerly these Negro workers could break a strike. And they did. But now both Negroes and whites are strong. We are learning.

Why is it that the British police seized Raj Anand's passport? Why is it that the State Department in Washington has not yet granted me permission to go to Spain as a representative of the Negro Press? Why is it that the young Negro leader, Angelo Herndon, was finding it most difficult to secure a passport when I last saw him recently in New York? Why? We know why!

It is because the reactionary and Fascist forces of the world know that writers like Anand and myself, leaders like Herndon, and poets like Guillen and Romaine represent the great longing that is in the hearts of the darker peoples of the world to reach out their hands in friendship and brotherhood to all the white races of the earth. The Fascists know that we long to be rid of hatred and terror and oppression, to be rid of conquering and of being conquered, to be rid of all the ugliness of poverty and imperialism that eat away the heart of life today. We represent the end of race. And the Fascists know that when there is no more race, there will be no more capitalism, and no more war, and no more money for the munition makers, because the workers of the world will have triumphed.

The Crisis, September, 1937; XLIV, 272.

49

VICTORIES IN THE SCOTTSBORO AND HERNDON CASES

by James W. Ford

The Communist Party played a decisive role in saving the lives—and finally gaining the freedom—of the Scottsboro Boys and of Angelo Herndon. At a milestone in those victories, in 1937, James W. Ford reviewed the history and tactics and meanings of these great campaigns.

After six and a half years of struggle, freedom was gained for four of the nine Scottsboro boys. This victory, although partial, serves as a lever to open the prison for the five remaining boys.

The Scottsboro case attracted world-wide attention. Millions of people in every part of the world, of all nationalities, of all religions, of every political viewpoint, people of all classes—writers, lawyers, doctors, artists, workers, trade union leaders, men and women of every walk of life—took part in this universal struggle to free the Scottsboro boys.

"The Scottsboro Boys Shall Not Die!" "The Scottsboro Boys Must Go Free!" "Help Save the Scottsboro Boys!" These slogans were written and read, spoken and sung, carried through the streets, painted on walls in almost every language known to man. It has been one of the most profound expressions of the human conscience against injustice and persecution.

The Scottsboro case established a sharp dividing line between two camps: those who would perpetuate the degradation of the Negro people and keep up endless exploitation and oppression, and those who are organizing to end this oppression and establish equality and freedom for the Negro people. Rival forces—justice against inhumanity, liberty and democracy against enslavement and reaction—fought for mastery. The Scottsboro frame-up was designed by the reactionary section of the officialdom of the state of Alabama as a signal for an intense terror campaign to frighten the Negro people. Every act of the prosecution in the case gave that signal. Each move was aimed to develop psychological intimidation. The incitements in the Scottsboro case were clearly for the purpose of developing a monstrous psychological setting to overawe the Negro people to "keep them in their place." It was the intent of the reactionary Alabama officials, in mass murder of nine Negro youths to stifle the spirit of struggle of the Negro people, to mortify their dignity and crush every noble, honest and forward-looking aspiration they might have.

The first trial in the little town of Scottsboro, Alabama, was held in the midst of a raving mob atmosphere, deliberately planned and executed. A band played "There'll be a hot time in the old town tonight," as an accompaniment to the death verdicts the jury brought against one after another of the boys.

Alabama jurisprudence, which was dominated by the reactionaries, took upon itself the historic mission of the Ku Klux Klan, that is, to help maintain the dog-eat-dog economic basis in the South. The Governor, most of the judges and the courts in Alabama intended not only to terrorize the Negro people, but to sow hate and distrust between poor whites and blacks so that exploitation might continue.

Alabama reactionaries posed as defenders of "white womanhood." They raved about saving the South from Bolshevism, from "Jew money from New York." They did everything possible to stir up sectionalism and the basest racial passions. The staging of the Scottsboro case was aimed to throttle the emerging organization of black and white labor, which is rising against economic slavery and feudalistic remnants. The trial was to serve as a springboard to attack trade unions and all other forms of organization of black and white labor. But the reactionaries reckoned without certain forces. They failed to reckon with the strength and indignation of the mass movement of progressive forces that was rising among the people, for justice and civil liberties in the United States. They ignored the maturing political consciousness among the Negro people and their determination to struggle for their rights.

Whence came the power and strength of these methods and tactics?

One must speak here of the methods and forms of struggle that have grown out of the experiences of the international working class and that have proved successful in countries where the rankest forms of persecution are practiced by powerful ruling reactionary cliques. The method consists in involving millions of workers, farmers, small business people, working intellectuals and those in whose interest it is to unite against reaction and fascism.

The Communist Party applied these experiences to the Scottsboro case. This method required international unity and leadership. It is this that distinguished our activities from all others. We fully realized that only struggle on a mass basis, only slogans supported by millions could bring success. In the main these forms of struggle may be summarized as follows: (1) The conduct of international campaigns of protest; (2) the conduct of national campaigns of protest; (3) the organization of committees applying the tactic of the united front, drawing in representatives of various organizations of the toilers (trade unions, cultural organizations, organizations of Negro people, etc.); (4) the organization of mass conferences, parades and demonstrations; (5) the sending of delegations to protest and to investigate the conditions of the prisoners; (6) the circulation of petitions, signed by thousands of people, demanding the freedom of the victimized; (7) the publication of facts, the exposure to the public at large of the whole system of terror; (8) the enlistment of scientists, writers, artists, etc.; (9) the popularization of the work rendered by the International Labor Defense in order to win wider and wider masses.

These fundamental forms of struggle of both the Communist Party and the International Labor Defense were not resorted to just when "something happened"; they have been a part of our day-to-day work and activities.

On March 25, 1931, the nine Scottsboro boys were arrested on a freight train in Paint Rock, Alabama. They were charged with rape of two white girls. They were railroaded through lynch trials. Eight successive death sentences were handed down. The boys were not permitted proper counsel. They were indicted by a grand jury, tried before a petit jury, on which no Negroes served; no Negroes had ever in the memory of living man been permitted to serve on an Alabama jury. There was a mistrial in the case of the ninth boy.

On April 1, 1931, the International Labor Defense stepped into the case. Combining its two-fisted tactics of the best court defense with the best mass defense, it challenged these convictions made by the Bourbon section of the South. The Communist Party developed the campaign on a national scale, and beyond the borders of the country, supporting the fight for the freedom of the boys, for vindication and defense of the whole Negro people.

Joseph Brodsky, chief International Labor Defense counsel, went to Scottsboro to demand retrial of the boys. This was denied. Appeals were taken to the State Supreme Court. The Alabama State Supreme Court upheld the verdict against seven boys, remanded the other two to the custody of the Probate (juvenile) Court.

The roar of protest rose, and extended around the world. Tours were organized for the Scottsboro mothers. One of them, Mrs. Ada Wright, toured not only in the United States, but in company with the late J. Louis Engdahl, chairman of the International Labor Defense and veteran Communist Party leader, toured through 26 European countries. Millions the world over participated in the struggle. In Chemnitz, Germany, police fired upon a demonstration called by the Communist Party and the I.L.D. of that country, resulting in the death of a Communist. A martyr to the Scottsboro cause, Engdahl collapsed from the strain of the tour, contracted pneumonia, died in a Moscow hospital on November 21, 1932.

On November 7 of that year the United States Supreme Court—to which the I.L D. had appealed the case, retaining Walter Pollack, noted constitutional attorney, to make the argument—reversed the death sentences on the ground that the Scottsboro boys had been deprived of proper counsel in their trial.

New trials followed, this time in Decatur, Alabama, following a change of venue from Scottsboro secured by the I.L.D. Ruby Bates, one of the white girls whom the boys were charged with having violated, dramatically appeared in the middle of the trial. She repudiated all charges and told a damning story of having been forced to testify to a lie in the first trial. From her experiences she learned of the trickery and deception used by the white ruling class to divide and exploit both the Negro and white working people. She saw these

Bourbons ready not only to sanction but to organize the mass murder of innocent boys in order to further their selfish interests. Her experiences have made a working-class fighter out of Ruby Bates.

It was proved that Negroes from Alabama juries were systematically and illegally excluded in violation of the United States Constitution.

Haywood Patterson and Clarence Norris were again condemned to death in a lynch atmosphere created by the now-deceased Attorney-General Thomas E. Knight of Alabama, who took personal charge of the prosecution. The campaign mounted to new heights of protest, under the leadership of the Communist Party and the International Labor Defense. On June 22, 1933, Judge E. Horton set aside the verdicts on the ground that "the evidence preponderates greatly in favor of the defendants."

For yielding to the dictates of justice expressed by the protest movement, the state put pressure against Judge Horton, who was defeated for re-election. Judge William Washington Callahan, Ku Klux Klansman, succeeded him in the new trials. Once again Patterson and Norris were condemned to death. And again the International Labor Defense appealed the case.

With the campaign mounting, the United States Supreme Court reversed the sentence a second time, on the grounds of illegal exclusion of Negroes from the jury. The lives of the Scottsboro boys had been saved again and a major victory won for the Negro people, whose right to serve on Southern juries was established for the first time by this decision.

In December 1935, the International Labor Defense, following out its policy of broadening and extending the defense on a united front basis, initiated the formation of a united Scottsboro Defense Committee. It included the National Association for the Advancement of the Colored People, the American Civil Liberties Union, the Church League for Industrial Democracy (Episcopal), the International Labor Defense, the League for Industrial Democracy and the Methodist Federation for Social Service.

The fourth trial opened in January, 1936. Judge Callahan and Knight sped through the trial of Haywood Patterson, excluding all vital defense evidence by pre-arrangement. Patterson was convicted, and was sentenced to 75 years in prison. The united front campaign had forced a break in the series of death sentences. The other trials were hastily adjourned.

Next day, as the boys were being taken back from Decatur to prison in Birmingham, a deputy sheriff beat and taunted Ozzie Powell, one of the boys, until in self-defense Powell struck back, scratching the deputy's throat with a small knife. Sheriff Sandlin of Morgan County, who was in the car, got out and deliberately put a bullet in Powell's head, paralyzing and crippling him for life.

On July 12, 1937, the trials opened in Decatur once more. Knight, who had died a few months previously, was replaced as prosecutor by Assistant Solicitor Tom Lawson. Callahan began to grind through the trials again.

In a sudden move the state dismissed the rape charges against five of the Scottsboro boys, explaining that the evidence against them was doubtful. In doing so, the state of Alabama indicted itself of murderous false prosecution against the four who had been sentenced, since the evidence in every case was precisely the same. It depended entirely on the perjury of Victoria Price, who had eighteen times sworn on the witness stand that she was raped by every one of the nine boys.

Four boys, Eugene Williams, Roy Wright, Olen Montgomery and Willie Robertson, were freed, under condition of exile from the state of Alabama.

The first partial victory in the Scottsboro case was won.

Other lessons gained in united front defense go back to the San Francisco general strike in 1934. At that time the International Labor Defense successfully initiated a united front of the most varied elements in the fight against vigilantes. A united committee, including the American Civil Liberties Union and Socialist organizations, was formed on the initiative of the I.L.D., as a national center for the fight against the vigilante terror which was unleashed against the strikers. This was the first step in the series of developments which have reached their greatest heights so far in the Scottsboro fight. For the first time the most diversified elements, some of them representing fundamental divergences in political viewpoints, were united on a specific defense issue.

The most outstanding complete victory of the united front has been the freeing of Angelo Herndon. Except for the Scottsboro and Mooney-Billings cases, broader forces—involving literally millions of people in specific united action through their organizations and individually—were brought into this united front than on any other issue.

This campaign forced the United States Supreme Court to free Angelo Herndon, and nullify the Georgia slave insurrection law under which he had been sentenced to from 18 to 20 years on the Georgia chain-gang. The national tour of the reproduction of the chain-gang, the circulation of the Herndon petitions which were signed by two million people through the agency of scores and hundreds of the most diverse organizations, involving the Socialist Party in united action with the Communist Party, the Young People's Socialist League with the Young Communist League, the American Federation of Labor, the National Negro Congress, the National Association for the Advancement of Colored People, all unemployed organizations, church groups and organizations, the Y.W.C.A., monster mass meetings held for Herndon in every part of the country, the formation of local Herndon committees on a scale even broader than the National Committee to Aid the Herndon Defense—these are highlights in the Herndon campaign which illustrate in the most graphic and dramatic manner the power of the united front. . . .

In the Scottsboro campaign we have an outstanding example of the effectiveness of united action in winning victory. The united Scottsboro Defense Committee undertook responsibility for the work of conducting the defense. The organizations supporting this Committee—although with varying degrees of energy and initiative, and at times with hesitations or reservations—on concrete measures brought much wider circles into concerted effort which has resulted so far in the freedom of four of the boys.

United action—continued, developed and extended with renewed vigor—is necessary for the winning of freedom for all the remaining boys. The National Association for the Advancement of Colored People's branches throughout the country, many of which were already involved in the campaign, were involved in larger numbers by the establishment of the united committee. Socialists, liberals, civil liberties groups, trade unions, fraternal organizations, church and religious organizations, and many others within the sphere of influence of the organizations in the Scottsboro Defense Committee, were brought into action through the establishment of the united front. The working relationship with the National Association for the Advancement of Colored People, established in the Scottsboro case, is an outstanding example, and the N.A.A.C.P. and its speakers in many cases have praised the key role of the I.L.D.

The most important lessons to be learned from our united front experiences in defense are the necessity for alertness and vigor in conducting this work; the need for patient, untiring effort to win to united action on specific issues the broadest elements of the people, no matter how sharply they may differ from us on other questions;

and the importance of a conviction of the correctness of our united front policies. These policies have been proved in action. The victories of united action in the Scottsboro and other cases were not accomplished overnight, nor was the work easy.

The partial victories gained in the fight for freedom of the Scottsboro boys stand before us. The Supreme Court was forced to affirm the right of Negroes to sit on juries, although this is still denied in practice, and can be realized only by the united struggle of progressive forces. Nobody can deny that among the white masses there is growing tolerance on the Negro question, that among large sections of whites the persecution of the Negro people as exemplified in the Scottsboro case has awakened strong ideals. They are beginning to see the Negro people as a noble and great people.

The Communist Party is proud of the leading part it has played in these achievements. Few have understood the contribution and the change that came over large sections of the South and particularly in Alabama. The best opinion of Alabama and of all of the South is not represented by the acts of the reactionaries. We must give credit to a change in attitude of an influential and large section of Southern opinion—workers, farmers and intellectuals—which finally saw through this shameful frame-up, and out of decency and honesty brought pressure to bear on the state and the courts, which helped to make possible the victories in the Scottsboro case.

Even the transformation in the life and outlook of Ruby Bates, who was born in an atmosphere of intolerance and prejudice, is a plainly-evident example of a maturing new attitude in the South. Those unfortunate utterances of Mr. Samuel Liebowitz at the conclusion of the first trials at Decatur, reflecting on the Southern people as a whole, were certainly not justified.

Following the freeing of four of the Scottsboro boys, the Birmingham *Age-Herald* said:

> The statement asserts that the prosecution is convinced of the guilt of the four Negroes who have been tried again and convicted, but in the view of the *Age-Herald* the doubt of the guilt of those who have been convicted will be greatly increased by the action of last Saturday, despite this statement of the prosecution and without questioning the good faith of those who issued it . . . that admission will inevitably deepen the opinion of many fair-minded citizens that the possibility has been more than "mistaken identity" in the cases of those who have been convicted.

This the admission will certainly do. The courts of Alabama stand convicted by their own statement of having tried to execute five Negro boys on a false charge. Why are not the others innocent, who were convicted on the same perjured testimony? This question must ring throughout the land!

A most significant development has been the expression organizationally of the liberal and progressive sentiment in the South. The Scottsboro Defense Committee formed in Birmingham a Southern committee, in which outstanding liberals and trade unionists in the South are joined together. This uniting of progressive Southern forces contributed a powerful lever to force the Bourbon reactionaries in their subsequent retreat in the Scottsboro case. It should be further developed into a broad movement for progress against reaction and for full rights for the Negro people.

The Scottsboro victory is not complete. The freedom of the remaining boys must be gained. The Scottsboro Defense Committee, the International Labor Defense, the Communist Party and all other organizations and the millions of supporters of the Scottsboro boys and the Negro people have said clearly and unalterably—*the fight is not ended*. It will never end until all the nine Scottsboro boys are free.

We cannot stop here. Scottsboro is a much broader issue. The Scottsboro fight, the issues around the Scottsboro case and the tremendous lessons learned in this struggle must be made a basis for a fight for all Negro rights. A fight against lynchings, mob violence, and police brutality; for the enactment of a federal anti-lynching law; for the right to vote, serve on juries and enjoy complete civil liberty—these are a part of this great struggle developed around Scottsboro.

The right of Negro youth to equal opportunity in education and in the economic and social life is a part of this struggle. Complete equality for Negro women, their right along with all women to equal pay for equal work, their right to a suitable environment for themselves and their children—an environment which demands adequate housing, good schools and recreational facilities—are all part of the struggle around the Scottsboro case.

The fight for the freedom of the Scottsboro boys must be considered as a campaign to fight for the democratic rights of the Negro people, the safe-guarding and extension of the democratic rights of the people as a whole, and against all forms of vigilantism, discrimination of Negroes, against fascist tendencies everywhere. It must be so organized as to develop the unity of Negro and white in the common struggle against reaction, for progress, and so as to bring the Negro people unitedly into the People's Front in the United States.

The Communist, September, 1937; reprinted in J. W. Ford, *Negro and Democratic Front*, pp. 95–107.

50

WHAT A NEGRO MOTHER FACES
by Cecelia Eggleston

Rare are the published essays considering the subject indicated in the title of this essay; especially rare are they when published in a magazine meant basically for a white readership. An example is published below, in full; its author had been educated in Roman Catholic and public schools in Washington, D.C., and then graduated from Howard University. For a time she was a social worker in New York City; at the time of the publication of what follows, she was a teacher in a Washington public school.

The Negro wife of today who is a thinking woman pauses and ponders deeply before she decides to assume what is to any woman the gravest of responsibilities—motherhood. Why?

Not because of the specter of poverty; for, although economic insecurity is widespread, it is the woman in fairly comfortable circumstances who hesitates most to have a child. Nor does the fear of hereditary taints trouble her more than any other intelligent layman of good education. Certainly she possesses the common instinct of motherhood. She must, or else, in these days of contraceptives, she would have no problem.

The Negro woman hesitates because she is faced most cruelly with the responsibility of bringing into the world a child victimized not by disease or extreme poverty but by that over which neither he nor his parents have any control—the color of his skin.

In fact white people are prone to regard the problems of Negroes in general very much as they do the grievances of children—disturbances of the moment, easily quieted, quickly forgotten. They know that Negroes may be blue or low-spirited or miserable, but it just does not occur to them that they are *people,* adults, capable of being deeply unhappy, torn by conflicting emotions, or weighted with problems that cannot be laid down by the river side.

A woman writer widely known for syndicated articles of opinion once wrote what she thought about the Negro woman.

The gist was that the Negro woman in what was described as her native habitat was a fine specimen of womanhood. It was only when she moved into the city and aped her white sisters that she became unworthy of anyone's interest or respect. Her native habitat was a cabin in which she was surrounded by the white folk's clothes and her own brood of seven or eight—of divers fathers. There she was a happy and an admirable character.

One might forgive this writer for her callous and superficial designation of her Negro woman as happy, because a certain sort of passive adjustment is mistaken for happiness in many situations. But to refer to her as admirable was not only unforgivable but absolutely disastrous to the ideals Negroes have been fighting for, all these years.

If this writer were to be honest with herself, she would admit that she would not dare to label as admirable that type of woman representing any other race of people under the sun. Indeed, if she were mentioned at all, she would be described as lazy, loose, unambitious, shiftless, and downright immoral. The question would be why did she not emulate her sisters, instead of being content to remain in her old environment. But, when the *Negro* woman attempts to better herself, then she is aping her white sisters and loses her charm.

Loses it for whom? Why, for white people who cannot relinquish this mental stereotype of the Negro woman, a relic of the days when no consideration was given the Negro woman's morality and her home ties were broken at the whim of the master.

This is a part of the slave heritage which my child, no matter what its sex, could not escape. Contrast it with our attitude toward foreigners who come there totally unacquainted with American ways and standards. They are encouraged by every means to adapt themselves to our life. The quicker their adjustment, the more desirable they are thought to be as citizens. Their assimilation is regarded as a promising sign of their versatility. But in an American Negro this is aping.

In considering whether I shall have a baby, my first thought is naturally of the child's health and physical well-being. Fortunately I live in a city where excellent medical attention is available and I feel sure that I should have prenatal care as fine as the nation affords for its great mass of citizens. But, were I in the deep South, my situation would be entirely different.

A Negro sorority I am familiar with has recently been operating a health project there. The women fled at the sight of doctors and nurses. A doctor at childbirth was unheard-of; prenatal attention was not even a myth. These mothers die in childbirth at the rate of three out of ten. The infant mortality is even higher.

Now I realize it is not because they are Negroes that these women and their offspring die. I know that their deaths are due to extreme poverty, ignorance, and neglect. Yet, when I read the cold, bare statistics, that the mortality rate for Negro women in childbirth is eight times that for whites, I am a bit panicky in spite of my personally favorable circumstances.

We Negroes teach our youth that the salvation of the Negro lies within the race itself; that, as soon as we become economically independent, educated, cultured, and skillful, we shall arrive. But wealth, education, culture, and technological advancement did not save the Jew in Germany.

Although Americans entertain no fears that the Negro in America will ever threaten a civilization which he lacks the inherent power, according to them, to sustain, they are nevertheless extremely careful to block all roads from the start.

The Negro child of today, then, must be imbued with more than a normal share of courage, for he has to clear the road before he starts on the journey. It is difficult to see from what source he can draw this courage.

Suppose I ask myself just what I have done as an individual to make this a better world into which to bring a child.

I have thought that one way of opening for my child doors that have been closed to me is via the interracial committee. The trouble is, I believed, that we do not know each other. If only we did, these mutual prejudices would melt away.

And indeed we do grow to know each other. The whites learn that all Negroes do not wait until Saturday to take a bath and that a high percentage of Negro women have a wholesome respect for their marital vows. The Negroes find that the white people on the committee are agreeable, well-meaning persons who feel that white people have a responsibility and that something must be done. So we chat pleasantly over the cups of tea and pass resolutions. But we get little further than the teacups.

Few, if any, lasting personal friendships develop from the association of the races on these committees. The white members are all friends of the Negro in a vague, impersonal sort of way. But real friendship in the sense that involves exchanging visits outside of meeting nights, showers for the bride, bridge, picnics, trips together, informal occasions where people really get to know each other—that is out of the question. After all, someone invariably protests, the purpose of the Committee is not to foster personal relationships and individual friendships. It is something much bigger than that—to create good will between two races, to break down prejudice and misunderstanding. Do not confuse the two interpretations of the term *social*. This is its more restricted use.

But, in spite of all resolutions passed for the social (in the larger sense) advancement of the Negro, I still cannot buy a house where I might wish to do so and I still would have to take my baby to the clinic on the special days for Negroes. And thus, before he left my arms, he would begin to live a lie, to learn day by day in a hundred subtle but nonetheless definite ways that he was different—somehow inferior. Thus he would grow to a manhood that could not make him a man, led on by first one mirage, then another, until at last the barrenness of the life about him met the nakedness of his own soul.

Why not try God? Surely, if anywhere, in the folds of Christianity I would find an approach to my problem.

Problem? I had no problem, only a duty clear and undivided. A married woman has no choice, according to the Roman Catholic Church, in which I was reared. I must bring my child, then, into the same kind of church world in which I grew up.

Should his baby feet stray in the house of God beyond the last three rows, frantic ushers would seize him and return him to his proper place—the last three rows or, it might be, the dusty gallery above the choir loft.

His baby ears would hear the same sermons that mine had listened to. He would learn how Christ had died to save all, rich and poor, high and low, black and white. He would swallow it all as I had swallowed it before him, until he, too, discovered that the Fatherhood of God and the brotherhood of man is a beautiful theory, harmless to believe in, dynamite to practice.

The parish priest inquires why you do not attend your duties. "That's the trouble with you people," he says. "As soon as you get a bit of education, you forget God."

As if God and the church were synonymous. I should not say that education makes us forget God but I do hold that it does for us what it is supposed to do for all exposed to its influence. It makes us think for ourselves and heightens our realization of the travesty that is carried on in the name of Christ.

From my last attendance at mass some years ago I have retained an indelible picture in my mind. I can still see the Negro communicants kneeling at the back of the church, waiting for the white faithful to leave the altar rail. A nausea came over me then, a nausea which now replaces the pious genuflection I used to make every time I passed a Catholic church.

Some loyal and devout Negro Catholics maintain that Holy Mother Church is much more liberal than the Protestant churches (at least in the South), for she does admit us within her doors—to the last three rows—and she will serve us communion—after the whites are served. Alas, the distinction is too fine for me to appreciate.

Some people may feel that it would not be fair for me to transmit to my child the discouragement and disillusionment my experiences with religion, as it is practiced in the Christian churches of America, have brought me. But I believe it might be kinder to prepare him for it in advance. Blessed are they who expect nothing, for they shall not be disappointed.

Since I find no encouragement in the faith of our fathers, I turn to other fields more practical and tangible. What are the prospects for my Negro child in industry, science, business, or the arts?

From latent ability on both sides of the family, this child, unborn, unconceived even, might develop marked dramatic ability. What would this mean for him?

If the child is a boy, it would mean, by present reckoning, buffooning, clowning. It might mean a variation of a character from *The Emperor Jones* or *Porgy* or a *Green Pastures* of a brighter hue but it most assuredly would not mean the rest of O'Neill—or Ibsen or Shakespeare.

If, still less happily, this Negro child should be a girl with dramatic ability, she might as well start learning her dialect in the cradle; for, in the years to come, Mammy will go marching on. Scarlett O'Hara may be gone with the wind, but good old Mammy—primitive, ignorant, stupid in every way save in her instinct to protect her li'l white lamb—Mammy will be the last of the stereotypes to go.

Here I interrupt with a timid song, "I Didn't Raise My Girl to Be a Mammy."

Sacrilege! screams the South. How dare you? She couldn't represent anything finer, more beautiful, more—.

Yes, yes. I know the rest.

In the business and scientific world the situation is different. It is much worse.

The chances of a Negro's getting proper preparation and training are growing slimmer and slimmer. Not only are increased costs in the great technical schools prohibitive, but the opportunities for Negroes to learn the practical side of this kind of work are extremely limited.

It is the same story in the matter of preparation for the professions. The colleges and universities pass the buck to the public. We are willing to accept you as students, they say to the Negroes, but we cannot force you on the public for practice.

It is interesting to note that these same educational centers feel duty-bound to take the initiative in guiding the public in its democratic duty in other situations. But, in a matter involving racial injustice, the cause of social reconstruction is politely laid aside, and the less provocative cloak of realism is assumed.

Even when the Negro youth manages somehow to acquire the necessary preliminary training for a career, he is not much better off. Several young men of my acquaintance who hold degrees from the business schools of leading universities are working on P.W.A. projects scarcely requiring an eighth-grade education. Furthermore, as the little business-man in all other groups yields steadily to the pressure of big business, the Negro businessman disappears altogether. In Negro shops of personal service, white syndicates are pushing out the few Negro owners and proprietors left. For the purpose of attracting the Negro trade they put in a Negro *front* in the persons of a few low-salaried Negro attendants.

In my frantic search for a desirable future for this child whose birth I debate so fearfully, I turn at last to the United States Government.

Is my answer to be found in longer relief rolls? Well, if Negroes are constantly denied admission to the openings compatible with their abilities, in all capacities from the lowest to the highest, they will have no choice but to become helots of the government.

The civil service offers no protection. With its photo requirement and the patronage dispenser's prerogative of choosing among the first three on the list, a Negro with a Sigma Chi Rho in chemistry is wasting his time taking an examination to qualify as even a laboratory assistant at $1,200 a year. When a few fortunate Negroes eventually succeed in receiving minor appointments as messengers or skilled laborers, they remain such, with no hope of promotion.

A few Negro lawyers in the North and Midwest, realizing how limited is their field in practicing in white courts, turn to politics as an outlet for their ambitions and energies. The returns are hardly worth the time and effort. It is lamentable that there is only one Negro congressman for 10,000,000 people. And Negroes really hold fewer important government positions than they did in the early part of the century. The so-called special assistant appointments made in the various departments and bureaus are merely sops to the Negro voters.

A white woman whom I met recently feels that I am unduly pessimistic. "For instance," she says, "I could just sit and worry about the things that could happen to my own child, natural catastrophes or a disastrous change in government. In such events my child would be no better off than yours."

I might have answered that, in the light of recent experiences of Negroes in flood and drought relief, sufficient evidence could be furnished to prove that, though nature was undeniably color-blind in delivering the blow, democracy was far from it in giving succor.

If, as some students of social and political trends maintain, we are drifting toward a fascist state, then indeed is the doom of the Negro sealed. Then what is now chronic would become acute, as Sinclair Lewis points out in *It Can't Happen Here.*

A change toward communism, on the other hand, appears to offer more hope of equal opportunity and protection under the law. But aren't *these same rights* guaranteed by our most sacred Constitution? Can we believe that another system will change the hearts of men?

Most Negroes are willing to struggle along under the palliative measures of the New Deal, which they believe will lead ultimately to a new day for themselves and their progeny. They naïvely trust that *new day* means *better day.*

Those Negroes who really wish to take an intelligent and active part in social reconstruction are looked on with suspicion by both Negroes and whites—by whites, because the thinking Negro does not conform to their stereotype of the happy, carefree Negro; by Negroes, because they feel that such individuals may jeopardize the slight gains already made.

There was a time when colored people living in some degree of comfort compensated for the limitation of their opportunities to get on in the world by saying that they would rather be high-class Negroes than poor whites. That time recedes further into the past, for Negroes now realize that nothing—education, wealth, culture, travel—can compensate for the lack of a white face. Any white person who believes that Negroes are oversensitive in this attitude need only black his face for a time. The Negroes, knowing they cannot, do not ask to be white. They do ask, however, to be *people.*

The Negro woman who asks her inner self, *Should I have a baby?* will find no ready-made answer. Before she responds to the question irrevocably, she might put it in another way: *Will my child rise up to call me blessed or curse the day that he was born?*

The Forum and Century, August, 1938; C, 59–62.

51

RESEARCH BARRIERS IN THE SOUTH
by L. D. Reddick

An incisive article on the racism permeating the United States scholarly establishment came from the pen of L. D. Reddick in 1937, when he was an associate professor of History at Dillard University in New Orleans and an assistant editor of *The Journal of Negro History*.

There seems to be a general lament on the part of professors in the Southern universities that uncommonly high and overwhelming barriers face the scholar in that section of the land. In this spirit Dr. Wilson Gee five years ago issued *Research Barriers in the South* for the Southern Regional Committee of the Social Science Research Council, and more recently has returned to the theme in the April issue of *Social Forces*. The thesis runs along in this fashion: The South is not really a cultural desert so far as creative scholarship is concerned. Because of the lack of facilities and opportunities found elsewhere, "a steady stream of the best intellectual and leadership qualities has been pouring from out the borders. . . ." Thus, by showing statistically that the equipment is inferior, the teaching load heavier, the appropriations for study inadequate or indifferent, the writers and speakers are in a position to "explain" the present degree of advancement and at the same time to plead for larger "recognition and support."

All this is very well and good. The last mentioned argument is especially laudable. From the standpoint of sectional patriotism, it may be important that some of the better minds "go North." However, despite the continuous plaint concerning "talent pouring out," this proves a little weak. The figures of this same Committee reveal that during the years studied, "there was a net loss to the South and hence net gain to the North and West of 31 (!) social scientists"; nevertheless, 770 men eminent enough to be listed in *American Men of Science* went into the South while only 660 left—a gain of 110.

But what makes the dissertations and discussions hollow to the core is that these supposedly scientific students of human affairs ignore absolutely the most dramatic part of their story, the much-less-imaginary barriers to the work of a body of men in their midst, the Negro scholars.

In *Research Barriers in the South* there does not appear the name of a single Negro, nor of such institutions as Fisk University in Nashville or Howard University in Washington, D.C., though ample space is devoted to Converse College, Agnes Scott College, Millsaps and Sweet Briar.

Every barrier faced by these others is encountered with increased difficulty by the Negro scholar. The inadequacy of buildings, books, and apparatus is so patent that the Negro deans and registrars in convention this year advised against the attempt to give graduate training in the publicly-supported institutions of the several states. As for salaries, the general condition may be suggested in the observation that the income of the presidents of these colleges is far above that of their faculties. Yet when the president of the state college for Negroes in Florida raised his pay in the budget, it is reported that the Governor vetoed the increase with the words, "No Negro is worth $4,000." In the government-supported Howard University and the three leading "privately endowed" schools—Fisk, Atlanta, and Dillard—the *average* income of the assistant-, associate-, and full-professors is $2,600.

Obviously, a research man can not work without data. Here special obstructions are met. It goes without saying that the doors to most private papers and collections are closed to black men. The same is largely true when it comes to public records. The state libraries follow a mixed policy. In Kentucky, for example, there is no interference. The more general practice is, as the Editor of the *Journal of Negro History* euphemistically puts it, to seat the Negro "somewhere in the building" and to bring to this place the materials he may wish. In other tax-supported libraries and those provided by philanthropy, the Negro is usually excluded. Sometimes use of the books, but not the building, is granted.

A stirring chapter could be written on the ingenious devices employed to gain access to the necessary books and documents. Ties of kinship are always useful. Often the old classmate in Harvard's "History 400," who may be teaching in the neighboring university, is helpful. The trick may be turned by a chain of letters to someone who knows someone who knows someone who knows the custodian. A good practice is to denounce a pro-Northern history book on the Civil War. The prize, no doubt, should go to the passionate devotee who entered into conspiracy with the Negro janitor (who alone knew the place of every book in the building). Every evening the required books were removed and returned early the next morning before the arrival of the political appointee (librarian).

There is, too, the outrage of downright vandalism. Any number of cases of the mysterious disappearance of source materials may be cited. In one of the largest cities of the South, the files of the Superintendent of Public Instruction during Reconstruction days were removed when it became known that a study was to be made of that administration. Dr. W. E. B. Du Bois reports a similar experience when a Negro professor planned to write an account of that highly efficient Jonathan C. Gibbs (Negro), Secretary of the State of Florida and Superintendent of Public Instruction, 1872–1874.

When it comes to the historical associations and other scientific or semi-scientific conclaves, their programs are arranged and executed without thought of the colored brother. This is not only true of the local or regional societies, but of important national associations which happen to convene in the South. Last February the Department of Superintendence of the National Education Association meeting in New Orleans (where there is, perhaps, less agonizing over the incidence of color than in any other southern city) was so indifferent to deliberate discourtesy to Negro members that the Julius Rosenwald Fund in a vigorous letter of protest withdrew. Some were sufficiently interested to go through the back door of the freight entrance to attend the sessions in the hotel. The American Historical Association has on occasion allowed such men as Professor Monroe Work of Tuskegee to appear. On the other hand, when one member of the committee on programs and arrangements suggested the names of Dr. Carter G. Woodson and Dr. Charles W. Wesley (both Harvard Ph.D.'s and authors of several volumes), who happen to stem from a more aggressive tradition, the committee was immediately reshuffled and this member was promptly dropped.

The effects of these impediments to the intellectual life are manifest. Here may be found one reason, at least, for the interminable round of faculty members' wives' bridge parties and the absorption in campus politics. One man came to a Southern Negro college well known as the author of two highly creditable monographs. Today he is better known as the auction bridge champion of the region. Another was known to babble in his sleep of the French Revolution; now his nocturnal murmurings are more related to the last fraternity initiation.

Across this darkness should be set the exceptions and what many like to believe are the rays of hope. Here and there, individuals may be found who go out of their way to aid in every manner possible. It is understood that professors, librarians, and other functionaries are not altogether free agents. The social environment is persuasive and persistent. In the light of custom and law a man is "experimenting" dangerously when he invites Negroes to use public facilities. Five instances are known where, informally and unofficially, Negro and white institutions exchange professors for certain classes. Dr. Guy B. Johnson is considered something of a wild-eyed radical because he has suggested a more general association of scholars irrespective of "race." In Chicago last December, some Southerners stated that they voted for Dr. Charles S. Johnson of Fisk when he was elected to one of the vice-presidencies of the American Sociological Society.

But when all this has been said and every instance of social intelligence has been recorded, it adds up (1) that the obstacles in the South to the un-"Uncle Tomish" Negro student are tremendous, and (2) that one of the most disconcerting of these is the indifference and occasional opposition of the white scholar. Without raising the question as to the obligation and necessity on the part of all thoughtful scholars to further the pursuit of learning, the conclusion can hardly be escaped that men who neglect to "universalize" their own problem by failing to include the more profound difficulties of their neighbors, have a flimsy basis to their appeal for "recognition and support."

The Social Frontier, December, 1937; IV, 85–86.

52

THE PROLIFERATION OF PUBLIC FORUMS

A distinct phenomenon in the nineteen-thirties throughout the Afro-American community was the appearance of forums for discussion and, at times, special forms of action. Two examples follow: Document [a] gives details concerning the Negro Forum Council of Richmond, Virginia, in 1937; public sessions were held twice a month at the Leigh Street M.E. Church. Its executive director was Milton L. Randolph and the Reverend Caleb Queen was its associate director. Among speakers were Dr. Du Bois, Phillip Murray, Dr. Charles H. Wesley, Dr. Mordecai Johnson, Dr. Rayford W. Logan, and others. Document [b] gives the history and the purposes of a young people's forum begun in 1938 in Lincoln, Nebraska. In 1938–1939 officers included Charles G. Blooah, Myron Stith, Charlotte Williams, and Yolanda Rogers.

[a]

NEGRO FORUM COUNCIL OF RICHMOND, VIRGINIA
A NON-PARTISAN, NON-SECTARIAN AGENCY FOR
CREATING AN ENLIGHTENED PUBLIC OPINION

Purpose of the Forum

Realizing that the greatest handicap of any racial group is the lack of proper information, understanding, and interpretation on present day subjects and problems, the Negro Forum Council was organized in January, 1937, for the purpose of filling this need of creating an informed and enlighted public opinion, particularly among the Negro citizens of Richmond.

The sessions of the Forum held since its organization have had an average attendance of 500 and have afforded Richmond some of the nation's outstanding personalities.

Progress is our destiny and we are asking that this be mutually desired and achieved. We are in the midst of a financial drive for $500.00 to assure the success of our expanded program and the appearance of the speakers' list.

WE CAN JUDGE THE SUPPORTERS OF THE CULTURAL PROGRESS OF RICHMOND ONLY BY THE EXTENT OF THEIR ATTENDANCE AND CO-OPERATION THROUGH THE PURCHASE OF SEASON TICKETS OR THROUGH DIRECT DONATIONS FOR THE MAINTENANCE OF SUCH AN INSTITUTION AS THE NEGRO FORUM COUNCIL.

Facts About Forum Council

1. The Negro Forum Council is not a Community Fund Agency.
2. The Council does not sponsor action on problems or questions but furnishes an agency for creating an enlightened public opinion as a basis for intelligent action by other existing organizations.
3. Speakers for the Forum sessions are selected without bias, by a democratically chosen committee and are selected according to their availability and our financial resources.
4. Discussions last rarely more than one and one-half hours.

5. Any duly appointed representative of any organized group in the community may become an Executive Member of the Negro Forum Council upon the payment of the required executive fee of $3.00 per year. From this membership group all officers and members of the executive committee are elected. Holders of Donor Season Tickets are eligible upon appointment for service on the advisory or other functionary committees.

6. The next election of officers and members to the Executive Committee will take place in January, 1939, and such persons elected will serve for a period of two years.

7. The fiscal year of the Negro Forum Council runs from September through May of the following year and season tickets available at $1.00 each will cover such public meetings as are held by the Forum during this period.

8. Persons not holding Patron's Season Tickets will be required to make a minimum donation at each public meeting of ten cents, such donations being collectable at the door.

9. Secure your season ticket today and help to raise the intellectual level of your Richmond neighbors. "With all thy getting, get Understanding."

10. We endeavor to create an enlightened public opinion on public questions through presenting authoritative speakers and discussions.

Four-page printed folder in editor's possession.

[b]

LINCOLN, NEBRASKA, YOUNG PEOPLE'S FORUM

Preface

The Lincoln Young People's Forum grew out of peculiar circumstances. A need for the young people of college age for an understanding of the various world problems in an age of confusion and shattered ethical standards, and the appalling ignorance and shiftlessness which has prevailed among young people of this day. To meet this need half way, Mr. Sidney Kennard, former student in the Lincoln Aeronautic School from British Guiana, and Charles G. Blooah of Liberia, met in a brief session to create a forum in which great-world problems might be discussed by men of wide and varied experience for the benefit of the general public.

About a week preparatory to the inauguration of the final plans for the creation of the organization, the Rev. Mr. Eugene A. Graham of the Newman Methodist Episcopal Church called together the students of the various schools and colleges in Lincoln, out of which grew the present "Lincoln Young People's Forum." The movement is a grand success under the leadership of Mr. Eldridge Leonard, then President, and Mr. Charles G. Blooah, Chairman of the Program Committee.

Origin

The rise of the "Lincoln Young People's Forum" among Negro Youth in Lincoln is due to many vital factors. A few of these are: (1) a desire for a better cooperation among all Negro students attending the various colleges, universities and schools of Lincoln and those of other cities, in order to make possible a better understanding and sympathetic appreciation of one another's problems; (2) a desire to afford some definite means of offering protection for each other by cultivating a more definite group consciousness not necessarily a desire to be clannish, but a means of providing a more effective way of protecting a minority group; (3) a desire to cooperate with the various university housing departments to provide better rooming quarters for both the male and female students who register each semester on the various grounds of the colleges and schools of Nebraska; and (4) a desire to bring about some financial aid to Negro students entering or contemplating on entering any school of higher learning in Nebraska after completing high school training. This point is regarded important for no student can do good work in college who must be compelled by unfortunate circumstances to worry about his finances or where the next dime is coming from in order to buy a sandwich for his next meal.

Nature

The Lincoln Young People's Forum was organized in September, 1937, by a nucleus of students from the different colleges, universities, high schools and laymen of the three Negro churches in Lincoln. While it was primarily organized by Negroes, the organization is non-racial, and non-denominational, but strictly cosmopolitan and a movement in which men of all races, creeds and classes can exchange their candid opinions.

The movement was first housed or sponsored by the Newman

Methodist Episcopal Church, located on the corner of Twenty-third and S Streets, under the sympathetic interest of Rev. Eugene Graham, Pastor, and Mr. G. B. Evans, Chairman of the Board of Trustees of Newman. At present, the Forum is sponsored by Rev. C. C. Reynolds, now pastor of Newman Methodist Episcopal Church.

Purpose

Aims—One of the primary aims of the organization is to provide means whereby there can be given clearer interpretation and better insight into the trends of contemporary thought, shifting standards of ethics and educational problems by an exchange of our candid opinions with those persons of our generation who have a better grasp upon those questions that affect our personalities, common life and conduct, as there is in every generation a need for an understanding of the world crisis.

The second primary aim is to create a scholarship fund for the sole purpose of aiding Negro students in their effort to educate themselves in the universities and colleges throughout the state of Nebraska by providing scholarships. The plans prepared by the organization for the acquisition and disposition of the scholarships by the Forum are listed as follows:

1. The goal—The Forum intends to raise at least ten thousand dollars or more eventually from which scholarships can be awarded to worthy students yearly. The money is to be raised on the basis of a five-year-plan.

2. The amount of money to be awarded in any single year to any deserving student shall be one hundred dollars. The award shall be made to any Negro graduating from any high school in the state of Nebraska, or in any other state, recommended by the Scholarship-Administrative Board, appointed for that purpose by the Forum, to enter any college he desires in Nebraska. There shall also be a scholarship of one hundred dollars awarded to any Negro graduating from the college of Liberal Arts and Sciences who wishes to take further work for an advanced degree in any institution in Nebraska.

3. Pre-requisites—Each recipient of a Forum scholarship is required to have a good Christian character; a keen interest in civic problems and activities; he shall be in the highest 25% of his class rating, and shall be so appointed after absolute proof of his needs has been established.

4. Time for the awards—Scholarships shall be made to candidates recommended by the Scholarship-Administrative Board during the last Monday in the May of each scholastic year. The one hundred dollar scholarship awarded shall be payable into the office of the registrar of any college or school the student chooses to attend by the Board in two separate halves. The said school shall refund to the student in cash the amount remaining after tuition for each semester is paid.

Eight-page printed pamphlet, in editor's possession, probably issued in 1938. Omitted are details concerning organizational framework and other administrative matters.

53

A CHALLENGE TO NEGRO COLLEGE YOUTH

by Charles H. Houston

The distinguished Afro-American attorney, Charles H. Houston, tells below of the struggles of Black people to crack the lily-white character of state university and professional schools throughout the South. It was not until the period after World War II that this battle was won—at least on the legal front.

In 1935 the National Association for the Advancement of Colored People, through a grant made possible by the American Fund for Public Service, Inc., began a legal attack on the established policy of the southern states not to provide at state expense any graduate or professional training for Negro college graduates.

No southern or border state admitted Negroes to the state university. Only two states provided out-of-state scholarships. West Virginia paid the tuition of Negro students in out-of-state universities to take graduate or professional courses offered to white students in the state university. Missouri, which in 1929 had begun paying full tuition scholarships, had amended its law in 1935 so that it paid the Negro student only the difference between the tuition charged at the out-of-state university and the tuition charged at the University of Missouri. Where the tuition at the out-of-state university was less than the tuition at the University of Missouri, the Negro student received nothing for his exile from home.

The first case filed was against the University of Maryland. That was won, and a Negro boy, Donald Gaines Murray, was admitted to the school of law. Subsequently a second Negro was admitted to the school of law of the University of Maryland. But reactionary forces in Maryland have increased the out-of-state scholarship provisions for Maryland Negroes and are trying to close the doors of the University of Maryland again. That is the first challenge directed specifically to the Maryland college youth.

The second case was against the University of Tennessee. That was lost on a technicality: that although the Negro student, William B. Redmond, II, had applied for admission to and been rejected by the dean of the school of pharmacy, the president of the university, and the executive committee of the board of trustees successively, nevertheless the court held his petition for writ of mandamus prematurely filed because he had not first appealed from the decision of the executive committee to the full board of trustees of the university. Prior to the Redmond case the Tennessee law had always been that while the board of trustees of the University of Tennessee was not in session, the executive committee of the board exercised the power of the full board. But the court ruled differently in the Redmond case.

An appeal was noted, but in the meantime Tennessee passed a scholarship act. It was then decided that as funds were so low, instead of pressing the Redmond case to its final conclusion, the Association would conserve its funds for a fight in a state which made absolutely no provision for graduate or professional study for Negro youth, coming back to Tennessee later if a worthy appeal for aid should be made.

The third case was against the University of Missouri where Lloyd L. Gaines sought mandamus to compel his admission to the university school of law. The lower court ruled against him, and this decision was affirmed December 9, 1937, by the Missouri court of appeals. At this writing counsel are studying the record and opinion with the purpose of seeking review before the United States Supreme Court as to what constitutes equality of opportunity in graduate and professional education under the equal protection clause of the 14th amendment.

The Gaines case, however, was not a total loss. The court affirmed the theoretical proposition that Negro Missourians are entitled to equality of education with white Missourians. It declared void the Act of 1935 paying only the difference between the tuition at the out-of-state university and the tuition at the University of Missouri and held that the state had to pay full tuition at the out-of-state university under the Act of 1921. But it also declared that where the state paid the full tuition at the out-of-state university, such payment constituted educational opportunity equal to that afforded white students at the University of Missouri.

This is one ground for asking the United States Supreme Court to review the Gaines case. The supreme court of Missouri said that a tuition scholarship for Gaines was an equivalent to education of white Missourians in the state university, regardless of any difference Gaines might have to pay in transportation or subsistence costs.

It may be true that white students have to pay tuition to go to the University of Missouri, whereas under existing arrangements Negro students can go to the out-of-state university free. But what do the white students get for their money? First and foremost, they preserve the rights and dignity of their citizenship. Second, they get the benefit of all the tax moneys which the state of Missouri year after year pours into the University of Missouri. Third, they have the advantage of any specialization which the University of Missouri gives to Missouri problems, and the advantage of associating with the future leaders of Missouri. In exchange for this the state banishes its Negro students with a hundred dollars or so for each as tuition in an out-of-state university where they enroll not by right, but by tolerance as strangers and outsiders.

There can be no true equality in a state educating its white students at home and exiling its Negro students beyond the state border. But if there could be a money equivalent it would not be tuition alone. The state would at least have to give the Negro student: (1) an allowance equivalent to the per capita expenditure for white students taking the same course in the state university, based not only on the current appropriations for running expenses but also on a computation of the annual income which a sum equal to the capital investment in university plant (ground, buildings, equipment) would produce; (2) plus an allowance for differential in transportation costs; and (3) an allowance for differential in subsistence costs.

At the outset of the campaign many persons believed the financial equivalent to Negro students excluded from the state university would be the total of the three differentials in tuition, transportation and subsistence. But reflection will show this basis is unsound. In the first place the full differential theory is based on the respective costs to the students, white and colored. But the 14th amendment does not measure costs between students; it measures state action: "No state shall deny to any person within its jurisdiction the equal protection of the laws." Therefore, the determining factor is what the state has done and is doing. The state of Missouri has poured and is pouring millions of dollars into the state university for the education of white students, which works out to a per capita expenditure of nearly a thousand dollars for the white students, while it banishes its Negro students with a pittance never over two hundred dollars per student.

A second objection to the full differential theory is that its application has no standard of certainty, but depends wholly on what out-of-state university the Negro student may happen to pick. There is no uncertainty, however, about the per capita expenditure on the education of white students in the home state university.

There were two great differences in the factual situations between the University of Maryland case and the University of Missouri case. Maryland had no provision for the graduate and professional education of Negroes, not even on paper. It had a scholarship law, but when the Murray case was tried there were three applications for every scholarship available, and the court ruled that Murray did not have to gamble on being in the lucky third.

In Missouri, however, the state in 1921 had passed an act changing the name of Lincoln Institution to Lincoln University, and on paper had given the board of curators of the new "Lincoln University" the same powers as the board of curators of the University of Missouri, with further proviso that pending full development of Lincoln University, its board of curators be empowered to pay the tuition of Negro students in adjacent state universities. The supreme court of Missouri ruled the scholarship provisions were intended as a mere temporary expedient during the transition period when Lincoln Institute would emerge as a real university.

But the tragic note in the Gaines case was that the Negro college youth of Missouri had not used up all the scholarship money as in Maryland. There was over a thousand dollars in the scholarship fund in Missouri left unallocated when the Gaines suit was tried, so no argument could be made that a scholarship for Gaines was not available. This is the second challenge to Negro college youth: that they grasp and cling to every bit of educational opportunity offered, and constantly clamor for more.

Oklahoma, Kentucky and Virginia also have out-of-state scholarship laws now. Such a law was introduced in the last session of the Texas legislature, but failed to pass. North Carolina, South Carolina, Georgia, Florida, Louisiana, Alabama, Mississippi, Arkansas, and Texas have no provisions whatsoever for the graduate and professional training of Negro youth. There is the third challenge to the college youth of the last named states.

This fight for graduate and professional training for Negro college youth has its difficulties. First is the question of time. The individual college youth cannot wait forever until the problem of his education is decided. For example Lloyd Gaines took his A.B. in 1935 and wanted to begin at once on a three-year law course. It is now 1937 but the question is still unsettled. If the United States Supreme Court reviews Gaines's case it will hardly be decided before the close of registration in September, 1938. So even if it is finally decided that the University of Missouri must admit Gaines, he will not be able to start on his three-year law course until 1939, four years after being graduated from college. These fights demand a continuity which the average individual student cannot give.

Here is a challenge to Negro college fraternities and sororities. The individual student's days are numbered; but the fraternities and sororities (graduate and undergraduate chapters) remain. The group student life represented by the fraternities and sororities has continuity; it can afford to wait, even to outwait the forces of reaction. Membership may change; but the fraternity or sorority can hammer at these educational inequalities year after year until equality is finally won.

Next, there is no established law concerning what is equality of graduate and professional training. Such law as exists the N.A.A.C.P. has made since 1935. Naturally, a certain amount of experimentation is inevitable. The program needs not only continuity, but also students and money so that if one experiment does not succeed, another experiment may be tried. No one need fear that the N.A.A.C.P. will make the same mistake twice. Here is the second challenge to the Negro college youth in their group life. Will the fraternities and the sororities furnish the students and the money for the necessary test cases to find the weak points in the reactionary lines? The students must be courageous; they must have good records which cannot be challenged on any ground except race; and they must have the support of their fellow students, both those in school and those who are out.

As to money, the grant from the American Fund for Public Service, Inc., has been exhausted. It never was the idea of the American Fund to finance this equal education fight through to the very end. The directors of the fund were interested only in pointing the way. Their theory was that if the Negro college youth were shown the pathway, they and their elders would then carry the fight on their own shoulders. If they do not want graduate and professional education enough to fight for it, the fund would not force it on them. Essentially leadership must develop from the aspirations, determinations, sacrifices and needs of the group itself. Another challenge.

A human note of encouragement showing that the fight for graduate and professional education is generating spontaneously out of the group itself is shown by the fact that up to date in the present educational campaign all the cases have been fought by the Negro lawyers who have practically donated their services. The Murray case was fought chiefly by Thurgood Marshall of Baltimore. Marshall's family pays taxes in Baltimore, but he had to go to the District of Columbia for his legal education. Sidney R. Redmond, now of St. Louis but formerly of Mississippi, and Henry D. Espy, now of St. Louis but formerly of Florida, were local counsel for Gaines. Both Redmond and Espy in their student days were and now are property owners and taxpayers in their home states, but they could not study law there. Redmond went to Harvard in Massachusetts, and Espy came from Florida to Howard university in the District of Columbia. Z. Alexander Looby of Nashville, counsel in the University of Tennessee case, had to get his legal education in New York.

A Negro has handicaps enough without having to pay taxes to support the education of white students to learn how to suppress him. The opportunities of education are not equal now; but if the Negro college youth of this generation accept the challenge, they can go far toward making educational opportunities equal, if not for themselves, then for the little Negro children now in the primary and secondary schools.

The fight will go on. It must. The Negro teachers have already picked up their fight for equal salaries and in Maryland, Virginia and Florida are financing the campaign themselves. The fraternities and sororities have all done their bit in the fight for graduate and professional education. But the real test of strength is yet to come.

The Crisis, January, 1938; XLV, 14–15.

54

JAPANESE "LAW AND ORDER" IN MANCHURIA
by The Negro Commission, C.P.,U.S.A.

The Japanese government, in the course of its conquest of a "co-prosperity sphere" in Asia in the nineteen-thirties, sought to justify this—in propaganda aimed at colored peoples throughout the world—as an achievement redounding to the glory of all such people. Five leading Black Communists—Theodore Bassett, Abner W. Berry, Cyril Briggs, James W. Ford, and Harry Haywood—on behalf of the Party's Negro Commission issued a pamphlet in 1938 contesting this claim. From it the following selection is made.

What is the fate of the peoples in these territories conquered by the Japanese militarists? How does Japan carry out her self-ordained mission of "liberator" of the Asiatic peoples?

We have before us the record of six years of Japanese militarist rule in Manchuria. The conquerors have completely taken over the governmental and economic life of the country.

The Japanese, in order to maintain their rule against a rebellious population, find it necessary to keep a permanent Japanese army of occupation, numbering 130,000 men, on Manchurian soil. But even under the protection of this mighty armed force they feel themselves insecure, and every Japanese official, merchant, and colonist is armed to the teeth.

The soil of Manchuria is one of the richest in the world, yet the peasants are completely ruined. Their cultivated land has been confiscated, and they have been compelled to break virgin soil. Forced labor has been instituted. The Manchurian peasants, like the natives of most of the African colonies, are forced to build roads and railways without pay. As the result of confiscation of their land, and the heavy burden of taxes levied upon them, thousands of peasants have been forced off the land to search for work in the cities. One-third of the land is now lying untilled.

The industrial workers are no better off. They are paid no more than a quarter the wages Japanese workers receive (which are low enough). While a Japanese worker gets thirty cents an hour, the Manchurian worker is paid seven cents.

All Manchurian universities were closed when the Japanese occupied the country. Special permission from Japanese-controlled Manchukuan authorities is necessary in order to pursue university studies. The number of secondary schools has been reduced. Students are forced to learn Japanese, and study in that language. According to the journal *Kweng Min* of November, 1936, a total of 300 children out of the entire population of Manchuria (30,000,000) were admitted to secondary schools in 1936.

The most damning indictment of Japanese imperialism is the rape and subjugation of the Korean people.

Since the time of its annexation by Japan in 1910, Korea has been governed by a series of notorious generals—the present one being the fascist-jingoist, General Jiro Minami. Under Japanese rule, the ancient culture of Korea, which has a history dating back to the twelfth century B.C., is being systematically destroyed. Freedom of speech, press, and assemblage is denied. The Korean language is forbidden in schools, the Japanese language being forced upon the population as the official tongue. Every city, village, mountain, river, and district has been given a Japanese name. It has been a relentless wiping out of every vestige of Korean culture and influence.

Thousands of students, workers, peasants, and national-revolution-aries have been thrown into prison by the Japanese police.

The blood of thousands of Koreans, massacred in the struggle for independence from Japanese rule, bears witness to the fact that imperialism knows no color.

But even worse than the fate of the Koreans is the "justice" meted out to the Formosans. In 1910, the Japanese government appropriated 9,750,000 yen for a five-year campaign of extermination of recalci-trant tribes in which thousands upon thousands of the island aborigines who refused to submit to Japanese rule were wiped out. For cold-blooded brutality, this wholesale murder of a people is paralleled only by the organized wiping out of the Australian aborigines.

Clearly the demagogic slogan, "Asia for the Asiatics," in the mouths of the Japanese war-lords is but a cloak to hide their predatory aim of making the whole of Asia a Japanese chattel.

With Japanese armies meeting increasing difficulties as a result of the heroic resistance of the Chinese people, sentiment for the resump-tion of Anglo-Japanese cooperation is gaining headway in the leading governmental circles of both Japan and Great Britain. *The New York Times* of March 24, 1938, commenting editorially upon the possibilities of a compromise between Britain and Japan for the partitioning of China on the basis of Britain's recognition of Japan's present con-quests, states:

Despite the barrage of bitter Japanese criticism of British policy in China, which has been featured in the Japanese press ever since the beginning of present hostilities, it is not improbable that Great Britain—as reported from Shanghai yesterday—is preparing to negotiate with Japan. Such action would be consistent with Prime Minister Chamberlain's attitude toward Italy and Germany. None the less, if London were willing, *Tokyo certainly would wel-come the opportunity to discuss the possibility of trading off Japanese assur-*

ances of fair dealings with British business and investments in Central China, in exchange for the participation of British capital in Japanese development of the vast resources of North China.

Thus while propagandists of Japanese imperialism attempt to rally sympathy for Nippon's aggression in China by prattle about her "mission" as a "liberator" of the Asiatic peoples from the yoke of "white" imperialism, Japanese rulers woo the Tory government of Great Britain—offering it a split in the spoils, in return for aid in the consolidation of Japan's conquest of China.

Is Japan The Champion of The Colored Races? The Negro's Stake In Democracy, by The Negro Commission, National Committee, C.P.,U.S.A. (New York: Workers Library Publishers, 1938), pp. 8-10.

55

BIRTH CONTROL IN HARLEM
by Isabella V. Granger, M.D.

The clinician of the Mother's Health Center, maintained by the Harlem Branch of the National Urban League, describes the functioning of that center during the depression.

When the word "Harlem" is mentioned, one immediately thinks of a densely populated section of New York City where the inhabitants are mostly Negroes. Pictures of The Savoy, noted dance palace, where the Negro enjoys his swing music, of Small's cocktail lounge, of The Big Apple and other night clubs are generally associated with thoughts of Harlem.

But Harlem has another side that is less well known—its family and community life. And in the midst of other typically Harlem landmarks is an institution which plays an important part in the life of this community. It is the Harlem Branch of the National Urban League, where are housed various social service activities which have proved invaluable in serving the needs of the underprivileged of Harlem's population. One of the newest and most valuable of these services is the Urban League Mothers' Health Center, doing birth control work exclusively. This center is one of twelve maintained by the New York City Committee of Mothers' Health Centers, and was opened under the Committee's direction in June, 1935.

The center has a preponderance of Negro patients, but its set-up is inter-racial, both as to staff and as to patients. Clinic sessions are held twice a week, for a period of two hours each. The Wednesday session is held in the afternoon, and the Thursday session in the evening, so that two types of mothers are accommodated—those who have small children and cannot leave them in the evening, and those who are working and therefore are not free during the day.

On Wednesdays the desk or clerical work is done by a volunteer who is white; the nurse and physician are Negroes. At the evening session, both the clerical work and the nursing assistance are done by registered nurses, one of whom is white and the other a Negro. The nurses alternate their duties so that both of them may be familiar with either routine. This makes for a high degree of efficiency, so that from twenty to thirty patients can be seen at a session.

Any woman who is married and whose economic status is such that she cannot afford a private physician is eligible to attend the center. When the center first opened, only mothers having one or more children were admitted. But recently the rules of admission have been liberalized to allow the childless wife to enjoy the benefits of the birth control service, when there is a health reason for giving her this advice.

During the two and a half years the center has been functioning, total attendance has greatly increased. This increase is due to several factors, but mainly to the more liberal interpretation of the laws governing the dissemination of birth control information and to the education of the public mind by means of free lectures and understanding newspaper publicity. Attendance has increased as follows:

	June through Dec. '35	January through Dec. '36	January through Dec. '37
Sessions	51	100	102
New Patients	123	294	369
Revisits and Renewals	514	1,469	1,797
TOTAL ATTENDANCE	637	1,763	2,166

A study of 675 active cases, based on the 1937 record, discloses some interesting facts about our patients. The greatest proportion, or 460, were between the ages of twenty and thirty, 169 were between the ages of thirty and forty, and fifteen were forty or more. We are all conscious of the need of the young mothers for the help that birth control gives them, but we often fail to consider the need of the older woman—the woman of forty or more—for the same help.

The average patient had had 3.5 pregnancies before coming to the center. The following analysis of pregnancies was made:

Living children 1,826
Dead children 112
Abortions
    Induced—153
    Spontaneous—301 454

    TOTAL NUMBER OF PREGNANCIES 2,392

One patient had had fifteen pregnancies; those who had had seven or more pregnancies totaled sixty-four patients.

Among these 675 patients, only six were not successful in using the birth control method prescribed for them at the center. A case is considered a "failure" if a patient has an unwanted and unplanned pregnancy. Of these six "failures," two did not use the method, one was negligent and only three were unexplained. The percentage of failure was less than one per cent, showing that, with careful instruction, more than 99 per cent of these patients were successful in being able to protect themselves from unwanted pregnancies, so that they could plan for the birth of their children as they wished. Since the largest percentage of these patients were colored, the record indicates that Negro mothers are able to practice birth control just as successfully as their white sisters.

The inter-racial character of the center demonstrates what an excellent piece of work can be done when staff members have caught the spirit of working together with a common goal—the betterment of humanity—without regard for race, creed or color.

Birth Control Review, May, 1938; XXII, 91-92.

56

ORGANIZING FOR JOBS: HARLEM, 1938

Black people not only faced discrimination in hiring in industry in general; in addition, within the ghettoes themselves Black people were not employed by the larger grocery chains, the banks, the transportation systems and the public utilities. Concerted efforts, often sparked and led by the Left, erupted during the depression years in many major cities throughout the nation to overcome this particular deprivation. By the late 1930's such efforts encompassed not only the Left but all political elements within the Black world. Illustrative are two documents that follow: one is from a weekly column conducted by

Adam Clayton Powell Jr. (1908–1973), who at this time was minister of the Abyssinian Baptist Church in Harlem and in 1941 was to be elected to the City Council and in November, 1945, to Congress; the other is the program of the Harlem Job Committee, which, jointly with the *Amsterdam News,* was one of the "responsible" groups battling on this front.

[a]

THE FIGHT FOR JOBS
by Adam Clayton Powell, Jr.

The Coordinating Committee for Employment is beginning a serious business in Harlem. It is beginning a fight for jobs. It has asked for work. It has pleaded for work. It has held work conferences. It has utilized every means at its disposal to get the employers of New York City to stop starving the Negroes of New York. These means have failed.

The Committee is now inaugurating a mass boycott and picketing of every enterprise in Greater New York that refuses to employ Negroes. The Gas and Electric Company has seen the light, the telephone company must also. The big department stores must follow suit. If Negroes can work at Ovington's, Wanamaker's, Macy's and Bloomingdale's, then an appreciable percentage must work at Gimbel's, Klein's, Hearn's, Saks and other stores.

The milk companies are next. No more subterfuges, no more passing the buck, but black faces must appear on Harlem milk wagons immediately or the milk concerns shall be boycotted.

Three hundred and fifty thousand consumers are not anything to be sneezed at and if anyone dares try to sneeze, we are killing him with the worst cold he ever had. The same thing goes for the Metropolitan Life. As long as we have Negro insurance companies there is no reason why Negroes should pay one cent to any other insurance company that refuses to employ Negroes.

From the column, "Soap Box," in New York *Amsterdam News,* May 7, 1938, p. 11.

[b]

PLATFORM FOR JOB CAMPAIGN

1. AIMS: To provide a greater measure of employment for Negro

workers in the institutions and establishments which are sustained by the purchasing power of the Negro.

2. All jobs obtained must provide for a standard living wage equal to that prevailing at the time of employment.

3. Wherever Negroes obtain jobs and union conditions prevail, the Negro workers must be, or must become members of the established union.

4. Workers are to be hired on the qualifying standards set by the employer.

5. Applicants for employment shall not be confined to any organization, or individual.

6. Employment of Negroes outside of the Harlem area must not be sacrificed for any possible local increases.

7. Any increase in employment of Negroes in Harlem must be accomplished without the victimization of white for black workers.

8. The Harlem Job Committee shall charge no fee or in any way exact profit of any kind from any employer or employee.

9. In pursuance of the above objectives the Committee will secure and utilize the cooperation and support of all responsible institutions and organizations in Harlem.

10. The Harlem Job Committee will cooperate with those employers recognizing the justice of the Committee's objectives. The Committee will, however, utilize every legal and recognized means to obtain its aims, in cases where employers either fail or are unwilling to cooperate.

New York *Amsterdam News,* May 14, 1938, p. 1. See *The New York Times,* April 29, 1938, p. 8, for a fairly full story on the work of Powell's Coordinating Committee for Employment, with the observation that "similar movements have been started in Boston, Philadelphia, Newark, Yonkers and in other cities."

57

CHEATING THE GEORGIA CHAIN GANG

by Jesse Crawford

The escape from a Georgia chain gang of Jesse Crawford, his arrest in Michigan, and his successful defense against extradition—conducted by a joint team of attorneys representing the N.A.A.C.P. and the International Labor Defense (I.L.D.)—attracted considerable attention in the nineteen-thirties. Below Jesse Crawford tells his own story.

If you have never served time in a Georgia chain gang, if you have never worn a seven-foot trace-chain around your neck, double shackles around your legs, broken rock with a forty-pound hammer from sun-up until sun-down, hung by your wrists in a stock and stood in a sweat-box until you were unconscious, you do not known the meaning of the word suffering.

But this is getting ahead of my story.

I was born in Atlanta, Georgia, 24 years ago. My parents were hard-working, God-fearing people and they tried to rear my three sisters and I to believe in their faith. It was their earnest desire for us to grow up and serve our people well.

I realized this at a very tender age and tried to prove worthy of the confidence my parents had in me. I obtained employment as a motor-cycle messenger in one of Jacoby's drug stores. At the same time, I carried registered mail for the Atlanta postoffice.

This work was hard and often painful, for the mail and medicine had to be delivered in the sleet, rain and snow, and there were no "off-days." But I stuck to it in hope of having the pleasure of hearing my parents say they were proud of me.

When the Georgia police accused me of stealing a model T Ford in 1931 my father, who had been a writer, mail carrier and school teacher was dead and my mother had become an invalid.

Even though the chief of police, Gunnie Brade, of Fayetteville, Ga., testified that he did not arrest me for stealing the T model Ford (which would not run), but for being in possession of it, they sentenced me to serve twelve months in the Georgia chain gang.

A few days after they sentenced me I was transferred from the Fulton County Tower, better known as "The Big Rock Jail," to Warden Charley Frank Collyer's chain gang camp. This camp was on Cleveland avenue, Atlanta, just across from the Rose Land cemetery. The inmates told me that the guards put it there so they would not have to carry the dead cons far to cover them up.

Before entering the chain gang I had heard a lot of horrible stories about it, but I never believed it was so bad. But now, since having served time in that prison, I can truly say the public have never seen a book or picture which actually described the terrible conditions of that infamous prison as it was when I was there.

Bad! I should say it was! We were aroused long before sun-up every morning, and rushed through the act of eating bad food, which usually consisted of fried sow-belly, hard corn punks and a rusty old pan full of black strap molasses that burned our throats badly. Then we were forced to walk to work, three miles away, with double shackles on our legs. The shackles cut our legs painfully and sometimes caused blood poison to set in.

Our work consisted of rock breaking with a forty pound hammer from sun-up until sun-down. And there was never a moment to rest or stall. The grim-faced guards saw to that. They kept their eyes on our every move, and to let us know that they were doing this, they would shout foul curses during the entire day. And ever so often they would stroll, swaggering up and down the line and wallop us across the back with a hickory stick they carried.

Whenever we wanted to get a drink of water we had to say, "getting a drink O'Boss." And whenever we wanted to attend to nature we had to say, "getting out over here, one time O'Boss," or, "Captain." If the guard yelled back, "all right, O'so and so, get out," we stepped out, but if he did not answer we knew that he meant for us to keep working.

At noontime we were given a pan of wormy, stock peas, a hunk of fat sowbelly and some hard corn bread. If we attempted to pick the worms out of the pea soup the guard would curse and flog us with his stick.

At sun-down we would start for the camp, soaking wet with perspiration, and so tired that we could hardly move one foot before the other one. Our supper, which usually consisted of corn meal grits, sorghum molasses and chicory coffee was always ready when we reached the camp.

After supper we were fastened to a filthy old bunk with a building chain. The building chain was a large log chain that ran from one end of the dormitory to the other.

Enraged with brooding hatred, rigid discipline, the constant menace of guns and merciless punishment, the convicts one day suddenly rebelled and turned the prison into an unholy place. They shouted at the top of their voices and hurled coarse and venomous epithets at the despised guards. Now and then one of the worst treated inmates would burst forth with bitter fury, ripping his bed clothing to threads; destroying everything that he could move, rip, burst or tear.

It was no longer a crowd of sane human beings. It was more like a mad house full of savages sending up an unholy cacophony to the sun-lighted sky. The rebels were raving and jumping frantically about like lost souls in a forever burning torment.

The riot started one morning when the guards ordered the inmates to work. Instead of marching out of the dormitory, the convicts sat on their bunks and gave vent to hatred loudly and long.

The county police force came to aid the guards in quelling that riot. When the large crowd of officers surrounded the camp with automatic shot guns, pistols and tear-gas bombs the warden and chaplain came to the window of the dormitory and pleaded with the men to be sensible.

The inmates could not or would not understand the plea advanced by the warden and chaplain. They continued to yell, "we want something to eat; we want a decent place to sleep and eight hours a day work, instead of 12 and 15," until the warden yelled, "I have given you hogs something to eat; now I am going to give you something else." At that, tear-gas-bombs came through the window.

Almost instantly the dormitory was filled with stifling gas. We were choking and staggering about like drunken men. The inmates fought back like cornered wild cats, but they did not have a chance to win. They were outnumbered many times and unarmed as well.

When most of the rioters had been beaten to a mushy pulp, they threw us in dump-trucks and carried us to the quarry. There, we were forced to work in the scorching sun which was so hot that it blistered our bodies raw.

When some of the boys refused to work because they were utterly disabled after the merciless beating, the guards sent for the warden and started to flogging the helpless creatures all over again.

They say the chain gang is changed now. "It is okay," the newspapers say. It is a modern prison with radio, clean dormitories, and shower baths, instead of the old barrel tub in which fifteen and twenty men used to bathe without changing water. The reports may be true, but I doubt it. Men who have left the prison recently tell me it is just like it was when I left there.

Knowing that I could not serve my sentence under such miserable conditions, I decided to escape. I knew when I thought of doing this that I would be taking a chance on being blasted to eternity by the guards, but I preferred that to the slow and torturous death that I was dying in that dreadful place.

For a while I discussed my idea of escape with a group of long-termers who were supposed to be okay and very tough. But I soon learned that this would not do, for somebody was telling the guards everything that I said about escaping.

After several weeks of constant plotting I chose five old-timers who I knew would make good pals and started cutting a hole through the dormitory floor under my bed, with crude tools we had stolen from the prison work shop. This work was slow and tedious, backbreaking, but each day it went on. Such is the perseverance of freedom-starved convicts.

Finally, the great day came. The hole had been completed and our time had come to go. It was at breakfast time one foggy morning when the six of us involved in the project crawled through the hole under my bunk, down into the basement of the dormitory and out a rear door. We continued to crawl and roll on the ground until we passed the bright searchlights surrounding the camp. We had only been gone from the prison a few minutes when the guards, trusties and bloodhounds came after us.

For almost an hour we plodded through the marshy swamp just ahead of the angry posse and flop-eared dogs. The guards were shooting so close to us that two of my pals wanted to surrender. I encouraged them to keep going until a piece of hot lead from the posse's gun passed through one of their shirts, slightly touching the skin. They just had to surrender then, they said, and stopped to wait for the pursuing posse. A few minutes later a high-powered rifle bullet passed between my arm and side, taking a small piece of my side with it.

It was about this time when my best pal, Lonnie Davis, who had been running beside me ever since we left the camp, stumbled and fell in a quivering heap upon the marshy ground with a back full of rifle lead. The officer who shot Lonnie told me when he came to the Michigan state capitol at Lansing to extradite me that the bullets paralyzed one side of Lonnie's body. I stopped to help Lonnie, but there was nothing I could do for him so I put on more speed in the snake-infested thicket.

It was indeed a matter of life and death now; two of my pals had surrendered; one had been shot, and the other two had left me.

I was just ahead of the aroused posse and the baying hounds were in sight and the bullets were flying so close that I could actually hear them singing as they passed me.

But somehow my luck held out. As I came out of the thicket, I saw a bicycle parked on the highway. I hopped on it and pedaled fast. I soon left the posse far behind and went to a friend's house. There I changed my prison uniform for a suit of civilian clothes and started out again.

I realized that I was a fugitive from justice, and a fugitive I intended to remain until my dying day.

I had gone into that living hell a young man, but now, two months later, when I re-entered the outside world, I felt and looked like an old man.

It was hard to force myself to believe that I had served only two months in that terrible place. Those two months seemed longer than all the rest of my entire life.

After having escaped I decided to go to some faraway place where I was unknown; anywhere, to hide, to forget that horrible place, and pretend that I was not a fugitive from justice. I was determined to carry out my idea and when the search for me had subdued considerably I came out of hiding and hoboed to Detroit, eight hundred miles away. In this strange city I took up life anew under the name of Joe Fisher, and Joe Fisher I remained until the dreaded day came.

Early one foggy morning, just as it had been on the morning I escaped, eight months before, I was arrested in Detroit and detained as a fugitive from the chain gang. It was time now, indeed, to mobilize, and believe me when I say that I did that with all the strength at my command. I sent out a startling true story in the newspapers about my experience in that disgraceful place.

At first, the northern public was shy of my story. It did not believe that such a horrible place existed on the face of the earth, let alone in free America.

I proved my story and got help from the Commonwealth. Several different organizations appointed attorneys to defend me after they read that story. At that time I did not have the slightest idea that there were so many attorneys in Detroit until they began to visit me, stating that some organization or club had appointed them to defend me.

For a while the attorneys bewildered me. I did not know which one to choose. Finally, however, I chose Harold E. Bledsoe, N.A.A.C.P. attorney, and also William V. Banks and Maurice Sugar, I.L.D. attorneys. All three of these men are well known for the good work they have done and are still doing for colored people. Mr. Bledsoe was appointed here recently to the Michigan Board of Corrections. This is the second time Mr. Bledsoe has been appointed by a governor. He served as assistant attorney general under the Comstock Administration.

Shortly after the attorneys took my case, three officers from Georgia came to Detroit to extradite me. They tried to persuade me to waive extradition and return with them. But my attorneys told me not to waive anything, so I flatly refused to yield to the southern officers and they left my cell in a huff, threatening to get revenge.

My extradition hearing was set for Friday the 13th, which is reputed to be an unlucky day for some people.

On the way to Lansing, the capital, I did not have very much to say, but the officers were very talkative and tried several times to get me to tell them what I was going to say at the hearing. They also wanted to know who was putting up the money for my defense; who was writing all the stories about my experience in the chain gang. I was in no talking mood and did not tell the officers anything.

They reminded me of it being Friday the 13th, and said that that surely meant bad luck for me. My reply to that was, "I am not superstitious, and the 13th might mean bad luck for you instead of for me."

The assistant attorney general, George Murphy, brother of the Governor of Michigan, presided at my hearing and requested me to show the court the scars on my legs which the chain gang shackles had made. He also requested me to described the condition of the infamous prison to the court. This was the chance I had been craving, and I explained to the best of my ability.

Finally, after an all-day hearing, the attorney general excused himself from the courtroom to talk with the governor. Shortly afterward, when he returned with a handful of legal papers, he asked me jokingly if I wanted to go back to the chain gang. When I assured him that I did not, he told me that I did not have to go: the governor had refused to extradite me.

When the southern officers heard that, they stalked out of the capital, eyeing me wickedly and chewing viciously on some mighty strong smelling Brown Mule.

After my release, I toured the state and told of my chain gang experience in churches, halls and theaters. Then my family came to me. I am North of the Mason-Dixon line and I am going to stay.

I realize I could not say this if the N.A.A.C.P. and the I.L.D. had not come to my rescue, so I cannot end this story without saying I do appreciate the help they so kindly extended me when I needed help most.

The Crisis, June, 1938; XLV, 168–69, 178.

58

SOUTHERN YOUTH MARCHES FORWARD
by Augusta V. Jackson

In April, 1938, the Second Annual Meeting of the Southern Negro Youth Congress was held in Tennessee. A first-hand account by one of the delegates was published in June of that year and follows in full.

Chattanooga, Tennessee, in the heart of the mountainous country at the base of the Shenandoah Valley, has always been an important center of Southern life. Yesterday, its mountain heights were the scene of some of the most intense struggles of the Civil War at Chickamauga, Missionary Ridge, and Lookout Mountain. Today, it dominates the region of the vast T.V.A. project, and promises to become one of the nation's great industrial and commercial cities. In this area, rich with historic associations, where traces of the old South are fading away since the triumph of present-day industry, some four hundred delegates assembled on April 1, 2 and 3 for the Second All-Southern Negro Youth Conference. They deliberated in the shadow of the lofty heights of Lookout Mountain where the struggle for freedom was carried on over seventy years ago—the new Negro youth of the South, carrying into the twentieth century the battle for freedom, equality, and opportunity.

These fighters for the new freedom know that their enemies are century-old institutions, prejudices, and inequalities which they must face with present-day weapons. They have determined that they must grapple now with those forces if they wish to spend their adult lives in some measure of happiness and security. Many of them are farmers from the lean regions of Arkansas, Georgia, South Carolina, and Alabama where sharecroppers can never be certain of even the bare subsistance the land affords, where heavy debts and fear of sheriffs and chain-gangs, or the prospect of certain starvation tie them in their bondage. Many are students, less concerned with the rah-rah than with the serious business of preparing a world in which to live. Some of them are lawyers and ministers, handicapped in their professions by the social and economic limitations of their people. Others are the youth who are building America in the fundamental sense of the word—

miners, factory and mill workers, most of them enthusiastic trade unionists, eager to see organized labor support the movement of southern Negro youth toward its freedom. They represent various strata of our race, but all alike realize that Negro youth in the South can have no divided interests; for race discrimination, disfranchisement, denial of opportunity for jobs and education begin at the color line without reference to class, training, or interest.

The delegates represented 383,000 southern youth. They came from every southern state. Among them were fifty white delegates. They personified the growing understanding between the whole of Southern youth. They spoke of the oneness of the nation's youth problems. And to them Negro youth extended a firm hand of fellowship.

The inter-racial aspects of the conference were made evident by the endorsement and support of leading southern white citizens. The Chattanooga *Times*, in a long editorial endorsement, stated that the conference should become a major factor in reducing crime and juvenile delinquency among southern youth. The *Times* suggested that the conference initiate recreational health projects, with government and private assistance, for Negro youth. The interest manifested in the conference by the Chattanooga *Times* was echoed by the executive secretary of the Central Y.M. and Y.W.C.A. of Chattanooga. The Chamber of Commerce secured the city auditorium for the final youth rally where 5,000 enthusiastic people participated in one of the largest mass meetings ever held by Negro youth.

They were no different from other young people. There was every evidence that they shared the enthusiasm of all other youth for gaiety, for sports, for social events; at another time the same group would have cheered lustily at a football game, and have danced until the last tune of a swing orchestra was played. Here they came on serious business; each had experienced his share of the world's injustice; each could have told some incident of discrimination, oppression, or terror which he had witnessed but which was so common as to merit no notice in the press of the nation.

A bright-eyed girl, who in appearance and manner does not differ from any girl seen walking down a city street, tells you that she teaches in a rural community where she conducts a school during the "season," that is during the six months of the year when neither the planting season, or cotton picking, or berry picking has emptied the school of its students. As she describes it, you can see her rough one-room schoolhouse, without enough textbooks, or enough teaching material, where most of her pupils come to school without shoes, where some who came last season must stay out this term so that another two or three from their large family can attend while the first is at work on the farm. Since her salary depends upon the attendance quota, she must walk many miles a week in all weather to recruit absentees. She is teacher, social worker, and the community model in morals, dress and speech. She earns twenty-five dollars a month—during the season. Another teacher from a school just in the suburbs of a large southern city tells a tale of different, but almost equal difficulties. She earns twice as much as her colleague in the rural community; her school has ten teachers, as many rooms and, in addition, offices for the staff and an auditorium. She has no trouble in getting her pupils to attend school; many are eager to come for they have no long miles to travel over the countryside. Her room is crowded to the door with sixty-five first grade children whom she must teach to read and write. She is responsible for obtaining teaching materials; she must either "raise" the money or give part of her fifty-dollar wage for this purpose.

The young people at Chattanooga were willing to tell you about themselves. An alert young man of about twenty says that he is a miner from Alabama. He never had a chance to finish school, even though the school in his community went no higher than the ninth grade. He left home when he was about fifteen to find more opportunities than working on his father's impoverished bit of farmland could allow him. He worked first in the mines, digging coal all day until the work weakened his young body, and the frequent occurrence of accidents frightened him. Later, he relates, he returned to the farm only to find the land no longer his father's; a few more acres had been added to the more than four million acres of farmland that Negro acres have lost during the last fifteen years. He drifted about for a while wherever there was work. In season, he has picked cotton for the comparatively "good" wage of *a dollar* a day. Now despite his father's protests he has gone back into the mines. A friend who is with him lives in the same industrial center. He can scarcely be over twenty; he supports a family of younger brothers and sisters by working in a cement factory. His father and two older brothers have died within and last three years of tuberculosis. Outside of the mine no work can be obtained except at the factory, and in the process of work a poison settles in the lungs. The death rate is high, and the men who work at the plant fear that before they are forty death or disability will have ended their days of earning a living.

A young social worker, burning with indignation and shame, describes how almost daily, in the city, she passes numbers of her sisters working on the roadway with pick and shovel, watched over by a foreman like a gang of laborers. These Negro women are the recipients of government aid, W.P.A. workers who face the necessity of taking unsuitable and degrading labor or of being left to starvation; for the recipients of relief cannot refuse work when it is offered them.

More than one spoke of a disgraceful traffic in Negro labor carried on in southern cities under the very eye of the law. They had seen young men who were sent from employment agencies in their own cities on promises of "good" jobs in Florida, taken into the turpentine camps of that state where low pay and the most wretched living conditions prevail. Armed guards prevent workers from leaving the camp and escaping across the state line back to their homes. In Florida such traffic in labor is not illegal; it is protected by statutory law. They tell, too, that intersate traffic in domestic labor between South and North is not unknown, and Negro girls also have been made the victims of false promises, and carried away from their homes to work for a wage too low to be anything but a mockery.

Thus, they came to Chattanooga from schoolroom and mine, from office and farm, from the churches and social clubs—each with a need, each from a community where others at home were faced with the same problems. Already in their local councils and clubs they had held many discussions, trying to contrive some way to meet their pressing needs. Now in this second conference they say that people of their own age from areas as far apart as Maryland and Louisiana, or Oklahoma and Florida were also looking forward to finding a way of bringing into the South the force of a new movement. They were not content with seeing extended into the future the chaotic uncertainty that the Negro faces today. Together they would determine what they could do in cooperation with each other, with their elders in their communities to help themselves.

They wanted jobs and economic security. The graduates of colleges and technical schools wanted opportunities to work as their training permitted. They endorsed the program of the Administration for the extension of P.W.A. projects, for the extension of N.Y.A. appropriations, the continuance and extension of relief measures to help the unemployed. The rural youth wanted to safeguard for the Negro farmer the ownership of his land, and to find in what way those forced to exist by sharecropping could raise their standard of living and could escape economic bondage. The conference advocated the passage of special farmers' legislation—the Jones Tenancy Act and the Boileau Amendment which offer the sharecropper an opportunity to purchase his land and pay off his debts.

The conference determined to mobilize its forces to secure citizenship rights for the Negro. Young people are aware that only when the disfranchised of the South have acquired the right to vote can there be a realization of democracy there. Thus, they ask for the repeal of poll tax laws, the abolition of accumulative poll tax, the right of Negroes to serve on juries. They have voted to return to their localities to establish institutes for citizenship where the people of each community may study the local election laws, and regulations for jury service, and the basic constitutional guaranties so that all may be equipped to insist upon their rights as citizens. They have planned to organize clubs for the payment of poll taxes throughout the year, and to establish registration centers, and to initiate drives to secure the maximum Negro vote in each community. Southern young people are aware, too, that over all of the South the terror of lynching hangs; they know that when the people move to alter their condition, when they attempt to unite with the forces of organized labor to strengthen their economic condition, or to secure an extension of the franchise, attempts will be made to keep them in abeyance with threats of lynching. So these young people add their voices and strength to the N.A.A.C.P. and those forces that work for the passage of the Wagner–Van Nuys anti-lynch bill. They know that thus not only can some dozens or hundreds of potential victims be saved, but that also the millions of Negroes in the South will be able to exercise their rights more freely without being intimidated.

Most of the delegates were products of the unequal educational system of the South. Any one of them could have told of the difference between the educational opportunities offered to white and to Negro children in every city and in every county of the South. Most of them had attended schools whose curricula were ill-suited to the needs of the young Negro boy and girl, many of whom must leave the grades and the high schools to seek some means to supplement the family income.

Some who have survived these schools and who have been fortunate enough to attend a college or a university return to teach, finding the ideals of education instilled into them in their academic training entirely inapplicable in poverty-stricken, understaffed schools and in overcrowded schoolrooms. These young people, students and teachers, do not need to be told that education is a weapon for obtaining democratic rights, or that securing the proper training is a first step in penetrating into the higher ranks of labor hitherto closed to them. So they have pledged themselves to work within their districts and communities for the equalization of funds appropriated for Negro and white education, and for Federal provision for education that could be impartially and extensively administered throughout the South. They ask for the co-operation of the school boards in making apprentice training for industry and trades a part of the curricula. They unanimously applaud the Urban League's initiation of National Vocational Guidance Week. They ask for vocational guidance not only in the public high schools, but also in the colleges where private foundations have made little attempt thus far to direct youth in mapping the future.

It was unusual and gratifying to find at the conference vitalizing interest in the cultural heritage of the Negro race. The attitudes expressed showed in every respect the vigor and the sanity with which the new Negro youth of the South is approaching its tasks. The old tendency to appraise and to rest upon what has already been done is replaced with the determination not only to preserve the culture of our forefathers but also to extend that heritage. Young artists at the conference spoke as one in favor of a conscious art, rooted in the lives, the struggles, and aspirations of the vast numbers of our race—an art for the people and of the people.

This is the idea upon which the Richmond Community Theater, under the leadership of Thomas Richardson, has been based, an experiment whose success last year has been noted. They will work and look forward to the establishment of people's theaters and art centers in large communities where the work of the artist may be consciously directed toward the social development of our people. There the artist himself may be strengthened by the knowledge that he has an audience, a purpose, and a goal which his understanding of his people can help him reach.

Every problem which these young people discussed reflected their most urgent needs and most cherished ideals. In singling out the problems which Negro youth face today, they gave prominent place to those which immediately concerned their intimate lives: religion, health, and marriage and home life. They urge adult leadership in the church to see the need of training young people for Christian leadership, and to cooperate with youth in making the church a force in the movement for social progress.

They want to preserve their homes, and to make successful married lives possible for Negro youth. They point to the high mortality rate in Negro communities; they know that the tuberculosis death rate among Negroes is double the figure for the white race, that among all American young people, one out of every six is a victim of venereal disease. Both as members of the Negro race and as young people, they will work for the eradication of these diseases, mobilizing the support of their communities for the national campaign against venereal diseases, and for the work of the National Tuberculosis Association. Even where health prevails, however, and there is some economic security, happy marriage and home life is not completely assured. They recognize the need of enlightened guidance for young people, and recommend the institution of required courses in marriage and homemaking for all young men and young women in high schools and colleges.

Again and again throughout the days of the conference, the observer was struck with the immediate practicality which these young people applied to the discussion of their situation and of ways of meeting the needs of the South. Abstract arguments and appeals were not in the order of the day. They had indicated that there was a practical means of meeting the employment situation and of securing the right to work, of remedying the inadequacies of their educational system and of extending the cultural heritage of the race.

There had been a marked development since the 1937 Richmond conference. The First All-Southern Negro Youth Conference had astonished the South: it was unique; it had no precedent. Among adult observers some were skeptical of this awakening of youth, and looked to see only a minor explosion of young people against the traditions and standards of their elders. None questioned the need of organizing for progressive action in the South, but many were openly pessimistic about its possibilities of survival and success. The young delegates, themselves, at last year's Richmond conference, experienced many uncertainties; they were groping in their deliberations for first, definite formulations to represent the hitherto unexpressed desire of Southern Negro youth for economic and cultural opportunities and for fuller citizenship rights. Secondly, they needed some form of unified organization to make possible the attainment of the goals they would establish for themselves. At Richmond these things were accomplished, and a permanent federation of organizations set up with overwhelming enthusiasms; the Chattanooga Conference was to be for the watching South a first test of whether the youth had deliberated wisely and planned with foresight. The test was met successfully.

The broader representation of the conference over last year; its penetration into every state in the South; the far greater extent of adult interest and participation in its work; and welcome extended to it by the liberal white elements in the South; above all, the concrete steps it has taken in the past year and its outlines for the next were the proof.

Now, with the initial period of experimentation behind it, the Southern Negro Youth Congress faces its second year. This year shall undoubtedly see a larger number of Negro votes polled in the South, the growth of a right-to-vote campaign among the disfranchised, the more rapid entrance of Negroes into the progressive labor unions, and an increasing collaboration between Negroes and progressive white Southerners. Southern youth realize more acutely than others can the importance of a related, but indigenous movement for a section of the country that has been the last to yield to the trends of the new day. The Southern Negro Youth Congress, then, is no separatist movement. From its incipiency its aims have coincided with those of all American youth. As it grows in strength and influence, it will become an inseparable part of the present day crusade of all American youth for democracy and opportunity.

The Crisis, June, 1938; XLV, 170–71, 188–89.

59

WOMEN OF THE COTTON FIELDS

by Elaine Ellis

Probably the most exploited workers in the United States were the Black women who labored on the plantations in the South. Below is an account of them written by a Black woman who lived in Austin, Texas.

Another cotton picking season has opened in the South. On the farms and plantations, tenants and croppers are harvesting the gleaming white crop with the hope that this year they will get enough from their share to live through the winter. In the cities, the relief agencies are following their annual custom of commanding thousands of undernourished families to go to the cotton fields and pick for what they can get, or starve.

Scenes showing pickers at work in these fields can be secured on post-cards throughout the South. Chambers of Commerce and other civic bodies use such pictures quite often in pamphlets which invite the summer tourist to visit Dixie and learn something about the picturesque region that formed the background for "My Old Kentucky Home" and other folk songs that will never be forgotten. The average tourist will drive through some of these states, visit a few capitols, shake hands with a few governors if he gets a chance to see any, and return home. The cotton fields will cease to be of much interest, for he will have seen too many of them.

Tourists are not told by the big-shot advertising agencies that these cotton fields tell the story of what Norman Thomas calls "probably the most depressed body of workers in America." The men, women, and little children who work in these fields under the blazing Southern sun create the great Cotton Kingdom for which this region is famed. In return for their labor, they receive only poverty, ignorance, and disease.

And it is the woman, Negro and white, on whom the burden is heaviest. In every cotton field one can see her type—a stooped woman dragging a heavy cotton sack. Usually she wears a slatted sunbonnet, and her arms and neck are swathed with rags to protect them from the blistering heat.

This is the woman whom civilization has passed by. But it is from her loins, no less than from the earth itself, that the world's greatest cotton industry has sprung. A slave, and a breeder of slaves, hundreds of thousands of her kind have been crushed in its gigantic and merciless machinery. And as long as the tenant system continues, she must be sacrificed to its greed.

In the past, this woman was compelled to reproduce a large number of children because a large labor supply was in demand. Large families also mean a cheaper form of labor; for children, as well as women, generally represent labor that does not have to be paid. Consequently, the "overhead" falls upon the family instead of the landlord. The landlord himself has enforced this monopoly by letting his farm go to the tenant or cropper having the largest family.

Now the tenant-croppers are charged with "over-population" by economists and agriculturists who disregard the unwholesome economic factors that have caused an increase in farm tenancy. This increase has amounted to sixty per cent since 1930 despite the fact that the A.A.A. drove approximately 300,000 tenants and sharecroppers from the land.

As one solution to this "over-population," proponents of the sterilization racket are endeavoring to work up an agitation for sterilization of these cotton workers. The now ex-governor of Arkansas, J. M. Futrell, and H. L. Mencken, the writer, have expressed themselves highly in favor of such a measure. Sterlization, one of the tenets of Fascism, makes women its chief victim. One can readily visualize its vicious application as a means of controlling the labor supply.

On the other hand, birth control information has been denied these women, although in some sections of the South there is a plan to introduce it by means of traveling clinics. Now that there is a surplus labor supply, this method that would be such a boon to women is beginning to be viewed in a most favorable light. But the most simple medical attention is still denied them. Even during pregnancy, a woman must work in the field. The fact that she is carrying a child does not excuse her from dragging and lifting the heavy cotton sack. Frequently, when the child is born, she does not have the assistance of a physician. Women in the neighborhood, or a midwife, must help her through her confinement. Very often she does not have even this inadequate aid. It is a common occurrence for a women who is pregnant to pick cotton until the labor pangs strike her. She may be able to drag herself to the shade of a tree, or to the wagon or car, to give birth to her child. But sometimes it is born among the cotton plants. After it is a few weeks old, it will be taken by its mother to the field. There it will sleep on a pallet with brothers and sisters too young to pick. As soon as it is old enough to carry a sack, it, too, will go into the field.

The mother, in addition to working in the home field, will "hire out" to a neighboring landlord as soon as this crop is harvested. In addition, she has the upkeep of the house, and further outside work. Her hours average from about twelve to fourteen a day, each being one of extreme toil.

There is an equally bad situation existing for young girls. Many have their health ruined for life because they are forced to drag and lift the heavy cotton sacks during puberty. While the landlords' daughters attend universities and join sororities, these daughters of the croppers help to pay the cost of their dinner dances, rush weeks, and dissipations.

In the lives of these illiterate farm women, there is mute evidence of a capacity for creation. During planting time, they will sow the seeds of zinnias along the outer cotton rows. After the day's drudgery, which ends late at night with the housework, they will return with buckets of water for the seeds. Often one of these women can be seen standing idle for a moment during the busiest part of the day to gaze across the even rows to where gaily colored zinnias flame among the white cotton. And the change in her is miraculous. This woman is suddenly straight and clear-eyed, and pushing back her bonnet, she shades her eyes with her hand as she looks across the field shimmering in waves of heat. But just as suddenly, she will droop, and turn again to her task. The cotton must be picked!

But the women of the cotton fields are awakening. It began back in 1931 when Estelle Milner, a young Negro girl, brought the tenants and sharecroppers of Camp Hill, Alabama, a little paper called *The Southern Worker.* The Organization of the Sharecroppers Union that followed, and the bloody battles of Camp Hill and Reeltown will never be forgotten. In the years that have followed, the Sharecroppers Union, Southern Tenant Farmers Union, and the Farmers Union have organized more than 300,000 tenants and sharecroppers throughout the South.

The bloodshed that planters and deputy sheriffs caused at Camp Hill and Reeltown, when mangled croppers were forced to flee for their lives, marked only the beginning of terrorism that breaks out wherever unions of these workers demand better conditions. But undaunted, they struggle on, frequently chalking up victories to their score.

And the women are standing by their men.

The Crisis, October, 1938; XLV, 333, 342.

60

WHAT I SAW IN SPAIN

by William Pickens

One of the decisive events in the twentieth century was the Spanish Civil War of the nineteen-thirties. Participating in the struggle against fascism were several thousand U.S. volunteers and they were Black as well as white. William Pickens visited Spain during the war and wrote the following account; among the Black men not mentioned by Mr. Pickens was Angelo Herndon's brother, Milton, who was killed fighting there.

When some one in a group of New Yorkers asked me in the summer what I intended to do in my month of vacation, "Perhaps go to Europe," I replied. "What for?" they asked.—"Just to see how many democrats are still left running loose there."—"Well," said Jimmie Harris, one of the group, "you better hurry, or you'll be able to call a mass meeting of them in a 'phone booth."

"Will you visit Germany?" some one challenged.—"No, sirree, for my opinions are so strong against dictators that they may stick out of

my pores, be discovered,—and I could be framed." Think of that,—
when only ten years ago, even six years ago, I had more friends in
Germany than in any other nation outside of the United States, and
when traveling about Europe I always felt "at home" when I got into
Germany. But today there is no law in Germany, only will and whim,
and there is no health for a democrat. I am going to die a democrat,—
and I do not want that end to be forced upon me by fascist dictators. The
last time I was in Germany was just a few months before Hitler; the
next time I go to Germany will be at least a few months after Hitler.

So this time I planned definitely to go to France and England, two
countries that might still be listed in the democratic column, and I left
the matter pending as to whether I should go to Switzerland and
Prague or to Belgium and Denmark also. This question was settled
when we had a dinner for the Medical Bureau of New York, which is
supplying medical aid and ambulances to the Spanish Government,
and they asked me to visit Spain. Well, visit Spain I would. Friends in
Paris had already been suggesting Spain. It was difficult, for in all
American passports there is a red stamp now, indicating that they are
not good for Spain. This is not to keep Americans free from French
and Italian bombs. It has no relation to the safety of Americans; it seems
part of the unconscious "plot" of the democracies to run out on all the
democracy that is left in Spain, and to aid what they ought to hate:
Fascism in Spain. For, note, these same passports do not forbid Americans to go to China, where bombs are thicker, nor to other places almost as dangerous to the individual. But Spain is cut out. That had to be
overcome. I would go legally, although many Americans, French and
English go illegally, or rather without the consent of their own governments. When I went into Spain an English woman went in, in spite of
her government, and an American woman came in the same evening,
without American o.k., and after two months of trying to get in from
southern France.

Perhaps I could never have got in illegally: it would have taken too
much time, too much pain, or both, and I had only a short time.
Accordingly, we got in touch with Secretary Hull's office, the American
State Department, with the straight request that I get permission to
enter Spain. In the few days before I left on the *Queen Mary,* the reply
could not be received, and the Medical Bureau was to cable me in
Paris and the State Department was to cable the American ambassador there. When I reached Paris, I soon received a cable from Mr.
Reissig of the New York Bureau office, saying that the matter was
"pending" in Washington, and suggesting certain Paris contacts. Think-

ing that the American government had not yet made up its mind, I went to the international organization in Paris that aids the Spanish Government and began to get ideas. The second day, I suggested that we call up the American ambassador and ask if he had heard from our State Department. Surprisingly he had; perhaps he had the cable when I arrived in Paris.

Now to the American embassy with my passport, to get the necessary notations made in it. It did not take the Americans as long as it takes Europeans: the Americans used only one hour and fifteen minutes, doing what could have been done in fifteen minutes. They cancelled the prohibition against entering Spain and entered a note from the embassy that I was permitted to enter.

But, not yet. The fight has just begun: the French authorities have to give their permission, since I am to enter Spain from France and over a closed French border. So next to the Prefect of Police. Now there is where it takes *time*. Not a gendarme nor a functionary in the place knew who the Prefect was. At least they would not say, but only referred one to the information window, before which a long line was already formed, waiting to ask the clerk perhaps similar questions, many of which could have been answered by the elevator boy, but for the official notion that all information must be secured from the information clerk. So there!

After entering this line and at long last getting up to the clerk and putting in my inquiry and stating briefly what I needed, the information clerk went away to find a personage for me, leaving me at the window and a long line behind me. This personage was finally secured and came out, learned my request, and told me of another line which I must enter in order to leave my passport (for two days!). One always has a reluctance at leaving his passport in European offices, outside of English offices. Once in Moscow I left my passport and when I went back it took the girl clerks what seemed like hours to find it. I actually waited painfully looking on while the embarrassed clerks went through baskets of jumbled passports, examining first one and then another, trying to find my precious American one. At that time, too, we did not have any official relations with Russia, and it was looking as if I were to be there for months, while the long red tape was being unwound, measured and cut and re-wound in America to "prove" my American citizenship. But at last the thing was found.

But I was determined to get into Spain, so I left my passport with the French. Two days later I went, got on the end of a que, and when I reached the window my passport was not ready, had not been sent back yet from some high-and-mighty place. I was asked by the very kindly girls to come back in two hours. So I walked for miles along the Seine, looking at the book stalls that are erected against the river wall, such as vegetable stands in America. In practically all of the stalls I saw many copies of Hitler's *Mein Kampf*. The French are reading that book. They are learning Hitler's intentions, and his opinion of the French. Almost to the Louvre in my walking, I hailed a cab and went to a restaurant near the Madeleine, where I had an appointment; left a note and took a cab back to the Prefecture. This time, after I negotiated another line, I was asked to wait "a few minutes," and was many minutes later called to the window and given my passport, with authority of France to cross the French border into Spain.

No, that is not all—not yet. There is still the Spanish ambassador's office, the long train ride to southern France, to Perpignan, the last French town, the seeing of the authorities and the Spanish consul there, the arrangements about money (very queer and uncertain in time of war), and then the tackling of the actual border, where the French military must pass you on one side and on the other the Spanish must receive you, both looking you over carefully. What a pain to enter Spain! But it is not the fault of the Spaniard; it is due to the false idea about "neutrality," a word I shall not respect so much in the future as I have respected it in the past. When there is a human fight going on, other humans cannot be neutral. They may act neutral, if they be afraid, but they cannot be neutral, ever. When a thug attacks the innocent, when a brute attacks the helpless, when a grown-up is beating a child, one certainly then is far from neutral. But in an effort to keep the peace with Italy and Germany, France has endeavored to follow England and act neutral. Those people of France and England do not want war, are afraid of a great war. What sane government heads are not afraid of war? Hitler is the only kind that does not fear it. But is war being avoided or its ultimate horrors lessened or increased by yielding to the bullying type of state heads?

From Perpignan to Barcelona we travel by road, auto and bus, for 125 miles, or a longer distance, into Spain. Trains are too dangerous, too visible to the eyes of war planes. Cars can take cover on the lovely highways that are canopied by the branches of the plane trees. In a Spanish town we stop for a bite of lunch and refreshments. What a monstrosity is war! In southern France are fruits, the best in the world, food in abundance, bread, sweets, vegetables, all begging to be sold. The shops and stalls are full of food. Just a few miles away is Spain, where this food would be worth its weight in gold, where people are smoking weeds for cigarette tobacco, where food is reduced to bare necessity even in the best hotels. That is "neutrality": the nations have closed their borders to these people who are on the defensive; they could not for a long time buy even anti-aircraft guns from France and England for the defense of Barcelona, which is open to frequent attacks from the Italian airmen from the Balearic Islands.

And this town in Spain in which we stopped was, unlike Barcelona, situated back from the coast, and yet it had been horribly bombed. Houses looked like skeletons, like ruins. These houses are not of wood. There is no wood for buildings in most of Europe, especially southern Europe. The houses are of rock and brick and earth, and that is why the whole city is not reduced to ashes when it is bombed and individual blocks set on fire. It is impossible to describe the wreckage from these powerful explosives that fall from the sky. Jupiter had no thunderbolt as terrific as these bombs.

We arrived in Barcelona, capital of Catalonia, great city on the Costa Brava, with more than a million inhabitants in normal times, but now with over two million, including the refugees from Franco areas, city of great Paseos and Boulevards, and of artistic buildings, with their stone and iron fronts carved or moulded into the flowing lines of sea waves or the foliage of trees. Life was not just something to go through in Spain: it was evidently something for the Catalonians to enjoy, "before the war."

It was just before night when we arrived, and were put out at the Majestic Hotel on Paseo de Gracias, great avenue with four walkways for pedestrians and three for vehicles, the central vehicular way being a two-way passage. The Majestic is (was) the leading hotel of the city. When we registered we were told: "The elevator is not running; you must walk up." Fortunately buildings are not sky-scrapers in Europe. The top floor here was the seventh. I had a room on the sixth floor up. No elevators; all energy being saved for the prosecution of war and defense.

Catalonia was evidently a very prosperous part of the world, and the most prosperous part of Spain. Why did we not go there when there was peace and when the travelers by foot on the highways went playing stringed instruments and singing? One Boston woman who came in the next morning told me that she was in Barcelona seven years before and that it was so prosperous that it was really wicked, and that she could hardly walk a block along the great Paseo Ramblas without "being insulted" every few hundred feet. But now in imminent danger of hellish attack at any hour, and more especially on any moonlit night, the men of Barcelona have no time to tease foreign women. And yet life goes on in Barcelona: hating, loving, having babies and planning futures. The air bombs have driven the people together against the enemy and forced them to construct underground refuges. These refuges are being built in many streets and under whole squares. Republican Square has one that can take in at least one thousand humans. All refuges have two exits or entrances, so that in case one is blown in by a bomb, the other may be open. But that is not all, for they have air vents in addition and picks and shovels stored inside for digging out.

The first day in Barcelona I set out to find the Internationale pour l'Enfance. It was not at the address given me in Paris, so I had a walk which was not wasted, for it carried me through much of the city that was being bombed about the time I set off from Paris, two days before I arrived: six story buildings, ripped from top to cellar by a single bomb, and in some cases demolished altogether; the Old Cathedral hit and blown into ruins, with its stark facade standing there like Kenilworth Castle remains. They call this cathedral "Old," because, before the present war started they were building on a new Cathedral, which they had got only so far with, that it too now stands there like a ruin. Windows blown out of the old and not yet put into the new. A German young man in his early twenties accosted me and made himself known, German in race but anti-German in sympathies. He said: "I would like to show you some of the ruinous work of some of my fellow countrymen here." Some of those planes were German. In one bombing earlier in the year, the planes had killed 800 and wounded 1,500 people. The bombs hit where life was crowded, at the markets and on the boulevards or Paseos. Later I found the International for Children on the same street as the Hotel Majestic, and a young Swiss doctor in charge, Dr. Jaeggy. The American young woman who had been in charge had left for home the same day on which I arrived.

Yes, there are American Negro boys in Spain, fighting with the Loyalist troops. All honor to those boys! They are making history. Among them are some of the greatest heroes of the war. There was McDaniels, of San Francisco, who drove back a whole company of Franco's troops by the use of hand grenades, when the Loyalists were re-crossing the Ebro. He is now a black god in Spain, with one explosive bullet in his left thigh. The bullet hit into the thigh, then exploded and moved in three pieces downward. But he is all right, and will be up soon and at 'em again, unless they send him to the States for propaganda purposes as they are thinking of doing. There is Oscar Hunter, once a student at West Virginia State, and one of the first group to go to Spain when the war opened. He is now Political Commissar of Hospitals, a very high officer. "How long do you think," he asked me, "it might take me to get up to such a position in the United States." "Well, not in the next hundred years," I replied sincerely. He has made it within a year in Spain.

There is no color question in Spain. People are just people. One of the tests for that: the Spanish girls and women who are interested in any colored man, do not sneak, as they often do in the United States, but they go along openly, naturally, and apparently without even any consciousness of being out of any conventions. They laugh and play and joke, and smack each other with their hands in public and in offices, and on the Paseos.

And there is also Abe Lewis; and there is Joe Taylor; also black boys like Luchelle McDaniels. McDaniels is as black all over his body as a well-shined pair of black shoes. When I saw him, he was undressed and his wound was being swabbed by an American nurse in Mataro Hospital, about 30 kilometers out of Barcelona. This is a great military hospital.

These boys, although they are risking their lives for the ideal of popular government, are rather happy in what must seem to them like a normal world. "It's not like the States here," said Joe Taylor, "for here I get some breaks perhaps just because I am colored." When I met Joe, it was first through his voice: going through the Mataro Hospital, which is located in a monastery, I heard singing before I came to the door of one ward, group singing,–Negro singing. "There must be the Negro boys," I thought, and felt that it was odd to find them segregated in Spain. But when we opened the ward door, there was but one Negro, Joe Taylor, and there were all the white patients and the nurses, and they were all singing, Negro songs under Joe's leadership. "Come on, mule!" was the refrain of the song which I had heard. Spanish and French, and American and German and Italian,–all were singing this song. Other songs followed, always led by Joe Taylor. It was not just a remark, but something that I meant and still mean, when I told the hospital authorities: "Joe Taylor is worth more to your patients than any surgeon in the place." They admitted it.

Strange how much we learn in a short period of contact: how cordial were these beleaguered people. It was a high privilege to visit this great military hospital, a privilege which they are reluctant to grant to those whom they know, let alone to a stranger. But they gave me this permit, and wanted to send me to other parts of Spain, if only I had had the time. French and English and American correspondents were being denied hospital permits at the same time my permit was being granted.

I shall long remember some of the Spanish leaders: people like Constancia de la Mora, a stateswoman, if ever there was one. She is head of the Foreign Propaganda Service, and is in charge of foreign correspondents in Spain. From her they must get their permits to write articles, and must submit to her censorship. Then there is San Marti, splendid Spaniard, dark and rather handsome. He it was who issued me a permit for visiting military hospitals, and he seemed to understand as soon as we had talked a few minutes. Immediately afterwards an American correspondent and hospital worker from France was denied any permit, even to go with me to Mataro. They took me in a state car, with guide and chauffeur. They made my short stay profitable.

One night the Italians from Mallorca, largest of the Balearic Islands, attempted to raid us, but were driven off by the defense planes. It was just after dinner, and we were seated in one of the hotel salons, conversing. Suddenly a whistle went by, a police whistling as he rode his motor-cycle. All lights of the city went out. It must be done by master switches at the power plant.

Were you ever in a dark hotel, in a great dark city, with all streets dark, and even the auto lights out, not a spark of fire or light to be seen, except the great searchlights playing on the scattered clouds and the sky, seeking out the enemy? "Were you afraid?" people ask. There seems to be no thought of fear in such a circumstance. There is a feeling of defiance. We, men and women, went out on the Paseo to watch the sights, with no more fear of being hit in the momentarily expected raid than we have hope of winning first prize in the sweepstakes. Of course, it was possible. Those searchlights are a beautiful sight, on a dark sky,—and the music of those planes! It was hours before the attempted raid was over. I actually got tired, and went in and felt my way up the stairs, six flights, in pitch-dark, and undressed and bathed and went to bed without so much as the light of a match.

Today these Spanish people, in their old, old home, antedating the Caesars there, are fighting on the front for popular government,—for self-government. It is our fight.

The Crisis, October, 1938; XLV, 319-21, 330.

61

BLACK PEOPLE, ANTI-SEMITISM, AND HITLER

The racism and barbarism of Hitler induced widespread condemnation in the United States, not least among the Afro-American people. Yet, given the virulence of the racist oppression suffered in the U.S. by Black people, there was a special quality to the response of the Afro-American. Two editorials from *The Crisis*—with Roy Wilkins as editor—on this matter follow.

[a]

ANTI-SEMITISM AMONG NEGROES

A number of inquiries has come to the N.A.A.C.P. in recent years about anti-Semitism among Negroes. Thoughtful Jewish leaders are concerned over occasional speeches and occurrences here and there.

We do not believe there is any real basis for their suspicions. Negroes do not hate Jews. Not only Negro leaders, but the Negro masses realize that race hatred is a vile and self-destroying thing. They have had this truth driven home to them through generations of treatment at the hands of a controlling section of the white majority in this country.

But that does not mean that Negroes have not been puzzled and disturbed at times over the actions of some Jewish individuals and groups. In general in the trade union movement and in the radical political organizations Negroes and Jews get along very well, with the Jews not only having sympathy for and understanding of the plight of the Negro, but actually doing something to ease the burden of prejudice.

Certain Jewish philanthropists have made substantial contributions to the financing of programs for Negro advancement and improvement, choosing, as is their right, the kind of movements they shall aid. But the Jewish middle class (upper and lower), the shopkeepers and merchants and the landlords, in many cases and in many localities, leave much to be desired. The story is still told in Harlem of the Jewish landlord who told his Negro tenants they ought to be glad to get an apartment with hardwood floors, tiled bathrooms and French doors—at any rental.

This middle class attitude is illustrated by a liberal Jewish rabbi who told the N.A.A.C.P. that members of his congregation informed him they did not want any sermons linking the plight of the Jew with the plight of the Negro. But this attitude ignores the fact that prejudice is virulent and uncontrollable; if it is condoned in one instance, it will fatten and intrench itself and shortly turn upon other victims.

Currently, the 165,000 Negro citizens of Baltimore, Md., are incensed over the flat refusal of department stores in that city to serve them—not ice cream sodas and luncheons, but clothing, furniture, and the thousands of other items sold by such establishments. It happens that the majority of these stores is either owned or managed by Jews. The question, of course, is economic, not racial, but the anger of a hurt people leaps to the racial aspect.

Another sore point is that of employment. Negroes are rigidly proscribed in many establishments owned or managed by Jews. In this the latter follow the pattern set by gentiles, but it does seem that Jewish employers might be peculiarly sympathetic to Negroes seeking to break out of the traditional jobs set aside for them. It is easy to forget, in this situation, that Jews themselves complain bitterly that in many businesses run by their own people, Jews either are refused employment or are hired on a quota basis.

The whole question is a complex one, not to be solved by set formulae or by recrimination. American Jews come from many lands and have vastly different heritages. They do not react racially as a unit on any question, except, perhaps, on Hitler. Neither do Negroes, except, perhaps, on lynching. But the matter of the attitudes of Negroes and Jews toward each other deserves thoughtful attention both for the sake of each race's individual happiness and progress, and for the sake of the larger ideal of making our democracy work at a time when the forces of fascism are on the march all over the world.

Editorial, *The Crisis,* June, 1938; XLV, 177.

[b]

NEGROES, NAZIS AND JEWS

Negroes, along with the rest of the civilized world, have been shocked at the crushing brutality which Hitler's Nazi Germany has visited upon the Jews in the latest outbreak of anti-Semitism in that country. As wide as has been the sympathy of the rest of the world with the plight of the Jews, it is doubtful if any section or race has sympathized more whole-heartedly and keenly with the Jews than Negro Americans, for they have known the same type of persecution ever since the beginning of America.

But it would serve no purpose to pretend that Negroes have given their sympathy and joined in protests without clear and often bitter insight into their own position as American citizens. They look around at the Americans who can be moved to protests against brutality in another land, but who cannot recognize and protest against the same conditions within our own borders.

In their hearts, the Negroes' feelings go out to the Jews. They know what Hitler means because they have known slave overseers, plantation riding bosses, high sheriffs, governors like Cole Blease (who shouted: "to hell with the Constitution when it interferes with lynching"); senators like Vardaman, Harrison and Bilbo, of Mississippi; Watson, of Georgia; Heflin, of Alabama; Ellender, of Louisiana; and "Cotton Ed" Smith, of South Carolina.

Negroes know what it is to have school doors slammed in their faces, churches and property destroyed, jobs denied, courts judging race instead of crime, insult and humiliation heaped upon them in parks, playgrounds, theatres, restaurants, hotels, beaches, trains, buses and airplanes. They have had their property and belongings confiscated and have been driven out of town between sunset and sunrise. They know ghettoes. They have read countless signs: "Nigger, don't let the sun set on you in this town." Unlike the Jews in modern Germany, they know lynching.

(As this proof is being revised news comes of the seventh lynching of 1938 in Wiggins, Miss., but the American humanitarians are so busy denouncing Hitler that they cannot find words for U.S.A. lynchings.)

They have been reviled and misrepresented in textbooks, from the kindergarten through the research seminar. The poison of racial hatred has been spewed forth in America for generations.

It is not to be wondered, then, that even while he feels most sincerely and most deeply for the Jews, he looks with a twisted smile upon the fervent protests of his white fellow Americans who have remained for so long insensible to the crimes against freedom, justice, humanity and democracy which have been perpetrated in the United States against a loyal minority.

He wonders that these people can become so stirred over raiding Storm Troopers in Germany and remain so quiescent over raiding mobs in Dixie. He wonders that white Americans can become so incensed over the ousting of Jews from German universities and yet not raise a whisper over the barring of Negroes from many American universities. He looks askance at American clergymen and bishops becoming aroused over Hitlerland, the while drawing a rigid color line in religion in America.

(Bishop Edwin Holt Hughes told a gathering of Methodist clergymen in Philadelphia that it would be an "injustice" to America to say that lynching is tolerated here. The gathering refused to endorse a federal anti-lynching bill. The bishop then assisted with the passing of a resolution condemning Germany's treatment of the Jews.)

He gazes in wonderment at the extraordinary measures being contemplated to admit and provide employment for refugees from Hitler, while he himself knocks at the door of a thousand businesses seeking employment in vain.

In the past few weeks, our papers and our radios have been full of articles and speeches about the necessity of preserving democracy in America. An endless procession of speakers and writers has thanked God for America. Like the ancient Pharisees, we are grateful we are not as other men.

Notwithstanding the hypocrisy of most Americans, *The Crisis* believes that Negroes should continue to protest against Hitler and all that he represents. The Nazi chancellor's treatment of the Jews is all the more despicable because he is using every instrument of the state against a helpless minority. That is the only difference between the treatment of the Jews in Germany and of Negroes in the United States. Over here the central government does not use its machinery against Negroes; it proceeds just as effectively by remaining indifferent to the plight of Negroes and using its machinery *for* white people.

We should join everyone in protest. We should take part in com-

mittees to combat fascism and the spread of anti-Semitism. We who
have suffered from this thing cannot degrade ourselves by harboring
prejudice and hatred. Hitlerism must not come to America and, if
possible, must be halted in Europe.

At the same time, we maintain—and we feel confident that the
vast majority of Negroes is of the same opinion—that the best way
for us to combat Hitlerism, the best way for us to strengthen democracy, and the best way for us to give dignity and honor and influence
to our protestations is to set to work immediately to see that in our
own country, under our own Constitution, democracy shall function
as a reality for all minorities of whatever race, religion or color.

Editorial, *The Crisis,* December, 1938; XLV, 12.

62

MORE SOUTHERNERS DISCOVER THE SOUTH

by Charles S. Johnson

In no part of the country did the nineteen-thirties result in more significant
developments than in the South. A pronounced upsurge in labor organization
—both in the cities and in the rural areas, and among both Black and white—
with powerful Left influence, and important stirrings in the churches were influential in producing, by 1938, the Southern Conference on Human Welfare.
Its organizational meeting—held in Birmingham, Alabama, in November of
that year—is described by a leading Black scholar of the time who was shortly
to become president of Fisk University.

Liberalism in the South is not a generalized social attitude; it is
rather, where it exists at all, an aggregate of specific liberal views,
some of which are mutually contradictory. This was one of the first
observable characteristics of the group assembled in Birmingham, November 20th to 23rd, for the Southern Conference on Human Welfare. It was a curiously mixed body which included labor leaders and
economists, farmers and sharecroppers, industrialists and social executives, government officials and civic leaders, ministers and politicians,
students and interested individuals. No one knew at the outset what
to expect, and no one was fully prepared for what actually happened
as this new front formed for attack on the South's chronic ills.

If liberalism means anything at all it implies a willingness to subordinate personal prejudices and relax traditional sanctions where neces-

sary in the interest of constructive social change. In this respect the Birmingham conference was as significant as it was historic. It drew together the largest group of liberals the South has witnessed. There were more than twelve hundred delegates present. It was the first bold emergence of the liberal South as a self-conscious group, inspired to action by the devastating government report on the region's economic and social plight.

In the South it is a form of liberalism, for example, to ignore the romantic tradition and face realistically the existence of a vast and backward peasantry. But this is not the same liberalism that seeks in the interest of struggling industry the abolition of differential freight rates. Similarly, it is a form of southern liberalism to advocate economic independence of the financial North and East, but not the same type that recognizes the necessity for wiping out racial differentials in industry and education. The most conspicuous contribution of the Conference was in achieving, first, a comfortable tolerance in diversity, and, later, in projecting a philosophy which revealed the organic relationship of many of the problems of the area, the solution of any one of which is conditioned upon the solution of the others.

The strategy of the Conference was sound. It aimed at being neither a labor meeting, nor a social work body, nor a race relations assembly. It sought to present the total regional configuration, with special elements and problems in their functional setting. The labor relations section, for example, attacked the encrusted opposition of the region to State wage and hour legislation. While encouraging southern industrial developments, it sought by proposals to reduce regional and racial wage differentials. Labor went on record as desiring greater unity in its programs in the area. It seemed unmistakably to be the feeling of the white labor delegates that the forward march of labor could not be maintained without according to the Negro worker full justice and fraternity. And it was not necessary in these discussions for a Negro to arise and ask for or demand such fraternity.

The question of suffrage, while acute for Negroes, is equally bad for that group described by President Graham, in his opening address, as the "underprivileged majority." In non-poll tax states 75 per cent of the persons of voting age actually vote, as compared with about 25 per cent in the poll tax states. The most effective way of extending the range of suffrage is by removing those artificial obstructions that have kept so large a part of the section virtually disfranchised. The Conference, accordingly, struck at the poll tax provisions which penalized most the economically handicapped and prevented them from voicing effectively their protest against their chronic predicament. The only major difference of opinion was on the method of repealing them. Some wanted Congress to enact uniform registration laws; others would go the slower route through the individual states and avoid the issue of States rights. The discussion of education moved inevitably into the problem of school finances and federal equalization aid and, aware of the customary mishandling of equalization funds in the past, the Conference found it expedient to work toward racial equalization within this framework.

There was a time when the problem of tenancy was regarded and promptly dismissed as a Negro problem. If it had been so discussed at this Conference it would have lost much of its significance for the South. Although most of the Negroes in southern agriculture are tenants and sharecroppers, most of the tenants and sharecroppers in the South are now white. Relief of the Negro situation is involved in relief of the general situation now so disastrously defective. The Conference gave its attention to the renovation of the ancient landlord-tenant statutes, to the extension of credit, to provisions for tenant farm purchase, and to essential rehabilitation. Implicit in all of this was the fact that the rationalization of southern agriculture could not proceed without including all farmers impersonally in the scheme.

One of the most significant features of the Conference was the presence and activity of southern youth, who came in large numbers. It is not without importance that it was in this section, rather than in the Race Relations section, that the discussion of the Anti-Lynching Bill reached its most dramatic heights. It precipitated a heated discussion between Congressman Patrick of Alabama and Mrs. Eleanor Roosevelt, and an inept answer by the Congressman to Mrs. Roosevelt's question why he opposed the Anti-Lynching Bill if he objected to lynching.

The race issue became the most conspicuous one of the Conference, and the concern about uprooting these traditions, obstructive as they have been to the development of the South, became so clamorous both in aggression and defense, it obscured much of really sound analysis and the proposals on other issues. The membership of the Conference, despite its diversity of specific interests, appears to have accepted the principle of full Negro participation and unrestricted seating. There have been, recently, other, though smaller meetings in Birmingham which did not invoke the segregation ordinances. After the first public meeting in the City Auditorium, police were sent to enforce the segregation ordinance, signs were posted and separate entrances designated for white and Negro delegates. It seems quite possible that other interests inimical to the Conference's program found it convenient to use the race issue, in the ancient manner, as the most effective means of confounding or perhaps nullifying the proceedings. A placid acceptance of the principle of segregation, even with knowledge of the ordinance, would, indeed, have nullified the spirit of the Conference. It would have been incumbent upon the sponsors of the Conference to explain why a city had not been selected that placed less stress upon racial separation in meetings. The hysterical efforts to enforce segregation with riot squads, however, dramatized the very purpose of the Conference, and seems to have aroused more indignation over the ban than would normally have developed otherwise. One result was a Conference pronouncement which went farther, perhaps, than any similar group has dared in reasserting its principles of action far beyond the usual generalized good intentions of such groups, in protesting the ban and, further, resolving not to meet again in cities in which such ordinances exist or are enforced.

Question has been raised about the selection of Birmingham for such a conference. It is a city in the South that has been more exacting than most in preserving the ancient etiquette of race relations; it has few public leaders among either white or Negro populations. Its labor policy has been criticized and its general lethargy toward progressive social programs is known. But it is the most thoroughly industrial city in the South, the locus of many of the problems attacked, thus challenging the forthrightness, or the faith of the Conference sponsors in the essential soundness of their cause. More significant, however, and possibly explanatory of the unexpectedly general resistance of the segregation ban, is the fact of its large labor group that has only recently discovered that class interests cut across race lines. For years white and Negro labor groups have divided and competed racially to their mutual injury. Over the past seven years there have developed more than a hundred mixed labor union locals, and through this solidarity they have made the first substantial steps toward security. It was undoubtedly this submerged but solid sentiment that supported the racial philosophy of the Conference.

The conspicuousness of the race issue will not only keep obscure other basic interests of the Conference but may, indeed, make more difficult a second meeting or, at least, a place for it. There will be, wherever possible, reprisals taken for the part played in the movement. The first Chairman, Judge Louise O. Charlton, for example, who lapsed, unfortunately, into a minor tradition in addressing Mrs. Mary McLeod Bethune as "Mary," found herself defeated for re-election, by a candidate, President Frank P. Graham of the University of North Carolina, named from the floor, and, for her role in the Conference, may lose her position as Democratic Committeewoman.

The raising of the racial issue was embarrassing and regrettable but not without its values. It gave emphasis, as did a current lynching, to the race tradition as the first major challenge to any movement aiming at social reconstruction in the South. Inevitably, the Conference will be accused of being politically inspired and may, indeed, have been. This, however, would not be wholly to its discredit. There is no evidence however, that this was the case.

A more serious apprehension might be entertained about its permanence. It lacks funds and, paradoxically enough, popular support, as do all other inspired social movements in the area. It will attract a fringe of whites and Negroes dangerous to its present objectives, and, at present its organization is still too weak and harassed for sustained defense either against such internal dangers or against more strongly entrenched conservative opposition from the outside.

In spite of the present confused state of public opinion on the wisdom of challenging at this time the racial traditions of the South, it seems likely that the dramatic test of these traditions will stand as an important precedent for any future meetings seriously concerned with southern welfare. The social maturity of the Negro delegates themselves, so well demonstrated in their own response to the situation, was a discovery of no little importance.

In all probability the impetus given by the Conference to Federal equalization of educational opportunity, and to the extension of suffrage, will stand out clearly as definite values. Labor's new position on the question of race undoubtedly found valuable reinforcement in the unsuspected number of supporters of this essential social philosophy. Moreover, the knowledge of the existence of a body of liberal opinion will serve to restrain some of the more demagogic appeals to the traditional prejudices of the area.

These values are open to the hazards of political distortion, and secret campaigns of reprisal and even vilification; and it remains a real question if these hazards can be sustained without the continued support of personalities and groups whose reputations are established for contributions to the South other than that of a point of view within the Conference itself. These personalities, in time, can and may achieve a substantial solidarity of liberal sentiment sufficient to constitute a real and moving force in the South. If the Negroes are to be most effective in the new strategy it will be necessary for more of them to be able to speak with knowledge and authority on issues other than the race problem. For they can never be presumed to speak wisely, or other than as special wards seeking group protection, unless they are known to be acquainted with the total structure of southern life and the confusing interrelationship of all of its problems.

The Crisis, January, 1939; XLVI, 14–15.

63

MARIAN ANDERSON SINGS

Early in 1939 the great contralto Marian Anderson was scheduled to offer a concert in Constitution Hall in Washington, D.C. The Daughters of the American Revolution, owners of the hall, on discovering that Miss Anderson was a Black woman refused its use. Eleanor Roosevelt, wife of the President, resigned from the D.A.R. as a result and this made the affair into a front-page matter. Rather unnoticed—hardly reported, at the time, or since—was the fact that after the D.A.R. had rejected the concert Miss Anderson was banned, on racial grounds, from using the auditorium of a public high school by the Board of Education of the District of Columbia. With the support of an aroused Black community and the active intercession of several Black organizations, plus the support of Mrs. Roosevelt and Harold Ickes, Secretary of the Interior, Miss Anderson's concert was given on Easter Sunday, April 9, 1939, at the Lincoln Memorial. Scores of thousands were present and millions heard the program via radio. A report of the event from a Black newspaper follows.

Never in the history of the nation's capital has such an enormous crowd gathered to pay tribute to any person as gathered in Potomac Park here Sunday to pay tribute to Marian Anderson, who was presented in a free concert at Lincoln Memorial by Howard University and Associated Sponsors.

Although Captain P. J. Carroll, in charge of the Potomac Park police, estimated the crowd at a little more than 75,000, other observers set the figure at nearer 100,000 and said that the crowd was even greater than that which greeted Col. Charles Lindbergh when he was honored here after his famous non-stop flight to Europe.

Beginning Saturday morning, excursion trains, buses and private cars began converging on Washington from New York, the New

England states, New Jersey, Pennsylvania, Delaware, Maryland, Virginia, North and South Carolina, and by nightfall every available room in hotels, the Y.M.C.A. and Y.W.C.A. was filled. Many, who had no friends in the city, slept in their cars all night.

Frost was in the air in the early morning, after a slight snowfall, and, for a time, it was believed that the weather would cause the concert to be postponed until Easter Monday; but before noon the sun was shining in a cloudless sky, and a little after noon, even before workmen carried the piano up the twelve marble steps to the memorial, a city-wide movement began toward Potomac Park.

People making up the audience were fifty percent Negro and represented every walk of American life. Here in the nation's capital, where discrimination is probably more acute than in any other city in the United States, black and white waited side by side in almost reverent silence and in complete harmony for as long as two hours, to hear the world's greatest singer.

Mothers carrying babies arrived early in order to find choice spots but by 4 o'clock—a full hour before the concert was scheduled to begin—the steps and wide landing before the Memorial were crowded and park police were having difficulty keeping the throng behind the roped-off sections reserved for the sponsors, the press and special guests.

Also before 4 o'clock the parking place on Constitution Avenue which the Police Department had reserved for 5,000 cars was completely taken and vehicles were parked as many as twelve blocks away, many passengers taking taxis from their parked cars to Potomac Park.

The crowd itself, thickest at the foot of Lincoln Memorial, stretched almost to the Washington Monument along both sides of the pool. As an evidence that the program was clearly audible to everyone, after each number persons as far as six blocks away from the singer could be seen applauding.

Although the crowd was unusually orderly, park police had great difficulty in keeping it from rushing Miss Anderson off her feet at the end of the concert. The signal to close in on the singer was seemingly set off by a small colored boy dressed in a lumberjacket who darted from the crowd after Miss Anderson's speech and shyly shook her hand.

New York *Amsterdam News*, April 15, 1939, p. 17; see G. J. Fleming's account of white southern newspaper coverage of this event in *Negro History Bulletin*, December, 1950, and the striking photo of Miss Anderson performing which makes up the cover of that issue.

64

THIRD ANNUAL MEETING OF THE
SOUTHERN NEGRO YOUTH CONFERENCE

While the first and second annual meetings of the Southern Negro Youth Conference met in Richmond and Chattanooga, the third met in Birmingham, heart of the Black Belt, center of heavy industry and notoriously racist in its official administrative and police apparatus.

At the time of this Third Meeting, the chairman of the conference was William F. Richardson; Edward E. Strong was executive secretary. Chairing the conference itself was Herman H. Long. Published below are: [a], the original Call of the Third Meeting, issued in March, 1939, and [b], an illuminating account by a participant published soon after the meeting itself which lasted from April 27 to April 30, 1939.

[a]

CALL TO
THIRD ALL-SOUTHERN NEGRO YOUTH CONFERENCE

"Hands locked together and with heads erect, we march into the future, fearless and unafraid. We are Americans. We are the hope of our people. We have the right to live." With these words 534 young men and women, assembled in Richmond, Virginia for the First All-Southern Negro Youth Conference, concluded their sessions in February, 1937. These youth then set out to improve the conditions under which they and theirs live and labor.

Since that day in February, 1937, when 534 representatives of Negro youth organizations resolved to join their efforts for the achievement of equal opportunities, the Second All-Southern Negro Youth Conference convened in Chattanooga, Tennessee in April, 1938. We could seek no better time than the present to assess the progress we have made and to memorialize ourselves, our friends and our national representatives, of our plans for moving onward with the task we have begun. For this purpose, we invite the Negro youth of the South, and all who love democracy well, to the Third All-Southern Negro Youth Conference, Birmingham, Alabama, April 28, 29, 30, 1939.

At this conference we will have an opportunity to accomplish certain well-defined objectives:

1. To consider the mutual problems and aspirations of Southern Negro Youth.
   a—Our economic status: the National Youth Administration, the Civilian Conservation Corps, vocational guidance, apprenticeship training, Negro business, labor movement.
   b—Citizenship rights: voting, anti-lynching legislation, the national defense program.
   c—Education: equality in educational opportunities, the content of Negro education, federal aid to education.
   d—The role of religion in the life of Negro youth.
   e—The special problems of rural youth.
   f—The development of a cooperative relationship with Southern white youth.
   g—Peace: the preservation of democracy, protection of the rights of racial and religious minorities at home and abroad.
   h—Special problems: marriage and home life, crime and juvenile delinquency, housing, recreation, health.
2. To provide a medium for cooperative planning and action in meeting our problems.
3. To develop a greater appreciation for the contributions of the Negro to our cultural life, through holding an All-Southern Art Exhibit and a Festival of Music in connection with the conference.

As the Third All-Southern Negro Youth Conference convenes, we recall that the history of the past few years has been filled with new currents of progress. We have just begun to estimate the importance of the growing movement of organized labor which marches apace with the rapid industrialization of the South. Its presence where feudal conditions once reigned supreme, gives assurance of a rising standard of living for all working men and women.

In addition, the special attention extended by the national administration has lent great impetus to the sober consideration of the South's problems. Not many weeks ago, the Supreme Court rendered a momentous decision. It held that Lloyd Gaines had an inalienable right, which the State must enforce, to enter the law school of the University of Missouri. What new horizons for winning complete equality in educational opportunities does this decision offer to Southern Negro Youth!

Of great significance as a sign of the times have been the recent efforts of Southerners from all walks of life, to think and work unitedly for the advancement of the South. Such an effort has given rise to the historic Southern Conference for Human Welfare.

The low economic status of our youth constantly reminds us of the urgent need of securing decent living standards. Five boys who languish in jail—the Scottsboro boys—call for our help, and are grim witnesses to the fact that our civil liberties are still to be achieved. The growing incidence of crime and delinquency among our youth; their scant educational play facilities; the presence among us of scores of thousands who toil in penury and degradation as tenant-farmers and share-croppers; the denial of our right to vote and participate in the ordinary affairs of government—these conditions fairly cry out for adequate remedy.

We invite Southern men and women to seek a solution to these problems through participating in the Third All-Southern Negro Youth Conference. The youth are the guardians of tomorrow's world. Let us assemble in Birmingham over the week-end of April 28th. Let us achieve the full blessings of true democracy for ourselves, our people and our nation!

Printed Call in editor's possession.

[b]

YOUTH MEETS IN BIRMINGHAM
by Augusta V. Jackson

"I can't believe this is Birmingham!"

Old inhabitants of the city and visitors to the Third All-Southern Negro Youth Conference April 27–30 were equally surprised. They had regarded Birmingham only as it was a few years ago, a grim slow-moving city where currents of modern progress were likely to be deflected immediately both by the unfriendly attitude of the authorities and the apparent lethargy of its people. For generations its furnaces had smoked and flared on the edges of the city, blackening the ramshackle little houses where most of the Negro population lives. For generations its miners, and workers in the steel plants, its maids, and laborers, and city teachers had gone to work, to church, and home again—an endless cycle. Nothing could happen in Birmingham, nothing ever did or ever would. Even a few months ago when the first preparations were being made by a courageous few to bring the conference of the Southern Negro Youth Congress to the city, people shook their heads at the unheard-of folly. "It might happen in Richmond, or Chattanooga, or Atlanta—anywhere, but," the final rejoinder always was, "Birmingham is different. Negroes here won't cooperate." Nevertheless, some of those who at first were doubtful and hesitant, became later the hardest workers in planning for the Conference and the most earnest believers in its message of uniting young Negro people for action on their own social problems. For the first time in the memory of its citizens a conference was held in Birmingham where Negroes freely discussed economic and social issues concerning them, without fear and without disturbance from outside groups. In fact, for the first time in the city white public opinion looked with approval and interest on a conference of this kind.

The conference opened its sessions the evening of April 27 with a festival of music. The delegates and observers who were already gathering heard four choruses of young people from Birmingham and from schools in nearby counties sing the songs of the Negro people, the traditional spirituals, and worksongs, and arrangements of contemporary Negro composers. They were sung not artificially, as we sometimes hear them, but with fervent feeling, communicating to their listeners the certain knowledge that even in the furthest corners of the deep South the spirit of the young generation has not been made dull by the circumstances in which they live. The festival was a fitting introduction to the days of the conference that followed. Just as much of the music of the Negro was created in times of severest stress, so Birmingham which has long been a city where opportunities for the Negro have been most denied became for the days of the conference, in the eyes of its Negro population, the cradle of a reviving faith in the Negro people's destiny in the South.

The delegates to the conference came from fourteen southern states and the District of Columbia. Their ages ranged from the very young to the very old, from twelve to seventy. The lone delegate from Houston, Texas, was a poised, serious-faced girl of fourteen years whose mother wired to the conference to be assured of her daughter's safety. There were many among the 650 delegates, not much older than she, who had been sent from their schools, for the first time in their lives making contacts with other young people like themselves from all parts of the South. Even the very youngest were eager to exchange experiences and to learn. Other delegates came from the few scattered mining and manufacturing centers of the South, from the tiny churches in poverty-stricken, half-rural areas, and from farm counties in the region known as the "black belt" thick with tenant and sharecropping farms. The students were a fresh and invigorating element. Every college in Alabama had yielded its crop of young men and young women—Alabama State, Selma University, Stillman Institute, Miles Memorial College, and Tuskegee, and numbers from the city and county schools. Into these institutions pour the native sons and daughters of the state, from some of the most typical areas of the South.

The delegates came already equipped with a first hand knowledge of the prejudices, problems, and assets of communities in the deep South. Already of necessity they had faced the question of coping with problems of health, education, recreation, and jobs in their home communities. The incidents they related formed the reservoir of actual human experiences in the South upon which the conference based its deliberations, and from which it drew the material for a program suited to the needs and moods of southern life. The freshness of their outlook told the conference in far more effective terms than statistical charts what is the status of Negro youth, and what Negro young people are thinking. A typical illustration of this occurred when in the course of general discussion a vote was taken on whether the group was in favor of according Negroes equal but separate accommodations in schools and all phases of life, or whether they desired a society in which race was completely disregarded. With but one exception the group of about two hundred voted in favor of the latter.

The vote that was polled on the question of separate institutions expressed a feeling that was present from beginning to end of the conference. The keynote was—working together; the organizations of the young people themselves, with the church, with adult bodies, and, where possible, with southern white youth. When Dr. Alain Locke, at the conference luncheon, praised the ability of today's youth to focus its collective attention on the problems before them, he summarized the attitude of the delegates. Community agencies of all types will be enlisted in carrying out the four-point program of Health, Jobs, Education, and Citizenship—which the young people at the conference indicated as the most vital needs of southern Negro youth.

As a complement to its four-point program for social action, the congress proudly espouses the cultural heritage of the Negro as its own. It seeks to widen an appreciation of the artistic and cultural contributions of the Negro in America, with the possibility of stimulating potential creators in the fields of art, music, and drama who now have only the most limited opportunities for expression. An ironic case (which has been repeated with variations in other southern communities) and which is well remembered is that of Augustus

Williams, the Birmingham colored lad who was denied admittance to the city's public exhibit where his entry had been awarded a prize. The work of this highly talented young artist was shown in the art exhibit held in conjunction with the conference where hundreds saw their first display of all-Negro art. The evening before the final session was devoted to Randolph Edmonds, the young Negro playwright, who presented the Dillard University players in dramas which he had written and staged himself. The cultural features of the conference program were a natural outgrowth of the activity Councils of the Southern Negro Youth Congress have been carrying on in working to establish Negro drama groups in their communities and in studying Negro art and culture. For the young people of the conference regard spreading the knowledge and love of Negro art as an essential part of their social program.

The tremendous success and prestige of the conference was due in a large measure to the support received from adult organizations and individuals. Adult leaders of Birmingham and of other cities had worked tirelessly to make the conference a triumph not only for the young people, but for the whole community. As speakers at the conference mass meetings they sensed keenly the heart of the difficulties that young people face, and the need for new methods where sometimes the approach of their own generation had failed.

Among the adult group was a delegation from a mining section of West Virginia which has been interested in the Congress since its founding. It was a mixed group of white and colored—several of them already past forty. It was at once strange to see their seamed and toil-worn faces among the young people, and still a sign full of meaning and hope. It symbolized the readiness of an awakening white South to do their share in the work of tackling the age-old problems of the Negro. The interest of the adult South was further indicated by the fact that from the schools came not only the students, but also their teachers; from the churches, not only the young people but also their ministers. Even the white press of the city believed the gathering an important enough event to editorialize favorably, seeing in the conference a potent force for good for both races.

The new outlooks and attitudes developing around the movement of southern Negro youth are helping to create a young Negro leadership that is both resourceful and energetic. The leadership comes from all ranks of the people—some are students, some young people with business and professional training, others are young working men and women who bring to the movement from their labor unions a consciousness of the power of organized, united action. The executive council of the congress presents a group of variously gifted, colorful personalities—from different sections and different backgrounds who have found one common aim. Their biographies are typical of thousands of young Negroes—tales of struggle to keep jobs, to stay in school, of work in "Y's" and the N.A.A.C.P., and of a lifelong, burning desire to see something done to extend opportunities for Negroes in the South. Two years experience organizing Congress councils of federated clubs, and actually achieving results, has widened their understanding of the possibilities of a movement among the South's 3,000,000 Negro youth. They think in terms of a lasting organization which will continue to hold dramatic and inspiring conferences, but which will more and more enter into the daily life of every city and county of the fourteen southern states where councils are now springing into existence.

The Third All-Southern Negro Youth Conference perceptibly strengthened the movement of Negro youth experimentally launched in Richmond in 1937. The conference revealed that the Congress has gone further than before into the deep South; that it has secured a wider cooperation of adult leaders; that its own leadership is maturing, and its role becoming clearer. Dr. F. D. Patterson of Tuskegee, speaking at the conference, listed the needs that progressive southern movements today must answer. One need, he said, is to establish a new view of life in the South—to end the too frequent recourse to the "dead end" outlook—to see, instead, that in the South a great opportunity exists to point the way to new horizons of life and liberty. With this perspective, the Third Conference of the Southern Negro Youth Congress has started the Negro youth movement on a new year of its life.

The Crisis, June, 1939; XLVI, 178, 180. Years later the author of the above, as Augusta Strong, wrote a helpful account of the history of the congress as a whole; this is in *Freedomways,* First Quarter, 1964; IV, 34–50.

65

THE MISSOURI SIT-DOWN STRIKE
OF SHARECROPPERS

In January, 1939, hundreds of sharecroppers—mostly Black—camped along highways in what is known as the "Bootheel" area of Missouri, consisting of seven counties in the southeastern part of the state. Cotton was the basic crop and peonage, indignity, and deception were the payments received by those who raised it. Led by a sharecropper and preacher, the Reverend Owen H. Whitfield, a Black man, and with the organizing work of the United Cannery, Agricultural, Packing and Allied Workers, C.I.O. (Missouri Council), these workers were united. Dramatically, they finally brought their struggle to the nation's attention by "sitting-down" in the heart of winter by the roadsides—men, women, and children.

One of those who visited these folks was Lorenzo J. Greene, then a young assistant professor of history at Lincoln University in Missouri (later chairman of its History Department); reporting what he saw to the faculty and students at his university produced among them an effective relief campaign. The movement led by the Reverend Whitfield and the union produced significant positive changes in the next few years.

Published below are letters which sharecroppers sent Professor Greene at the time, herewith published with Dr. Greene's kind permission.

Wyatt Mo.
5/17/1939

Dear Prof.

I am Writing you in regards Of My eviction from the Farm. I Was on Mr. O. A. Reeves Farm about 1½ Miles south West of Deventer, Mo. Mr. O. A. Reeves sent Me a Written Notice to Me At Night About 9 oclock by A deputy Constable of Wyatt Mo. Mississippi Co. The notice telling Me To quit Procession [sic] . . . Written Jan. 3 1939 [and] to give [up] Prossession [possession] by the 15th day of January 1939. I felt it to be unlegal and I carry The Notice to the State Atorney [sic] and ask him About it and he told Me That he, Mr. Reeves, did Not Need to gave Me but 10 days and said That Mr. Reeves had give me plenty of time and That he Would Advise Me to Move, That I have got 12 days and I should give Mr. Reeves his house and not have no trouble, for a share Cropper did Not hafter have but 10 days, so I begin to Walk looking for a place and I could Not fine no place and I had no Money for Mr. Reeves had Not settle with Me and a deal of others. . . . he also put our Cotton in The government loan and Ask none of us anything bout it . . . I begain to Protest to Mr. Reeves about my Cotton. I Made 9 bails of Cotton and Mr. Reeves Would not allow Me to put my part of cotton in The government loan so I Could be entitle to father [further] Payment should Cotton go up on the Market. And also Mr. Reeves in 1938 tryed to get Me to sign Over My 1937 government Payment and because I Would Not do it he was Very hard to get alonge With. now I made 2 crops of Cotton on Mr. O. A. Reeves Farm, one doring [during] 1937–1938. I Work 15 acerage of cotton in 1937. and When I received My government Payment Mr. Reeves Just turn in For Me 5½ acerage [acres] of cott⟨n When he should have turn in 15 acerage for Me. I tryed to get Consideration from Washington D.C. from the Department of Agriculture; they defored [referred] My letter to Jefferson City Mo. and Jefferson City defored [referred] it To Columbia, Mo. and they Just Continure To hold for The landlored and I just Could not get but $11.52. . . . I pick and gin 15 bails Of Cotton and My 1937 payment Just come to $11.52 when they got Throu. . . . now I has Not yet got My 1938 Payments. Now it is more harder To get what You Make in This County after making [it] than it is To Work and Make it. Now Mr. O.A. also Charge Me $2.50 for gardin[1] after The Crops Was laid by, and he also Charge 75 cent per bail [bale] for To hall it to the gin and he should Not have Charge anything. The many landlords had come to an agreement they Was goning [going] to Work the farms On a ⅝ Bases . . . that Mean That the share croppers Would not get but 3 bails of Cotton out of 8 Bails, so all of the farmers begain to give they labor notice To Move, and you could not go To No other place and get no sheair Crop other than on a ⅝ Bases. . . . Then mooven [moving] taken place On about Jan. 9–10–11–12 And . . . Highway 62 and 61 begain to get busy and I and My group Came To This Church (sweet home) . . . And have been here ever sent [since] That time. We Came To This Church and it begain to snow and sleat and rain. . . . We stayed here at This Church, sweet home, and it has been the Only home for us up until Now . . . We have been threaten by The White peoples of This County and We also have been treated Verry Cool by our Own County laws. And Now We are faceing A lawsuit. 3 of this group have allready got summons to Court The first Monday in June. They are Trying To get us out of this Church. I am unable . . . to no whate Will be The result. We are Just [ready?] for Just What ever Come. We are here and it I guss [guess] This is Where We Will be untill they sue us Off this ground. so I shall close For . . . Tractors and preduction [production] have put a Many farmers out of work and off the farm; so they want we Poor peoples to work for .75 cent and $1.00 per day and We just Cant live at Those prices . . . this bein all From sweet home Church Camp

Walter Johnson Wyatt Mo.

---

[1] (Each sharecropper often had a plot of ground to raise vegetables for his family.)

Wyatt Mo. May the 12, 1939

I Will Write the Cause of Me be [ing] out doors in 1937. I had to Move in house [that] Want fit to live in. the in [end] of 1938 I had to give it up and I move out here. I Made a Sharecrop With Henry Claycomb. in 1937 I had to by my on hoses [hoes] to chop With. I had to pay to have my collon [cotton] haul. We fosted [were forced to] Clean out his barn far nothing and he told me I had to sell my hog cause, he did not want no body to have hog but him on the place. I had live on $8.00 a month for 4 month and then I had open a count at the store to live. I made 13 bale on 20 Acres. he haul people out of caird [Cairo, Illinois] and pick [my cotton] an I had to pay for crossing the bridge an did not have nothing to live on. I got $16.60 of the 1937 government

IKe Wright age 28

I made a small crop in 1938. I had 8 Acres an he [the landlord] put picker in my field that look [took] al of Mine and I had to pay tax [of] $5.00 on [each] bale. I had to pick by the hundred for my living. I had to [pay] 35¢ a load for my half. I need food an colth [clothes]. after all, the man said he want his house an if I could stay there on nothing, I can stay here.

Eaty May Wrigh 24

According to Mamie Sweetenberg, 50 year old mother of three children, and widow of an ex-serviceman:

I was a day labor, [laborer] $1.00, 90, 80 per day. I left Because I could not get no work. he gave me Notice to move. I read [received] No Government Money 1938. I am a union woman I experence a Better life in camp Life. Very good at camp I need food, an Money, I an fighting for libity

My name is Gladys Fields. I am 17th Years old and Me and My Mother and Father move out on the Hi Way The 10th of January and We have suffered . . . from the Tiem we come out until Now. we have had a hard time every since We Been out on The hiWay. Some Time Mother To earn [?] and half necket [naked] and Treated like a Dog from White Focks [folks]. We was Drove from The hiway and The state Petrolems Move us in The Jail house Yard and They made us Move in a old Colored Man gardin Spot and The Women the [they were] renting from Made us Move from Their and We Move Down to The School house, and looking To hafter Move from Their pretty soon. We is hungry Now and no Way To get nothing to Eate. In [I'm] closing May letter But Not My heart and Still leaving Me hunyry and out Dorse.

Lorenzo J. Greene, "Negro Sharecroppers," *Negro History Bulletin*, February, 1968; XXI, 18–19. See L. Cantor, "The Missouri Sharecropper Roadside Demonstration of 1939," *Journal of American History*, March, 1969; LV, 804–22.

66

THE PROGRAMS OF ORGANIZATIONS DEVOTED TO THE IMPROVEMENT OF THE STATUS OF THE AMERICAN NEGRO

by Ralph J. Bunche

As a professor at Howard University and a consultant for the Myrdal study sponsored by the Carnegie Corporation, the late Dr. Bunche made an analysis of the directions and needs of Afro-American organizations. Omitted in what follows are the opening pages which describe the programs of earlier groups and leaders—as Booker T. Washington, Marcus Garvey, and W. E. B. Du Bois. Published is the concluding section of the essay where Dr. Bunche projects his own suggestions.

It is a sad but true commentary that despite the universal grievances endured by the harshly buffeted Negro, there is no single organization, save the church, the school, and in lesser degree, the fraternal order, which can boast any intimate contact with and support from the common man who represents the mass Negro population. The Negro church has consecrated itself to the spiritual salvation of its charges, and has leaned heavily on the side of social reaction and racialism whenever it has concerned itself with the black man's worldly life. The Negro lodges and fraternal orders have contributed little of a constructive nature to the social thought of their Negro membership, though they indulge abundantly in ritual and social activity. The Negro schools are socially vacuous and have shown no disposition to meet the challenge offered by the problems of the group whose interests they are designed to serve. The Negro school, its principal or president and its teachers, are content to seek refuge in the tranquil atmosphere of the academic cloister and to look down upon the problems of the group and its neglected masses, in "scholarly" detachment.

The students are infected by this false isolation and are not equipped to understand nor to attack the social problems with which they are confronted in their post-school life. It is not surprising that the narrowly racial conceptions of the Negro have caused him to be seduced by anti-Semitism. He thinks only in terms of jobs for Negroes, business for Negroes, Negro landlords, bankers and employers, and vents his emotional spleen on the Jewish shop-keeper in the Negro neighborhood, who exploits the black trade quite as enthusiastically as would the black shopkeeper. The Negro anti-Semite does not reason, nor does it matter, that all Jews are neither shopkeepers nor prejudiced. It is sufficient that the Jew makes profit from a store in a Negro section that Negroes ought to own and work in, or that a Jewish professor holds a position at a Negro university that a Negro, if even a less competent one, should occupy. Such bigoted attitudes are deliberately nurtured by the self-seeking, sensitive Negro middle-class—the business and professional groups, who seek an economic base for their middle-class aspirations.

In view of the obvious social implications for the Negro of this sort of blind, suicidal emotionalism, and the certain truth that racial generalizations and prejudices are luxuries which the Negro can ill afford, it is a bitter indictment of Negro organizations that none has been rational or bold enough to wage a vigorous campaign against Negro anti-Semitism.

Again, in a world in which the major issues affecting the future of humanity are increasingly defined in terms of fascism, with its fundamental racial and totalitarian dogmas, versus democracy, imperfect as it has been for minority groups, no Negro organization makes any serious attempt to define these issues in terms of Negro interest, or to align the full power of Negroes with those forces which are struggling heroically to preserve the last vestiges of human liberty in a world gravely threatened with enslavement. Negro organizations herald the Gaines Case and the anti-lynching bill while the eyes of the rest of the world are turned on Munich, Prague and Memel, Albania, Spain and China.

It is typical of Negro organizations that they concern themselves not with the broad social and political implications of such policies as government relief, housing, socialized medicine, unemployment and old-age insurance, wages and hours laws, etc., but only with the purely racial aspects of such policies. They are content to let the white citizen determine the expediency of major policies, and the form and direction they will assume, while they set themselves up as watch dogs over relatively petty issues, as whether the Negro will get his proper share of the benefits and whether the laws, once made, will be fairly administered. They thus demark for the Negro a residual function in the society.

There is no coordination of thought or serious collaboration in action among these several important Negro organizations and their numerous satellites. Each has marked off its little sphere of action and guards it with professional jealousy. No effective use has ever been made of the numerical strength of the Negro population, nor of its economic importance in labor and consuming power. Race pride does not permit most Negro organizations to make intelligent and practical overtures to the white working population, since a rebuff would result in loss of dignity.

The Negro is sorely in need of organization and leadership which is sufficiently independent and intelligent to give courageous orientation to the group and to guide it rationally through the bewildering maze of social forces which characterize the modern world. This organization and leadership would presumably adhere to some such policies as the following: (1) it would place less emphasis on race and more on economics and broad political and economic forces; (2) it would understand that the major problems of Negroes are not entirely attributable to race but are intimately linked up with the operation of the economy; (3) it would attempt to gain a mass basis among Negroes by a simple program designed to raise the economic level of the Negro worker; (4) it would devote its full energy toward the incorporation of Negro workers in labor unions, and would carry on incessant educational propaganda among both black and white workers toward this end; (5) it would attempt to throw the full support of Negro workers behind the movement to organize labor on an industrial basis, since the vast majority of Negroes are unskilled workers; (6) it would not cease to fight on the political and judicial fronts but would subordinate this to the fight on the economic and union fronts; (7) it would recognize that the future interests of Negroes are closely related to every general effort to improve the lot and increase the security of the working man of whatever color, and it would back every such measure to the limit; (8) it would include Negro labor leaders in its leadership and among its most influential advisers, and avoid dependence on professional Negro leaders and professional white interracialists; (9) it would interpret for Negroes, and relate their interests to, every world event and every foreign policy of importance; (10) its interpretations would be less in terms of race and more in terms of group economic interest; (11) it would recognize that the problems of the Negro cannot be solved in the courts, nor yet by the ballot, even under American democracy; (12) it would take its cue from the share-croppers' and tenant-farmers' unions formed in the South in recent years, and realize that above all, these successful efforts have broken down once and for all the stubborn legend that prejudice between white and black in the South is invested with a mystical quality and is insurmountable; (13) it would recognize that under oppressive conditions identity of economic interests can overcome racial prejudices, and that black and white unity is possible.

Existing Negro organizations are philosophical and programatic paupers. They think and act entirely in a black groove. In a world in which events move rapidly and in which the very future of themselves and their group is at stake, they are unable to see the social forests for the racial saplings. They, like Hitler, even though for different reasons, think that "all that is not race in this world is trash."*

Because of the extreme provincialism of its organizations and leadership, the Negro population of America suffers from stagnation in its social thought. The traditional stereotypes and clichés of Negro thought have become outmoded and a new set of values, tooled to fit the political and economic conditions of the modern world, are indicated. Negro organizations should take close inventory of their policies and discard shop-worn doctrines; and should realize that freedom in the modern world is not to be bought at bargain-basement prices. Unless the Negro can develop, and quickly, organization and leadership endowed with broad social perspective and fore-sighted, analytical intelligence, the black citizen of America may soon face the dismal prospect of reflecting upon the tactical errors of the past from the gutters of the black ghettoes and concentration camps of the future.

The Journal of Negro Education, July, 1939; VIII, 547–50.

67

WASHINGTON FIGHTS

by John Lovell, Jr.

A very revealing essay disclosing the realities of mounting militancy in the nineteen-thirties—and specifically some of the details behind an event such as the Marian Anderson concert—came from the pen of a person who, as

* Adolf Hitler, *Mein Kampf* (Reynal and Hitchcock unexpurgated edition, 1939), p. 406.

part of this process, had been elected, in 1938, secretary of the then newly reorganized District of Columbia branch of the N.A.A.C.P. It is published in full herewith.

Washington is a giant awakened. For years, people have known of her strength—financial, social, scholarly. Washington is the town where thousands of Negroes enjoy good salaries, and are sure to be paid. It has no industrial life, but that doesn't matter much. Money circulates; men and women buy fine cars and good houses in large numbers. Washington clubs and societies are the snootiest in the nation among Negroes. Her lawyers and doctors are acknowledged leaders. At Howard, you will find over one-half of the living Negro Ph.D.'s. Around the town, you will bump into Negroes whose ancestors had forgot what slavery meant long before 1865.

When Du Bois wrote his *Quest of the Silver Fleece,* he selected Washington society as representative of the best Negroes had. He was not far wrong. The Negroes who "were somebody" may have been comparatively few but they were noisy and colorful. They had 11-room and 13-room houses. They had maids and chauffeurs, and they still have. They did not vote, but they supplied the country with the wiliest and smoothest politicians. They spawned first-rate tradesmen and business men, even architects and theatrical impresarios.

With all this surface power, you would suppose that Washington Negroes were fully able to take care of themselves. But the great majority of these who were whitewashing the slave-besmirched Negro by imitating the raucous American bourgeoisie never thought about fighting for their rights. They had the equipment with which to fight. And here and there, an individual would shake off an insult in a way the insulter never forgot. But fighting was the wrong thing for their technique of growth. They wanted to be "accepted," and that was no way to get "accepted." White people had to be asked for things. You couldn't ask favors of a man if you were always bristling up to him or shaking a fist in his face.

Washington Negroes, in spite of their phenomenal culture, would have moved very slowly but for the so-called rowdy element. Let any one who wishes to deny this read the records of the 1919 riot before he enlists on the negative side. The highfalutin' Negroes would have taken 50 years to get the self-respect the boys from the bucket-of-blood got in a few days. The boys had always questioned the method of soft blandishment. They still do. When the riot burst the capital city open, and the bigwigs started holding conferences to determine how best to ameliorate and pacify, "the boys" merely went to work and set a machine gun or two on top of the Howard theatre.

A few years later, a really militant Howard professor moved into a "restricted" area. He was told to get out and get out fast. When he failed to comprehend the warning, his new home was given a battering. Others reported the matter to the police; the professor merely took the pains to build a barricado that even the Japanese would respect. Some of his friends at the university recommended to him some interesting court procedures. One of them got his guns together and installed himself in the barricado. The two, fortified further by sandwiches and milk, quietly sat, watched and waited. "The boys" heard about it and were powerfully elated at this vindication of their technique. They sent word that their scouts were keeping an eye on the place, and that when help was needed, help would come. Evidently they got a similar message over to the enemy, for absolutely nothing happened after that. The professor, using a rowdy principle, had opened up a new and decent area for Negro habitation. Thousands of fine Negroes live there now.

After the riot, a new lethargy descended upon the town. Negroes gained 50% in self-respect, as they had done in riot-educated Houston, Tulsa and Chicago. The upperclass Negroes were thankful for the enhanced position—the better seats down front—but they did not change their method. They went on conciliating white folks and hoping for the day of interracial understanding. When a thing became intolerable, they would send a spokesman down, and he would come back with five barley loaves of promises and two small fishes of good cheer. The rowdy Negroes were once more glowing in disgust. Washington policemen began a target practice in the Negro districts. In "self-defense" or in "the line of duty," they shot a Negro every two months. Many of the Negroes were shot in the back. When within a few short days a Negro youth had his spine splintered by an officer "defending" himself and a demented Negro war veteran was struck with bullets like a savage beast, little as Washington knew it, she was on the verge of another 1919.

A new element, though, had risen up in the Washington community. They came from the high and the low. They boasted of barbers, day laborers, Howard and Terrell professors, preachers, and even the middleclass business men and lawyers. Their job was to find a technique in which both elite and rowdy could participate. They decided that they would begin on a middle course, but they did not rule out the machine gun high over 7th and T streets if all else failed.

A host of organizations had come together to form the Washington Council of the National Negro Congress. With encouragement from John P. Davis, national executive secretary of the Congress, they grew and waxed. They brought in fraternities, medical societies. and guilds of government workers. On June 25, 1938, the date of a killing, they opened fire on police brutality in the District of Columbia. They kept pouring their fire upon city officials, civic leaders, and Congressmen. They brought every civic pressure to bear, not softly nor wildly, but with an unswerving militancy and a remarkable use of intelligent planning. They did not use actual machine guns, but their aim was just as deadly, and their power just as penetrating. Police killing stopped! In a mass meeting on June 25, 1939, they celebrated one year of blustering city life in which no policeman found it necessary to defend himself by cutting down harmless citizens.

On the same June 25, 1938, an organization, founded in 1933, called the New Negro Alliance, threw a picket line around two Peoples Drug Stores. Peoples Drug Stores are one of Washington's largest corporations and operate 44 stores of predominantly Negro trade. The Alliance was not exactly a fledgling David meeting a stubby-bearded Goliath. They had brought another of Washington's first-line corporations, The Sanitary Grocery Company, to its knees, by means of a decision from the United States Supreme Court, and by a great corralling of public support. The Alliance's Administrator, Eugene Davidson, has a list of dozens of jobs which white business men in Negro areas have turned over to Negroes in the past five years, as a result of Alliance pressure. Peoples have not yet surrendered, though many similar warriors have as a result of the Peoples fight. But that is not so important as the fact that here in Washington, lethargy has been killed to the extent that a picket line has been maintained 15 hours a day since June 25, 1938, without a moment's interruption. Washington Negroes are finally proving to themselves that they can *last.*

In January of this year, and again in February, March, and April, Marian Anderson was insulted by the local D.A.R. and the Washington School Board. Such an insult had been visited upon Roland Hayes 13 years ago—denial of the same Constitution Hall which was denied Miss Anderson—and Washington Negroes had responded with some spirit. But the spirit they showed this year was beyond the recollection of the oldest old-timer. They flooded the newspapers with letters, bitterly and skilfully written. They got their friends from outside to shower Congressmen with petitions. They hung from the rafters when the Board of Education met to try to find some way to grant the Central (white) High Auditorium without losing face completely. Hundreds of Washington school teachers sgined the petition to the Board, asking that they reverse themselves, in the face of the known pettiness and vindictiveness of Frank W. Ballou, the Superintendent of Schools.

They demanded a picket line against the D.A.R. national Convention, and shouted for the opportunity of being the first to ride in the Black Marias, if Black Marias were going to materialize. Sixty-five Negro organizations, of every description and social status, joined thirty-two white and mixed ones in one of the most brilliant displays of mass action this nation has seen. The national press put the credit for the furore upon Mrs. Roosevelt and Secretary Ickes; but it was the Marian Anderson Citizens Committee which first notified Mrs. Roosevelt and which got her first response. It was the same Committee which asked for an expression from Secretary Ickes nearly two months before he granted Lincoln Memorial. The 600 newspaper clippings from Singapore to London would never have been possible if the Marian Anderson Citizens Committee had not set off the explosion. Had not Negroes accepted the Constitution Hall business silently for years?

The 75,000 who heard Miss Anderson on Easter Sunday were a tribute to fighting Negroes in the District of Columbia as much as to democracy and the preservation of art. Believe it or not, the Marian Anderson Citizens Committee is far from dead. They are determined that their School Board shall interpret the dual school laws so as to grant the community use of school buildings to all, regardless of race, during non-school hours and on non-school days. To this end, they are gathering ammunition for hearings this fall. Moreover, it will be the proverbial hundred moons before the D.A.R. hears the last reverberation of the Marian Anderson case.

And the fighting on all fronts is going to go on! In the midst of the Marian Anderson struggle, the Norms presiding over social justice for the Negro tossed into the lap of Washington a new baby N.A.A.C.P. Branch to replace the branch which died three years ago. It is now a strapping youngster with nearly 2500 members. Its new membership chairman, Wendell Erwin, a fiery young business man, says that the District of Columbia Branch is marching to Philadelphia next June at the head of N.A.A.C.P., where it formerly was, and where it belongs. Its president, C. Herbert Marshall, Jr., is a perpetual whirlwind. It is making plans to fight not only current difficulties of Negroes in

Washington but also the deep-seated accumulations in prejudice and discrimination of the last 50 years.

Some shrewd commentators on Negro life have said that the Negro will not gain salvation by making his fight along racial lines. He must recognize, they say, the economic virus at the core of it all. Let this writer be recorded as agreeing with them. Let him also be recorded as finding a real hope in the picture of bourgeois aspirants and regular workers in Washington joining hands. and then making fists at their enemies. Let him testify that many of these very fights have sponsored makeshift seminars on the economic structure of American society. Let him take pride in the fact that Washington Negroes have been sensible enough, in every one of these fights, to get the support of white and Jewish working and worker-minded people. Let him express, above all, the view that the man who has determined to fight, without ever stopping, for his social and political rights is a good beginning for the new world we all look forward to. And let him be thankful that in the past year, Washington Negroes by the thousands have learned that much.

The Crisis, September, 1939; XLVI, 276–77; see also V. R. Daly, "Washington's Minority Problem," *The Crisis,* June, 1939; XLVI, 170–71.

68

CONDITIONS IN ATLANTA, GEORGIA

In 1939 the Senior and Young People's Departments of St. Mark's Methodist Church in Atlanta set themselves the task of undertaking a careful study of the social conditions of the Black people in their city. In January, 1940, a summary of those findings was published; it is given below in full.

In His Steps

The youth groups at St. Mark's Methodist Church of Atlanta, Georgia, *"want to be loyal followers of the Master."* In order to do this, these groups took two important *"steps."*

First, they studied the life and teachings of Jesus and found *"the essential thing in Jesus to be the intense love he had for every man. That love proved itself to be genuine by being concerned about every phase of any man's life which was harmful to him, or in any way prevented the full expression of his personality."*

Second, they studied the phases of life among Negroes and white people of Atlanta in an effort to learn to what extent the *"intense love of Jesus"* was applied in forming the community pattern of life. What these young people found stirred them to plead thus with the older citizens of Atlanta:

"Many of these conditions are beyond our control. As we look at them, however, we see plainly that some of them are not beyond the control of our fathers and mothers. In the name of our Master, the Master that you taught us to love and follow, we demand of you a deeper consecration to Him and His purposes, a more thorough understanding of un-Christlike conditions in Atlanta, a sense of personal responsibility, and untiring effort to make right as many wrongs as possible under Divine guidance and power."

I.—Education

"(a) There are 12,000 Negro children in Atlanta who go to school. 10,000 of these go to double-session school. No white children go to double-session schools.

"(b) Only one Negro school in Atlanta has a gymnasium and only one has an auditorium."

Salaries

Teachers	Av. College Status	No. of Pupils	Salary per Year
White	3.39 yrs.	30.31	$1,950
Negro	3.15 yrs.	75.5	1,275

Textbooks

Pupils	Average per Person	Equipment
White	$6.11	$19.00
Negro	0.73	4.59

II.—Recreation in Atlanta

(According to the standards of the P.T.A. study on recreation, parks and playgrounds must not be more than one mile from the neighborhood which they are to serve. Atlanta has one park for Negroes—acreage 16.42—located almost two miles from the center of the population of the Negro group.)

Park and Playground Space

	Acres	Evaluation
White	1,323.58	$3,000,000
Negro	16.42	40,000

III.—Health in Atlanta

"(a) Two-thirds of the births of colored children in Atlanta are at Grady Hospital. Negro mothers are returned to their homes in three days, while white mothers are normally returned seven days after the birth of a child.

"(b) The greatest number of Negro deaths are between the ages of 23–50 years; the greatest number of white deaths between 55–75.

"(c) Negro deaths out-number Negro births 1.9 to 2.1; white births out-number white deaths 3.1 to 2.4."

IV.—Housing in Atlanta

(The Statistics given in this section include housing conditions of both races but *"The Negro housing situation due to his low income is by far the greater problem."*)

1. Over half of our population cannot afford to pay more than $15 per month for rent.
2. 2,274 families live in houses situated on alleys and streets 20 feet or less in width, or in structures in the interior of blocks.
3. Cost of Police Department in the area of bad housing is $6.10 per capita; in the remainder of the city it is only $3.23 per capita.
4. Juvenile delinquency, as indicated by police arrests and convictions, is traceable to this bad housing area and corresponds closely with adult crime. Though this area covers about 5% of Atlanta's territory and contains 17% of Atlanta's population, yet it produces 32% of the crimes which reach Atlanta's courts.

"We are not proposing a sudden change of social, economic and political systems as a solution. Neither are we satisfied with slow change. We are demanding of ourselves that we do everything possible at the present moment, and continue always to bring better conditions for every man as speedily as possible."

From a four-page brochure, in editor's possession. The title page states, "Edited by Fulton-DeKalb Interracial Committee [in Atlanta], January, 1940." The officers of the committee were the Reverend Nat G. Long of the St. Mark's Methodist Church, Dr. Rufus E. Clement, president of Atlanta University, and Mrs. M. E. Tilly, the committee's secretary.

69

AGAINST JIM CROW
IN PROFESSIONAL BASEBALL

by William L. Patterson

Commencing with the struggle to save the lives of Sacco and Vanzetti in the 1920's, no single person has been more significant in civil rights and anti-racist efforts than William L. Patterson. In his autobiography, he describes one moment in one such effort, when he was living in Chicago, shortly before World War II.

By 1940, when we were winding up the affairs of the newspaper, the Black community had pushed back the walls of the ghetto beyond Garfield Boulevard, beyond Washington Park. Westward and northward sizable Black neighborhoods had been established. The *Record* had left at least one heritage, a campaign to get Black baseball players into the Big League ball clubs. The campaign had also been persistently pursued by the New York *Daily Worker*.

I myself had pushed the campaign vigorously, and not only in the pages of the *Record*. Leaflets were distributed in white and Black neighborhoods. Communists everywhere were active.

This talk of baseball was not the usual statistical chit-chat of earned runs, runs batted in, home runs and fielding averages. There was a side of baseball more important to the Blacks on the Southside than the pitching of Bob Feller of the Cleveland Indians and the bats of the famous "Murderers' Row" of the New York Yankees. Black sport fans were talking about the conspicuous absence of Black ball players. Jimcrow had kept Black Americans out of its higher and most lucrative echelons. Black Americans were aware that there were players among them who were the peers if not the superiors of any white player. Black fans following the Negro League teams knew players like Satchel Paige, Josh Gibson, lanky "Bullet" Rogan and others whom they recognized as being better players than many white professionals drawing five-figure salaries in the Big Leagues.

A group of us, including Paul Robeson, Gil Green and Claude Lightfoot, discussed carrying the issue further. The decision was reached that we had to intensify the campaign. To this end, we would confront directly one of the Big League club owners or Baseball

Commissioner Kenesaw Mountain Landis, or both. I was asked to handle this phase.

I wondered whether I should seek a conference with William Wrigley, owner of the Chicago Cubs, or Charles Comiskey, owner of the American League team, the Chicago White Sox. The White Sox home grounds, Comiskey Park, was on the Southside. Wrigley Field, the Cubs' home ground, was located on the Northside, outside the Black community, but this did not exempt the team from pressure, picket lines, leaflets and letters. The campaign, when it went into full swing, was fed by articles and editorials in the *Daily Worker* and a number of Negro weekly newspapers.

After consultation, I wrote for an appointment with William Wrigley and at the same time sent a letter to Baseball Commissioner Landis, outlining the issue I wished to discuss. Favorable replies came back from both offices.

I spoke by telephone with Paul Robeson in New York and with Earl Dickerson, an acquaintance of many years before, who was now chief counsel for the Liberty Life Insurance Company of Chicago. With their agreement and in their names, I arranged the conference with Judge Landis. I decided, however, to speak with Wrigley myself.

I arrived promptly at the appointed time and entered Mr. Wrigley's suite after getting a breath-taking view of the city and Lake Michigan before being ushered into his private office. I had expected to see an office that could have been used as a Hollywood set—and I did. Mr. Wrigley's greeting was cordial; he invited me to sit down and indicated that I "had the floor."

It was high time, I told him, that the jimcrow pattern of baseball was changed. Black baseball fans were no longer willing to support a national game from whose ranks one-tenth of the nation was excluded. . . . If Black players were brought into the Big Leagues, an untapped reservoir of Black baseball patrons would be opened up.

I reminded him of the calibre of the Black players in the Chicago American Giants, a Black team, and of players in other Negro league teams; their exploits had not gone unnoticed in the metropolitan press. He nodded agreement. And he listened without an outward show of irritation. He knew the value of the perspective I had outlined—perhaps he saw a pennant or two in the offing. Yet he was afraid to commit himself. Here was a new angle—white racism could be a barrier to greater profits. And yet, business afraid of the juggernaut it might create.

When he spoke he expressed agreement with what I had said and deplored the existing situation. He buzzed for his secretary and asked her to get "Pants" Rowland on the telephone. Rowland was manager of the Los Angeles Angels, a Cub farm team in California. He informed Rowland of the discussion that we had just had and asked him to come to Chicago. As he hung up the phone, he turned to me and said he would give the matter his sincere attention. He invited me to return upon Rowland's arrival; I assured him I would be there and left the office feeling I had accomplished a good first step. I then returned to the Communist Party office and reported what had happened. There was some feeling that reporters should have been present, but Wrigley did not want them.

The next order of business was to set up a date for Robeson and Dickerson with Judge Landis. That meeting took place before Rowland could come to Chicago. It turned out that Dickerson did not appear so we decided that Paul should talk with the commissioner alone. Judge Landis gave him more than an hour. Paul later told us that he had raised two questions: the absence of Black players from organized baseball and the Commissioner's responsibility to remedy this situation. The Commissioner acknowledged the first point but said that while he might not have been sharp enough, he had raised the question at the club owners' meeting. Robeson replied that it was not enough to have discussions—"it was time to act." The Commissioner promised to "see what could be done."

My second meeting with Wrigley was most interesting. Wrigley introduced me to "Pants" Rowland, and the talk opened with Wrigley asking Rowland if he knew of any Black baseball players who were ready for the big time. Rowland replied bluntly that there were probably several, but the person he regarded as having the greatest potential was a young man who had been a most outstanding athlete at the University of California at Los Angeles. His name was Jackie Robinson.

There was talk of Jackie Robinson being acquired by the Angels, but that was not what we wanted. He had all the qualifications of a Big League ball player. Wrigley did not openly discuss any decision he had made to secure Jackie's signature to a contract. What would Rowland do when he returned to Los Angeles, I wondered? We didn't know. But within a few years from that conference in Wrigley's office, Jackie Robinson was playing in Ebbets Field with the Brooklyn Dodgers, after a short probationary period with Montreal, Brooklyn's farm club. And just as quickly as one could say his name, Robinson was established as one of the country's outstanding baseball players.*

I am not saying that Jackie Robinson got to the Big Leagues only through the good offices of the Communist Party. But I say, without fear of refutation, that the *Daily Worker,* under the direction of its sports editor, Lester Rodney, and the Chicago *Daily Record* were second to no other voices in the United States in the fight to get Negroes on the rosters of Big League baseball clubs.

What was most important was the repeated proof that democracy in every sphere of human relations had to be fought for. Where Negroes were concerned, they had to lead that fight and help educate white Americans to their responsibilities.

From: William L. Patterson, *The Man Who Cried Genocide: An Autobiography* (N.Y., 1971, International Publishers), pp. 141–47.

70

THIRD ANNUAL MEETING OF THE NATIONAL NEGRO CONGRESS

The Third Annual Meeting of the National Negro Congress took place in the Department of Labor Building in Washington, D.C., April 26–28, 1940. The officers at this time were A. Philip Randolph, president; John P. Davis, secretary; U. Simpson Tate, treasurer. A highlight of the congress was the call for Black-white unity—especially labor unity—from the President of the Congress of Industrial Organization (C.I.O.), John L. Lewis. The full text of the Call to this meeting is published below.

The First and Second National Negro Congresses were called together to deal with grave problems facing the Negro People. At these two great meetings thousands of the best representatives among us met together and worked out a program of action. Now in a world ridden with war it is time again to summon the Negro People and the friends of Negro freedom to close ranks, lock hands and courageously deal with the crisis which today threatens the security of every section of Negro America. It is out of this crisis that the need for a Third National Negro Congress arises.

* Robinson played for the Brooklyn Baseball Club of the National League from 1946 through 1956.

We state in plain words the problems which must be solved if the Negro People are to live as free men.

Millions of Negro People in America are hungry and jobless. Eleven hundred thousand Negroes who used to work in mills and factories, on railroads, as building mechanics, in mines, stores, hotels, and other enterprises today have no jobs. More than half of them have had no steady jobs for years. They have led a hand-to-mouth existence. For a few there has been occasional help through relief or a W.P.A. job. But the amounts of such relief aid and the number of such jobs have dwindled from month to month. In the last twelve months more than 125,000 Negroes have been fired from W.P.A. jobs. And most of these have been driven back to the ranks of the unemployed. At least another 75,000 Negroes now on W.P.A. will lose their jobs in the next six months under the proposed reduction in W.P.A. money for the coming year.

No one knows how many tens of thousands of Negro families have been cut off relief. But there is not a Negro center in America where hundreds of such families have not been dropped from relief, despite the fact that they have no other way to live.

There are fewer chances for Negro youth to find work in industry. Industry more and more demands skilled labor. But the door to skilled training remains closed to Negro boys and girls. For tens of thousands of trained high school and college youth who graduate each year there are but a few paltry hundreds of jobs open.

Even the millions of Negro industrial workers who still have jobs are working for the lowest wages at the longest hours. They are robbed of a chance to advance on the job, to secure raises in wages. Serfdom of cook and maid, of long hours, low wages and intolerable working conditions is still the lot of most Negro women workers.

From the throats of more than five million Negro wage-earners there comes today a single cry: *"Give us a chance to earn our daily bread at a steady job."*

The masses of Negro People in America live in structures unfit for human beings. They live in firetraps. Nearly four hundred of them burn, smother or suffocate to death every year because of this. They live crowded together in unsanitary and enforced squalor. Because of this the death and disease rates in each thousand of the Negro population are greater than those for whites.

Landlords squeeze families with unfairly high rent on rundown houses they refuse to repair. City officials refuse to improve Negro communities. Real estate owners mark out small slum areas for Negroes to occupy; and then make contracts among themselves to prevent Negroes living anywhere else. And these contracts are enforced by the courts.

In the Negro communities of America ther. are always too few hospitals, too few playgrounds, clinics, schools The Negro child—in no place in America—has half a chance to grow up healthy, wholesome, or properly educated. In hundreds of counties of the South there are *no* hospitals, *no* playgrounds, *no* high schools, *no* clinics for the Negro population.

An economic cancer has eaten at the heart of Negro farm families in America for ten years. Each year larger numbers of them have lost their homes, have received less cash income, have had less to eat. Each year a larger number of them have been driven from plantations as sharecroppers onto the roads as landless, homeless wage hands getting 40 or 50 days' work a year at less than a dollar a day. At the very moment this is written tens of thousands of them have not a roof over their heads, not a dime they can call their own.

Underlying all of these problems is the denial to large masses of the Negro People of their fundamental rights as American citizens. Three million Negro citizens are still denied every effective means of exercising the right to vote in democratic America. The mob and the rope still rule large sections of the country. In October and November of 1939 hooded mobs of Klansmen literally flogged and beat at least 100 Negroes in South Carolina alone. In other states the Klansmen have carried on a persistent reign of terror against thousands of Negroes to deprive them of their citizenship rights. And these acts of violence have gone unpunished by federal or state authority.

And these are but examples of hundreds of ways in which evil forces in America oppress, Jim Crow and intimidate the Negro People —rob them of their civil liberties and seek to destroy their heritage as free men.

Thus to those who love America we address this Call for the Third National Negro Congress to meet in the city of Washington, D.C., April 26, 27, 28, 1940. We invite to this great national meeting the representatives of trade unions, churches, civic groups, women's and youth clubs and every other kind of organization concerned with the well-being of the American People. The Third National Negro Congress will unite for action thousands of progressive groups of American People. It will unite these groups in the noble effort to bring peace, prosperity and complete democracy to our country.

The Third National Negro Congress—as has been true of the first and second congresses—will remain a great non-partisan body not dominated and not controlled by any political group. It will not duplicate the courageous efforts of other groups, but rather will weld together the strength of these groups into one powerful expression of the will of the Negro People and their friends for justice. Through the Third National Negro Congress the Negro People will continue to march to freedom.

The battle lines are forming in America today. Make no mistake about it. Already such men as Vice President Garner and Senator Tom Connally of Texas are scheming ways to defeat the anti-lynching bill in the United States Senate. Already reactionary forces of *both* parties in Congress are plotting—and sometimes successfully—to curtail vital social services and destroy progressive labor legislation—thus robbing the people of every gain they have made in recent years. This gang is playing for high stakes: for control of the national elections. They are seeking to drive the American People toward war; and to use the threat of war as a smoke screen behind which to attack our living standards and civil liberties.

They can be beaten. Our job is to unite Negro People as never before in a struggle to beat back these attacks upon us. Our job is to join with the great labor movement and the many progressive-minded white Americans in a combined effort to defend democracy in America. We are not just beginning this job. The first and second congresses have shown America that through unity real victories can be won for the Negro People. We need more such victories. And we will win them through unity.

That is why every organization has the solemn responsibility to heed this call by electing its representatives to attend this important national meeting. The United States Congress will be debating the fate of major national issues. And seated in Congress are hundreds of Congressmen and Senators who owe their seats to the Negro vote. They should be made to feel the strength of the Negro People. National political leaders will be planning for their party conventions. They should be made to feel the urgent needs of the Negro People. Never before was there so rich an opportunity for the Negro People to win their democratic rights. Every organization which sends delegates to the Third National Negro Congress will be helping to realize this opportunity.

The month of April in Washington is a symbol of freedom to the Negro People. For in this month in 1862 slavery was forever abolished in the Nation's Capital. Washington is at the very heart of America.

It is fitting that the combined voice of the Negro People should be heard in the highest forum of our land.

We conclude this call to liberty-loving organizations of the American People with the words of the matchless leader of the Negro People, Frederick Douglass:

The whole history of the progress of liberty, shows that all concessions have been born of earnest struggle. If there is no struggle there is no progress. Those who profess to favor freedom yet deprecate agitation are men who want crops without plowing ground. Power concedes nothing without a demand. It never did and never will.

Forward to liberty for the Negro People. Forward to the Third National Negro Congress.

From the original Call, in oversized poster form; in editor's possession.

71

I AM A DOMESTIC

by Naomi Ward

Millions of Black women, down through the centuries, have been the domestic workers in white households throughout the United States. In the midst of the Great Depression one such woman, after three years' experience at this kind of labor, wrote as follows.

They just can't be as bad as they seem to me—these women I have worked for as a domestic. After all, I knew many fine women in various capacities before I was forced, as a penniless widow of forty, to go out to service in order to earn a living for my child and myself.

No, she can't be as bad as she seems, this average woman who hires a maid—so overbearing, so much a slavedriver, so unwilling to grant us even a small measure of human dignity. But I have had three years of experience in at least a dozen households to bear eloquent witness to the contrary.

Of course I am speaking of the average woman. There must be many exceptions. But in my experience the only exception I encountered was a woman whose friends thought her a trifle crazy.

It was true that she employed me by way of astrology—that is, of all the many applicants she figured that my date of birth showed that we would get on well together. I cooked for her one week by astrology and by a color chart the next. That is, our dinner would be entirely purple one day—eggplant, purple cabbage, and beets; and next it would consist of golden corn, yellow squash, carrots, and oranges. And sometimes, poor dear, she would ask me to sit by her bed and talk to her all night to keep her awake because she feared dying in her sleep.

Take this matter of inconsiderateness, of downright selfishness. No other women workers have the slave hours we domestics have. We usually work from twelve to fourteen hours a day, seven days a week, except for our pitiful little "Thursday afternoon off." The workday itself is often nerve-racking. Try broiling a steak to a nice turn in the kitchen while a squalling baby in the next room, in need of a dry diaper, tries to protect himself from his brother, aged two, who insists on experimenting on the baby's nose with a hammer. See how your legs can ache after being on them from 7:00 A.M. until 9:00 P.M., when you are finishing that last mountain of dishes in the pantry! Know how little you care for that swell dinner you cooked when it comes to you, cold, from the table at 8.00 P.M.

Our wages are pitifully small. I doubt if wages for domestics average higher anywhere than in New York City; and here $45 a month is good for a "refined woman, good cook, and fond of children." I often wonder just what they mean by "refined." I remember one woman to whom I applied saying: "Say—Wadda ya mean? Usin' better English 'an I do askin' me fer a job! Git out."

Then there was the old lady in "reduced circumstances" whose sick husband tried to earn a living as a door-to-door salesman. I'm sure she could not afford a maid, even a part time one at $6 a week. She was unhappy, had little to do, and took it out by standing over me at each little task.

One day I was glad to see she had borrowed a book from a lending library. I thought that now, engrossed in her book, she would leave me alone. Unwisely I said: "I see you are reading ——— ———. I read it last year and enjoyed it." Mrs. S——— looked at me forbiddingly and merely grunted. Later she followed me to the kitchen and whispered: "Naomi, do you read?" I looked at her bewildered. "Read? Why, of course I read!" Then the point of the question dawned on me. I had to laugh. "You mean, Mrs. S———, do I read instead of getting on with my work when you are out? No, I don't do that."

Then there was the grandma in the household of Southern folk, a fat old lady who would call me away from anything I was doing to help her dress. "Naomi, please fasten my garters—I can't reach," or

"Tie my shoes—I hate leaning over!" After I had been in that household a week I found the three-year-old calling me "Naomi Noble" instead of my own name. Grandma explained: "Down South we always call our niggers by our own last name, so here we'll call you 'Naomi Noble.'"

These women are so contradictory. They want someone "good with children"; yet when we turn out to be really good—that is, interested, kindly, and intelligent in our handling of their spoiled offspring—they are likely as not to resent the fact that we have succeeded where they failed. They hate the feeling that a "low" domestic worker can do anything better than they.

It is not only the long hours, the small pay, and the lack of privacy—we often have to share a room with the children—that we maids find hardest to bear. It is being treated most of the time as though we are completely lacking in human dignity and self-respect. During my first year at this work I was continually hopeful. But now I know that when I enter that service elevator I should park my self-respect along with the garbage that clutters it. Self-respect is a luxury I cannot retain and still hold my job. My last one was a good example of this.

As such jobs go, it was a good one. It was "part time." That is, I worked as cook nine instead of the customary twelve to fourteen hours per day. My Sundays were free. My wage was $40 per month, and I "slept out." After my last ride down with the garbage I could hurry home to the furnished room I shared with my schoolgirl daughter. My employer, Mrs. B———, was the wife of a fashionable doctor. And another person worked with me as a chambermaid. She was a little French girl, new in America, and just learning our language. We two got along splendidly.

Mrs. B———'s apartment was huge. But Lucille and I together kept it immaculate. However, no matter how much we scoured and dusted on hands and knees Mrs. B——— could always find imaginary dust. "Now Naomi," or "Lucille—you know you're lying when you say you cleaned under that settee!" Mrs. B——— was a hypochondriac who drank too much. One day she would be maudlin, the next vindictive. "Now you know I'm no slavedriver and you know there's little work to do around here—why can't you do it *well* instead of just trying to get by?" Or, "What's happened to all that butter I got yesterday?" The idea being that I had stolen some of it. And I would answer respectfully, minutely accounting for the disposal of the butter. We domestics, whatever our background, are supposed to be natural born thieves. "Lucille! You took my box of candy!"

"No, madame!" with a flash of peasant temper, banging open several bureau drawers, "here is your candy where you yourself put it, madame!"

No apology. Why apologize. We needed our jobs, didn't we?

Mrs. B——— was forever giving me orders as to just how many minutes to cook a certain dish—corned beef, for instance! Of course the only way to get around this was to listen respectfully, say: "Yes, Mrs. B———," and then go ahead and cook it as it should be cooked. I had learned early that Mrs. B——— would tolerate no discussion on such matters. That was "talking back" or "impudence." She was always talking about a legendary Negro cook she had once had for six, eight, or ten years (the time varied according to the low or high of the whisky bottle) who in all that time had never "answered back."

"Mrs. B——— is the one beeg liar," Lucille would whisper at such times. Lucille, by the way, in learning English, had also acquired some fine cusswords. She enjoyed muttering, when Mrs. B——— had been especially trying: "Son o' de beech! Son o' de beech!"

Healthy Lucille came down with a heavy cold, and finally, after trying to conceal her misery had to go to bed for three days. Mr B——— berated her soundly for not having told her. The truth was Lucille knew that when I had been sick for two days my pay had been docked, and she feared the same thing happening to her. While she was ill I did her work as well as my own; but there was no extra pay in my envelope at the end of the month.

When Mrs. B——— had hired me my hours were to be from noon until after dinner. Dinner was to be at seven. But soon dinner was set ahead to seven-thirty and then to eight. Which meant that I did not get through till nine or ten. Mrs. B——— would say: "Now, Naomi, don't rush yourself to have dinner just on the dot—it doesn't matter to us whether it's at eight or eight-thirty. We like to sit around and sip our cocktails."

We dared not say: "But it matters a lot to us whether we finish at eight or ten!"

Lucille and I both met our Waterloo in the following fashion. I had cooked a huge dinner for many guests—we always had company besides the ordinary family of five—and it was 9:00 P.M. before we two sat down to our meal, both too tired to eat.

Suddenly the bell rang furiously and Lucille came back, flushed with anger. "She say to put the cake right on the ice!"

Soon the bell rang again. "Is that cake on the ice?" called out Mrs. B———.

I sang out. "We've just started our dinner, Mrs. B———."

Later I said to Lucille: "Does she think we're horses or dogs that we can eat in five minutes—either a coltie or a Kiltie?" (Kiltie was the dog.) Lucille, who loved such infantile jokes, broke into peals of laughter.

In a second Mrs. B——— was at our side, very angry. She had been eavesdropping in the pantry. "I heard every word you said!"

"Well, Mrs. B———, we're *not* horses or dogs, and we *have* been eating only five minutes!"

"You've been a disturbing influence in this house ever since you've been here!" Mrs. B——— thundered. "Before you came Lucille thought I was a wonderful woman to work for—and tonight you may take your wages and go. Tomorrow, Lucille, your aunt is to come, and we shall see whether you go too!"

I wanted to tell her what I thought of her, but for Lucille's sake I kept quiet. At last at the door I offered my hand to Lucille, saying: "Here is my address."

"I am not interested!" she cried dramatically, throwing the paper to the floor.

I felt suddenly slapped. But from the pleading look in Lucille's eyes, I understood. Mrs. B——— was still in the pantry, and poor Lucille was thinking of her stern French aunt and that she would get no references after ten months' work.

They have us there! For a petty whim they can withhold that precious bit of paper without which it is hard for us to obtain another ticket to slavery. I knew, in my case, I would never get a reference from Mrs. B———. So I did not ask for one, but rode on down for the last time with the garbage.

Jobless, and with only $15 between us and starvation, I still felt a wild sense of joy. For just a few days I should be free and self-respecting!

New Masses, June 25, 1940; XXXV, 20-21.

72

DEMOCRACY AND THE NEGRO PEOPLE TODAY

by Max Yergan

At the General Convention of the Episcopal Church, in Kansas City, Missouri, on October 16, 1940, a meeting was sponsored by the Church

League for Industrial Democracy. The speaker of the evening was Dr. Max Yergan, who had been elected president of the National Negro Congress at its Third Annual Meeting. The text of Dr. Yergan's speech on that occasion follows in full.

The present status of thirteen million Negroes in the United States is the most serious challenge to and the sharpest indictment of our democracy. A policy and practice have been adopted in America which strike at the root of the well-being and progress of the Negro people. Those who still regard democracy as a way of life and as a goal demanding man's best thought and effort must see in the status of American Negroes our great national failure and our immediate task.

We Americans ought to address ourselves to the task of an inclusive democracy because our country is a great country. Anything less than full democracy for all is unworthy of us. The stature of American manhood, the extent of its resources, the magnitude of its achievement and the breadth of its spirit represent the quality of our country. We must address ourselves to this task of complete democracy if any democracy in America is to survive.

Because America is so great, it seems well-nigh unbelievable that there can be such a descent from our national heights to the depths we know in the experiences of the Negro people. Yet, the actual descent is here for us all to behold. May I sketch it briefly by discussing the issues confronting the Negro people of America.

First, with regard to the right to work. Basic in the life of any people is the necessity and the right to gain by work the means to meet their economic needs. The social right to a job, as well as the right to a job for which one is by natural gifts and training best fitted, is inherent in any concept of an efficient society and is the only means to a good society. It is an untenable theory and an indefensible practice that consign a large proportion of a race or group to joblessness. It is equally as indefensible to limit those who are at work to certain kinds of employment. Yet, that is precisely the experience of the Negro people within America.

Earning a living becomes, therefore, a double burden for the Negro worker. He is faced with the problem of unemployment common to all workers in America plus the handicap of restricted employment due to racial prejudices. The most devastating fact in the United States facing Negroes is this: with the exception of those few communities where enlightened and progressive organized labor policies prevail, there is no part of our country where Negroes may participate normally and naturally in the available employment in that community. The humiliation, the frustration and the actual suffering, due to this fact, play havoc in the life of Negro youth and work a grievous hardship upon the great mass of Negro workers. This is an unbearable situation and is the most bitter denial of democracy.

In every city in America the ratio of unemployed among Negroes is far in excess of that among Whites. The great bulk of those employed have marginal jobs, demanding the longest hours with the lowest pay and affording the least security.

The problems of unemployment, of "blind alley" jobs and restriction of Negroes to unskilled occupations call for the highest form of social and economic statesmanship and for the most courageous mass action. The organized life of each community ought to deal with it. Great utilities in the large cities, with which Negroes spend millions of dollars, employ all too few Negroes. In municipal, state and federal civil services, the heads of departments and personnel directors have various ways of keeping Negroes, with high ratings, out of the services.

The basic problem in unemployment among Negroes is of course a problem common to all unemployment in America. The need is for job security in the broadest sense. To provide that, hundreds of thousands of new jobs must be made available and existing jobs opened up to Negroes. Unorganized Negro workers must be brought into trade unions. The mass strength of Negroes and their allies must be directed toward breaking down barriers to jobs. The social intelligence of all America must be aroused to seek a solution of the problem. The Negro people want work with decent wages.

The second issue facing Negroes is that of increasing their political strength by abolishing the poll tax and other restrictions of the right to vote. This is absolutely necessary as a means towards an improved standard of living and is the most powerful evidence of a democratic status.

The southern states are notorious in their denial to Negroes of the right to vote. Indeed, Mr. Barry Bingham, president and publisher of the *Courier-Journal* of Louisville, Kentucky, shows that in the eight poll tax states, less than 25 per cent of the adult population, White as well as Negro, voted in the 1936 presidential election. Mr. Bingham describes this as, "the worst voting record shown anywhere in the world under even a pretense of a democratic system of suffrage."

The existence of the poll tax places the political control of those states, where it operates, in the hands of a few politicians who form the most reactionary bloc in America. Each election returns practically the same men from these southern districts because the Congressmen are responsible to only a small part of the electorate. By the seniority rules many of these Congressmen are made chairmen of committees and become the most active supporters of all anti-labor and anti-Negro legislation.

The President of the United States delivered a resounding address in Philadelphia on September 20th, extolling the privilege of free elections in America. Was Mr. Roosevelt unmindful of the fact that four million Negroes and a larger number of white people are effectively denied their voting rights because of the existence of the poll tax and other voting restrictions? Democracy in America calls for the enforcement of the 14th and 15th Amendments, for the abolition of the poll tax and other franchise restrictions and for elections which are really "free." The National Negro Congress, the Southern Negro Youth Congress and other organizations are determined to work persistently to this end.

The third side of the triangle of disabilities to which Negroes are subjected is related to the two already mentioned. Economic and political limitations necessarily lead to the public social discriminations which limit and starve the life of Negro Americans. American democracy is a partial and sometimes ineffective institution precisely because it has failed to observe the one principle necessary to the building and maintenance of a democratic state. That principle is the scrupulous respect by the majority for the rights of the minority. Failure to observe this principle has made it possible for the clever and powerful among the majority to set up a status of cheapness for the Negro minority. Deny Negroes free access to jobs, deny them the right to vote, and other social evils follow. These evils are inadequate and inferior educational and hospital facilities, second-rate, often unsanitary, and always expensive housing accommodations, restricted recreational facilities and limited use of public institutions and services.

I call attention to the indivisibility of democracy. In its policies, aims and services, democracy must be a whole, inclusive, complete thing or it may become a hypocritical, disappointing, sometimes shameful thing. This contention is borne out by the social weaknesses and economic wrongs within the poll tax states. You cannot permit the existence of political power in the hands of a few without having the feudal and otherwise oppressive conditions found in those states. The National Negro Congress has set forth the slogan that the only reason and the only secure basis for *total defense* is *total democracy*. This leads me to a discussion of current and further basic issues confronting the Negro people.

On October 9th, President Roosevelt made public a statement of policy of the War Department. Among other matters, that statement set forth War Department policy affecting Negro draftees, Negro troops now in the regular army, and Negro officers for the enlarged as well as the existing armed forces of the country. I list below some of the important provisions in that statement.

The War Department's policy, with the President's approval, continues the practice of segregating Negro troops, of providing white officers, excepting chaplains and medical officers, for Negro regiments in the regular army, and of making inadequate provisions for training Negro officers and for recruiting Negroes for the aviation services. Bluntly the statement declared:

The policy of the War Department is not to integrate colored and white enlisted personnel in the same regimental organizations. This policy has proven satisfactory over a long period of years and to make changes would produce situations destructive to morale and detrimental to the preparation for national defense.

This statement is a shameful slander against American citizens, Negro and White. It is an acceptance of an age old system of Jim-Crowism in American life. And its endorsement by the President of the United States is the most shameful act of all.

In releasing the War Department's statement, the United Press account declared the following:

"White House secretary, Early, said the segregation policy was approved after Mr. Roosevelt had conferred with Walter White, president of the National Association for the Advancement of Colored People, and two other Negro leaders." The two other Negro leaders referred to were Mr. A. Philip Randolph, president of the Brotherhood of Sleeping Car Porters, and Mr. T. Arnold Hill, an assistant in the National Youth Administration.

This statement of War Department policy affecting Negroes as approved by the President has stunned the Negro people. There is not a Negro man, woman or youth who does not feel the shameful stigma which Negroes suffer under that policy.

Upon the publication of the War Department's statement, Messrs. White, Randolph and Hill are reported to have sent a telegram to the White House declaring: "In a written memorandum we specifically repudiated segregation." I quote further from that telegram as referred to in the press service of October 11th of the National Association for the Advancement of Colored People:

"We are inexpressibly shocked that a President of the United States at a time of national peril should surrender so completely to enemies of democracy who would destroy national unity by advocating segregation. Official approval by the Commander-in-Chief of the Army and Navy of such discrimination and segregation is a stab in the back of democracy."

Negro Americans will always resent and oppose Jim-Crowism wherever it is practised. The Negro people protest particularly this approval, by the President, of one of our country's most degrading customs. The Draft Act declares: "There shall be no discrimination for or against any person because of his race, creed or color." Once more the law of the land is violated and gives way to prejudice. Once more a law becomes for Negroes, like the 14th and 15th Amendments, a promissory note upon which collection has yet to be made.

The President's approval of Jim-Crowism and discrimination against Negroes in the army must be regarded as a part of the Administration's policy whereby it has refused to support and pass an anti-lynching law. On behalf of the National Negro Congress and the millions, whose views it most certainly represents on this matter, I wish here to raise the sharpest protest against the President's approval of the principle of segregation and discrimination. In this respect the President and his Administration take their place alongside of previous Republican and Democratic administrations. They have in their action, or failure to act, regarded the Negro people as a cheap people, void of sensitivity to violation of their individual and corporate personality and unfit to be members of a democracy. Once more, a President is not chief executive for all the people. Again, in the Senate and in the House can be found those enemies of democracy, those traducers of the Negro people who hold and decide the fate of one-tenth of the American population. It is for Negroes and those other millions of Americans, who are also victims of political domination, never to forget these degrading acts and, in their strength, work to make them forever impossible.

The possibility of our country entering the present war as an ally of the British rulers is perhaps the most urgent and far-reaching issue the Negro people face today. Among some Negro spokesmen and in some Negro circles there is a disposition to regard the chief issue in our relation to the war as one of securing the more lucrative positions for a relatively small number of Negroes in the armament and war-making program. Now naturally it is essential that, with defense plans already far advanced, masses of Negro workers be given equal opportunity to share in the training and job program created under these plans. But such a consideration should not make us unmindful and uncritical of the danger of involvement in the present war. Such involvement can solve no problems for the people of America.

There are, among our group, those who, in their justifiable hatred of Hitler and Hitlerism, feel it to be our country's duty to send military aid to Britain. Thus they approve the present policy of our government of so-called "steps short of war."

To each of the attitudes mentioned above, as President of the National Negro Congress and in terms of my own personal convictions, it is my duty to take exception. We desire to see our country kept out of this war.

The American Civil War, for instance, was a conflict involving the extension of democracy. That cause had the support of the Negro people and it is undoubtedly true that in a similar war today Negroes would be found overwhelmingly on the side of the democratic cause. The present war, however, is for no such cause. Hence our demand that we keep out of it.

We do not believe we have any business allying ourselves with either of the belligerent sides now responsible for the war. We believe *that* to be the basic question for the masses of Americans both White and Negro. In this question are involved all other questions confronting the Negro people and, for that matter, all the people of America. On the eventuality of peace or war depends the possibility of carrying forward the struggle for fuller democracy or turning to fascist dictatorship in America.

It need hardly be pointed out here that the question of defense of our country is not involved. The Negro people have defended and will always defend our country and its democratic institutions. This is true of Negroes as it is of all the liberty-loving people of America. No section of the American population has greater traditions of loyalty than my people. On Boston Common during the American Revolution, at New Orleans in 1812, at Fort Pillow and in other engagements, from 1860 to 1865, fighting to destroy slavery and to preserve the Union, and on through subsequent wars, Negro Americans have distinguished themselves in defense of their country. No traitor to his country disgraces the Negro people.

For these reasons, it is clear, that Negroes need no lesson in patriotism or Americanism from the army of paid propagandists for war. The Negro people take their Americanism from Abraham Lincoln and from Frederick Douglass. Negroes, like all other Americans, must not be precipitated into war measures and war-making by the hysteria manufactured by those who desire to make America an ally of any nation already at war or who desire to make huge profits from war ventures. Nor must Negroes confuse defense of their country with imperialist aggression or political ambitions certain to lead to dictatorship or a worsening of their already limited political and economic privileges.

The concern and the conviction referred to have found expression among us in an organized and representative form. At the Third National Negro Congress held at Washington in April of this year, a resolution was adopted which expressed the conviction of that representative gathering on the issue of American involvement in the present war. I quote from that resolution as follows:

The National Negro Congress declares that the Negro people have everything to lose and nothing to gain by American involvement in the imperialist war and sharply condemns the Administration for the steps it has taken towards involvement and the partiality it has shown.

This resolution declared firmly the conviction of the delegates assembled; and, they believed that the resolution was representative of Negro opinion throughout the country. Today, with America nearer the war, that conviction against involvement in this war stands more firmly as an expression of the attitude of the Congress. We believe, further, that it still represents the overwhelming conviction of all the American people. We have an anxious concern about those forces of war and destruction which grip and overrun the world today.

In the first place, we are aghast at the horrors of the regimes of Hitler and Mussolini. We utterly condemn their destructive aggression which has left such indescribable suffering in its path. We denounce their inhuman, brutal persecution of the Jewish people and we hope (with some basis for our hope) that the yoke of these oppressors will be thrown from the shoulders of the German and Italian people. We are completely and unreservedly opposed to the destructive power personified in the Nazi and fascist dictators. That is part of our concern and our conviction. But we cannot stop there.

We Negro people, out of our long experience and observation, must likewise condemn, and desire to see ended the destructive and oppressive imperialism personified in the ruling forces of Great Britain,

France and the other imperialist countries. If fascism is the acute manifestation of brutal ruthlessness in high places, imperialism with its long-standing abuses at home and abroad is its basic cause.

It must never be forgotten that Hitler and Mussolini owed their rise to power as much, if not more, to the imperialist masters of Britain, France and other countries as they did to the objective circumstances and the imperialist rulers of their own countries. There can certainly be no doubt that fascist aggression into China, Ethiopia, Austria, Spain and Czechoslovakia was not opposed but was aided and abetted by the forces of imperialism still powerful in Britain and active elsewhere in Europe.

In this war, as in the last, there is much talk of "saving the world for democracy." Negroes of America observe, however, the persistent and shameful denial of every vestige of democracy to their blood brothers in Africa and the West Indies. Even today the conflict between Britain and Germany reveals itself to be a greedy struggle for domination of African lands and peoples. We need only look at the recent actions at Dakar and in the Cameroons. India has struggled in vain to win self-government from her British rulers for 360 million Indian people. The same can be said of the action of imperialist powers in all other colonial countries. The war aims of the conflicting powers have nothing to do with saving and extending democracy.

It becomes clear that the similarities between fascist and imperialist rule are numerous and strong. Both resort to ruthless territorial expansion; both seize the goods of other people; both exploit racial, cultural and religious differences. Both are destructive of human rights and depend upon undemocratic, anti-social methods for their expansion and their maintenance.

What then, is to be said of a war waged by such forces as have been described? What can be said, save that by their very nature neither Nazi Germany nor imperialist Britain and France can wage a war for democracy or for freedom and justice. There is no other conclusion to arrive at save that this war like the last Great War is a conflict between rival imperialist forces, each striving to enrich itself at the expense of the other.

It must be further pointed out that the very nature of the rivalry and conflict between Nazism and Imperialism makes for war and more war. Like the American slave system of pre-Civil War days, Imperialism and Nazism must expand or die. Imperialism in its battle against democracy builds up a Hitler, a Franco, a Mussolini and thereby sets the stage for the conflict which brings such destruction upon the world.

The goal and the possibility in America are an ever-increasing democracy. Therefore a war between fascism and imperialism offers no choice to our country. The Negro people, as all Americans, want nothing of imperialism or fascism. Their choice is for *democracy*. America most certainly will not aid Nazi Germany. America must not become an ally of imperialist Britain. To help either of these powers is to use the tremendous manhood and material wealth of this country in the support of the forces of human exploitation, for war and misery. Let us build a strong democratic country which no foreign power will dare touch. Let us not become involved in outworn imperialism which breeds war and fascism. *Let America become a mighty force for peace throughout the world by becoming a great democracy here at home.* That, we are confident, is the overwhelming view of the Negro people on the question of American involvement in the war.

If the question is asked what it is that American Negroes want today, the answer comes with swiftness and clarity. We want security in employment; freedom to exercise our constitutional right to vote and relief from the debasing discriminations imposed upon us in the public social life of our country. To ask for or accept less than this minimum standard of Americanism would be unworthy of the Negro people. For this reason I know that our struggle for full-fledged American democratic rights will take on an increasingly effective form.

Finally, what are the means open to us for reaching our goal of democracy within the American framework? What path must we take? The answer to these questions obviously involves political parties.

To the two major parties of long standing, Negroes have this to say:

Since 1875 you have both permitted and given aid to the policy of Negro disfranchisement through the poll tax and other unconstitutional and illegal methods.

You have both permitted the crime of lynching to continue by refusing to place an anti-lynching law on the statute books.

You have both sanctioned widespread discrimination against Negroes in state and federal services and you have thereby endorsed the debasing practice of Jim-Crowism in America.

You have both failed to provide a single meaningful answer to the vital social and economic problem of unemployment. And today, you are both prepared to exploit the instinct of defense of our country by resorting to unconstructive and fascist substitutes for the political and economic reforms necessary to remove unemployment from our land.

Let these political parties that now seek the support of the Negro vote bear in mind their failures. The Negro people will not forget these failures. We must not again permit ourselves to give unqualified support to any political party. In this election and those to come the Negro voters must support men and measures and not party labels. In this election and those to come it must be our task to show politicians that they cannot trample upon our rights and win our support. Intelligent non-partisanship is the course we must follow.

Meanwhile an awakening Negro people is becoming increasingly conscious of where its interests lie. There are mighty forces in our land, in factories and mills, on farms and in mines, among youth and the aged. Organized labor, militant minorities in the churches and in the southland—these are also among the overwhelming millions in America who have struck their tents and are on the march towards a national status of peace, of democracy, of the good life for all.

The National Negro Congress, expressing the deep feeling of the Negro people, is also on the march. We have made common cause with these great forces for progress in America. Perhaps no single step so clearly indicates this as our acceptance of the statesmanlike invitation of John L. Lewis to our Congress to enter into a working agreement with Labor's Non-Partisan League—the great legislative arm of the labor movement.

The significance of this cooperation to Negroes may best be seen by this clear and unequivocal statement made by Mr. Lewis at the Third National Negro Congress:

> You know, I am one American who believes in equality of opportunity for the Negro people. I do not try to conceal that fact. I am rather anxious that a great many people find out about our views in this country and I am doing what I can to educate them on that particular point. I want the help of the Negroes of this country. I want their help and their cooperation with the labor movement of America that stands for the principle of protection and security that affects every American.

It is for the Negro people of America to work intelligently, patiently, and yet with all possible haste, to strengthen their own ranks. It is likewise imperative for them to cooperate with all other sections of the American people whose welfare depends upon an ever widening democracy. These are the goals of the National Negro Congress.

From a sixteen-page pamphlet published by the National Negro Congress in New York City late in 1940; in the editor's possession.

73

JIM CROW IN THE ARMY CAMPS

Anonymous

The building up of a vast army for subsequent use in the already flaring beginnings of what, within a short time, was to be World War II, commenced late in 1939. From then to the end of the war in 1945, the U.S. armed forces at home and abroad maintained an overwhelmingly jim-crow arrangement—with some slight concessions in the last months. A year before Pearl Harbor, a Black enlisted man wrote the following characteristic piece, published anonymously.

I am a newly enlisted soldier, stationed in the Northwest. I volunteered, as I knew I would eventually be forced into the Army by the draft, and I wanted a better chance than the draftee would have.

But, after being in the Army a short while, my militarily-inclined enthusiasm turned to a feeling of disgruntled surprise and sorrow. Why? I'll tell you why!

I had envisioned the Army as being a vast military machine, working with utmost precision. Instead I found it to be, for the Negro, a place impregnated with suppression and racial prejudice.

We have a War department theatre which shows the latest pictures. It is the size of a medium-class city theatre. It is for the military personnel and their families.

We have a Negro regiment stationed here, composed of approximately 300 men. And in the theatre, size aforementioned, there is a row of seats, seating not more than fifteen men, which is set aside for the Negro soldiers.

I ask you, is that the proper spirit for an army training to fight for democracy?

Whenever a Negro soldier sits in any seat other than the row set aside for Negroes, as I and many others have done upon their first visit to the theatre, he is rudely and loudly asked to move to the *Reserved For Colored* section. This practice arouses hatred where there would be none if we were treated as we should be treated.

Also in the library and the Post Exchange, and on the Post in general, the Negro is treated as if he isn't wanted. Many of the young men enlisted in the U.S. Army are thoroughly disgusted because of segregation. Many were faithfully promised, before enlisting, that they would have an opportunity to learn a trade, or continue with their previous studies. As yet there are no educational facilities for the Negro. Young men have enlisted to do their patriotic duty to America, and to learn some useful trade. The men have done their part. The question is: Will Uncle Sam do his part?

Last, but far from least, is the way a Negro soldier is treated on the Army bus when he goes to town. It is far from any idea I ever had of Army life! When the Negro regiment was first organized here (it has only been stationed here a little more than a year) the Negro soldiers were asked to sit in the back of the bus, but since more have begun to ride the bus, they have begun to move forward and sit any place they please. Yet hardly a week passes without an altercation resulting from the word so many of the white race deem necessary to label us by.

Why is it we Negro soldiers who are as much a part of Uncle Sam's great military machine as any cannot be treated with equality and the respect due us? The same respect which white soldiers expect and demand from us?

This is the age of science, of steel—of speed and modernization. It is no time to let petty indifferences stand in the way of a nation in great need of defense, on the brink of a great crisis! There is great need for a drastic change in this man's Army! How can we be trained to protect America, which is called a *free* nation, when all around us rears the ugly head of segregation?

The Crisis, December, 1940; XLVII, 12.

74

NEGROES AND DEFENSE

by Metz T. P. Lochard

An outstanding Black journalist, for years a senior editor of the *Chicago Defender,* offered the following general estimate of the Black people's relationship to the world crisis represented by the war in Europe.

The attitude of the Negro toward national defense and the European war must be examined in the light of a growing, subtle nationalism that conditions the thought-process of the leadership of America's thirteen million blacks. Unable to integrate himself fully into the social and economic pattern of American culture, the Negro has attempted to formulate a doctrine of separatism as a rational escape from the rigors of race prejudice and discrimination. The very nature of the social situation has forced him into acceptance of the fallacy that his people are a "nation within a nation." This may explain why the strident cry for national preparedness leaves him unresponsive; he fears that he may be unable to exact appreciable guaranties from the national government as a condition for his support. His habitual emotionalism is conspicuously restrained in the midst of a contagious war hysteria.

The Negro is nevertheless fully aware of the dangers that threaten democracy, and he is not disposed to minimize the gravity of the circumstances that call for defense and unity as measures of national security. Isolationist propaganda has had no effect on him. He believes in some form of intervention in the European war as an inescapable alternative to actual engagement. Aid to Britain is conceived to be a necessary expedient in the present emergency, though the Negro nurses no inborn love for England. The unmitigated exploitation of black labor in the Crown colonies in Africa, the suppression of fundamental political rights in the West Indies, the refusal of the Secretary for the Colonies to place before the British Parliament the aspirations of the natives of West Africa with respect to universal education, political suffrage, and abolition of child labor—these and many other instances of rapacity and imperialism have not endeared Britain to the hearts of black men. Realizing, however, that the fall of England, in this crisis, cannot but foreshadow a total eclipse of democracy and of representative government, the Negro is willing to cast aside his tra-. ditional Anglophobia.

More than any other racial minority, Negroes have a stake in democracy. Under a system in which they could not exercise the power of the ballot they would lose every vestige of human rights. Certainly they could cherish no hope in a fascist society that relegated them to the status of "auxiliary" or "subhuman" race, as Hitler puts it in *Mein Kampf*. The Italian invasion of peaceful Ethiopia and the ruthless dismemberment of the last independent African kingdom in 1935, the recent expulsion of all people of African descent from German-occupied France, the Nazis' destruction of all French monuments to black soldiers as "insults to the dignity of the white race" have thoroughly awakened the Negro masses to the dangers of fascism. While the absorption of Austria, Czechoslovakia, Poland, Norway, Denmark, Holland, and Belgium excited little emotional feeling among American

Negroes, the invasion of France brought quite a different reaction. For France, with its historic declaration of the Rights of Men, with its traditional liberalism and racial tolerance was, in the sight of all black men, the living symbol of democracy.

The Negro sees in the conflict between fascism and democracy a serious challenge to those political principles through which he has been hoisted out of chattel slavery and through which true social justice may eventually be attained in America. He recognizes, therefore, that the present emergency imposes upon his race the necessity of retreating from the untenable position of a "nation within a nation." But if he is willing to forego the defensive attitude into which he has been forced, he does so in order to secure a more equitable participation in the affairs of this republic. The determination not to surrender his democratic rights even under the stress of a national emergency is based upon past experience.

In October, 1918, a month before the signing of the Armistice, the War Department sent Dr. Robert R. Moton—the late principal of Tuskegee Institute—to France to advise Negro soldiers who had had a glimpse of real democracy not to press the government upon their return for extension of hard-earned democratic rights. In fact, Secretary Baker informed Dr. W. E. B. Du Bois, then editor of *The Crisis,* "We are not trying by this war to settle the Negro problem."

The Negro problem is a major problem of American democracy. If the black man is called upon to defend this democracy, he has a legitimate claim to those rights which are guaranteed by the fundamental laws of the form of political government which he is urged to protect. If this be an incorrect view, the Negro has no reason, except human compassion, to be exercised about a war fought by white folk, for the exclusive benefit and glorification of white folk. He should be given the unconditional choice between fighting as a slave for the perpetuity of a nefarious system and fighting as a free man for free institutions.

In 1917 the War Department, after tenaciously refusing to train Negro officers in established military centers, finally provided, upon the plea of Joel Spingarn, chairman of the board of directors of the National Association for the Advancement of Colored People, a Jim Crow officers' training camp at Des Moines, Iowa. The man eminently qualified to head this camp was Charles Young, a black man, then lieutenant colonel in the regular United States army. He had a splendid army record. He had accompanied General Pershing in the Mexican foray and received high commendation from the man who later became commander-in-chief of the American Expeditionary Force. He was in good health, and only forty-nine years of age. In the accelerated scheme of war-time promotion he would have attained the rank of a general in the army by 1918. But a black general in the United States army was too much of a nightmare for the brass hats in Washington.

The Des Moines camp was established in May. When Young came up in June for examination for promotion to a colonelcy, the medical board retired him for "high blood pressure." An entire corps of white officers was appointed to train the colored cadets.

Fear of a repetition of a chain of ugly incidents led recently to a White House conference at which Walter White, secretary of the N.A.A.C.P., A. Philip Randolph, president of the Brotherhood of Sleeping Car Porters, and T. Arnold Hill of the National Youth Administration submitted a seven-point memorandum to President Roosevelt. This memorandum urged that Negroes be used as reserve officers and that the same training opportunities be given to Negroes as to others. It requested that existing units of the army be required to accept officers and enlisted personnel on the basis of ability instead of race or color. It asked for the abolition of racial discrimination in the navy and recommended the appointment of competent Negro civilians as assistants to the Secretaries of War and the Navy. Some of these requests have been granted, but in the main the War and Navy departments are still clinging to their policy of discrimination—a policy based on traditions of caste and social life in a professional army and navy.

In the hope of lifting his status beyond the limitations of a theoretical citizenship, the Negro has made sacrificial offerings in every major struggle in which this nation has been engaged. Four thousand Negro soldiers served with the Continental army during the American Revolution. Andrew Jackson had no compunction about mobilizing black men in the War of 1812. He said in his proclamation to them, "Through a mistaken policy you have heretofore been deprived of participation in the glorious struggle for national rights in which your country is engaged. This no longer shall exist. As sons of freedom you are now called upon to defend your most inestimable blessing." Some 178,000 Negroes served in the Civil War. Black troops acquitted themselves creditably at Las Sussinas, El Caney, and San Juan Hill in the Spanish-American War. Of the 400,000 Negro soldiers mobilized for action during the first World War 40,000 were on the firing line.

Despite this impressive record, black men are still discriminated against in the caste-ridden United States army. Not a single Negro officer is on duty with regular-army troops. Not a single Negro reserve officer is serving in the regular army. Under the Thomason Act Congress this year made provision in its regular appropriation for training 650 reserve officers, drawn from schools and colleges, with units of the regular army. Howard University in Washington, D.C., and Wilberforce University in Ohio are two Negro institutions with senior R.O.T.C. units. The War Department has completely ignored them.

The only Negro troops in the United States army with full combat status are in the Twenty-fifth Infantry, the Twenty-fourth Infantry and the Ninth and Tenth Cavalry, which have distinguished themselves in many engagements, are serving in training schools as laborers and personal servants. At present, of the total strength of 229,636 officers and enlisted men only 4,451 are Negroes. There are fewer Negro troops in the National Guard today than there were on the eve of the first World War. The first separate Negro battalion of the 372d Infantry, assigned to the District of Columbia, is kept on a skeleton basis with only Company A mustered in and that company denied the facilities of training and housing. Companies in Tennessee and Connecticut have been dissolved. The Negro citizens of West Virginia have been attempting to form a National Guard regiment in their state but have had, so far, no success. In the case of an established battalion in New Jersey, the War Department has flatly refused to grant it federal status.

According to General George C. Marshall, Chief of Staff, the National Guard has a shortage of men. Yet the army refused to take additional Negro units, which could have been inducted into the service in the new categories required in the program of expansion. All these facts and figures were presented recently to the House Subcommittee on Military Affairs by two eminent Negro scholars—Dr. Rayford Logan, of the Department of History of Howard University, and Dr. Charles Houston, former dean of the Howard Law School.

On June 5, 1939, the Secretary of War, testifying before a subcommittee of the House Committee on Appropriations, stated that the War Department was studying ways to provide training for Negro pilots. As yet no Negro is being trained for service in the army air corps as either a flying cadet or an enlisted mechanic. The Secretary of War designated a school at Glenfield, Illinois but the War Department has refused to accept Negroes in that corps. On October 11, Garland F. Pinkston, a Negro, received the following letter signed by Herbert M. West, Jr., First Lieutenant, United States Air Corps, Recorder:

Dear Sir: Through the most unfortunate circumstances, your application was allowed to be completed because of our ignorance of your race. At the present time the United States Army is not training any except members of the white race for duty as pilots of military aircraft.

Thirteen million Negroes, representing a vast reservoir of possible war material, are being ignored and in some instances openly humiliated. It is therefore not surprising that Negro citizens are without enthusiasm for national defense. They can have no faith in the leadership of an army or a navy that denies them the right to serve their country on an equal footing with other citizens.

The Nation, January 4, 1941; CLII, 14–16.

75

JIM-CROW ARMY

by Henry Winston

In a vein somewhat similar to that of the preceding essay, Henry Winston, early in 1941, denounced the racism characteristic of the armed forces of the United States and related this to that nation's general stance on a global scale. At the time this was written, Henry Winston was national administrative secretary of the Young Communist League and a member of the National Committee of the Communist Party.

Jim-Crow discrimination against the Negro conscripts has already become a national scandal. In Jamaica, Long Island, the appeal of a Negro youth for deferment because of his mother's dependency upon him for financial support was rejected with the following insulting memorandum:

This particular case is common in our board. We have a large colored population and there seems to be no regard for moral or financial responsibility. . . . This type of registrant knows very little about the truth.

The leadership for the insulting Jim-Crow policy was given by the national Administration in legalizing the maintenance and formation of Jim-Crow regiments. On October 9 [1940], an ominous statement was issued from the White House through the President's secretary, Stephen Early:

The policy of the War Department is not to intermingle colored and white personnel in the same regimental organization. This policy has proven

satisfactory over a long period of years, and to make changes would produce situations destructive to morale and detrimental to preparations for
national defense. For similar reasons the War Department does not contemplate assigning colored reserve officers other than those of the medical
corps and chaplains to existing Negro combat units of the regular army.

Think that statement through. It was issued for the Commander-
in-Chief of the Army and Navy, the President of the United States.
The statement says that this policy has proven satisfactory over a
long period of years. Satisfactory to whom and for whom? To the
Negro men and women who are waging a ceaseless battle against
Jim Crow? To the wide masses of white toilers who are in ever
increasing numbers participating in the fight to storm the citadels of
Jim Crow? *No,* to them this policy has been highly *unsatisfactory* over
a long period of years. Then for whom has it been satisfactory? Only
to that small group in Wall Street whose interest such a policy serves.
The Jim-Crowism felt by young Negro Americans in civilian life is
here reflected in the military forces with the public sanction of the
President.

Two questions automatically arise in the minds of young Negro
Americans: Is this tremendous draft army being created for national
defense? Are the Negroes who are now being placed in Jim-Crow regiments considered a part of the nation? The simple truth is that the
purpose for which this armed force is being created is not for the
defense of the nation, but rather for profits and empire to benefit
the rich. Negroes are excluded in this concept of the nation in the eyes
of Wall Street.

The ruling circles of this country, who pursue a policy of national
oppression of the Negro people, fear the prospect of intermingling "colored and white personnel in the same regimental organization." This
fear is based not on the premise that it may be "destructive to morale"
or "detrimental to preparations for national defense." What they fear
is that such intermingling may spill the beans and expose the real
intent of this headlong drive toward full participation in the present
war. They fear a fusion of the common problems, a recount of common experiences in civilian life, a growing collaboration and understanding between Negro and white. They well know that the possibility
of such intimate contact may well result in recognition of their common destiny, directed not alone against the present war, but against
imperialist oppression in general.

There will be not only Jim-Crow regiments, but these regiments will
be officered by white personnel. Why white officership over the Jim-

Crow regiments? To impress upon the minds of the Negro people the pernicious idea of white superiority, the idea that only whites can lead. The mailed fist of the imperialists in our country has placed the Negro people in a special position. Is it not clear that when the President announced his intentions to maintain the Jim-Crow system, this was being done for purposes alien to the spirit, tradition and common interest of the Negro people? Every Negro man and woman has been taught that he is part of the nation. Now, once again, he is being told otherwise. Yet, the Negro people are asked to make equal sacrifices, indeed, if not greater. Can you see any difference between this enunciation which comes from the White House and that of Jefferson Davis, Chief Justice Taney, Tom Heflin, Bilbo, or the Ku Klux Klan? The only difference is that Roosevelt speaks in the name of "national defense" while those dark forces of yesterday spoke of defending "white civilization." They really mean national offense. How dare the President of the United States speak in the name of "civilization," "democracy," "freedom," "culture," and "world order"! What can better expose this entire set-up than the reactionary attitude of the Administration toward one-tenth of America's citizenry?

From a fifteen-page pamphlet, *Old Jim Crow Has Got To Go!* (New York: New Age Publishers, March, 1941), pp. 9–11.

76

THE MARCH-ON-WASHINGTON MOVEMENT

The Afro-American people were fiercely determined to seek significant changes in the racist nature of U.S. society, especially as involvement in the European and Asian fighting seemed more and more likely. An important phase in this effort was the March-on-Washington Movement—under the leadership of A. Philip Randolph—the purpose of which was to force anti-racist action on the part of President Roosevelt. After prolonged resistance and maneuvering this was finally forthcoming, on June 25, 1941, with Roosevelt's Executive Order 8802, which declared it "the duty of employers and labor organizations . . . to provide for the full and equitable participation of all workers in defense industries, without discrimination because of race, creed, color, or national origin" and appointed a Committee on Fair Employment Practices to administer the Order. With the issuance of this Order, the March—to have reached a climax on July 1, with one hundred thousand Black people in Washington—was called off. The page one report of this in a Black newspaper follows.

By telephone early Thursday morning [June 26, 1941] the *Star News* was informed that President Roosevelt had issued an executive order prohibiting discrimination in the National Defense program, and that director A. Philip Randolph, who organized the "March-to-Washington" movement, had notified members of the committee that the proposed pilgrimage is off.

Mr. Randolph, in Houston, Tex., attending the annual convention of the National Association for the Advancement of Colored People, could not be reached for a statement before the *Star-News* went to press.

The President stated that he had acted on evidence that workers had been barred from defense jobs solely because of considerations of race, creed, color or national origin to the detriment of workers' morale and national unity.

Plans had been completed for a march of some 100,000 Negroes from all sections of the country. They were to converge on Washington July 1. The *Star-News* having initiated the demand for an executive order from the President to check discrimination in National Defense, has also supported the "March-to-Washington" idea since its inception.

Three weeks ago Mr. Roosevelt issued a statement to Messrs. [William] Knudsen and [Sidney] Hillman, chairmen of the O.P.M. [Office of Production Management] in which he urged them to integrate Negroes into our National Defense program. The demand for an executive order continued, and Mr. Randolph, at a White House conference last week, told the President the march would go on unless more effective action was taken to stop discrimination.

New York *Amsterdam Star-News,* June 28, 1941, p. 1; for a good account of F.E.P.C., see Louis Ruchames, *Race, Jobs, and Politics* (New York: Columbia University Press, 1953).

77

BARRIERS TO NEGRO WAR EMPLOYMENT

by Lester B. Granger

To further develop the history of the executive order of June, 1941, and to indicate something of the realities of its impact, there is published below an account by the executive secretary of the National Urban League. Mr. Granger at this time was also first vice-president of the American Association of Social Workers.

On June 18, 1942 several thousand white Detroit workers, members of the United Automobile Workers, CIO, went on a wildcat strike shutting down 60 per cent of the Hudson Naval Ordnance Arsenal. The strike occurred because eight Negro employees, in accordance with their union seniority rights, had been assigned to machines formerly operated by white men. Prompt action by R. J. Thomas, president of the union, ended the strike after seven hours. The strikers were told to return to work or be expelled from the union. The walk-out was described by the UAW head as sabotage of our war effort that played into the hands of the enemies of our Nation. "Our constitution," declared Mr. Thomas, "provides for safeguarding the rights of all our members irrespective of their race or creed."

In New York City a group of Negro college graduates protested to the War Department and the President's Committee on Fair Employment Practice against what they charged was flagrant racial discrimination by the New York Office of the War Department in selection for employment of translators from a list of qualified candidates. Negroes were refused appointment no matter what their qualifications, stated these protests.

In Atlanta, Georgia, a committee formed by the Urban League of Atlanta, and representing numerous Negro organizations of that city, vigorously attacked policies of the local educational authorities in denying training to Negro workers who wished employment at the Bell aircraft plant near Atlanta. Promises had been received from the Bell officials that Negroes would be employed if trained. Five thousand Negroes had registered to show their desire for training and employment. Instructions have been given to local educational officers to set up training classes for Negroes at once to match the fifteen classes already in operation for whites. But on June first, Atlanta officials were still refusing to move.

On June 18, 1942 the President's Committee on Fair Employment Practice cited two Chicago labor unions—Steamfitters' Protective Association Local 597 and Chicago Journeymen Plumbers Union Local 130—as being guilty of racial discrimination in preventing Negro steamfitters and plumbers from working on defense projects. This discrimination, the Committee stated, violated Executive Order 8802 and constituted a hindrance to the war effort.

During September 1941 the United States Employment Service inquired of selected defense industries throughout the country how many jobs would be opened to qualified Negroes out of the new jobs that management expected to produce during the following six months. Out of 282,245 prospective job openings, 144,583 or 51 per cent were absolutely barred to Negroes, the answers holding good for northern and southern states and for unskilled as well as skilled jobs. They showed how seriously Executive Order 8802 had failed of its purpose, which was to eliminate racial discrimination from defense employment.

The history of the Executive order is more than interesting. It throws a searching light on some of the difficulties standing in the way of solving one of America's most serious social problems—economic discrimination against minority groups, chiefly the Negro population.

At the very opening of the National Defense Program in 1940, it was apparent that employment discrimination against Negro workers, long a general policy of industrial management, was erecting formidable barriers against effective use of American industrial manpower. Thoughtful leadership instantly recognized that industry faced a production assignment far beyond the existing resources of skilled and semi-skilled labor; before the quotas tentatively set by Government could be reached, many more millions of workers would be employed than ever before in the Nation's industrial history.

For this reason, the Advisory Commission to the Council of National Defense addressed special instructions to holders of defense contracts, calling their attention to the unprecedented drain on labor reserves that was anticipated, and urging full consideration of the training and employment of Negro workers in all occupations for which they could be made available. In the congressional bill that appropriated funds for vocational training of defense workers, there was a provision that the benefits of such training must not be denied to any worker because of his race, religion, or place of birth.

But not Government's urging nor even the threat of war could persuade many employers to drop old habits of thought. Persisting in ideas handed down from a plantation economy, employers still regarded Negroes as a wholly unskilled rural group. They ignored the fact that as early as 1930 there were over a million Negro workers experienced or trained in skilled and white-collar work; that in one year over fifty thousand young Negroes had completed trades and industrial courses in vocational and technical schools; and that nearly five thousand others were awarded college degrees in chemistry, engineering, other sciences, and the liberal arts.

Management officials usually shrewd in sizing up labor resources held onto old ideas because it was easier to retain an old mental error than to make the effort involved in a new outlook. Continuance of these attitudes produced a virus of discrimination that infected nearly every area of the Negro's living. Commercial employment offices and public employment services reflected the unwillingness of employers to use Negro workers by refusing to refer or even to register Negro applicants except in domestic or unskilled jobs. Vocational schools also took their cue from industry by discouraging or rejecting Negro youth seeking training for industrial occupations. White workers readily accepted their employers' designation of industry as an "economic white man's country" and regarded the employment of Negroes with hostility. Their labor unions frequently formalized this attitude by adopting constitutional clauses, ritualistic practices, or tacit policies barring the membership of Negro workers.

Here was the picture that had long been familiar to students of social problems. Nothing in the picture had been changed by the fall months of 1940 when industry began to recruit trained labor on a scale unprecedented in two decades. The recommendation of the Advisory Commission to the Council of National Defense had stirred not a ripple of interest among employers to whom it was addressed. Ominous portents of what was to come were seen when construction of army cantonments began all over the country. Contractors were frantically seeking skilled building trades workers; building trades unions were summoning delinquent members to reinstatement and re-employment; there were over seventy-five thousand Negroes experienced as carpenters, bricklayers, painters, electricians, plasterers, and cement workers. But when these dark-skinned craftsmen moved forward to take their places at the hiring gates they were met with outright refusal by contractors who, in the same breath, continued to shout for more workers. Or they were referred to business agents of local unions, to be told in one way or another, "Sorry, no Negroes!" It was the exceptional construction job where employment could be found by the skilled Negro worker for the seeking.

Against this forming pattern of defense discrimination, Negro leadership bestirred itself, taking advantage of experiences suffered in the days of the last World War. The Negro public was forewarned by disappointments of those times, and had moreover received thorough training during the depression period in developing mass weight of public opinion. The national Negro press came out with one sustained roar of protest against the sin of racial discrimination in a country preparing to defend democracy. Organizations representing Negro welfare, such as the National Urban League, addressed memoranda to government agencies and held frequent conferences in Washington offices. Negro labor, church, medical, legal, dental, fraternal, and political groups swelled the volume of protest. Emergency committees in nearly every important Negro community gave the masses of people a chance to express themselves. A mass meeting called by the Urban League of Kansas City, Missouri, attracted five thousand persons, the largest protest meeting of Negroes in the history of that city. The more angry Negroes became, the longer grew the names of their "co-ordinating committees."

Careful surveys, as well as impromptu investigations, were made in various parts of the country so as to "get the goods" on discriminating employers. The Curtiss-Wright and Bell aircraft plants of Buffalo, New York, employed no Negroes at production jobs; Standard Steel of Kansas City, Missouri, declared, "We have never had a Negro worker in twenty-five years and don't intend to start now." North American Aircraft of the same city stated that Negroes would be employed only in custodial jobs. Of all the companies manufacturing war planes, only the Douglas Corporation of California employed even a handful of Negro production workers. Similar reports of racial discrimination piled up regarding Sperry Gyroscope of New York; Pratt and Whitney of Hartford, Connecticut; Budd Manufacturing of Philadelphia; New York Shipbuilding Corporation of Kearney, New Jersey; Buick, Chrysler, and Packard of Detroit and Flint, Michigan; Bethlehem Shipbuilding of Los Angeles; Stewart-Warner, Majestic Radio, Studebaker, and White Motors of Chicago; Julius Heil and A. O. Smith of Milwaukee; and hundreds of other large manufacturers in every part of the country.

The reasons given for the nonemployment of Negroes were of infinite variety, often mutually contradictory. Most common were the following: Negroes never applied; whites and blacks can't mix on the same job; haven't time or money to build separate toilets; no trained Negroes are available; they are racially unequipped for skilled work; the union won't have them; don't like Negroes and don't want them around; this is a rush job and we haven't time for experiments.

And so Negro spokesmen, realizing the futility of trying to break past employer resistance without heavier weapons, turned their attention to Washington again. Some defense agencies were now lumbering into motion on this matter, in response to the proddings of public opinion. The Labor Division of the National Defense Advisory Commission had already added to its staff an experienced Negro member, Dr. Robert C. Weaver, previously consultant on racial problems with the United

States Housing Authority; but the small size of the staff assigned to him at first was an indication of how little the National Defense Advisory Commission realized the importance and magnitude of the job that had to be done.

But realization gradually came. The National Urban League brought to Washington in October 1940 a group of local league secretaries from different parts of the country to undertake the job of educating key defense officials. Over several days they sat in conference with staffs of the United States Office of Education, charged with carrying out much of the defense training program; the Bureau of Employment Security, responsible for public employment services; the Division of Defense Housing Coordination, entrusted with plans for housing defense workers; and the Labor Division of the National Defense Advisory Commission.

Other organizations made pilgrimages to Washington to lay their complaints directly before central authority. Waves of telegrams and letters of protest began again to sweep over defense officials, who now realized that they dealt with an aroused Negro population. When the Office of Production Management superseded the Defense Council, Sidney Hillman, as co-director, brought over the Weaver Staff, bag and baggage, and enlarged it to establish a Negro Labor Training and Supply Branch of the Labor Division of O.P.M. It is true that William Knudsen, Hillman's fellow director, was never sympathetic to a program for increasing effective use of Negro labor, but one-half of the authority in this strategic government agency was in support of the Weaver program.

The Office of Education came in for sharp criticism over continued discrimination in defense training. State educational officers, through whom vocational training funds were disbursed, almost completely ignored the new law that stipulated equality of training opportunity. Negroes in southern states reported that training classes for whites were being set up in such trades as welding, sheet metal work, aviation mechanics, machine operation, and blueprint reading, while "defense" classes for Negroes were in nonindustrial occupations. In several states no provision at all was made for Negroes. The training-within-industry program of O.P.M. followed the same pattern. Employers who were unwilling to employ Negroes at production jobs were doubly resistant against admitting them to training classes established in their plants. Even the Newport News Shipbuilding Company, 35 per cent of whose workers were Negroes, refused to train their dark-skinned labor for such jobs as machinists. Since O.P.M. supervision for this program was recruited directly from industrial corporations, there was slight chance of serious pressure being brought to bear on such employers by government representatives. Thus by the winter of 1940 the whole pattern of racial discrimination in defense industry lay clearly exposed. The employment gates of an estimated 75 per cent of defense industry were closed against all Negro labor. Exclusion of skilled Negro workers was even more widespread. Absence of any real defense training for Negroes in most southern cities and discrimination against Negro trainees in most northern cities reduced this group's chances to find jobs in the future.

State employment services either refused to register skilled Negro workers at their trades or failed to refer them to jobs when they were registered, or referred them only when employers clearly specified preference for Negroes. In only two states, New York and Illinois, did state employment services adopt constructive steps to induce employers to accept Negro labor, and these steps were usually tentative. In typical northern states, employment interviewers were instructed to fill job orders as they came in, without attempting to persuade employers to change discriminatory specifications. In all states, north or south, the fate of the Negro job applicant depended to a great extent upon the personal interest or prejudices of the interviewer regarding the Negro's "place" as an industrial worker.

The situation created by racial policies of labor unions was familiar to students of American social problems. Eighteen international unions, A. F. of L. and independent, still maintained constitutional or ritualistic restrictions against Negro membership. Most important among these in the defense field were the International Association of Machinists, holding closed shop contracts with twelve major aircraft companies; the Brotherhood of Boilermakers, Iron Shipbuilders and Helpers of America; and the railway unions. In addition, thousands of local unions openly excluded Negroes from jobs, whether in defiance or with the tacit consent of international officers. Practically none of the officials of these unions showed any indication that the threat of war had influenced their contemptuous attitude toward black labor. Aeronautical Mechanics Local No. 751 of Seattle, International Machinists Association, made a public issue of its refusal to admit Negroes to closed shop employment in the Boeing aircraft plant. The union's general organizer for the district declared to the press, "Organized labor has been called upon to make many sacrifices for defense and has made them gladly, but this [admission of Negroes] is asking too much." Thus was completed the vicious circle of defense discrimination against

Negroes. No training and therefore no jobs; no jobs and therefore no union memberships; employer and union opposition and therefore no training.

Only one force could break this circle, and that was government action backed by enlightened public opinion. In developing such opinion and securing such action within a space of ten months, Negro leadership accomplished what will eventually be recognized as a feat of social statesmanship. The repeated protests of Negroes developed support from liberal white citizens. The daily press took notice and not only reported the opinions of Negroes but also presented strong editorials in their behalf. An interracial committee of 160 distinguished Americans, under the leadership of Dr. Anson Phelps Stokes, made public a signed protest against the intolerable evil of racial discrimination in a democracy preparing for defense. The Council for Democracy issued a special pamphlet on the subject. Governors in several states appointed committees to find some way of attacking the problem. State legislatures considered bills for banning racial bias in defense employment.

In some cases Federal officials welcomed this aroused public opinion; in most cases they responded to it. Sidney Hillman issued an emphatic memorandum on April 11, 1941 calling employers' attention to the wastefulness of importing labor from distant areas or raiding the employment rolls of competitive firms when unused Negro labor remained available at their plants' very doors.

The United States Employment Service adopted in its entirety a plan of reorganization offered by the National Urban League for improving services to Negro workers. An impractical "Division of Negro Employment" in the U.S.E.S. was eliminated. Experienced Negro employment service officials were placed in regional posts to advise on state service functions as they related to Negro labor. An able Negro economist, Dr. Ira DeA. Reid, was appointed as assistant to the Director of the Bureau of Employment Security, of which the U.S.E.S. is part.

Now, under constant prodding, the United States Office of Education addressed another communication to state educational officers, instructing them to make defense training available to Negroes, either by their admission to existing classes or by setting up classes for them similar to those established for whites.

O.P.M. had already conferred with heads of A. F. of L. and C.I.O. unions in the building and shipbuilding trades so as to gain official trade union support for Negro employment on jobs in these fields. Results of these conferences, combined with the efforts of civic groups, were seen in a gradual increase of Negro building trades and ship-building workers on defense contracts in the South as well as the East and the Midwest. The more progressive union leadership, especially in the C.I.O., secured the passage of resolutions at labor conventions demanding an end to the color line in defense industry. Several C.I.O. unions, such as the United Automobile Workers, the United Electrical, Radio and Machine Workers, the National Maritime Union, and the Steel Workers' Organizing Committee, made equal job opportunity for Negroes a part of their agreements with management.

The next move came from the White House. The President, urged for months to take official cognizance of a serious national problem, broke silence on June 17, 1941 with a memorandum addressed to O.P.M. directors Hillman and Knudsen. The President stated:

. . . I place the full support of my office behind your statement that "all holders of defense contracts are urged to examine their employment and training policies at once to determine whether or not these policies make ample provision for the full utilization of available and competent Negro workers. . . ."

But this statement, well-directed as it was, proved insufficient to stem the tide of Negro resentment which had risen by now to truly formidable proportions. The White House found itself faced with immediate prospect of a mass demonstration by Negroes unparalleled in national history, scheduled for July 1. All over the country racial organizations were preparing for a march on Washington similar in size and scope to the Bonus Army demonstration of 1932. The movement was spontaneous in that numerous groups had been urging such a step for months; it was deliberately organized in that the prestige of A. Philip Randolph, president of the Brotherhood of Sleeping Car Porters, made it possible to put the idea into action. A March-on-Washington Committee was organized under Randolph's leadership, including many well-known Negro spokesmen. One hundred thousand Negroes prepared to "meet in Washington."

The administration emphatically did not desire this. It would have been notice to foreign critics of our domestic disunity at a time when a semblance of unity was most essential to national prestige. It is significant that arguments to this effect, addressed to Randolph, had no effect on his committee's plans. For possibly the first time in history, Negroes were willing to make an issue of their citizenship rights, even to the point of delaying plans for military and naval defense. A delayed start that is sound, they argued, is better in the long run than a hasty start based on the fatal error of racial discrimination.

The President summoned Randolph and members of his committee to Washington. Flanked by Cabinet members and other advisers, the President first requested cancellation of the march, then agreed to issue an Executive order forbidding racial discrimination in defense industry. The march was canceled; Executive Order No. 8802 was issued on June 25, 1941, stating, in part:

. . . It is the duty of employers and labor organizations to provide for the full and equitable participation of all workers in the defense industries without discrimination. . . . All departments and agencies of the Government of the United States concerned with vocational and training programs for defense production shall take special measures appropriate to assure that such programs are administered without discrimination.

All contracting agencies of the Government of the United States shall include in all defense contracts hereafter negotiated by them a provision obligating the contractor not to discriminate against any worker.

There is established in the Office of Production Management a committee on fair employment practices, which shall consist of a chairman and four other members to be appointed by the President.

So ended the long fight of Negroes for direct action by the highest executive authority of the land. But they soon found that this action of itself did not solve their difficulties. The Committee on Fair Employment Practice was appointed, with Mark Ethridge, liberal Louisville newspaper publisher, as chairman. Its remaining membership consisted of William Green, president of the A. F. of L.; Philip Murray, head of the C.I.O.; David Sarnoff, president of R.C.A.; and two Negro members—Earl Dickerson, attorney from the city of Chicago, and Milton Webster, vice-president of the Brotherhood of Sleeping Car Porters. After several months of plan-making and preparation, the Committee began a series of investigations and public hearings on defense discrimination in Los Angeles, Chicago, New York, and Birmingham. On the basis of facts uncovered, firms found guilty of discrimination were cited, ordered to correct their practices, and in case of failure to comply were certified to the President as violating Executive Order 8802.

The record of the Committee on Fair Employment Practice is worthy of special study because it constitutes a new approach by the Government of the United States to an old problem. It is the first time since the Emancipation Proclamation that a Presidential Executive order has been issued especially in behalf of Negroes and similarly disadvantaged groups. This may be the first step toward a permanent action, to act in the sphere of racial discrimination, just as the National Labor Relations Board does in the field of union discrimination.

It must be confessed that without such authority the role of the Committee on Fair Employment Practice must be largely exhortatory and persuasive. At present it must exert its punitive authority through the President. It can recommend cancellation of the contract of an offending employer; it cannot assess fines or apply other intermediate punishment. The "all-or-none" nature of its recommendations to the President exposes the Committee to a fatal weakness which employers have been quick to seize upon. They can persist in discrimination, possibly less openly, knowing that the administration will hesitate long before canceling any important contract for ships, planes, tanks, or guns. This is the policy that many employers have followed with impunity. But the net results of the Committee's work have been good, because the larger firms investigated have not desired the unfavorable publicity that comes from citation for racial discrimination at such a time as this. The pressure exerted on some of the larger industrial corporations has been reflected in relaxing discrimination by their smaller competitors.

Meanwhile, war's outbreak and the merger and reorganization of key agencies into efficient warmaking bodies brought important changes in the Federal race relations program. The War Production Board swallowed O.P.M. The War Manpower Commission took over the United States Employment Service as its recruiting agency. Robert Weaver was appointed a member of the War Manpower Commission as director of the Negro Manpower Service. The staff had been greatly enlarged with regional field representatives assigned throughout the country. Weekly reports poured in emphasizing the extent to which jobs were being opened for Negroes in war industry. The Curtiss-Wright plants now reported more than 3,000 Negro workers employed. Glenn L. Martin, North American Aviation, Consolidated, Brewster, Bell Aircraft, and Lockheed Vega plants were all using Negroes at production jobs. Thousands of Negroes were at work in ordnance plants throughout the country. The number of Negro shipbuilding workers at skilled and semiskilled jobs had doubled in one year, with over 14,000 employed in Navy yards and with more than 5,000 employed in the Newport News Shipbuilding Company alone. The Sun Shipbuilding Company of Chester, Pennsylvania, announced that it would open a new shipyard manned entirely by Negro workers at all skills. The Higgins Industries of New Orleans, applying the assembly line to shipbuilding, planned an all-Negro assembly line with skilled and semiskilled Negro workers. In the shipbuilding field Negroes were now employed in 37 different crafts, including first-class machinists. Auto plants converted to war industry, such as Kelly Hayes, Chrysler, Oldsmobile, Murray, and Briggs, were upgrading skilled and semiskilled Negro workers who had formerly been confined to unskilled and custodial work.

Activity of the Federal Government had been matched by similar special efforts in several states. In New York and Illinois, state laws had been passed forbidding racial discrimination on war contracts. In New York a special committee was appointed by the Governor as part of the State War Council to make this policy effective.

Refusal of public officials to train Negro workers for war production jobs remains a serious stumbling block. The United States Office of Education has been ineffective in handling the situation. Figures produced by this Federal agency show that in eighteen southern and border states, where 22 per cent of the total population are Negroes, only 3,215 Negroes, or 4 per cent of the total trainees, were enrolled last January in pre-employment and refresher training courses. Out of 4,630 training courses in southern states, only 194 were open to Negro trainees. In Florida, Negroes are 27 per cent of the state's population, but only .17 of 1 per cent of its trainees. In the state of Texas, where Negroes comprise 14.3 per cent of the population, only 206 Negroes were admitted to training courses out of 12,472 persons trained in defense production last February. This is a confession of almost complete failure by the Office of Education to enforce the provisions of the law that there shall be no racial discrimination in defense training.

When this barrier is cleared away, as it must be, the prospects for Negroes in war and postwar industry will be brighter than ever. The first World War brought about initial entrance on a large scale of Negroes into northern industry. The second World War is already providing them a chance to move up the occupational ladder. Whether this is a permanent advance or only a temporary perch "for the duration" will depend upon the efficiency that Negroes show in the jobs they are now doing, the extent to which they find and master training at skilled trades, and the readiness of employers to evaluate American workers on a basis not of their color but of their ability to do the job. It will depend, also, upon whether organized labor learns the lesson that labor in England has mastered too late—that white workers can never be free while their fellows are in chains.

Annals of the American Academy of Political and Social Science, September, 1942; CCXXIII, 72–80. See also by Lester B. Granger, "Negroes and War Production," *Survey Graphic*, November, 1942; XXXI, 469–71, 543–44.

78

WHY SHOULD WE MARCH?

by A. Philip Randolph

Though the March on Washington set for the early summer of 1941 was called off with the President's Order, a March-on-Washington Movement remained and through much of the war exerted anti-racist pressure upon the national and state authorities. Its leader tells of this development in the following essay, published late in 1942.

Though I have found no Negroes who want to see the United Nations lose this war, I have found many who, before the war ends, want to see the stuffing knocked out of white supremacy and of empire over subject peoples. American Negroes, involved as we are in the general issues of the conflict, are confronted not with a choice but with the challenge both to win democracy for ourselves at home and to help win the war for democracy the world over.

There is no escape from the horns of this dilemma. There ought not to be escape. For if the war for democracy is not won abroad, the fight for democracy cannot be won at home. If this war cannot be won for the white peoples, it will not be won for the darker races.

Conversely, if freedom and equality are not vouchsafed the peoples of color, the war for democracy will not be won. Unless this double-barreled thesis is accepted and applied, the darker races will never wholeheartedly fight for the victory of the United Nations. That is why those familiar with the thinking of the American Negro have sensed his lack of enthusiasm, whether among the educated or uneducated, rich or poor, professional or non-professional, religious or secular, rural or urban, north, south, east or west.

That is why questions are being raised by Negroes in church, labor union and fraternal society; in poolroom, barbershop, schoolroom, hospital, hair-dressing parlor; on college campus, railroad, and bus. One can hear such questions asked as these: What have Negroes to fight for? What's the difference between Hitler and that "cracker" Talmadge of Georgia? Why has a man got to be Jim-Crowed to die for democracy? If you haven't got democracy yourself, how can you carry it to somebody else?

What are the reasons for this state of mind? The answer is: discrimination, segregation, Jim Crow. Witness the navy, the army, the air corps; and also government services at Washington. In many parts of the South, Negroes in Uncle Sam's uniform are being put upon, mobbed, sometimes even shot down by civilian and military police, and on occasion lynched. Vested political interests in race prejudice are so deeply entrenched that to them winning the war against Hitler is secondary to preventing Negroes from winning democracy for themselves. This is worth many divisions to Hitler and Hirohito. While labor, business, and farm are subjected to ceilings and floors and not allowed to carry on as usual, these interests trade in the dangerous business of race hate as usual.

When the defense program began and billions of the taxpayers' money were appropriated for guns, ships, tanks and bombs, Negroes presented themselves for work only to be given the cold shoulder. North as well as South, and despite their qualifications, Negroes were denied skilled employment. Not until their wrath and indignation took the form of a proposed protest march on Washington, scheduled for July 1, 1941, did things begin to move in the form of defense jobs for Negroes. The march was postponed by the timely issuance (June 25, 1941) of the famous Executive Order No. 8802 by President Roosevelt. But this order and the President's Committee on Fair Employment Practice, established thereunder, have as yet only scratched the surface by way of eliminating discriminations on account of race or color in war industry. Both management and labor unions in too many places and in too many ways are still drawing the color line.

It is to meet this situation squarely with direct action that the March on Washington Movement launched its present program of protest mass meetings. Twenty thousand were in attendance at Madison Square Garden, June 16; sixteen thousand in the Coliseum in Chicago, June 26; nine thousand in the City Auditorium of St. Louis, August 14. Meetings of such magnitude were unprecedented among Negroes.* The vast throngs were drawn from all walks and levels of Negro life—businessmen, teachers, laundry workers, Pullman porters, waiters, and red caps; preachers, crapshooters, and social workers; jitterbugs and Ph.D.'s. They came and sat in silence, thinking, applauding only when they considered the truth was told, when they felt strongly that something was going to be done about it.

The March on Washington Movement is essentially a movement

* In view of charges made that they were subsidized by Nazi funds, it may not be amiss to point out that of the $8,000 expenses of the Madison Square meeting every dime was contributed by Negroes themselves, except for tickets bought by some liberal white organizations.

of the people. It is all Negro and pro-Negro, but not for that reason anti-white or anti-Semitic, or anti-Catholic, or anti-foreign, or anti-labor. Its major weapon is the non-violent demonstration of Negro mass power. Negro leadership has united back of its drive for jobs and justice. "Whether Negroes should march on Washington, and if so, when?" will be the focus of a forthcoming national conference. For the plan of a protest march has not been abandoned. Its purpose would be to demonstrate that American Negroes are in deadly earnest, and all out for their full rights. No power on earth can cause them today to abandon their fight to wipe out every vestige of second class citizenship and the dual standards that plague them.

A community is democratic only when the humblest and weakest person can enjoy the highest civil, economic, and social rights that the biggest and most powerful possess. To trample on these rights of both Negroes and poor whites is such a commonplace in the South that it takes readily to anti-social, anti-labor, anti-Semitic and anti-Catholic propaganda. It was because of laxness in enforcing the Weimar constitution in republican Germany that Nazism made headway. Oppression of the Negroes in the United States, like suppression of the Jews in Germany, may open the way for a fascist dictatorship.

By fighting for their rights now, American Negroes are helping to make America a moral and spiritual arsenal of democracy. Their fight against the poll tax, against lynch law, segregation, and Jim Crow, their fight for economic, political, and social equality, thus becomes part of the global war for freedom.

PROGRAM OF THE MARCH ON
WASHINGTON MOVEMENT

1. We demand, in the interest of national unity, the abrogation of every law which makes a distinction in treatment between citizens based on religion, creed, color, or national origin. This means an end to Jim Crow in education, in housing, in transportation and in every other social, economic, and political privilege; and especially, we demand, in the capital of the nation, an end to all segregation in public places and in public institutions.
2. We demand legislation to enforce the Fifth and Fourteenth Amendments guaranteeing that no person shall be deprived of life, liberty or property without due process of law, so that the full weight of the national government may be used for the protection of life and thereby may end the disgrace of lynching.
3. We demand the enforcement of the Fourteenth and Fifteenth Amendments and the enactment of the Pepper Poll Tax bill so that all barriers in the exercise of the suffrage are eliminated.

4. We demand the abolition of segregation and discrimination in the army, navy, marine corps, air corps, and all other branches of national defense.
5. We demand an end to discrimination in jobs and job training. Further, we demand that the F.E.P.C. be made a permanent administrative agency of the U.S. Government and that it be given power to enforce its decisions based on its findings.
6. We demand that federal funds be withheld from any agency which practices discrimination in the use of such funds.
7. We demand colored and minority group representation on all administrative agencies so that these groups may have recognition of their democratic right to participate in formulating policies.
8. We demand representation for the colored and minority racial groups on all missions, political and technical, which will be sent to the peace conference so that the interests of all people everywhere may be fully recognized and justly provided for in the post-war settlement.

Survey Graphic, November, 1942; XXXI, 488–89.

79

THE DURHAM STATEMENT OF 1942

Expressions of mounting discontent and militancy evoked a response of concern from some of the relatively older and more moderate among the Black leadership. Significant in this connection was an article, "Interracial Hypertension," written by Dr. Gordon Blaine Hancock of Virginia Union University in 1941 and widely reprinted throughout the Black press. It caught the attention of Mrs. Jessie Daniel Ames, a liberal white woman of Texas and Georgia, who was a member of the Commission on Interracial Cooperation. The result was a meeting between Dr. Hancock and Mrs. Ames; it was agreed that if prominent southern Black figures would confer and draw up a statement of concern and intent, an analogous group of southern whites would respond favorably and quickly. The result was a meeting in Durham, North Carolina, in October, 1942, with Dr. Hancock, Dr. P. B. Young, editor and publisher of the Norfolk *Journal and Guide,* and Dr. Benjamin E. Mays—then dean of the School of Religion at Howard University—among the outstanding figures (numbering fifty-nine) who adopted "A Statement by Southern Negroes" entitled: "A Basis for Interracial Cooperation and Development in the South." The Durham meeting was followed by a statement from southern whites issued out of Atlanta in April, 1943; then a joint meeting of Black and white southerners in Richmond in June, 1943—and from this, the next year, the birth of the Southern Regional Council. Published below is the preamble to the Durham Statement of October, 1942.

The war sharpened the issue of Negro-white relations in the United States, and particularly in the South. A result has been increased racial tensions, fears, and aggressions, and an opening up of the basic questions of racial segregation and discrimination, Negro minority rights, and democratic freedom, as they apply practically in Negro-white relations in the South. These issues are acute and threaten to become even more serious as they increasingly block, through the deeper fears aroused, common sense consideration for even elementary improvements in Negro status, and the welfare of the country as a whole. With these problems in mind, we, a group of southern Negroes, realizing that the situation calls for both candor and wisdom, and in the belief that we voice the sentiments of many of the Negroes of the Nation as well as the South, take this means of recording our considered views of the issues before us.

(1) Our Nation is engaged in a world-wide struggle, the success of which, both in arms and ideals, is paramount and demands our first loyalty.

(2) Our Loyalty does not, in our view, preclude consideration now of problems and situations that handicap the working out of internal improvements in race relations essential to our full contribution to the war effort, and of the inevitable problems of post-war reconstruction, especially in the South where we reside.

(3) The South, with its twenty-five million people, one-third of whom are Negroes, presents a unique situation, not only because of the size of the Negro population but because of the legal and customary patterns of race relations which are invariably and universally associated with racial discrimination. We recognize the strength and age of these patterns. We are fundamentally opposed to the principle and practice of compulsory segregation in our American society, whether of races or classes or creeds; however, we regard it as both sensible and timely to address ourselves now to the current problems of racial discrimination and neglect, and to ways in which we may cooperate in the advancement of programs aimed at the sound improvement of race relations within the democratic framework.

(4) We regard it as unfortunate that the simple efforts to correct obvious social and economic injustices continue, with such considerable popular support, to be interpreted as the predatory ambition of irresponsible Negroes to invade the privacy of family life.

(5) We have the courage and faith to believe, however, that it is possible to evolve in the South a way of life, consistent with the principles for which we as a Nation are fighting throughout the world, that will free us all, white and Negro alike, from want, and from throttling fears.

See Benjamin E. Mays, *Born to Rebel: An Autobiography* (New York: Charles Scribner's Sons, 1971), pp. 213–19. The full texts of all statements referred to above are in *The Durham Statement, October 20, 1942; the Atlanta Statement, April 8, 1943; the Richmond Statement, June 16, 1943* (Atlanta: Commission on Interracial Cooperation, 1943).

80

NATIONAL COUNCIL MEETING, S.N.Y.C.

The highest governing body of the Southern Negro Youth Congress—the All-Southern Conference—met annually from its beginning in 1937, but the war prevented such meetings commencing in 1941. However, its Advisory Board and National Council regularly met; one such joint meeting was held in November, 1942, in the Administrative Building of Atlanta University, with Dr. Frederick D. Patterson—chairman of the Advisory Board and president of Tuskegee Institute—presiding. The minutes of that meeting are printed below.

The meeting convened at 10:30 A.M. The morning session was a joint session of the Council and the Advisory Board. Dr. F. D. Patterson, Chairman of the Board, presided.

Those present were:—Council Members: William Y. Bell, Jr., Charles A. Davis, Phillip Harloy, Esther V. Cooper, Louis E. Burnham, James E. Jackson, Jr. Advisory Board Members: Dr. F. D. Patterson, Charles G. Gomillion, Jesse B. Blayton, Dr. W. E. B. Du Bois, Miss Susie A. Elliott, Dr. R. O. Lanier, Dr. Ira De A. Reid. Visitors: Joseph Bostic, Dorothy Burnham, Lucy Graves, Theodore Johnson, Lucille Lewis, Mrs. Willie Lewis, Anne M. Mayfield, Mildred McAdory, J. B. Sims, William Spooner, Ida Wood.

Reports on perspectives, organization, and job training and placement were given by Esther V. Cooper, Louis E. Burnham and James E. Jackson, Jr. After brief discussion of the first two papers, the group centered its attention on the jobs and training report of Dr. Jackson. It was agreed that the local councils should use the report as the basis for concentrating on winning more opportunities for training and jobs in war industries in their communities. It was agreed that the suggestions contained in the report should be strengthened by more factual material on the availability of training under all government programs.

The group recessed for lunch at 1:00 P.M. and reconvened at 2:30. The afternoon sessions of the Council and the Advisory Board were held separately. James E. Jackson, Jr. presided at the afternoon session of the Council. The first points for discussion were reports from the local councils.

William Spooner, Chairman of the New Orleans Council, said the

Council there is cooperating with groups such as the N.A.A.C.P., local labor unions, the Urban League, and churches in a program to win job opportunities. Members of the Council initiated the fight to free three Negro soldiers sentenced to die in Alexandria on a framed-up charge of rape. The Council recently held a successful dance and is planning to open a community youth center.

Mildred McAdory, S.N.Y.C. field worker, and Lucille Lewis, secretary of the Fairfield (Alabama) Youth Council, reported that the Council there opened a Youth Center on October 1st, and has launched a program of activities of interest to the entire community. Seventy-five members are enrolled at present, and other organizations are cooperating.

Theodore Johnson of the Tuskegee Council reported that his group has elected officers for the school year and started an educational program. He also reported on the Internal Student Assembly held in Washington, D.C., September 2–5, which he attended as a representative of the Southern Negro Youth Congress.

There followed a discussion of the policy of the S.N.Y.C. as formulated at the 5th Conference and as reiterated in the report of the executive secretary in the morning session. There was some discussion as to whether the emphasis of the policy of the organization should be placed on the winning of the war or the winning of democracy at home. Mr. Bell asserted that more emphasis should be placed on democracy and less on the war. Mr. Spooner stressed that if we fail to defeat the Axis, what democracy we now have will be lost. Considerable discussion led to general agreement that the two objectives, victory over the Axis and full citizenship rights for Negroes, are inseparably linked. The consensus was that our efforts on behalf of the one will necessarily advance the cause of the other.

Following this discussion, the proposals contained in the organizational report of Louis E. Burnham were discussed and voted upon as follows:

1. S.N.Y.C. to concentrate in building a limited number of active councils in Alabama, Tennessee, and Louisiana in the months immediately following. (Passed)
2. Initiate a drive for three thousand new members in these areas of concentration by February 14th, 1943, the 6th Anniversary of the S.N.Y.C. (Passed)
3. To conduct a special project of establishing at least six industrial youth centers during 1943 in Fairfield, Alabama; Inslev, Alabama; Pratt City, Alabama; Mobile, Alabama; Bessemer, Alabama; and New Orleans, Louisiana. (Passed)

4. To establish Councils on the college campuses in the states of concentration, and in Atlanta, Georgia. (Passed)
5. In regard to program, to concentrate on three campaigns: (1) expand opportunities of Negro youth to serve in flying services of Army and Navy; (2) extension of the franchise and further development of education for citizenship; (3) and further development of opportunities for jobs and training in war industry. (Passed)
6. To substitute mass conference in the selected areas of concentration for an All-Southern Youth Conference in the spring. (Passed)

Mr. Spooner proposed that the local councils keep in closer touch with the national office and that they be urged to send in full quarterly reports of activities. (Passed)

The Advisory Board members returned from their session, and Mr. Charles G. Gomillion, Secretary, reported on their discussions. Dr. Patterson resumed the chair at this point.

The financial statement and the budget were then discussed. Dr. Jackson proposed that each Council member raise the sum of $10.00 by Feb. 14th through coin gleaners to be mailed from the national office. (Passed)

It was pointed out that, due to the war emergency, three vacancies among the officers exist: President, one Vice-President, and Treasurer. It was proposed that National Council members be asked to submit nominees for all these offices and then on the basis of the nominations ballots be mailed from national office. (Passed)

Dr. Patterson expressed appreciation and, with common consent, instructed the secretary to direct a letter of appreciation to Dr. R. Clement, President of Atlanta University.

Meeting adjourned at 5:00 P.M.

Mimeographed minutes in editor's possession.

81

BLACK VIOLATORS OF THE DRAFT

There were many Black and white men who violated the Conscription Act. In most cases, no doubt, these resulted from failure to understand its requirements and/or religious and pacifistic reasons. But with the Afro-American another major reason was objection to a racist society. Three outstanding cases of this nature, occurring in 1942 and 1943, are summarized below in a handbook contemporaneously compiled and edited by a Black woman then living in New York City.

Winfred W. Lynn Case

The most outstanding case asserting violation of the Selective Service Act, and the only case which sought to test the legality of the racial quota practice of the War Department in connection with the act was that of Winfred William Lynn, a gardener of Jamaica, L.I., New York.

In September, 1942, Mr. Lynn, 36, was notified by the induction board of his locality to report for induction. The order was issued pursuant to a requisition by the New York City Director of Selective Service which informed the local draft board of Jamaica that "Your Quota for this Call is the first 90 White men and the first 50 Negro men who are in Class 1-A. . . ."

Mr. Lynn refused to report, having earlier stated his position in a letter to his board in which he said:

I am in receipt of my draft-reclassification notice. Please be informed that I am ready to serve in any unit of the armed forces of my country which is not segregated by race. Unless I am assured that I can serve in a mixed regiment and that I will not be compelled to serve in a unit undemocratically selected as a Negro group, I will refuse to report for induction.

The draft board and government officers, tried to persuade Mr. Lynn to change his mind, but failing to do so, he was ordered to report for induction on September 18. He failed to do so, and two months later he was indicted by a Federal grand jury on charges of disobedience of the induction order.

Conrad Lynn, the gardener's brother, was his counsel. On November 16, 1942, Winfred appeared before Judge Abruzzo in the Federal criminal court in Brooklyn and pleaded "not guilty." He was held under bail of $2,500. The next day, his brother filed a petition for a writ of habeas corpus, basing his plea on the grounds that the induction order was invalid, "having been issued to your petitioner as a part of a 'Negro quota' and your petitioner was not bound to obey said order."

The legal question raised by the Lynns was not one of discrimination in training, but of discrimination in the selection of draftees. This course was chosen because they believed it to be the only legal grounds on which the case could be successfully fought. They pointed out that under the separate quotas for white and colored it was impossible to draw on the two racial quotas in exactly equal ratios, therefore discrimination exists because the speed with which a man is called to service depends upon his race, as well as his draft number.

In this manner, they contended, Section 4 (a) of the act was violated. This section states: "In the selection and training of men under this Act, and in the interpretation and execution of the provisions of this Act, there shall be no discrimination against any person on account of race or color."

The hearing on the habeas corpus petition was set—after a number of postponements—for December 4, 1942. It was held before Federal Judge Mortimer Byers, who after reading the petition, dismissed it without argument, saying that he would not consider the merits of the case so long as Winfred refused induction.

Meanwhile the case had attracted nation-wide attention. The American Civil Liberties Union became interested and assigned Arthur Garfield Hays, white, and Gerald Weatherly, a white Texas lawyer, associated with Mr. Hays, to assist in the case. The National Citizens' Committee for Winfred Lynn was organized to finance the case.

In order to get a court test on the main issue rather than on the question of whether a draftee could bring a habeas corpus action while resisting induction, counsel persuaded Lynn to submit to induction.

Mr. Lynn followed their advice and was subsequently inducted. The criminal charge against him for refusing induction was then dismissed. Another petition for a writ of habeas corpus was filed, and on January 4, 1943, a hearing was held before Judge Marcus B. Campbell in the Brooklyn Federal Court.

The government argued that the record did not show that the appellant was inducted under a Negro quota, nor that he was directed to report for induction ahead of men whose draft numbers were lower than his own, and that therefore there was no proof of discrimination against him on the grounds of race.

To this argument Lynn's counsel replied that the existence of separate quotas for whites and Negroes made it incredible that he was called for induction precisely in his turn under the draft; and that there was discrimination against him if he were called either sooner or later than would have happened in the absence of separate quotas.

Losing out in this court, Private Lynn was sent back to camp and counsel appealed the case. He was subsequently sent to a camp in California and while awaiting his appeal was promoted to corporal.

On December 8, 1943, the appeal was heard before the U.S. Circuit Court of Appeals in New York, and on February 3, 1944, the court decided against Corporal Lynn in a two-to-one decision, with Justices Thomas W. Swan and A. N. Hand writing the majority opinion and Justice Charles E. Clark, former dean of Yale Law School, dissenting.

The majority opinion held that "if the appellant was called for induction later than his turn, his grievance seems to be that the military custody in which he now finds himself should have begun at an earlier date."

The opinion continued:

"Delay in calling him may have resulted in discrimination against others who were called ahead of their turn, but we find it difficult to regard it as a discrimination making illegal the Army's present custody of him. Even if the induction practice had been conducted without separate quotas, as he claims it should have been, he would now be, as he is, in the Army."

Saying, however, that the broader question in the case was an important one, they then discussed the question of statutory construction of Section 4 (a) of the Selective Service Act which prohibited discrimination against any person on account of race or color, stating that Congress did not intend, in passing that section, to interfere with racial segregation either in selection or in training of men for the Army. They cited the Army's "long established practice of segregating enlisted men into separate white and colored units" as part of their justification for the separate draft quotas.

"If the Congress had intended to prohibit separate white and Negro quotas and calls," they wrote, "we believe it would have expressed such intention more definitely than by the general prohibition against discrimination appearing in Section 4."

In his dissenting opinion, Justice Clark declared that the legislative intent "does not seem to me disputable on the words of the statute itself; but if any doubt exists, I think it must be dispelled by a consideration of the legislative history."

He then gave his interpretation of the reason for the insertion of the non-discriminatory amendment in the act, pointing out that the clause was inserted "to quiet the doubts of representatives of the colored people.

"In fact, I find it difficult to think of more apt language to express the Congressional intent," he continued. "The suggestion that Congress should have said something more, or amended the statute, means in effect that it should be watchful to see how a statute is violated and then expressly negative such violation or be assumed to sanction it.

"This registrant asserts his desire to serve and his willingness to do so if inducted according to law. I think it unsound to overlook a violation of law as to him on a premise which we ourselves would reject as patriotic citizens and which is contrary to the whole spirit of the act, namely, that avoidance of service is to be desired."

The case was scheduled to be appealed to the U.S. Supreme Court.

Lewis Jones Case

Lewis Jones, 28, of New York City, was arrested on a charge of violation of the Selective Service Act for refusing to report to his draft board for induction in the Army. Arraigned before Judge Samuel Mandelbaum in the Federal court in New York in October, 1942, he pleaded guilty.

Mr. Jones is a native of Texas and a graduate of Morehouse College in Atlanta, Ga. He was employed at Macy's Department Store when arrested. He had lived in New York for three years.

Following his plea of guilty Mr. Jones was released on his own recognizance pending final disposition of the case.

At the trial, the young man reiterated his stand in refusing to serve in the Army on the grounds that its policy was one of discrimination. He was not a conscientious objector, he said but a "constitutional" objector.

The judge tried to persuade him to change his mind and others also sought to do so, but he was adamant, saying that he could fight the enemies of democracy by protesting the policies of race discrimination at home, instead of serving in a segregated Army.

Among those who interested themselves in the case was John P. Lewis (white) editor of the Newspaper *PM*. He devoted an entire page of one issue of the paper to conversations and letters that passed between him and the young draft violator, stating his arguments and those of Mr. Jones.

In attempting to persuade Mr. Jones to change his mind, Mr. Lewis stated that the war was a "two-front" one—the military front and the political front. He contended that the military front was the more urgent, because if "that fight is lost, any gains made on the other front would be meaningless." Mr. Jones contended that both fronts were equally important.

After all attempts at persuasion failed, the judge sentenced Jones to three years in prison, but extended him a three-month period in which to change his mind if he wished to do so. The young man did not change his mind, and at last report (in January, 1943) he was serving his sentence.

Donald W. Sullivan Case

A case which attracted wide interest was that of Donald W. Sullivan of Orange County, N.J., who was arrested for refusing to report for induction in the Army as a protest against injustices practiced against Negroes.

When he was arraigned before Judge Philip Forman in a U.S. district court in Trenton, N.J., in 1942, the judge first argued with the defendant in an effort to get him to change his mind, giving to him a copy of Hitler's *Mein Kampf* to read and extending to him a period of eight weeks in which to think things over.

Efforts of Harold A. Lett, executive secretary of the Newark Urban League, and other social and civic workers in the community failed to shake the youth from his conviction. When he re-appeared in court after eight weeks of grace, he persisted in pleading guilty.

Mr. Sullivan's insistence, he said, grew out of his resentment at being rejected when he tried to enlist in the Navy five years previously and was refused because of his color. He also had been refused employment in a war industry.

After reading to him certain sections of Hitler's book, the judge asked: "How can you sit idly by and say, 'I will not raise a finger against a man who thinks that my race is only half human'?"

Mr. Sullivan answered: "There are a lot of people here who agree with him."

"Don't you think there are a lot of people here who don't agree with him?" the judge asked; and Sullivan replied, "I haven't seen so many of them."

Telling the defendant that his resentment was justified, the judge said that his form of resentment was not wise and would harm his people, and called the attention of the youth to the progress his race had made since its emancipation, naming various ones who had accomplished outstanding work, and ending with the words: "but with this you don't agree, do you?"

"With a lot you say I do agree," he replied, "but I can't see it that way."

Judge Forman then reluctantly sentenced him to three years in the penitentiary.

Florence Murray, ed., *The Negro Handbook, 1944* (New York: Current Reference Publications, 1944), pp. 130–33.

82

NEGROES ARE FIGHTING FOR FREEDOM

by Shirley Graham

The writer of the essay that follows was active in theatre and musical work in the nineteen-thirties, had contributed to various periodicals and, during World War II, was in charge of the U.S.O. at Fort Huachuca in Arizona where tens of thousands of Black troops were stationed.*
    Shirley Graham (Mrs. W. E. B. Du Bois) is the author of several biographies—that of Frederick Douglass is perhaps the best known—and at the present time resides in Egypt.

The virtual silence that shrouded the important role played by Monsieur Felix Eboué, black Governor of Equatorial Africa in opening Africa to the Allies, was characteristic of a major paradox of World War II. In many parts of the United States such news is still regarded as "propaganda." It was Governor Eboué who refused to accept the armistice terms imposed by Germany and Italy on the Chad Territory. It was he who turned over to the Free French that vast belt of territory stretching from the Atlantic Ocean to the borders of Anglo-Egyptian Sudan and the Libyan desert. His story, with graphic pictures, was published December 6th in "This Week," Sunday magazine section of the *New York Herald Tribune*. It could not be found on that date in the newspapers of Washington, D.C., which carry the same feature section. Apparently, the syndicate putting out the story carefully deleted it from all papers sold below the Mason and Dixon line.
    The opening of a "second front" on this ancient continent of black peoples has accentuated certain aspects of the war. It is not, happily, a race war. Alignments of friend and foe cut diametrically across race lines. Yet the whole question of color and of the freedom of colored races is becoming more and more acute. It is significant that nowhere are colored peoples fighting to maintain or to advance white supremacy. The determination of India has strengthened all dark peoples. Regardless of what may be the objectives or aims of other groups, colored people are fighting for freedom. And every act either of commission or omission on the part of nations pledged to that aim is weighed in the balance.
    Much has been written of the loyalty of the American Negro, of his

* See the comments on Fort Huachuca in the essay by Grant Reynolds in this volume, p. 501–04.

patience and faith as glorified in beautiful spirituals. Perhaps you have drawn a picture of him from stage or screen. Somewhere there may be Negroes like the ones depicted in *Green Pastures, Porgy and Bess* or *Cabin in the Sky*—just as somewhere there are probably whites like those shown in *Tobacco Road*. But I assure you that the acknowledged leaders of thirteen million American Negroes are neither as long suffering as "De Lawd" nor as naive as "Little Joe" nor do they wear Ethel Waters' wide smile. These leaders speak clearly and emphatically in the rapidly expanding Negro press, on platform, in labor unions and from the pulpit. There are those who say they speak too loudly, that their newspapers are "inflammatory." On this charge the *Pittsburgh Courier* has on several occasions been barred from certain army camps.* But you need not long be in doubt about what the Negro wants. He merely wants the citizenship granted him years ago by the Constitution of the United States.

There are today some 380,000 colored soldiers in every branch of the United States Army. By the end of the year it is estimated there will be more than half a million. According to figures released December 27, 10.1% of the entire army is colored. Until April 7, 1942 Negroes were admitted to the Navy as messmen only, but following constant bombardment by the Negro press and organized leadership, and in the face of the award to Messman Dorie Miller of the Navy Cross for exceptional conduct at Pearl Harbor, Secretary Knox announced that Negro volunteers would be accepted for enlistment as "reservists." Since then, nearly 1,500 Negroes have enlisted in the Great Lakes Naval Training School for basic training. They have not yet been admitted to the Marine Corps.

The announcement of an all-Negro Division brought rejoicing from many quarters. Many saw here an opportunity for proving what Negroes could do in united effort and under Negro leadership. The chagrin, disappointment and humiliation which swept the country twenty-five years ago upon the forced retirement of the late Colonel Charles E. Young had not been forgotten. Admittedly, there was no officer in 1941 who equaled this West Point graduate in rank or in years of exceptional service with the regular army, but it was hoped that from

---

* Bureau of the Census, 1940, reports 339 newspapers, magazines and bulletins published in the United States by Negroes. 155 of the listed newspapers have a total circulation of 1,276,600; 18 newspapers published in the Middle Atlantic States report 24.4 percent of total circulation of all newspapers in this section. Negro newspapers have been severely criticized by thoughtful Negroes for playing up crime and sex and for sensationalizing color prejudice. This period in their development is now passing. Papers which appear each week in every section of the country are *The Afro-American, The Chicago Defender, The Norfolk Journal and Guide* and *The Pittsburgh Courier.*

among Negro Reserve Officers would be chosen men for further training. Since 1802, twenty Negroes were admitted to West Point. Five of them were graduated. There were a few hastily trained Negro officers in World War I, but after the war only one Negro regiment, the 25th, was left bearing arms—and all its officers were white.

When the 93rd Division was activated last year these reserve officers were not assigned. Scores of young college graduates, however, were rushed through the nine weeks training course at Fort Benning and sent to the division as lieutenants. From R.O.T.C. and other sources came a few captains. Promotions were made rapidly. Practically all the senior officers in this division are now white but a large percentage of the junior officers are colored.

Because it was impossible to set up separate Officers Training Schools for a comparatively small number of colored cadets, they are now being trained for the Infantry together with the white candidates at Fort Benning, Georgia. Contrary to all the arguments once given for segregation, not an "incident" has occurred. Black and white soldiers march elbow to elbow across the dusty expanse of south Georgia soil, eat in the same mess hall, sleep in the same barracks, sit together in classroom, compete for honors. I have never heard of any white officer expressing the opinion that because of this experience he is any less an "officer and a gentleman." Yet when the graduated colored officers arrived to take their places in the Negro Division everything changed. Even the simple intelligence of Negro soldiers understands the rigid system which separates officers from enlisted men. But they were bewildered and insulted by the spectacle of officers of the same rank, in the same regiment, occupying separate barracks, eating at separate tables, being shaved in separate barbershops (often the colored officer forced to use the enlisted man's barbershop) and going to separate reading rooms. The entire picture was one of a force divided against itself.

Segregation in the Army is as expensive as it is everywhere else. But if segregation were the only unpleasant aspect of Negro army life there would be little immediate danger. Negroes have become stoical in this matter. Some of them accept it as a blessing which forces Negro solidarity, independence and racial expression. But segregation leads to discrimination, persecution and injustices on a mass scale. Equipment in Negro units is often inferior and commanders of these units must wait until last for requisitioned needs to be filled. The efficiency of Negro soldiers is delayed. The great bulk of these Negro soldiers are in camps located in the South. The 93rd Division was activated in Arizona, which geographically as well as sociologically is bound to Texas. The way certain communities have treated Negroes in uniform has grown to the proportions of a national crime. Negro MP's have been killed in the performance of their duties. Negro soldiers have been dragged off jim-crow buses and beaten when trying to return to camp on time. The National Association for the Advancement of Colored People is now investigating the beating of a young second lieutenant by an Indianapolis policeman. This lieutenant, passing through the city, went into the restaurant at the Terminal Station for lunch. . . .

The Army, it is said, cannot be held responsible for these attacks by individuals in the communities. Does the Army become less powerful in time of war? What happens in any country in the world when a citizen of the United States is mistreated? Yet instead of protection we have the humiliating experience of hearing members of Parliament and the British press speak out in criticism against the treatment by the United States Army of its colored soldiers in England and Ireland. Labor groups in Australia have become aroused and are making serious charges. These charges have been printed in detail in the United States only by the Negro Press but they are in possession of colored peoples outside the United States. They should be investigated, because until proved false they will continue to be believed by the dark peoples of the world.

What can be expected of the morale of the Negro soldier or of his family at home? True, he has with him the Red Cross and U.S.O.— morale builders. But, since the Red Cross is serving as an official auxiliary of the Army itself it is helpless to shape or change policies. The U.S.O., though maintaining its independence as a civilian organization, feels obligated at times to observe the "mores of the community." Pamphlets are sent out and speeches made at conferences on the "education and broadening" of these communities, but when a white or colored U.S.O. worker takes these things seriously and sets up a local inter-racial program that worker is rather firmly told that such "activities" are undesirable and "outside the U.S.O. program." The "mores of the community" continue to force club houses for Negro soldiers to the outskirts of town or into slum areas. Wholly inadequate transportation prevents the soldier from getting to them. He still can't buy a cup of coffee at the restaurant just around the corner—nor does he dare enter the near-by movie house. But the U.S.O. continues to spend thousands of dollars for ping-pong balls and badminton birds and for fine rugs upon which the embarrassed soldier, with his muddied shoes, is afraid to walk.

The great bulk of Negro population, of course, is not in the Army. Of the thirteen million Negroes in this country more than five million are workers—men and women of all trades and skills. Over 650,000 of them are equipped for skilled work. In 1941, 4,964 Negroes received college degrees in engineering, chemistry, sciences and the liberal arts. More than 56,000 completed trade, industrial, professional and clerical courses. An additional 56,000 enrolled in defense-training courses. This, in spite of the fact that "of the 4,630 training courses in the country, only 194 accepted Negroes; yet all defense training courses are financed out of the $60,000,000 fund appropriated by Congress in 1940 for the defense program. In a bill that forbade discrimination!" (*Public Affairs Pamphlets,* No. 71, 1942)

On April 14, 1942, the *Baltimore Evening Sun* pointed out that 'despite the ever increasing demand for war-industry labor in the neighborhood, despite the acute housing shortage caused by the coming of war workers, despite the fact that the city's water and sewage systems are unequal to the task of serving the swollen population, no attempt has been made to hire any of the 167,000 Negroes already living in our city." In a recent survey of the hiring schedules of selected defense employers, the Bureau of Employment Security reported that 51 percent of 282,245 future job openings were barred to Negro workers.

Unions that discriminate against Negroes fall into four classes:

(1) Those that have color clauses in their constitutions or rituals, such as the four powerful Railroad Brotherhoods, together with all but one of the railroad organizations in the A. F. of L. (2) Unions that have a color bar in their constitutions, but provide jim-crow auxiliary locals for Negroes that give the Negro workers the doubtful privilege of paying initiation fees and dues. In this category are the musicians' unions in most of the large cities. (3) Unions that do not have color clauses in their constitutions but practice discrimination against Negroes as a matter of policy. It is well known, for instance, that the International Machinists' Union is keeping Negro machinists off defense jobs. In Chicago there are a good number of licensed Negro plumbers who are not taken in by the union or allowed to work on union jobs. The Electrical Workers' Union now gives Negro electricians probation cards to work on certain jobs, but does not permit them to join the union. (4) Unions that do not have color clauses in their constitutions and accept Negro workers as members, but which have locals that refuse to let them work on union jobs. An example is the San Antonio local of the carpenters' union which refused to take Negro workers in as mem-

bers and threatened to strike if Negro carpenters were permitted to work on a housing project built for Negroes.

One of the chief reasons for the establishment of the C.I.O. was the growth of the mass production industries with their large percentages of Negro workers. The constitutions of the new unions contained no color bar. The A. F. of L. accuses the C.I.O. of increasing labor difficulties by encouraging the Negro to become militant. While there are some unions in C.I.O. which resist the organization of Negroes, the weight of the national officers is consistently thrown against discrimination. At the Fifth Convention of C.I.O. held in Boston last November, President Murray called on labor the world over to enlist the potential power of black workers. Resolution No. 18 reiterating "firm opposition to any form of racial or religious discrimination" was actually criticized from the floor for its weakness.

The relative success of the Communist Party in assuming leadership of Negro protest movements during the '30's is attributable to this delayed response on the part of organized labor. The championship of Odell Waller by the Workers Defense League in 1941 and the organization of the March on Washington movement by A. Philip Randolph the same year marked a new phase in Negro insurgency. Randolph, perhaps the outstanding Negro leader in America today, is President of the Brotherhood of Sleeping Car Porters (A. F. of L.) and a Socialist. His March on Washington movement was supported by the Negro churches of various denominations as well as by Negro labor and professional groups.

News of this planned march was broadcast in early June of 1941 and Washington became alarmed. About three weeks prior to the date set (July 1st), Mr. Randolph wrote President Roosevelt a letter requesting that he address a throng of 100,000 Negroes at the Lincoln Memorial in Washington. The reply came in the form of a request made through Mrs. Anna Rosenberg of the Social Security Board that Mr. Randolph and Walter White, Secretary of the N.A.A.C.P., meet with Mrs. Roosevelt and Mayor La Guardia at the New York City Hall on Friday of that week. At this conference Mrs. Roosevelt and Mayor La Guardia argued that a march on Washington was entirely too drastic a form of action for Negroes to take during this national crisis. Mr. White and Mr. Randolph explained to them that conditions were growing worse instead of better and asked that the President issue an Executive Order banning discrimination in defense industries and the government. A few days later, a conference was held in the White House. Present at this conference, in addition to the Secretaries of War and the Navy, were the Negro leaders, Layle Layne, Frank R. Crosswaith, Walter White, and Mr. Randolph. There was little said by anyone but the President. But out of this meeting came the President's Executive Order No. 8802. "Because the executive order," says Mr. Randolph, "was granted, the march on Washington was called off but not abandoned." Actually, it was the threat of this march of protest which secured the only official and concrete realization of the Negro demands—Order No. 8802. After affirming the "policy of full participation in the defense program by all persons," it provides for full and equitable participation of all workers in defense industries and states that "all contracting agencies of the Government of the United States shall include in all defense contracts a provision obligating the contractor not to discriminate against any worker because of race, creed, color or national origin."

Hardly was the ink dry on this document when planned and organized efforts were made to defeat its execution. The breach between Congress and the President, between conservative Democrats and New Dealers, widened. The South lined up its forces. When the Committee met to hold hearings in Birmingham it was openly condemned by Governor Dixon. One of its own members, Mark Etheridge, of the *Louisville Courier Journal*, described the Order as an emergency war measure which was "not a social document and which had no concern with racial segregation." It was his next statement which caused his subsequent retirement from the committee: "All the armies of the world, both of the United Nations and the Axis, could not force upon the South the abandonment of racial segregation." Georgia papers published pictures of the white and colored members sitting together. Governor Dixon, speaking at the fifty-seventh annual dinner of the New York Southern Society at the Waldorf-Astoria, accused the Administration of endangering American democracy by "stupid tampering" with the racial problem of the South. He gave as examples the United States Employment practices and the F.E.P.C. which enforces them. Both, he said, are a challenge to "the basic principle of segregation, without which there can be no orderly society below the Mason-Dixon line."

In spite of opposition and even curtailment of its budget, the F.E.P.C. continues to meet and hold public hearings in the major war cities. Many employers, rather than become involved in federal investigation, now employ Negroes. Objections are being met by facts and figures. White and colored workers can and do work together amicably. The path of the Fair Employment Practices Committee has not been easy. A typical test case has just been settled in Washington, D.C., where the Capital

Transit Company has been ordered to discontinue its discriminatory practice of refusing to hire Negro bus drivers and conductors. In its reply, the Company filed an amazing 10-point brief defending its position. In condensed form it reads:

1. Negroes are not qualified for work as operators of common carrier public vehicles. (Most of the chauffeurs in the United States are Negroes.)
2. The policy proposed by F.E.P.C. would seriously impair the service of the company and be detrimental to the war effort. (Washington has hundreds of busy colored taxi drivers.)
3. The company believes that overtime work of present staff, employment of part-time operators, and women will provide necessary personnel for operating its expanded service. (Service now in Washington is most inadequate. But the company would rather over-work its present employees than employ Negroes.)
4. The company employs 523 Negroes as of October 31. (Janitors, laborers, trackmen, cleaners, etc.)
5. Great difficulty would be experienced with the public. (This statement is expanded, pointing out the chagrin of white people in having a Negro make change for them and tell them when to get off the bus! For years Pullman cars have been run throughout the South in charge of colored Pullman porters.)
6. The present street car and bus operators have a definite feeling against the employment of Negroes. (Is it not the responsibility of intelligent employers to show that only by cooperation of all the people will this war be won?)
7. The Congress of the United States has seen fit to separate the schools and social institutions in the District of Columbia, which results in separate theatres and restaurants. (One up for the Company!)
8. There are no adequate toilet facilities for use of Negroes while away from their barns and garages and no eating facilities where colored operators have time off for a meal. (True—in the Capitol of the United States.)
9. When reporting after a day's work, it would be necessary for white men and Negroes to be jammed into stations at the cashier's window, and undoubtedly a decision would often have to be made as to whether the white man or the Negro reached the window first. (!)
10. A large proportion of Washington's inhabitants come from areas where they are accustomed to segregation. Their inborn emotions would lead to serious objection at the mingling of the races which would result from employment of Negroes as operators. (Will bus drivers and conductors come in closer "contact" than the traditional nurses and cooks without whom the South would be lost?)

These ten reasons have been seriously set down by a board of "intelligent" business men and drawn up in the shadow of the White House.

The line between tragedy and comedy is often easily crossed. This was going on in Washington at the same time that Harlem's ridiculed Father Divine was voluntarily turning over his 250-room hotel at Atlantic City to the Coast Guard. This is believed to be the first such free grant of a hotel. And the Coast Guardsmen who will use it are all white.

What opportunity does the Negro have for shaping or administering policies in his own federal government? Practically none. From a period before the Civil War down to twenty years ago some Negroes held positions of real influence. One was paymaster of the United States Navy. Until it was recently abolished, the position of Register of Treasury, signer of all United States money, was held by Negroes. Numerous Negroes have been in foreign service in Europe, Asia, Africa and Latin America. In Honolulu, at one time the Collector of Internal Revenue was a colored man. But a few months ago Lester Walton, colored U.S. Minister to Negro Liberia, was recalled. It had become apparent that the Monrovia post would become important in the war and that high U.S. British Army and Navy officers might find themselves under his jurisdiction. (What are they doing about the Negro President of Liberia?) Today, the only remaining Negroes in governmental positions are handling strictly "Negro affairs." They act for the most part as "interpreters" of policies already laid down. Dr. William J. Thompkins, Recorder of Deeds for the District of Columbia, is an isolated exception.

Is it the intention so to encircle and encompass the Negro by segregation and discrimination that finally we will have a separate and distinct "nation within a nation"? Even if this were possible, is it desirable —in a Democracy?

The first soldier killed in the American Revolutionary War, on Boston Common, was Crispus Attucks, a Negro. In World War II the first American soldier killed at Pearl Harbor was Robert Brooks, a Negro. Now the American Negro is beginning to ask questions. "What does it take to make me a citizen of the land in which I was born? I have been loyal. My father was loyal before me. We have fought in every war, we have worked—performing the most menial and hardest of tasks. My children are educated. I have paid taxes. Now, I am called to die for freedom. What of my children's future?" Two-thirds of all the peoples in the world are waiting for the answers.

Common Sense, February, 1943; XII, 45–50.

83

JAMAICANS IN THE UNITED STATES:
A CONFERENCE

Ever since the years of World War I, the West Indian component of the Black population in the United States has been increasingly consequential; among these, those from Jamaica have been especially significant. In February, 1934, the Jamaica Associates was organized with Eric L. Jackson as president and Mrs. Enid M. Nelson as vice-president. During World War II, activities looking toward the postwar world intensified; indicative was an "All-Jamaican Conference" held May 30–31, 1943, at the Ebenezer Baptist Church in Boston; chairing was Alfred Haughton, editor of the Boston *Chronicle,* while the secretary was William Harrison, associate editor of that weekly paper. A summary of the conference, appearing in its Proceedings, follows, as document [a]; document [b] consists of the remarks on "Labor Movements" made at the conference by the secretary of Local 370, Dining Car Employees Union (A. F. of L.).

[a]

SUMMARY

National and indeed international attention was focussed upon the two-day All-Jamaican Conference on the *"Four Freedoms for the Island of Jamaica, British West Indies,"* which was held on May 30 and 31, 1943, under the sponsorship of the Jamaican Associates, Inc., of Boston, Massachusetts, with the cooperation of the Jamaica Progressive League and of the British-Jamaicans Benevolent Association of New York, other organizations of people of Jamaican birth and ancestry. Evidence of the widespread interest was afforded not only by many notices in the press throughout the United States, but also by the broadcast which the Office of War Information beamed to the Caribbean countries. It appeared that the Conference assumed greater significance because of the then recent decision of the United States Department of Agriculture to import 10,000 Jamaicans to relieve the manpower shortage in agricultural labor. There are already 15,000 Jamaicans in the United States, according to the most reliable estimates, and nearly 3,000 reside in the Greater Boston area.

As previously announced, the purposes of the Conference were mainly (1) to unite all Jamaicans resident in the United States for effective, organized action; (2) to consider the ways and means whereby Jamaicans can make their most valuable contribution to the victory of the United Nations; (3) to discuss and relate the meaning of the Atlantic Charter in terms of self-government for the Jamaican people; and (4) to inform Negro and white American public opinion of Jamaica's social, economic, and political problems in order to provide the basis of knowledge for improving relations between the Jamaican people and the peoples of the Americas. It was stated: "No narrow exclusiveness animates the conference, for the Jamaican people know that the *Four Freedoms anywhere and everywhere means victory for the United Nations.* Hence they are concerned with the defense and extension of democratic freedom in the West Indies, in all the United Nations."

[b]

LABOR MOVEMENTS
by R. Neale Thompson

It is generally agreed that 99 per cent of colored people in these United States are working people. In order to live we must sell our labor, in return for which we are vitally interested in getting the best price.

Experience has shown that the most effective way of doing this is to organize into labor unions. What, you may ask, is a labor union and how does it function? A labor union is an assembly of persons who work who meet to discuss all problems affecting working conditions and agree upon means to improve working conditions. The setting up of By-Laws, election of officers, affiliation with other organizations or support of political issues are all the outgrowth of the meeting of workers in their meeting-halls. To operate a labor union effectively requires mastery of the technique of organization. It requires study and participation of the membership. We have to do this, however, because our future demands that every man of color join the labor union where he works.

It is a fact that some labor unions have color clauses in their constitutions which exclude the colored man from membership. This situation must be overcome by agitation from within the Labor movement and other liberal organizations to break down the color bars wherever they exist. I don't think it will be disputed that most unions in the United States will accept the membership of persons of our race.

Wherever we are accepted in a union, we must attend meetings, and fight for racial tolerance and understanding as well as the higher objectives of the union.

Especially since the passing of the Wagner Act, we have seen a tremendous growth of Organized Labor. Many promising leaders of our race are in the vanguard of the battle. For instance, there are such leaders as Ferdinand C. Smith, Secretary of the National Maritime Union. In the railroad industry we have such figures as A. Philip Randolph, President of the Brotherhood of Sleeping Car Porters; George E. Brown, Chairman of the Negotiating Committee for Dining Car Employees and Willard Townsend, President of the nation's Red Cap organization.

As an illustration of progress through labor organization let us take the record of Dining Car Employees over the past six years. During the depression of 1933–1937 Dining Car men discovered that more and more work was being demanded by the boss and conditions of work were getting worse and worse. The independent union which represented us locally was completely ineffectual to do anything about the situation. A few of the younger men met and decided to do something about it. We found that our employers do not respect any group which is not strong enough to demand respect, and, furthermore, to improve our lot we must affiliate with the Labor Movement. We found that although we were weak numerically, when allied with the millions of other workers our lot can be greatly improved.

In New York City a charter had been obtained from the Hotel & Restaurant Employees International. Dining Car men of the Boston & Albany and the New Haven joined that Union. During the depression, Dining Car men all over the nation had applied for and received charters from our International. By their belonging to the American Federation of Labor, the basis was formed for a national headquarters and a national spokesman. Through the help of our International Union was set up the Joint Council of Dining Car Employees Unions in Chicago which handled our share in the recently successful fight to get a raise in pay from the railroads.

Before we reached this development the boss could hire and fire as he pleased. To-day the boss must give the employee a hearing at which minutes are taken and must prove his charges or pay time claim for time lost from work. Having to pay claims for charges which could not be proved made the boss respect his men. Along with this has gone better regulation of seniority and improvements in working conditions all along the line. And where wages are concerned, in 1937 a waiter was getting 25¢ per hour, a senior chef 65¢ per hour. In 1936 a waiter received 30¢ per hour, a senior chef 70¢. In 1941 a waiter received 40¢ per hour, a senior chef 80¢ per hour. After July 1st of this year, a waiter will receive 48¢ per hour and a top chef 88¢ per hour.

Some of our fellow workers tell us that the American Federation of Labor is a prejudice-ridden organization which does not want us. Seven years of work in the field of dining car labor have convinced me that prejudice can be overcome in the labor movement by fighting from within. For three years dining car employees were barred from the Railway Labor Executives Association, the national organization which handles the affairs of the A. F. of L. unions in the railroad industry. In reply to our requests for affiliation they told us, "Negroes won't support a labor organization, they won't pay dues regularly." Or this one, "You fellows can't pull your own weight, you are of no advantage to us." Well, when they wanted a unanimous vote to strike in 1940, dining car men all over the nation voted to strike. When the R.L.E.A. saw Negro labor unions functioning all over the nation and getting results for their membership, they accepted us and today dining car men have achieved national representation. We are on our way to better conditions.

I offer this as proof that it is to the advantage of every working man, especially members of our group, to join a labor organization.

Proceedings of the All-Jamaican Conference, May 30–31, Boston, Sponsored by Jamaican Associates, Inc. (Boston, 1943), foreword and pages 11–13. The pamphlet is in the editor's possession.

84

THE DETROIT RACE RIOT OF 1943
by Earl Brown

The worst pogrom of the World War II years occurred in Detroit in June, 1943. From 1940 to 1943, due to war production, its population leaped from about 1.6 million to 1.8 million and of the newcomers perhaps fifty thousand were Black people while the incoming whites emigrated in their majority from the South.

Earl Brown had been a special correspondent for the New York *Herald Tribune;* at the time he wrote what follows he was the only Black person on the editorial staff of *Life* magazine.

On Sunday, June 20, 1943, one of the most serious race riots in American history broke out in the city of Detroit. Before it was brought under control some thirty hours later, twenty-five Negroes and nine white persons were killed and property worth several hundreds of thousands of dollars had been destroyed.

The forces which led to the outbreak in that city exist, to a greater or lesser degree, in most of our cities. Similar outbreaks have occurred elsewhere. A study of the factors leading to the outbreak in Detroit is important because it can show us how to avoid similar outbreaks, not only in Detroit, but in other cities. . . .

My first visit to wartime Detroit occurred in July, 1942. I found that although Detroit is the munitions capital of the United Nations and its war production is essential to victory, there was a disturbing lack of unity of effort. The atmosphere was tense, and the tension was increasing. There were sudden gusts of strikes for unimportant reasons—a strike occurred at the Chrysler Tank Arsenal because the men were not allowed to smoke during work.

But racial feeling was the most alarming of all. Groups of Negro zoot-suiters were brawling with gangs of young white toughs; the determination of Negroes to hold the war jobs they had won was matched by the determination of numerous white groups to oust them. There were many signs of trouble.

Eleven months later, in June, 1943, came the Detroit riot, the most serious racial conflict in this country since the East St. Louis riot in 1917. Said Mayor Jeffries: "I've been conscious of the seriousness of the race problem here for more than a year." "We felt the riot coming," said William E. Dowling, the Prosecuting Attorney of Wayne County. "Race tensions have been growing here for three years."

Here is something of a mystery. If these responsible officials had reason to fear riot, why didn't they take steps to prevent it? Since continuous production of munitions is vital to the prosecution of the war, why didn't the federal government act? In March, 1943, a local newspaperman wrote to Attorney General Biddle about the critical state of affairs in Detroit. Mr. Biddle replied: "Your letter has received careful consideration, although it does not appear that there is sufficient evidence of violation of any federal statute to warrant action by this department at this time." The federal government did not act until nearly midnight on June 21, when President Roosevelt declared a state of emergency and troops began to patrol Detroit—long after the murder, the burning, and the pillage began. . . .

One of the features of Detroit that in many ways sets it off from many other cities is the presence of great numbers of religious and political fanatics. Even before the last war Detroit was known as the city of "jazzed-up religion." Today all shades of opinion are to be found in the city, all races, all creeds, all political attitudes and beliefs. The first figure to attract national attention was Father Charles Coughlin. Railing against Hoover and Wall Street from his radio pulpit, he soon attracted a great following in Detroit and through the Middle West. Next came the Black Legion, an organization of native white Americans and an offshoot of the Ku Klux Klan—with hoods, grips, and passwords. It was organized originally for the purpose of getting and holding jobs for Southern whites, but it quickly developed into an elaborate "hate" organization—its enmity directed against Catholics, Jews, Negroes, and "radicals." After the conviction of the Black Legion leader, Virgil F. Effinger, a former Klansman, for the murder of a Detroit Catholic named Charles Poole, the police had the clues to a long series of unsolved crimes which included several murders, arson, the bombing of Father Coughlin's house and the Workers Book Store as well as the homes of a number of labor organizers. An investigation by a grand jury resulted in the listing of eighty-six persons as members of the Legion. In this list were found the names of a member of the state legislature, the manager of the state sales tax, a city treasurer, sheriffs, and other officials.

By the middle 30's, Detroit had a representation of every kind of panacea, political nostrum, and agitation. There were the Anglo-Saxon Federation and an anti-Negro organization called the National Workers League. But the most steady, day-in and day-out exhortation came from the sensational preachers. Of these the best known are the Reverend J. Frank Norris and the Reverend Gerald L. K. Smith. Norris was born in Alabama and has held pulpits in a number of Southern towns. He was an energetic politician and brought his brimstone gospel clear to New York City, where he teamed up with the Reverend John Roach Straton and preached in a gospel tent west of Central Park. In 1935 he came to Detroit and took over the Temple Church, commuting to Fort Worth by plane in order to shepherd two flocks.

Gerald Smith has been even more active in politics than Norris. Smith was a minister and had a number of midwestern congregations before he went to Shreveport, Louisiana. He was great for muscular good will; he harangued luncheon clubs; he loved the radio; and then he fell for Huey Long. He fell so hard that he quit pastoring and became one of Huey's lieutenants, only to have his Share-the-Wealth ambitions paralyzed when Huey was killed. There followed a dismal period when the shepherd was busy looking for a flock among the Townsendites and other unhappy souls. Finally he showed up in Detroit as the founder and manipulator of The Committee of One Million, and in Detroit he has stayed ever since. Last year he ran for the Republican senatorial nomination on a "Tires for Everybody" platform and corralled comparatively few votes. But that has neither dampened his restless ambition nor stopped his noise. In April, 1942, he brought out the first issue of a monthly periodical called *The Cross and the Flag*. The magazine announced that its slogan was "Christ First in America" and recounted Smith's fight for justice and his numerous escapes from death by violence. Now he is trying to round up the remnants of the Detroit America First membership into an American First Party.

These three men—Coughlin, Norris, and Smith—are the best known of the Detroit religious-political demagogues, but there are thousands of others. Some have been in Detroit for years; others came during the recent migrations. It is estimated that there are more than 2,500 Southern-born evangelists of one kind or another in Detroit alone, not counting those in near-by communities. This war has caused an upheaval among the little shouting sects in the South; they have split and split again, and new sects have been formed. When the flow to the war industry towns began, numerous piney-woods and sandy-bottom clerics went along representing the Last Days Church of God, the Church of God (Reformation), all brands of the Assemblies of God, the Firebrands of Jesus, the Pillar of Fire, the Pentecostal Baptists, the Christian Unity Baptists, the Two-Seed-in-Mind Baptists, and various splinters of the Holiness sects. One of the militant sects in Detroit is the American Bible Fellowship headed by a former Methodist preacher who refused to accept the merger of the Northern and Southern Methodist churches. Some of these pulpit-thumpers have gospel tents (complete with oilcloth signs, saxophone, and microphone); some have regular churches; some are radio preachers; the humbler ones have "storefront" churches or work in war plants and preach in their spare time.

There is a connection between the apocalyptic doctrine of these sects and religious and racial intolerance. The appeal is not only highly emotional but is grounded on old traditions—which in the South mean White Protestant Supremacy. A local preacher described it this way: "Their forerunners for generations preached from the crossroads and schoolhouses that 'Christ came to His Own and His Own received Him not'—'His Own' being the Jews." On a Friday night in January, 1943 at Missionary Tabernacle, the Reverend R. H. W. Lucas said that Jesus had destroyed Jerusalem because it was a Christ-crucifying city. The next Sunday morning it was stated over a national radio hook-up that the history of the Jews for the last 2,000 years is proof that God punishes a nation because of its sin. Many of these exhorters are members of the Klan off-shoot organizations, defiantly "American," suspecting "radicals," and completely at home with White Supremacy. For more than a decade—and increasingly during the past three years—these rustic preachers have been spreading their brand of the Word. As feeling in Detroit became more aroused over the race issue, the effect of this kind of preaching was like pouring gasoline on a bonfire.

Feelings also have been kept on edge by labor conflicts. Detroit had never been a union town, but in the bad days of the depression a number of attempts were made to organize the auto workers. The Communists, through their Trade Union Unity League, led four little strikes of auto workers in January and February, 1933. Other groups made several attempts, mostly futile, to organize the auto industry. These moves excited the alarm of the local manufacturers, and the Detroit Union League called for strong measures against labor agitation. Many prominent industrialists were members of the Union League and its utterances were judged to be the voice of business.

Efforts to organize automobile unions—in the shape of the Associated Automobile Workers, the Automotive Industrial Workers Association, the Mechanics Educational Society of America, and others—were increased after the passage of the National Recovery Act. Gradually, the results began to show. The early unions were consolidated into the United Automobile Workers (affiliated with the C.I.O.), and in October, 1936 the Chrysler Corporation recognized the union. Early in 1937 General Motors also made a contract with the union.

Ford was left as the only big open-shop employer in Detroit. In order to assure its position with the other firms, the new auto workers' union had to organize Ford. It hesitated to act, however, not only because of the size of the job but because of Ford's Negro employees. There were thousands of Southern whites in the union, and it was too clear what their attitude toward Ford's Negro workers would be. Further, many of Ford's Negro workers were anti-union. They were loyal to Ford as the one big industrialist who would hire Negroes.

When a Negro migrant from the South arrived in Detroit looking for a Ford job, he generally discovered that it was a good thing to get a letter from one of the Negro preachers before applying. Many of these pastors warned the migrants against listening to talk about unions and urged them to remember at all times that the one powerful friend the Negro had in Detroit was Henry Ford.

For years Ford had maintained a private police and detective system, and a part of the system was devoted to the oversight of Negro employees. What Ford's colored workers did at home and during their hours of recreation were matters of great interest to these Ford detectives. Organization of Ford's colored employees by the union meant not only overcoming their devotion to Ford, but also combating the influence of the spy system. Finally, in 1940, the campaign was undertaken. The C.I.O. sent money and its best organizers to help in the campaign. The full strength of the U.A.W. was enlisted in the effort, and the color line was declared to be a thing of the past.

The thing that eventually brought success in this campaign was an unexpected strike, which was not initiated by the union at all. Once the strike had developed, it became a question of whether Ford's Negro help at the River Rouge plant would go out or stay at work and break the strike. The union decided to make the strike official and redouble its efforts to win over the Negroes. A group of prominent Negro citizens of Detroit urged the Ford Negro employees to stand by the union. The result was a tremendous victory for the union in the ensuing National Labor Relations Board election and the collapse of the last opposition to the U.A.W. Today the largest union local in the world is U.A.W.–C.I.O. Local 600, the River Rouge Ford plant local. It has about 90,000 members, of whom 18,000 are Negroes. . . .

It is interesting to note that despite the racial collisions and the frequent enforcement of Jim Crow practices in Detroit, Negroes have succeeded in getting some political preferment. There are two Negro assistant prosecuting attorneys, the State Labor Commissioner is a Negro, and one of the State Senators is a Negro. The Detroit Street Railway Company, which is owned by the city, employs about a thousand Negroes—both men and women—as motormen, bus drivers, conductors, and workers of other kinds. With the police it is another matter, and this has been a burning issue. Out of 3,600 policemen, only forty are Negroes. In addition, Southern whites have been taken into the force freely, and they have frequently shown a hostile attitude toward Negroes.

The local political machine was perfectly willing to cooperate with Negro gamblers, but they had no interest whatever in the fact that most of Detroit's Negroes lived in two wretched slum areas. The two principal Negro districts in Detroit cover about thirty square blocks on the West Side and a larger district on the East Side called Paradise Valley. This latter name goes back to First World War days and the wonder of $5 a day. "Goin' to Paradise" meant going to a job that paid more money than there was in the world. But the section did not look like Paradise in the beginning and it does not now. There are few city areas in the United States more jam-packed. Hastings Street, a dirty thoroughfare lined with dives and gin mills, is filled from dawn to dark and until the small morning hours with a dense crowd. Here—on the East Side—live most of Detroit's Negroes. Almost everybody now has plenty of war wages to pay for lodging, but decent houses simply do not exist. The only recourse the Negroes have is to cram themselves into the filthy valley tenements. . . .

The war naturally aggravated Detroit's underlying instability. Anti-Negro sentiment was particularly strong in the Polish districts of Hamtramck, a suburb. As early as July, 1941, gangs of Polish youths provoked a series of minor riots. An editor of a Polish paper reports that anti-Negro handbills were distributed on the steps of St. Florian's Church in Hamtramck during the Sojourner Truth riots.

For many months the Negro press in Detroit and elsewhere busily promoted a "Double-V" campaign for victory at home as well as abroad. This campaign was based on the assumption that victory in the war against the fascists abroad did not mean much if there was Jim Crow at home. Colored soldiers had told a thousand bitter stories of discrimination and lack of respect for the uniform. The killings of colored soldiers at Alexandria, Louisiana, and in other Southern communities were taken to heart. The hopes roused by President Roosevelt's Executive Order 8802, issued June 25, 1941, forbidding job discrimination in plants with war contracts slowly faded. The Committee on Fair Employment Practice, set up by the President shortly after the issuance of the Executive Order, was left to pine away without money or authority and was finally placed under the War Manpower Commission. If the government would do nothing, there was nothing left but the union and the determination of the Negroes themselves. Colored workers who had been promoted to more skilled jobs were ready to hold on for dear life to their new jobs, and the brimstone evangelists, viewing with alarm this resolution of the Negroes, whipped up resentment.

Shortly after the beginning of 1943 a series of anti-Negro strikes broke out in the plants. Aside from fights between individuals, there was no violence in the plants, but much bitterness was aroused. The U.S. Bureau of Labor Statistics lists anti-Negro strikes in the following plants from mid-March until the end of May: United States Rubber

Company; Vickers, Incorporated; Hudson Motor Car Company; Hudson Naval Arsenal; and the Packard Motor Car Company. In the Packard strike, which brought the climax, 26,883 men left work when three Negroes were upgraded. The circumstances of this strike were so peculiar that union leaders were convinced that it had been engineered by one of the anti-Negro groups in the city, but nothing was ever proved

Shortly after the Packard strike Mayor Jeffries called together the editors of the three local dailies, the *Free Press,* the *News,* and the *Times,* to take counsel. The conference over, nothing was done A procession of Negro leaders and a few prominent white citizens besought the Mayor to take heed and act before the explosion. The Mayor listened, but appeared to be more confused after these visits than before. Then everyone relaxed to await the inevitable. It came on the evening of June 20, 1943.

Belle Isle lies in the Detroit River, connected with the city and Grand Boulevard by a bridge. There were probably a hundred thousand persons in the park that hot, humid Sunday, and the greater number seem to have been Negroes. The atmosphere was anything but peaceful. Tension had increased to the breaking point. An argument between a Negro and a white man became a fist fight and the fighting spread.

A hurry call was made for the police, but by the time they arrived the brawl, involving some two hundred white sailors by this time, was eddying across the bridge into the riverside park on the mainland near the Naval Armory. The news that fighting had broken out traveled like the wind. A young man in a colored night club on Hastings Street is supposed to have grabbed the microphone about 11:30 and urged the five hundred customers present to "come on and take care of a bunch of whites who have killed a colored woman and her baby at Belle Isle Park." This rumor was, of course, false. It was matched by another story, which spread through the white districts, that Negroes had raped and killed a white woman on the park bridge. By midnight fighting and looting had spread into a dozen different districts and Paradise Valley was going crazy. By two o'clock that morning a crowd of Negroes stopped an East Side street car and stoned white factory workers who were passengers. White men coming from work at the Chevrolet Gear and Axle plant, three miles away from the center of Paradise Valley, were attacked by a Negro mob.

Alfred McClung Lee, chairman of the Sociology Department of Wayne University, and Norman Humphrey, Assistant Professor of Sociology at the same institution, have pieced together a remarkable timetable of the violence in *Race Riot,** a report on the riot. Both the authors were present and moved about the city while the fighting was in progress. Their report shows that:

At four o'clock in the morning (Monday, June 21) there was a meeting in the office of Police Commissioner Witherspoon to determine action. Mayor Jeffries, Colonel Krech (the U.S. Army commander of the Detroit area), Captain Leonard of the Michigan State Police, John Bugas (in charge of the local office of the F.B.I.), and Sheriff Baird were present. Colonel Krech told the Mayor that the military police could be on duty in Detroit in forty-nine minutes after a request from the Mayor had been cleared through the Governor and the proper U.S. Army officials. Nothing was done about this at the time, and by 6:30 A.M. Commissioner Witherspoon decided that there was a let-up in "serious rioting."

But there was no let-up. At 8:30 in the morning a Negro delegation asked the Mayor to send for troops. At nine o'clock Commissioner Witherspoon asked the Mayor for troops. Mayor Jeffries telephoned to the Governor, who transmitted the request by telephone to the Sixth Service Command Headquarters in Chicago. By eleven o'clock it was known that troops could not come unless martial law was declared. Governor Kelly hesitated to do so. By this time gangs of white hoodlums were roaming the streets burning Negro cars.

The police had already shown themselves to be helpless or negligent. On the previous night, police had been stationed outside the all-night Roxy movie theater. A witness reported that a threatening white crowd assembled at the entrance and every time a Negro came out of the theater the mob went for him. When the witness asked the police to get Negroes a safe-conduct through the mob, the officers replied, "See the chief about it!"

At four o'clock on Monday afternoon Major General Aurand arrived from Chicago. By that time, according to Lee and Humphrey, "the crowds of whites were increasing in size on Woodward Avenue. Milling packs of human animals hunted and killed any of the easily visible black prey which chanced into the territory."

At 6:30 Monday night, just as Mayor Jeffries was going on the air with a plea for a return to sanity, four white boys, aged 16 to 20, shot down Moses Kiska, a middle-aged Negro, "because we didn't have anything to do." Still no troops, and all through the evening, after even the Mayor had admitted that the city administration and police were unable to deal with the situation, there went on an endless amount

* New York: Dryden Press, 1943.

of official confusion until, at last, it was discovered precisely what had to be done to get federal intervention. Just before midnight President Roosevelt proclaimed a state of emergency, and by Tuesday morning 6,000 troops in trucks and jeeps were patrolling the city. The hold of the city authorities had so completely collapsed that it took the United States Army to get twenty-nine Negro members of the graduating class of Northeastern High School away from the closing exercises in safety.

Two days later Governor Kelly decided to ease restrictions a little, and by degrees the city began to breathe again. On Monday, June 28, Commissioner Witherspoon made a report to the City Council justifying his conduct and that of the police. "This was not believed to be the proper time,' he said, "to attempt to solve a racial conflict and a basic antagonism which had been growing and festering for years. Such a policy could well have precipitated a race riot at a much earlier date and one of much more serious proportions. The fact remains that this department did not precipitate the riot."

Councilman George Edwards urged that a grand jury be called to investigate fifteen unsolved murders. Both the Council and Police Commissioner rejected the idea.

"Don't get the impression that I'm afraid of a grand jury," Commissioner Witherspoon said, "but it would be an unfair position to put any judge in." In the end the Council smothered any action likely to uncover unpleasant facts, but it did appoint a five-man committee to plan and finance new housing and recreation facilities.

In the succeeding days and weeks there was much dodging of responsibility. The easiest "out" was to blame the Negroes, and this was done. On June 30, Mayor Jeffries said that he was "rapidly losing patience with those Negro leaders who insisted that their people do not and will not trust policemen and the Police Department. After what happened I am certain that some of these leaders are more vocal in their caustic criticism of the Police Department than they are in educating their own people to their responsibilities as citizens."

Shortly after this, Prosecutor Dowling was visited by some members of the Mayor's Interracial Peace Board. Apparently unaware that a reporter was in the room, the Prosecutor not only announced himself as opposed to a grand jury but declared that in his opinion the National Association for the Advancement of Colored People and the *Michigan Chronicle,* the local colored weekly, were responsible for the riot. The report of the Governor's investigating committee, issued August 11, also attempted to whitewash the local authorities. In the official statements about the riot no real effort has been made to deal directly with the more obvious reasons for it.

One of the most extreme proposals for meeting the situation came from Attorney General Biddle—a proposal that has cropped up in other circles. It will be recalled that in the previous March he had written to a Detroit reporter that he, the Attorney General, could see no basis for action by the Department of Justice. But on July 15, he wrote a letter to President Roosevelt in which he suggested "that careful consideration be given to limiting, and in some instances putting an end to Negro migrations into communities which cannot absorb them, either on account of their physical limitations or cultural background. This needs immediate and careful consideration. . . . It would seem pretty clear that no more Negroes should move to Detroit. Yet, I know of no controls being considered or exercised. You might wish to have the recommendations of Mr. McNutt as to what could and should be done."

In commenting on this statement, John Chamberlain, economic and political specialist, declared that: "Only a severe case of emotional shell-shock could have pushed Attorney General Biddle into suggesting that Negroes be chained to their places of abode, for all the world as if they were serfs on medieval manors, or slaves on the Roman *latifundia*. In Booker T. Washington's day the Negro might have taken Biddle's suggestion lying down. But no longer. Every Negro leader of any importance stresses the necessity of being polite but firm in insisting on the full protection of the Bill of Rights. This time the Negro is not going to be smacked down without making a fight of it."

Earl Brown, *Why Race Riots: Lessons from Detroit* (New York, 1944), Public Affairs Pamphlet No. 87, pp. 1–3, 6–11, 14–15, 18–24. See also, Louis E. Martin, "Behind Detroit's Terror," in *New Masses*, July 6, 1943 (XLVIII, No. 1, pp. 4–6).

85

WE WHO HAVE KNOWN DEPRIVATION (TO THE UNITED JEWISH APPEAL)

On September 9, 1943, Lester B. Granger of the National Urban League sent a letter to Sylvan Gotshal, a New York attorney, then president of the United Jewish Appeal, enclosing a contribution from a committee of seventy-seven Black people and from Hampton Institute and the Kansas City *Call*.

The text follows.

Dear Mr. Gotshal:

With this letter I am presenting to you checks in the total amount of $755.00 as a contribution from a committee of 77 Negro Americans to the United Jewish Appeal. Our committee has no formal title, neither is this contribution the result of any special campaign. Many of those sharing in this effort have contributed before and will contribute again to the cause of suffering Jewry overseas. We wish, however, to make this special expression of the deep sympathy felt by members of our race for a people whose extremity of anguish is unmatched in the history of modern civilization.

Daily we read with growing horror of the ruthless savagery unleashed against helpless Jews in Nazi-occupied Europe. We who have known deprivation and suffering in our native land, America, stand aghast at the maniacal fury and bestial atrocities practiced against the Jewish people by Hitler and his foul associates. Those crimes of Nazi leadership constitute one further reason why Negroes must remain wholeheartedly committed to this war until the last vestige of Nazism is driven from the earth.

Negroes share the tremendous debt which the world owes to the descendants of Israel—for your scholars and soldiers, scientists and judges, teachers and workers have enriched the living of every nation on the globe. But as Negroes we owe a special debt to those Jews of great spirit who have through the years brought such important material and moral support to the cause of Negro advancement and interracial understanding.

The contribution which our committee makes to the United Jewish Appeal is not so much an acknowledgment of that debt as it is a reaffirmation of our conviction that we are under one God, one people united in one cause. May this small gift stand as additional testimonial to the bond of friendship that must grow between two peoples with a glorious history, and a still more glorious future.

Sincerely yours,
Lester B. Granger

Opportunity, January–March, 1944; XXII, 18–19. On page 19 was published the letter of acceptance and appreciation from Mr. Gotshal.

86

WRITERS CONGRESS, 1943

Under the auspices of the Hollywood Writers' Mobilization and the University of California, a congress was held in Los Angeles, October 1–3, 1943. Two of the speakers were Walter White of the N.A.A.C.P and William Grant Still, composer of "Afro-American Symphony," "Kaintuck'," and the theme music for the 1939 World's Fair. Their remarks are published below.

[a]

COMMUNICATIONS MEDIA AND RACISM
by Walter White

No truer statement has been made than the theme of this Congress— "the spoken and written word and the image on the screen are of crucial importance in developing civilian and military morale, in bringing the promise of victory to the countries under Axis tyranny, in cementing the unity of the United Nations, in clarifying the conditions for a just and lasting peace."

In a sense, the importance of these media by which ideas are formed and propagated is more crucial than the making of guns and planes. Men shoot guns and fly planes because of ideas, good or evil, which the spoken and written word and the image on the screen have planted in the minds of the gun-shooters and plane-flyers. Because of this fact, an enormous opportunity—and an appalling responsibility—faces the coiners of words and the makers of media which will help to shape the world to come.

Unhappily, we face this task with a huge handicap—the correction, if possible, of sins of commission and omission we have wittingly or unwittingly committed in the past. We have also the pressing obligation to try to reeducate vast numbers of the people of the earth who have been allowed to hear and see. An entire generation of Nazi youth and many generations of Japanese youth will have to have their minds de-poisoned and purged of the fantastic lies upon which they have been fed. If the democratic way of life is to survive, so also will countless other youth have to be convinced not only by the written and spoken word and the image on the screen, but by the narrowing of the gap between our practice and our profession of democracy, that it, and not totalitarianism, is the way of peace and prosperity, and of racial equality. I speak particularly of the one thousand million brown, yellow, and black people of the Pacific among whom radio Tokyo is industriously and gleefully playing up every "zoot suit" riot in Los Angeles, every mob murder in Mississippi or Detroit, every manifestation of racial or religious prejudice in the United States or Great Britain as examples of what will happen to them should the United Nations win the war. I have in mind as well the swarthy-skinned youth of Latin America who have heard the unfortunately true story which Axis agents have helped to spread of the United States band playing as farewell to the President of Haiti not long ago a popular tune of the 'twenties, "Bye, Bye, Blackbird."

Is there any wonder that many of our eloquent radio and screen and printed assertions that this is a war for the freedom of all men everywhere are received with somewhat less than complete faith and enthusiasm in some parts of the world, including our own country? Especially when the leader and spokesman for one of our allies bluntly asserts that: "We intend to hold on to what we have," and "I was not appointed His Majesty's first minister to preside at the liquidation of the British Empire"; or when our own country permits the mistreatment of religious and racial minorities without restraint or rebuke?

On my way here I purchased a newspaper in Chicago, in which there appeared a story illustrative of the task before us. An interned German officer in guttural English demanded, "We want to see the ruins of Chicago. . . . We would like to take a trip there and see the smashed buildings like there are in New York and Washington."

It will be simple to refute the falsehoods of this character which have been fed to the German people by a pathological liar like Hitler. But what will we do about the Nazi officer's bewilderment that Jamaican Negroes at work on an adjoining assembly line in a canning plant sang lustily as they worked? "Why should these conquered black people sing?" the German asked. "It is simple to know why we sing. Although we've been captured, Hitler will soon be here and set us free!"

We can place only part of the blame for this concept on Hitler and Goebbels. The producers and writers of Hollywood and of the Anglo-Saxon world who have made pictures and written books glorifying empire and colonial imperialism and race superiority were preparing the ground for the evil machinations of the madman of Berchtesgaden long before he came into power. And unless we revise our concepts and practices we are inevitably going to build future and even more evil Hitlers to plague mankind for generations yet unborn.

Fortunately, a mild change in the treatment of minorities in fiction and on the screen has begun to take place. But even yet one hundred and fifteen million Americans each week and moviegoers in other countries have been fed pictures which, in their portrayal of certain groups, have created resentment among those so pictured and smug convictions of their own "superiority" among the white people of the world. Chinese were shown as laundrymen, South Americans as gigolos, Negroes as fat, funny, and feebleminded. In fairness, it must be said that white people weren't treated much better—as gangsters, unscrupulous politicians, and business pirates. But they were portrayed also as normal human beings at times and occasionally even as noble and heroic; yet today this is rarely true of the cinema treatment of such a minority as the Negro.

Let me tell you of a recent episode which illustrates one of the by-products of this practice. A distinguished Negro poet was invited to lecture at one of our great universities. During a lull in the conversation at dinner, the six-year-old daughter of the president of the university asked the poet, "Will you teach me how to shoot dice?" Startled, the poet had to admit that dice-shooting was not among his talents and asked the child why she had selected him as her teacher of the art. She innocently and promptly replied: "In the movies, all Negroes shoot dice!"

The correction of the miseducation of the Nazi officers and the university presidents' children of the world concerning human beings of other races, religions, places of birth, language, and concepts different from our own is a task of herculean proportions. But correct it we must if any of us are to survive in a world free from war. In the hands of the creators of "the spoken and written word and the image on the screen" are the tools for this process of reeducation. Tackling the problem will cost you headaches and heartaches and money. Some of you will not have the fortitude or the vision to undertake the task. But if this Writers' Congress does nothing more than extend the mental horizons of some of us to comprehend the world picture of racial and economic self-interest in Wendell Willkie's *One World*, or in the President's statement of last Tuesday that "We cannot stand before the world as a champion of oppressed peoples unless we practice as well as preach the principles of democracy for all men," the Congress will have justified its convocation and made a measurable contribution to the winning of the war and the peace.

However, the steadily brightening promise of victory is one of our gravest dangers. Powerful forces of greed and reaction, both at home and abroad, recovering from their fright during the days of unbroken military successes by our enemies, have emerged from their storm cellars and today work arrogantly and feverishly to take over again control of the war and the postwar years. They would reestablish the prewar status quo which plunged us into this terrible conflict. Their ruthless drive has stilled by sheer weight the voices of many enlightened liberals who see the folly and peril of the old order. A determined block of unscrupulous Southern Democrats and reactionary Northern Republicans today dominates the Congress, virtually imprisons the President in the White House, and viciously sabotages every attempt to translate our announced war aims into reality, here and abroad.

If this powerful minority succeeds in capitalizing on our naive assumption that the war is virtually over and the apathy to what is going on about us growing out of that assumption, we may win the war in a military sense but lose it morally and ethically. If this should come to pass, we will not abolish war but merely purchase for ourselves a brief armistice until the nations of the earth are strong enough to begin World War III.

How can the practices of these dangerously misguided forces be checked? Only by the force of enlightened public opinion, which the makers of the spoken and written word and of the image on the screen, above all others, have the power to create. If we liberate our own minds of half-truths and misconceptions and use our own media to build a world free of racial and religious hatred, a world free of vicious and fictitious notions of the superiority of one race over another, a world free of imperialism and colonialism, we can then help immeasurably to insure a durable peace. But should we choose instead, through blindness or greed, to continue to follow the stereotypes of the past, there will be no security or peace for any man, of any race, anywhere. Which will we choose?

May we here resolutely resolve to do our part in choosing the kind of world Stephen Vincent Benét, just before his death, pictured in the prayer he wrote for last year's United Nations Day:

Yet most of all grant us brotherhood, not only for this but for all our years—a brotherhood not of words but of acts and deeds. We are all of us children of earth—grant us that simple knowledge. . . . If our brothers are oppressed, then we are oppressed. If they hunger, we hunger. If their freedom is taken away, our freedom is not secure. Grant us a common faith that man shall know bread and peace—that he shall know justice and righteousness, freedom and security, an equal opportunity and an equal chance to do his best, not only in our own lands but throughout the world. And in that faith let us march toward the clean world our hands can make. . . . AMEN.

[b]

THE NEGRO AND HIS MUSIC IN FILMS
by William Grant Still

When one discusses the Negro "stereotype," one speaks of something that colored people have been fighting for many years—something that extends to almost all art expressions in which colored people are portrayed. Films, up to now, have rarely been an exception to this rule. And because all the elements in a film are interdependent, it is impossible to isolate Negro music in films, generally speaking. Without a doubt, when the films begin to portray a different sort of colored person, the accompanying music will improve accordingly, both in quality and authenticity.

If people will scan the vast panorama of American life, they will see colored people of a great variety of types: professional people, intellectuals, creators, shopkeepers and teachers, as well as the folksy Negro and the stage personalities so often portrayed in the past. All of these people have drama in their lives, drama that could be made into stirring films. Music for such films would naturally parallel their emotional content.

Such an innovation would be a distinct contribution to the war effort. It would create increased respect for the colored man abroad, wherever films in which only colored actors participate. Such films are not only home by bringing mutual understanding to all Americans. Backward people can and should be educated, not pampered.

Some colored critics have seen a danger in the glorified, segregated films in which only colored actors participate. Such films are not only undemocratic; they are false. Negroes are not and never have been an imprisoned group which has had no contact with people of other races. Negroes are a part of American life, just as other racial groups are a part of it. They should be portrayed honestly, in their true relationship to other people.

To my mind, the Negro "stereotype" in films results more from closed minds and lack of imagination than from racial prejudice. The blind following of tradition is something that extends to films in general. Actually, each different film, each different episode, needs a fresh approach. Yet this is impossible, because neither the established craftsmen nor the hopeful newcomers are permitted to introduce innovations. Music for a certain scene, a character, a plot development—all must move according to old formulas.

In many respects, I must confess that I don't know exactly where the line of demarcation comes: what is racial prejudice and what is inherent in the business of film-making. The music director today regards himself as teacher and critic. It is he who decides what should go into a film at certain spots and then expects the composer to translate, by some secret psychic communion, what is in his mind. He wants only traditional things, such as battle music for battle scenes, and so forth. He closes his mind to any new ideas the composer may present, and it goes without saying that more effective background music, enhancing the mood of the film rather than each specific action, is out of the question.

Consequently, each musical director has decided what Negro music should be in films and, right or wrong, he will stick to it. Unfortunately, in the majority of productions, no account is taken of the richness and variety of Negro music, music which ranges from an untutored folk expression to the most sophisticated symphonic forms. Invariably, the type of music selected to represent the colored man is the folksy sort or the jazz element, and all too often this is performed crudely in an effort to give what is amusingly termed "authenticity." A Negro choral director told me that film people always criticized her choruses on the ground that they were "too refined." Yet she employed colored people, singing Negro music without affectation. Colored people now wonder why if there must be a "stereotype," it is not a "stereotype" based on the best in Negro life and all its art phases?

Very often Negroes are engaged to work on music for Negro films and their opinions are then discarded in favor of what other people think it ought to be. A recent experience of my own is significant. Employed as supervisor of music on an all-Negro film, I found that every suggestion I made was disregarded, everything I did was thrown out with the statement that it was "too good." One particular orchestration, designed for the period immediately following the first World War, was not used because "Negro bands didn't play that well then," according to the musical director. I protested that at that period I was playing in Negro bands and that the men played better then than they do today. My comment was simply ignored, and the orchestration never got into the picture.

On another occasion, a strong Negro theme was needed for a Negro film. I wrote one, based on an authentic folk song. Some people connected with the film were enthusiastic over it, but soon they began to ask for the opinions of many others, most of whom knew nothing about music and some of whom knew nothing at all about American traditions and art phases. By the time all these people finished tearing the music to pieces, we threw it out and compromised on a hymn. In short, I, who for more than thirty years have been intimately associated with Negro music, have had to give way to the hasty verdicts of people who cannot possibly be as familiar with the subject as I am and who calmly doubt my "authenticity."

Naturally, there have been many colored people who do what the men in charge command, for financial reasons. If there had not been, there would be no problem today. Nor is it true that every Negro musician is capable of turning out something at once authentic and good. On the other hand, there is something so fundamentally Negroid about genuine Negro music, whether it be folk or symphonic, that no white man can imitate it. No matter how extravagant the claims made for white imitations, how pleasing they may be as music, or how much similarity there is in their external aspects, they are at best imitations.

There are as many different kinds of Negro music as there are different types of colored people. When the films depart long enough from accepted formulas to present to the public a finer type of Negro and more sophisticated Negro music, even colored people will be able to enjoy the cruder aspects of Negro life unashamedly because they will know that the public, here and abroad, no longer will have a one-sided view of the race as a whole.

The present war and its attendant crisis at home should wrest two major concessions from Hollywood: an open mind with regard to minority groups and their art forms, and the will to make a positive contribution to interracial understanding.

Writers' Congress: Proceedings of the Conference Held in October, 1943 (Berkeley: University of California Press, 1944), pp. 14–18, 277–79.

87

THE ELECTION OF A
BLACK COMMUNIST LEADER
TO THE CITY COUNCIL OF NEW YORK

The struggle against Hitlerism and the war-time alliance with the Soviet Union brought about an upsurge in the acceptance of the Communist Party within the United States. A striking reflection of this were the local elections in New York City in November, 1943. At that time Peter V. Cacchione, Communist, was re-elected to a two-year term to the City Council, from Brooklyn, receiving the highest number of first choice ballots (in a proportional representation vote) of any candidate. Michael Quill, the leader of the Transport Workers Union, also was elected to the Council. Most striking, however, was the election for the first time of a Black Communist leader to a major political office. This was the election of Benjamin J. Davis, Jr.—with 44,000 votes. While Mr. Davis was re-elected in 1945, it was the results of this 1943 election and particularly his own successes which led to the finally successful movement to repeal proportional representation in New York City voting.

Two documents on Mr. Davis' 1943 election follow. The first is the account of his press conference, written by J. J. Adams and appearing in the New York *Amsterdam News,* November 20, 1943; the second is the editorial in that leading Black newspaper appearing on the same date.

[a]

BEN DAVIS, SR.–G.O.P. STALWART
BEN DAVIS, JR.–C.P. RADICAL

by J. J. Adams

Stocky Georgia-born Benjamin J. Davis, whose early life was imbued with the tradition of the Republican party, but who in recent years has been a true member of the Communist party, told a news conference Saturday morning what he believes was responsible for his election to New York City Council on November 2.

Ben's father, Benjamin J. Davis the elder, once a most powerful figure in the Republican Party of which he was National Committeeman from Georgia, is mighty proud of his son. When informed of young Ben's victory, the aged politician said feebly:

"Communists didn't elect him."

"Quit kidding, the Communist Party never elects anybody. All it does is run candidates." But Ben wasn't kidding. He had won, thus becoming the first Negro Communist ever to win an elective office in the United States.

During the press conference Davis didn't bother to go into his personal history. He said little about the time he was suspended from college at Morehouse in Atlanta, Ga. where he was born, because he led a strike, nor would he do more than smile when questioned about his proficiency as a violin virtuoso.

On the other hand the councilman-elect was somewhat moody as he discussed his experience at Harvard Law School where he had gone following his graduation at Amherst college. It seems that his scholastic record had made him eligible for membership in one of the exclusive campus societies, but his color blocked his admittance.

In spite of his early background and the fact that many of his friends as well as powerful friends of his father are conservative in their politics, Ben's own experience has been such as to cast his life and career in an entirely different mold. He is Communist through and through.

Davis first gained public prominence when he defended Angelo Herndon who was charged by an Atlanta Ga. grand jury of inciting an insurrection. Herndon was convicted but Davis and others fought the case all the way to the Supreme Court and Herndon was eventually freed from the chaingang. Since that time Ben Davis has been almost synonymous with Communist.

Of his election Ben believes it is an achievement of all the progressive people of New York County of all national and racial origins, religious and political beliefs who saw in his candidacy an opportunity to be represented by a councilman fully devoted to the defeat of Hitlerism abroad and to the defeat of all fascist manifestations at home. Jim Crow, anti-Semitism and racial discrimination of all forms must be outlawed in our city, as a necessity for victory, he said.

The councilman-elect said that his work in the council will be carried on through a broad program, principal parts of which will be the drive for jobs and for better housing for Negroes and other low-level minority peoples. In addition, he said, he will be ever ready to stop jim crow in its vicious track wherever and whenever he encounters it.

On the question of the war Davis said it is useless to talk about post-war problems unless we win the war. He then emphasized the imperativeness of effecting the unity necessary for victory.

"I shall support every genuine win-the-war measure introduced in the council, no matter with what party it originates," he said. "I shall work tirelessly in the fight against Jim Crow and anti-Semitism, for the elimination of racial discrimination from the Stuyvesant Project, in fighting discrimination against Negroes on the faculties of our city colleges, in fighting discrimination in Nurse Training, in fighting for a Public Market in Harlem and for better educational and recreational facilities."

Davis said also that he will press for the investigation of the text books used in the schools and colleges and for an investigation of the Public Utilities and all other industries which discriminate against workers because of race, creed, color or political affiliation.

Calling himself the choice of the people and indirectly taking a slap at the charges that his campaign was based on race and class issues, Davis said:

"I was elected by a coalition of Negro and white citizens affiliated with the Communist, Democratic, Republican and Labor Parties, as well as by the independent voter. This unity of the people cut through old established Party labels." He attributes this unity to what he stands for and not the result of party affiliation.

"It is crystal clear," he said, "that it cannot be said that I was elected by Harlem alone or by the Communists alone. Therefore, I consider myself not only the Communist Party representative in the Council, but rather the representative of all the people." The council post is for two years and pays $5,000 a year. Mr. Davis is a bachelor.

[b]

THE BENJAMIN DAVIS ELECTION

(An Editorial)

The election of Benjamin Davis to the City Council is, in many respects, the most outstanding feature of the recent councilmanic contest. Following as it did closely behind the election of Justice Francis E. Rivers to the City Court, it proves conclusively that white voters will vote for qualified Negroes for political offices. Of course, some white and colored politicians have often denied this; either because of ignorance or because of their own selfish motives.

Another important point to make about the election of Mr. Davis is that a well organized minority can elect its candidate to the City

Council (under proportional representation), particularly if its candidate can win the support of another group of voters. The support thousands of non-Communist Negroes gave to Mr. Davis is what did the trick for him. Conversely, the support the Communist Party gave Councilman Powell two years ago greatly aided in his election. Rev Powell was almost solidly supported by colored voters.

The most important of all points to make about the election of Mr. Davis, however, is that he is thoroughly qualified for his membership in the Council. A close student of social problems, courageous, honest and highly educated, Mr. Davis, son of a former Republican National Committeeman from Georgia, should be a real asset to the entire citizenry of New York as a member of its legislative body. At least we think he will be and congratulate him upon his whopping victory.

88

A DECLARATION BY NEGRO VOTERS

In preparation for the 1944 elections, and at the invitation of the N.A.A.C.P., a meeting on political tactics for Black people was held in New York City on November 20, 1943. Twenty-seven men and women, representing twenty national organizations and unions, issued the following "Declaration" which produced much discussion in the Black press and some notice in major white newspapers.

The Negro voter has not yet chosen sides for 1944.

His vote cannot be purchased by distributing money to and through party hacks. It cannot be won by pointing to jobs given to few individual Negroes, although the recognition of the Negro as an integral part of the body politic through the selection of qualified Negroes for appointive or elective offices is included among the Negro's demands. The Negro vote no longer can be won by meaningless generalities in party platforms which are promptly forgotten on election day.

The Negro voter will support a political party which by words and deeds shows its determination to work for full citizenship status for thirteen million American Negroes and to better the lot of all disadvantaged people in this country. The Negro knows that his voting strength in 17 or more states with 281 or more votes in the electoral college gives him the potential balance of power in any reasonably close national election and in many state and local elections. His vote no longer belongs to any one political party. Although the Negro has largely supported the Democratic Party in recent years, it is highly significant that in 1943 the Negro vote played an important part in the election of a Negro Communist to the New York City Council, a Negro Republican as Judge in the same community, a Democratic mayor in Cleveland and a Republican Governor in Kentucky with phenomenal manifestations of independent voting in many other important centers. Public officers who have not made a record of liberal and democratic action may expect the Negro to help remove them from office. If their successors are no better, they may expect the same fate at the next election. For if the Negro does not always find any satisfactory candidate to support, he can and will continue to help remove unsatisfactory officials until truly democratic forces shall come into power.

The undersigned are officers of church, fraternal, labor, civic and educational organizations with a total membership of more than 6,000,000. Though we speak as individuals, we shall recommend to the membership of our respective organizations that Negroes shall measure all appeals for their support made by political parties and by presidential and other candidates according to the following yardstick:

The Negro people, like all other Americans, recognize the war as the chief issue confronting our country. We demand of any political party desiring the support of Negroes a vigorous prosecution of the war. We are opposed to any negotiated peace as advocated by the Hitler-like forces within our country. Victory must crush Hitlerism both at home as well as abroad.

In evaluating the merits of parties and candidates we must include all issues—those touching the life of Negroes as a group as well as those affecting the entire country. The party or candidate who refuses to support a progressive public program for full post war employment, or opposes an enlarged and unsegregated program of government-financed housing, or seeks to destroy organized labor, is as much the enemy of the Negro as is he who would prevent the Negro from voting.

We insist upon the right to vote in every state, unrestricted by poll taxes, white democratic primaries, the gerrymandering of districts, or any other device designed to disfranchise the Negro and other voters. Any political party in power, or aspiring to power, must demonstrate its determination through legislation and through vigorous criminal prosecution by the Department of Justice to protect and secure voting as a fundamental right of citizenship.

The ever-serious evil of lynching and mob violence has become more critical as a result of unrestrained violence against Negroes in the armed services. No national administration can merit the support of the Negro unless it is committed to a legislative and administrative program for the elimination of this national disgrace.

Republican and Democratic members of the Senate alike have attempted to delude us by alleging that they favor anti-lynching, anti-poll tax, and other legislation against which filibusters by southern Democrats have been waged but on which these Republican and Democratic Senators, from states where Negroes vote, refuse to vote for cloture. We refuse to accept such subterfuges any longer. A vote against cloture or failure to vote for cloture will be construed by us as opposition to whatever legislation for the benefit of the Negro and other minorities against which a filibuster is waged. The Senate rule requiring a two-thirds majority to end debate, combined with the refusal of senators to vote for cloture, is one of the greatest obstacles to liberal legislation in general and to legislation for the betterment of the Negro's status in particular. Negroes insist that national parties and individual candidates for senator pledge in advance their support to the abolition of this two-thirds rule now required for cloture.

The program now being carried on through the Fair Employment Practice Committee to secure and protect the right to work without racial or religious discrimination must be continued and expanded during and after the war. No party or candidate for the Presidency or Congress can deserve the vote of the Negro without supporting a liberal appropriation for a Fair Employment Practice Committee when that issue shall be presented in the spring of 1944 and such legislation as is needed further to secure the right of minorities to work without discrimination.

No injustice embitters Negroes more than continued segregation and discrimination in the armed forces. The policy of the present administration with reference to the Negro in the armed forces is bad in principle and has failed. Any party which hopes to win the support of Negroes must adopt a new and democratic program for their integration into the armed forces, including the following provisions:

Full integration of the Negro into the armed forces without segregation.

The abolition of quotas by race in the medical corps, the nurse corps, the technical and all other branches of service throughout the armed forces.

A vigorous and purposeful program of education in decent and democratic race relations to be carried out throughout the Army and Navy.

A radically revised Navy program which will include the acceptance of Negroes as commissioned officers, the use of Negroes in general and technical service on seagoing vessels, the elimination of restrictions preventing capable messmen from transfer and promotion out of that service and the acceptance of Negro women in the WAVES, SPARS, and nurse corps without segregation.

The abolition of segregation in recreational and other facilities at army posts and naval shore installations as well as the abolition of segregation of blood plasma for the armed services.

The progressive removal of Negro troops from those areas where they are treated with violence, abuse, and disrespect in the civilian community in view of the demonstrated inability of the federal authorities, military and civil, to cope with such behavior.

Negroes now largely denied the right to serve in combat forces must be given the same opportunity as others to serve in this field as well as all other branches of the service.

We are concerned that this war bring to an end imperialism and colonial exploitation. We believe that political and economic democracy must displace the present system of exploitation in Africa, the West Indies, India, and all other colonial areas. We insist that all parties and candidates formulate a foreign policy which will resolutely and unequivocally oppose either perpetuation or extension of exploitation based upon "white superiority" or economic or political advantage to "white" nations at the expense of the two-thirds of the people of the earth who are brown, yellow, or black of skin. The United States must point the way by including Negroes among its representatives at the peace conference or peace conferences and among its diplomatic, technical, and professional experts engaged in international post war reconstruction.

Negro Americans are fully aware of the forces in this country which are now attempting to effect the nomination of reactionary or vacillating candidates for the Presidency and Vice-Presidency in both major political parties.

Negro voters are also distrustful of most candidates who come from those states which deny Negroes opportunity to vote and confine them to rigid patterns of segregation and inferior status. No candidate from any section of the country will be acceptable to Negro voters unless he has clearly demonstrated opposition to and departure from the prevailing anti-Negro traditions.

We hereby serve notice that if either major political party shall nominate for President or Vice-President a candidate of vacillating or reactionary character, or with an anti-Negro record, it will be vigorously opposed by the Negro vote.

We repudiate all venal politicians, Negro and white, who attempt for personal profit to "deliver the Negro vote." We hereby serve notice that the Negro has come of age politically.

This statement is designed both to make clear the Negro's present attitude of resentment against the shortcomings of both major political parties and to serve as a guide in measuring the future intentions of parties and candidates. The first test of the honesty of these intentions will be to vote upon the pending poll tax bill and cloture, if necessary; and we serve notice on all Senators and their party associates that we will vigorously oppose all Senators who refuse to vote for cloture on this bill. We call upon enlightened labor, church, farm, and other groups to oppose actively the current wave of reaction. We will combine on a minimum program with such enlightened groups. Together these groups constitute a majority of the electorate. Together we will beat back the tide of reaction and build a more decent world now and in the post war years which can insure a durable peace.

Signed:

Elsie Austin, Delta Sigma Theta Sorority

Mary McLeod Bethune, National Council of Negro Women

Dr. R. A. Billings, Phi Beta Sigma Fraternity

Oscar Brown, Chicago, Illinois, National Association for the Advancement of Colored People

Dorothy Hobday Bryant, National Association of Colored Graduate Nurses, Inc.

Walter Hardin, International Representative, United Automobile Workers–C.I.O.

Judge William H. Hastie, National Association for the Advancement of Colored People

Dr. D. V. Jemison, National Baptist Convention, U.S.A., Inc., and Alabama Baptist State Convention, Inc.

Carl R. Johnson, Kappa Alpha Psi Fraternity

Belford V. Lawson, Alpha Phi Alpha Fraternity

Dr. Rayford W. Logan, Alpha Phi Alpha Fraternity

Z. Alexander Looby, Omega Psi Phi Fraternity

Thurgood Marshall, National Association for the Advancement of Colored People

George W. Millner, International Longshoremen's Association

Leslie Perry, Washington Bureau N.A.A.C.P.

Adam C. Powell, Jr., People's Committee

A. Philip Randolph, Brotherhood of Sleeping Car Porters and March on Washington Movement

Dr. Leon A. Ransom

Mabel K. Staupers, National Association of Colored Graduate Nurses, Inc.

Ferdinand Smith, National Maritime Commission

Dr. Channing H. Tobias, Social Action Committee of the Colored Methodist Episcopal Church

Ashley Totten, Brotherhood of Sleeping Car Porters

Bishop W. J. Walls, A.M.E. Zion Church

George L-P Weaver, National C.I.O. Committee to Abolish Racial Discrimination

Beulah Whitby, Alpha Kappa Alpha Sorority

Walter White, National Association for the Advancement of Colored People

Dr. Max Yergan, International Committee on African Affairs and National Negro Congress

The Crisis, January, 1944; LI, 16–17.

89

PITFALLS THAT BESET
NEGRO TRADE UNIONISTS

by George L-P Weaver

The director of the National C.I.O. Committee to Abolish Racial Discrimination argues in the following essay against any special provisions or arrangements for Black members of the trade union movement, in terms reminiscent of Eugene Debs' insistence upon the same idea and for the same alleged reason—that Black workers were simply and solely members of the working class.

The Congress of Industrial Organizations, like other forward-looking groups, began to demand the full utilization of all available manpower as soon as the defense program got under way in 1939 and 1940. That demand, backed up by unremitting efforts, has broken down many barriers that have been a half-century in the making. A great number of industrial plants now hire Negroes that had never hired them before. Similarly, Negro workers are joining unions in greater numbers than ever before. But even with this decided progress, the job that must be done has just begun.

One direct result of this new union membership of Negroes is an increase of problems that grow out of our varied racial community practices. Another result is the emergence of a new Negro trade-union official, particularly in the C.I.O. These officials are operating on all levels of authority with a growing number of Negro local presidents, local grievance committeemen, and members of other key local committees. In the larger Internationals we tend to have an ever increasing number of Negro International Representatives. And this thread of progress leads up to the highest councils of the C.I.O., where there are now two Negro members serving on the C.I.O. Executive Board. The first to be placed was Willard S. Townsend, President of the United Transport Service Employees, who blazed the trail for other Negroes to follow. The second was Ferdinand Smith, Secretary of the National Maritime Union, who was selected by his union at the 1943 C.I.O. Convention.

Willard Townsend's service on the C.I.O. Board has been marked by his interest in all trade-union problems, instead of problems that can be considered as solely "Negro problems." In this Mr. Townsend offers the key that all Negro trade-unionists must use in order to advance their racial as well as their general interests in the labor movement. All of us need to realize that so-called racial problems are in reality only part of a worker's problem. The Negro neither wants nor needs special attention—he is looking to his trade-union for equal opportunity and the right of an American worker to advance up the ladder in whatever industry he may be employed. One of the most dangerous pitfalls that Negroes in the labor movement can fall into is that of allowing themselves to be maneuvered into a position of demanding special racial rights and consideration. In far too many instances, Negroes have fallen into this very pitfall.

The National C.I.O. Committee to Abolish Racial Discrimination has received complaints from Negro workers, Mexican workers, Jewish workers, Japanese-Americans, and the largest minority of all—women workers. Investigation discloses that each one of these groups thinks its problem the most important of them all. Our Committee's approach to all minority problems follows the theory that they are all *workers'* problems—part and parcel of the same fabric. As long as one of these vexing racial or cultural problems remains unsolved, the rights and privileges of all other workers are threatened.

If we Negro trade-unionists allow ourselves to become engrossed in the Negro's problem to the exclusion of the others, we run the risk of creating a dangerous racism, an evil that no one has ever been able to control and direct constructively. There are dangerous trends leading in this direction. The March on Washington Movement is the most outstanding manifestation of this "black chauvinism." And this writer has been puzzled and alarmed at the attitude of many local Negro trade-union officials. Too frequently ordinary trade-union grievances are blown up into charges of discrimination. Every local problem involving a Negro is laid on the doorstep of discrimination, regardless of the attitudes and principles of the white officer or brother union member involved. Such an approach robs the complainant of the necessary objectivity that he must possess to be a useful trade-union official in his local. A Negro elected to a post in a local union is expected to function as an officer for all the members, not for a Negro minority —or even majority. Then, too, by placing primary emphasis on the whole trade-union point of view, Negroes are much more apt to win the support of white members who recognize the trade-union approach, but who might become opponents if the issue were presented as a race issue.

The recent convention of the United Auto Workers, held in Buffalo, furnishes an example of this kind of danger. That union's race relations record is second to the record of no other American union. Its convention was thrown into an uproar by a minority report on an amendment to the constitution which would create a Minorities Department in the International, headed by a Negro who would also have a seat on the Executive Board.

Thoughtful observers must agree with the position of R. J. Thomas, U.A.W. President, who firmly opposed this proposal. If Negro workers are entitled by race alone to a special place on a union Executive Board, that same argument could be used to justify segregation on a streetcar, in a hotel, and in a restaurant. To carry this principle to its logical conclusion would mean insuring places on the Board for women, Poles, Jews and Catholics, since there is a sizable representation of each group in the U.A.W. Many union officials would be strongly tempted, if this proposal were adopted, to pass on to the Negro Board member problems that should be solved by the whole Board.

A number of Negroes took this position at the U.A.W. convention because they recognized the inherent dangers contained in the proposal. Oddly enough, they were castigated as anti-Negro and reactionary. Horace Sheffield, a Negro International Representative, was bitterly condemned and several Negro delegates have stated to this writer that "they are out to get him." Paul P. Shearer, labor editor for the *Ohio State News,* and an officer in Local 927, U.A.W., Columbus, Ohio, lumped together all opponents of the plan as members of anti-Negro factions and reactionaries. His list included Victor and Walter Reuther. When Shearer had pointed out to him the dangers and inconsistencies of this line of reasoning, he agreed and unconsciously explained the predicament that many Negro trade-unionists are in. They ride into office on the race issue in locals with large Negro memberships, and their thinking and approach to most trade-union questions constantly starts off from the point of "how do they affect Negroes?"

Negroes are also pushed along toward their pitfall by certain kinds of white support. For example, at the recent National C.I.O. Convention in Philadelphia, Abram Flaxner, President of State, County and Municipal Workers, in speaking on the anti-discrimination resolution, said, in part, that he felt it would be in the interest of the C.I.O. to elect a colored Board member to the International Executive Board—not from any one organization, but as representing all of the organizations on that Board. When the Flaxner proposal is examined, it seems patronizing, to say the least. Why should a Negro be elected to the Board, floating around without any anchor when all other members of the Board represent their International Unions? If the Board lacks Negro membership, there is nothing to stop Brother Flaxner's organization, or any other organization from electing a Negro to represent it.

To think clearly on this question, we must keep firmly before us our long-time objectives. If we are working towards the goal of complete economic equality and are using the trade-union structure toward that end, it seems a tragic paradox to consider any kind of proposal that dignifies separation. It may be held axiomatic that anything which separates people into sharply distinguishable groups—whether it be a racial difference, a difference of religious groups, or a class distinction—will produce between the groups thus separated: first, ignorance of one another; then, suspicion growing out of that ignorance; then, misunderstanding growing out of that ignorance and suspicion, and finally conflict. A safe general approach for Negro trade-unionists is one that considers questions affecting the black worker's welfare from the standpoint of sound trade-unionism, rather than the much narrower one of race. Time will prove the wisdom of this view. What harms the Negro harms all workers. But what harms workers in general also harms the Negro. Trade-union leadership has come to recognize today—certainly in the C.I.O.—that if the rights of Negro workers are not made secure, exploitative management will not long hesitate before pushing white workers down to the Negro's level. Just as white workers through their leaders have rapidly come around to this point of view, so Negro workers and members of their race who aspire to leadership in the trade-union movement must accept their responsibility for protecting the interests of organized labor itself.

Opportunity, January-March, 1944; XXII, 12–13.

90

WHITE SUPREMACY AND WORLD WAR II
by Walter White

The 1944 meeting of the N.A.A.C.P. was called a War Emergency Conference; it was held at the Metropolitan Community Church in Chicago, July 12–16. On its final day, Executive Secretary Walter White, having just returned from a tour of several war zones, delivered the following address.

On this 952nd day of America's participation in a war to save the world from the military aggression and racial bigotry of Germany and Japan, the United Nations with a comparable master race theory of its own moves on to victory. The growing certainty of that victory intensifies determination to permit no fundamental change in the attitude of "white" nations toward the "colored" peoples of the earth.

This is the harsh reality of the report I must unhappily bring you from visits to battlefronts stretching from England to the Middle East. In that reality lies not only continued misery and exploitation for black and brown and yellow peoples who constitute two-thirds of the population of the world. In it exists as well the virtual certainty of another and bloodier and costlier world war in the not too distant future.

The white world has not yet learned the danger and folly of its racial greed and intransigence. The wholesome and becoming humility of the dark days of the early part of the war when Hitler seemed unstoppable has passed. The certainty of "white supremacy" is hastily wrapped again like a mantle about the shoulders of the United Nations as their citizens emerge from bomb shelters into the comforting light of victory, a little ashamed of the panic they had felt. Only a few wise men and women like Wendell Willkie and Henry Wallace, Edwin Embree and Sumner Welles, Marshall Field and Pearl Buck are discerning enough to see that the old world is gone and that a new one must take its place or else we all may perish.

Though the voices of the thousands here today may be only as one crying in the wilderness, nevertheless it is our duty to cry aloud unceasingly and, whatever the price we have to pay, doing so not for our own selfish interests but to save the world from destroying white and colored together.

But there is comfort in the fact that today ours is not a lone voice. The hundreds of millions of China and India, of Africa and South America and the Caribbean are neither silent nor inactive. A vast and unstoppable seething moves them. They take literally the shibboleths of the Four Freedoms. They intend to secure and enjoy those freedoms and to put an end to the old order in which men, solely because they are colored, can be worked to exhaustion, exploited, despised, spat upon and derided by those whose chief right to sovereignty is whiteness of skin. And Russia with a passion not only for economic equality but for racial and cultural equality is committed to the fight against prejudice and discrimination.

It is highly significant that the eyes that see and the voices that speak are not solely those of the oppressed. I was in England when four by-elections were held in which the people repudiated the old order of Winston Churchill and his class who would perpetuate imperialism for the benefit of the few. In North Africa and the Middle East I talked with Maquis just escaped from Nazi-controlled France whose gaunt figures and tense faces bespoke the strain of the underground resistance movement, who are determined that the old order shall not be restored where a decadent class lives in luxury on the exploitation of colonials and working class white French men and women. In London and Algiers and Cairo I talked with men and women who had escaped from Balkan countries all the way from Estonia on the north down to the Black Sea and the Aegean. Almost without exception they favor,—distrustful as they are of the old order which brought on the terrible misery of this and the last war,—alliance with a steadily more powerful Russia than further reliance on an Anglo-Saxon capitalist world. Mind you, they do not wholly trust Russia. But they place slightly more hope in the Soviet as perhaps the lesser of two evils.

Meanwhile, a similar process proceeds with even greater speed to the east of Russia in Asia and the Pacific. This is less Russia's doing than it is England's and America's. A high official of the British Empire's India Office told me bluntly that Nehru and Gandhi and the other leaders of the fight for freedom of India's three hundred and fifty million people would never be freed from prison until they confessed guilt of treason and insurrection for daring to demand that India's millions receive as well as fight for freedom. Lest he be made a martyr by dying in prison, Gandhi has since been nominally freed. But the brilliant Nehru and other Indian leaders remain in jail to furnish the Japanese propagandists with superb material to convince the one thousand million colored peoples of the Pacific that the white nations of the world are liars and hypocrites when they say that this is a war for the freedom of all men everywhere.

In this shameful program, the United States is doing her full share to create cynicism and skepticism. Every lynching, every coldblooded shooting of a Negro soldier in Louisiana or Mississippi or Georgia, every refusal to abolish segregation in our armed forces, every filibuster against an anti-poll tax or anti-lynching bill, every snarling, sneering reference by a Mississippi Senator like Eastland to "burr headed niggers" in fulmination against an appropriation for the Fair Employment Practice Committee builds up a debit balance of hatred against America which may cost countless lives of Americans yet unborn.

Capitalist America and Great Britain fear and distrust Communist Russia, despite all the oleaginous talk nowadays about "our Russian Ally." If they hope to preserve a capitalist economy, would they not be wise enough to stop virtually forcing the oppressed of the world—white, black, brown and yellow—into desperate alliance with Communism or a racial war which would destroy white and colored peoples? Would not such a course be dictated at least by enlightened self-interest?

Instead of such a course what has recently happened and what will likely happen right here in Chicago during the next week? Three weeks ago the Republicans adopted here a weasel worded platform plank on post war international relations which is so meaningless that even the isolationist *Chicago Tribune* approves it. The same platform favors increased international trade and "a fair protective tariff"; opposes government subsidies and favors grants to farmers; pledges reduction of taxes and at the same time a reduction in the public debt and an abundant income for everybody. Since the Congress voted only a two and a half billion dollar tax bill with the war and the running of the government costing us nearly one hundred billion dollars a year one wonders what feat of legerdemain the Republicans plan to perform to achieve such a miracle.

But the height of double talk was reached when the Republicans came to the Negro question. Painfully aware that they could not reoccupy the White House unless they can corral the 2,500,000 Negro voters who hold the potential balance of power in seventeen or more states with a total of 281 or more votes in the Electoral College, the Republicans set about to lure the Negro back into the Republican fold. They included one plank pledging Congressional establishment of a permanent Fair Employment Practice Committee which, on the surface, was fair and unequivocal. But elsewhere they pledged "the return of the public employment office system to the states at the earliest possible time. . . ." Shades of consistency!! Eight of the thirteen million Negro citizens of the United States still live in the South. Imagine,—if you will subject yourself to such torture,—the chances of a Negro getting a post-war job in a state controlled employment system in a Mississippi controlled by Bilbo and Rankin!

Let's look at what the G.O.P. proposes to do about housing—the direst of all needs of the ghetto-doomed Negro. They propose to stimulate "state and local plans to provide decent low-cost housing properly financed by the Federal Housing Administration"—the agency which has done more than any other body in the history of America to enforce restrictive covenants as a means of perpetuating, extending, and giving Federal sanction to the unholy pattern of condemnation of Negroes to slums forever.

The Republicans say they favor "legislation against lynching," but they neglect to specify whether they mean federal, state or municipal legislation. If they mean state legislation their gesture is both silly and dishonest in the light of the number of Republicans in the states where lynchings are most frequent. If they mean federal legislation they are even more dishonest when they fail even to mention, much less pledge, to vote for cloture to stop filibusters by Southern Democratic Senators. I speak from more than a quarter of a century of experience with Republican majority and minority leaders including the late Senator Charles McNary and the present Minority Leader, Senator Wallace A. White of Maine. Both of these men smiled sweetly but delivered a sufficient number of Republican votes to estop cloture. We Negroes are finished with being treated as nitwits and dolts.

The Republicans promise Negroes an "investigation" of "mistreatment, segregation and discrimination against Negroes who are in our armed forces . . . and the adoption of corrective legislation." In 1941 the N.A.A.C.P. secured introduction of a resolution for a Senate investigation of mistreatment of Negroes in the armed services. It got little support from either Republicans or Democrats. Now three years later, on election eve, an investigation is promised. The Congress is in recess until August and, in effect, will be so until after the election. Only a miracle could effect the passage of a resolution for such an investigation by the end of the present Congress in January. Do the Republicans believe us to be completely stupid to think such an investigation will be put through by them in time to be effective in this war? Or are they thinking of World War III?

The whole procedure is redolent of the evasion practiced by Mr. Dewey in New York State in connection with the commission to investigate discrimination in war industries. The commission, composed of distinguished Negro and white New Yorkers, devoted eight months to its work and recommended remedial legislation. This was pocketed by Governor Dewey and a new commission appointed to traverse the same ground and report some time in 1945—well beyond the 1944 election day. Dewey could find but two Negroes in the whole of New York State to serve on his new commission—one of them a political appointee. The Negro's coming of age politically is evidenced by the courage of men like Channing Tobias who refused to be deluded or kidded.

But most shameful of all is the Republican proposal to abolish the poll tax by a constitutional amendment. Southern Democratic Senators, aided by reactionary Northern Republicans, have time and again blocked by a filibuster a vote on Federal legislation against the poll tax which required only a majority. How much more impossible will it be to pass a resolution for a constitutional amendment which requires a two-thirds vote of both houses of the Congress, and approval by thirty-six, or two-thirds of the state legislatures, of the amendment. After twenty years only twenty-eight state legislatures have approved the child labor amendment which most certainly is less venomously opposed than would be one to enfranchise ten million white and Negro Southerners whose disfranchisement perpetuates the Eugene Coxes and Rankins, the Bilbos and Tom Connallys in power. As a Negro I bitterly resent the Republican implication that we Negroes are as feeble-minded as they appear to believe us to be.

But if you think the G.O.P. platform dishonest and stupid as I do, we "ain't seen nothin' yet" until the Democrats get going here Wednesday. Playing a brazen game of bluffing, the sub-Potomac Democrats have been "revolting" for the past three years. They threaten to throw the election into the House of Representatives, to "secede from the union," and to do a host of other dire things, not one of which they have the slightest intention of doing. Their strategy is not nearly as fantastic and bombastic as it seems. It is, instead, shrewdly and calculatingly conceived. They demand that Vice President Wallace be replaced as the President's running mate because his views on racial, social and economic questions are "fantastic" and "impractical." They conveniently forgot that what Wallace advocates today the President himself preached in 1933 but now no longer preaches— namely, a world of the common man.

But Wallace is only a pawn in the hardboiled game the Southern revolutionists play with more than a fair chance of succeeding. Their real goal and purpose is to force the nomination as vice president on the Democratic ticket of a reactionary Southerner. They count on the President not surviving another four years in the White House or, more likely, his resigning when the war ends to head some sort of international peace commission and thereby turning over to the vice president the reins and powers of office.

Let me solemnly warn the Democratic convention that if it nominates a Southerner as vice president it can kiss the Negro vote goodbye. This is not a sectional issue. There are a number of Southerners, white and Negro, who would make excellent vice presidents. But none of them has a ghost of a chance to be nominated by the ruthless political machines of the South which perpetuate themselves in power by disfranchisement of from ninety to ninety-seven percent of the voters, white and Negro.

Let me make crystal clear at this point that what I say today is not the opinion of a single individual or even of a single organization, even though it be the N.A.A.C.P. with 783 branches and a membership of 400,000. What I say is instead what is deep in the hearts and minds of thoughtful Negro citizens all over this country. As evidence I submit excerpts from the statement, drafted and adopted with striking unanimity on June 17th by the spokesmen of the twenty-five most important mass organizations of Negroes in the United States with a combined membership of six and a half million.

Here is what these men and women ask of their country:

In the coming November election, the Negro voter will judge political parties, as well as candidates, by their words and deeds as to whether they show a determination to work for full citizenship status for thirteen million American Negroes and to better the lot of all disadvantaged peoples. Political parties and candidates that seek the votes of Negroes must be committed to the wholehearted prosecution of the war to total victory, must agree to the elimination of the poll tax by Act of Congress, the passage of anti-lynching legislation, the unsegregated integration of Negroes into the armed forces, the establishment of a permanent federal committee on fair employment practice, and a foreign policy of international cooperation that promotes economic and political security for all peoples.

The votes of Negroes cannot be purchased by distributing money to and through party hacks. They cannot be won by pointing to jobs given a few individual Negroes, although the recognition of the Negro as an integral part of the body politic through the selection of qualified Negroes for appointive or elective offices is included among the Negro's demands. Negroes are no longer persuaded by meaningless generalities in party platforms which are promptly forgotten on election day.

Later in the same statement, the twenty-five organizations declared:

In evaluating the merits of parties and candidates we must include all issues—those touching the life of Negroes as a group as well as those affecting the entire country. The party or candidate who refuses to help control prices, or fails to support the extension of social security, or refuses to support a progressive public program for full post war employment, or opposes an enlarged and unsegregated program of government-financed housing, or seeks to destroy organized labor, is as much the enemy of Negroes as is he who would prevent Negroes from voting.

We insist upon the right to vote in every state, unrestricted by poll taxes, white primaries, or lily-white party conventions, the gerrymandering of districts, or any other device designed to disfranchise Negroes and other voters.

We hereby serve notice that if either major political party shall nominate for President or Vice-President a candidate of vacillating or reactionary character, or with an anti-Negro record, it will be vigorously opposed by Negro voters.

Let me emphasize here that what is asked is not asked solely of national political bodies nor of the South alone. It is directed as well at Northern Democratic and Republican organizations which have all too often played ball and made deals with Southern reactionaries, using the Negro vote as the vanishing plea in a political shell game.

Though the Republicans are little if any better—particularly in the recent years of the Congressional coalition of death composed of reactionaries of both parties—we may have to submit to the temporary defeat of seeing Tweedledum replace Tweedledee. There are disturbing rumors that the Southern bluff is likely to succeed and that the President plans to "leave to the convention" the choice of a vice president. Negroes have reason to be grateful for much during the Roosevelt administrations. We have deep respect and affection for the courage and integrity of Mrs. Roosevelt. But we cannot run the risk—so desperate is our plight—of an anti-Negro figure as heir apparent to the most powerful position in the world today.

The South—or certain political elements in it like Senator "Cotton Ed" Smith of South Carolina and the Democratic State Committees of Texas, Mississippi and South Carolina—declare that they will secede unless they have their way. Let me say here quite seriously that a far worse fate could come to America than to have this happen. Just as the proverbial one rotten apple spoiled the barrel of apples, so democracy itself is being destroyed by the anti-democratic forces in the South today. They utilize hatred of the Negro precisely as Hitler used prejudice against Jews, Catholics and Christians. Through disfranchisement and the seniority rule, they head or dominate more than sixty percent of the Senate and House Committees which determine not only domestic legislation but foreign affairs and the shape of the post war world. Southerners constitute 28 percent of the nation's population but less than ten percent of them are permitted to vote. Thus approximately three percent of the population of America control, through the men they elect and who chair Congressional committees, the destiny of America. Perhaps democracy in America can be saved only by letting the rebels secede until the South is ready to obey the Constitution and the laws of human decency. Our nation's plight is far too precarious not only now but even more in the years to come to risk being jeopardized even more by the racism and bigotry of the Rankins and Bilbos.

Permit me to put race aside for the moment and point out how much a menace this bloc is to the interests of Americans generally. Between eleven and twelve million American men and women are serving in the armed forces, nearly six million of them overseas. If any citizens are worthy of the privilege of participation by voting in a democracy, it should be those who are sacrificing most in defense of that democracy. But certain people in and outside of Congress feared that soldiers and sailors might upset their political apple carts by voting too intelligently and liberally. They got Eastland and Rankin of Mississippi, McClellan of Arkansas and McKellar of Tennessee to sponsor a substitute measure, shameless in its ineffectualness. Why did they select these four men to put over disfranchisement of men facing death? For the simple reason that these four legislators were invulnerable to the wrath of an aroused electorate because the overwhelming majority of that electorate is disfranchised.

Or consider another example from among many which could be cited—the Bankhead amendment to the price control act which would have added three hundred and fifty million dollars a year to the cost of clothing—not only, mind you, of the cost of clothing to the people of Senator Bankhead's state of Alabama but to the cost of clothing to the people of Illinois, California, New York and of every other state of the union. Fortunately, this barefaced attempt to add greater profits to the textile interests was blocked. But hamstringing amendments on the Office of Price Administration were affixed as the basis of compromise. How neatly Bankhead's amendment fits in with the Republican platform's pledge to "terminate rationing, price fixing and all other emergency powers." Inflation, thar she blows!

This kind of legislative sabotage of all that we are fighting for in the war illustrates an obligation upon American voters, particularly those who belong to racial, economic and religious minorities, which cannot possibly be stressed too strongly. Never forget that it is vitally important that we elect a president and vice president at this crucial stage of the world's history who by record and promise symbolize the march towards genuine democracy and freedom for all men everywhere. But it is equally important that we elect a Senate and a House of Representatives equally intelligent and liberal. In the October, 1943, and June, 1944, issues of the N.A.A.C.P. *Bulletin* we published the voting record of every member of both Houses of the Congress on issues which affect your interests. Study those records. Cast your ballot according to what that record shows; not by what candidates promise in some vague future. "By their fruits ye shall know them." Pay no attention to their party affiliations. Party labels, as we have seen in the Congressional coalition of reactionary Southern Democrats and Northern Republicans, mean nothing to the enemies of progress. They should mean even less to us.

Continue to repudiate venal, slippery politicians who claim to be able to deliver—for a price—the Negro vote. Make this particularly true of Negro charlatans who jump from candidate to candidate, from party to party which has the largest campaign fund, who are able to fool only gullible white candidates because the latter know so little and take so little trouble to learn what the masses of Negroes really think. But while we repudiate purchasable politicians, we must also vigorously support those political leaders who fight for principle and the rights of all.

Permit me now to report tersely to you on my trip overseas since last we met in annual conference and to tell you how your sons and fathers and husbands and friends are faring. I covered as a war correspondent more than twenty thousand miles in the European, North African, Italian and Middle East Theatres of Operations. I talked with many thousands of officers and soldiers, white and Negro, ranging in rank from G.I.'s of engineering units who had just stepped off the boat from America to the Supreme Allied Commander, General Eisenhower. I shared with them the unique fraternity of enemy bombs dropping nearby and the ultimate democracy where race or color do not count—when men huddle together in a slit trench as enemy planes strafe at the rate of 3200 fifty-calibre bullets per minute per plane.

I wish it were possible for me to tell you truthfully that the alchemy of war and fighting to destroy Nazism had transformed the racial behavior of Americans in the armed services overseas. I cannot do so.

We have merely transplanted to other lands the American pattern, both good and bad. As is true at home, there are some officers and enlisted men, from North and South, who are decent human beings who believe in and practice democracy. A decidedly encouraging note is the number of G.I.'s who, brought face to face with death, are re-examining their racial and other opinions. Some of them are beginning to realize that race is a global question which must be faced and solved. Unfortunately, our War and Navy departments, threatened by Congressional reactionaries and bigots, have manifested but slight and grudging recognition of the existence of this enlightened minority in the armed services. Basically, the root of all our difficulties overseas is in insistence on racial segregation.

As long as our government insists on segregation in an army, and navy allegedly fighting for democracy, the chasm between the races will be perpetuated and broadened with resultant bitterness on both sides. When ten or eleven million men return after the war is over, our government cannot escape responsibility for whatever happens since it is in large measure responsible for immatures racial, political, economic and social thinking among these men whose every act they have directed for the period of their army and navy service.

What some of us like to believe is that a minority of American soldiers overseas have deliberately fomented brawls with colored soldiers, and spread malicious falsehoods about Negroes among the citizens of countries where these men have been stationed. Among them are that all Negroes have tails, that they are illiterate and diseased and inferior, and even that Negroes are so sub-human that they cannot speak English but communicate their thoughts, if any, by grunting and barking. It is fortunate for America that colored soldiers had self-control and sense enough to treat this campaign as a joke. In some areas Negro soldiers, learning on arrival of the fanciful tales about themselves which had been spread in advance of their coming, barked at the English people of the neighborhood. Belying their reputation of being slow to catch on to a joke, the English soon began to bark back in a kind of warm, friendly language of friendship.

In Italy I ran across a deliberate printed campaign of vilification of Negro American soldiers. Large green placards appeared mysteriously one day on billboards in Naples, allegedly put out by the "Comitato Italiano-Americano," whose full name, translated, is the Italian-American Committee for the Preservation of the Italian race. The Placard vilified Negroes, declaring them to be inferior because their skins were black and warned Italians that they would not receive much consideration or help if they treated American Negro soldiers as equals.

As your representative, I investigated these and other attempts to spread prejudice against the Negro and reported my findings to Major General David G. Barr, Chief of the North African Theatre of Operations. I am happy to read you the following excerpt from a letter recently received from General Barr:

As a result of your letter calling my attention to the conditions which you came across during your visit to Naples, I directed that an immediate investigation of the conditions . . . be instigated so as to enable us to take remedial action, if necessary. I have delayed answering you until such a time as I might have the benefit of the report submitted as the result of this investigation.

The "Comitate Italiano-Americano" poster referred to by you appeared in Naples on 12 January 1944. The investigation revealed that an American soldier of Italian extraction was fully responsible for its posting. This soldier, and two others who had assisted in financing and distributing the poster, have subsequently been tried and convicted by court martial under the 96th Article of War.

General Barr's prompt and effective action in this instance is matched, fortunately, by some of the other high officers of the United States Army overseas. Lt. General John C. H. Lee, Deputy Theatre Commander of the European Theatre of Operations, has recently written, "My staff has been instructed to implement wherever possible your many fine suggestions. It should be a source of great satisfaction to you to know that you have played a definite part in the preparation of our men for the primary mission—combat operations against the enemy. Suggestions such as promotion for Negro officers; the placing of certain officers in positions where they can be of most value are being gone into thoroughly, and, I know, will bring beneficial results."

In General Lee, I found a real friend of fair play and justice for the Negro. When the War Department published an excellent pamphlet, *The Command of Negro Troops,* General Lee had many thousands of copies printed in England for distribution to every officer in the European Theatre of Operations.

When I was in England, virtually all of the Negro soldiers there were so-called service troops—members of quartermaster, engineer, port battalion and trucking units. It was strongly urged that Negro combat troops as well be brought to the European theatre and given opportunity to participate in the invasion of the Continent. You have recently seen Army photographs of Negro combat troops on the Normandy beachheads, and you heard at the opening session of this conference General Eisenhower's tribute to the part Negroes are playing with other Americans in beating Hitler.

One of the most galling practices to Negro soldiers overseas is the designation of certain towns and other places as "off limits." This practice sorely limited already greatly limited areas in which soldiers could find diversions while on leave. An order has been issued by General Eisenhower forbidding such practices.

Some prejudiced officers have utilized court martial to intimidate Negro soldiers. This has been true both here and overseas. It has been strongly urged upon the War Department that special boards of review of such cases be established and that on them shall serve able Negro lawyers, appropriately commissioned, to insure justice. It is our intention to follow up this recommendation to the end that no officer of the United States Army will dare utilize the machinery of the court martial to implement his prejudices.

Another source of dissatisfaction I found was the tendency to transform Negro combat units into service units. We have reason to believe that facts presented on this issue will check this process.

These are but some of the specific problems and the specific action which your Association attempted to take on them. There are others which are in process of correction. But all of these and other problems are but the surface manifestations of the basic evil—segregation. If I were asked to state my most fundamental criticism not only of our Army and Navy, but of our whole governmental attitude, it would be this—that white America has so little faith in the inherent decency of white Americans. Wherever I went overseas, I found many young, intelligent, decent Americans, both northern and southern, who are disturbed by the race problem. They would like to bring their practice of democracy into line with their profession of it. But they fear that to do so would get them into difficulties with their superior officers. I believe the time has come for our government and all its agencies to stop basing their racial patterns on the lowest common denominator of American thought and action on this question. Unless it does so, I predict broadening of the chasm between the races which can only result in greater hatred, more friction and a weakening of the whole democratic structure.

One final word regarding the framing of the peace and the post war years. I am happy to announce that the distinguished American scholar, Dr. W. E. B. Du Bois, will return to your N.A.A.C.P. on

September 1 as Director of Special Research. His first and chief responsibility will be the preparation of material, in cooperation with a distinguished committee of Negro and white Americans, for presentation of the Negro's cause to the peace conference or peace conferences. If the peace treaty is based on the perpetuation of white overlordship over the peoples of the earth, another war is inevitable. On behalf of the Negroes not only of America, but of Africa, the West Indies and other parts of the world, we shall make our voice heard in an effort to save the framers from the folly of another Versailles Treaty.

We have just completed the most active and successful year in the Association's history. Ahead of us lie tears and heartaches, problems and hard work. But also there lies ahead greater strength out of which will come inevitably greater victories. We must, in the wise words of C. C. Spaulding, teach America that "It cannot play the Star-Spangled Banner without using both the black and the white keys."

Address delivered at closing meeting of Wartime, N.A.A.C.P. Conference, Washington Park, Chicago, July 16, 1944; mimeographed copy in editor's possession.

91

BEATEN HALF TO DEATH

by Nat D. Williams

The editor of a Black newspaper, the Memphis (Tenn.) *World*, was witness to a particular incident of characteristic racist brutality. He sent off a brief letter about it to a liberal Protestant magazine, as follows:

I saw a Negro soldier beaten half to death in the Grand Central Station at Memphis last Tuesday night. I did not have a chance to find out his name. The shore patrol police were beating him too fast. He was standing in line holding his luggage when a patrolman said something to him. They didn't like his answer and in a matter of seconds jumped on him. I asked why and they told me to "shove off." I wonder if they would have been so brave if the poor black soldier boy had been in a company of black folks. My God! What is democracy?

Christian Century, September 13, 1944; LXI, 1060.

92

WHAT THE NEGRO SOLDIER
THINKS ABOUT THIS WAR

by Grant Reynolds

Captain Grant Reynolds resigned as an army chaplain in January, 1944, in protest against the persistent and blatant racism in the armed forces. He then became administrative assistant, Washington Bureau, N.A.A.C.P. In that capacity he addressed the July, 1944, conference of the N.A.A.C.P. on "What the Negro Soldier Expects." An expanded version of that speech was published in three issues of *The Crisis* later in 1944. Arthur Hale, in a popular nationally broadcast radio program, "Confidentially Yours," stated on September 16, 1944, that the text of this article was being studied by key figures in the Roosevelt administration. It follows in full.

I

For the past two years and ten months I have been a Chaplain on active duty with the United States Army. I have found Negro soldiers bitterly resentful of their lot in this war. My having served with Medical Troops in Virginia, Infantry Troops in Massachusetts, raw recruits at a reception center in Michigan, sick and wounded soldiers from both Negro Divisions at a hospital in Arizona, and the troops comprising a Station Complement in California, has given me a broad picture of the conditions which affect our men from coast to coast. In each instance, regardless of the geography, the net result has been the same . . . Negro soldiers are damned tired of the treatment they are getting. This dislike cannot be attributed to the natural antipathy of the majority of soldiers, white and black, developed out of their efforts to adjust themselves to the rigors and uncertainties of war. Now the Negro soldier is as easily adaptable as any other American soldier. I'd even go as far as to say that he is more adaptable. His lifetime of adjusting himself to the whims and inconsistencies of the American white man substantiates this claim. His resentment then goes much deeper than this. It grows out of the unamerican treatment which plagues his every day while at the same time having to listen to loud voices telling him what a great honor it is to die for his country.

The Negro soldier needs no one to remind him that this is his country. He knows this. But he knows also that there is a lot of unfinished business about individual human decency that he would like to see cleared up before he becomes a corpse for *any* country. To deny him food when he is hungry, dignified transportation when he has to travel, a voice in choosing those who rule him, or just the most fundamental aspects or our proclaimed method of living, and then propagandize him daily into becoming a hero for democracy, is nauseating, to say the least. As one Negro soldier asked me in this respect: "Chaplain, do the white folks who are running this war think we are fools? Or, are they a pack of damned fools themselves? Excuse me, sir, for being profane, but this mess makes a man say a lot of nasty things."

My tour of active duty which began in Virginia and ended in California, after periods of service in Massachusetts, Michigan, Ohio, and Arizona, has provided me the opportunity not only of observing the Negro soldier under the varied *Jim-Crow* conditions which make life miserable for him, but because I am a Negro too I have lived under the same conditions and shared his resentment to them. Then too it must be remembered that a chaplain who tries to do a real job does more than sermonize on Sundays. His activities extend into areas concerned with the thoughts and lives of the thousands of men he serves.

How do I know what the Negro soldier thinks? Until a few days ago I was one myself. I have lived with him in his barracks because white officers in Virginia would not permit a colored officer to occupy quarters built by the War Department for its officers. Interesting, to say the least, is a personal experience which grew out of this insult. By a sudden jolt of fate I began my military career at Camp Lee, Virginia. There I immediately discovered the South more vigorously engaged in fighting the Civil War than in training soldiers to resist Hitler. And what was obvious, though nonetheless disturbing, this war was being won . . . as far as the Negro was concerned anyway. Because of the few officers needed with my small outfit less than fifty percent of the available rooms in the officers' barracks were occupied. But there was no room for me. I was therefore assigned quarters with the enlisted men in their barracks. What did it matter that such an assignment infringed upon the freedom of Negro soldiers during their leisure moments? What did it matter how this personal embarrassment and humiliation impaired my morale? My job, it seemed, was to *build* morale, not to *have* it. Anyhow, of what importance is the condition of the Negro soldier's morale to the proper performance of his duty? But of equal importance, what did it matter that army policy prohibiting officers and enlisted men from sharing common quarters except under field conditions was deliberately ignored? The Negro soldier has learned that army policy, binding upon whites, far too often relaxes to his disadvantage. This separation of officers and enlisted men is supported on the grounds that the familiarity involved is destructive to proper discipline. There are other methods of maintaining discipline among Negro soldiers, some of which make Gestapo Chief Himmler look like a rank amateur. What *did* matter in this situation was the doctrine of white supremacy which had to remain undefiled regardless of the cost. To assign a Negro officer quarters in an officers' barracks which housed white officers was unthinkable! Entirely ignored was the fact that this officer by virtue of his military status indicated the same willingness to die for American fair play . . . for democracy.

After some weeks of this humiliation, which the Negro soldiers resented as much as I did, I was called to meet with the Post Construction Officer. To my utter amazement he showed me the blue prints of plans for the construction of an officers' quarters for my exclusive use. As an added favor to me I was given the privilege of selecting the site where the quarters of the "untouchable" would be erected. But here I made my usual mistake, a mistake which was to plague the remainder of my military service. I did not say: "Thank you white folks for being so kind and generous to this nigger." Instead I summoned the effrontery to remark that this was an unnecessary waste of the taxpayers' money. For this I was immediately labelled as a Negro who not only did not "know his place," but one who was also a base ingrate.

I have been on occasion the only colored officer in the Negro soldier's outfit and therefore the one most likely to hear both his gripes and his legitimate complaints. I have marched with him in the heat of a southern sun, shivered with him in the wake of a New England blizzard, and with him I too have breathed the scorching dust of an Arizona desert. I have laughed with him in his moments of pleasure, heard his confession of the worthlessness of his former life as he embraced the Christian religion, sorrowed with him in the loss of loved ones, and suffered with him under the heel of the dehumanizing demon of American race prejudice. I know what the Negro soldier thinks, not only because he has told me, but because I know my own thoughts.

Not long ago Secretary of War [Henry L.] Stimson revealed in no uncertain terms what the War Department thought about the Negro soldier. I propose to relate in like manner what the Negro soldier thinks about the War Department's War. In the next installment I shall relate what the Negro soldier thinks about the War Department itself. But a word about Mr. Stimson's insult. Negroes throughout the nation along with other decent Americans were scandalized and they were prompt in making their protests known. But let us not be too harsh on a man who is the victim of the "logic" of his own thinking. Anyone sharing the traditional American regard for the colored citizen, and being party to that regard as it daily segregated the Negro soldier and citizen, could not have reached any other conclusion. This is especially true if he had given ear to reports of Army Intelligence on the Negro Soldier.

Mr. Stimson must have been told that the Negro soldier is demoralized, that he does not want to fight—unless a second front is opened in Mississippi, Texas, Georgia, South Carolina, Louisiana, or just *anywhere* below the Mason and Dixon Line—that his heart is not in this war. Such a soldier cannot be depended upon to offer up his life against German or Japanese soldiers who know why they are fighting and demonstrate each day their willingness to die for their beliefs. Where are the American soldiers, of any color, who would destroy their own lives rather than fall into the hands of a hated enemy? The Japs did this on Attu. Incidentally, the record of our forces at Anzio and Cassino for 4 months showed that American white troops with only one enemy to fight were hardly super men in face of their German opposition. We might just as well realize that the Negro soldier has two enemies to fight, one foreign and the other at home. Now since public opinion forced the Secretary of War to give some reason for the War Department's refusal to allow Negro soldiers to die for America in some appreciable manner other than in labor battalions and in the "high-falutin Engineers," which is a camouflaged term meaning practically the same thing, Mr. Stimson's hand was called. Those who expected the unvarnished truth about this matter were either dreamers or drunks. Who among our military authorities would admit that the nation's indecent treatment of the Negro soldier had rendered him unfit for combat with a foreign enemy? So following the traditional point of view, since this point of view led to the creation of the dilemma in the first place, the Negro soldier was promptly discredited. Not because he could not master the technique of modern weapons of war—this was the Secretary of War's claim—but because this is the logical stand that the traditional race haters were bound to use in defense of their hypocritical and infamous conduct. Talk about impeding the war effort! What *is* treason anyway?

Out on the Pacific Coast I found young Negroes holding key positions in the industries—the airplane industry to be exact—which produce the most difficult of weapons to master, the army bomber. Other young Negroes are now flying these planes. Still other young Negroes are now prepared to be their navigators. Now it is a commonly accepted fact among honest men and women that no racial group has cornered the market on either intelligence or native ability. This is what the celebrated pamphlet *The Races Of Mankind** would have told a few thousand army officers had it not been banned by stupid people who refuse to recognize the obvious. All Negro soldiers are not graduate engineers. Nor are all white soldiers. All Negro soldiers were not born in that section of the nation, which because it seeks to keep the Negro in the educational gutter, directs that white youth too must wallow in the pig sty of ignorance. But the Honorable Secretary of War has not claimed that white soldiers cannot master the techniques of modern weapons of war. His blanket statement about the Negro soldier's inability in this respect not only insults the thousands of intelligent Negro youth in our armed forces from all sections of the country, but by indirection it classifies them as morons incapable of attaining the intelligence level of the most ignorant southern cracker. What does the Negro soldier think about this? He considers it a vicious attack upon his manhood. And what is more he thinks that the Administration continues to insult him as long as such men are allowed to control his destiny in this war. The Negro soldier will not give his life for the perpetuation of this outright lynching of his ability, nor for the right of domestic nazis to make of him a military scapegoat.

Every factual pronouncement which falls from the lips of Anglo-Saxon war leaders in this conflict lays foundation for the Negro soldier's conviction that this is a war to maintain the white man's right to keep the colored man in social and economic bondage. The Negro soldier is not so dumb as far too many people in authority lead themselves to believe. He is asking a lot of questions. Does the Atlantic Charter apply to colored people now enslaved by the British, Dutch, Portuguese, and other imperialistic powers? Why is our ally Britain silent about the fate of Hong Kong and Singapore in the post-war world? Why are the great leaders of India, especially Nehru, kept in prison at the very moment when all India should be rallied against the Japanese invader? Why does our foreign policy fail to make clear America's stand in regard to spilling the blood of its sons to dictate the destiny of people who admittedly have a right to self-determina-

* By Gene Weltfish and Ruth Benedict (New York, 1943).

tion? But most important of all, the Negro soldier is asking how he can be expected to give his last full measure of devotion for his country when each day, while he wears the uniform of his country, he is insulted, humiliated, and even murdered for attempting to be an American?

My experience with Negro soldiers has led me to oppose the idea that the majority of them consider this a "race war." One must confess, however, that at times they are given strong evidence to the contrary. To say that all Negro soldiers share this or any one point of view is to engage in deliberate falsehood. Many of them think that this is a white man's war, "lock, stock, and barrel." This conclusion is reached in spite of Hitler's treatment of the people in the occupied countries and what the Chinese have suffered at the hands of the Japanese. Like countless thousands of whites this group has listened too intently to the expressed convictions of the "white supremacy boys." Responsibility for their conclusion can be traced to the ravings of such misrepresentatives of the nation as Bilbo, Rankin, "Cotton" Ed Smith and many others of the same litter. "But what about Russia?" you ask them. The immediate answer is that there are good betting odds that Russia will have to fight Britain and the United States before peace actually comes. This group knows too well that everyone willing to face reality knows —that there are far too many people in high places who love Russia less than they hate Nazi Germany. If Russia were not killing so many German soldiers and therefore the only hope at the moment for an Allied victory, the anti-Red voices in this country would be reaching a deafening crescendo. But Russia, these soldiers will tell you, is merely a tool to be used until it can be safely cast aside. Anglo-Saxon pride and a sense of imminent danger make strange bedfellows.

Much more strongly entrenched in the Negro soldier's thinking is the firm conviction that Soviet Russia's expulsion of the nazi race-haters from Russian soil and the herculean struggle of the Chinese people are evidence that something far more valuable than concepts of race is involved in this struggle. The freedom of millions of men and women, and countless generations which follow them, is involved . . . possibly his freedom too. The realization of this, however, does not lessen in any great degree his state of confusion and bewilderment. What man who has worn the shackles of slavery would not gladly strike a blow for freedom? The Negro soldier is prevented from striking that blow, at least with great enthusiasm, because freedom for his race during the past eighty years has not gibed with its definition in the dictionary. The march of daily events convinces the Negro soldier that his efforts in the struggle for freedom might well result in solidifying the control with which the South now directs and determines the national welfare and vigorously thwarts every effort of scientific progress in the field of human relations. A struggle for freedom which materialized in such a goal would not be worth a single drop of sweat . . . to say nothing about a single drop of blood. As a result the Negro soldier sees himself a miserable pawn in the inexorable hands of a fate which has already stacked the cards against him. He will fight if ordered in contact with the enemy. But this will be a fight for personal survival, a fight for his own life. His fight will hardly be characterized by that spark of enthusiasm which in war raises men to the heights of glory and heroism to which normally they would not dare aspire. Yet who knows but that the absence of this mysterious, though highly essential quality, in the Negro soldier may some day explain the difference between defeat and victory for a potentially great nation? The Negro soldier deplores the existence of such a probability.

One of the great soldiers which has emerged from this war is Lt. Col. Evans F. Carlson, famous for his development of that group of super-marine fighters known as *Carlson's Raiders.* This man not only built this extraordinary fighting outfit but led it in the Makin Island raid which resulted in complete destruction of all enemy military emplacements and annihilation of more than eight hundred Japanese soldiers which constituted the island garrison. Only eighteen of Carlson's Raiders lost their lives. Col. Carlson borrowed the fighting slogan, *Gung Ho,* from the Chinese Red Army with which he spent many months as a military observer. This experience convinced him that men, although they were hungry, nondescript, and poorly equipped could by living the full meaning of this slogan become unconquerable in the face of overwhelming odds. When he was called upon to train a group of American soldiers in the technique of guerilla warfare he not only made *Gung Ho* their battle cry but insisted that the deeper significance of this battle cry become the philosophy which undergirded every thought and action of every man. *Gung Ho* means: *Work Together . . .*

Work in Harmony.

The nation's utter lack of this essential spirit would seem to direct that it be made our national battle cry on both the military and home fronts. In fact *Gung Ho* could with great wisdom be extended to comprise the entire war effort of the United Nations. It would pay far greater dividends than the existing pattern of suspicion and dissension. Hats off then to a great soldier who was first a great man. The inspired feats of Carlson's Raiders have made military history, and with the passing of time will take on legendary dimensions. Said Col. Carlson: "My men, who are professionally competent, *know* why they are fighting."

The young Americans who followed this leader were not Negroes. How could they have been if honest answers were given to the following questions which Col. Carlson asked each man before accepting him: "Do you know why this war is being fought? What do you expect the world to be like after this war? Do you think the American dream of the post war world is worth suffering for as much as you will probably have to suffer?" Can't you hear the Negro soldier ask the Colonel: "Sir, are you all right?" The answer contained in this contemporary colloquialism would not be a flippant answer. Negro soldiers want to be heroes just like their white comrades; they want to distinguish themselves for the land they love. But most of all they want to be given the opportunity to become *real soldiers;* they want to be able to find clarity out of the maze of confusion and contradiction from which this love for country grows.

In spite of his frustration the Negro soldier sees a New World A-Coming. But he hasn't read about it in anybody's book. He sees its light beginning to break across the dark and distant horizon of time and events. It won't dawn tomorrow, nor on any tomorrow for a long time to come. This knowledge makes him sad. But that light has begun to shine, dimly 'tis true, and the darkness of man's inhumanity will not prevail against it because it is the light of determined millions of men and women marching toward freedom. That light is burning in the hearts of Russia's intrepid millions and brightens the path of the victorious Red Army. That light has provided the spark of warm hope which has kept the valiant millions of Chinese from capitulating to a superior military power. That light is slowly penetrating the darkness of India's miserable millions, causing an unmistakable urge toward freedom that will ultimately destroy all opposition.

That light now burning weakly will on some not too far distant tomorrow burst into a consuming flame in the hearts of more than a billion darker people. Thus will be created a power for good so intense in our rapidly shrinking world that human debasement can no longer exist anywhere. The Negro soldier sees this light and it quickens his pulse . . . yes, in spite of little minds now wielding big clubs trying to hold back the dawn.

The Negro soldier thinks . . . !

II

The War Department has sold the Negro soldier a rotten bill of goods. The Negro soldier not only resents its putrid odor but equally resents being made the victim of what many soldiers consider a foul and debasing trick. This great war brain should have as its primary objective the winning of this costly war as soon as possible and with the least possible loss of life. In pursuit of this objective the War Department should declare traitor every human being who by direction or indirection prolongs this war a single day. I further suggest that such treason be dealt with by the firing squad. But if the tree itself is rotten it can hardly be expected to bear good fruit. The Negro soldier thinks the War Department itself is prolonging this war and he is convinced by multitudinous evidence that he is right.

In the first instance he observes his daily treatment which is both lamentable on the one hand and unsupported by decency on the other. Having a record of loyalty and devotion to the nation that is unequaled as well as unquestioned, he sees the War Department destroy his love for his country by making him a military "untouchable." All other American citizens, irrespective of racial origin, serve in American units—all except the Negro. He serves in a jim crow unit, separated from other Americans, giving stark evidence each day of the War Department's unqualified disrespect for his status as an American citizen. In this sorry situation the Negro soldier has witnessed the most foolish and tragic game ever played by a so-called enlightened people. In this game of homo sapiens' folly multitudes of human beings lose their lives each day. This is especially true as Allied forces now approach the German border. The game, as you might have guessed, is war. The goal, as far as we are concerned, is civilization itself. Yet each day the War Department by its stupid refusal to recognize ability and merit, when these qualities are not inclosed in a white skin, flirts dangerously with doom as it renders ten percent of its soldiers incapable of doing their best. Civilization therefore becomes secondary to the preservation of the very corruption which will eventually destroy it.

The Constitution and its accompanying Bill of Rights have been literally torn up and the bits insultingly thrown into the Negro soldier's face. Yet these sons of American mothers are expected to die and are dying in the face of such indignity. It is a widely known fact that Nazi prisoners of war receive better treatment in this country than do hundreds of thousands of Negro soldiers. Stripped of his constitutional rights, bereft of any particular concern for his welfare, denied the right to die honorably in his country's crusade, subjected each day to conditions which contradict every claim of democratic principle, the Negro soldier has been betrayed by the very agency which controls his destiny —the War Department. As it prepares him for death on the foreign battlefields of the world, and actually sends him to his death, it winks at conditions which torture him physically and which mob and lynch his spirit. Under these conditions the War Department sends the sons of American mothers into battle ill-prepared indeed. It is small wonder that among many Negro soldiers, there is the feeling that the War Department itself is helping to destroy their lives.

"Chaplain, how can we get a decent break in this war when our bitterest enemies are running the show?" Such was the question put to me by a group of Negro soldiers who followed me to my office one Sunday morning after my sermon.

"What do you mean by such a statement?" I asked.

"Well, just take a look at the military big shots. Practically every one of them comes from the south. In fact the Army and Navy are lousy with southerners and their leaders give us reason to believe that they would rather lose this war than see us have equality. And judging from the way these cracker officers treat us, they're not fooling either. Now, sir, can you say that these people are not our enemies?"

I found words difficult as I stuttered and sputtered in an effort to provide the right answer. Before I could do so another soldier opened up with still another broadside. Declared he: "The War Department is running a plantation as far as Negroes are concerned. Just look at this post. The commanding officer by his disregard for us soldiers is an excellent example of a plantation boss. And don't forget, he's a 'red-neck' from Tennessee. That's bad enough, but anyone who is not blind will immediately recognize how subordinate every Negro must be in order to stay here. It makes me sick!"

"Listen, fellows," I said, "don't let such things get you down. And if I were you I would be more careful about expressing such thoughts."

Immediately one of them spoke up: "Chaplain, you haven't turned 'long-coat,' have you?"

There was a dreadful silence as each man glued his eyes upon my face. "Now, what do you think?" I replied. After a pause the expressions of wounded suspicion left their faces. I, too, felt relieved.

"Run along now, fellows, it's near chow time and I've got some work to do. I'll expect you at the evening service."

The work I had to do was not nearly so important as my desire to be alone with my thoughts. Here was a group of ordinary American Negro soldiers, intelligent but not a college graduate in the group. Yet each man gave unmistakable evidence that he knew the score. I knew how one such man in a barracks was enough to evangelize all others even if they had not given serious thought to such matters. As I sat and gave thought to their statements I became disturbed. I knew they were right and they knew it too. Another disturbing factor was how narrowly I had escaped losing status by merely suggesting a contrary point of view or even demonstrating displeasure with such conversation.

The statement charging the War Department with running a plantation returned to my mind. I began to make mental notes about the Negro's treatment on that particular post. I thought about how rigidly the doctrine of white supremacy was upheld there, making itself manifest in the jim crow school system and in the post commander's refusal to place a white officer in any position where he might be subordinate to a Negro officer. In fact a bulletin was published on one occasion by this post commander declaring that a white officer in the grade of 1st Lt. would be superior to a colored officer in the same department who had the rank of captain. The white officers on the post who were numerically inferior to Negro officers, could find comfort from the Arizona heat by cavorting in a beautiful swimming pool. Moreover, their families, as well as the poor white civilian trash that worked on the post, could enjoy this luxury. But Negroes, regardless of their educational background or their outstanding achievements in the professions, could do no more than pass by and see the white folks enjoy themselves. These were but a few among the many features of the operation of this post which gave credence to the soldier's claim.

One more illustration, however, will suffice. One of the bulwarks of the plantation system was the belief that Negroes were a happy and simple group of children. These light-hearted people therefore were deserving of special understanding as well as special treatment. They must be given adequate opportunity to dance and sing and, of course, to indulge occasionally in an overdose of religion. Any outburst among them, regardless of its nature, was attributed to the emotional instability of the group and was therefore classified as hoodlumism. On one occasion I had made myself *persona non grata* with the commanding officer of this post when I refused to accept this explanation as the reason for the stoning by colored soldiers of an automobile carrying high military officials. He had just made a speech to an assemblage of the post chaplains, directing that we use extreme care in listening to soldiers who complained about having been abused by their officers. I told the officer about the case of Pvt. Tommie Thompson, who died before he could learn to shoot a gun, because I had been unable to convince his white company commander at another post that the man was sick. Tommie, supported by two soldiers, was sent to my office because he was thought to be "gold-bricking." After a brief talk with him I was convinced that he was a sick man in spite of the fact that he had just been discharged from the hospital. I therefore called the company commander by telephone and recommended that the soldier be sent back to the hospital at once. But, following the prevailing attitude too frequently found among white officers that all Negro soldiers are lazy, this company commander sent Tommie away that night on a troop convoy. When the train, carrying him to Fort Leonard Wood, Missouri, reached its destination Tommie Thompson was dead. I tried to describe how this experience had seared itself upon my consciousness and how I had promised my Creator that in the future I would listen to every story a man had to tell me. And what was more, if upon investigation the story was found to be true, I intended to press for punishment of the officer concerned.

Vainly I attempted to reveal how resentful Negro soldiers were about their treatment and to point out the danger of misleading himself by contributing all acts of violence to hoodlumism. I further suggested that as long as the cause of such unrest prevailed, it constituted a daily threat to those guilty of its perpetration. I was promptly admonished with the kind of tongue lashing a Tennessee cracker can so adeptly dispense. In other words, I was wrong, and what was more, my attitude was detrimental to the best functioning of that post. Not long afterwards, however, a white officer was taken to the hospital beaten almost to jelly. Some "hoodlums," who grew tired of his abuse, crept into his tent one night with the avowed intention of murdering him. They almost did, although 'tis said they got into this man's tent by mistake. The object of their wrath, according to the grapevine, was their company commander.

The Negro soldier charges that the War Department destroys his morale each day as it maintains southern white officers in control of his destiny, many of whom admittedly declare that the Negro soldier has no place in the Army at all. Apart from thus insulting him, many of these Negroes now find themselves embarrassed by intraracial conflict incited by such officers. In this respect southern Negroes, many of whom accept silently jim crow conditions in the Army similar to those they have known in civilian life, are given preferential treatment over northern Negroes who resent this treatment and speak out against it, and this preference with no regard for other qualifications, such as educational background and technical training. White soldiers from the North will testify that they, too, have suffered from this despicable policy.

Under such officers the Negro has seen officers of his own color held up to shame and ridicule and in many instances unjustifiably persecuted. He has seen the positions of command in the various companies of his regiment so shuffled about that Negro officers were not only denied positions commensurate with their training and ability but were handicapped by lack of opportunity for promotion to the next higher grade. In this respect Negro soldiers read with great interest the following statement made by the Archbishop of York as he spoke to the students of Union Theological Seminary: "There is nothing more disheartening for a man than to find no one wants to use his talents. It breaks him in spirit and engenders bitterness in him."

Historians of the future when writing the history of this war will undoubtedly include the great sociological changes which took place. Much of these phenomena will be the result of direct War Department initiation. In this respect it will be seen how the entire educational system of the United States has been revolutionized to meet the immediate military needs. Further, the War Department has not only built and manned numerous technical schools but has instituted courses in now-existing schools taught by its officers and instructors in which the course of study has been accelerated to an extent hitherto unknown. This has resulted in the development of new skills for thousands of men which points to an incalculable influence on post-war employment. Vast population changes will have resulted not only from the deployment of soldiers into many sections of the nation hitherto unfamiliar to them, but from the creation of the incentive whereby thousands of women and children have followed these men. Scores of such families will never return to their native communities and will thus influence by virtue of their regional culture whatever area they settle.

Millions of American soldiers will have been trained in the geography, customs and psychology of vast numbers of peoples of whom they previously had no knowledge. They have been taught to respect methods of activity which in comparison to their own cultural background seemed altogether strange or even ludicrous. The provincialism of untold millions will have been changed because of the vast geographical nature of the military undertaking. And also the very nature of war itself induces within men a restlessness and dissatisfaction which leads to serious changes in their modes of behavior and which in themselves make serious inroads into previously existing community patterns.

Thus when War Department spokesmen plead their inability to change contemporary practices in such instances as the creation of a mixed division, the very facts themselves deny the validity of their claims. When they state that the War Department is not "running a sociological laboratory" the Negro takes such an excuse for the continuation of military segregation as so much poppycock. And if War Department officials are stupid enough to make such an excuse for their un-American behavior, the Negro soldier is not stupid enough to believe them.

One of the pillars of democratic government is the fair administration of courts of justice. Without fair judicial procedure the democratic principle of equality before the law becomes a farce. Too often military justice as it has affected the Negro in this war has shown the same color prejudice which characterizes the behavior of the degenerate group of American demagogues who have been bred south of the Mason-Dixon Line. The Negro soldier is no more of a saint or a sinner than the white soldier. Members of both groups will at times behave in a manner which is condemned by military regulations, thereby creating the necessity for trial and punishment. This is an accepted characteristic of any community organization and administration. In all fairness it must be said that these military courts are usually found to be of greater efficiency and dispatch than corresponding civilian courts. Personally, all things being equal, I should prefer trial by military court if I were innocent and trial by civilian court if I were guilty. However, the treatment accorded too many Negroes in this respect holds up to mockery and shame the ideal of judicial behavior. Too often these courts, which correspond somewhat to civilian juries, are comprised of prejudiced officers with preconceived notions of the guilt of Negro defendants, which outweigh any testimony to the contrary. The Negro soldier considers such maladministration of justice a direct reflection of War Department policy, and implores the conscience of the nation that such utter disregard for his welfare be immediately investigated and proper corrective measures instituted.

The Negro soldier holds the War Department responsible for the daily un-American treatment he receives in the surrounding villages of most Army camps. Any agency which can completely uproot an entire racial group and place it in concentration camps but which cannot insure him elementary protection well deserves his condemnation. Negro soldiers know that these conditions could be changed by a simple order from the post commander. Such an order placing communities guilty of abusing American soldiers off-limits would immediately engage the local chambers of commerce and merchants associations in a crusade for better treatment of these soldiers. Why then, the Negro soldier asks himself, has not the War Department sent out such an order to its post commanders? Is it part of War Department policy to perpetuate these insulting conditions?

Colored soldiers are being trained each day to the latest and most diabolical techniques of destroying life that the mind of man can evolve. He not only learns to kill with the rifle, the hand grenade and the bayonet, but with his bare hands is taught to mutilate and dismember the body of an enemy. The War Department thus is making deadly killers of Sam Jackson and Henry Jones and the nice boy who once lived in the next block.

When these men return from participating in the global struggle they will have paid the price of freedom and decency. If they are denied these privileges guaranteed all American citizens and if such denial prompts them to engage in bloody conflict, much of the responsibility must be laid at the very door of the War Department.

III

The War Department has at long last done something which will bring joy to the hearts of Negro soldiers. It has announced that it is discontinuing its *"Foreign Legion"* outpost, Fort Huachuca, Arizona. Thousands of our colored fighting men in all theatres of combat will say when this news reaches them: "Well, it's about time."

These men will remember how the War Department not only isolated them in the middle of a desert thirty-four miles from the nearest railroad junction, but placed their destiny in the hands of an unreconstructed southerner from Tennessee as Post Commander. They will remember how devotedly homage was paid to the sacred cow of race prejudice on a post which was referred to as "The Home of the Negro Soldier." In this respect those who had children out there will remember how their children were insulted and humiliated by the Jim-Crow school system which was maintained on this United States Army military reservation. Children of Negro and Indian parentage (these

Indians representing the last of the old Apache Scouts of the U.S. Army) were directed to the "colored school." On the other hand "white" Mexicans (white in this instance referring not to the color of skin, but rather to the absence of Negro blood), Chinese and Caucasians attended the "white school." A Mexican widow with children who by chance married a Negro soldier would thereby be forced to send her children to the "colored school."

Still others will remember, and this is especially true in the case of a Negro chaplain of my acquaintance, how a white officer drove a Negro officer and his wife from a table in the only restaurant on the post which was supposed to cater to all races alike. Interestingly, but nonetheless unforgivable, the restaurant was operated by a Chinese.

Burned indelibly into the minds of thousands of Negro soldiers will forever remain the insult which was manifested in the "protection" given white girls on the post. An electrified barbed wire fence surrounded their dormitory, but no such "protective device" was provided for the colored girls who lived on the same post.

Negro soldiers will never forget the famous "Hook," and thousands of decent men will never forgive the War Department for allowing its existence. This little disease-infested area lay just south of the main entrance to the fort. Comprised of ramshackle huts, tents, and vermin-infested adobe structures, this disgraceful community did a thriving though deadly business in prostitution. Electric lights, pavement, running water, or any other signs of sanitation were entirely unknown. Yet this pest-hole of venereal disease was allowed to flourish at the very front door of the "Home for the Negro Soldier."

Due to his deplorable environmental conditions the Negro, more than any other segment of the American population, has suffered from the ravages of social diseases. The War Department has gone to great expense and considerable effort to protect its soldiers from this deadly killer. There was a time when Fort Huachuca apparently did not come within the purview of this program.

Any calculation of the cost in terms of treatment and training hours lost due to the prevalence of venereal disease at Fort Huachuca must have reached a staggering figure. Add to this the psychological cost in terms of employment for Negroes and the total becomes incalculable.

While I was stationed at this fort I did not fail to give full expression of my disgust with the Post authorities for allowing this place to operate. In my sex morality lectures I not only painted the "Hook" as an insult to the decency of colored soldiers and a threat to their physical well-being, but did not fail to contend that it could not have existed adjacent to any other post in the nation. I have a strong feeling that my crusade did little to win for me the esteem of my superiors. After having served in a southern army camp and having been literally driven out I was used to being held in the contempt of those who mistreated Negro soldiers. When I was finally driven from this post my wife was told that if I had kept my mouth shut I could have remained there for the duration. Could this have had reference to my crusade against the "Hook"? I wonder. On the other hand the answer to my question might be found in a statement which was directed at me by one of the white chaplains when he rebuked me saying: "You are too enthused over the solution of the race problem on this post." Now, I ask you!

Negro soldiers who were inhabitants (prisoners would perhaps be a more descriptive word) of this post will never forget the makeshift type of entertainment which was provided for them. The army has gone to greater lengths in this war than in any other to build good morale. Millions of dollars have been spent in providing American soldiers with good entertainment. In this respect I hasten to add that I do not share the belief of those who state that the American soldier has thus been coddled. I think that our soldiers of all races are entitled to all the entertainment they have received and more.

To accomplish this purpose big advertisers have helped both the men and themselves by making available the various radio shows which delight the American radio public. So profitable to morale have such shows as Bob Hope, Eddie Cantor, Red Skelton and others been that they have played the same military camps on several occasions. Nor has the best that radio, Hollywood, and the legitimate stage have to offer been restricted to men training in this country. Luminaries of the entertainment world have carried their specialties to the far-flung battlefields of the world in an effort to keep the American soldier "on the beam." That this has been an heroic undertaking no one will doubt.

With this excellent record as a background it is interesting to observe what happened at Fort Huachuca. The list of entertainment features offered for the enjoyment of the Negro soldier is conspicuous by the absence of any such talent as I have just described. The one exception to this, and upon which hangs the supposed reason why white troupes of entertainers passed Fort Huachuca by, was the visit of a Hollywood blonde and a white comedian. It was dubiously claimed that on this occasion an attempt was made to molest the blonde. It was also admitted that no one ever saw the supposed prowler and therefore his identity will forever remain a mystery. It was immediately assumed, however, that a Negro soldier was responsible for the disturbance. Her partner in giving account of what happened suggested that perhaps no· one molested her and that the incident was undoubtedly the result of a figment of her imagination since she was possessed of an unstable and highly emotional personality.

Regardless of what happened in the above mentioned situation it cast poor reflection upon the post authorities and the entertainment world for thus penalizing Negro soldiers. It must be said in the interest of the performers, however, that they could not force themselves upon the military authorities. The War Department then must assume the responsibility.

Negro performers alone were permitted to entertain at Huachuca. Such stars as Lena Horne, Rochester, and Hattie McDaniel gained entrance to the desert outpost. Special praise is due Miss Horne for the many visits she made and for giving generously of her best in the interest in the morale of the men of her race. Under these circumstances it is entirely fitting and proper that she was crowned "queen of the 92nd Division."

There are scores of other reasons why Negro soldiers will rejoice over the announced closing of Ft. Huachuca. They will hardly shed a tear over its demise nor offer a prayer for its resurrection. In fact their joy can be measured in the same degree as their disappointment over the recovery of Senator Bilbo from his recent operation.

Headlines in the press a few days ago carried news of a clash between Negro soldiers and Italian war prisoners. In the melee it was reported that several of the prisoners were severely hurt and one was found hanging from a tree. The locale of this unfortunate incident was the state of Washington in the far Northwest. A few days later the headlines again informed the nation of still another revolt among Negro service men. At Mare Island, California, Negro sailors refused to load and unload high explosives and a mass court martial was conducted during which fifty of their number were tried for mutiny. About the same time news from reliable sources revealed that Negro casuals at Camp Gordon Johnston, Florida, had refused to obey orders and faced punitive military action. Add to this the uprising at Camp Claiborne, Louisiana, in which a Negro soldier was killed and a white officer badly wounded and we get still another example of the thought patterns of Negro soldiers during this war.

To an observer unacquainted with the inhuman treatment so often accorded Negro soldiers such news comes not only as a shock but suggests that Negro soldiers are letting their country down. On the contrary, it is the country that has let the Negro soldier down. To prove this let us look behind the scenes and discover the reasons for this strange conduct.

In the state of Washington, far removed from the traditional race bitterness so characteristic of the South, one hardly expects to hear that Negro soldiers, during a period of war have thus jeopardized their very lives. Unfortunately the United States army has carried southern racial hatred and backwardness wherever it has gone. George Goodman, writing in the Fall number of *Common Ground,* describes the result of this viciousness. Englishmen were actually told that Negro soldiers possessed long tails. The English families were therefore warned that if these men sat on hard-bottom chairs it would irritate their curious appendage to such a degree that they would be driven into a state of rage. The intent of spreading such malicious and damaging falsehoods was to drive a wedge between the English people and the very American soldiers who came to defend them and their homeland. This explains how the army has spread the infection of color prejudice throughout the bloodstream of both the nation and the world.

Within the broad ramifications of such evil lies the reason for the clash at Walla Walla, Washington. Negro soldiers had put up with humiliation and abuse to the extent that their patience reached the breaking point. They could no longer endure seeing prisoners of war, many of whom had possibly killed their comrades on foreign battlefields, enjoy in this country the very facilities which they were denied. It is inconceivable that Negro soldiers under normal circumstances would develop anti-Italian sentiments. One must therefore place credence in the report that the Negro soldiers involved in the clash did so only because in their opinion it was the only way to focus American public opinion upon their unhappy plight.

This explanation, however plausible, cannot be accepted as justification for mob action. Moreover, the Negro who has been traditionally the American victim of such brutality can ill-afford to embrace it as a means of assuaging his bitterness. America would do well, however, to interpret this deplorable situation in the light of what it portends for the future. Negro soldiers are reaching a state of desperation. They will hardly accept their former status of second class citizenship when they are returned to civilian life.

The case involving the refusal of Negro sailors to load and unload high explosives is also worth examining. While the general reasons for this mutinous conduct lie in the traditional Navy policy of relegating Negro sailors to the insulting categories of menial service there is a specific reason in this case which becomes understandable to those who have a trace of human sympathy and understanding. Many of these men had been among the survivors of the Port Chicago tragedy during which more than two hundred of their comrades had been blown to bits in an explosion. They had gathered up the fragments of the mutilated bodies of their former buddies. The psychological strain produced thereby, aggravated by the general resentment they have built up against the Navy for the way they have been treated, must be considered in passing judgment upon such men. To expect this is to expect the inconceivable. The American military establishment has long since demonstrated that it is totally lacking in both decency and conscience where the Negro service man is concerned. The traditional beast of burden has no right to complain. When he does the whip and the lash are applied and the white military mind finds justification for its application.

United States Navy policy, in spite of the spasmodic commissioning of a handful of Negro ensigns, is far more vicious than that of the army, if that is possible. The navy has never established a Negro civilian aide to whom Negroes could carry their grievances. (There are many Negroes who think that they suffer no loss if the establishment of such a position would be as innocuous as that of the civilian aide to the Secretary of War.) This does serve to convince Negro mothers and fathers that the navy gives not a tinkers dam about the just grievances of their sons in uniform. These men have been rendered psychologically unfit to give their best service to their country. When the immortal Shakespeare wrote: "The fault, Dear Brutus, is not in our stars that we are underlings, but in ourselves" he most certainly did not contemplate the application of the same to Negro sailors. The gods of justice might better be served if those responsible for the miserable plight of the Mare Island mutineers were tried in mass court martial instead of the innocent victims of their despicable policies.

The Florida Soldiers

At Camp Gordon Johnston, Florida, where Negro soldiers refused to obey military orders, they were faced with conditions that must shock the sensibilities of the most callous. White soldiers training on this primitive reservation, which was without modern facilities for waste disposal it is said, could not be induced to work the "sugar detail" in spite of the added remuneration of three ($3) dollars per day in addition to their regular monthly pay. On the same post, it was reported, there were resident large numbers of war prisoners. There is no way of knowing whether these former killers of American soldiers were ordered to work the infamous "sugar detail" or not. Negro soldiers, however, many of whom were casuals (men declared physically and mentally unfit for regular military duty) were ordered to work the aforementioned detail as a matter of routine. Because they expressed resentment for such a filthy assignment they were brought face to face with the dire consequences inherent in disobedience to military orders. For the enlightenment of the uninitiated the term "sugar detail" refers to the assignment of soldiers to dispose of ten (10) gallon cans of human body waste.

I must repeat again, in order to free myself of any charge of encouraging poor discipline among Negro soldiers still in the army, that this does not imply any attitude on my part to condone or encourage any actual or contemplated refusal on the part of Negro service men to obey given military commands. However, Almighty God himself must look with pity upon American soldiers receiving such treatment from the nation they stand ready to defend with their lives. God, if He is just, must also look with wrathful indignation upon the perpetrators of such indecencies who visit their beastly debasement upon His children simply because in His wisdom He chose to give them dark skins. That American soldiers, many of whom are paying with their lives for the fundamental concepts of simple fair play, should be thus dehumanized must come as a shock to the conscience of humanity.

Let us assume that you are a colored service man and that you were faced with any of the aforementioned insults. If after your white commanding officer had in a lecture declared that he was going to see to it that Negro soldiers suffered their full share of casualties in this war, what would be your attitude? If after you had been abused and insulted and then expected to demonstrate a high degree of *esprit de corps* and you found that you were incapable of being a super man, what would be your state of mind?

The Crisis, September, October, November, 1944; LI, 289–91, 299, 316–18, 328, 352–53, 357.

93

THE NEGRO SOLDIER

by Charles H. Houston

Under the auspices of *The Nation,* a "Conference on America's Opportunity to Create and Maintain Lasting Peace" was held in New York City, October 7–8, 1944. A sixteen-page supplement to the magazine's issue of October 21 carried excerpts from the main speeches; one was that which follows, by the distinguished attorney who at this time was a member of the President's Committee on Fair Employment Practice. *The Nation* promised that the full text of Mr. Houston's speech "will be printed in a future issue," but this was not done.

I want to speak particularly on the subject of the armed forces. Here, after nearly three years of war, Negroes are still insulted by the Navy's barring all Negro women, except those now passing for white, from the Waves, the Marines, and the Spars. We have officers in the Army and the Navy; but there is still not a single Negro lieutenant in the United States Marines. The Army puts Negroes in uniform, transports them South and then leaves them to be kicked, cuffed and even murdered with impunity by white civilians. In places, Negro service men do not have as many civil rights as prisoners of war. In at least one Army camp down South for a time there was one drinking fountain for white guards and German prisoners, and a segregated fountain for Negro soldiers. And Negroes know that just as soon as the shooting stops many Americans will give the same Germans, Austrians, Italians, Rumanians and others who were trying to kill them preference over Negroes who were defending them, simply because these Germans and others are white.

Many white service men are talking about what they are going to do to put the Negro in his place as soon as they get back home. Many Negroes are getting to the point of disgust and desperation where they had just as soon die fighting one place as another. Meanwhile enemy propaganda is carrying the stories of racial dissension in the United States to all corners of the earth, and the colored peoples of Asia, Africa and India are getting an eyeful of how white Americans act abroad.

I advocate immediate enlistment of Negro women as Waves, Spars and Marines; assignment and promotion of Negroes in all the armed forces strictly according to service, experience and merit; and the organization of non-segregated combat units on a volunteer basis. The administration of the G.I. Bill of Rights and all other veteran rehabilitation programs must be administered impartially with absolutely no discrimination.

The American color bar unless speedily removed will be the rock on which our international Good Neighbor policy and our pious claim to moral leadership will founder. The moment the peoples of Asia, Africa and India become convinced that our true war aims are to perpetuate the old colonial system with the white man's heel on the colored man's neck, and that we are fighting Japan merely to substitute European imperialism in place of Japanese imperialism—that moment we might as well begin preparing for World War III, and World War III will not necessarily be to America's advantage. The Negro problem gives the United States the opportunity to practice what it preaches, and it is time the country awakens to the fact it is guaranteeing its own salvation by making a substantial down payment on the Four Freedoms at home.

The Nation, October 21, 1944; CLIX, 496–97.

94

A BLUEPRINT FOR
FIRST CLASS CITIZENSHIP

by Pauli Murray

While it is widely affirmed and believed that "sit-downs" made their appearance in the anti-racist battle only in the nineteen-sixties, a then recent graduate from Howard University tells of similar activities in which she and other Black students participated in the early nineteen-forties.

Howard University traditionally has been called the "Capstone of Negro Education." When 2,000 young Americans, fresh from 45 states and students from 24 foreign countries arrived there two years ago, their futures uncertain, their draft numbers coming up every day, and their campus surrounded by the dankest kind of degradation they were tempted to call their alma mater the "keptstone" of education. More than half of these students had come from northern or border states or western and middle-western communities. Many of them had never tasted the bitter fruits of jim crow. They were of a generation who tended to think for themselves as Americans without a hyphen.

Thrown rudely into the nation's capital where jim crow rides the American Eagle, if indeed he does not put the poor symbol to flight, these students were psychologically and emotionally unprepared for the insults and indignities visited upon them when they left the campus and went downtown to see the first-run shows, or stopped in a café to get a hotdog and a "coke." The will to be free is strong in the young, and their sensitive souls recoiled with a violence that reverberated throughout the war time campus.

The revolt against jim crow started with a mutter and a rumble. It was loudest in the Law School where men students, unprotected by any kind of deferment, were being yanked out of their classes and into a G.I. uniform. "I don't want to fight in a jim crow army." "I'd rather die first!" "I'll go to jail first." were some of the remarks daily. During the first tense days of war time conscription, classes were almost entirely disrupted by the feeling of futility and frustration that settled over these young men.

And then the spirit of revolt took shape. It started in the fall of 1942 with the refusal of Lewis Jones, Morehouse graduate, to be inducted into a jim crow army and the editorial comment of John P. Lewis of *PM* on Lewis' stand. Stung into action, a letter signed by 40 Howard University students, supporting the spirit which led Lewis to take such action, was sent to editor Lewis. He did not print the letter although he wrote the students a courteous reply.

In January, 1943 three women students were arrested in downtown Washington for the simple act of refusing to pay an overcharge for three hot chocolates in a United Cigar store on Pennsylvania avenue. The young women sat down at the counter and ordered hot chocolates. The waitress refused to serve them at first and they asked for the manager. They were told the manager was out, and they replied they would wait, keeping their seats at the counter. After hurried legal consultation the "management" ordered the waitress to serve them, but upon looking at their checks they were charged twenty-five cents each instead of the standard dime charged for a packaged hot drink. The young women laid thirty-five cents on the counter and started for the door where they were met by a half dozen policemen, hauled off to a street corner, held until the arrival of a Black Maria, and landed in prison in a cell with prostitutes and other criminal suspects. It was not until they were searched and scared almost out of their wits that the dean of women at Howard University was notified and they were dismissed in her care without any charges lodged against them.

The flood of resentment against the whole system of segregation broke loose. Conservative administration members frowned upon this "incident" and advised the three young women they should not stage individual demonstrations against jim crow. It was suggested they should work through an organization concerned with such matters.

These young women of Howard were determined. Others joined them. They took the matter to the student chapter of the N.A.A.C.P. In the meantime from the Law School issued a new trend of thought. The men had spent hours in their "bull sessions" discussing attack and counter-attack upon jim crow. One second-year student, a North Carolinian and former leader in N.A.A.C.P., William Raines, had agitated for months for what he called "the stool-sitting technique." "If the white people want to deny us service, let them pay for it," Raines said. "Let's go downtown some lunch hour when they're crowded. They're open to the public. We'll take a seat on a lunch stool, and if they don't serve us, we'll just sit there and read our books. They lose trade while that seat is out of circulation. If enough people occupy seats, they'll lose so much trade, they'll start thinking."

While Raines was arguing another student, Ruth Powell, from Boston, Mass., later chairman of the dynamic Civil Rights Committee, was doing just this. She would sit for hours and stare at the waitress who had refused her service. She reported it disconcerted the management and sometimes she might even be served.

When this point of view percolated the campus, the students went into action. Raines went into the army but his idea went on. A temporary Student Committee on Campus Opinion was formed. A questionnaire was distributed throughout the campus on February 3, 1943 testing student and faculty reactions to an active campaign against segregation in Washington, D.C.

292 students answered the questionnaire. 284 or 97.3% of those said they did not believe Negroes should suspend the struggle for equal rights until the end of the war. 256, or 97% of those answering this question said they believed Negro students should actively participate in the struggle for equality during war time. 218 said they would actively join a campaign to break down segregation in Washington; 38 indicated they would not join but would support others who did. Only 6 disapproved of the idea.

A Civil Rights Committee was formed in March under the sponsorship of the Howard Chapter, N.A.A.C.P. The students unearthed an "Equal Rights Bill for the District of Columbia, No. 1995," introduced by Congressman Rowan of Illinois and a companion bill introduced in the Senate by the late Senator Barbour from New Jersey.

The Civil Rights Committee undertook a campaign to bring equal accommodations to the District of Columbia. They set up five sub-committees, publicity and speakers' bureau, program and legislative, committee on correspondence, finance, and direct action. They lobbed in groups with the representatives and senators from their states. They made ingenious little collection cans out of hot chocolate cups and collected pennies from their classmates to pay for paper and postage. They held pep rallies around campus and broadcast their campaign from the tower of Founders Library. They sponsored a Town Hall Meeting at Douglass Hall and brought in community speakers to lead a discussion on "Civil Rights" and the techniques by which they were to be attained.

Their most interesting project, and the one to draw the most fire, was the Direct Action sub-committee. There the "stool sitting" idea combined with the "sit-it-out-in-your-most-dignified-bib-and-tucker" idea to make a fundamental thrust at the heart of jim crow.

A committee of students surveyed the accommodations of the immediate Negro community on northwest U Street. They reported four stores which still excluded Negroes and catered to "White Trade Only." One of these cafés, the Little Palace Cafeteria, run by a Greek-American, was located at 14th and U Streets, N.W., in the heart of the Negro section, and the stories told by Negroes of their embarrassment and mortification in this cafeteria were legion.

The direct action sub-committee spent a week studying the disorderly conduct and picketing laws of D.C. They spent hours threshing out the pros and cons of public conduct, anticipating and preparing for the reactions of the white public, the Negro public, white customers and the management. They pledged themselves to exemplary behavior, no matter what the provocation. And one rainy Saturday afternoon in April, they started out. In groups of four, with one student acting as an "observer" on the outside, they approached the café. Three went inside and requested service. Upon refusal they took their seats and pulled out magazines, books of poetry, or pencils and pads. They sat quietly. Neither the manager's panicky efforts to dismiss them nor the presence of a half dozen policemen outside could dislodge them. Five minutes later another group of three would enter. This pilgrimage continued until the Little Cafeteria was more than half-filled with staring students on the inside, and a staring public grouped in the street. In forty-five minutes the management had closed the cafeteria. The students took up their vigil outside the restaurant with attractive and provocative picket signs, "There's No Segregation Law in D.C.—What's Your Story Little Palace?" "We die together—Why Can't We Eat Together?" and so on. The picketing continued on Monday morning when the restaurant reopened its doors. The students had arranged a picketing schedule and gave their free hours to the picket line. In two days the management capitulated and changed its policy.

In the spring of 1944, the Civil Rights Committee decided to carry the fight downtown into the heart of Washington. They selected a Thompson's cafeteria at 14th and Pennsylvania in the shadow of the White House. They took off a Saturday afternoon, dressed in their best, and strolled into Thompsons in two's and three's at intervals of ten minutes. They threw up a small picket line outside. Three white sympathizers polled the customers inside and found that only 3 out of 10 expressed objection to their being served. They scrupulously observed the picketing laws, and neither the jeers of undisciplined white members of the Armed Forces, nor cheers of W.A.C.s, W.A.V.E.s and other sympathetic members of the public brought any outward response. When 55 of them, including 6 Negro members of the Armed Forces, had taken seats at the tables, and the Thompson's trade had dropped 50 percent in four hours, the management, after frantic calls to its main office in Chicago, was ordered to serve them.

Before the Civil Rights Committee was able to negotiate with the local management of Thompson's with reference to a changed policy, the Howard University Administration, through the office of Dr. Mordecai W. Johnson, requested them to suspend their activities until there was a clarification of Administration policy. A hurried meeting of the Deans and Administrators was called and a directive issued requesting the students to cease all activities "designed to accomplish social reform affecting institutions other than Howard University itself."

The students were quick to take up this challenge. They then directed their efforts at "social reform" toward the Administration itself. They had already requested a discussion with representatives of the faculty and administration. They indicated their unwillingness to give up their direct action program, and appealed the ruling of the Administration to the Board of Directors which meets in October, 1944.

Out of the struggle, however, issued a new level of student responsibility and interest in campus affairs. The students did not win their total battle against Thompson's, but they achieved a moral victory for student-administration-faculty relationships. They learned interesting things about their University—for example, that 60 percent of its income is a grant from the Federal Government, that 22 percent comes from student fees and that 13 percent comes from campus enterprises, and that only 9 percent comes from gifts other than governmental aid. They learned that the enemies of Howard University in Congress seek to destroy it every time the voting of appropriations arrives. They also learned that Howard University is a beacon light to the Negro community and a significant contribution to the total community, and that everything done there is watched with intense interest. A Student-Faculty-Administration Committee has been set up to make recommendations on student affairs.

The question remains to be settled during the coming months whether Howard students shall participate in social action directed against the second-class citizenship to which they have been victimized. There are those who believe the energy and the dynamics of social change must originate in democratic institutions which form test-tubes of democracy and that there must be a realistic relation of one's activities in the community to one's studies in the classroom. There are others who believe that education is a static affair and must not be related to the community at large. Between these two points of view Howard University must make a choice.

But whatever the final outcome, Howard may be proud of those students who have led the way toward new, and perhaps successful techniques to achieve first class citizenship in one area of life in these United States.

The Crisis, November, 1944; LI, 358–59.

95

AN INDEPENDENT PARTY

by A. Philip Randolph

The idea of a mass political breakaway from the two dominant political parties in the United States is at least one hundred years old, and was widely discussed during the closing months of World War II. A characteristic expression of it comes from the Socialist, A. Philip Randolph, in an article appearing in a magazine whose policy itself reflected the same idea.

I suggest that a national study conference on the formation of a third party be called early in 1945. At such a conference I should like to present for discussion this point of view.

A third party, geared to independent political action, not to support candidates of the old parties, must be organized without delay if America is to face with assurance the difficult problems of peace and postwar reconstruction. The Cooperative Commonwealth Federation in Canada furnishes an excellent model.

The new party must be dedicated to a well-defined set of principles, not to any man. Its cardinal principle should be production for use, not for profit. Until that principle is adopted, we shall be unable to achieve full employment without war production.

The new party must stand for full equality—economic, political and social—for all peoples, at home and abroad. Unlike the Republicans and Democrats, it must win the deep loyalty of minorities at home and the hope of people all over the world by adopting an honest program against racism. It must come out for passage of the Scanlon–Dawson–La Follette Bill for a Permanent Fair Employment Practice Commission, and must state specifically that it will not tolerate emasculation of this economic Bill of Rights for all minorities by amendments as to coverage or enforcement powers. It must be clearly committed to passage of a federal poll tax repeal bill and a federal anti-lynching bill. It must stand for abolition of race segregated education in border states such as Missouri and Maryland. Passage of the federal aid to education bill, without which millions of children must grow up lacking decent educational opportunities, should be another major concern of the new party.

Its minimum program on the economic front might well be that of the Canadian C.C.F. which calls for the socialization of key industries and enterprises—banking, transportation, electric power and large monopolies—as soon as possible after taking office. The C.C.F. urges establishment of a National Planning and Investment Board, as an overall public planning agency. It offers to farmers a guaranteed minimum price for their products. An American C.C.F. should urge drastic upward revisions of the minimum wages under the Fair Labor Standards Act, and a thirty hour week.

An American C.C.F. should attempt to unite labor and farm groups with the millions of unorganized teachers and other professional people, who, like the small shopkeepers, face low income and insecurity under capitalism. It must exclude fascists and communists, the totalitarians of left and right, as persons whose beliefs are incompatible with building either a democratic party or a democratic society. Such groups as the Liberal Party in New York, the Political Action Committee, the Socialist Party, the Michigan Commonwealth Federation and the Social Democratic Federation should be urged to unite with the trade unions and liberal farm organizations in building the new party. If some of these groups do not agree to cooperate in the new political alignment, they will find that an important section of their support comes from forces that do believe the time is ripe for independent political action. From farm and factory, from kitchen and classroom will come people ready to work hard to build a party which carries hope of a better social order, a new society such as cannot be built from deals with Tom Pendergast's machine or that of Joe Pew.

The great problem of our day is the maintenance of human freedom while ending our Alice-in-Wonderland system of poverty because we produce too much. Civil liberties must be a prime concern of the new party, which should recognize the grave menace to plans for universal democracy in peacetime military conscription, now being advocated by the anti-labor proponents of the Austin-Wadsworth labor draft bill. It must oppose imperialism—including American imperialism—everywhere in the world, and support the democratic aspirations of the common people of all countries.

We need an American C.C.F. now to create a society of abundance. Unless we start now to build a party free from humbug and hypocrisy, we will wake up on the eve of an important national election to find that by failure of American liberals to have their own party, the only choice for voters is between slightly varied shades of reaction.

The time available for building such a party is short. It will not do for us to say that the job is one that must be done, but this is not the time to do it. Decisions are being made today which will irrevocably influence the future of the United States and the world; in the absence of such a party as I have here outlined, almost insuperable obstacles to the building of a better world in our time may be erected in the next few years.

Common Sense, December, 1944; XIII, 421.

96

LET'S LOOK AT THE RECORD

by Madeline L. Aldridge

At the end of 1944, an editorial assistant of the organ of the National Urban League produced a very long, largely statistical survey—based on official releases of the various armed services—of the participation by Afro-American men and women in the war effort. Much of the basic data is given in the extract that follows.

There were 701,678 Negroes serving in the United States Army on September 30, 1944. These included, in the infantry, 49,483; coast and field artillery, 36,302; cavalry, 867; engineers, 133,180; air corps, 73,686; and all other branches, 408,160. Commissioned officers numbered 5,804; dental corps officers, 101; nurses, 247; other medical corps, 463; and chaplains, 236. Negroes serving overseas totaled 411,368.

The highest ranking Negro officer in the United States Army is Brigadier General Benjamin O. Davis of the Inspector General's Department, who rose to his present rank from a private in the Regular Army. The present war is the third during which he has served.

Other high-ranking officers include: Colonel Howard D. Queen, commanding officer of the 366th Infantry; Colonel Edward O. Gourdin, commanding officer of the 372nd Infantry; Colonel Benjamin O. Davis, Jr., who commands an all-Negro fighter group in Italy. Also Colonel Midian O. Bousfield, commanding officer of the Station Hospital No. 1, Ft. Huachuca, Arizona; Colonel Anderson F. Pitts, Colonel Chauncey M. Hooper, and Lieutenant Colonels Wendell T. Derricks, Anderson F. Pitts, Benote H. Lee, Theophilus M. Mann, John B. West, Wilmer F. Lucas, and De Maurice Moses, serving both in this country and overseas.

While a small percentage of Negro troops are in actual combat service, their record has been creditable and they have received commendation from high sources. On the other hand, those serving in the less glamorous, less publicized, arms of the service are playing a vital part toward winning the war.

"Let's look at the record." The first Negro heroes of World War II were Dorie Miller, of the Navy, who received the Navy Cross, and Private Robert H. Brooks, who was killed on December 8, 1941 in the Philippines—the Armored Forces' first casualty. In his honor the main parade ground at Fort Knox, Kentucky, was named "Brooks Field." It was dedicated by Major General John L. Devers, Chief of the Armored Forces.

The Negro soldier is serving in all the spheres of action all over the world. And since the road-builders, the "ammunition passers," the supply handlers, et al., may be considered the "unsung heroes," let's reverse the usual order and start with them to travel to some of these places and "look at the record."

From the Aleutians to Australia, from Alaska to Africa, in the China-Burma-India Theater and the Middle East, in England, France, Italy, and the South Pacific, Negro engineers, port battalions, and truck companies have served or are serving; in short, wherever the Army is engaged, the Negro does his share.

On April 7, 1942, the Navy Department announced that Negro volunteers would be accepted for enlistment for general service in the reserve components of the U.S. Navy, the U.S. Marine Corps, and the U.S. Coast Guard. As of June, 1942, more than 93,000 Negroes had joined the Naval Service. On April 28, 1943, the Navy Department issued a press release announcing that an increasingly greater number of Negroes would enter the Navy through the Selective Service procedure.

Camp Robert Smalls Naval Training Station, Great Lakes, Ill., and the U.S. Naval Training Station, Hampton Institute, Hampton, Va., were established to train Negro recruits. Commander Daniel W. Armstrong, U.S.N.R., Assistant Recruit Training Officer, was in charge of the Negro Recruit Training Program at Great Lakes from June, 1942 until September, 1944, when he was succeeded by Lieutenant Vance A. Kauffold, U.S.N.R. The first group of Negroes to complete basic training —222 in number—left Camp Robert Smalls on September 3, 1942. Of these, 102 were chosen for advanced training to become specialists. Ninety-seven completed instruction in various trades offered by the Navy and graduated from the Service School at Great Lakes on January 7, 1943. Subsequently, similar classes have graduated at regular intervals.

On Feburary 23, 1944, the Navy Department announced that Negro candidates would be selected for commissioning as officers in the U.S. Naval Reserve to fill approximately 22 available billets, with twelve qualified enlisted men to be selected as line officers, with the rank of

Ensign; ten professionally qualified men as staff officers, with the rank of Ensign or Lieutenant (Junior Grade), depending upon ages and professional qualifications; and two officers for each of the following: Chaplain Corps, Dental Corps, Medical Corps, Civil Engineer Corps, and Supply Corps. It was anticipated that the staff officers would be appointed from civilian life. The announcement stated that the enlisted men commissioned as line officers would be given a special three to six months' training course and the staff officers a short indoctrination course at the Great Lakes station.

Latest figures available (September 1944) show Negroes in the Navy, Marine Corps and Coast Guard as follows: Navy, 23 officers, 142,628 enlisted men; Marine Corps, 15,771 enlisted men; Coast Guard, 4 officers, 3,657 enlisted men.

Negroes are serving with the fleet and at advance bases in all parts of the world. They hold a wide variety of ratings, including radioman, radarman, electrician's mate, machinist's mate, quartermaster, coxswain, signalman, storekeeper, yeoman, and motor machinist's mate.

Two combatant ships have already been manned by Negro crews—the destroyer escort U.S.S. *Mason,* launched in March 1944—and a patrol chaser. And it is expected that other combatant ships will ultimately receive Negro crewmen in a variety of ratings. It is pointed out that all ratings and rating branches in the Navy are open to Negroes, and that Negroes are being trained in the V-12 program, the Navy's present principal source of young officers.

Opportunity, December, 1944; XXIII, 4–5, 36–37.

97

FULL EMPLOYMENT AND THE NEGRO WORKER
by Willard S. Townsend

In 1944 at Fisk University, from July 3 to July 21, an Institute of Race Relations studied the present and projected the future. One of those who spoke was a leading Black figure in the C.I.O.; his paper follows.

It may perhaps occur to you that it requires a certain amount of temerity for a labor leader to appear before a distinguished gathering of scholars such as this, with the purpose of considering a topic which in a large measure involves the whole field of our national economy.

I would not have had the courage to undertake the task had I not, after long and serious consideration, concluded that it is highly essential that constant and intimate exchange of views by scholars and teachers in universities on the one hand and those of us at the grass roots of the nation's economic problem on the other, is fundamentally necessary.

It is indeed my hope that instrumentalities may be devised by our universities through which such discussions may take place to the end that labor may achieve a measure of the objective and scientific point of view of the scholar and that the scholar and educator may understand more fully the purposes, aspirations and problems of the laboring man.

The subject I have elected to discuss, Full Employment and the Negro Worker, is one that has ramifications so broad that the question naturally arises: How can this be made possible? Since I firmly believe that economic security is a forerunner of social and political impartiality, it would follow that the Negro must look to organized labor for economic security. Assuming this as my premise, it is reasonable to point out that the so-called racial problem is a workers' problem and must be solved by the organization and education of workers.

In support of this theory, we might view with interest the frank statement made by Senator John C. Calhoun in the defense of slavery debating in the United States Congress during the 1840's: "There has never existed a wealthy and civilized society in which one portion of the community did not live on the labor of the other. The person who works for wages is more severely exploited than the chattel laborer. What does capital do with its 'wage slaves' when it does not happen to need them? Let them starve."

In a word, Calhoun laid bare the exploitative roots that bound the black chattel slave and the white "wage slave." With the emancipation, the black chattel slave joined with the wage slave class.

Basically then, the so-called racial problem is a workers' problem. For as long as the Negro workers' rights are insecure, all workers' rights are in jeopardy. Labor's program for the security of all workers is maintaining full employment.

This summer more than a million Negroes were in war plants. The vast majority entered war work during the latter half of 1942 and the first quarter of 1943. Unemployment among Negroes has reached a new low, and occupational progress has moved steadily forward. Full employment for Negroes in war time, in certain selected war industries, means that the total number employed is 5 per cent for agricultural machinery; 5 per cent in aircraft; 12 per cent in steel; 25 per cent in iron and steel foundries; 4 per cent in communications; 2 per cent in electrical equipment; 10 per cent in smelting and refining of non-ferrous metals; and 10 per cent in shipbuilding.

A recent survey of important war industries in Pennsylvania, New Jersey and Delaware revealed some interesting developments. One hundred and thirteen firms studied in January, 1492 employed 358,285 workers of whom 4 per cent were Negroes. In October of the same year, this percentage had increased to 7 per cent. From May to December of the same year, non-white employment in important war industries (outside of shipbuilding) in the Los Angeles area increased almost fourfold while the total labor supply only grew 50 per cent.

The above examples illustrate what can be achieved toward full employment for Negroes under the compulsion of war needs. These examples serve to highlight how Americans can overcome age-old fears and prejudices in many industries and occupations under the demands of full production. Many of the occupations and industries referred to always erected bars of one sort or another to the Negro workers. Tragic as it is to admit, the obvious conclusion is that the war seemed to accelerate our pace toward economic democracy.

These gains, however, were not achieved without cost. One example of the cost is the bloody clashes between the races last summer (1943). Some people argue that the price was too high—but was the "Little Steel" massacre of 1937 too high a price to pay for the successful organization of the little steel industry? These clashes of interest in an unplanned society, such as ours, are inevitable. When the forces of progress meet the forces of reaction, in the absence of intelligent planning, there is bound to be a clash, generally a resounding clash. This is part of the price we pay for neglect and our habitual ostrich philosophy when the question of races is concerned. We will continue to have clashes if we continue the hit or miss policies.

The Negro worker is definitely worried. He is worried about today. He is worried about tomorrow. He is restless. He remembers only too well the stirring slogans of the last war. He remembers too well the broken promises. He is more grim today in his determination to enjoy some of the freedoms so glibly mouthed. The Negro remembers World War I, when he was introduced into industrial employment only to be dismissed in the depression of the thirties. He also remembers the unfortunate and uncomfortable position he was in as the pawn between labor unions—labor unions in which he was not welcome—and management during the twenties, when capital embarked upon its "union-busting" campaign. He remembers the riots, the rise of the Ku Klux Klan, the ugly head of restrictive covenants, the period of reaction during the twenties. He remembers the period of black disappointment when he awoke to the fact that economic democracy was an illusion in the North. His dreams of a peaceful, democratic environment in which to live and rear his family became a figment of his imagination —the North became like the South that he had so recently left.

That is why the Negro has pressed for upgrading; pressed for training; pressed to become a truly American citizen in the fullest sense of the word. The fight for equal job opportunities, the fight for economic democracy, is not the agitation of a few Negro radicals—it is the will of the enlightened working people. Intelligent labor leaders, white and black, know this.

Labor is probably more aware than any other group, that the steps taken to insure orderly integration of Negroes, have been partially effective as emergency wartime measures only. But remove the compulsion of wartime production and they become palliatives only. A long-run national program directed toward economic freedom must dig down to the basic causes. We must insist upon sound planning. It is an imaginative project, but absolutely necessary. Otherwise, we will pay a price greater than the riots of last summer.

The unplanned migration of large numbers of people into already overcrowded industrial centers will exact a larger toll. In the South the problem is shifting from the "cabin in the cotton" to the "quarter across the tracks." Hundreds of thousands of Negro workers have moved to war production centers—most of them to stay after the war is over. The Negro population of Mobile, Alabama, which witnessed the first serious clash last May, has increased by more than 50 per cent since 1940 according to census estimates. The Black Belt of Norfolk, Virginia, has grown more than 200 per cent; that of Charleston, South Carolina by 39 per cent. Outside the South the increase has been 30 per cent in Los Angeles; 19 per cent in Detroit and more than 20 per cent in Chicago.

An intelligent plan must give due consideration to the economic fears that the white workers possess. According to [Robert C.] Weaver's "The Negro Comes of Age in Industry": "The black worker has become a symbol of potential threat to the white worker, and the Negro's occupational advancement is consciously or unconsciously feared." This fear has been woven into the economic fabric of America. Its origin lies in the unfavorable position of the "poor whites" during slavery, and under the intense competition for employment in the South during

Reconstruction. The repeated introduction of the Negro as a strike breaker, particularly in the industrial North and West, was instrumental in spreading the fear geographically and infecting organized labor with its germ. It has grown out of the American workers' experience with our economy which has seldom had enough jobs to absorb the labor supply. In such an economy, its development was an inevitable consequence of a system that perpetuated the concept of white men's jobs and black men's jobs; while at the same time it was used to secure the support of the white worker for such a system.

Resistance to advances in the economic and occupational status of the Negro persists even in periods of full employment, because better jobs for him represent a direct challenge to the accepted color caste system. To some, the changes represent a loss of Negro servants and laborers; by others they are interpreted as a threat to the white man's job in the post war economy. The tradition of white men's jobs and black men's jobs is being challenged and actually being broken down in a score of tight labor markets outside the South. In the South itself, there is unmistakable evidence of economic advances among Negroes and this fact has been dramatically brought to the attention of the white community by the scarcity of Negro domestics.

Intelligent planning by organized labor, must recognize that the Negro in the United States has developed more rapidly than his opportunity for participation in American life. Although he has been conditioned through exposure to education and propaganda to seek the goals of Americans, he is denied these goals and accused of being impatient and unduly militant when he exerts pressures to achieve them. As a matter of fact, in demanding fully recognized citizenship, the Negro is being a typical American, seeking accepted American objectives, in characteristic American ways. He is demanding for himself more of these freedoms which the nation is dedicated to secure for people all over the world. When in his quest for more of the rights of American citizenship, the Negro encounters occupational limitations, and he is again reminded of his inferior status in America. He realizes that job discrimination is a part of a general picture which emphasizes that he does not belong—that his position is outside the main stream of American life.

The big question—what of the Negro worker after the war?—is causing as much concern among Negro workers as any other segment of our population. Will peace destroy the gains toward full employment of the Negro? What will be his status at the end of hostilities? A depressed economy has always meant but one thing for the Negro worker

—widespread unemployment. If we have an economy of full employment, it will establish a framework favorable to the continuing occupational advancement of the black worker; and to the removal of the white worker's fear of him as an economic rival.

Full employment in the post war period will not remove racial tensions. It will, however, set the economic stage for effective educational programs designed to reduce the frequency and intensity of one of the basic causes for race conflict. In such an economy, trade unions can, as some of them have so well done in the past few years, take the lead in establishing cooperation between white and black workers.

There will be important results flowing from full employment. Such an economy should provide better housing for all people, better educational and recreational facilities and more adequate transportation. Most important, however, is the fact that economic success will offer practical experience in relaxing the caste system which prevents democracy from becoming an accomplished fact in America.

The courage that forces one to move toward the goal of full employment, with all the resources at our command, must be that courage born of a thorough understanding of the problem and motivated by our ideals and convictions. Full employment is not a visionary Utopia. It is possible of achievement. It was achieved for destruction and the labor movement must be the force that directs our economy toward full employment for consumption.

Those who plan for an enduring peace must be capable of hope—must be capable of trusting the people. As Orson Welles said: "To be born free is to be born in debt; to live in freedom without fighting slavery is to profiteer." This debt can only be paid by service.

Who can say that both whites and blacks in the South are not slaves yet? The white enslaves himself in trying to keep the black worker in economic bondage. You can't keep a man in the ditch without descending in that ditch with him. You can't have unencumbered and prosperous white workers and unemployed black workers—for, if you let that happen, the white worker will have to carry the black worker on his back through relief or dole. Already a large majority of labor unions and their leaders are reporting that sentiment to abolish race discrimination is on the increase and look approvingly upon it as a safeguard against the possibility of exploiting their membership through union-busting tactics.

Basically the objective of labor's full employment program is one of high moral values, whose possibilities of rehabilitation for different races of workers will dispel the fears of hunger and need. As a matter of sober fact, labor leaders realize that such steps to relieve dire need are the best possible insurance against racial conflicts; and that the future of the white and black worker alike will be determined by this understanding as well as by the power of collective bargaining.

The Journal of Negro Education, July, 1944; XIII, 6–10. Weaver's article, mentioned above, appeared in *Atlantic Monthly,* September, 1943, pp. 54–59.

98

SOME MUTINIES, RIOTS, AND OTHER DISTURBANCES

by Florence Murray

The late Florence Murray, in her *Negro Handbook, 1946–1947,* compiled the most complete record so far produced of the outbreaks and assaults by and upon Black men and women in the armed forces during World War II.

Introduction

As in the earlier years of the war, there were in the last two years a number of disturbances in which Negro servicemen and servicewomen were involved aggressively.

These disturbances grew out of what the participants regarded as unfair or prejudicial treatment which they sought to remedy or to resist in one form or another.

Many of the disturbances might be called in dictionary terms "breaches of tranquillity"; a few, however, were of such proportions as to be referred to as mutinies or riots.

A considerable number of cases were based on charges of disobedience or insubordination, which, although the accused probably were not aware of it, are classed among serious offenses, in many instances tantamount to mutiny.

While some of the riots brought death or injury to participants and to others, none of the mutinies were accompanied by violence.

A few cases in the various categories follow.

The Port Chicago, Cal. Mutiny

On July 17, 1944, two ships that were being loaded with ammunition exploded at the docks at Port Chicago, a small town on San Francisco Bay about 35 miles northeast of San Francisco.

Over 300 persons were killed and several hundred injured. Of those killed, about 250 were Negro seamen who were engaged in loading the ships. Others killed were nine white officers in charge of the loaders, seventy members of the mixed crews of the two ships, fifteen Coast Guardsmen on vessels nearby, and several civilians.

The injured were mostly Negro seamen loaders who were at that time (10:30 P.M.) in their barracks a mile from the docks.

On August 9, the survivors, who had been scattered about in various camps, were assembled at Vallejo, a few miles from Port Chicago, with the view of resuming the loading. However, the men expressed strong reluctance. Various reasons were given, but the principal reason was fear of another disaster.

After three days of persuasion and urging, the commandant of the Naval district was called in, but his efforts, too, were largely unavailing. Of the 400 men, 258 were unable to overcome their fears and they were put in virtual confinement on a barge at the docks.

Several days were consumed in persuading and interviewing the men by the post chaplain and others with the result that all but 44 of the 258 expressed willingness to resume the loading.

These 44, plus 6 others who balked after a few days of work, were formally charged with mutiny.

On September 14, the "mutineers" were put on trial before a naval court-martial. The trial lasted six weeks, ending on October 24 with a verdict of guilty. Three weeks later they were given sentences ranging from 8 to 15 years at hard labor, and dishonorable discharges.

The initial sentence in each case was 15 years, but Rear Admiral Carleton H. Wright, commandant of the district, ruled that forty of the men were entitled, because of mitigating circumstances, to reductions of sentences. Because of youth, previous clear record or short period of service, terms were reduced to eight years for five men, ten for eleven men and twelve for twenty-four men. (Court-martial sentences are subject to further review by the Judge Advocate of the Navy, the Bureau of Personnel and the Secretary of the Navy.)

Sections of the Negro press, following their investigations, took exception to the mutiny charges. They contended that officers of two of the three divisions to which the men belonged did not give direct and explicit orders to go to work; that in the one division which received such orders there were no recalcitrants.

Thurgood Marshall, an attorney representing the National Association for the Advancement of Colored People, who was an observer at the trial, stated the matter thus:

"The men actually don't know what happened. Had they been given a direct and specific order to load ammunition and had refused to obey that order, then the charge would be legitimate. But they say no direct order to load was issued them. They were asked whether they would load, and they replied that they were afraid.

"They have told me that they were willing to go to jail to get a change of duty because of their terrific fear of the explosives, but they had no idea that verbal expression of their fear constituted mutiny."*

There was considerable testimony to indicate that such was the case. Some of the men testified that while they were in confinement on the barge had they been ordered to work they would probably have done so. Others testified to the contrary, while at least one of the accused testified that he had asked permission to resume the loading but his superior officer had refused on the ground that he had had his chance and did not take advantage of it. The officer in question confirmed this.

Concerning the opportunity given the men to explain the reasons for their actions, it was brought out that the statements made in interviews—which statements were put in evidence—were not couched in the men's own words but purported to be a recording of what was relevant and important in the conversations as the interviewers recalled them from their notes.

The accused men were ably and conscientiously defended by white Naval officers appointed by the court. They sought to establish that under the circumstances the men were in no mental condition to make sound and considered decisions and statements.

No official psychologist was called to testify in the case, but statements were made by several specialists supporting the arguments of the defendants' attorneys as to their mental reactions.

Immediately after the sentences were announced, efforts were begun to have the reviewing bodies set aside the convictions or reduce the penalties. Mr. Marshall asked for permission to file a brief and personally appeared before the Navy's board of review on April 3, 1945.

On July 13, the Navy Department, through Acting Secretary Ralph

* See the editorial, "The 'Mutiny' Trial," in *The Crisis,* November, 1944; LI, 344.

A. Baird, announced that it had been determined that the sentences were legal and that the trial had been fair and impartial.

Request was made then by Mr. Marshall for permission to file additional briefs and for opportunity for personal presentation of the case before Secretary of the Navy Forrestal. He did not get the opportunity, but the Secretary sent a letter dated August 13, saying that the sentences "have not yet come to me for final review."

In the meantime, petitions and appeals for clemency were coming from many sources, including the daily press; and Lester Granger, then on loan from the National Urban League as special aide to the Secretary, was giving the case attention along with his inspection of Naval installations on the West Coast.

The first week in January, 1946, it was announced that the convictions had been set aside and that the men were restored to duty on probation and were then "presumably overseas."

The Freeman Field Case

A disturbance which originated at Freeman Field, near Seymour, Ind., in April, 1945, had wide ramifications and repercussions.

At this field, where the only Negro bombardment group, the 477th, was stationed, technically there were no separate recreational facilities for white and Negro servicemen, but there was an officers' club for instructors and one for trainees, or students. However, all of the teachers were white and all the trainees were Negroes.

NOTE: Of the trainees, those who were pilots or bombardiers ranked as officers.

The 477th Bombardment group had been recently moved to Freeman Field from Godman Field, Ky. When they learned of the "white" officers' club, they decided to boycott all recreational facilities, contending that they were Jim-Crowed in violation of Army Order No. 97. This order is cited in the topic "The Anti-Jim-Crow Order of July 8, 1944."

On April 5, sixty men of the group attempted to enter the officers' club. They were refused entrance and were ordered to be confined to their quarters. Later, 57 of the men were released and 3 were held for court-martial on charges of "jostling" a superior officer and refusing to obey the command of a superior officer.

A few days later, 101 of the group were arrested and confined to their quarters for refusing to sign a statement that they would confine themselves to the trainees' facilities allocated to them.

As the news of the affair spread, and Negroes protested to the War Department, the Department sent a directive to the Freeman Field commander, Col. Robert R. Selway, Jr., ordering him to withhold further disciplinary action pending the completion of an investigation by Washington authorities.

Within a few days, all were freed from detention in a trial at Godman Field, Ky., to which place they had been moved, except the three held in the original flare-up. These three—2nd Lts. Roger C. Terry and Marsden A. Thompson, of Los Angeles, and Shirley R. Clinton, of Camden, N.J.—were ordered to face a court-martial.

Meanwhile, Col. Selway had been relieved of command of the group and Col. Benjamin O. Davis, Jr., (Negro) put in command.

The court-martial detail of ten Negro officers which heard the case on July 22 and 23 was headed by Col. Davis. However, he did not actually preside at the trial, having been excused from the panel under challenge by the defense.

Clinton and Thompson were exonerated of all charges on the first day of the trial. On the second day, Terry was exonerated of the charge of disobedience, but was convicted of using violence in pushing aside a white officer. His penalty was forfeiture of $50 pay for three months.

The Hawaiian Mutiny

The morning papers of February 1, 1945, carried a dispatch from United States Army Headquarters in Hawaii which said that 73 Negro soldiers in that area had been sentenced to hard labor terms ranging from eight to 30 years for refusal to report for work at an airport on Oahu, the night of July 31, 1944.

During the seven months preceding February 1, 1945, Army censorship had prevented any news of the revolt or of the trial from reaching the States.

Later information disclosed that 74 men were involved. There had been two trials by court-martial. In one trial, 69 were convicted and sentenced—two men to 17 years, the other 67 to 15 years. In a separate trial of five men, said to be the ring-leaders, two had been given 35 years, two 25 years, the other, 20 years.

On review by the commanding general, one man of the 69 had been granted a new trial and the sentences of the other 68 had been reduced—the 17-year sentences to 15 years; of the 15-year sentences, seven to 12 years, 48 to 10 years, and 11 to eight years. The 35- and 25-year sentences given the ring-leaders were reduced to 30 and 20 years respectively. The 20-year sentence stood.

The men involved were members of a company of engineers. They had become disgruntled, it was said, when their Negro officers were replaced by white officers because the enlisted men had complained of unfair promotion practices.

Describing the occurrence, a correspondent of the *Chicago Defender* stated that twice on the night in question, the regimental colonel had read to the company the articles of war dealing with mutiny, after the men had refused to leave their barracks for a lumber-moving task, but the reading failed to move them.

Later, he said, the men responded to the appeal of another colonel whom they regarded as less hostile. They also complied with his request to make up the time lost. Several days later, the mutiny charges were preferred.

The case came to the attention of Walter White, executive secretary of the N.A.A.C.P., while he was in Hawaii in December, 1944. Upon his return to the States in April, he conferred with the then Under Secretary of War, Robert Patterson, on behalf of the men. On June 17, Mr. White was advised that 67 of the men had been assigned to a rehabilitation company "where they were undergoing special training with view to restoration to duty."

On September 4, 1945, 52 of those undergoing rehabilitation were recommended for restoration to duty. In the *Chicago Defender* of October 13, 1945, the Hawaiian correspondent of the paper reported: "With few exceptions, these 'graduates' have made successful and enthusiastic soldiers, two having received the Bronze Star Medal and one the Silver Star. A third has been recommended posthumously for the nation's highest military award, the Congressional Medal of Honor, for valor far beyond the call of duty during the Okinawa campaign."

The status of the other convicted men had not been disclosed at the end of the year.

Mutiny at Mabry Field

The first week in May, 1944, a trial in a mutiny case at Dale Mabry Field near Tallahassee, Fla., ended with the conviction and sentencing of five Negro privates—two to 15-year terms and three to 13 years.

The offense with which they were charged occurred at the field on

March 23, at which time the men, all of whom were prisoners in the guardhouse, refused to turn out for work until they could "see the colonel" and present certain grievances based, they felt, on racial discrimination.

Later, on June 21, the case was heard and taken under advisement by an Army board of review in Washington.

On September 6, Attorney David Levinson (white) who had voluntarily represented the men at the hearing, received notice that the sentences had been greatly reduced—the 15-year terms to five years, one 13-year term to three, the other two 13-year terms to two years.

A few days later, the remaining terms of two of the low-term men had been waived and the men sent to a rehabilitation camp.

At the review hearing, four mothers of the accused men made pleas, one of whom, mother of Leo M. Jones, of Philadelphia, said to be ringleader, recited a long story of humiliations and injustices which she said her son had endured, beginning with his rejection when he sought training as a pilot, because "Negroes were not (then) wanted in the air force." He did, however, later enter the air force as a mechanic and completed his course at Chanute Field, Ill., after which he was sent South where he was soon in difficulties because of his militant attitude.

Persecution and discrimination, she said, finally caused a nervous breakdown and a series of violations which finally landed him where he was at the time of the mutiny.

The Brookley Field Mutiny

On the night of May 24, 1944, a disturbance occurred at Brookley Field near Mobile, Ala., in which Negro soldiers and white military police exchanged shots, and one Negro sergeant, who was not a participant, was seriously wounded.

The sergeant was shot in crossfire when he attempted to move a jeep at the command of a white officer. That was the only casualty, although an estimated 1000 rounds were fired.

At the court-martial which followed a month later, nine Negro privates, charged with mutiny and failure to suppress mutiny and rioting, were convicted and three received sentences of 25 years, the other sentences ranging from 16 to 22 years.

At a board of review hearing in the Judge Advocate General's office in Washington in September, all sentences were confirmed.

Versions of what occurred on the night of the disturbance differ, but the most acceptable account indicates that the trouble originated when white military police sought to permit a white civilian to explore the Negro soldiers' quarters ostensibly to identify a soldier who had allegedly robbed him outside the gate.

When the soldiers learned that it was intended to turn over to civilian authorities whoever was "identified," they revolted and drove the MP's and the intruder out. The exchange of shots followed. The melee was quelled by unarmed superior officers who were not fired on.

Subsequent information indicated that the white civilian who alleged he had been robbed really had been beaten by a soldier in defense of a Negro woman.

The Fort Devens Case

This case, arising at the Lovell General Hospital, at Fort Devens, Mass., was not generally referred to as a mutiny, but as a case of disobedience or a sit-down strike.

The trouble came about through the refusal of four Negro members of the Women's Army Corps (W.A.C.s), to do certain work assigned to them which they felt was menial and was assigned to them because of their color.

At the court-martial which followed their refusal, they testified that white W.A.C.s were not required to do the type of work assigned to them. They also recited other acts of discrimination and quoted the commanding officer of the hospital as saying that he didn't want "black W.A.C.s" in the motor pool or as medical technicians.

The matter came to a head on March 10, 1944, when, despite the reading of the articles of war bearing on disobedience to the sixty Negro W.A.C.s on duty by Maj. Gen. Sherman Miles, in command of the military district, the four persisted in their refusal, while the 56 others went back to duty.

On March 20, a two-day trial ended in their conviction for disobeying a superior officer, and sentences of dishonorable discharge and a year at hard labor were given them. The trial board was composed of two white W.A.C.s, two Negro captains, and five other officers.

Protests and demands for reversal came from Congressmen and other sources. Two weeks later, on April 3, General Miles voided the court-martial proceedings and the four were restored to duty.

The War Department announced that the proceedings were vacated because the court was improperly convened. This decision turned on a finding that the commanding general, Miles, was "technically the accuser . . . and therefore not authorized to convene the court."

The Camp Claiborne Riot

At Camp Claiborne, near Alexandria, La., where a clash between Negro soldiers and white military and civilian police had occurred in January, 1942, an outbreak on the night of August 16, 1944, in which two soldiers and a white lieutenant were wounded, brought a death sentence to one soldier and long prison terms to twelve others.

There had been reports of incitements and provocations, including the killing of a soldier nine days previously by a white policeman in a town a few miles away.

During the previous week, armed white civilian and military police, accompanied by bloodhounds, for three days had searched the camp and nearby area for an unidentified soldier who had allegedly raped two white women a few miles from the post. No one was arrested but the manner of the invasion and search caused strong resentment.

On the night of the uprising, a rumor had spread that the soldier wanted, or one who supposedly looked like him, had been killed just outside the camp. Thereupon—in the language of one account— "incensed soldiers broke into the arsenal, took several carbines, it is reported, and started showing their resentment."

Just how the firing began or who were engaged was not brought out except that one soldier (the one later given the death sentence) had led in "firing shots through an orderly room which houses the company commander and other officers." (These officers were presumably white, for there were no Negro officers in the area.)

Twenty-seven soldiers were arrested and in a series of court-martial trials six weeks later, thirteen of fourteen that were tried were convicted. The death penalty was given to Leroy McGrary, of Chicago; six received life sentences; two, 30 years; three, 25 years; and one 9 years.

The charges included mutiny, attempt to incite mutiny, disobedience, attempts to storm the supply room to secure ammunition, and holding two officers prisoners.

The one given 9 years, Sgt. Conway Price, of New York, was accused of failure as a non-commissioned officer to attempt to suppress a mutiny.

Price's case was presented to a review board on November 9, 1944, by E. R. Dudley, attorney for the N.A.A.C.P., and later his conviction was voided by the board and he was sent to a rehabilitation camp. The sergeant's attorney contended that, not only was there not a mutiny in the presence of the accused, but that Price was conscientiously seeking some sort of instructions from the officers as to how best he could help in the situation.

The N.A.A.C.P. was later successful in having the death sentence of Pvt. McGrary commuted to dishonorable discharge, forfeiture of all pay and allowances, and confinement for forty years. The charges against him were participating in a riot, mutiny, and lifting arms against an officer.

What might be regarded as an aftermath of the case was the conviction and death sentence by a court-martial at Camp Claiborne, in November, of a Negro soldier, Pvt. Lee R. Davis, for the alleged assault on the women which gave rise to the searches of the camp just prior to the August riot. He was said to have confessed both crimes.

The Fort Lawton Anti-Italian Riot

On the night of August 14, 1944, a group of Italian prisoners of war at Fort Lawton, Wash., were attacked in their barracks by Negro soldiers. Thirty of the prisoner group were injured seriously and a few of the soldiers slightly. In addition, the body of an Italian prisoner was found hanged near the scene of the riot the following day.

On November 16, forty-three Negro soldiers were put on trial before an Army court-martial—forty charged with rioting and three with the murder of the prisoner found hanged.

The trial ended December 17, with twenty-eight convicted and thirteen acquitted. Two had been exonerated before the trial ended.

A few days later, sentences for twenty-seven were announced. The three men originally charged with murder were given 25, 20, and 15 years, respectively, the murder charge having been dropped during the trial, when evidence was presented which indicated that the prisoner who was found hanged had committed suicide. Other terms were: 10 years for eight men; eight years for six; five years for three; four years for four; three years for one; one year for one, and six months for one. The sentence of one man who was hospitalized was not announced.

In a release from the N.A.A.C.P. dated November 1, 1945, it was stated that a petition for clemency had been filed for the men then remaining in confinement. Earlier it had been disclosed that the reviewing authority had suspended the dishonorable discharges of ten of the men and placed them in rehabilitation centers, with a view to early return to duty; and that the sentences of the others had been reduced so that the maximum was 15 years.

The cause of the clash was not explicitly brought out, but it appeared to have been due primarily to favored treatment of the Italian prisoners in the matter of work assignments, also fracases in which individual Negro soldiers were worsted, and ganging up on one soldier who was seeking to protect a white soldier from an Italian prisoner.

The Guam Disorders

Disturbances in which Negro Navy men on the Island of Guam claimed they suffered unprovoked annoyances and assaults by white troops began in the summer of 1944 and came to a climax Christmas night.

No publication of the matter was made in the States until six months later in a radio broadcast, July 7, 1945, by Walter White, secretary of the N.A.A.C.P. In the meantime 45 Negro Navy men had been convicted by court-martial and given sentences from 4 months to 4 years for participating in the final uprising.

On Christmas Eve, according to Mr. White, a group of white servicemen had fired on a group of Negro seamen and run them out of the main town on the island. That same night a truckload of white Marines invaded the Negro camp making threats, charging that one of their number had been hit by a stone.

On Christmas Day, he said, a Negro serviceman was killed and another shot by white servicemen. That brought matters to a head, and that night, according to reports, twenty or thirty Negro naval men left the depot in two trucks, without permission, to seek revenge.

They were intercepted by Negro masters-at-arms and white military police who found arms and ammunition in the vehicles. Later in the night, according to one version, white M.P.'s, who were patrolling near the base, were fired on and one was wounded in the leg.

It developed that Mr. White, while in Guam in January, 1945, had, as a correspondent of the New York *Post,* written an account of the occurrence for this paper which Navy censors held up, but later sent on, marked "For release July 11, 1945."

The charges at the court-martial included riot and unlawful use of United States property, and lesser offenses. Three men received terms of less than two years, 33 got two years, the others 26 months to four years.

Efforts in behalf of the men were at once begun and continued through 1945. Early in January, 1946, it was announced that the 36 men still remaining in confinement would be released and cleared within a few days.

Seabees' Hunger Strike

A two-day hunger strike of a Navy Construction Battalion (Seabees) was staged at Camp Rousseau, Port Hueneme, Cal., March 3 and 4, 1945, in mass protest against Jim Crow conditions and lack of promotions. There was no violence and the thousand men involved continued work as usual during the strike.

For more than two months complaints and charges had been pouring into Washington, aimed mainly at the commander of the unit, Comdr. P. J. McBean, from Mississippi. There were complaints of segregation carried to extremes, of inequalities in quarters and food, and, above all, of injustice and discrimination in promotions.

The outfit had served overseas for 21 months and had made an outstanding record at Tulagi and Guadalcanal, which even their allegedly prejudiced commander had praised.

Prior to the strike, the Navy Department had submitted to the N.A.A.C.P. a denial by McBean and by the commander of the base, who had commended McBean as having "an enlightened and fair attitude toward the colored race" and as being "genuinely interested in their welfare." Nevertheless he was removed from command, and after a period of rest and rehabilitation, the outfit went back overseas.

Seabees Discharge Case

On April 5, 1945, the Office of War Information announced that the Secretary of the Navy had approved the decision of the department's board of review that the discharges of 14 of the 15 Negro Seabees who were discharged as "undesirable by reason of unfitness" or because of "inaptitude" be changed to discharged "under honorable conditions."

Thus ended a case that had aroused uncommon interest and had been agitated by the press and many organizations for over a year.

The case grew out of the discharge in October, 1943, of 19 men who were members of the 80th Naval Construction Battalion (Seabees) under the conditions cited above.

At the time of the discharges no specific grounds for the action were made public; however, certain occurrences that had preceded the action were regarded as the cause.

A few days before the action, a dozen men, all of whom were in the group that was later discharged, were called into the office of the commanding officer and invited to give their views about racial conditions at the base, which was located on an island in the West Indies. According to the testimony of the men, they were told to talk man-to-man, that the conference was off the record.

Thus reassured, they were frank in stating their grievances, they said, and in airing conditions that they regarded as biased and unfair, especially the lack of up-grading.

They pointed out that of the 80 percent of Negroes in the battalion, none were rated above second class petty officer, while all of the 20 percent of whites ranked higher.

Before the meeting broke up, the commander said that he would ask the chaplain to form a committee on interracial matters and that further meetings would be held.

The next day the superior officer at the base called the group together, and upbraided them for "griping," and announced that there would be no more conferences. A few days later, the twelve men in the original conference and seven others were discharged, sixteen as undesirable, and three on grounds of unfitness and inaptitude.

These three later, upon appeal, were given honorable discharges.

When the discharges and the conditions became known, there was a vigorous protest. The matter was taken to the Secretary who decided there were no grounds for relief. An appeal for reconsideration met no favor.

But efforts and agitation continued. Several national organizations, including members of both races, interested themselves in the case.

In June, 1944, the so-called Bill of Rights for servicemen had been made into a law by Congress. In this act there is a provision that discharged persons can have their discharges, such as the ones at issue, reviewed by a board. Fifteen of the sixteen men still without relief joined in a petition for review.

A review was granted and the date for a hearing set for December, 1944.

At the hearing on that date, attorneys representing several organizations pleaded the Seabees' case. Among the organizations represented were: the American Civil Liberties Union, the Winfred Lynn Committee,* the N.A.A.C.P., and the C.I.O. The results were as stated above—fourteen of the fifteen petitioners were given discharges that stated, "under honorable conditions." One petitioner was refused relief because of a bad record prior to the incident preceding his discharge.

* This committee was originally organized to press the case of Winfred Lynn, which had, on completion of case, changed its name and purpose. For the Lynn case, see earlier document, pp. 426–28.

VIOLENCE AGAINST NEGRO SOLDIERS

The Durham, N.C., Murder

On July 8, 1944, a Negro soldier, Pvt. Booker T. Spicely, formerly connected with the business department of Tuskegee Institute, was killed in Durham, N.C., by a white bus driver.

The killing, like so many other cases of violence involving Negroes, grew out of a segregation law. Spicely entered a bus which was crowded, with Negroes seated toward the rear as the law required. As was customary when there were no seats available in the rear for Negroes, Spicely sat in a vacant seat well toward the front.

When some passengers had gotten off, making seats available toward the rear, the driver ordered Spicely to move back to make room for white passengers entering the bus. Some of those entering were white soldiers who engaged in good natured banter with Spicely, agreeing with him that, since all were in the same uniform, it was ridiculous that he should make room for them.

Spicely moved to the rear, but the banter had angered the driver, and he had uttered a veiled threat. As Spicely was about to get off, he attempted to placate the driver by saying to him, "If I have said anything to offend you, I apologize."

However, it is said that on leaving the bus by the rear, he said to the driver, "If you weren't a lousy 4-F, you wouldn't be driving a bus." Thereupon, the driver got out, accosted Spicely, and shot him twice. He died in a few minutes.

The driver was indicted for second-degree murder, and the governor promised a fair trial.

The trial, which ended September 15, resulted in a jury verdict of not guilty. The driver had pleaded self-defense, saying that the soldier had advanced on him with his hand in his pocket.

The case attracted wide attention and interest. The Department of Justice at one time announced that it was studying the case to determine whether federal civil rights statutes had been violated. It did not enter the case.

W.A.C.s' Beating Case

While waiting in a bus station at Elizabethtown, Ky., on July 9, 1945, three Negro members of the Women's Army Corps (W.A.C.) were set upon and beaten by civilian policemen. The beating occurred when they did not move promptly enough on orders to leave the "white" waiting room where they had sat down because the "colored" room was crowded.

When accosted by a policeman, they sought to explain the situation. While the parley was in progress, other police joined in and the parley was cut short when one policeman was reported to have raised his club, saying: "Down here, when we tell niggers to move, they move," and brought the club down on the head of one of the two younger women.

The oldest of the three tried to shield the younger ones, and was badly mauled, dragged across the street and jailed.

After a few hours she was released to join the younger ones and resume their journey to Fort Knox from which post they were on leave. In the meantime, though bleeding and suffering severely, the injured one received no treatment for her wounds.

At Fort Knox, it is reported, the three were called into the office of the commander of the post and lectured and reprimanded for violating the state's Jim Crow laws, and informed that they would have to appear before a court-martial.

However, when investigation disclosed that Kentucky has no law requiring separation of the races in bus terminals, railroad stations, or other public buildings, the originally proposed charges were dropped, and they were charged with disorderly conduct. On that charge the three were arraigned before a seven-member board a month later and acquitted.

The hearing was held behind closed doors. The names of the officers who were appointed to the board were not disclosed, but it was learned that two of them were excused because they had formed opinions. These two acted as defense counsel.

Pending the trial and later, the War Department was urged to institute proceedings against the policemen involved in the assault, but no action was reported.

The Bohannon Case

On October 9, 1944, the Department of Justice announced the filing in the United States District Court in Dublin, Ga., of an information charging James Mitchell Bohannon, police chief of the town of Summit, Ga., with violation of the federal civil rights statute in the killing of Willie L. Davis, a Negro soldier. The information stated that Bohannon, "acting under the color of law," shot Davis without provocation, July 3, 1943.

The police chief had been called to a roadhouse to restore order, the information stated, and after order had been restored, he had "wilfully and unlawfully" shot Davis with a pistol.

No action was taken by the state authorities. The case was then referred to the Department of Justice by the War Department, but it was later dropped, for lack of evidence, according to an official statement.

Florence Murray, ed., *The Negro Handbook, 1946–47* (New York: A. A. Wyn Pub., 1947), pp. 347–56. See H. Sitkoff, "Racial Militancy and Interracial Violence in the Second World War," *Journal of American History,* December, 1971; LVIII, 661–81.

99

THE NEGRO AND THE POST-WAR WORLD

by Rayford W. Logan

In a rather brief and sorely neglected book, Professor Logan of Howard University outlined his views on the relationship of the status of Afro-American people and the role of the United States in the world that was to follow the war. An extract from that book conveys the essence of its argument.

The United States has emerged from this war the most powerful nation in the history of the world. Only Russia can compete with the United States from the military point of view. Economically, Russia at the present time is far behind the United States even though its vast resources and larger population may make her in a relatively brief period the equal if not the superior of the United States. This world preeminence of the United States makes it necessary that she adopt a social and economic policy commensurate with her power. Otherwise, we can not hope that other nations will cease their racial discrimination, and we all recall that one of the reasons for the hatred against Nazi Germany was its persecution of the Jews.

Negro Americans hardly know what to say about the statement in the Potsdam declaration demanding the abolition of racial discrimination in Germany or the insistence by Secretary of State Byrnes that there should be free elections in Bulgaria. When Byrnes was a member of the House of Representatives in 1919, he declared that "neither social equality nor political equality is essential to the happiness of the Negro." There has been no indication that he has called for free elections in his own state of South Carolina where Negroes are most effectively disfranchised. We see Negroes sent to direct welfare work among Germans when those same Negroes would be limited to work among the Negroes in the United States. The American press hails the fact that a Negro, Rudolph Dunbar, by his able conducting of the Berlin Philharmonic Orchestra, changed the attitude of some Germans about Negroes. We wonder whether Mr. Dunbar would have been allowed to conduct a white orchestra in the home state of the Secretary of State.

Not only Latin Americans but many persons in other parts of the world know that our ideals do not always square with our practices. No greater evidence of the patriotism of the American Negro can be found perhaps than the fact that skilful Japanese propaganda reminding soldiers at the front about current acts of injustice in the United States failed to produce the desired effect. When an American delegate at an international conference took France to task for her colonial administration, he was reminded that when the United States had appointed a colonial governor like Félix Eboué or had a vice-president of its house of representatives like Gratien Candace or an under-secretary of state for colonies, protectorates and mandated areas like Blaise Diagne, then the United States would be in a better position to criticize France.

In brief, if the United States is going to assume a position of moral leadership in world affairs, it behooves her to clear her own house first. We must not be blind to the fact that this housecleaning is not an easy job, for the dust and dirt have been accumulating for a long time. . . .

Today, at the end of the second war "to make the world safe for democracy," the Negro is still effectively disfranchised in most parts of the South except in occasional bond elections and in presidential elections in which a majority for the Democratic candidate is assured. In seven Southern states a poll tax is a prerequisite for voting. While in some of these states, the tax is as small as one dollar, in some others it is cumulative so that a person who has not voted for over a period of years may have to pay as much as fifty dollars for the privilege of voting. Even when the poll tax has been paid, there is the greater obstacle of the Democratic "white primary." Since the Democrat nominated in the primary is almost assured of election, participation in this primary is necessary if the Negro vote is to express their wishes. The United States Supreme Court in the case of *Smith* v. *Allwright* in 1944 declared that Negroes should be allowed to vote in the Texas primary, but it is not yet known whether the decision is applicable to all states that have barred Negroes from the primary. South Carolina has taken new steps to assure non-participation. On the other hand, the state supreme court of Florida has reaffirmed the decision as far as that state is concerned. Meanwhile, Negroes voted freely in the Texas primary in November, 1944.

Perhaps as the "shadow of the plantation" grows dimmer and Negroes when allowed to vote in the South show themselves as good citizens as others, this determination to exclude Negroes from the primary will gradually weaken. In the meanwhile every legal effort to bar Negroes from the primary must be fought just as it has been up to the present time and the fight must be continued to abolish the poll tax by both federal and state action.

In the North Negroes vote freely and, in the opinion of some observers, hold the balance of power in some of the most important states. In recent years Negroes have voted in large numbers for Democrats rather than for Republicans as they had done traditionally since Lincoln and the Republicans gave them freedom from slavery during the American Civil War. They had come to realize first of all that in city and state elections party labels had little significance as far as racial attitudes were concerned. And then the liberalism of Franklin D. Roosevelt on some measures and the outspoken friendship of Mrs. Roosevelt led many of them to vote the Democratic ticket in national elections. But we are still faced with this dilemma. While the Republicans pay lip service to friendship for the Negro, their economic and social policies are frequently opposed to the advancement of workers in general. On the other hand, Northern Democrats frequently favor liberal social and economic legislation, but they are held back by the anti-Negro and anti-labor policies of most Southern Democrats. At the same time the history of the United States shows convincingly how difficult it is for a third party to win a national election even though it may have the "nuisance value" of making one of the two major parties adopt a part of its program in order to keep it from winning wide support.

The increasing role of organized labor, especially as represented by the Congress of Industrial Organizations, may prove to be the best hope of the Negro not only in politics but also in social, economic and educational problems. We do not yet know how much of the greater participation of the Negro in industry has been due to the C.I.O. and how much to the war. It is clear, however, that Negroes in the C.I.O. unions have fuller rights than do those in the unions of the American Federation of Labor. Some of these latter still bar Negroes from membership; others grant them only limited rights in auxiliary unions.

This second world war has not only brought the Negro many opportunities in industry that were formerly denied them. It has finally made the Negro problem a national problem. During the first world war about a million Negroes migrated from the South to the North and many of them remained there after the war was over. No accurate estimate of the number who similarly migrated during this war is yet available, but according to virtually all reports many of them intended to remain in the North and on the Pacific Coast. Some idea of the changing complexion of the North and the Pacific Coast may be seen in the fact that the Negro population of Detroit has increased by about 65,000 during this war and that of San Francisco has risen from about 4,000 to about 40,000. Along with these Southern Negroes came many Southern whites.

In the presence of this influx most white Northerners found that they had no real convictions about any kind of equality, social, political, or economic, for the Negro. Negroes in the North had in all too many instances assumed the contrary. Moreover, many of these Southern Negroes had been denied, generally through no fault of their own, opportunities for public education and for home training equal to that of Negroes in the North. Hostile Southern whites therefore found it relatively easy to convince Northern whites that Southern patterns of segregation should be adopted. In Detroit this hostility culminated in a riot. Rumors of riot were current a few years ago in Washington, Baltimore, Columbus (Ohio), Los Angeles and other cities. The fact that none occurred in them is one of the most hopeful developments in recent American history. It is still being predicted that riots will break out when the soldiers return. On the other hand, many white soldiers are angry because of the friendly reception given to Negroes in some foreign lands—large numbers of English girls openly wept when colored soldiers left one port. Even in Germany it appears that Hitler's racial propaganda had not influenced many of the German people against the Negroes. On the other hand, many Negroes have declared that they did not intend to risk their lives and see their "buddies" killed and maimed only to have to come back to the same old discrimination. Even though a riot might break out while this book is in the press, we can still find encouragement in the fact that as yet none has been reported. Indeed, according to a poll by *Yank*, the army weekly, on "What changes would you like to see made in post-war America," the soldiers "mentioned, above everything the need for wiping out racial and religious discrimination."[1] If the soldiers keep the faith after they have returned to the United States, this war will not have been fought entirely in vain.

Second on the list of the soldiers was the need for a better educational system. Negroes would heartily endorse this need, especially those who live in the South. The report of the Harvard Committee points out that "Mississippi, for instance, is able to pay its teachers and principals an average annual salary of $559 against New York's, $2,604. . . . Indeed, if South Carolina spent its entire state budget for education, it would still be spending less per pupil than do several states."[2] This excellent report thus emphasizes the relative poverty of the Southern states. But, strangely enough, it does not call attention to the disparity between the per capita expenditure in these Southern states for white children and for colored children. Mississippi, for example, spends six times as much for the education of each white child as for that of each colored child. Even in one of the most advanced states, North Carolina, where equalization of salaries is being achieved, Negro children still do not have equality in length of school term, curriculum content, transportation and school facilities.

This war has demonstrated that education is also a national problem. Dr. Martin Jenkins of Howard University and his associates have convincingly demonstrated that the greatest number of Negroes rejected for the army because of the inability to meet educational standards came precisely from those states that provided the least opportunities for education. Now, if these Southern states can not meet their quotas, then an added burden falls upon the Northern states that afford better education. In other words, white boys from Northern states have given up their life because Negroes from Southern states were denied educational opportunities that would make them good combat troops. Even South Carolina came to realize this fact and demanded better opportunities for Negroes in education in order to reduce the number of white soldiers drafted from that state.

As a consequence, there should be more support for a federal bill for public education, especially if adequate provisions are retained that will assure an equitable distribution of federal funds in those states that have separate schools. But, it should be remembered, equitable distribution of federal funds will not assure complete equality of expendi-

[1] *New York Times,* Magazine Section, August 5, 1945, p. 10.
[2] Buck, *et al., General Education,* p. 16.

tures. The states must be induced to allocate their own funds equitably. Perhaps the experience of this war will make them see the error of their ways in the light of their own "white" self-interest.

If the best results are to be achieved, education must be interpreted in the broadest sense and not merely in terms of instruction in the classroom. The plan adopted in Springfield, Massachusetts, points the way in both the classroom and out of it. There is really nothing new in the "Springfield Plan." It is unique only in the sense that it tries, and very successfully, to do what all persons of good-will know must be done. Its success rests upon the facts that it has a mixed school population, a mixed staff, and community activities that embrace all members of the population. It should be noted also that, however valuable Negro History Week may be, Springfield's "I Am an American" Program embraces not only Negroes but also Jews, Poles, French Canadians and other foreign-born. Here is democracy not only in theory but in practice. The extension of this program in cities that have a mixed student body should be one of the most constructive steps in the realization of the dream of American democracy.

Any discussion of education leads naturally to the question: How far can education change the established practices in a community? Some students, especially followers of William Graham Sumner, are convinced that "Stateways can not change folkways." On the other hand, Dr. Clyde Miller is sure that "Prejudice is a Disease: It *can* be cured." I am convinced that Dr. Miller is right. In my boyhood days I had many prejudices against Catholics. I had picked up in some way practically all the vile tales about Catholics the origins of which Dr. Ray A. Billington traces in his *The Protestant Crusade*. Today, while remaining critical of some practices of the Catholic (and of the Protestant) Church, I do not bother about the religious affiliation of anybody. How much of this is the result of an intellectual emancipation and how much the result of indifference to religion in general, I do not know.

I had also had a prejudice against the invasion by girls of boys' sacred precincts. When the girls in our high school first played basketball, we boys looked on with as much astonishment as a white man once did when I correctly used a finger-bowl in a dining car. Today I am almost willing to admit that women are the equal of men, even though when women first began to drive street cars in Washington I waited until a man-driven car came along. Once, however, when I was in a hurry I *had* to board a car driven by a woman. Now it makes no difference. In the same way, many white persons have doubted the ability of Negroes to meet the tests of white men. (I myself felt better when I went down to Tuskegee and saw Negroes actually flying aeroplanes.) Necessity is not only the mother of inventions but also one of the most potent factors in improving race relations. It is a pity that a world war that has killed 25,000,000 men and cost a trillion dollars has been necessary to prove that Negroes can do jobs that many persons previously denied they could do.

The experiences of some "emancipated Southerners" further prove the value of education in its broadest sense as a curative for prejudice. One of the most valuable contributions to better race relations in the United States and elsewhere would be a summary of case histories on "Why I Stopped Hating Negroes." One acquaintance said that she was reformed when she saw a Negro girl who was more chic than she was. Another was emancipated when a colored girl made better grades than she did. Still another Southerner saw the light as a result of his conversion to Christian Science. One young Southern girl, with "typical feminine perversity," became intellectually interested in the Negro problem when her parents tried to steer her away from it and definitely determined to do something about it when she saw a Southern white lady, without provocation, slap a Negro college president in Atlanta, Georgia, in a vain attempt to provoke a race riot because colored and white students were meeting together to discuss America's most difficult problem.

Even when such radical eradication of race prejudice is not always possible, discrimination can be removed. Ohio, for example, has long had one of the most rigid civil rights laws. But it has been allowed to fall into "innocuous desuetude." But a group of young people organized the Vanguard League to encourage the fullest enjoyment of the law. Their success has been almost phenomenal. Today Negroes may obtain accommodations in the best hotel in Columbus and eat in the restaurants and go to the theaters whereas a few years ago they would have been denied. The fact that in a few establishments the management still passes out a mimeographed sheet with the quotation from the law when a colored customer comes in is simply added proof that stateways can change folkways.

These experiences by no means prove that all conditions can be changed by law or legal decision. We must regretfully agree with Mark Ethridge, a so-called liberal Southerner, who said in substance that not all the armies of the world could now make the South abandon segregation. But white admitting the impossibility of changing overnight the pattern in the South and in some places in the North, we should not give up the ultimate goal. We should always declare that, the Supreme Court to the contrary notwithstanding, there is no such thing as "separate but equal accommodations." For even when the physical facilities are equal, as they rarely are, *the very fact of segregation constitutes the inequality.*

The question of segregation raises the most difficult problem in Negro-white relations. The abolition of segregation, many persons in both the North and South argue, would mean social equality. Of course, this term has never had a precise meaning except opposition to intermarriage. But many persons who believe that they oppose social equality themselves are guilty of some participation in what other persons call social equality. Many Southerners, for example, employ Negroes in personal family roles that in the North would be reserved for only whites. Some Southern restaurants and theaters have special sections reserved for Negroes whereas in a border city like Washington, for example, Negroes are not admitted at all to any white movie (if they are recognized) and to some restaurants. Washington, indeed, affords a most interesting example of the inconsistencies of this phase of social equality. In certain places, not indicated here for fear that the white purists might start a campaign to remove them from the list, Negroes are served with every courtesy. But in a restaurant right across the street, they would be charged with trying to practise social equality. Only two hotels refuse to serve Negroes when they are guests of a group meeting in a private dining room; none will serve a Negro who goes in as an individual guest. Many Negroes have spoken to white audiences and have eaten with persons in the audience who have declared their willingness to grant Negroes equal economic opportunity but not social equality.

Since the publication of the excellent sociological treatise, *An American Dilemma,* by Gunnar Myrdal and his associates, practically all "authorities" on the race question have accepted the dictum that economic equality is more readily granted than is social equality. I seriously doubt this is true as far as the North is concerned. It is not unusual for Negroes to be entertained either in hotels or in the homes of their white friends in the North who have only white servants in their home and who would not give a decent job to a Negro in their bank, office or factory. Indeed, Doxey Wilkerson, who follows rather closely the Marxist principles of economic determinism, argues that opposition to social equality is only a subterfuge for opposition to economic equality since economic equality would inevitably lead to social equality including even intermarriage.

While I do not agree that opposition to social equality is only a subterfuge, although I have seen some "professional Southerners" not even bat an eye in the presence of an occasional Negro at social affairs, we realize that many persons, North as well as South, oppose and deny equal opportunities in industry and education for fear that ultimately they will lead to social equality, that is, intermarriage. As I have elsewhere stated, we will all be dead a hundred years from now and Americans will do then what they wish and not what we decree in 1945. But this should be said now. Opposition to intermarriage purely on racial grounds is an assertion of the "inferiority" of the Negro. Opposition because of realization of the fact that marriage is a difficult institution even under the best circumstances and an exceedingly difficult one when it flies in the face of the established pattern of the community should not be lightly dismissed. But acceptance of this fact does not mean that when the community is ready to accept intermarriage, as it is in some parts of the United States today, the laws should be changed to prevent it.

The fact that today the Negro problem is a national problem rather than a sectional problem, while temporarily resulting in an increase of segregation, should in the long run mean a more intelligent approach to the problem. So long as the South was treated as the "problem child" of the nation, it resented any suggestion for improving race relations in the South, especially if these suggestions involved "social equality." Now, however, that the North has to meet problems similar to those in the South instead of looking at them through a long-range telescope a national solution to the problem is necessary.

An indication of this national approach is seen in pending legislation. On the one hand, a law to establish a permanent Fair Employment Practice Committee, while necessary primarily to prevent discrimination against Negroes (and incidentally against Catholics and Jews), is almost as necessary in the North as it is in the South. Similarly, the extension of social security to include domestics and farm workers would primarily benefit Negroes, and bills for full employment, a minimum wage of sixty-five cents an hour and a maximum of twenty-five dollars a week for twenty-six weeks for the unemployed would benefit many Negro workers.

In the meanwhile, action by states should be sought, for there is such a thing as "social climate." If any considerable number of states had followed the example of New York in enacting a state Fair Employment Practice Law, it would be easier for Congress to do likewise.

Negroes must be unified, of course, if a national approach to the question is to produce the best results. Some Southern Negroes have been just as antagonistic to "interference" by "furriners" as have Southern whites. But fourteen Negroes, so-called conservatives, liberals and radicals, Southerners as well as Northerners, have expressed an unlooked for unanimity in their desires for first-class citizenship. These desires, set forth in *What the Negro Wants* may be summarized as follows: Equality of opportunity; equal pay for equal work; equal protection of the laws; equality of suffrage; equal recognition of the dignity of the human being; abolition of public segregation. When these aims shall have been achieved, the United States will be in a position to assume the moral leadership in world affairs that her military and economic power merit.

R. W. Logan, *The Negro and the Post-War World: A Primer* (Washington: Minorities Publishers, 1945), pp. 62–75. The Editor is grateful to Professor Logan for consenting to this republication.

100

RACE RELATIONS IN PUERTO RICO AND THE VIRGIN ISLANDS

by Eric Williams

At the time of the publication of the following essay, the present Prime Minister of Trinidad was an assistant professor at Howard University and a research member of the Anglo-American Caribbean Commission.

I

The islands of the Caribbean differ in size, political affiliation, religious beliefs and language; but the basic difference is ethnic. Racially, the Caribbean falls into two distinct groups: the territories with a comparatively large white population, and the territories with a predominantly black or colored population.

In the 1940 United States census, the population of Puerto Rico was given as 76.55 percent white; the corresponding figure for the Virgin Islands was 9 percent. There are further divergencies within the Virgin Islands group. Only 3.2 percent of the population of the island of St. Croix was given as white, as compared with 15.8 percent for the island of St. Thomas. Charlotte Amalie, the chief city of St. Thomas, had a white population of 12.1 percent; the two chief cities of St. Croix had white populations of 2.2 and 4.3 percent respectively. This ethnic difference is the consequence of the particular economy developed in the various regions. Where the plantation economy based on sugar predominated, Negro slavery was essential and the territory automatically became black. The Virgin Islands fell in this category, together with Haiti and the British, French and Netherlands possessions. Where the small farmer survived, in a coffee or tobacco or livestock economy, white labor was predominant. Puerto Rico, Cuba and, to a lesser extent, The Dominican Republic were in this group. . . .

In Puerto Rico today a population of close to two million people is crowded on a small island of slightly more than two million acres, less than half of which are arable. The population has doubled twice in the last century and is increasing at a net rate of 30,000 a year. The chief means of subsistence is the land, and the principal crop sugar. The sugar industry accounts for 60 percent of the total export trade, occupies 40 percent of all farm lands, employs 40 percent of the working population, and accounts for 90 percent of the freight hauled by the public railways. The industry achieved this supremacy by reason of tariff protection in the United States market, and without this tariff protection the crop would be almost eliminated. Its further expansion is prohibited by the quota system. Sugar has brought to the island a phenomenal increase in wealth, but the average Puerto Rican is today a landless wage earner, ill-fed, ill-housed and ill-clothed, living on an income of $341 a year. Puerto Rico today has a subsidized economy. Federal contributions, direct and indirect, amounted to $57,000,000 in 1942, or approximately $30 per capita.

In the Virgin Islands a population of 25,000 people live on 85,000 acres, of which less than one-sixth is crop land. With 11,600 acres of cropland and 8,000 acres in cultivation, St. Croix, the agricultural center of the group, supports a population of nearly 13,000. Yet the population has declined by more than 50 percent in the last century; the decline in St. John is more than 70 percent, while for the group as a whole it is more than 40 percent. Large-scale emigration represented an unconscious effort to achieve some equilibrium between population and means of subsistence. In spite of such emigration, the Administrator of St. Croix estimates that the present population of that island is 25 percent greater than the island can support. The National Resources Planning Board is even more pessimistic. In its "Development Plan for the Virgin Islands," the Board frankly confesses its inability to see a way of providing for more than 60 percent of the population of the area. Sugar, the main crop of St. Croix, yields 10 tons per acre as compared with 30 in Puerto Rico. Without tariff protection the industry would collapse overnight. Before the war, tourist expenditures were the chief supplementary source of revenue. National defense projects have taken their place during the war. The average income in St. Croix is $400 per year; the income of the working classes is much lower. Even this standard of living is achieved only by subsidies. Federal contributions in 1942 amounted to nearly $1,000,000, or $39 per capita.

It is in this concrete economic setting that we must view the question of race relations. The struggle for survival, by the community and by the individual, is a grim one.

II

Legal discrimination in the two countries is unknown. Children of all colors meet on equal terms in the public schools, though discrimination is prevalent in private schools, even those which receive government grants. There are no segregated housing areas. Whites, blacks and mulattoes sit side by side in theaters, churches and public vehicles, and lie side by side in the cemeteries. The law recognizes no differences based on race, color, creed, national origin or previous condition. Lynchings are unheard of.

This absence of legal discrimination against the Negro arises from the fact that racial differences are subordinate to those of class. Muñoz Marín, Puerto Rico's distinguished statesman and popular leader, tells the story of the white voter who was asked by a colored lawyer to vote for a certain candidate. The white voter replied: "You *blanquitos* ["little whites," not to be confused with the American term "poor whites"] have too much." The story is very revealing. "White" denotes class and status rather than color and race. In the Caribbean generally a man is not only as white as he looks. If by virtue of his position or his wealth he moves about in white society, he automatically becomes "white." An American student, Dr. Charles C. Rogler, has made an intensive study of a small Puerto Rican town, Comerío. He found that social distinctions were based on class and not race, and that the two coalesced merely because the Negro is never found in the upper class. "However," he adds, "if, to take a hypothetical case, a dark mulatto were to belong to the upper class, he would be socially defined as a white person." There is no unanimity as to who are Negroes and who are not. Some Puerto Rican families may have one child classified in the census as white, another as colored. It is well known that, in order not to antagonize some prominent family which does not wish to be identified with Negroes, the census officer would classify its members as white, and perhaps change the classification later. For this reason some observers believe that the percentage of colored people in the Puerto Rican census has been grossly underestimated. It is a notorious fact that these "white-minded Negroes," as they are called in St. Thomas, have colored ancestors. The mulatto in the United States Caribbean possessions thus has a much greater social mobility than his kinsfolk in the United States. It must be emphasized that this mobility is very largely a result of historical causes.

The mulatto's concern with color is understandable in a society where his handicaps increase more and more drastically as the pigmentation deepens. But the consciousness of legal equality tends to give the colored people confidence in social relationships. For example, within the last 70 years numbers of French people have migrated to St. Thomas from the French island of St. Barthélemy. Today this French colony has more than a thousand members, concentrated in a fishing village three miles west of Charlotte Amalie and in a community of farmers on the northern side of the island. They keep very largely to themselves, speak a French patois though they understand and speak English, and are easily identified by the obvious signs of malnutrition they reveal. The islanders derisively call them *Chachas*. The attitude of the colored people to this French community is, indeed, one of unveiled contempt. Some of the French people send their children to the schools, wearing shoes. Some of the adults have taken to trade, and own grocery stores and liquor bars in the French district. But the prejudice against them remains, and the marriage of a colored girl to one of these Frenchmen is an occasion for endless gossip. The children, it is said, will always have "the Chacha look." The feeling is unmistakable in St. Thomas that "the Chachas are all right in their place." It is a complete reversal of the relationships that would prevail in other countries.

The Negro enjoys equality with the white man politically as well as legally. Negroes in Puerto Rico vote not as Negroes but as Puerto Ricans identified with one of the major parties. The Republican Party was founded by a colored Puerto Rican, Dr. José Celso Barbosa, one of the great names in Puerto Rico's history. Today colored Puerto Ricans are found in the Insular Congress and in municipal government, as well as in high administrative positions. Ramos Antonini, the colored deputy leader of the Populares Party, was elected as representative-at-large in the 1942 elections and polled the largest vote. In other words, he does not represent a Negro constituency nor are his supporters Negroes only. His color debarred him from becoming Speaker of the House of

Representatives, however. Dr. Leopoldo Figueroa, another colored Puerto Rican, head of the maternity section of the Municipal Hospital, is one of the chief stalwarts of the Coalition Party. Until recently a prominent Negro lawyer sat on the Public Service Commission; another is Chief Examiner of the Civil Service Commission. In the Virgin Islands in recent years, very dark men have taken positions that were reserved, under the Danes, for Europeans or light colored people.

Thus it is that, by virtue of the absence of legal discrimination, the high degree of social mobility, the emphasis on class, and the political equality that prevails, unity among Negroes on the race question does not exist in Puerto Rico and the Virgin Islands. The word "Negro" is seldom used in the Caribbean, and, when used, is not a "fighting" word. All over the Caribbean it is either synonymous with "slave," or is a term of endearment, used colloquially by both whites and Negroes. The Spanish word for slaveship is, significantly, *negrero,* but there is no Spanish equivalent for "nigger" or "damned nigger." The militancy of American Negroes has no counterpart in Puerto Rico and St. Thomas. To repeat—the issue in the Caribbean is not one of race but one of class. Puerto Ricans talk not so much of "the colored race" as of "the colored class." The conflict is not between white and black but, as in St. Thomas, between those who live on one of the three hills on which the town is built and those who do not. Muñoz Marín puts the same idea in different words: there are in Puerto Rico only two classes, those who wear neckties and those who don't. The situation is the same in the British West Indies, where the mark of differentiation is the wearing of shoes rather than of neckties. It is to be noted that similar conditions prevail in Haiti where there is no considerable number of white people.

III

Legally, the Negro is on a footing of equality with the white man. On the social level, however, race prejudice antedated the American occupation, exists today, and is increasing. It will be readily appreciated, however, that in the nature of things social discrimination does not affect the large majority of colored people. The entry of foreign capital has brought the practices associated with the countries of origin. It is not the influx of Americans as individuals but of American capital that has resulted in the recrudescence of the race problem. Social discrimination is most obvious in private employment in the upper brackets Conventionally, none but white people or the fairest-skinned among the colored are employed by banks, sugar corporations, airlines and shipping companies, and the large department stores.

Discrimination is common in all the better hotels and restaurants. A few years ago a well-known restaurant in San Juan, then under non-local management, refused to serve people of color. The issue was taken to the District Court, where a decision in favor of the management was given. The Supreme Court upheld the verdict, and the practice continued until the establishment passed into Puerto Rican hands. In the leading hotel in Puerto Rico the patronage is almost wholly composed of whites from the United States. Colored people are never seen in the dining room or at the bar unless they are foreigners traveling on government missions. The outstanding hotel in St. Thomas, government-owned, and leased on a contract which specifically prohibited racial discrimination, refused to admit colored people until recently, when it was turned over to a new manager who is colored. There is, however, another hotel which still refuses to serve colored people, on the plea that it is reserved for service men. Clubs in Puerto Rico are customarily classified as "first class" and "second class." Whites belong to both types of club, but Negroes belong only to "second class" ones. Cases have arisen in recent years of refusal by night clubs to serve colored people; in one instance the establishment was fined $25. Such small fines are locally considered a joke. In the University of Puerto Rico, colored students, the majority destined to be schoolteachers, are freely admitted. Yet two members of the faculty, in a special study of the Negro in Puerto Rico, have brought to light a number of sayings about the Negro common to university students. The saying, "God made the Negro so that animals can rest," is an example.

Social discrimination has increased in Puerto Rico to such an extent that the legislature passed a Civil Rights Act in 1943 guaranteeing the right of all persons irrespective of differences of race, creed or political affiliation to enjoy the facilities afforded by public places, businesses and any agency of the Insular Government. The penalties decreed are a fine of from $25 to $100, or a jail term of from ten to a hundred days. Despite this law, however, colored people in Puerto Rico are very reluctant to visit certain hotels or night clubs.

IV

The lower classes of Caribbean society look to America as the land of opportunity. They are the underdogs now, since they are black, and the left-handed racial egalitarianism of the United States, where one drop of colored blood makes one a Negro, gives them that feeling of equality with the colored aristocracy which is ruled out at home by the emphasis on status. To these people contact with the United States means material benefits, the opportunity of education and the monthly remittances from emigrants who have made good.

But the islanders are even more aware of racial distinctions than they were before American rule. This is not to say that the presence of large numbers of American troops, mostly colored, in the area has produced any serious change in the racial situation, as far as the masses are concerned. The rank and file of American troops have fitted into local society. Barred from officers' clubs, looked down upon by white and colored aristocracy, the enlisted men have gravitated toward the people of their own social milieu, the colored middle and lower classes. Left alone, white soldiers and colored population can and will work out an adjustment of their own. It is particularly important that they should do so. One instance taken from Jamaica suggests the problem. On December 8, 1943, an advertisement appeared in *The Gleaner* of Jamaica for "help" at the American base. The advertisement specified: "White, Male and Female." The next day the same advertisement appeared, minus one word: "White." But Kingston was in an uproar. Letters and protests poured in, the Corporation met and passed a resolution vigorously condemning the "insult," and voted that a copy of the resolution be sent to President Roosevelt. The United States Base Commander made a public apology, but the tension continued. Discriminatory notices are, in fact, a common feature of the West Indian press. But the incident is a reminder of Caribbean sensitiveness on the race question and of the perils inherent in the situation.

The constituents of the race problem in Puerto Rico and the Virgin Islands are, in short, a historical background that emphasizes class rather than race; an economic setting in which the problem of the Negro is merged in the larger problem of the community; the absence of legal discrimination against the black masses; and the pressure of social discrimination on the lighter-skinned middle class minority. There is no "solution" to such a problem. With the economic and social forces as they are it is difficult to see how there can be any substantial changes in race relations in the two communities. Ultimately, the shape of race relations in the United States will be the decisive factor in the relations between races in these colonies.

Some Puerto Rican sociologists advance as a solution the long tradition of interbreeding, which will, they believe, "whiten" the Puerto Rican Negroes in 75 to 100 years. But this is quite ridiculous, since the essential character of the present relations would prevent this "whitening" even if it were desirable and, within reasonable human expectation, possible. On the occasion of the Jamaican incident referred to above, a publicist advanced a more serious proposal. Americans, he said, must learn West Indian psychology. "It will not be enough for the Americans to say they followed the local custom."

There are many Americans in the islands who take these questions seriously. They must seek to understand that conditions in the West Indies are not like conditions at home. President Roosevelt's directive to United States forces in the Caribbean to respect local customs has had good results, in this regard. All Americans in the area must recognize the particular racial background and historical development of the islands. The Administration must try to formulate policy and practice in accordance with the history and patterns of the area, and not allow itself to be influenced by the national traditions of the interests which it represents. Given the history and social sentiments of the island, it is not at all impossible for the United States Administration in Puerto Rico to strike blows at race prejudice and to try to develop an official attitude toward race relations in harmony with the aspirations and practice of the colonial areas. There are already signs that the American and British authorities recognize the necessity of action on this question. It is interesting to note that a special correspondent of the London *Times,* in two articles on the West Indies published on October 29 and 30, 1943, said that "it is time to consider whether Colonial Office officials should not in future be forbidden to belong to clubs which impose a color bar . . . sooner or later, the color bar which at present surrounds the higher administrative posts must be broken down."

Asked his views on the subject, Muñoz Marín replied simply: "More democracy." Even the colored opponents of this Puerto Rican leader agree that he and his party have given Negroes a square deal and opened positions to them, especially in the teaching profession and the higher ranks of the police force, from which they were conventionally debarred. The popular movement in these island possessions of the United States stands for "no discrimination," as opposed to what it considers the American trend toward greater discrimination. Similarly the Communist Party has consistently opposed racial discrimination. Recent events in Europe have shown that even liberty and racial rights which have been exercised for centuries are not safe except in a fully democratic order. In trying to base the struggle against racial discrimination upon the democratic aspirations of the people, Muñoz Marín is in harmony with the best thought and increasing practice of the age.

Foreign Affairs, January, 1945; XXIII, 308–17.

101

COLONIALISM, PEACE,
AND THE UNITED NATIONS

by Board of Directors, N.A.A.C.P.

On March 12, 1945, the Board of Directors issued the statement which
follows, in connection with the founding meeting of the United Nations,
then being held in San Francisco. Its chief author was Dr. Du Bois, who,
in 1944, had returned to the N.A.A.C.P. as Director of Special Research
with his main task—as he saw it—to develop a global approach to questions
of colonialism and racism.

The National Association for the Advancement of Colored People
earnestly desires the prevention of war and the future preservation of
peace in the world. It believes that one step toward this would be an
international military force to curb aggression; but it also believes that
beyond and above physical force must stand spiritual faith. For this
reason it demands the following steps to make war at once unlikely
and unprofitable:

1. A declaration at San Francisco of the racial equality of the great groups
   of mankind in international law.
2. A further declaration that the ownership of colonies, protectorates and
   dependencies, by any country, has been and still is a frequent and repeated cause of war and oppression; and that therefore it be the sense
   of the United Nations that the ownership and control of colonies and
   dependencies be recognized in international law only on the following
   terms:
   a. That the dominating country solemnly engage to give the peoples of
      such areas immediately a voice in their own government.
   b. That it solemnly declare its intention that by a given date these peo-
      ples shall either be integrated into the polity of the mother country
      with full rights of citizenship; or shall be allowed to become inde-
      pendent and autonomous countries, as the peoples themselves shall
      decide.
   c. That the natural resources of these countries including mines, forests,
      land and its materials shall be owned by the colonies and used pri-
      marily for the benefit of the inhabitants of the area; that the organi-
      zation of industry, the control of labor and investment of capital
      shall be ordered for the benefit of the people of the area and not
      simply for profit of invested capital or primarily for the welfare of
      people outside the colony.

d. That an international Mandates Commission be established and implemented under the supreme authority of the United Nations with the right to supervise the government of territory mandated after the First World War and any such enemy territory acquired in the present war and to investigate, report and recommend action in the case of countries who do not keep their commitments in colonies or will not make such commitments; and that in such cases the conduct and administration of these colonies be placed under control of the Mandates Commission, backed by the authority of the United Nations.

The National Association for the Advancement of Colored People points out that every demand on colonial powers here made has at some time or other been declared by these powers as an integral part of their policy. Lacking only in these promises was any method of checking their sincerity or accomplishment by international supervision. Peace and civilization, humanity and religion today demand this sacrifice of independence on the part of the world's great powers for social progress and democracy. We sincerely believe that no action less than this is going to rescue this world from continued war and the persistent exploitation of a large portion of mankind if not indeed the majority of human beings.

Mimeographed release.

102

NEW YORK ANTI-COLONIALISM CONFERENCE

With Du Bois' inspiration, the N.A.A.C.P. called a Conference on Colonialism, which was held in the auditorium of the 135th Street Branch of the New York Public Library on April 6, 1945. Cooperating were the Council on African Affairs and the West Indies National Council. Participating, in addition to Du Bois, were Kwame Nkrumah (then of Lincoln University in Pennsylvania), Charles A. Petioni, W. Alphaeus Hunton. Kumar Goshal, Richard B. Moore, L. D. Reddick, Rayford W. Logan, and scholars from Puerto Rico, Nigeria, Burma, Korea, India, and Indonesia. This conference adopted the following Resolution.

The ownership of colonies, protectorates and dependencies, by any country, has been and still is a repeated cause of war and oppression; and is causing extreme poverty, predominant illiteracy and widespread famine, undernourishment and disease. Out of these colonies comes large income to increase the power and excite the greed and intensify the envy of great modern nations. For this reason we demand that immediate steps be taken towards ending the ownership and control of all colonies and dependencies.

Naturally so momentous a change cannot be immediately achieved but we demand that the United Nations at San Francisco establish an international Colonial Commission.

This Colonial Commission should be composed of representatives of all permanent members of the Security Council, additional representatives elected by the General Assembly, and members who represent directly the several broad groups of colonial peoples. The Commission should appoint its own staff of colonial experts and advisors, including the services of qualified persons of all races, and particularly persons indigenous to the colonies.

This body shall be empowered to oversee and facilitate the transition of peoples from colonial status to such autonomy as colonial peoples themselves may desire.

To this end all territories mandated after the first World War and all territory seized and internationalized after this war shall, except as military necessities require, be under the direct control of the Colonial Commission.

The minimum functions of the Colonial Commission, in addition to those mentioned, shall be:

1. To establish economic, social, and political standards to be maintained in the administration of all colonial territories.
2. To use the powers of the United Nations to insure adherence to these standards by all colonial powers. No state which practices legally sanctioned discrimination against any body of its inhabitants because of race, creed, or color should be regarded as qualified to serve as a mandatory power.
3. To establish the time necessary for each colonial territory to develop to the stage at which it can exercise political self-determination, and to declare the date on which this right is to be exercised.
4. To promote the fullest measure of international cooperation in securing the industrialization; economic advancement; improvement of education, health and other social services; transportation; communication; and other similar matters in all colonial areas.

The future of colonial peoples and territories is a world problem. World security cannot be achieved unless international responsibility is assumed for the rapid advancement of all dependent peoples so that they may exercise self-determination and be integrated with other peoples in the general progress of the world toward a higher and more stable civilization. From the point of view of the needs of both the colonies and the industrially advanced nations, economic progress in the dependent areas is immediately and imperatively essential.

The welfare of developed and undeveloped countries alike depends upon the realization of a far greater exchange of goods and services between them than has existed, and this in turn necessitates the general leveling up of the living standards of hundreds of millions of colonial subjects. Such economic progress is possible only within a framework in which the restrictions upon social development, democratic rights, and self-government—restrictions which are characteristic of the colonial world as a whole—are removed.

> W. A. Hunton
> Council on African Affairs
> Francis N. Nkrumah
> Gold Coast, West Africa
> Rayford W. Logan
> Association of Colleges and Secondary Schools
>   for Negroes
> John R. Andu
> Netherlands Indonesia
> Maung Saw Tun
> Burma
> Akiki Nyabongo
> Uganda, East Africa
> L. D. Reddick
> Schomburg Collection, 135th Street Branch of
>   the New York Public Library
> Kumar Goshal
> India
> W. E. B. Du Bois
> National Association for the Advancement of
>   Colored People

Du Bois Papers, formerly in editor's custody.

103

APPEAL TO U.N. FOUNDING MEETING
ON BEHALF OF THE CARIBBEAN PEOPLES

In April, 1945, individuals and organizations from the West Indies and the Guianas and British Honduras, having met in New York City, submitted the following appeal to the San Francisco Conference establishing the United Nations. The actual signers of the appeal did so on behalf of the West Indies National Council; they were Charles A. Petioni, M.D., president; Richard B. Moore, vice-president; and Leonard Lowe, secretary.

To this historic Assembly of Delegates of the United Nations met to lay the foundations of World Security and Peace, the Caribbean Peoples which are still held as colonial dependencies now look with eager hope and confident expectation. In this Conference these peoples see the great opportunity never before afforded by history for the adoption at last of those democratic principles and the establishment of effective means of enforcement which will enable them to realize their long sought goal and inalienable human rights to freedom, security, and self-government along with all the liberty-loving nations of the world.

Events preceding and during this war have shown that security and peace depend upon organization which will ensure justice, equal rights and protection to all peoples, to small and weak nations as well as to great and strong, and which will provide guarantees for the effective exercise of genuine democratic rights by all people who cherish and defend democracy.

It is therefore essential that the voice of dominated peoples, seeking justice and the exercise of those democratic rights for which they have fought and bled, should be heard and accorded due consideration by this World Conference upon which the solemn responsibility rests to rescue mankind from the ravages of war, insecurity, and slavery.

Because the very status of colonial dependency imposes onerous restrictions which render it extremely difficult if not impossible for these peoples to make direct representation, it is necessary for the West Indies National Council to present this Appeal on behalf of the Peoples of the British, French, and Dutch West Indies, the Guianas and British Honduras. This Council, organized by natives of these areas and supported by liberty-loving individuals and organizations irrespective of nationality, creed, or race, reflects the fundamental aspirations of these peoples based upon original ties, constant contact and knowledge, and the statements of responsible democratic representatives of the peoples of these areas.

This Appeal is therefore respectfully and earnestly presented together with seven proposals, adopted by this Council and endorsed by a public meeting assembled on April 16, 1945 at the Renaissance Casino in New York City and further endorsed by the Paragon Progressive Community Association, Inc., the Congress of Dominated Nations, and other organizations and prominent individuals. The Council requests that this Appeal be duly considered and urges this World Conference to adopt its recommendations and proposals in the form appropriate to secure their enforcement. The Council further desires to assure this World Conference that the peoples of these Caribbean areas may be depended upon wholeheartedly to support every measure necessary to the establishment of security, peace, and democracy, as their record amply demonstrates, and also to assume and discharge all duties and responsibilities in furtherance thereof.

The Declaration of Rights of the Caribbean Peoples to Self-Determination and Self-Government was presented by the West Indies National Emergency Committee to the Pan-American Foreign Ministers' Conference at Havana in July 1940. As a result, the Act of Havana while providing for concerted action by American Powers, recognized certain democratic rights of the Caribbean peoples.

Nevertheless, the Act of Havana was never invoked, though the French and Dutch Empires failed to provide protection and ceased in fact to exist as effective governing heads for these colonies. For a period indeed the people of the French West Indies and Guiana found themselves subject to the control of the fascist Vichy regime against their will and profound democratic conviction.

Despite the debilitating hindrances and galling yoke of colonial domination, the Caribbean peoples have loyally and unstintingly supported the United Nations in the present war against Nazi barbarism and fascist domination. In proportion to their size and numbers and the meager actual resources left to them after centuries of colonial retardation and impoverishment, they have made notable contributions to the armed forces and in labor power, finance, and essential materials such as oil, bauxite, etc.

Situated around the approaches to the Panama Canal, which was built mainly by their labor, at the strategic centre of the defenses of the Americas, the peoples of the West Indies have suffered and withstood savage attacks by German submarines. Sites for vital bases and labor for their construction have been willingly furnished for the defense of the Americas and the United Nations, even though the rights of these peoples to consultation were not considered.

The Anglo-American Caribbean Commission has conducted broadcasts, made studies, and held conferences, but has done nothing practically to implement the rights of these peoples to self-government and self-determination. These fundamental rights are contravened by the very composition of this Commission which does not include a single direct representative of the Caribbean peoples or any one allied with them by ties of origin, feeling, and contact, in spite of repeated requests for such representation.

The economic and social conditions prevailing in these areas are inhuman, tragic, and unbearable. The overwhelming majority of the population must labor when employment is available at wages far below the level of human subsistence. Housing and health conditions are among the worst in the world; illegitimacy, illiteracy, and the death rates are appallingly high. These dire conditions, resulting directly from centuries of slavery and colonial rule, have been intensified by the war to the point of "almost famine conditions in some places," as acknowledged in a recent bulletin of the British Information Services. Yet the Secretary of State for the Colonies of Great Britain in a recent statement publicly laments that the British taxpayer will be called upon to contribute to a small proposed fund for social development in the colonies.

The West Indies National Council respectfully but firmly submits to the United Nations' Conference that such colonial conditions constitute a major menace to World Security and Peace. The resolute liquidation of these menacing economic conditions should therefore be begun immediately. For this it is imperative to raise the level of living standards and purchasing power of the Caribbean peoples, as of all peoples still subjected to colonial rule, in order to transform them into free and valuable participants in that increased production and exchange of goods and services which is no less essential to the security and peace of the people of the industrially advanced nations than it is to the welfare and progress of those now retarded colonial peoples.

The Council also submits that such economic rehabilitation and progress, so essential to World Security and Peace, can be achieved only by breaking the fetters of imperialist domination and colonial dependency. For in no other way can the free political relations of mutually co-operating, self-governing peoples, fully respecting the democratic rights of each and all, be realized as the indispensable condition for social development and for the full release and stimulation of the energies of all in that increased production and exchange so vital to the security and peace of all mankind.

The Council further submits that the abolition of imperialist domination and colonial dependency will at the same time eliminate those conflicts over colonies which constitute the major source of war in the modern world. The logic of history now demands that imperialist control and colonial subjugation must cease that men may live and attain security and peace. A definite time in the immediate future should therefore be set in agreement with these peoples for the realization of full self-government and democratic rights for the Caribbean peoples and for all other colonial peoples.

In accordance with the foregoing, the West Indies National Council earnestly recommends that a Fund adequate for the economic rehabilitation and social development of the Caribbean areas should be established under international supervision through the proposed International Bank for Reconstruction and Development or some similar agency. This Fund should be open to private and government subscription and substantial contributions to this Fund should be made by the British, French, and Dutch Empires. Since a large share of the vast fortunes and immense wealth of these Empires has been derived from the forced labor of the Caribbean peoples, these contributions would not only be in accord with justice but would also materially spur the increase in production and exchange which is recognized to be necessary to world prosperity, security, and peace.

In respect to their readiness for self-government, it is undeniable that the Caribbean peoples possess all the characteristics of nationality and have many times proclaimed their demand for self-government. To settle this question it is necessary only to point to the numerous West Indians who have occupied and now hold administrative posts in every branch of government and to the late Governor General of Free French Africa, Felix Eboué, a native of the West Indies, whose administrative genius and timely action saved the greater part of Africa, and perhaps all Africa, from falling into the barbarous hands of the Vichy regime and the Nazi hordes in the darkest hours of the present war for the United Nations.

Present discussion and renewed proposals affecting the sovereignty of the West Indian peoples render it our duty to call attention to the following statement affirmed in the Declaration of Rights presented to the Havana Conference and to the supporting evidence adduced therein.

Reflecting and expressing the profound sentiments of the people of the Caribbean areas, this Committee declares that it is firmly opposed to any sale, transfer, mandate, trusteeship, or change of sovereignty of these peoples without the exercise of their inalienable human and democratic right of self-determination.

In view of the urgency with which various proposals for mandates and trusteeship are being pressed upon this World Security Conference, it is imperative to affirm with renewed emphasis the following protest contained in the Statement of the West Indies National Emergency Committee on the Address delivered by Secretary Hull at the Havana Conference.

For, however well intentioned such a proposed collective trusteeship might appear, it cannot be forgotten that this device of trusteeship or mandate has been used and is now being used by imperial governments of the Old World as a means of maintaining control over various peoples and subjecting them to tyrannous oppression and unbridled exploitation. It cannot be conceded for a moment that this discredited formula of trusteeship could be successfully employed in connection with the Caribbean peoples, when it is well known that it has signally failed either to ensure the democratic rights or to preserve the vital interests and welfare of the many down-trodden peoples to whom it has been applied.

In the opinion of this Council however, no truly representative objection might be expected from the Caribbean peoples to an International Commission specifically established to supervise the transition from colonial dependency to full self-government, provided their rights to self-government and self-determination were unequivocally recognized and a definite time mutually agreed upon for the realization of such complete self-government, and provided also that adequate and effective representation on such an International Commission were accorded to bona fide natives of these areas truly representative of the majority of these peoples.

This Council would fail in its sacred duty if it did not urge this World Security Conference to give serious consideration to the grave menace to world security and peace which stems from racial, national, and religious prejudices. This venomous ideology was developed to its monstrous height in the "master race" mania with which the Nazi imperialist butchers, the Italian fascist slaughterers, and the Japanese military war mongers incited their followers to plunge the world into the present holocaust of slaughter and terror. Full cognizance must therefore be taken of the existence of racial, national, and religious prejudices and of the fact that such poisonous prejudices have already reached alarming proportions within most of the democratic nations themselves, with dire results to minorities therein and to colonial peoples controlled by these states.

Moreover, it is imperative to be aware of the fact that these vicious prejudices are inherent in the system of imperialism in which they are rooted and from which they inevitably develop. It is likewise salutary to mark that the horrible atrocities perpetrated at Belsen, Buchenwald, Dachau and elsewhere, at which mankind is now properly aghast, differ only in detail and degree from similar atrocities perpetrated upon colonial and semicolonial peoples. The security and peace of mankind require that the lesson of history be now practically drawn that terror and torture developed at first in colonial areas inevitably reach back to the dominating peoples and menace all mankind.

The resolution adopted at the Chapultepec Conference, recognizing the existence of racial, national, and religious prejudices within the frontiers of any country to be a matter of international concern, is an important step forward. This Council earnestly recommends that this World Conference adopt such a resolution, as a vital principle for the organization of world security and peace, requiring that all nations shall enact and enforce laws with adequate penalties against any and all overt manifestations of such racial, national, and religious prejudices, and shall undertake a vigorous campaign of education for the extirpation of such prejudices and animosities.

The West Indies National Council earnestly and finally urges this World Security Conference to consider and to adopt the following seven proposals in the interests of the Caribbean peoples and of World Security and Peace.

1. Forthright recognition of the inalienable right of the Caribbean peoples to self-government and self-determination.
2. Practical recognition of the age-long objective of the West Indian peoples for voluntary federation.
3. Integration, on the basis of equality, of the Caribbean peoples into the regional organization of the American nations and for their representation in the making of all plans for the political, military, economic and social security of all the peoples of the Americas.
4. Specific inclusion of the Caribbean peoples in the plans of the Conference for post-war rehabilitation and social security in view of the dire economic conditions of these peoples, resulting from colonial rule, which have been intensified by the war and which have reached almost famine conditions.

5. Recognition of the right of the Caribbean peoples to representation at the United Nations' Conference by delegates of their own choosing, as a matter of democracy and justice and by virtue of the vital contribution which the Caribbean peoples have made to the war effort and to democracy in this hemisphere and in the world.
6. Guarantees for the abolition of all discriminatory laws and practices based on race, religion, color or previous condition of servitude or oppression, and for the assurance of full protection of life and liberty for the Caribbean peoples, for the African peoples, and for all peoples without regard to race, creed or color.
7. Genuine equality of rights both in fact and in law for all peoples everywhere and full democratic citizenship rights, including universal adult suffrage, for all people.

The West Indies National Council sincerely hopes for the success of this World Security Council and for the adoption of these measures which will enable the Caribbean peoples to take their rightful place among the nations of the world in a new era of freedom, security, peace and prosperity.

Printed folder, in editor's possession.

104

THE PRESIDENT LEAVES A LEGACY

by The Chicago Defender

The death of President Franklin Delano Roosevelt caused world-wide grief; among Afro-Americans this was deep. A fairly typical reaction was the following editorial in a leading Black newspaper.

Negro America has suffered its greatest loss since Abraham Lincoln in the sudden, shocking death of President Franklin D. Roosevelt.

Perhaps no other single segment of the land will feel his passing as much as the thirteen million colored step-children of this nation.

It is grim, significant symbolism that his death should come almost 80 years to the day since the Great Emancipator was assassinated in Ford's Theater in Washington.

President Roosevelt, like Lincoln, was a Great Emancipator for the darker brother. If Lincoln set the Negro physically free from slavery for the first time in history, it was Roosevelt who pioneered in the struggle to win economic emancipation for the Negro.

By executive order, Lincoln ruled that a man could not be held in servitude because of his color. By executive order, Roosevelt ruled that a man could not be held in economic servitude because of his color.

If only for the beginning of the principle in government that racial discrimination in employment is illegal, President Roosevelt would live in history as a champion of Negro America. But the creation of the Fair Employment Practice Committee was but one of many precedent-shattering moves by the late Chief Executive in the field of racial relations.

Negro America knew and recognized Roosevelt as their most outstanding friend since Lincoln. At the polls colored voters shattered tradition and cast their ballots "overwhelmingly" for a Democrat in 1944 for the first time since Reconstruction. The *Chicago Defender* is proud of its place in the people's movement that returned Roosevelt to office for a fourth time.

Now that the great humanitarian is gone to his final resting place, Negro America joins with a saddened world to mourn his passing, to bow in tribute to the world's greatest citizen.

President Roosevelt is gone, but he has left in his legacy a challenge to America to carry on his stalwart fight to win the war and the peace to come. A vast void has been left by his passing and in the grim first flush of tragedy, America cannot but feel his loss an irreplaceable one.

But America must go on to the promise of the future. President Roosevelt has opened the high road to us, he pointed the way and now the people, the common men and women of this great country, must take up the challenge.

No doubt the greatest challenge of all falls on President Harry S Truman. To most Americans he is an unknown, as are too many Vice Presidents.

Doubtlessly many Negroes will find the man from the jim crow state of Missouri suspect. The unabashed, vulgar efforts of the reactionary camp to claim Truman as their own will be disheartening. Already some liberals have compared President Truman to Andrew Johnson, who detoured Lincoln's blueprint for freedom into devious paths after he succeeded the Great Emancipator.

Negroes cannot but view with alarm his first official move in making James F. Byrnes, South Carolina Negro-hater, one of his chief confidants and closest adviser. We cannot but be sickened by the reports that Truman may replace Secretary of State Edward Stettinius with Byrnes, making the Dixie race-baiter the next in line for the Presidency if Truman should die.

But for all our misgivings, the progressive camp cannot afford to surrender the nation to the reactionaries by default in this crucial, critical hour. Truman has shown that he will not be the strong independent that was Roosevelt, but he will be subject to many pressures.

It is the job of progressive America to demonstrate to Truman beyond a doubt that it is the people's will that the new President follow the straight and narrow path to full democracy that Roosevelt charted.

President Truman has at this early hour pledged his efforts towards carrying out Roosevelt's policies. He goes into office with a sacred obligation to continue the progressive program to which the voters of the nation gave their support last November. Truman was elected to office on the same platform as Roosevelt and has a mandate from the people to follow the liberal path.

Negro America will remember Truman's pledge to support a permanent Fair Employment Practices Committee. They will recall his promise to assure the Negro a full and equal role in the post-war employment picture. They will keep in mind his renunciation of racial intolerance.

They will solemnly hope that Truman can prove himself another Justice Hugo Black, who although he is from Alabama and once was a Klansman has proven himself one of the outstanding progressives in the U.S. Supreme Court.

But above all, Negro America will stand adamant to work for and carry out the ideals of their great champion, the late President Franklin D. Roosevelt. It is our staunch hope that Truman will live up to the faith that was placed in him by the late President and the American people.

President Truman can be assured of the full unrelenting support of the tenth of the nation that is Negro as long as he keeps faith with the ideals of the late President Roosevelt.

Chicago Defender, April 21, 1945.

105

"MISSING THE GREATEST OPPORTUNITY"

by W. E. B. Du Bois

Dr. Du Bois and Walter White—representing the N.A.A.C.P.—were accorded Consultant status to the U.S. delegation at the San Francisco founding meeting of the United Nations. In that capacity, on May 16, 1945, Dr. Du Bois sent the following prophetic memorandum to that delegation.

The attempt to write an International Bill of Rights into the San Francisco Conference without any specific mention of the people living in colonies seems to me a most unfortunate procedure. If it were clearly understood that freedom of speech, freedom from want and freedom from fear, which the nations are asked to guarantee, would without question be extended to the 750 million people who live in colonial areas, this would be a great and fateful step. But the very fact that these people, forming the most depressed peoples in the world, with 90% illiteracy, extreme poverty and a prey to disease, who hitherto for the most part have been considered as sources of profit and not included in the democratic development of the world; and whose exploitation for three centuries has been a prime cause of war, turmoil and suffering;—the omission of specific reference to these peoples is almost advertisement of their tacit exclusion as not citizens of free states, and that their welfare and freedom would be considered only at the will of the countries owning them and not at the demand of enlightened world public opinion.

To insist, therefore, upon this flagrant omission would, Sir, as it seems to me, be missing the greatest opportunity of our age. For the first time in modern history it is possible for three great nations which do not depend upon the exploitation of colonies for their development, to unite and open a new path of progress. We all know that the opposition of Great Britain to any international action on the colonial problem has made the United States refrain from this step and make no allusion to the festering problem of India, of the Netherlands Indies and of West and South Africa.

But is this wise, not only for our own sakes but for the future of the people of Britain, many of whom have denounced the colonial system? We have allowed ourselves in this conference to be estranged from Russia by the plight of a dozen reactionary and Jew-baiting Polish landlords, and have made no comment and taken no action on the great words spoken by Molotov: "We must first of all see to it that dependent countries are enabled as soon as possible to take the path of national independence."

May I beg of you in the name of 13 million Americans who are blood brothers of many millions of these colonists

First, to make a preliminary statement on the essential equality of all races, the same statement which the United States and Great Britain once refused to grant Japan; and identical with the suppressed proposal of the Chinese delegation at Dumbarton Oaks; and that

Secondly, the United States delegation propose this article for the

Charter of the United Nations: "The colonial system of government, however deeply rooted in history and customs, is today undemocratic, socially dangerous and a main cause of wars. The United Nations recognizing democracy as the only just way of life for all peoples make it a first statute of international law that at the earliest practical moment no nation or group shall be deprived of effective voice in its own government and enjoyment of the four freedoms. An international colonial commission on which colonial peoples shall have representation will have power to investigate the facts and implement this declaration under the Security Council."

Respectfully yours,
W. E. B. Du Bois

Mimeographed sheet, Du Bois Papers.

106

THE POSTWAR WORLD BEGINS

Soon after World War II commenced, the Social Science Institute at Fisk University began publishing *A Monthly Summary of Events and Trends in Race Relations.* From its Volume III, numbers 1–2 (a combined issue) and 3, 4, and 6 (August–September, October, November, December, 1945, and January, 1946), selections are offered as a fitting conclusion for this documentary survey of the life and history of the Afro-American people from the beginnings of the New Deal to the beginnings of the postwar world.

I

NEGRO VETERANS RETURN

One of the most important race relations jobs of the next ten years will be the full integration of minority group veterans into a post-war world. There are 900,000 Negroes serving today in the armed forces. By the end of the war well over a million will have been in uniform. Large scale demobilization is now taking place. Ultimately then, a million Negro GI's, each with three or four dependents or close family connections, will be discharged. This means that a third of the entire Negro group will be directly affected by the post-war opportunities available to Negro veterans and the use they can make of their rights and benefits.

What are the opportunities open to the Negro veteran and what are his plans? Using the reports on the "Post-War Plans of the Soldier" compiled by the Armed Service Forces and data as to the number of Negroes serving in the Army released by the Adjutant General's Office, it is possible to get a good picture of what Negro GI's are planning and to estimate the number of men falling into the various types of plans.

First of all, there will be a substantial amount of post-war migration, the pattern of which will correspond roughly to movements already made by the Negro worker during the war. The net effect of these movements will be a heavy out-migration from the agricultural regions of the South with a considerable increase in the Negro populations of the Northeast and Pacific Coast states. While it is difficult to estimate the numerical volume of such migration, it should total about 300,000 men. Most of the migration planned is from one region to another, involving long distances, and hence will tend to be permanent.

Education

Almost every Negro veteran will be entitled to at least one year's education at any type of school he chooses, on any academic level, and may take this schooling wherever he wishes throughout the United States. He may also attend approved schools in foreign countries. Among Negro enlisted men 43.5 percent, an aggregate of 522,000 men, have made some plans for returning to school after the war. This total includes men with a very wide range of plans for full-time schooling, 32,000 of whom will be returning to the South. These are the men who will wish to resume high school or college studies broken off by the war. While the majority of these men are young—eighty-eight percent are under twenty-five years of age, and eighty-five percent are single— nearly a third, 17,000 men, have had less than four years of high school education.

Although some Negro veterans will take advantage of specific vocational training rights, most men will receive their benefits under the general education clauses in the GI Bill of Rights. The Bill has two qualifications particularly important for Negroes. First, the veteran must be acceptable to the school and meet its academic standards. Second, the school he chooses must be on the approved list submitted by the state to the Veterans Administration. Let us see what these two qualifications mean for the Negro veteran.

Because of the formal segregation in education in the South, the Negro veteran will be subject to the differential in the quality and quantity of education available for Negroes and whites. The facts of this differential treatment have been told and retold for years. The 112 Negro colleges, having a present over-crowded enrollment of 50,000 students, will be expected to absorb, at the minimum, about 22,000 Negro veterans. The southern Negro veteran will probably not be told by his sources of information that he may go to any college outside the South. Neither will the counselors at Negro colleges be likely to urge him to go elsewhere, as these colleges have a vested financial interest in his attendance.

The 10,000 men who plan to return to full-time school below the college level in the South, must find their education in the very few, inadequate, and already crowded high schools provided for Negroes.

Outside the South the Negro veteran will be confronted by a high informal barrier; although there is no formal segregation, the majority of schools either will not take Negro students or do it grudgingly and often on a quota basis.

Since many states are lax about their standards of approval, all veterans will be exposed to the danger of being exploited by opportunists who start new schools or use their control of existing institutions merely to make money from government tuition payments. The Negro veteran, because he is mainly excluded from attending old and well established institutions, is highly susceptible to the inducements offered by these "sheepskinners." This will be especially true in the South where approval standards are very low, particularly where Negro education is concerned.

Business

About twelve percent, 144,000 men, have some fairly well formulated plans for owning a business after the war. Contained in this group are 84,000 men with definite plans, 49,000 of whom will be returning to the South. The type of establishment that Negro GI's are predominantly planning is the small one-man retail or service business having a low capitalization met partly out of savings and partly by borrowing.

There are very stringent requirements that must be met before a veteran can get a government guaranteed loan. The veteran must satisfy the lending agency, governmental or private, that his ability and experience, and the conditions under which he proposes to pursue his business, are such that there is a reasonable likelihood of success. Of the Negro GI's definitely planning business, only an eighth, 13 percent, were self-employed before the war. However, half of the men with definite plans have had previous experience as employees in the type of business they wish to own. It is doubtful whether this previous experience is adequate, in many cases, to enable the men to obtain a loan, or to operate a business of their own effectively. In general, it may well be that the widespread myth of the Negro's inability to operate a successful business will bar him from obtaining loans.

While 84,000 Negro GI's are definitely planning to own a business, mainly in the retail and service fields, the number of establishments in these fields owned by Negroes before the war was only 29,827. Moreover, it is exactly in these types of establishments, regardless of the color of the owner's skin, where the rate of failure is high.

There is a paradox facing the prospective Negro businessman whose success is largely dependent upon Negro patronage. Outside the South credit is relatively easier to obtain but he must compete fiercely with white-owned business for customers; in the South, credit will be difficult to get, but his clientele will be far more assured.

Agriculture

Almost all the ten percent of Negro GI's, 120,000 men, who have either definite or tentative plans for full-time farming will be returning to the South. Of the men with definite plans, a group of about 84,000, a very high proportion were full-time farmers before they went into the armed forces. Most of these men received their previous experience working on the family farm. Over half of the Negro GI's who plan to operate a farm intend to invest not more than $1,000; less than ten percent intend to invest as much as $4,000. This small investment indicates that most of the men will be operating farms at the subsistence level.

In obtaining guaranteed loans for farms, Negro veterans are faced with much the same restrictions as confront them in getting business loans. The processing of farm loans is handled by the Department of Agriculture, and the Negro veteran interested in agriculture must go to the local office of the Department's county extension agent. The county agents in the plantation South often have an attitude on economic, social, and racial questions similar to that held by the large landowners. The question is, will the county agent and the local community in the South be more interested in a square deal for the returning Negro veteran than they have been in the past for Negro civilians?

A ray of hope for the Negro veteran desiring a loan is that the GI Bill of Rights also makes each veteran eligible for a loan under the

Bankhead-Jones Farm Tenant Act to the same extent as if he were a tenant. This act is administered by the Farm Security Administration which has been the main federal agency helping Negro farmers in the South.

Southern agriculture has long been greatly overcrowded and during the war more crops than were grown in the pre-war years have been produced by fewer men, using larger farms, more machinery, and increased capitalization. With the close of the war, the trend toward increased mechanization of farming in the South will be accentuated. Only by mechanization and large scale farming can the South hope to compete with the price of cotton determined in the world market. These new large farms will be owned by wealthy white landowners. In cold fact this means that the Negro in agriculture is at the very bottom of the economic heap.

Other Employment

A surprisingly large group, twenty-one percent, constituting 252,000 Negro GI's, have plans for public employment after the war. Of this group, 108,000 men have definite plans.

Because of the sweeping advantages granted veterans under the Veterans' Preference Act of 1944, the Civil Service for many years to come will be made up largely of veterans. Government jobs hold particular attraction for Negro veterans owing to the relative lack of racial discrimination. Due to the impetus given to public employment of Negroes by the policies of the Roosevelt administration, it is not surprising to find that eight percent of the Negro veterans want federal jobs rather than state or municipal. A large majority of the men planning federal employment have worked for the government before the war and a third of these men desire a job in a different occupational group than the one they were in before joining the armed forces.

While the Negro veteran's chances for a job are better in the Civil Service than at almost any point in the employment structure of our society, the number of jobs available in the post-war period will meet only a fraction of the demand. The total number of Negroes in public employment in April, 1944, was about 200,000 in contrast to fewer than 60,000 in the same month of 1940. It is obvious that with the contraction of public employment after the war, Negro veterans will experience considerable difficulty in carrying out their plans.

Of the 700,000 Negro veterans who plan to join the general labor force as workers after the war, 400,000 will be returning to the South.

Almost all of these men were employees before they joined the armed forces. However, their re-employment rights will be of little benefit to them as only a fifth of the men have definite plans for returning to their old job and employer. Further, only a third are even planning to return to the same kind of work they did before the war. Negroes have been trained in many skilled fields—as pilots, mechanics, radio technicians and operators—and will not be content in the menially unskilled employment of traditional Negro jobs.

The single basic issue confronting Negro veterans who plan to enter the labor market as workers is whether or not there will be a reasonably high level of employment in the reconversion and post-war periods. Between April, 1940, and April, 1944, the employment of Negroes in civilian jobs increased by almost a million, the occupational shift being mainly from the farm to the factory. But, looking to the post-war period, it must be noted that the Negro worker has made his greatest employment gains in occupations such as semi-skilled factory jobs, which will suffer the highest rate of lay-off once the war is ended. Further, the Negro's occupational gains have been in those industries—iron and steel, munitions, aircraft and ship building—which will experience the greatest decline and most radical reconversion adjustments.

For the 400,000 Negro veterans returning to the South as workers there may be no jobs of any kind. The South remains industrially underdeveloped despite the emergency aid of defense industry, and even during the war there was a surplus labor force. This surplus will be swelled now that the war has ended by the closing of defense plants and the coming home of millions of veterans looking for jobs.

The theory behind much of the administration, evolved to give the veteran adequate aid in re-establishing himself, is based on the belief that the local community can best handle the problems of its own veterans. The right to decide whether a veteran may enroll in a school rests with the local school he wishes to attend. Whether the veteran may make a loan for a business or farm rests with the local bank or other agency which will decide whether he meets the requirements for a loan. The veteran's re-employment in his old job is handled by the re-employment committeeman of his local draft board. A new job will depend upon the policies of local industry and the local United States Employment Office.

For the white veteran the theory of allowing each local community to take care of its own has a certain validity. It is true that with federal and state aid providing the channels through which local decisions are implemented, the community can give individualized special service to its own veterans. And the Negro veteran will receive individualized and special treatment in an ironical sense; it is at the level of the local community where he had always suffered the most discrimination.

At three points the Negro veteran will have difficulty not encountered by the white veteran. First, he will have less access to places in which he may obtain information about his benefits and where he should apply for them. In the South he will have to utilize "jim-crow" veterans' information centers, or no information centers at all. Second, once he has obtained information, he will be subject to careless treatment and possible discrimination in the offices where his rights are administered. Lastly, he has the very special problem, particularly in the South, that, even if he were to obtain sufficient information, if he were to meet absolutely no differential treatment in the offices of administering agencies, he would still not have the wide choice of schools, loan institutions, or jobs open to the white veteran.

Therefore, at many points of contact with society where veterans must act to change their plans into reality, the white GI will be considered first a veteran, secondly and incidentally a white man; the Negro GI will often be considered first a Negro, secondly and incidentally a veteran.

August–September, 1945.

II

POLITICS

Marion, South Carolina

Rather than permit a group of Negroes to register, all offices in the Marion County Courthouse were closed on Monday, October 6, 1945. Negro citizens from all over the county, under the leadership of the Progressive Democratic Party, came in to Marion on a date designated by F. M. Boatwright, county registration officer, as an official day for registration. When the group arrived they were informed that Mr. Boatwright was not in. A "searching party" was sent out to look for the missing registrar. It is reported that they spied him at one point, but that he quickly took to his heels. Meanwhile, the door to the office in which the prospective registrants were waiting was closed. They remained, however, for five hours. Later they learned that all offices in the building were vacated soon after they had come in.

Columbia, South Carolina

Negro Democrats from all over the nation were represented at a recent meeting of the National Council of Negro Democrats held in Columbia. Aside from going on record in favor of the Norton-Chavez F.E.P.C. bill, the Murray-O'Mahoney Full Employment Bill, Federal aid to education, the Anti-Poll Tax Bill, and anti-lynching legislation, the meeting served to demonstrate the essential unity of political aims of Negroes from all sections. Prominent among the leaders of the conference were Emmet S. Cunningham, Council President, from Detroit, John H. McCray and Osceola McKaine of the Progressive Democratic Party, convention hosts, Emory O. Jackson, editor of the *Birmingham World*, and C. A. Scott, editor of the Atlanta *Daily World*.

Civil Rights

Davenport, Iowa

Mr. and Mrs. Charles W. Toney have won the first civil rights case to be tried in Davenport. The couple swore out a warrant for the arrest of the proprietor of an ice cream parlor after the latter had refused to serve them. The assistant county attorney and S. Joe Brown, a Negro attorney from Des Moines, prosecuted the case. Mr. Toney is president of the local N.A.A.C.P.

Cincinnati, Ohio

A new pressure group, which is as yet without a name, has been exerting considerable energy toward securing service for Negroes in Cincinnati's restaurants. The persistent efforts of the group have been characterized by frequent and systematic visits to recalcitrant establishments, negotiation through conferences with managers, and threats of court action under Ohio's civil rights statutes. So apparent has the activity been in recent weeks that a hurried meeting of the Restaurant Owners Association was called. An unexpected turn of events came when a member of that body provided practical and convincing arguments in favor of serving everyone. As a result of these arguments a "gentlemen's agreement" was reached whereby most members of the Association pledged themselves to abide by the spirit of the civil rights law. This agreement is, of course, not binding on all members. The manager of one large chain of eating establishments is reported to have been gratuitously inciting his customers against the possible presence of Negro customers.

Police Administration

Portland, Oregon

At two o'clock in the morning of August 21, three police officers and a deputy district attorney, seeking an alleged murderer, came to the house of Ervin Jones, a Negro war worker living in the Guild's Lake Housing project. The officers did not have a warrant to search the premises and there is considerable doubt that they clearly identified themselves as officers of the law. Members of the Jones family report that they thought them to be burglars. Mr. Jones fired at least one shot. (Police say that he shot twice *through* the door. Later investigation by disinterested persons disclosed evidence of only one shot having been fired *over* the door.) While two of the officers were trying to enter the front door, the third went to the rear of the house, broke out a window pane and shot Jones in the back with a sawed-off shot gun, fatally wounding him. The alleged murderer was not even known to the Jones family.

Superior officers called the shooting "justifiable homicide" and attempted to close the case. The Council of Churches, the N.A.A.C.P., and other civic groups demanded that further investigations be made. Forming an Ervin Jones Committee, a group of citizens demanded a coroner's inquest. The District Attorney's office scheduled such a hearing and the Ervin Jones Committee raised five hundred dollars with which to return Mrs. Jones and her two sisters who, in the meantime, had gone back to Shreveport, Louisiana, to live. The coroner interpreted his obligation to select his jury from "the community in which the death occurred" broadly; and chose all members from the St. John's district across the river from Guild's Lake. The six coroner's jurors were all white. From the type of evidence permitted and rejected by the coroner, the hearing seems to have been heavily weighed in favor of the officers. From this hearing came a verdict that Jones had died as a result of a shot fired by Detective Purcell in defense of himself and his fellow officers.

Following the coroner's jury verdict the Ervin Jones Committee requested a grand jury investigation of the shooting. A grand jury was convened on the case and "found insufficient evidence to warrant an indictment." The efforts of those who worked on the case are reported to have had two positive results. Under the stigma of her husband's having been the victim of justifiable homicide, Mrs. Jones and her five children could not easily have collected his two thousand dollar group insurance policy. Negroes and whites of many political persuasions were able to unite around this *cause célèbre*.

Albany, Georgia

Sheriff Claude Screws and his deputies Jim Kelly and Frank Jones, whose sentences of three years in prison and one thousand dollar fines were ordered reconsidered, have been placed on trial again in the Middle Georgia District of Federal Court. The peace officers are charged with having conspired to deprive a person of his civil rights (in this instance his life) under the cloak of law enforcement. They are alleged to have fatally injured Robert Hall, a Negro, in a beating administered while Hall was handcuffed and under arrest on a charge of stealing an automobile tire.

Chattanooga, Tennessee

The policemen's union of Chattanooga, negotiating for a contract with the city, made several proposals discriminatory to Negroes. The limitations demanded by the union caused such a great protest among Negro and white citizens that they have subsequently been withdrawn. The original contract submitted to the City Commission provided that there be at least fifty white police to each Negro employed, that the latter be restricted in authority to the arrest of Negroes, and that Negro policemen be confined to the detective branch and that none wear uniforms. Chattanooga has had Negro policemen for several years.

Brooklyn, New York

The Brooklyn N.A.A.C.P. is pressing three charges of assault against Police Sergeant George Neff in magistrates court and is supporting a civil suit for twelve thousand dollars in damages on behalf of the victims. William Hudnell was returning to the home where he was house guest when Sergeant Neff of the 77th Precinct stopped him and searched him. The Sergeant, who was apparently under the influence of liquor, threatened to beat Hudnell "only a little" and struck the latter across the eye with his night stick. Hudnell then fled toward home. Ruth Hemmings (winner of "Miss Negro Victory" title for 1945) sister of Hudnell's hostess, opened the door but was not able to close it before Neff entered, knocking her against the wall. This representative of New York's finest then rushed to the kitchen, manhandled an eight-year old child, and threatened to shoot everyone.

The policeman is under investigation and has been transferred to Queens.

Johnson, South Carolina

The vulnerable position of Negro women in many parts of the South is reflected in the arrest and subsequent release of Miss Annie L. Smythe, a teacher in the Edgefield County Training School. While returning from a visit at the home of the school principal, Miss Smythe was approached by a local police officer who is reported to have given her the alternative of being seduced by him or being arrested. Resisting the officer, she was arrested and booked on charges of disorderly conduct. When her colleagues received word of her predicament, they interceded with local officials and refused to teach until the matter was settled. Faced with this courageous (for South Carolina) action on the part of the principal and other teachers, the police released Miss Smythe, claiming that it had been "a case of mistaken identity." There is no report of any action being taken against the offending policeman.

The Courts

Selma, Alabama

J. D. Booker, local police officer, was acquitted by an all-white jury on charges of murder in connection with the fatal beating of Mrs. Nicey Brown, seventy-year-old Negro resident of Selma. The officer alleged to have come to Mrs. Brown's home and demanded the whereabouts of one of her daughters. The policeman was off duty at the time and is said to have been inebriated. When Mrs. Brown was either unwilling or unable to give him the desired information, Booker began beating her over the head with a bottle. Her husband, attracted by the disturbance, came and fired on the peace officer with a shot gun. Booker's attorney, James Pitts, held that he had acted in self-defense. Pitts is quoted as saying during the trial, "If we convict this brave man who is upholding the banner of white supremacy by his actions, then we may as well give all our guns to the niggers and let them run the black belt." The jury "deliberated" for only a few seconds.

Memphis, Tennessee

After five hours of deliberation, an all-white jury in the First Division of the Shelby County Criminal Court returned a verdict of not guilty in the case of Leotha Palmer, a thirty-one-year-old Negro charged with assault and attempted rape of a white woman. Palmer's attorneys definitely established the fact that he had been in the company of several friends during the entire period in which the assault was alleged to have occurred. According to the defendant he had been picked up by the police and taken to the woman's home for identification. In the police line-up the next morning he was again pointed out as the culprit. A. A. Latting, Negro attorney of Memphis, was joined in the defense by a white attorney, Wallace Lopez.

Lynching

Madison, Florida

A Madison County Grand Jury has made the usual report that its members were unable to discover the guilty party or parties in the lynching of Jesse James Payne. Stating that "stupidity and ineptitude" are not sufficient grounds for the removal from office of Sheriff Lonnie Davis, Governor Caldwell noted: "A crime of this nature is not essentially local in its character. Its significance transcends the borders of both county and state and draws unfavorable attention to Florida. . . . Florida and Madison County have suffered a loss of standing in the country as a result of this affair. There was no excuse for it."

General

Louisville, Kentucky

Articles of incorporation for the Mason-Dixon Society have been issued at Frankfort. According to these articles, the Mason-Dixon Society is organized to promote "the American Way of Life and to improve our standard of living." These objectives are to be achieved by "maintaining free enterprise, by fostering individual initiative, by preserving our established freedoms, by respecting human and property rights, by creating greater national unity, by encouraging more active and intelligent participation in public affairs, and by supporting the Constitution of the United States." According to the Washington correspondent of the Louisville Courier-Journal, however, the sub-title of the name of this organization is "The National Association for the Advancement of White People," and its main purpose is that of lobbying all legislation aimed at granting equality to Negroes.

Lexington, Oglethorpe County, Georgia

William Henry Huff, Chicago, attorney for several peonage victims in the past, has entered a complaint with the Attorney General of the United States charging two cases of attacks against Negro women by white merchants in Oglethorpe County. The one case involves Mrs. Hattie Cantrell, whose son was inducted into the Army while in debt to George Walter Paul. Mrs. Cantrell, who is reported to have paid seventy-nine dollars of the debt, went to Mr. Paul and informed him that she was going to move. The man picked up a feather duster and beat her brutally with the wooden handle.

Walter Matthews, another merchant of Oglethorpe County, is charged by Attorney Huff with having kicked Mrs. Maggie Appling out of his store without cause. When Mrs. Appling attempted to swear out a warrant for Matthews' arrest, Herbert Whitehead, a local peace officer, refused to issue the order. The Guardian of the Law is alleged to have stated, "I will not give any nigger a warrant for a white person." Assistant Attorney General Caudle has replied to Mr. Huff on Attorney General Clark's behalf, assuring him that he is "taking appropriate action in this matter."*

The National Pastime

Brooklyn, New York

President Branch Rickey of the Brooklyn Dodgers has announced the hiring of Jackie Robinson by the Montreal Royals, Brooklyn's International League "farm team." This marks the first time that a Negro has been given a contract to play in organized baseball. The agitation for fair play in America's Favorite Sport has been increasing in recent years. Writers in the Negro press, who have been calling for an opportunity for Negro players for many years, have been joined in later years by sports writers for such politically diverse journals as the Philadelphia *Record,* the New York *Daily News,* the New York *Post, PM,* the *Daily Worker,* and the *News Leader.*

Lieutenant Jackie Robinson (late of the United States Army) is at present a player for the Kansas City Monarchs, one of the more profitable all-Negro clubs. He achieved All-American mention while playing football at the University of California–Los Angeles, his alma mater, where he also played basketball. The hiring of Robinson has been commended by the majority of those sports writers who have commented upon it—Southern and otherwise.

* For data on peonage in general and in Oglethorpe County, Georgia in particular, see the editor's *Afro-American History: The Modern Era* (N.Y.: Citadel Press, 1971), pp. 191–201.

The Heritage of Lincoln?

Springfield, Illinois

The Chicago Civil Liberties Committee and the Springfield Junior N.A.A.C.P. chapter have recently reported instances of serious abridgement of civil liberties in the hometown of the Great Emancipator. The former organization has released a report by its minorities secretary of an investigation into police brutality and other instances of discrimination. According to this report, Mrs. Willie Bradley, the sixty-four-year-old widow of a minister, Mrs. Bradley's daughter, and Kenneth Scruggs were arrested at the home of Mrs. Bradley on September 21. The arrest was made by six policemen (including one Negro policeman) who, without a warrant of any kind, forcibly entered the coal-shed that served as home for the woman. Scruggs, who was visiting the home, and the two women were booked on charges of vagrancy and placed under five thousand dollar bond. At the jail, the older woman is reported to have been beaten into a state of unconsciousness by the turnkey, and left on the floor without medical attention. Other women prisoners put her to bed. The next morning she was taken to the hospital and found to have two broken ribs.

(It was September 22, 1945—the eighty-third anniversary of the writing of the Emancipation Proclamation by Springfield's most famous son!)

Miss Anna Bee Bradley was present in the jail when her mother was attacked. Unable to raise bond, she was retained in jail until October 6. According to her affidavit, the Chief of Police asked, "Are you going to have anything to do with your mother's case?" When she replied that she would tell what she had seen, Police Magistrate Conway, before whom she was appearing, gave her thirty minutes to get out of town.

Some other indices of the state of race relations in Springfield, Illinois are:

Although there are mixed schools, there are no Negro teachers.

Poolrooms provide the only recreation usually available to Negroes of all ages. So many children frequent poolrooms in the Negro area that the proprietors carry milk in their refrigerators.

Drug stores, restaurants, and taverns, even in the heart of the Negro district, refuse to serve persons of color.

When a local N.A.A.C.P. officer reproached a school principal for pushing a Negro girl down a flight of steps, the educator is said to have quoted Senator Eastland's slander of Negro soldiers in rebuttal!

A physician in a public clinic reportedly told a Negro mother, "I will not attend a Negro baby. If I had to prescribe for her it would be arsenic."

(A letter-to-the-editor in a Chicago daily recently observed that Lincoln's tomb has been allowed to fall into a state of ill repair.)

October, 1945.

III

THE INDUSTRIAL FRONT
Fair Employment

Aside from the emasculation of the Full Employment Bill, led by Congressmen Whittington (Mississippi) and Manasco (Alabama), the most dramatic occurrence in the fight for fair employment was the resignation of Attorney Charles H. Houston from the Committee on Fair Employment Practice (F.E.P.C.). Significance was added to Mr. Houston's action by the fact that it came as part of the ground-swell of bitter criticism which the Administration has received from liberal forces. The letter of resignation said, in part:

On November 23, 1945, in the Capital Transit Company Case, No. 70 on the committee docket, the committee voted to issue its decision which directs Capital Transit to cease and desist from practices and policies which have resulted in the denial of employment policy declared for industries essential to the prosecution of the war by Executive Order No. 9346.

Without notice to the committee or a chance for the committee to present its views, on November 24 you ordered the committee not to issue the decision. November 25 on behalf of the committee I wrote you asking that you give the committee opportunity to confer with you. The return registry shows the letter delivered to The White House November 26. . . .

The President's Committee on Fair Employment Practices was created by Executive Orders Nos. 8802 and 9346 as an independent agency responsible directly to the President, and charged with effectuating on his behalf the national policy of full utilization of the nation's manpower in war industries, government contract operations and government service, without discrimination "in regard to hire, tenure terms or conditions of employment, or union membership because of race, creed, color, or national origin."

Since the effect of your intervention in the Capital Transit Case is not to eliminate but to condone it, to that extent you not only repudiate the Committee but more important, you nullify the Executive Orders themselves. . . .

Your action in the Capital Transit case means that you do not hesitate to seize Capital Transit when employees strike in violation of a private collective bargaining agreement, but will not move, or permit the committee to move, to effectuate the national non-discriminatory employment policy declared in Presidential Executive Orders. . . .

The issue of the Capital Transit case far transcends the question whether a few Negro workers shall be placed on the platforms of street cars and buses and as traffic checkers on the Capital Transit system.

It raises the fundamental question of the basic government attitude toward minorities. The failure of the government to enforce democratic practices and to protect minorities in its own capital makes its expressed concern for national minorities abroad somewhat specious, and the interference in the domestic affairs of other countries very premature.

November, 1945.

IV

THE FRONT PAGE

The *Afro-American's* columnist, J. Saunders Redding, commented during the month upon the fact that the restraints of war are off and reaction has again set in. "The paradoxes and contradictions in American life are again in evidence," he says. Nowhere do these paradoxes seem more apparent than in the field of race relations; nowhere is the evidence more conclusive than in the patterns of segregation and discrimination, more familiarly, and collectively known as "Jim Crow." These facts of American life give the Negro press its chief news of the month.

This month's diet of race disorganization and maladjustment may seem a little less unsavory if the *pièces de résistance* are served first. Much to everyone's amazement, and to the general satisfaction of the Negro community, President Truman named a Negro, Irvin C. Mollison, to a judgeship in the U.S. Customs Court of New York. Mr. Mollison is capable beyond any doubt and has achieved the appointment through professional and political merit, despite the fact that the chairman of the Democratic Party apparently had to force Congressional action on the appointment. Less spectacular but of greater moment to the masses of Negroes, perhaps, was the employment of five Negro workers in the New York City Office of the Metropolitan Life Insurance Company after years of public pressure to achieve that end. Likewise the successful use of Negro operators in New York's telephone system was indicated by the fact that they now number more than one hundred. Sports lovers thrilled to learn that Jack Robinson, former U.C.L.A. crack athlete, had been signed as the first Negro player in big-league baseball. Educators continued to be elated over their inching-along-toward-amity efforts as Webster College in Missouri admitted its first Negro student.

To these credits might be added the usual upon-second-thought actions which follow the fighting phases of wars. The armed services reconsidered the penalties inflicted upon three Negro officers at Walterboro Army Air Field in South Carolina and reduced their sentences. Major Homer Roberts who so successfully publicized the doings of Negro troops was given the Legion of Merit upon resigning from the Army. An hitherto unpublished report of the War Department is released and indicates that Negro troops fought "very well" in mixed racial units, according to General Eisenhower. And the fifty-two Negro soldiers who last year were convicted of mutiny at Fort Shafter, Hawaii, because they refused to obey orders and report in work formation, have been restored to duty with original sentences suspended. Meanwhile, the Secretary of War has formed a committee to study the possibilities for full implementation of Negro troops in the Army, and Admiral Nimitz has been cited by the *Defender* as "OK"ing a mixed Navy. All in all, the Negro press regarded this as good evidence of a better situation. In its more colorful aspects such stories as that told by Gordon Hancock in the *Journal and Guide,* made good copy. In essence the story is that white and Negro troops were not adjusting so well in a certain camp. The white troops had set up rules and barriers segregating Negroes. The situation had become so tense that the Commanding Officer had to take over. He did so in these words: "I cannot end segregation in the U.S. Navy, but I can end it in this camp and it is hereby ended."

But all of the government's vestments had not gone to the cleaners. *People's Voice* took great issue with President and Mrs. Truman over the D.A.R.'s refusal to let Hazel Scott, wife of Congressman Adam Powell, the paper's editor, play in its Constitution Hall. The President wrote a formal reply, the issue was raised in Congress. Mr. Powell started his own D.A.R. (Drive Against Reaction) and a southern daily labelled the Daughters of the American Revolution the "Daughters of Asinine Reaction." The issue is neither resolved nor solved to date. More far reaching, of course, was the failure to get constructive action on F.E.P.C. out of the Congress, as well as that body's failure to act on the poll tax. Likewise, a tactless statement from an official of the Veterans Bureau was headlined in one of the papers, VETERANS BUREAU TO REMAIN J.C. The fine words of our foreign policy for overseas democracy were pitted against democracy as practiced in the states represented by our policy spokesmen, and became the subject of wide editorial comment. Senator Bilbo's home in Washington was picketed because of his undemocratic statements, and the T.V.A. took editorial spankings for declaring that its policy for housing Negro workers would be within the framework of the South's established practices of law and order—"separate but equal." None too favorably received was the Army's announcement that charges against the former commanding officer at Freeman Field, Indiana, who sought to separate the facilities provided for white and colored officers, had been dropped.

State and local governments faced situations no less serious than did the federal agency. Judge T. Hoyt Davis' decision in Macon, Georgia, which cleared away one legal barrier to Negroes voting in that state was widely acclaimed. But when Governor Ellis Arnall announced that the decision should be appealed, the *Courier* and the *Journal and Guide* wanted to know "How Liberal is Governor Arnall?" The state courts of Alabama dismissed the franchise suit brought by citizens in that state, while Texas politicians were continuing to seek ways around the Supreme Court decision which outlawed its white primary.

The most serious race-ruckus of the month, however, was in the public schools. New York, Chicago and Gary were faced with race situations that reflected the general social tenor of their communities as well as community-school relations. The Negro press was of one accord in believing these strikes adult-prompted. One commentator dolefully pointed out the fact that once we thought youth would solve the problem of race relations. On these and similar problems the *Defender*'s headline, PEACE: IT'S TRULY FASCIST, indicated the editorial reactions.

Beneath the level of officialdom, there was a lynching in Madison, Florida; the banning of a motion picture *Imitation of Life* in Atlanta, Georgia, because it was "contrary to the order of the community in its handling of the race question" (though it has been almost a perennial in that city's Negro theatres); the threatened dispossessing of one-fourth of the Negro families in Cranbrook, New Jersey, because they live in slums and whites will not rent to them; the revival of the K.K.K. in Atlanta as it burns its faggot cross from Stone Mountain; the accusation of discrimination against Negro pupils in the Williams Township school near Paoli, Pennsylvania; the fight between a discharged Negro sailor and a train conductor on a southern railroad, the sailor being ejected from the train because of his "sassy talk"; the cigar manufacturer who requested one thousand "white only" workers; the cigarette manufacturer who did the same thing; the southern policemen who arrested and jailed a Negro teacher on charges of disorderly conduct when she refused his "proposition," and the thirteen teachers who struck in protest until the teacher was released and the charge withdrawn; the revelation of Dr. Frank Kingdon that there is a systematic racial and religious bias in all of the nation's medical schools. All of this was news and grist for the racial press's mill.

November, 1945.

V

THE FRONT PAGE

An editorial in the *Afro-American* on "Our Bill of Rights Today" points out that after 154 years of the Bill of Rights the Negro's right to be treated as a human being is still challenged. A review of the month's news not only supports that conclusion but makes it a neat understatement. It is utterly and completely impossible to read the Negro weekly without having disturbed emotions, and, at year's beginning, without musing on the shape of things to come. The shadows were cast in politics and education, war's end and peace's labored birth, in fact, in all aspects of human relations.

The Negro press headlines did not feature the maladroit handling of the country's social legislation, but the contents of its news stories did. The disruption of F.E.P.C., the Labor-Management fiasco, the national health program's legislative collapse, the return of U.S.E.S. to the Department of Labor and state supervision, the butchering of the full employment bills, were all roundly criticized in editorials and news stories. Even more, the papers gave forthright criticism to the national and international policies of the United States. P. L. Prattis, writing in the *Courier,* points out that according to almost any standard of measurement used, our State Department is "lousy." Mr. Prattis maintains that outside of the Navy the State Department is one branch of our government which is least responsive to the wishes of the people, which cares less for what the people think, cares nothing about serving the public and has been rotting for years.

George Schuyler, also writing in the *Courier,* maintains that our troops and administrators stationed abroad are creating thousands of enemies daily "not only by their arrogance, callousness, and brutality, but by the uninterrupted series of diplomatic, administrative and psychological hogs they have cut. Instead of democratic liberators, Germany and the Far East got chucklehead oppressors. . . . Our racially intolerant policies in the Caribbean, Panama and South American countries have made enemies there. In our smear campaign against her, Latin America's sympathy is with Argentina, whose government is more democratic than the government of South Carolina, or of any State between the Potomac River and the New Mexico boundary." He concludes that the religion of race prejudice and color prejudice, "American Shintoism," will be spread all over the earth wherever our forces and agents are stationed.

Horace Cayton, writing in the same paper, says that before subscribing to the Eighth War Loan he wants to know where and how the money is going to be spent to "complete the job."

And though these samples of comment have been taken from one paper, they are typical of the forthright, bold attacks that have been made upon the current portents indicated in the month's news. First of all, there is question of racial discrimination against Negroes in transportation. In Virginia, Mississippi, South Carolina, Alabama and Georgia, there were court suits and administrative rulings that were affecting the whole fabric of discriminatory practices in services and facilities for Negro passengers. On a Southern branch of the Rock Island Railroad the dining car waiters struck when two Negro sailors were denied service. They were dismissed from the service.

Veterans were having their problems, too. No Negro member of the armed forces received the coveted Medal of Honor, though one unit, the 92nd Division, received 12,096 decorations. The development of pressure groups among veterans in the form of veterans organizations may be measured by the fact that there were sixty-five of them in December, 1945, according to a survey made by the *Afro-American.* This paper found that only a few of these organizations were free from racial bias. The American Legion refused to tell its Southern State Departments to lower their racial bars. The courts of California told the Disabled American Veterans, Inc., that it could not discriminate against veterans on the basis of race, color or religion.

In education there were portents of schemes designed to adjust the inequalities toward the nether side of justice. From England came the plan for a British West Indian University, a plan which is opposed by many hard-thinking students of colonial policy. From the Conference of Southern Governors came a plan for a regional university for Negroes in the South, a plan which is opposed by many hard-hitting exponents of an equal-education-for-all policy in the South. From Tampa, Florida, came a case in point for that opposition. In the summer of 1945 that city spent $80,000 for the improvement of schools for white children and $1,000 for schools for Negro children. The *Afro-American* called this "Skimmed Milk Education."

In California, the restrictive covenant was at the nonce rendered illegal as an instrument for removing colored tenants. In Dade County, Florida (Miami is the county seat), restrictive covenants based on race were declared illegal. In Chicago, the American Council on Race Relations was criticized by the *Defender* because its program for eliminating the racially proscribing restrictive covenants substituted an equally offensive class restriction program. In Le Havre, France 123 colored soldiers were kept off a home-bound ship because of their race. There were three lynchings in the last three months of 1945, one in boom-seeking Florida, two in Bulgaria-saving-for-democracy South Carolina. San Francisco's Negro population had leaped from 4,846 on April 1, 1940, to 32,001 in December, 1945, an increase of 560 per cent. Negro troops cannot be sent to Panama and the British Islands of the Caribbean, because of the possible color complications. Australia's Department of the Interior has ruled that only those members of the United States armed forces who are of "European race or descent may remain in Australia after discharge." No wonder the Negro press queries editorially "Is the United Nations Charter Dead?" Is there wonder that Dorie Miller's father said his son had died in vain?

Of course, there was a brighter side to the news. Negroes voted in a primary election in Georgia for the first time in forty years. A Negro professional man became a Democratic committeeman in Roanoke, Virginia. The national government named January 5, 1946, as George Washington Carver Day. The University of Indiana uncovered a Negro football star and began to crack the Big Ten's racial provincialism. The Anglo-American Caribbean Commission invited France and The Netherlands to discuss and plan with it on the future of the West Indies. Frank Sinatra crooned his throatiest to combat what the *Journal and Guide* called the "mass insanity" of public school strikes. *PM,* the *People's Voice,* attacked the indiscriminate arrest of Harlem residents in an editorial "Raising Hell." The *Defender* praised Bill Mauldin for his cartoons of social significance and named twenty-one persons who had gloriously served the cause of human justice during 1945. And President Frank Graham of the University of North Carolina supported the North Carolina Student Legislative Assembly in its 110–48 vote to invite Negro students to participate in its 1946 meeting.

A Selected Bibliography for Afro-American History 1933-1945

OF SOME SERVICE to readers may be a brief bibliography of significant works in the history of the Afro-American people during the period covered by this volume. Titles mentioned below do *not* include works mentioned in the body of the text; they are those considered to be indispensable for a knowledge of the subject.

The best single-volume overall text in the field of Afro-American history is John Hope Franklin's *From Slavery to Freedom: A History of Negro Americans.* The fourth edition was published by Knopf in 1974; this volume contains an excellent bibliography.

Also to be especially noted is *The Journal of Negro Education,* which began its distinguished career in 1932. This quarterly, issued at Howard University, is an indispensable source of information.

DRAKE, ST. CLAIR and HORACE CAYTON. *Black Metropolis: A Study of Negro Life in a Northern City* (Chicago, 1945).

DU BOIS, W. E. B. *Dusk of Dawn: An Essay toward an Autobiography of a Race Concept* (1940).

DU BOIS, W. E. B. *The Autobiography: A Soliloquy on Viewing My Life from the Last Decade of Its First Century* [edited by H. Aptheker] (1968).

FAUSET, ARTHUR H. *Black Gods of the Metropolis: Negro Religious Cults of the Urban North* (1944).

FRANKLIN, CHARLES L. *The Negro Labor Unionist in New York: Problems and Conditions among Negroes in Manhattan, with Special Reference to the N.R.A. and Post-N.R.A. Situations* (1936).

FRAZIER, E. FRANKLIN. *The Negro Family in the United States* (1939).

GRUBBS, DONALD H. *Cry from the Cotton: The Southern Tenant Farmers' Union and the New Deal* (1971).

JOHNSON, CHARLES S. *Growing Up in the Black Belt: Negro Youth in the Rural South* (1941).

LEE, ULYSSES. *The Employment of Negro Troops* [in World War II] (1966).

LERNER, GERDA, ed. *Black Women in White America* (1972).

LOGAN, RAYFORD W., ed. *What the Negro Wants* (1944).

MYRDAL, GUNNAR. *An American Dilemma* (1944); and see H. APTHE-KER. *The Negro People in America: A Critique of Myrdal's "Dilemma"* (1946).

NORTHRUP, HERBERT R. *Organized Labor and the Negro* (1944).

POWDERMAKER, HORTENSE. *After Freedom: A Cultural Study in the Deep South* (1939).

STERNER, RICHARD. *The Negro's Share* (1945).

STERNSHER, BERNARD, ed. *The Negro in Depression and War: Prelude to Revolution, 1930–1945* (1969).

WEAVER, ROBERT C. *Negro Labor: A National Problem* (1946).

WHITE, WALTER F. *A Man Called White: The Autobiography* (1948).

WILKERSON, DOXEY A. *Special Problems in Negro Education* (1939).

WOLTERS, RAYMOND. *Negroes and the Great Depression: The Problem of Economic Recovery* (1970).

WRIGHT, RICHARD. *Black Boy: A Record of Childhood and Youth* (1945).

ZANGRANDO, ROBERT L. "The N.A.A.C.P. and a Federal Antilynching Bill, 1934–1940," in *The Journal of Negro History,* April, 1965 (50:106–117).

Index